THE PALLISER'S LATE VICTORIAN ARCHITECTURE

A facsimile of George & Charles Palliser's
Model Homes (1878) and American Cottage Homes (1878), as
Republished in 1888 under the title American Architecture,
   and
New Cottage Homes and Details (1887)

With a new introduction by
MICHAEL A. TOMLAN

PUBLISHED BY THE AMERICAN LIFE FOUNDATION *in*

The Athenaeum Library of Nineteenth Century America

1978

The advertisements which originally appeared with the two books reprinted herein appear at the back of this edition. Those inclusive from "Palliser, Palliser & Co., Architects, ... Bridgeport, Conn., After November 1, 1882, New York City" though the two pages of advertisements for "Lucas' Ready Mixed Paints" (a total of twelve pages) appeared in *American Architecture*. The others are from *New Cottage Architecture*.

Production notes: This new edition was seen through the press by Walnut Grove Graphics and Book Production Associates in Watkins Glen, NY. Printing and binding was performed by Valley Offset, Inc. in Deposit, NY.

This is a book of 312 pages, printed on 70-pound Finch Opaque Smooth, sewn in signatures, and glued into a cover of 25% cotton Strathmore Appian Gold Rhododendron Antique. One thousand copies were printed.

We gratefully acknowledge that Earl G. Shettleworth, Jr. of Augusta, Maine provided us with his copy of *American Architecture* for this facsimile.

The Palliser Brothers and Their Publications

IF ANY ONE FIRM in American architectural history might be cited as contributing most to the democratization of late nineteenth century domestic ideas, that firm must surely be Palliser, Palliser and Company. Through over twenty publications from 1876 to 1908,[1] the English emigrants George Palliser (1848 ?–1903) and his brother, Charles (1854– ?),[2] were among the foremost disseminators of architectural designs of their time. Perhaps even more important, their desire to raise the level of popular taste and practical understanding of design led the Pallisers to perfect a method which would provide architectural services to anyone within reach of the post office.

The method was simple: address the building public directly by distributing inexpensive illustrated paperback booklets describing the latest available designs. When the prospective client found an appealing scheme, he would be encouraged to answer a series of questions regarding cost, size of lot, orientation, etc. These particulars, along with the appropriate fee, were to be mailed to the architects, who would transform them into sketches and plans. The client was then given the opportunity to alter or correct this initial design before the firm would produce a complete set of plans, elevations, details, and specifications for the use of the local builder. The attempt, in essence, was to provide the client with a modicum of architectural guidance where the traditional architect-client relationship was deemed too expensive, too time-consuming or too difficult to obtain. The results were truly remarkable. Thousands of buildings throughout the United States, and many abroad, were designed in this manner not only by the Palliser firm, but also by the numerous other carpenter-architect-publishers who soon adopted the Palliser method as their own.[3]

As George Palliser himself had found upon arriving in Newark in 1868,[4] most architectural books were comparatively expensive and the available building journals were few. His experience in the burgeoning suburbs with a wide variety of clients, first as a master carpenter and then as co-owner of a sash, blind and door manufactory,[5] convinced Palliser that a method should be found whereby more people could benefit from the talent and experience of an architect. This became all the more obvious when, having moved to Bridgeport, Connecticut, in 1873,[6] Palliser was commissioned to design block after block of speculative housing backed by the entrepreneur-mayor P. T. Barnum and others.[7] The firm grew busier, being responsible between April, 1874, and September, 1875, for designing buildings whose aggregate cost was nearly a quarter of a million dollars.[8] It was during this time that they first turned to the idea of duplicating plans, with but minor alterations, for various clients.[9]

Because of his "increasing business, supplying parties in every section of the United States with designs, plans, specifications, etc.,"[10] Palliser published his first booklet, *Model Homes for the People, A Complete Guide to the Proper and Economical Erection of Buildings*, which first appeared in October, 1876.[11] This was a thin octavo work (5″ x 8″) which sold for only twenty-five cents. Its low cost was made possible by the fact that almost half of its forty-four pages were advertisements, solicited from Bridgeport's leading craftsmen and prominent building material suppliers. Forty-eight designs were presented, the majority in the Gothic mode, such as the charming Centennial Villa [Fig. 1], while others were in the Italianate and Mansardic styles. With this booklet the practice of mail order architecture was established. The information about each design included not only the cost of the building and where and for whom it had been constructed, but also the price of plans and specifications, a fee significantly lower than an architect's customary percentage.

The response to the first book was so encouraging that a second, larger work was soon on the drawing boards, to be known as *Palliser's American Cottage Homes*. This is also the first publication of the firm Palliser, Palliser and Company, for by the time it was advertised for sale in January, 1878,[12] Charles had been made a full partner. At $5.00 this quarto volume (10¾″ x 14″) was considerably more expensive than *Model Homes*, although it was comparable to many architectural works of similar size. The featured design on its cover, identified as Plate 1, was a cottage

[FIG. 2] THE BORIGHT HOUSE, RICHFIELD, VER-
MONT (1887–88), A COPY OF GEORGE PALLISER'S
BRIDGEPORT RESIDENCE. (PHOTOGRAPH BY M. A.
TOMLAN)

[FIG. 1] "THE CENTENNIAL VILLA" BY GEORGE
PALLISER. FROM SCOFIELD, H. G. ATLAS OF THE
CITY OF BRIDGEPORT, CONNECTICUT (NEW YORK:
J. B. BEERS & CO., 1876).

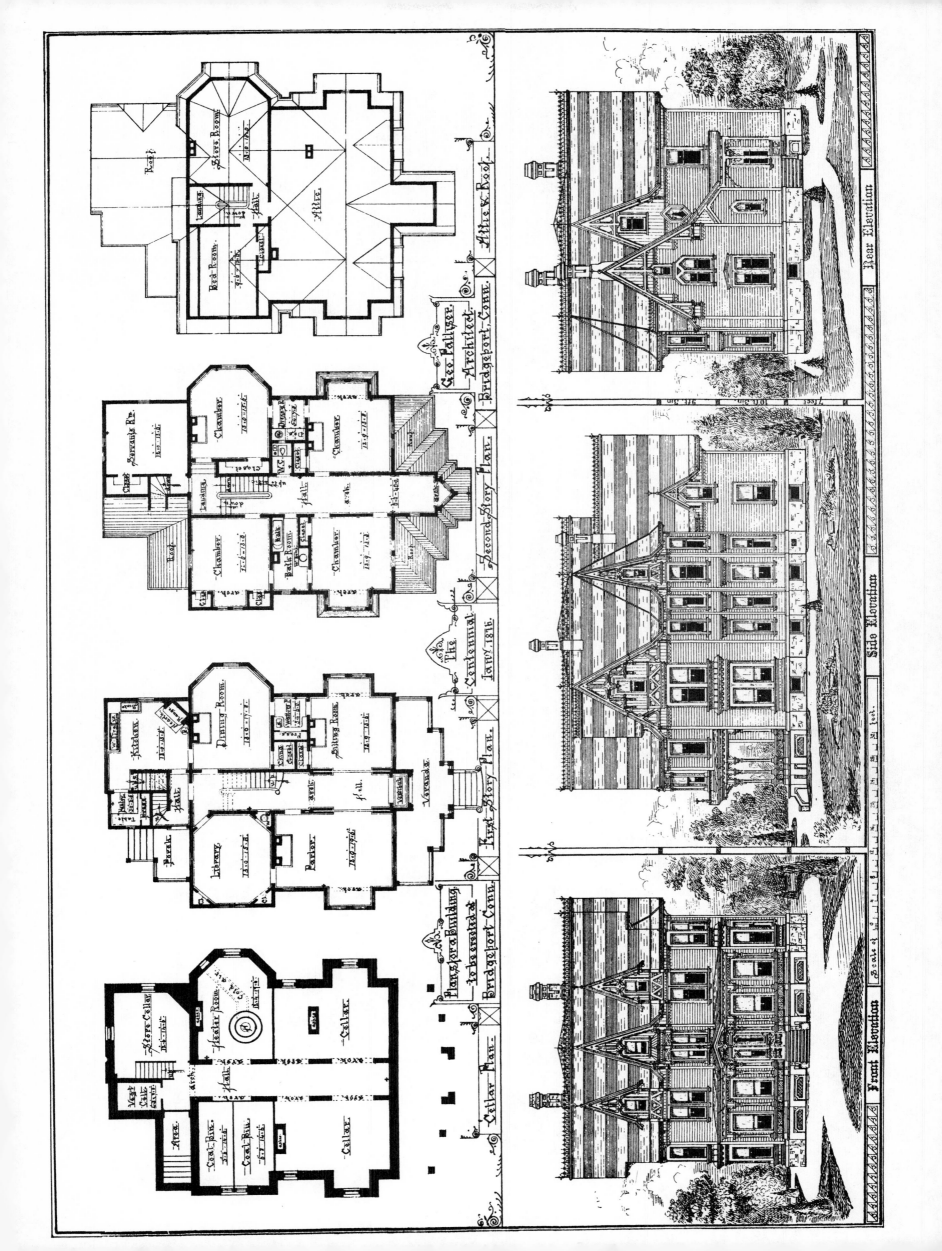

Attic & Roof.

Second Story Plan.

First Story Plan.

Cellar Plan.

Geo. Palliser, Architect. Bridgeport, Conn.

The Centennial. Jany. 1876.

Plans for a Building to be erected at Bridgeport, Conn.

Rear Elevation.

Side Elevation.

Front Elevation.

which George Palliser was building for himself at Seaside Park, Bridgeport's then-fashionable residential suburb. This house is no longer extant, but a copy of the design, the Boright house (1887–88) in Richford, Vermont [Fig. 2], still stands as witness to the architect's imaginative capabilities.[13] The majority of the designs were not as imposing, for most were "low and medium priced houses suited to the masses of our country." Most had decidedly vertical proportions, all the more pronounced for their simplified gothic detailing and thinly enframed, grouped Queen Anne sash.

Having sold nearly all 5,000 copies of the first book, *Model Homes*, the brothers undertook another work of the same size with a similar title. *Palliser's Model Homes. Showing a Variety of Designs for Model Dwellings* first became available in November, 1878.[14] This publication had a much more professional air, with larger, engraved illustrations instead of simple woodcuts. The buildings were primarily frame dwellings of much the same character as those in *American Cottage Homes*, but with an increasing dependence upon Queen Anne massing and details. One of the most popular works of the period, it was published twice in Bridgeport and twice in New York, reaching a total of 15,000 copies. By November, 1883, the authors could boast that many of the designs had been "built as often as twenty to fifty times to our certain knowledge,"[15] and the reader could easily see by the geographic distribution of the designs that the influence of the Palliser firm was by now nationwide.

The first volume reissued here contains all the designs which were first presented in *American Cottage Homes* and in *Model Homes* of 1878. The former had, perhaps, been overpriced for its intended audience and hence was less than well-received. The latter, however, had been an exceedingly successful work, so that by interleaving the plates of both books and having them republished in 1888 under a new title, *American Architecture; or Every Man a Complete Builder*, the Pallisers attempted to extend the life of their earlier designs. This "new" work was quite successful, for at $1.00 paperbound and $2.00 clothbound, its sales ultimately approached 35,000 copies.[16]

While the mail-order method was intended for client and builder alike, the firm specifically addressed the latter by issuing a series of more practical works. *Palliser's Specifications* was published, in various forms, in 1878, 1880 and again in 1886, and *Palliser's Useful Details* appeared in 1881, 1883 and 1890. The latter, a folio volume which included designs for gates, posts, walls, inside doors with casings, mantels, bookcases, gables, and tables, would, at 50,000 copies, top the circulation record of any of the Palliser works.[17] Hardly a woodworker in the country could have failed to hear of the Palliser firm.

The second volume reissued here, *Palliser's New Cottage Homes and Details*, continued the mail order method of the books of the late 1870s. This publication reflects the firm at its apogee. Many of the designs date from the period before the firm moved in the summer of 1883 from Bridgeport to New York City.[18] This book was not published until 1887, however, and thus must be seen as a very selective portfolio. By careful examination of the plates it is possible to distinguish a variety of layouts and several techniques of illustration, suggesting the contributions of a number of designers, for by this time the office was dozens strong.

Stylistically, *New Cottage Homes* is in the mainstream of architectural fashion, and reveals the more popular aspects of the English and American Queen Anne modes. Indeed, some of the designs resemble quite closely previously published works by well-known architects. Design 78, for example, could easily have been inspired by the cottages of Bruce Price,[19] while the general massing of Design 159 might be compared to the contemporary country houses by Lamb and Rich or Cabot and Chandler. Even in this later case, however, the Palliser effort is to transform this massing into a double house.

As the subtitle indicates, the designs include "low-priced, medium and first-class Cottages, Villas, Farm Houses, Town and Country Places, Houses for the Seashore, the South, and for Summer and Winter Resorts, etc.," and the variety of forms and materials reflects this range in class and price. For while the Pallisers were providing a great volume of plans by mail, they continued to believe in the principle that each design must be tailored to the individual client's needs. This point was stressed by the authors in their "Prefatory" and "Introductory" comments as they reviewed their own success and the rise of their imitators. The authors may well have had in mind a firm such as that of R. W. Shoppell[20] when they cautioned, "Please bear in mind that we are not in the ready-made plan business, and in all our experience, serving as we have upwards of two thousand clients all over the United States by correspondence, we have not found two persons wanting to build just the same house . . ."[21]

In the succeeding years the Pallisers broadened their efforts to aid client and builder alike. Whereas the firm's earlier publications had included only a few institutional designs, these building types were now featured in separate volumes, such as *Palliser's Commonsense School Architecture* (c. 1889, 1892), and *Palliser's Court Houses, Village, Town and City Halls, Jails, and Plans of Other Public Buildings* (1889). The firm offered numerous opportunities for self-improvement in architecture and the building trades, acting as a clearing house for hundreds of architectural publications, both foreign and domestic,[22] as a commercial outlet for drafting instruments and supplies,[23] and as an educational facility by providing "A Thorough, Practical System of Home Study." [24] The last-named endeavor may well rank as the earliest architectural correspondence school in the country.

Early in his career George Palliser had recognized the opportunity of providing tastefully designed, practical housing at moderate cost. As a carpenter-turned-architect, he identified with the needs and desires of the lower and middle classes, and, in the democratic spirit of his adopted country, Palliser developed his method of individualized, mail-order design. Thus, the importance of the two books presented here lies not merely in representing the Pallisers' approach to high-style design, but in demonstrating the method by which their buildings, and others like them, came to be built in villages, towns and suburbs throughout the country.

Michael A. Tomlan
Muncie, Indiana
July, 1978

NOTES

1. Twenty-one publications have been identified. The most comprehensive list of works by the firm and by the brothers individually remains *The National Union Catalog of Pre-1956 Imprints* (Volume 438). Even this, however, does not cite the following works by Palliser, Palliser and Company:

Palliser's Improved Form of Building Contract with Bond (Bridgeport, Conn.: [1881]).

Palliser's Full Working Plans and Specifications for Modern Eight-Room Cottage with Tower (Bridgeport, Conn.: 1882).

Palliser's Model Homes. Showing a Variety of Designs for Model Dwellings. Fifteenth Thousand. (New York: 1883).

Palliser's Specification Blanks, Consisting of Masons', Carpenters', Painters', Slaters', Tinners', Plumbers', Heaters', and Gas-Pipers' Specifications for Brick and Frame Houses at Any Cost (Bridgeport, Conn.: [1886]).

In addition, it would be well to point out that *Palliser's Model Homes for the People* (Bridgeport, Conn.: 1876) should be attributed to George Palliser and not to the firm, which was formed only in late 1877.

2. The birth date of George Palliser and the death date of Charles remain uncertain. In the case of the former, while 1849 has been generally accepted, census data in this country and a check of the registration of births in the General Register Office in London both seem to indicate a birth date in mid-1848. As for the latter, no obituary has yet been located. His last known works, however, are dated 1908.

3. Even before the Civil War the authors of the most prominent architectural stylebooks—Downing, Wheeler, Vaux, Sloan, Elliott, and Holly—all had suggested to their readers that an architect be consulted before building. H. W. Cleaveland and the Backus Brothers had even gone so far as to lithograph their drawings for designs illustrated in their book *Village and Farm Cottages* (1857). None of these authors, however, openly solicited or emphasized mail order design. After the Civil War, while designs were occasionally provided

by mail, the idea of openly developing a mail-order practice was not fully realized until undertaken by George Palliser. Thereafter several carpenter-architect-publishers entered the field, the most prominent being R. W. Shoppell of New York, W. J. Keith of Minneapolis and G. F. Barber of Knoxville. Others included: F. P. Allen and D. S. Hopkins, of Grand Rapids; F. L. Smith, J. F. & G. H. Smith, of Boston; W. K. Johnston and W. A. Radford, of Chicago; Child and DeGoll, and W. H. Abbott, Jr., of New York; E. E. Holman of Philadelphia; H. C. Chivers of St. Louis; and J. Rice of Clinton, Iowa.

4. "Obituary," *The Greenburgh Register*, April 10, 1903, p. 4. My thanks to Mrs. George Graham of Dobbs Ferry, New York, for providing me with this information.

5. *Holbrooks Newark City Directory for the Year ending April 1, 1870* (Newark, N. J.: Stephen A. Holbrook, 1870).

6. "Obituary," *The Greenburgh Register, op. cit.* The first contemporary reference to George Palliser in the *Bridgeport Daily Standard* appears on September 20, 1873, p. 3, which notes he is designing "a block of houses, eight in number, from a style of English basement houses in Jersey City..."

7. *Bridgeport Daily Standard*, November 7, 1874, p. 3; December 17, 1874, p. 3; December 18, 1874, p. 3; and January 26, 1876, p. 3.

8. *Bridgeport Daily Standard*, September 15, 1875, p. 3.

9. *Bridgeport Daily Standard*, January 21, 1875, p. 3.

10. Palliser, George, *Palliser's Model Homes for the People. A Complete Guide to the Proper and Economical Erection of Buildings.* (Bridgeport, Conn.: Gould & Stiles, Steam Job Printers, 1876), p. 1.

11. *Bridgeport Daily Standard*, October 14, 1876, p. 3. Succeeding advertisements by Palliser in the paper urge the reader to send for the booklet.

12. *Bridgeport Daily Standard*, January 2, 1878, p. 3 and January 3, 1878, p. 3.

13. My thanks to a recent owner of the house, Mrs. Lenox White of Canaan, Vermont, for providing this information.

14. *Bridgeport Daily Standard*, November 4, 1878, p. 3.

15. Palliser, Palliser & Co., *Palliser's Model Homes, Showing a Variety of Designs for Model Dwellings...* (New York: Palliser, Palliser & Co., 1883) [p. 4].

16. Palliser, Palliser & Co., *Palliser's Memorials and Headstones* (New York: J. S. Ogilvie Publishing Co., 1891), inside front cover.

17. "Obituary," *The Greenburgh Register, op. cit.*

18. See the Bridgeport City Directories for 1882, 1883 and 1884, published and compiled by Price, Lee & Co.

19. This comparison is all the more interesting when one notes that eight of the thirty-two plates collected in Palliser's *Selected Details of Interior and Exterior Finish for Architects, Carpenters and Builders* were by Bruce Price.

20. Robert W. Shoppell of New York City was probably the first to mimic Palliser's method, by offering mail order designs through his Co-operative Building Plan Association, which began about 1880.

21. Palliser, Palliser & Co., *Palliser's New Cottage Homes and Details* (New York: Palliser, Palliser & Co., 1887) [p. 9].

22. See for example, the advertisement pages in Palliser, Palliser & Co., *Palliser's Model Dwellings* (New York: J. S. Ogilvie, Publisher, 1891).

23. *Ibid.*, p. 93.

24. *Ibid.*, p. 91.

Please note: For the sake of comparison and to put the first facsimile into proper chronological perspective, we have reproduced, on the next two pages, the original title-page from *American Cottage Homes* and its "Preface." Then follows the original title-page from *American Architecture* and the balance of this volume in facsimile.

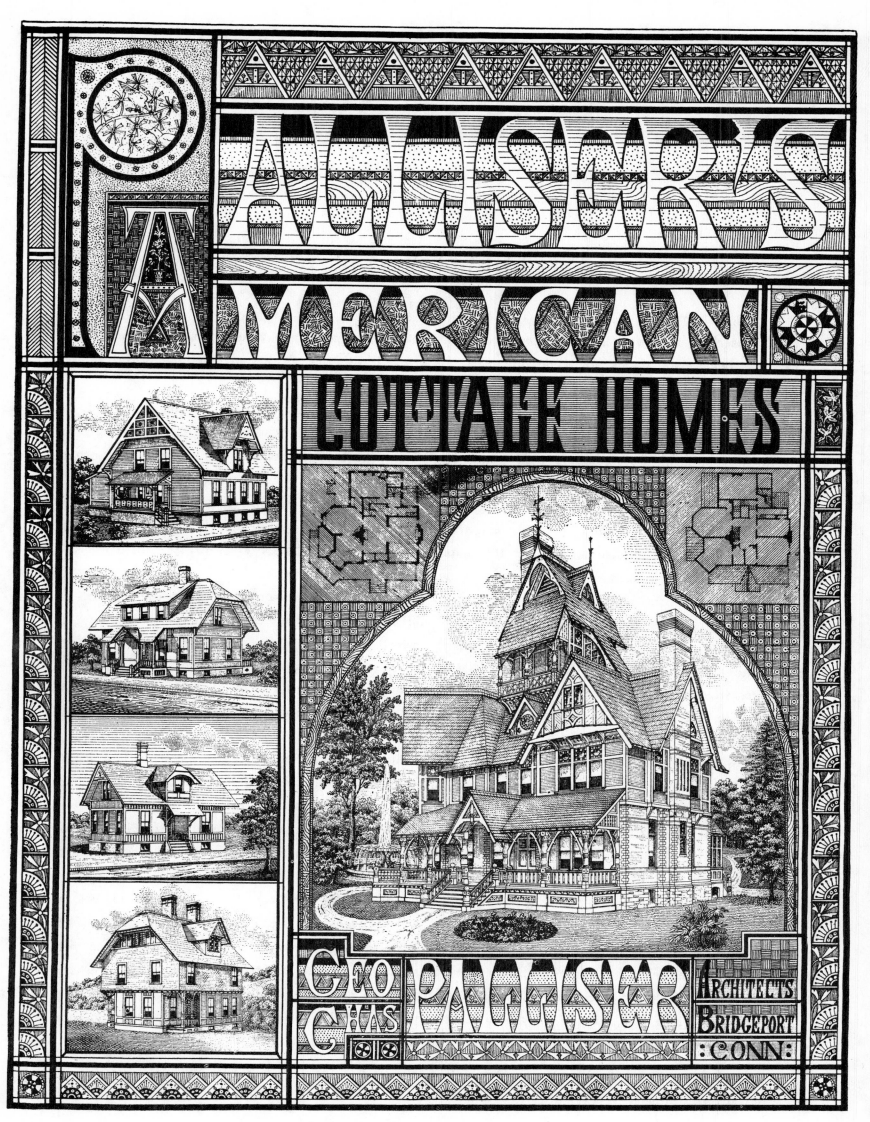

PALLISER'S AMERICAN COTTAGE HOMES

GEO. PALLISER CHAS. PALLISER

ARCHITECTS BRIDGEPORT CONN.

Copyright 1878, by Palliser, Palliser & Co., Bridgeport, Conn.

PUBLISHED BY PALLISER, PALLISER & CO., ARCHITECTS, BRIDGEPORT, CONN.

PREFACE.

IN presenting to the public a new work on Architecture, we have endeavored to meet a demand that has been made on us, for some time past, for practical designs of low and medium priced houses suited to the masses of our country.

We have endeavored, by careful study of proportion and distribution of parts, to combine good design with practical, convenient plans and sound construction; in fact our aim has been, to get the best effect in design in the simplest, most common sense, and least expensive manner, as it is not expense and ornate decorations, which so many ignorantly believe to be the highest attainment of architecture, but design, which produces true beauty and graceful appearance. The same materials and expense thrown away on an ugly, ill-proportioned building, if guided by good design, would produce an elegant building, and this is why the architect is brought into requisition, to treat the materials placed in his hands so as to give an expression of beauty to the simplest form.

It is an erroneous idea, that it is necessary to enclose convenience and comfort in the internal arrangements with ugliness, or that it is impossible to obtain a pleasing and effective design with a good plan and a modern construction. We have seen buildings which, externally, were perfect, but their plans of interior arrangement were absolute failures, being without a closet or pantry and devoid of the comfort and conveniences which one would expect to find. The first and main object of consideration should be the plan, the design being of a pliant nature and easily adapted to the ever-varying forms of comfortable and convenient plans.

One of the objects of this work is to show, that in the erection of buildings the last named principles may be combined; also, we hope that it may prove suggestive to those intending to build and to mechanics engaged in the erection of buildings. We are inclined to think that, in many instances, the ideas contained will be something more than suggestive, and they will no doubt be found useful in assisting those who propose the erection of buildings, to decide on the character of the building they wish to erect.

It has not been stated on the Plates where and for whom the buildings have been erected, yet the greater portion of the designs have been executed, or are in progress of execution in different parts of the country. In this we hope to have shown what can be done in obtaining good and convenient plans, with tasty and effective exteriors, at very low prices; the present state of the country has made this a necessity, and has been one of the chief considerations in preparing these designs.

The prices given will only do for the same specification the designs were executed by, and the same locality, and will vary according to location and style of material and finish used in construction.

PALLISER, PALLISER & CO.,

BRIDGEPORT, CONN., January 1, 1878.

PALLISER'S
AMERICAN ARCHITECTURE;

OR

Every Man a Complete Builder.

BY

PALLISER, PALLISER & CO., ARCHITECTS,

NEW YORK.

Authors of " Palliser's Useful Details,"   " Palliser's New Cottage Homes and Details,"   " Palliser's
Building Specifications and Contract Blanks," etc., etc.

(Copyright 1888, by Palliser, Palliser & Co.)

J. S. OGILVIE, PUBLISHER.
57 ROSE STREET, NEW YORK.   182 WABASH AVENUE, CHICAGO.

" When we mean to build,
We first survey the plat then draw the model;
And, when we see the figure of the house,
Then must we rate the cost of erection ;
Which, if we find outweighs ability,
What do we then but draw anew the model
In fewer offices ; or, at least, desist
To build at all?   Much more in this great work
Which is almost to pluck a kingdom down,
And set another up should we survey
The plat of situation, and the model ;
Consent upon a sure foundation ;
Question surveyors ; know our own estate,
How able such a work to undergo ;
To weigh against his opposite : or else
We fortify in paper and in figures,
Using the names of men instead of men ;
Like one that draws the model of a house
Beyond his power to build it ; who, half through
Gives o'er, and leaves his part created cost
A naked subject to the weeping clouds,
And waste for churlish Winter's tyranny."

KING HENRY IV., Act 1, Scene 3.

"If half the thought which is given to
obscure questions in theology or metaphysics
had been given to the question of making men
more comfortable by building better habitations
for them, what a much happier and more comfortable world it would have been !"

SIR A. HELPS.

PREFATORY.

The title of this book sufficiently indicates its character to which we may add that the aim has been to present a variety of plans which, with few additions and changes, can be adapted to the requirements and individual tastes of those about to build, whether living in town or country.

The plans have been built from and their practicability proven, giving also correct figures of cost, but, owing to the variation in prices of materials and labor in different localities and at different times, they should be accepted with caution and as not adapted to every circumstance and locality.

The plans shown give a great variety of arrangement and style, and are well adapted to meet the wants of the masses for tasty, convenient and economical buildings ; in fact, this book is offered as a plain and practical aid to people who desire to build at moderate cost, though it is not supposed that everyone will be able to find exactly the very thing he needs, but he will be able to learn what at least are his requirements, and gather ideas so as to be able to meet them, and he can procure from us at reasonable rates working plans and specifications with any changes desired for any plan shown in this work, or for that matter in any book, periodical or journal ever published.

Very respectfully,

PALLISER, PALLISER & CO.

PLATE 1

Represents the title-page of this work, which has been deemed best to be made a useful plate, by showing the perspective views of Designs 1, 2, 3, and 23, these designs being without views on the plates where they are illustrated.

The large perspective view is of a neat cottage erected at Seaside Park, Bridgeport, Conn., one of the most charming places in New England. The first story is built of fine Trenton pressed brick, trimmed with buff and chocolate-colored brick and Longmeadow brown stone, the second story being of timber construction; roofs covered with black slate, ridges of terra cotta; upper part of all windows filled with stained glass; windows fitted with rolling Venetian blinds. The first floor is finished in ash, with paneled ceilings and hardwood floor; second floor in pine, finished in natural color. All rooms have open fire-places, built of buff brick and furnished with hard-wood mantels.

First floor contains main hall, ten feet wide, having tiled floor and with large open fire-place in same, and is connected with parlor by sliding doors, so that on special occasions they can be thrown together. The dining-room and library are connected in like manner, and have a handsome conservatory with tiled floor adjoining on south side. A toilet-room is placed in rear of main hall, which is convenient to the stairs and back hall. The kitchen is in rear wing, and communicates with dining-room through waiter's pantry. Store pantry and ice-closet are on the north side, the ice being put into ice-tank from outside, through a door provided for that purpose. Back hall contains back stairs, also communicates with cellar, kitchen and main hall.

Second floor—Five chambers, three dressing rooms, bath-room, cedar and linen closets. A fine room on third floor is provided for servant and there is also a large attic for storage.

The room in tower is 10 x 12 feet in size, with large open fire-place; is designed for use, and commands an excellent view of Long Island Sound and the surrounding country.

Laundry and drying room are placed in basement under kitchen.

This cottage is intended for a first-class residence, is furnished with all modern improvements and conveniences, and heated by indirect heat.

This handsome and popular residence has been adopted and erected with modifications by many people all over the United States and Canada at various cost, ranging from $4,750 to $13,000.

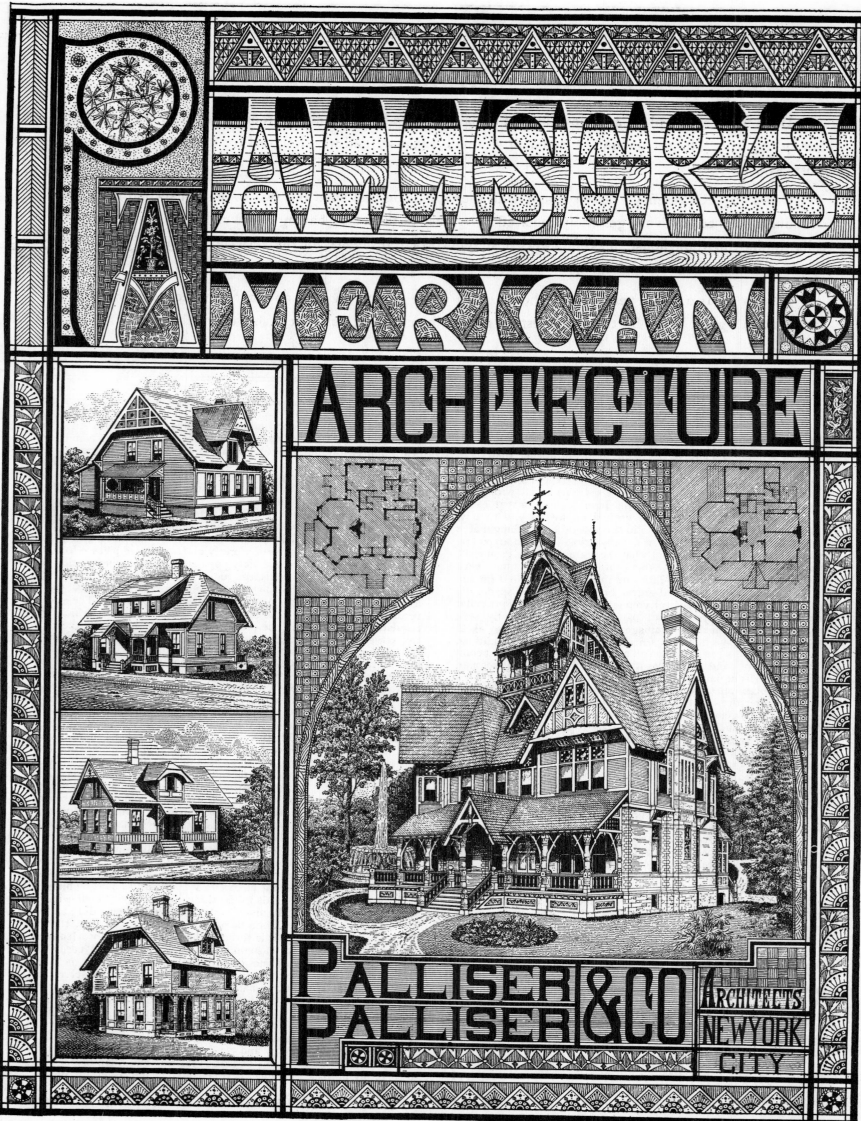

PALLISER'S AMERICAN ARCHITECTURE

PALLISER, PALLISER & CO. ARCHITECTS NEW YORK CITY

PLATE 2.

DESIGN 1—Shows plans and elevations of a plain cottage house of eleven rooms, suited to the wants of a family requiring a large amount of room at a small expense, and was designed for a Western farm house. Cost, $1,500.

DESIGN 2—Represents a tasty cottage, with four rooms on first floor and two rooms on second floor, and contains all the convenience generally required in a house of this class, having good closets and pantry, with cellar under the whole house, making a very desirable cottage residence for the very small sum of $850. (See specifications in latter part of book.)

DESIGN 3—Is a small, neat cottage house, with three rooms on first and two on second floor, which would make a good house for the southwestern part of the country; estimated cost of which is $800.

HINTS ON BUILDING.

One of the first and most important things to be settled in the erection of a home is a site, and it is not at all surprising that there are so many who never give the matter of location the first thought, further than, is it a good neighborhood; are there good neighbors; and is the price reasonable. To such we say this is all wrong and we speak from actual experience. John Jones, who is a real estate agent, and has the sale of a piece of ground he wishes you to buy, will not point out to you the defects in the ground or anything that is detrimental to the property, but will fully explain its good points. The first thing to do is to find out what the nature of the ground is, as some locations are resisting—others soft and compressible to various degrees; is it made ground? for you must only build on firm and solid ground; or is it a sand and gravel bottom? Take a spade, dig down four or five feet and see for yourself what it is. If your cellar bottom is placed in a layer of hard pan, as we have frequently seen them, then the treatment of drainage should be different, so as to keep it dry; and while it makes a firm foundation for the building, yet sand or gravel is preferable on all accounts, for if the weight compresses the bed of sand and forces it to settle, the settling is regular, and hence free from danger.

The alluvia formed by sluggish water courses that naturally flow through the interstices of a hard or clayey soil are very injurious to the health of the occupants of a house erected over such ground; and in the erection of such great care should be exercised in the matter of drainage, so as to keep the cellar bottom dry and free from moisture; the foundation walls should descend below the cellar bottom sufficient to allow a drain to be laid on and around the outside of walls, and the bottom part of this drain should be one foot below the level of cellar floor: this drain should entirely encompass the building at a distance of a few inches from walls and the water as it sinks through the soil will be thus arrested in its progress by the drain and drawn off from the building, leaving the entire ground under your house free from moisture. This drain will carry the water where you wish, and can have branches connecting with roof leaders to carry off the waste water from the roof; also the necessary branches can be connected from inside, so as to carry away all surplus and waste water from all parts of the house.

We strongly advise this method of draining all houses, no matter what the soil may be; and even if it costs a little more to put in the drains this way it is preferable to any other. The leader pipes from the roofs form a series of ventilating shafts for the drains, a feature that is desirable and necessary, as they will carry the gases generated in the sewer up above the roof of the house where it will pass away and do no harm; care should be taken not to have any leader openings in roof near to or under upper story windows; there should also be a running trap between the connection to the house and the sewer in main pipe; this should be put as near the house as practicable and a leader branch or vent pipe connected as near to it as possible—this for proper ventilation, as the trap is liable to syphon dry if not ventilated.

A cellar bottom should be thoroughly cemented tight with cement concrete, which should be not less than two inches in depth to obtain a good bottom, and should not be made of nearly all sand or gravel—as some masons try to do, presuming to save cement—but should have a proper proportion of good cement thoroughly mixed in with it and properly laid.

When the people who build homes have had the experience the writer of this has, and had to fight scarlet fever and diphtheria and grim death himself through the want of a proper system of sewerage, then they will perhaps begin to realize that this is indeed one of the first and most important things to be taken up in the planning and erection of a home, and one which will not bear a saving at the spigot and wholesale waste at the bung hole.

What is architecture? What is anything? If we look out of our windows what do we see? perhaps nothing but the verdant fields covered with their vegetation and dotted here and there with green trees, which at this time form a pretty and attractive picture to look upon, or we see perhaps a thickly populated district where little else is to be seen but brick walls, tin roofs, skylights to light down into bodies of stores where fine displays of fancy and useful goods of every description are seen, to meet the wants of all classes. The green verdant fields we see are the natural results of the seasons, which are regulated by the hand of the divine architect, and constitute the motive power whereby all living creatures on land move and have their being; the houses, walls, roofs and skylights we see are a necessity that we must have to shelter us from the wind and rain and allow us to see and act in places where but for them it would be cold and dark; and as we look out and see these things, and reason, we find that these forms are an expression of our wants and thus have good reason for existence.

As the ancients found at the commencement of the world that it was necessary to protect themselves from the wind and the rain and cold, they undoubtedly went to work with such materials as they had at hand and erected for themselves huts or tents, made probably with sticks or leaves, or perhaps mud, and as they progressed in civilization they thus were educating themselves to better supply their wants, and as one improvement was made it suggested another; and so on, *ad infinitum*, until we have now reached an era of civilization that one hundred years ago was never dreamt of, nor would have been credited. As the erection of the humble abodes in ancient times was a direct result of necessity, so it is now; and as the times have so changed and men's ideas with them, we have architecture on an improved scale. If anyone doubts this we advise him to betake himself to the woods, and look about and see what he can do with regard to housing himself with the means and materials found there, and no doubt in nine cases out of ten he would not do much better than the ancients did; and as it is a necessity that we should be housed and protected from the inclemency of the weather, it is through this necessity that we learn to reason and to apply our reasoning powers to each special case, for what answers one case will not do for another. There is no method, no recipe, no procedure that can be applied, for we must observe circumstances, facts, habits, climate and hygeian conditions as well as the individual wants of the occupants. And as the materials and means of execution are every day modified or changed, we must follow these variations, and a good practitioner in the art must have a working power and independence of character, a thorough knowledge of business, enough energy and tenacity, and assert his authority—saying I will only accept this or that so far as I find them useful, and to serve my purpose; he must have character, and ascertain by his reasoning and working, and not allow himself to be seduced by attractive appearances; must express his thoughts clearly and reflect

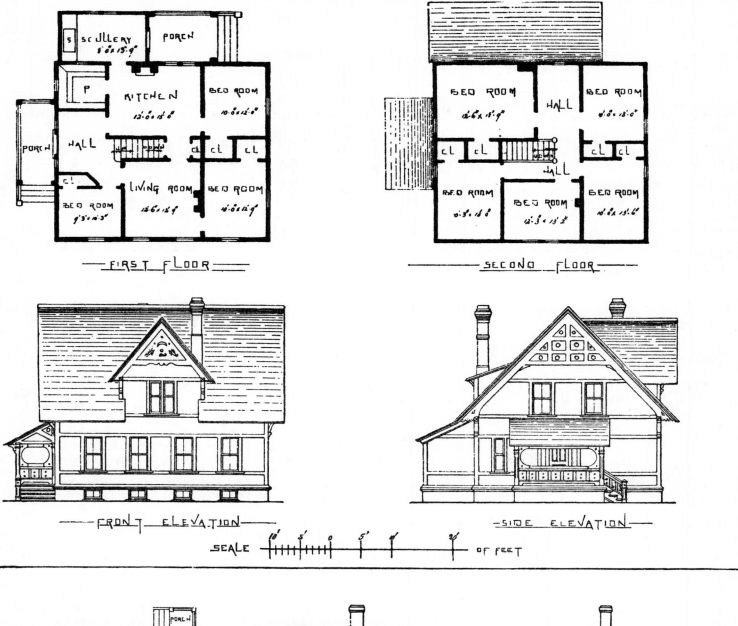

FIRST FLOOR

SECOND FLOOR

FRONT ELEVATION

SIDE ELEVATION

SCALE OF FEET

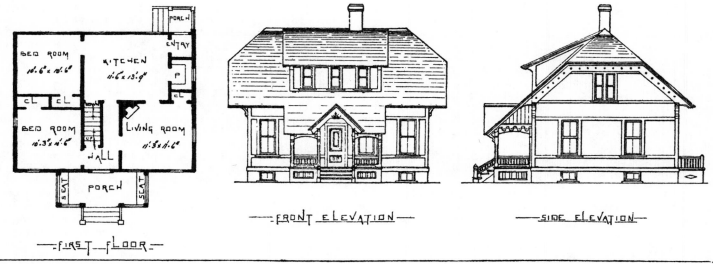

FIRST FLOOR

FRONT ELEVATION

SIDE ELEVATION

FIRST FLOOR

SIDE ELEVATION

FRONT ELEVATION

PLATE 3.

DESIGN 4—Illustrates a one-story cottage, having four rooms on first floor and room for two bedrooms in attic, which, for convenience and economy, speaks plainly for itself, and when executed makes a home which no one need be ashamed of ; it is equally adapted to city or country and can be erected in a neat and substantial manner for $700.

DESIGN 5—Six-room cottage, suitable for erection on a small city lot.   Cost, $900.

DESIGN 6—Is a small cottage of two rooms on first floor, with good pantry and closet : stairs to loft over and cellar under.   Cost, $325.

before speaking, and if nature has endowed him with genius, such will be—if his reasoning powers are properly applied—a splendid compliment to his faculties.   But without reasoning, genius would only serve as a stumbling block and had better lay dormant.

What has been done before our time must not be ignored, as it is a good acquired, a common storehouse filled with the reasonings and works of our predecessors, and which has been handed down to our own time for us to start from. Architecture is an art, and the true architect should so wield this art that it be but the faithful expression of the times as we see them, that the building may be in truth the envelope of that which it contains.   To be a good architect is to be a good reasoner, and to reason well is to work well, for the one is subservient to the other.   All the essential conditions must be thoroughly reflected on—the client's needs fully known.   Then the result can be placed on paper, for nothing must be left to chance ; every function must know and fill its place, and every particle in value must be in relation to the whole, so as to render them intelligible to those who execute them.   This is what is commonly meant by Architecture.

The simplest way to study architecture is by practising it, and though many are taught to conceive and plan buildings that cannot be constructed, only on paper, under the shallow pretext of preserving high art, they soon tire of putting these conceptions on paper, when they see the success that attends the working and practical architect, whose buildings are daily growing more and more beautiful the more difficulties he has to encounter.   Construction outside of a certain scientific and practical knowledge can only be studied by experience, a habit of reasoning and obedience to the rules of good sense, and he who disdains this natural faculty under the pretence that it hampers inspiration, will always see his conceptions applied to paper where they hurt nobody ; for to carry out such whims costs dear, and as practical men always exercise their reasoning powers and good sense in erecting a home, they then have a right to consider it inopportune and stop before they begin.

There are a great number of people who, intending to build for themselves homes, have an idea that only symmetrical houses look well.   This class of people are to be met with almost every day in the week in the experience of an architect who is consulted by a large number of clients, and we have frequently been very much tried in our patience and labors in preparing plans to suit the wants of such people, therefore we now propose to have a few words to say to this class of clients.

A close observer in traveling through the country towns and villages in almost every portion of our country, cannot fail to notice the sameness and monotony of most country residences, which are nearly all built after one order, and very frequently a large number in each village all just alike, presenting symmetrical aspects.   There is the country house of, say, from 36 to 40 feet front ; the front door in the center, two windows on each side, two story high, and roof about 1-3 pitch, with that same old box cornice—we presume they copied from what Noah had on the Ark.   This matter of symmetry is a very grave question, and one which may work well enough on large public buildings but should have nothing to do with the design and arrangement of private dwellings. Fancy your building a house with the sitting and dining room on the south side, to which you want bay windows ; and as the kitchen comes on the north side, as it is necessary to have a symmetrical house, it must have a bay window there also, or else dispense with the bay on south side.   There are undoubtedly a great

many people who are willing to satisfy their vain pleasure of displaying outside, regular and monumental exteriors, by sacrificing the everyday conveniences which are so essential to the comforts of a home.

Symmetry applied to private architecture is an invention that has had its day and is completely run out, except in rare cases, where old fogyism holds the sway and rules supreme.   The most convenient homes are those which are planned with a special reference to satisfy the needs of its occupants and so as to avoid all useless expenditures —and we might add these are the most pleasing in point of aspect, for the simple reason that they clearly show the purposes for which they are built.

The ancients never troubled themselves about symmetry in their residences ; the houses at Pompeii are not built with any regard to it, and the villa or country house, of which Pliny has left us a full description, does not give us any appearance of symmetry.

In designing homes we must follow the laws of common sense, and not sacrifice interior comfort for the satisfaction of displaying an outside show which is offensive to the cultivated eye.   But let us have homes wherein nothing whatever is conceded to a false luxury, and where harmony says that though here is a small and there a large opening to suit the interior requirements, they are so grouped and blended together that they produce a pleasing and picturesque exterior and which, when finished, will cost us no more, as we shall have nothing concealed, nothing artificial, nothing useless ; all the details throughout, though modest, being direct results and a necessity of the structure and requisite to suit the needs of the occupants, so that the structure when built will always permit you to see its organs and how these organs work.   This sort of construction is the only satisfactory one to people of sense and taste, there being a good reason for it.

In building, every detail is worthy of close attention and everything should be taken into account.   In all things the way to avoid an evil is to analyze and search for its cause and to determine its effects, for we can only appreciate what is good by a knowledge of what is bad ; so much so that in the absence of the bad we cannot admit that the good exists.   And it requires a large experience to know what must be avoided in building, while if you are born an architect you will readily discover in what the good and beautiful exists ; and if not, all the examples that the world contains will not give you talent. A sight of the finest achievements of the art may pervert the minds of some, if when they see them no one is there to explain how the authors succeeded in making them beautiful, because they avoided falling into such and such faults.

An exact mind and experience is only acquired by long and tedious study, and the observation and experience aid us to recognize what is bad and avoid it ; besides what is good in one place is bad in another, by reason of climate, habits, and the quality of the materials and their adaptability to this or that local circumstance.   You cannot establish absolute rules in building, since experience, reasoning and reflection must always intervene when building is undertaken ; all the special circumstances which come up in an architect's career have to be dealt with and worked out in a certain method to solve the problem, and it requires no small amount of intelligence and observation to work out these cases in a manner that no given rule ever yet invented could foresee.

There is in every community a class of persons who sow broadcast their advice to any and every one with whom they come in con-

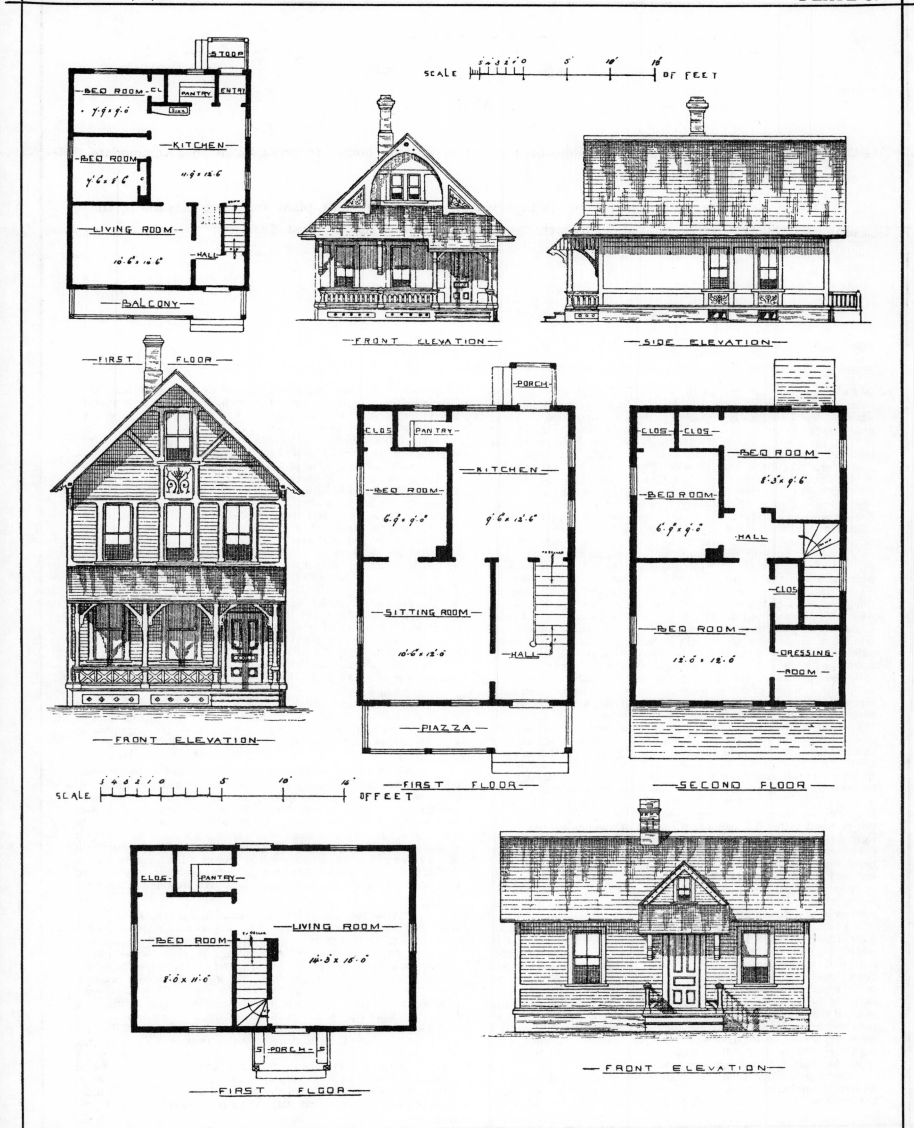

BED ROOM–CL · 7'·9"x9'·0"

PANTRY ENTRY STOOP

Sink

BED ROOM 7'·6"x8'·6"

KITCHEN 11·9"x12·6"

LIVING ROOM 10·6"x12·6"

HALL

BALCONY

— FIRST FLOOR —

— FRONT ELEVATION —

SCALE 5 4 3 2 1 0   5   10   15   OF FEET

— SIDE ELEVATION —

CLOS PANTRY

BED ROOM 6'·9"x9'·0"

PORCH

KITCHEN 9'·6"x12·6"

SITTING ROOM 10·6"x12·6"

HALL

PIAZZA

— FIRST FLOOR —

CLOS CLOS

BED ROOM 6'·9"x9'·0"

BED ROOM 8'·5"x9'·6"

HALL

CLOS

BED ROOM 12'·0"x12·6"

DRESSING ROOM

— SECOND FLOOR —

— FRONT ELEVATION —

SCALE 5 4 3 2 1 0   5   10   15   OF FEET

CLOS PANTRY

BED ROOM 8'·0"x11'·0"

LIVING ROOM 14·5"x15·0"

PORCH

— FIRST FLOOR —

— FRONT ELEVATION —

PLATE 4.

DESIGN 7—Shows plans and elevations of a two-story cottage house, so arranged as to accommodate either one or two families. Cost, $1,000.

DESIGN 8—Illustrates a neat six-room cottage, giving two sets of floor plans for same elevations, the changes in plans being brought about by a change in the location of stairs. Cost, $875.

tact who may be interested in the erection of buildings—men who have read and traveled and who know a little of everything, and whose opinions are greatly respected in their neighborhoods. These men always pretend to give a simple solution to everything, whether politics, science, commerce or even the arts ; they have themselves built houses, and were their own architect, making their own plans and contracts, treating directly with suppliers and supervising the works—men who are by themselves regarded as infallible judges on every subject that comes up ; they are honest, polite, and sometimes even generous to those who may, through interest or conviction, flatter their eccentricities. Such are some whose experience has cost them dear, and having had such misadventures are ever ready to try help snatch one—a brand from the burning as it were—and who are ever ready with "Will you permit me a few remarks ;" and they proceed after this wise : "Now really this all looks very nice on paper, and seems to be excellent ; still as I have seen and compared a good deal, I tell you frankly I don't think that this is really just the thing for you ; excuse me, but do you see the size of this room ? why, it don't come in to suit carpets ; now when I have built a house, I have always made it so as to fit carpets, and I should strongly advise the making of this room eight inches wider, so as to accommodate five breadths of carpet. Now this I think is an indispensable feature, as it never seemed to me right to turn the carpet under ;" still, when you inform him that the floor in question is to be of hardwood with a border of darker wood around it, he is never taken back but still insists that the change should be made, as it may be carpeted some time. " Yes, there are some very good ideas in the plan, but I think if I were you I would throw those two small rooms into one and have one large room. I have seen houses something like this arranged that way ; then I think instead of passing through this closet from dining-room to kitchen, a direct communication would be better, as you would not have but one door to pass through"—he never thinks why there are two doors—" my house is that way and it is very handy "—perhaps so ! " then I cannot say that I like this large roof—it seems to me there is too much of it ; now I would stop this part and flatten this porch-roof instead of running the main roof right down, as it would not look so long ; it is well enough for English houses, but it never seemed to me right to have it so here—and besides, you seldom see such roofs here." These men don't know why such a roof is better for this climate than for England, nor does he see why you should be so foolish as to go and erect anything that is in accordance with what he does or has done ; you must share his opinion or you do not know anything.

You may be very inexperienced yourself in building, but if so your architect should know enough for both himself and you, and while your busy neighbor may ply you with his wholesale advice, you need not sacrifice yourself to any whims or suggestions he may make. Never mind how much he don't like your large roof, your gables, or your internal arrangements, if they are what you want ; go straight ahead in the path you have marked out and let your advisers go their way ; if they want their ideas carried out let them do it themselves at their own cost—let them produce their own works of vanity erected for vanity's sake, or for desires of their own misapplied talents, reaping the reward of their folly, which will only be admired by themselves for their own lives and then abandoned.

Our experience has been very large with this class of advisers ; we have stumbled across them in our professional path so frequently that we now have a formula ready to salute them with, and while we

firmly believe that we shall never agree with such, we presume they have a reason of existence and a right to be heard, and if they would always let those who know more than themselves hear them, we should have no fault to find.

We feel it would be no trouble for us to fill a volume of 200 pages with advice given to our clients and criticism of the uninformed. Only a week or two ago one of our clients, 1,500 miles away, wrote us that he was not aware how many disinterested friends he possessed until he commenced building ; almost every one he met had something to say about what he was erecting—people seemed to think he was spending his money to suit them instead of himself. When we forwarded him the drawings, etc., we put him on guard against his friend's advice, and told him to go by the drawings and specifications and not to deviate from them, no matter what advice he got, and if he wished any information to communicate with us. He has done this, and says he threw overboard seven tons of everybody's advice and took only ours in the erection of his home ; if he had taken most of his friend's advice he would have built the usual large dry goods box with a flat roof ; but the result is very different, and as the press in speaking of it says : "It is a pretty residence, and Mr. and Mrs. ———— may well feel proud of their new and comfortable home."

Let your architect do the thinking for you which you pay him for, and you will save time, trouble—and most of all, expense.

"GENTLEMEN :

"I have been advised by some of my neighbors to dispense with the stone foundation for my house, and to cement the sides of the ground to form walls, starting the brick underpinning upon the ground. What would you advise me to do about it ?

"Yours, etc., W. J."

The above letter was received from a gentleman we had furnished with plans for a Cottage Home, and as we had given him full plans, working drawings and specifications for construction, we could not understand what he was driving at, and we had to think twice before attempting to answer it. In the first place we came to the conclusion, here is a gentleman who is troubled with the advice of his neighbors, which he probably thinks considerable of, who no doubt flocked around him like so many moths around a light, and he has no decided mind of his own, or else he would consult his drawings and specifications and be governed accordingly. We answered in this wise:

"DEAR SIR :

"Yours of the 2d inst. is at hand and contents noted. In reply would say we never yet in all our experience heard of such a mode of construction as referred to in your letter, and should certainly infer that your neighbors are strange people to advise you to do any such thing and we should think very ignorant in these matters and incapable of giving advice. We will suppose that you construct your wall in this way and watch the result say for one year. It is now an excellent time to build, the weather is fine and building operations can be pushed to good advantage. You get your cellar dug, but do not dig close up to the walls, to avoid the dirt falling in, and probably slope them to counteract this trouble. You level the top all around, so as to start your underpinning and run up the brick work from the ground line the proper height to receive the frame above. Well, this all looks very nice, everything going along pleasantly ; the frame is raised and sheathed and enclosed in good time, the floors are laid, partitions set, the walls plastered, and you pro-

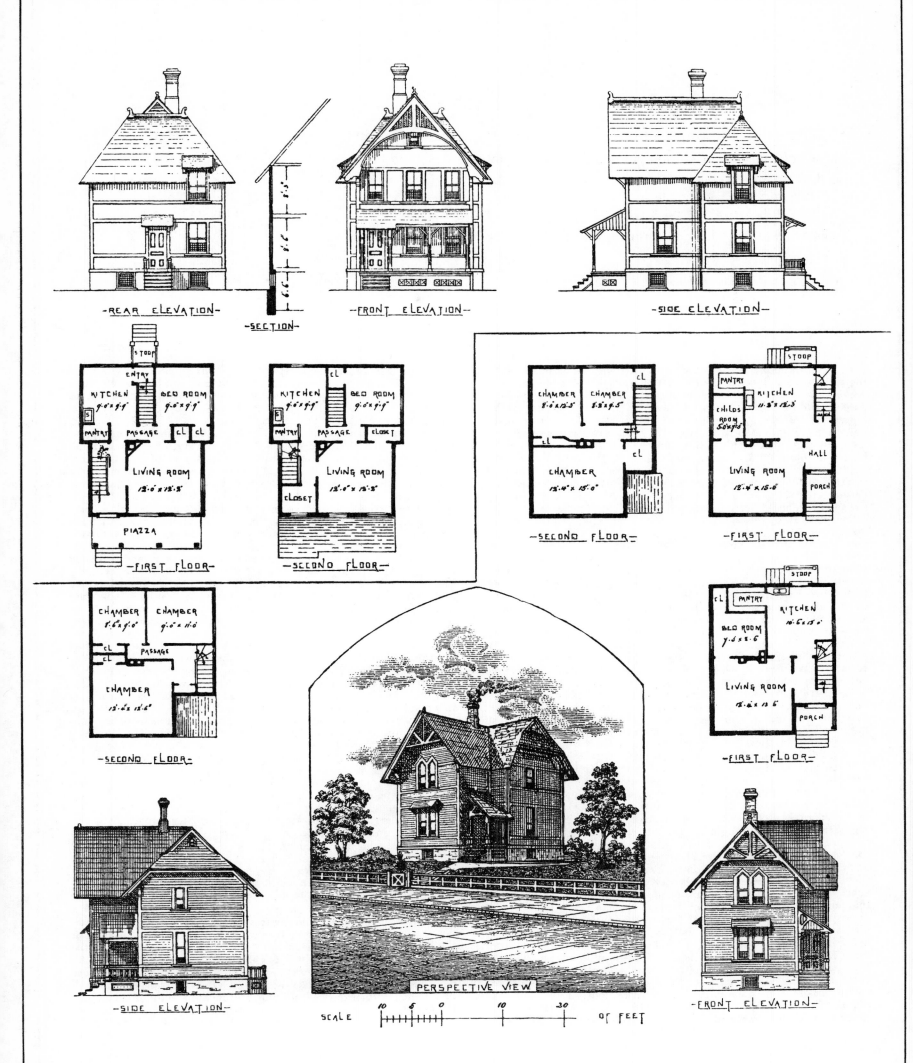

-REAR ELEVATION-

-SECTION-

-FRONT ELEVATION-

-SIDE ELEVATION-

KITCHEN 9'-0"x9'-9"

ENTRY

BED ROOM 9'-0"x9'-9"

PANTRY

PASSAGE

CL   CL

LIVING ROOM 12'-0"x12'-8"

PIAZZA

-FIRST FLOOR-

CL

KITCHEN 9'-0"x9'-9"

BED ROOM 9'-0"x9'-9"

PANTRY

PASSAGE

CLOSET

LIVING ROOM 12'-0"x12'-8"

CLOSET

-SECOND FLOOR-

CHAMBER 8'-0"x12'-5"

CHAMBER 8'-5"x9'-5"

CL

CL

CHAMBER 13'-4"x15'-0"

CL

-SECOND FLOOR-

STOOP

PANTRY

KITCHEN 11'-3"x12'-3"

CHILDS ROOM 5'-0"x9'-5"

LIVING ROOM 12'-4"x15'-0"

HALL

PORCH

-FIRST FLOOR-

CHAMBER 8'-6"x9'-0"

CHAMBER 9'-6"x11'-6"

CL

CL

PASSAGE

CHAMBER 13'-6"x12'-6"

-SECOND FLOOR-

STOOP

CL

PANTRY

KITCHEN 10'-6"x15'-0"

BED ROOM 7'-6"x8'-6"

LIVING ROOM 12'-6"x13'-6"

PORCH

-FIRST FLOOR-

PERSPECTIVE VIEW

SCALE ├┼┼┼┼┼┼┼┼┼┤ 10 5 0   10   30   OF FEET

-SIDE ELEVATION-

-FRONT ELEVATION-

PLATE 5.

DESIGN 9—Illustrates a two-story and attic cottage the floor plans of which explain themselves. The exterior is very plain yet neat in design. The mantel is designed to be of wood and the cut work picked out incolor. Cost, $1,400.

DESIGN 10—Is a good study for a four-room cottage, suited to the requirements of a small family, and was designed for a farm laborer's cottage. Cost $600.

ceed to finish up the inside work ; all still going along nicely, nothing to be seen amiss with the foundation walls, they are as firm as a rock, no cracks in the underpinning visible, and you begin to prepare for and do the cementing in the cellar, all the time congratulating yourself what a sensible man you are to take your friends' advice and save all that stone work, though it does take considerable cement to cement the sides ; why, how nice it looks! Certainly you have a far more solid appearing wall than rough stone would make, besides it is pleasanter to the eye. You get your house finished, painting done, and now you are moving in, putting down carpets and getting everything set to rights generally. All this time you have been busy as could be, and had no time to think further about your cellar walls ; however, Mrs. —— calls your attention to the door opening into the parlor ; it don't shut and catch properly—would you just fix it ; and upon examination you find it strikes the top corner of the casing. You think this strange ; why, it was all right a day or two ago ; and while you are casting your eyes up to examine the door you notice a crack in the angle of the wall and ceiling on both sides of the partition in the hall and parlor, which you think to yourself is only the natural result of slight shrinkage of timber, and something that always happens to a new house ; you get your carpenter to plane off the top corner of the door, the painter to touch it up, and all is straight again—no, not exactly. There is trouble with the windows in the rear angle of the dining room—they don't seem to fit as they did when you first moved in ; the sash locks bind and you cannot lock them. You begin to think the carpenter was not as particular about the fitting of the windows as he should have been. Of course this must be fixed, the windows must be locked ; and in the meantime you insert a stick from top of meeting rail of lower sash to lower edge of top rail on upper sash, as you have seen the carpenter fasten the windows before the locks were in place. Well, you wait a day or two and see your carpenter, he calls and looks at your windows, sees what is the matter and wonders how that came to fit so badly, as he fitted those very sash himself and knows full well he did not leave them in any such state as he now finds them ; he takes out the sash, planes off the corners where they bind, and makes them lock, although he cannot make the lock rails come together level as they ought to, yet they work all right, so that will do ; but stop ! Mrs. —— says will he just fix the pantry door—it touches on the bottom and shuts hard ; he lifts it off its hinges, eases it and replaces it. What he took off the bottom corner is wanting now on the top. Nothing like plenty of play you think—better have them small enough than be all the time troubled this way. Well, you think that now as you have the carpenter here you had better look over all doors, etc., and have a general fixing up ; you go all over the first floor and fix a catch here and a bolt there, and then pass up stairs to find the two windows in the rear gable over dining room don't work as well as they might ; you fix them. This closet door, which is just over pantry door, seems to bind a little, and the door into front chamber binds on the bottom. This door is over the parlor door, and as it is hinged on contrary side to parlor door, it binds on bottom in place of the top. You get everything put in working order, touch up your painting, and find you have considerable cracks in the wall ; you get a mason and have them all fixed, and now you think you can be at peace and have no more trouble ; you have often heard it said that the lumber will shrink and cause walls to crack, doors to sag and things to settle generally, and suppose your house is no worse than any other in this respect.

"You commenced building in spring ; the summer is passed and the leaves fallen from the trees—you have everything as you think made snug for winter ; you start up your fires, and all goes as merry as a marriage bell until Christmas morning, when you come down stairs and find you have three doors in your house that won't open. They seem to be loose enough on one end, but really it looks as if they were grown in on the other end. Finally you succeed in prying them open, only to find they cannot be shut again, and upon opening the window of your parlor you find the sash lock very hard to turn, and when it has been opened you cannot lock it again. It is impossible for you to understand what all this means, and it is such a bitter cold morning you cannot bother about it. Upon passing out of your front door you find that also troubled in the same way and don't operate properly ; the key turns hard in the lock, and when turned you cannot relock the door. You don't know what has got into your doors and windows, and with the thermometer at zero you don't feel like investigating the matter. Then what is it ? Why, dear sir, it is Jack. Don't you know him ? Jack Frost ; he has been in an elevating mood the last night or two, having now penetrated some fifteen inches into the ground, and as he burrows into the ground he expands, and as there is only one way for him to grow, and that upwards, why up he comes, and up your house comes with him ; and as the verandas keep off a good deal of frost from walls, where they are so covered up, there Jack has not gone as deep ; consequently one part of your house is raised somewhat higher than the others—hence the confusion among doors and windows. Things go on rising and falling, the doors shut and then they don't, and you are all the time fluctuating with the weather, now up and then down.

"When winter is over and Jack is leaving for foreign parts, you are in a general uproar. The water soaks through your beautiful and economical cellar wall, the cement flakes off in big pieces, bringing with it large pieces of earth, the water is oozing and trickling into your cellar and your whole house is in a general dilapidated condition, roof leaking at chimneys, and you are entirely discouraged. At this time, one year from commencement of building, what have you ? a rickety tumble-down house, not fit for man to live in and not safe. The way to avoid this trouble—the same old story we have repeated to our clients hundreds of times—is to keep both ears open; one to take in the advice from your neighbors and the other to let it out. Read, mark, learn and inwardly digest the drawings and specifications we sent you. Go by them, deviating neither to the right or the left and the general result will be as directly opposite from the result as here described as it is possible to be—for as a sure foundation is the keystone of success in everything, so must every house have a sure foundation under it, so that all its parts when built will be retained in their proper position, and insure a harmonious working of the whole. Yours very truly,
"PALLISER, PALLISER & CO."

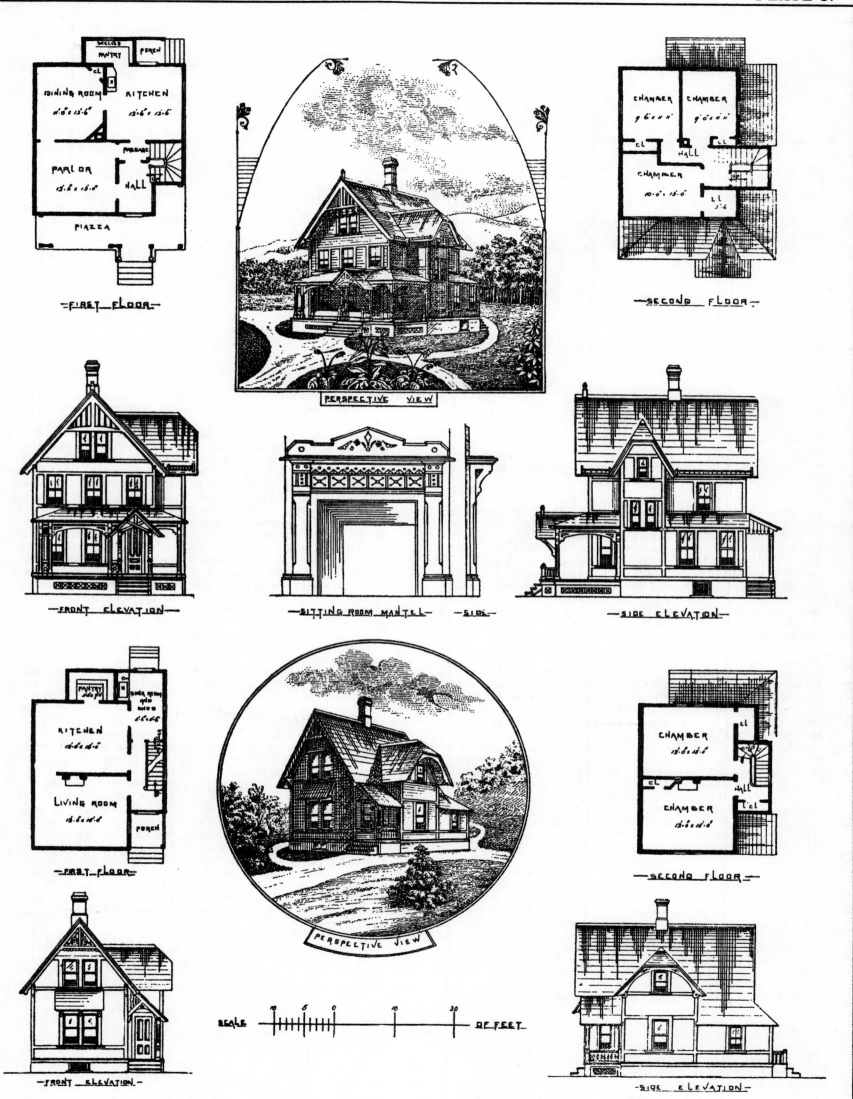

-FIRST FLOOR-

-PERSPECTIVE VIEW-

-SECOND FLOOR-

-FRONT ELEVATION-

-SITTING ROOM MANTEL- -SIDE-

-SIDE ELEVATION-

-FIRST FLOOR-

-PERSPECTIVE VIEW-

-SECOND FLOOR-

-FRONT ELEVATION-

SCALE OF FEET

-SIDE ELEVATION-

PLATE 6.

DESIGN 11—Is a six-room cottage, of a very plain and neat design.   Cost $850.

DESIGN 12—Shows a cottage with two rooms on first floor, with room for two bed-rooms on second floor, and which would make a neat house for anyone requiring the amount of room and conveniences here illustrated.   The sink it is designed to enclose, shelves being arranged above it.   Cost, $375.

EMPLOYMENT OF ARCHITECTS.

The American public only require to be shown what well qualified architects really can and ought to do for them, to appreciate and remunerate them accordingly.

Verbum sap Sapienti.

When any one contemplates building, no matter whether it is a building to cost but $500, if he is wise he will consult an architect with reference to its design, construction, etc., and this is usually done, except with those who cannot be taught anything in architecture, or that other class who are ignorant and think they cannot afford to pay an architect. If the latter is really true they certainly cannot afford to build.

Some people have an idea that it is useless to employ an architect unless for an important building and that for ordinary dwelling houses a builder is all that is necessary to carry out their wishes. But it must be remembered that a builder is not an architect and that he has no convictions unless in regard to the mechanical mysteries of his trade, where his employer cannot follow him ; and, not finding them in his way, is content to leave them uncrossed. The employer, knowing that the mechanic expects to be directed, does not hesitate to watch him and follow him up with instructions. He ends by securing at least the particular things on which his mind is set ; and if he fails of a good many conveniences and elegancies which the skillful adjustment of an architect would give him, he does not know it and so does not miss them.

It is a well known fact that when a builder has complete drawings to work from, that he will save a large amount of time that he would otherwise have to spend in thinking up every detail of the work as it progresses, to say nothing of the time the employer would have to spend with him.   The possible alterations in the work caused by advice from his friends or his study by practice, is money saved, by having a thoroughly studied and prepared design from which no deviations are made and which would enable the builder to go through with the work with the utmost dispatch.

Architects, like other professional men, come in contact with all sorts of clients. Perhaps the best are those who have in mind an ideal house, which they wish, with the assistance of an architect, to put into a tangible shape.   One who has given the subject thought can easily describe the arrangement of rooms that would best please him, and what adjuncts seem to him indispensable ; and if he has a partiality for any particular style, the architect would be glad to know it. With this information before him, and knowing what the client would be willing to spend on the house, the architect can work understandingly ; and you may rest assured he will perpetrate nothing that will be in violation of good taste.   When we say this it is understood that the architect is one of ability and standing and worthy his client's confidence.

Some people are in the habit of forming a vague idea of what they want, founded merely on what they have seen, with such changes, omissions or additions as their education and circumstances suggest; they give their ideas and instructions to the architect, while at the same time they impress upon him the necessity of adhering to a certain limit of cost, as if it were in his power to give them what accommodation he pleases for their money, when it can only buy so much material and labor according to their prices, and he can only exercise his ingenuity and judgment in such a way as to make the most of them.

The architect at the outset identifies himself with his client's interests ; and they should not lose sight of their relative position. The architect should be frank and the client should give the architect his confidence the same as he would his physician. If the sum the client is willing to invest is not sufficient to pay for the building that he requires and expects to have, the architect should tell him so ; and it is much better for the architect's interest as well as the client's that the disappointment should be suffered because the project must be modified or abandoned than because it has involved an unexpected expenditure.   There should be a thoroughly confidential relation between an architect and his client, a relation which is not like an ordinary business negotiation, but is rather like that of a legal adviser.   It is to the client's advantage to use the utmost freedom of consultation, and to take care that his work is not made less satisfactory by hurrying it, nor by taking for granted things that might be explained.

There are many difficulties that might be obviated by the architect, and there are many that require the coöperation of the architect and client to remove.

There are few persons who do not intend to build some time in their lives, and people should always live in a home of their own, no matter how humble that home may be.   Better only to have two rooms to live in than be without a hearthstone of their own, leading a life which is destined to be fraught with all that lacks an interest in practical things, and leads to a life which is sure to warp and run into the quicksands of nonchalance and a don't-careism for all occupation and responsibility of the home pleasures and comforts that surround the happy possessors of homes.

The custom which is becoming a general one—for each one who contemplates building to mark out some idea of the arrangement of rooms, etc., suited to their wants is a good one, and should be studied more by those about to build than is usually the case, and then submitting your ideas to your architect to be by him worked up into practical shape. If by making an effort to express in this way an idea you think good, or as inexperienced people often have it, perfect and cannot be bettered, you hesitate to submit this expression to your architect because he is better informed than yourself, in the fear of provoking more criticism than praises, such would not be modesty, but a sentiment of ill placed pride that frequently deprives you of advice which could not fail to be valuable. When one has done the best he can he must not shrink from criticism, for that is the only means of finding out what is deficient, and consequently the best way to ascertain what is really wanting in the work. People cannot begin too early to discuss their plans and think the matter over before committing themselves to what they may wish otherwise when it is too late.

The usual way of employing an architect is to wait till the last moment, and then tell him that the building must be completed by a certain short time.   How much wiser it would be to commence consulting and planning six months or a year before building actually begins, study drawings and designs ; in fact, educate one's self to know what one does want, and as far as possible what one ought to want.   Such a course would often result in discouragement. But even suppose that a man pays a considerable sum for advice, sketches,

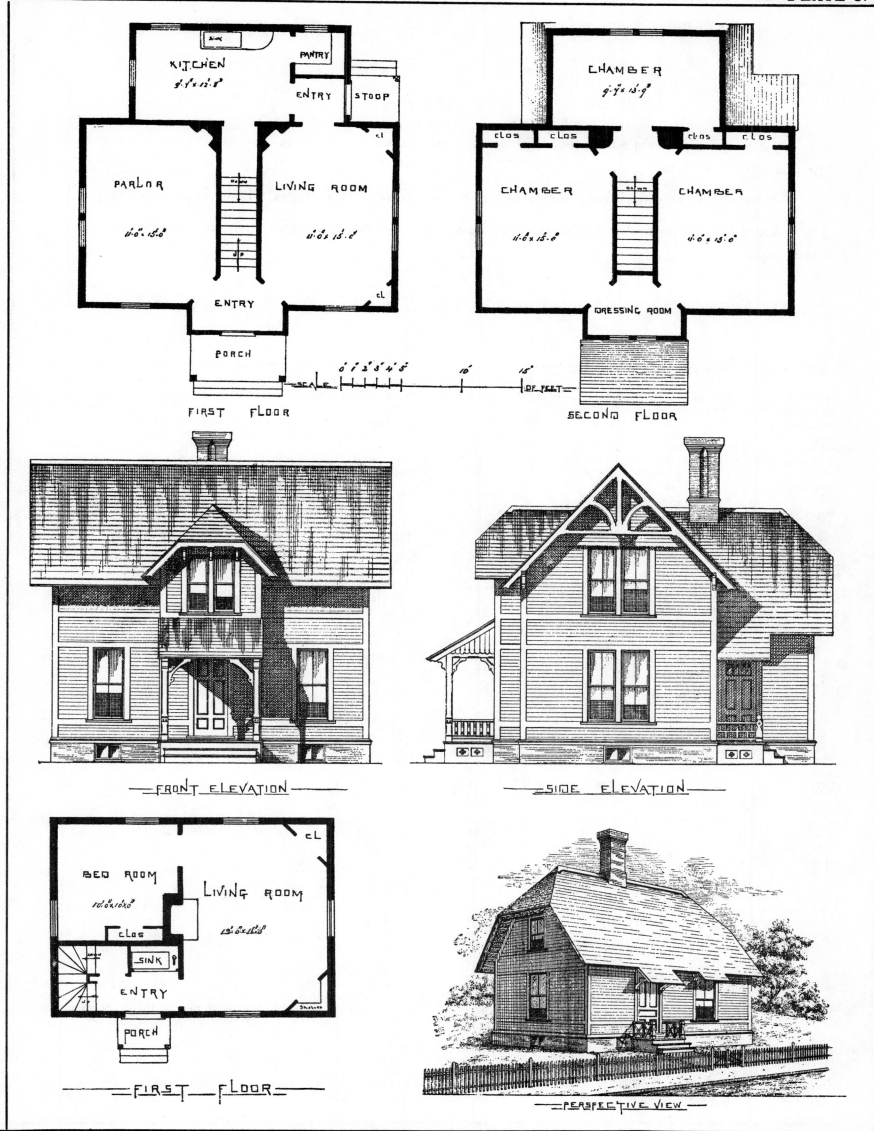

FIRST FLOOR

SECOND FLOOR

FRONT ELEVATION

SIDE ELEVATION

FIRST FLOOR

PERSPECTIVE VIEW

PLATE 7.

D<small>ESIGN</small> 13—Illustrates a fire-proof brick cottage, proposed for erection in blocks of five or six together. Estimated cost, $1,150.

D<small>ESIGN</small> 14—Represents a view in elevation of five fire-proof brick cottages. Plans similar to design 13.

D<small>ESIGN</small> 15—Plans and front elevation of two-story five-room fire-proof cottage, for erection in blocks. Cost, $850.

etc., and spends some of his time in artistic and practical study and discussion. We say suppose he does this, when, after all said and done, he concludes not to build ; has he wasted his time and his money? Not at all. He has spent both in gaining a piece of mind and confidence in his convictions that are worth much more in comparison to the dissatisfaction that so often follows building, to say nothing of the increase of his general information and consequent enjoyment.

How many men are saying at this time : "If I build again, I should know better than adopt this or that, or plan or build in this way!" There are only two ways to avoid this disappointment—either to take the trouble to educate one's self as we have suggested, or, as most Englishmen do, to select an architect on whose taste, ability and character you can rely, and let him alone. The former of these alternatives will not always prove successful, because there are those whose natural inclinations are not artistic, and again, those whose natural inclinations are not practical.

The second alternative is undoubtedly the one for most persons to pursue, although it may be, that, however competent and tasteful an architect may be, he still may not produce a work that is to your taste. But, with few exceptions, is it not your taste at fault? A person cannot be said to have an opinion upon a matter of architecture, any more than upon a composition in music, without more or less special study, according to the bent of his mind ; because architecture, like music, is an artificial art ; not pretending to represent any natural object.

In architecture, taste is governed by several well defined excellencies ; and a building in whole or in part, is good or bad as a matter of fact, dependent upon no individual judgment. In the first place, there is the excellence of plan to meet certain requirements, which is indisputable ; and this is closely allied to the æsthetic ; for the best plan is that one which, while it fulfills the practical needs of the project, also admits of an artistic treatment, expressive of the purpose. A plan may be admirably adapted to the purpose of a building, while the building has no other merit ; but this only shows that another disposition should have been made of the plan, retaining its fitness, while it should be the most economical one consistent with mechanical and scientific principles. In regard to expression, there is the traditional, the practical, and the sensual ; sensual meaning the expression due to form and color, without regard to the purpose of the building.

Sensual beauty in architecture, at all events, is not a matter of opinion. There are combinations and relations of form and color that are disagreeable to the eye for scientific reasons, and those reasons the same for which some combinations of musical notes are painful to the ear ; and combinations of form and color can be refined to the same extent that those of musical tones can be. There are millions of people who derive more enjoyment from listening to a hand-organ playing a popular air, than they could possibly appreciate from hearing Beethoven's Seventh Symphony; but do we doubt for an instant that this preference is due to a lack of education or of a sense of music?

To judge of the practical excellence of an architectural design, one must unquestionably know something of materials, and their uses and possibilities, to determine whether the result has been achieved with economy and in the best manner. This excellence, then, must be a fact, and not an opinion.

Then, as to expression ; a building, or any part of one, should suggest its uses as far as possible ; for it would be absurd, manifestly, to be unable to decide, even at the distance of half a mile, which of three buildings is a church, a prison, or a dwelling house ; and on a nearer approach, the detail and disposition, external and internal, should carry out the first impression. These distinctions, again, can be refined *ad infinitum* ; and good taste should forbid an attempt to deceive, and should avoid shams and impositions as an element of vulgarity.

There are too many buildings assuming the air of Grecian or Roman temples, with the aid of sham decoration that is as vulgar as false jewelry. Sham decoration may be made up of expensive materials, and still be sham as decoration ; for all decoration should be functional æsthetically ; that is, its use should be to emphasize the natural expression of the work. In short, if a building is founded upon the best plan for its purpose, its exterior and interior follow as a matter of course, either intimating the other dispositions, and explaining them ; the detail being confined to the explanation of parts, and being in some instances phonetic.

Clients should bear in mind that the responsibility of saying they do not like that or this design can only be indulged in by those who have acquired a knowledge of the art ; and these seldom express themselves until they have endeavored to fathom the artist's intention, knowing that a good work does not show itself in all its advantages at a glance, and that to condemn a work, without knowing why, is to confess one's self a child in discretion.

It is astonishing what ridiculous suggestions and objections clients will have when a design is being prepared for them. For instance, a case we had a short time ago. A client came to us to prepare him a design to cost $2,500 ; the floor plans were laid out and made to his satisfaction ; then we made the elevations, but he objected to an open timber cornice on his house, because he thought it would look like what they always put on barns. We talked with him a long time, and after seeing other and more costly houses than his with the same finish, he concluded that we were right, and that if he had known at first what he learned by a little study, he would not have been so foolish as to make such an objection. The party also made many other objections, in some of which we showed him he was wrong, while in others our arguments were useless and he would have his own way. This is one of the many instances that has come under our notice, though they are of rare occurrence nowadays. Finally, we ascertained where the trouble lay—it was with an old fogy of a carpenter who was to erect the building, and from whom our client was receiving his education in architecture—from an ignorant village carpenter, who did not know how the cornice or any other part of the work—as designed by us—was constructed until he received the working details ; all he knew was what he had done before over and over, and he had never studied anything outside of the village in which he lived, and in which the houses are made up of white boxes with green blinds Such men as these are stumbling blocks in the way of architecture in the village and country, and we would strongly advise anyone who intends to build to let such men severely alone.

Had this builder been any sort of draughtsman, we presume our client would never have come to us, but would have had his builder scratch out his ideas on paper, or perhaps on a board, and then commenced building without any regard to taste or proportion or any-

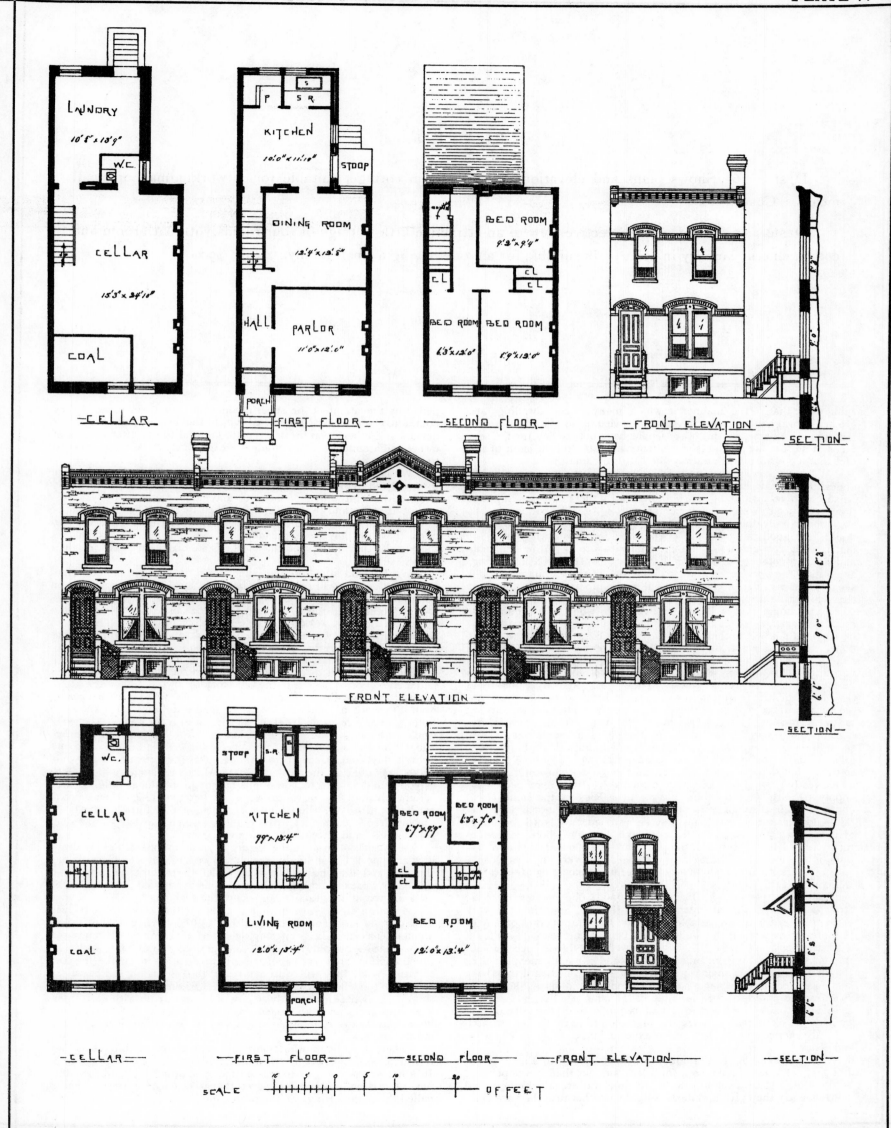

LAUNDRY
10'5" x 18'9"

W.C.

CELLAR
15'3" x 24'10"

COAL

— CELLAR —

KITCHEN
10'0" x 11'10"

STOOP

DINING ROOM
13'4" x 12'5"

HALL   PARLOR
11'0" x 12'0"

PORCH

— FIRST FLOOR —

BED ROOM
9'3" x 9'4"

CL   CL
CL

BED ROOM
6'3" x 12'0"   BED ROOM
6'9" x 12'0"

— SECOND FLOOR —

— FRONT ELEVATION —

— SECTION —

— FRONT ELEVATION —

— SECTION —

W.C.

CELLAR

COAL

— CELLAR —

STOOP   S.R.

KITCHEN
9'9" x 18'4"

LIVING ROOM
12'0" x 18'4"

PORCH

— FIRST FLOOR —

BED ROOM
6'7" x 9'9"   BED ROOM
6'3" x 7'0"

CL
CL

BED ROOM
12'0" x 13'4"

— SECOND FLOOR —

— FRONT ELEVATION —

— SECTION —

SCALE ⊦⊦⊦⊦⊦⊦⊦⊦ OF FEET

PLATE 8.

DESIGN 16—Shows plans and elevations of a six-room cottage, suitable for a workingman of small means. Cost, $860.

DESIGN 17—Plans and perspective view of an attractive little cottage of four rooms, with bath-room and conveniences; laundry in cellar. Is suitable for anyone having a small family. Cost, $900.

thing else ; that is the manner in which many of the dwellings are erected throughout the country, and why we see so much bad architecture. Of course, in this way people have not to pay for the services of an architect, and some clients are apt to lose sight of the fact that a poor article can always be had for a small price.

We have known instances where several builders, irresponsible and without credit, have been at work preparing drawings for the same person who was thinking of building, with the understanding that they were not to receive any remuneration for their drawings, but they were simply doing this to try and get the work. This would no doubt be a good thing for the client, provided the drawings were of merit, as they would assist him in some measure in getting his ideas and wants together ; but we warn the public against such a proceeding, as no man can work for nothing, and if one of these builders should secure the work, depend on it he will make up for this in a manner that will not be noticed by the owner.

Care should always be taken by parties who have buildings to erect to ascertain the standing and character of the builder about to be engaged ; it would be well to examine some of the work he has done, and question the owners of buildings recently erected by him as to the manner in which he did his business and work. When a competition for work is opened it would be well to allow only reliable builders—either of whom would do the work well—to estimate on the work, but it is too often the case that the client gives every applicant a chance, especially those who have the reputation for turning out work at a low figure. One of these men, without capital and with little or no credit, is sure to get the job, and the client sees only the difference in figures. And yet it is vain to hope that a builder will give his employers a dollar's worth for ninety cents ; he may contract to do so, but depend upon it, that, as the grocer who offers to sell coffee ready ground for less than he asks for the green berry, will supply us with anything but Java or even Rio, so the builder will contrive to cheat in some way to avoid a loss he would otherwise sustain—no matter how much he may be watched, frauds will be smuggled in by a man who is forced to make himself whole. The moment one's back is turned, the foreman—like master, like man—puts in inferior stock where it can be speedily covered up, and scanty nailing where it cannot be detected till a future seasoning of the woodwork reveals the fraud.

Take for example the laying of a floor ; one may examine the stock, and have the good separated from the bad, and when the work is done his eye may not be able to detect the introduction of any of the inferior quality, if the builder has been smart enough to lay it with the sappy side down. It all looks well, but how about the nailing ? One comes in from time to time suddenly and unexpectedly ; the men keep on with their work, and put down the board they have just squeezed into its place, nailing it properly and as it should be. Another and another board is nailed in the same manner, but immediately one's back is turned, one nail is made to do the duty of four or five. A client who expects the architect to have his design satisfactorily carried out by such men, expects him to make bricks without straw.

We have had a great amount of experience with this class of builders, who have taken work for a less amount than it was possible to do it at, and with whom it was a terrible warfare all through, and consequently they give architects a hard name because they are compelled by the architect or superintendent to do their work as they contracted to do it, and they lost by it, to the disadvantage of lumber dealers and others who furnished material, and to the utter disgust of owner and architect. Such builders are not likely to be recommended to others.

We have taken down rod after rod of what appeared on the face to be a good foundation wall, for the reason that the mason had only used mortar on the face of the wall and had left the rest dry. Dishonest at heart, and this feeling intensified by the desire to get out of the job without loss, he and his men become lynx-eyed ; and the moment they see anyone approaching who would be likely to inspect their work, they hurry on the mortar and strive to cover up their tracks.

We have no intention of crying down the honest and conscientious builder, who will do his very best whether he is doing work from an architect's drawings or trying to carry out his employer's ideas , to such we hold out the right hand of fellowship, and say keep on in your path, do good work and you will always be busy. The day is not far distant when responsible builders and good work will be employed more than they have been hitherto.

There are a thousand frauds that are practised by dishonest builders, who resort to every measure to enable them to underbid reliable and good men. It is the old story of trying to get the maximum of show for the minimum of outlay. Everything is cheapened, even the work of building dams to retain millions of gallons of water, which we know if let loose, by the giving way of the wall, would carry loss and distress to hundreds of homes. We want to know from our own experience if it be possible for a horse to live on a straw a day, and to see if we cannot solve the problem that would make one dollar do the work of two. We say let such builders alone as you would an architect who has had no professional training, who is impracticable and of whose work you know nothing ; then you will not be heard to say, when the work is completed, " I would have given two hundred dollars more to so and so—some one they know does good work—and have him do the work."

We need not discuss the absurdity of an architect making drawings for approval by individuals, and yet we know of architects making sketches and drawings for parties under the alternative sometimes offered by quacks—no cure, no pay. This is adopted by some architects in their daily practice, to secure their clients by a sort of trap. These same architects, when they hear of anyone about to build, will flock around him and offer to do this, although they know that an architect has already been employed—while common decency requires that they should refuse to have anything to do with work with which another architect is engaged, unless called in by him for consultation—and they will ofttimes resort to the basest means to try and have the client dismiss the architect whom he has already consulted. It is needless to advise any one what to do with such interlopers, as any man can at once read their character. Fancy a number of physicians running to a house where some one is ill and acting in this wise.

There are clients who think they may try on architects as they try on hats, not expecting to pay for any but the one they like best. It is unnecessary for us to waste time in showing the unreasonableness of this notion, and we regret that it is encouraged by what is called the ragged fringe of the profession.

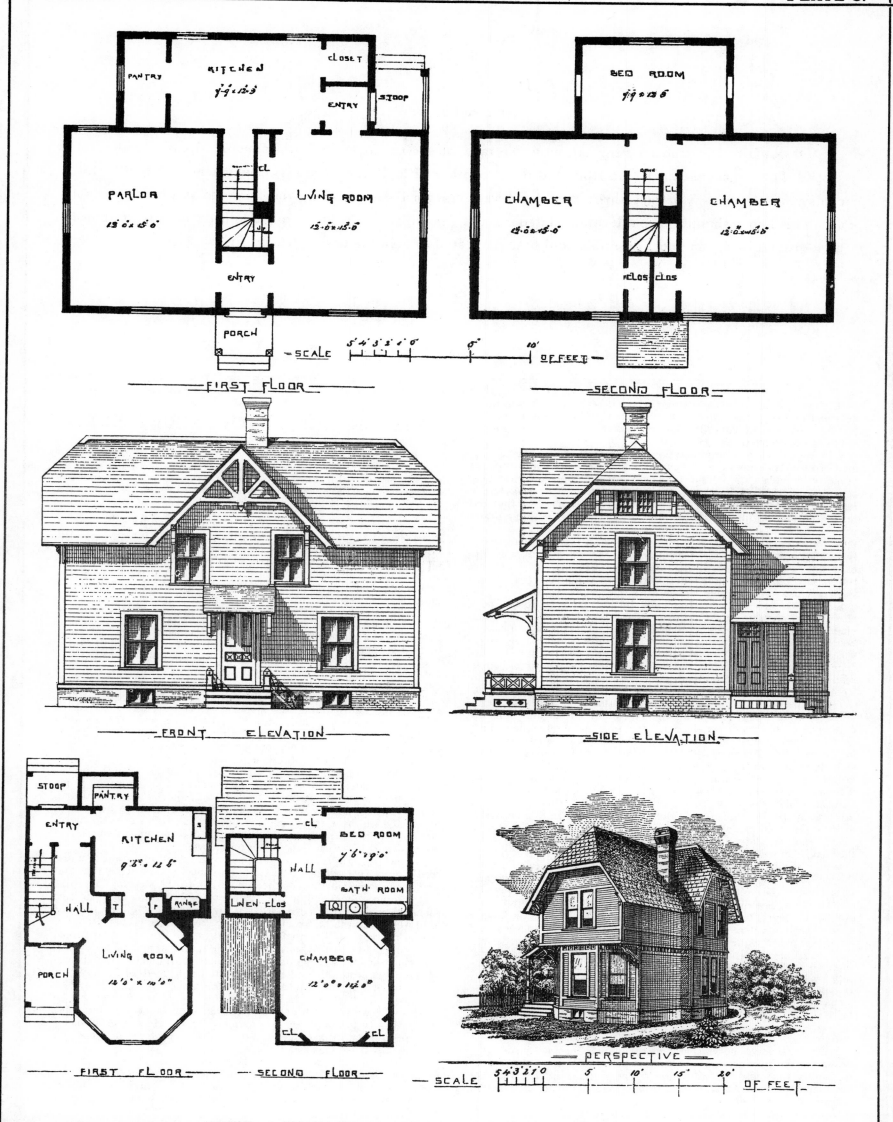

PANTRY

KITCHEN
9'9" x 12'3"

CLOSET

ENTRY

STOOP

PARLOR
13'0" x 15'0"

CL

LIVING ROOM
12'0" x 15'0"

ENTRY

PORCH

BED ROOM
9'9" x 12'6"

CHAMBER
13'0" x 15'0"

CL

CHAMBER
12'0" x 15'0"

CLOS CLOS

— SCALE — 5 4 3 2 1 0   5'   10' — OF FEET —

— FIRST FLOOR —

— SECOND FLOOR —

— FRONT ELEVATION —

— SIDE ELEVATION —

STOOP

PANTRY

ENTRY

KITCHEN
9'8" x 12'6"

HALL

T   F   RANGE

LIVING ROOM
12'0" x 10'0"

PORCH

CL

LINEN CLOS

BED ROOM
7'6" x 9'0"

HALL

BATH ROOM

CHAMBER
12'0" x 14'0"

CL

CL

— FIRST FLOOR —   — SECOND FLOOR —

— PERSPECTIVE —

— SCALE — 5 4 3 2 1 0   5'   10'   15'   20' — OF FEET —

PLATE 9.

DESIGN 18—Illustrates a very attractive cottage of six rooms, with bath-roomand dressing-room on second floor, spacious piazzas on front and rear, together with all the necessary conveniences required for comfort and economy, making this a very desirable house for those requiring the comforts of a home.

This house should have a location suited to the design, to be in harmony, a hillside or mountainous back-ground being the most desirable, and best calculated to give the desired effect.   Cost, $1,500.

It is astonishing to see so many, who are otherwise intelligent business men, offering their architects every temptation to rob them, by driving bargains which a little thought would convince anyone cannot afford a competence.

In regard to just remuneration for professional services, any man of business knows that to have your business conscientiously and properly attended to, one must engage persons who are honest and capable, and that such cannot be had for nothing. It must be remembered that an architect's fees are earned rather more by the protection he affords his client, than for his design and working drawings, with their accompanying specifications, though this latter is a most important document, and is too often inexplicit and dangerously general in its provisions, entailing extras for which there is no excuse but the ambiguity of the description. In fact, it requires a thoroughly competent architect to draw up a complete specification —an exhaustive description of the work in every particular.

Some time ago we were employed by a committee to design a church, and they informed us that an architect had offered his service for nothing, but even at that they said his services would have been dear. Also in the matter of a large public building on which we were engaged, an architect offered his services for 1½ per cent less than we were paid, and no doubt there are plenty of people ready to take a position without remuneration beyond what they can steal.

So little does the public appreciate the difference in the skill and labor of one architect and another, that they often allow a paltry difference in charges of one-half per cent of cost—a difference which he would think trivial in comparing the merits of two existing buildings if he were purchasing—determine the choice between architects, without regard to the qualifications on which the whole success or failure of the building will depend. It should be borne in mind that it requires from seven to ten years of study and close application to be reasonably admissible to practice, and for this time and cost of preparation the architect is entitled to as fair a return as any investment of time and money can be had.

If you get cinders in your iron, it is because there is cinders in the pay ; there is always good iron to be had.

Our advice to everyone who contemplates building is : secure the services of a really well-trained and capable architect, pay him properly and be guided by his judgment and experience—-this will also be the advice of anyone who is experienced in such matters, and others who regret that they built without such aid. Of course every one has their peculiar wishes to be provided for, and all these should be presented to your architect before he commences the design. Architects have their own ideas as to what form the building ought to take, and should be allowed to use their own cultivated taste, which it has taken years of constant study to acquire, and this should not be thrown away for any momentary caprice, which the client would be sorry for in the end.

An architect is one who prepares the plans, conceives the designs, draws out the specifications ; in short supplies the mind ; the builder is merely the mason or carpenter. The builder is, in fact, the machine ; the architett, the power which puts the machine together and sets it in motion.

RESPONSIBILITY OF ARCHITECTS.

The architect has far more to do with the health and usefulness, and long life of the family which he shelters, than the physician can ever have, and he is in far greater degree answerable for its ailments and its weaknesses, and its early deaths.

Pro bono publico.

It is the legitimate claim of an architect, that his skill enables him not only to contribute his own ideas of comfort and beauty, but to satisfy the special wants of his client—to carry out his wishes, and even whims, if need be, more successfully than another, provided he is made fully acquainted with these wants and wishes ; and the architect's claim is pretty generally acknowledged nowadays where his profession is well established.

Who is responsible for the hideous structures which are daily erected throughout the country, staring good taste out of countenance ? The architects are not alone responsible for the crudities that take shape under their hands. It is the client who is really to blame, in a majority of cases, for giving birth to these monstrosities ; but it is the architect whose name is associated with them who has to bear the odium.

Some one has said that nearly every man thinks he knows something about both building and finance. It is true, but the views of the wiseacre are not equally strong on both subjects ; for, while he hesitates to invest his money without the advice of those who are more experienced in such matters, he never questions his ability either to plan a house or to criticise a design. If he has sickness in his family, he does not presume to advise his physician as to the proper mode of treatment ; nor would he feel warranted in suggesting to his lawyer how to carry on an important suit ; but, when it comes to house building, that is wholly a different thing. There he feels at home, and will have everything his own way. In his eyes the architect is but little more than one employed to carry out his views, and not to thwart him with suggestions of his own.

How galling it is to the architect who is full of enthusiasm and ready to give his client his best, to be called upon to construct that which will be in violation of the simplest rules of his profession, to be asked to put up and father the crudities that even the owner will be ashamed of when they are criticised by his better informed friends ! Men who ask these things are as set in their views as they are ignorant of the laws of harmony and proportion. You will hear people say, "when I build my house I will have it as I want it or not at all." The client has it as he wants it, the architect's argument being thrown away on one who thinks he is the better informed of the two ; his efforts to lead his client into the right channels are wasted, and he sees now as he has seen before, and will see in the future, that he must do the work as laid out or throw up that which will be worse than drudgery to him, from beginning to end. He would be wise if he were to throw up his pencil rather than accept the blame which in a great part belongs to another.

When will the world learn the truth of the adage "He who would be his own architect will have a fool for a client ?" He who would trammel his architect after he has given him his general instructions, would so dictate to him that the work when completed

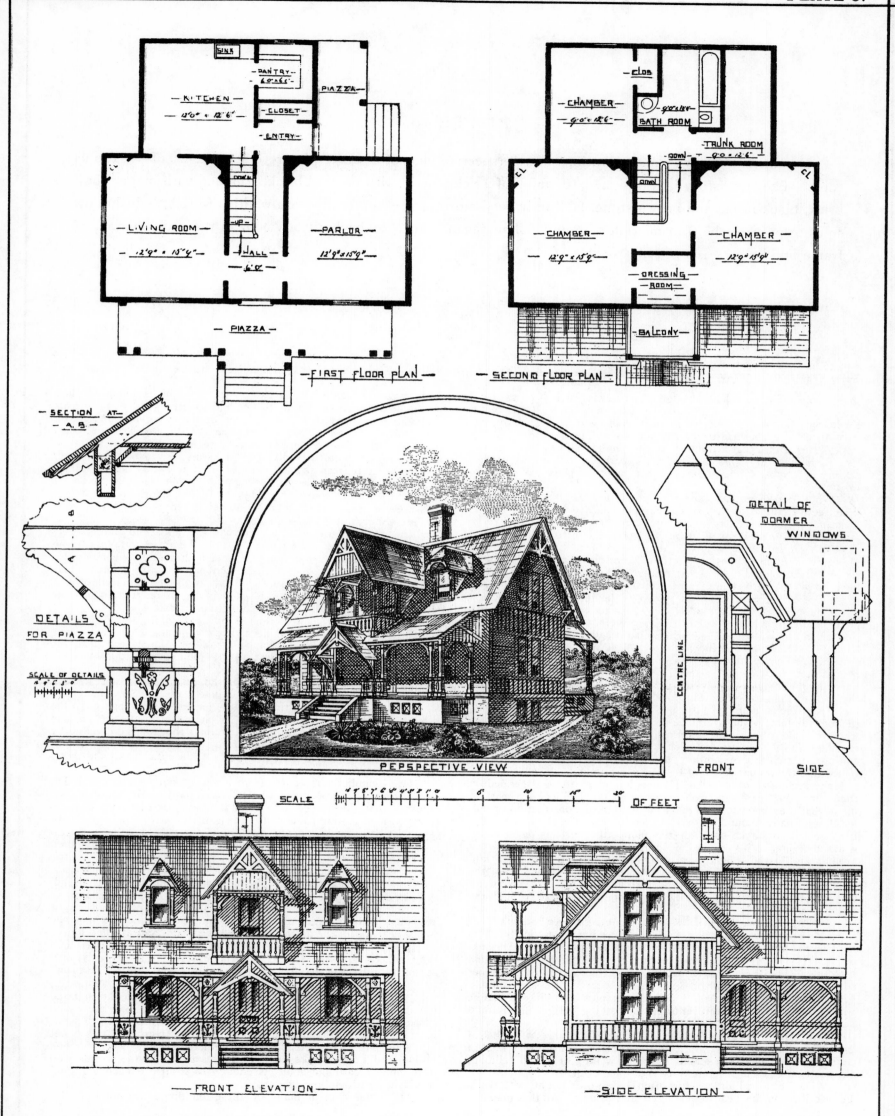

KITCHEN
13'0" x 12'6"

SINK
PANTRY
6'0" x 6'5"
CLOSET
ENTRY
PIAZZA

LIVING ROOM
12'9" x 15'4"

HALL
6'0"

PARLOR
12'9" x 15'9"

PIAZZA

— FIRST FLOOR PLAN —

CHAMBER
9'0" x 12'6"

CLOS
BATH ROOM
9'0" x 12'6"

TRUNK ROOM
9'0" x 12'6"

CHAMBER
12'9" x 15'9"

DRESSING ROOM

CHAMBER
12'9" x 15'9"

BALCONY

— SECOND FLOOR PLAN —

— SECTION AT A.B. —

DETAILS FOR PIAZZA

SCALE OF DETAILS

PERSPECTIVE VIEW

DETAIL OF DORMER WINDOWS

CENTRE LINE

FRONT   SIDE

SCALE   OF FEET

FRONT ELEVATION

SIDE ELEVATION

PLATE 10.

DESIGN 19—Shows plans, elevations, and perspective view of a pair of picturesque cottages, of five rooms each. The first story it is designed to build of brick, faced with pressed brick, trimmed with molded buff brick, black brick, and brown stone, laid up in read mortar; the center division wall is of brick, built hollow so as to prevent the transmission of sound. The second story to be built of wood, in the usual manner of frame buildings. Cost, $1,400 a side.

must of necessity be a hodge-podge, is as unwise as he who calls no professional aid. Nay, of the two the latter does the least mischief; for he only holds up to the world the evidence of his own folly, instead of shifting the load to the shoulders of another.

We are aware that a fraction of the public still regard an architect as a mere draughtsman—an artist perhaps, but a sort of necessary evil whose duty is to make upon paper the picture of a building.

What do people realize of the actual responsibility which rests upon their architect or the extent to which their lives are in his hand? Talk of the responsibility of a physician; that is indeed great. If your friend falls ill he calls upon his good doctor to lead him back to health; and if possible this is done: if not one man dies. The physician was not responsible for the illness; he did his best to counteract it but failed, and he is not blamed. But suppose your friend, being in good health, takes tickets for himself, his wife and children, to the opening of some new room, hall or theater, which an architect has built. He goes with hundreds, perhaps thousands, under the excitement of the pleasure of an opening night. Does he, or any of that audience, realize for an instant what they have done—that they have placed their lives in the architect's hand and he has accepted the trust? We know that if by some error or oversight of the architect, or had he miscalculated in this or that or the other direction, the lives of your friend and family, with scores of others, are not worth the price of their tickets. But do they know this? Probably not; and it may be a merciful dispensation of Providence which blinds them to the fact. But ignorance or parsimony upon the part of those who are responsible for the erection of such buildings, leading them to trifle with their safety, to employ incompetent builders, or if consulting an architect of ability, to restrict him or in any way limit him within the proper scope of his office is criminal.

Many architects have allowed their judgment to be overruled by their client, for fear they would lose their employment by insisting upon what they know to be right as a matter of construction or material, and many a building has settled or failed in some particular because the architect had not the pluck to assert his *locus standi*, while the injury to his reputation is greater than if he had stood his ground, and lost his client; or still more, if his client had left him and found an architect less scrupulous. In either case, when the failure finally occurs, his judgment and integrity would be apparent, and would gain as much prestige for him as his having built the building successfully.

In France an architect is held responsible to the whole extent of his means for work under him, and this gives him an authority which his client is bound to respect; while it insures his conscientious exertion. If this were the case in this country there would be less building accidents reported through the daily press, and the number of unqualified persons advertising themselves as architects would greatly diminish. One should no more employ an architect than he would a physician without knowing something of his ability and standing.

The profession of an architect is closely identified with that of public health, and as sanitarians in the construction of every kind of building, whether it be a stable, private dwelling or public building, the vastness of their responsibility is at once evident.

"Died of a bad air." How often these words might, with truth, be inscribed on the headstone of old and young. All that man can do to make our modern houses warm and air tight, is done, and then we kindle a monstrous fire in the cellar, so arranged that all the air we breathe must pass over plates of iron heated to a cherry-red before it reaches us. Day and night is the same. We are warm and comfortable, nothing freezes in the house; we have, nevertheless, taken a viper to our bosom that will certainly sting us. No man can rob his lungs of pure fresh air, and not pay for it in bodily health. Pure air, and in large quantities, is as essential to our health and comfort as animal food and nourishing drinks. In our efforts to perfect our creature comforts, we have not only shut out the cold from our dwellings, but with it the vitalizing air.

The architect must see to it that the house he builds is so arranged that not only the temperature of the air in it can always be regulated—at least to such a degree as advancing science enables him to do—but also that the air be fresh and pure. In its sanitary character architecture must, therefore, look to the combination of heat with pure air or ventilation. The architect in his relation to his client is either a practical sanitarian or the reverse.

Our forefathers knew nothing of diphtheria and kindred diseases, traced to what we term "modern improvements." Our plumbing and sewers, if not properly trapped and ventilated, will lead the poison into our dwellings, instead of removing it to a distance, where it can do no harm.

It is only a few years ago that the whole British empire was filled with anxiety on account of the illness of the heir-apparent to the throne—an illness said to be due to imperfect drainage. To the same cause is attributed the death by plague in London of 100,000 persons, and in the cities of our own country thousands die yearly by the same cause. No nation can afford, by the untimely making of the graves of thousands of its producers, to lose its wealth and thereby its greatness.

Dr. Chamberlain reports from a recent conversation with Dr. Richardson, acting Secretary of the State Board of Health of Massachusetts, that they never have a fatal case of scarlet fever or diphtheria without finding some cause for it in defective drainage, ventilation, or bad sewerage of the dwelling.

The contents of the vault saturates the whole of the surrounding earth, poisons the springs and the wells, and finds its way in little currents through the interstices of the foundation walls of our houses; there it throws off gases too slight to attract attention, but too deadly to be inhaled by the inmates with impunity. The soil pipe is an improvement on this; but if it be not tight in all its parts, if there be any imperfectly soldered or caulked joints, woe betide the man who sleeps near it; for the destroying angel is abroad, and will find him as surely as he lies down and rises up in an atmosphere so charged with the germs of disease. He may not be conscious that the foe is near at hand; for the leak may be slight, and during the day its effects will be neutralized, in part, by open windows and doors; and, moreover, as "evil communications corrupt good manners," so the habitual inhaling of a noxious atmosphere dulls the senses: and they soon cease to detect the odor that would have startled them, had they not gradually become habituated to it. Anyone may test this. Let him enter into a crowded and badly ventilated theater or other public building, and he will take no more notice of it than the crowds who have inhaled carbonic acid gas enough to insure to each a raging headache for the following day.

Of course a great many of these buildings are not built by

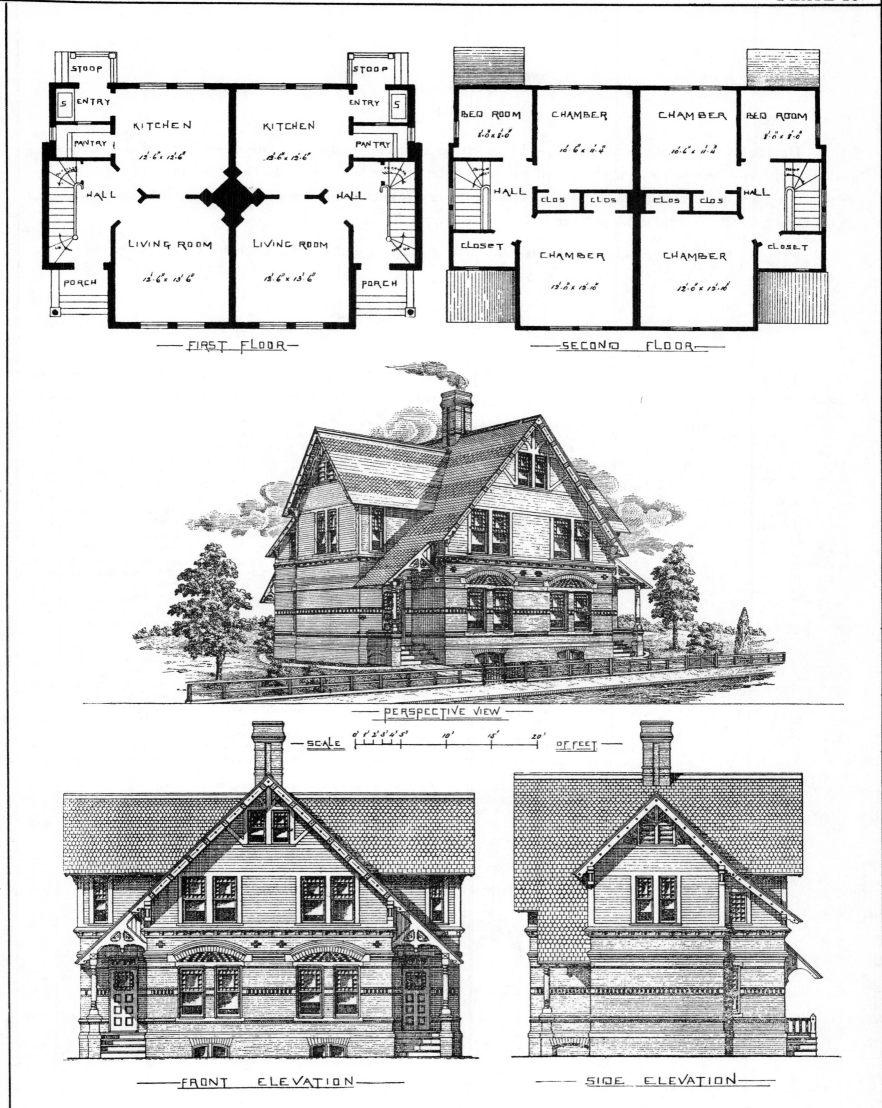

FIRST FLOOR

STOOP
ENTRY
KITCHEN 12'6" x 12'6"
PANTRY
HALL
LIVING ROOM 12'6" x 13'6"
PORCH

STOOP
ENTRY
KITCHEN 12'6" x 12'6"
PANTRY
HALL
LIVING ROOM 12'6" x 13'6"
PORCH

SECOND FLOOR

BED ROOM 8'0" x 8'0"
CHAMBER 16'6" x 11'4"
HALL
CLOS CLOS
CLOSET
CHAMBER 12'0" x 12'10"

CHAMBER 16'6" x 11'4"
BED ROOM 8'0" x 8'0"
HALL
CLOS CLOS
CLOSET
CHAMBER 12'0" x 12'10"

PERSPECTIVE VIEW

SCALE 0' 1' 2' 3' 4' 5'   10'   15'   20' OF FEET

FRONT ELEVATION

SIDE ELEVATION

PLATE 11.

DESIGN 20—Illustrates a house adapted to a site on a hillside, the kitchen and offices being placed in the basement, and on rear, is entirely out of ground. The dumb-waiter, from the closet in kitchen to waiter's pantry on first floor, connected with dining-room, is a very desirable and convenient feature. Second floor contains four sleeping rooms, and there is a good attic over the whole house. Cost, $1,700.

DESIGN 21—Is a two-story seven-room and attic cottage, suitable for a mechanic's home, and can be erected on a lot of small frontage. Cost, $1,600.

architects at all, but by the "practical builders" who do so much of the bad building the whole country over.

There is only the excuse of public indifference to shield the modern builder in view of his almost universal disregard of simple and well known methods of wholesale house-drainage. He would consider himself blameworthy if his roof leaked so badly as to destroy the wall paper of a single room; but he expects no blame— he would often scout the idea that he should be blamed—for a condition of interior drainage which lays the whole household open to an ever-threatening danger. At present not a man in ten thousand— literally not one in ten thousand—cares or thinks anything about this matter, beyond satisfying himself that his house has as good plumbing as other people's houses. His accustomed nostrils detect no odor—even where to one fresh from the country the very entrance hall is tainted with air from the drains; and where he can neither see nor smell offence, he is quiet and content. He has yet to learn that the most serious danger is often unattended by any marked warning to the senses.

Where the battle rages fierce and long, are the dead and dying —but the plague and pestilence is not announced by the clashing of arms and booming of cannon.

The architect, who is the creator of the sanitary condition of the house, must give to its drainage and water supply system the same intelligent and educated skill which he now applies to its arrangement and beauty.

Architects have not been held to any real accountability for these things, and the people themselves are thus far at fault. The demand creates the supply, and thus far it has been for handsome houses, or for cheap houses, or for convenient houses, and these have been supplied; the time is now at hand when the demand will be for healthy houses first of all.

We say the responsibility of the architect is great indeed, but how much more is the responsibility of those who erect buildings without the aid of an architect? What is the responsibility, we ask, of one who sets his irresponsible and crafty builder at work to erect a building, which is usually the case when no architect is consulted, the owner only studying parsimony--although the fees of a competent architect are not so much additional as he thinks; but on the contrary a saving of at least five times the amount. This builder knows nothing of design or the harmony of parts, neither the owner who follows him up with his instructions, and they gather their ideas from this and that or the other which they have seen; fancy looking for a harmonious whole in a house built after this fashion. The builder will turn an arch, and build a wall above it, ignorant whether it will stand or fall when the center is struck; while his brother will frame together a combination of timbers, innocent of any positive knowledge whether his structure when finished will bear a locomotive, or fall of its own weight; and the plumber, who has so much to do with the health of the occupants, will get the impression that a cheap job is required, and no one will take any interest in how he does it, and the whole of the work will be scamped from beginning to end, and the question arises will this building be fit for occupancy of man when finished, and should not something be done to prevent the erection of buildings that will be a lasting injury to society?

It is very much to be deplored that in many of our cities the public has delivered itself over a willing victim, body and soul, to the speculating builder. Stupidly housed in ugly, inconvenient and monotonous brick boxes, with holes cut symmetrically in them, the public stays contentedly until a fever breaks out or frost sets in. Then, however, it immediately raises an insensate howl against the architectural profession, which was never consulted, because sewer gas was laid on to and fresh air carefully kept out of its dwellings, and because all the pipes were left exposed to the elements.

We have no desire to claim infallibility for the capable members of our profession, but will remind our readers that where such things occur as we have here referred to, usually an architect was not at all concerned, or if there was, he was probably limited in the scope of his office.

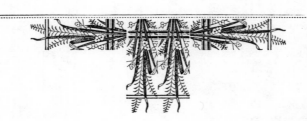

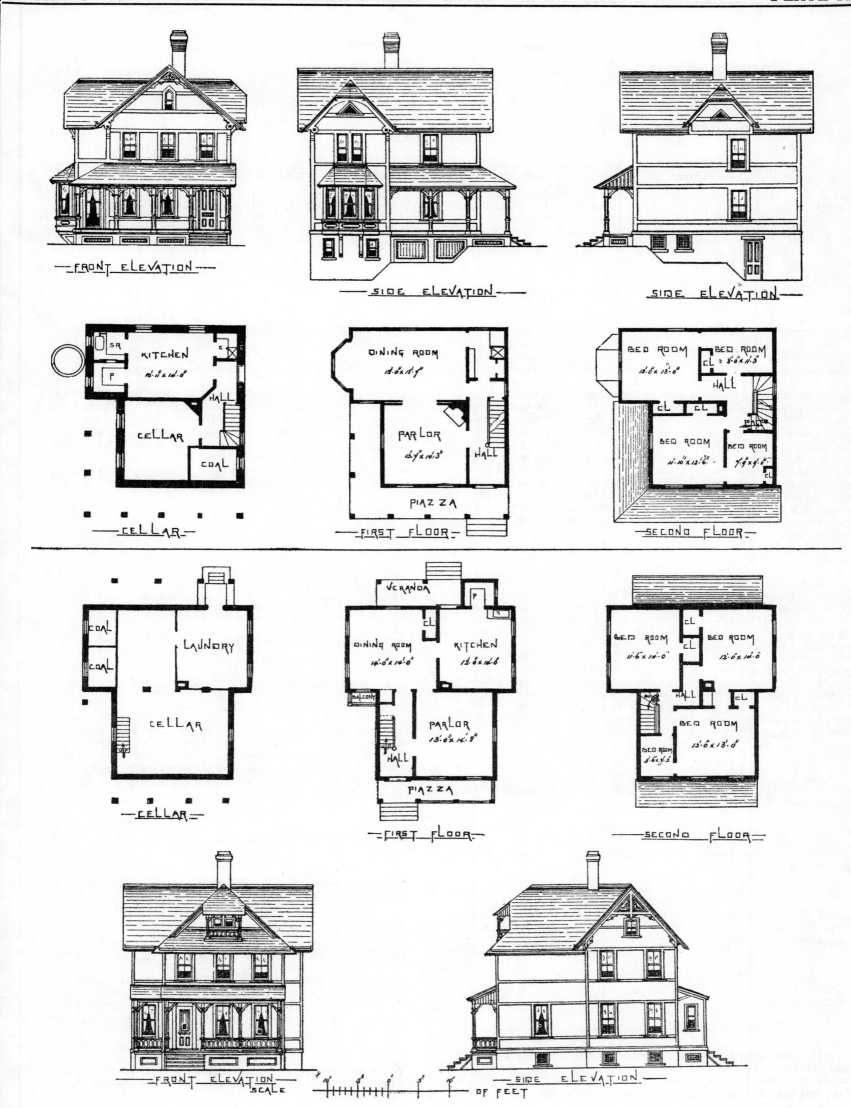

FRONT ELEVATION

SIDE ELEVATION

SIDE ELEVATION

CELLAR

FIRST FLOOR

SECOND FLOOR

CELLAR

FIRST FLOOR

SECOND FLOOR

FRONT ELEVATION

SCALE OF FEET

SIDE ELEVATION

PLATE 12.

DESIGN 22—Shows a pair of frame cottages, of seven rooms each, which, when executed, make a very attractive home for anyone requiring the amount of room this plan gives, and which can be erected for $1,200 each.

A permanent home should be built with care and planned with a special reference to the wants and necessities of the family; it should be neat and attractive and in harmony with the lives to be spent under its roof. A house or stopping place may be all external show, with the larger part of the conveniences omitted internally, thereby cheapening the cost, and which enhance the chances of many birds filling the nest for a short time, and ultimately the place becomes the half-way house between nowhere and home. Let us have permanent homes, built in accordance with the times and of modern styles, homes where the manly virtues may grow strong and flourish, and which our children will ever remember in after years with pride.

It is quite surprising what a number of people there are who will get about half a dozen hieroglyphics o. a piece of paper and then think they are all ready to commence building, and that there is nothing more to do but put hands to the work. But, softly, how about the lettering and figuring of plans ; are the sizes of all rooms figured out, the frame, the location and size of all doors and windows; where are the specifications, the details of execution, the contracts and a host of minor things which must be properly prepared and attended to, if your building affairs are to be conducted in a practical manner, for as sure as the compass is indispensable to the mariner to steer by, so are the plans, specifications and details, requisite for the builder to work by to obtain satisfactory results and to reach the goal of proper construction and harmony of parts.

It is on the architect that the public must rely for the proper construction of the building.

It is only a penny wise and pound foolish policy that says : " Do not employ an architect."

People who have tried to be the architects of their own buildings have instead been the architects of their own misfortunes and emptied their pockets.

A simple suggestion from a competent architect is sometimes worth his fees.

The intelligent public are convinced that architects who have had every advantage by their training and experience can meet their wants with practical contrivances and arrangements for their comfort, and that they can do this better than anybody else.

The faculty of inventing, designing and giving shape to conceptions so as to make them living realities, is a talent as indispensable in the true architect, as a thorough knowledge of the strength of materials and the proper and most economical mode of their use, and anyone who dabbles in architecture without these talents is an amateur, and an amateur architect is the worst of all amateurs, for he not only builds structures that are hideous, but also wastes people's money.

Do the public want good architects ? Men show but little care to get the best that are to be had.

An architect should be thoroughly practical and know how to use material with economy, so as to carry out a proper construction in building and not waste material, and consequently his client's money.

An architect is a confidential and responsible adviser.

Children and fools should never see anything half done.

Critics of architecture will hate a thing with all their might, but they cannot substantiate their dislikes by telling one why—simply because they don't know. and are not versed in architecture. These kind of critics are heard a good deal nowadays and it seems as if everyone were critics, though they don't know the first principles of what they are talking about.

It requires the same training to choose a design that it does to make one.

When people ask you as to what you are doing, say to them what the Japanese said when asked about the building they were erecting at the Centennial—" Wait, till comes time, you then see?"

John Smith was building him a boat, and everyone who came along and saw what he was doing found fault with it and offered their suggestions. Some said it was too shallow, others too deep, and so on. Finally Mr. Smith got mad and informed his friends he was building the boat for himself, and if after he was through they would call on him he would be happy to build one to suit them all and then he would chop it up.

People want to live in more comfortable and attractive houses than they used to, and the designs shown in this book pleasantly indicate their demand.

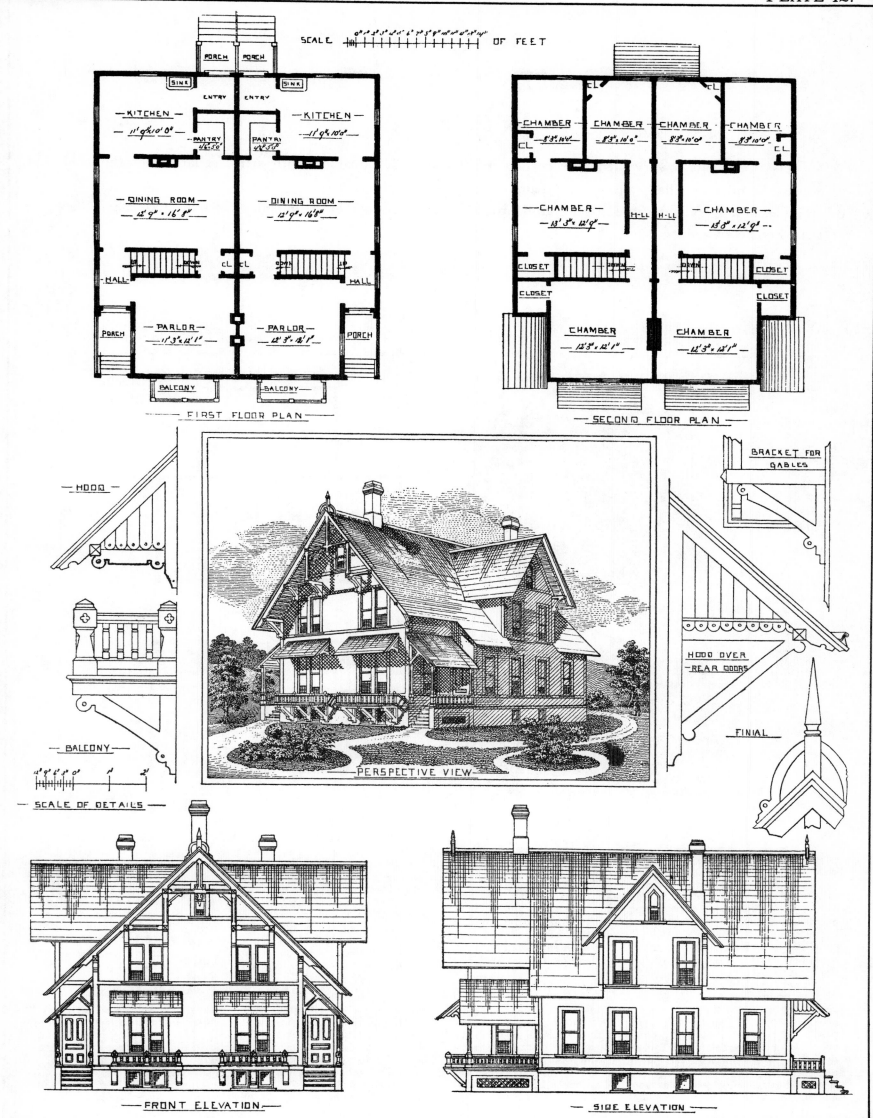

SCALE OF FEET

FIRST FLOOR PLAN

KITCHEN
11' 9" x 10' 0"

KITCHEN
11' 9" x 10' 0"

PORCH   PORCH

SINK   SINK

ENTRY   ENTRY

PANTRY
4'6" x 5'0"

PANTRY
4'6" x 5'0"

DINING ROOM
12' 9" x 16' 8"

DINING ROOM
12' 9" x 16' 8"

CL   CL

HALL

HALL

PORCH

PORCH

PARLOR
11' 3" x 12' 1"

PARLOR
12' 3" x 12' 1"

BALCONY   BALCONY

SECOND FLOOR PLAN

CL   CL

CHAMBER
8' 3" x 10' 0"

CHAMBER
8' 3" x 10' 0"

CHAMBER
8' 3" x 10' 0"

CHAMBER
8' 3" x 10' 0"

CL   CL

CHAMBER
13' 5" x 12' 9"

CHAMBER
13' 5" x 12' 9"

H-LL   H-LL

CLOSET   CLOSET

CLOSET   CLOSET

CHAMBER
12' 3" x 12' 1"

CHAMBER
12' 3" x 12' 1"

HOOD

BALCONY

SCALE OF DETAILS

PERSPECTIVE VIEW

BRACKET FOR GABLES

HOOD OVER REAR DOORS

FINIAL

FRONT ELEVATION

SIDE ELEVATION

PLATE 13.

DESIGN 23—Is a. very attractive cottage residence of seven rooms with attic; cellar under the whole house; laundry in cellar; gives a large amount of room for the cost.

The first story is designed to be clapboarded and the second story shingled. Cost, $1,300. (See Plate 1 for Perspective View.)

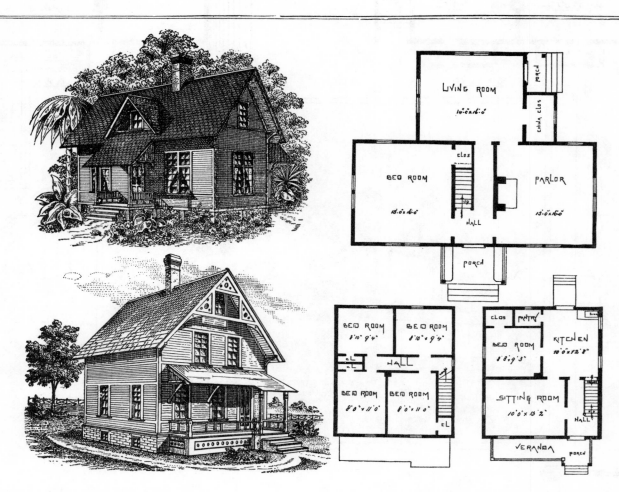

COTTAGE AT SCOOBA, MISS.

In a Southern climate the requirements for houses, either great or small, are very different from what they are at the North.

Special attention must be paid to keeping cool in summer rather than warm in winter; therefore the rooms must be large and the ceilings high. Cellars are not among the requisites. Neither is it necessary in some parts to build solid foundations, there being no frosts to get clear of; and in some instances houses are set on logs stood on the ground. In this case the frame is supported on brick piers, and a large open space is left under the floor, which is properly prepared so as to keep down damp.

It will be observed there is no kitchen provided, the cooking being done in a small out-house provided for that purpose, so as to keep the heat out of the house as far as possible. It is, however, necessary at some seasons of the year to have a fire, and for this purpose a large open fire-place is provided in the parlor. This fire-place is built of brick, with an arch turned in it, and the brick breast continued up; the brick being left exposed in the room, and in this fire-place it is intended to burn large logs on the hearth. The second story or loft is merely a lumber room and air space between the roof and rooms below.

The arrangement of the windows is one of the principal features in the design. The lower sashes are arranged to slide into the walls and the transom sash to swing. In this way the whole of the windows can be opened instead of half, as is usually the case. The rooms are well supplied with windows, and from their arrangement, if there is a breeze, a good draft will be obtained. The front porch is arranged with a seat on each side, so that one may sit out of doors, and yet be in the shade, which is a very desirable feature. This cottage was designed for the residence of a laborer on the estate of J. A. Minniece, Esq., at Scooba, Miss., to be built of yellow pine throughout. Cost, about $500. We also give on this page

A COTTAGE AT BIRMINGHAM, CONN.,

designed for a workingman of large family, and is a neat little cottage, and well adapted for the purposes intended and the requirements of its occupants. The first floor contains living-room, kitchen and bed-room, and on the second floor four bed-rooms, with the necessary closet room. There is a cellar under the whole. Interior finished in a plain manner, and painted in tints. Color on exterior are: clapboards, light slate; trimmings, light brown, and trimmed up with red; blinds, olive green. Cost, $900.

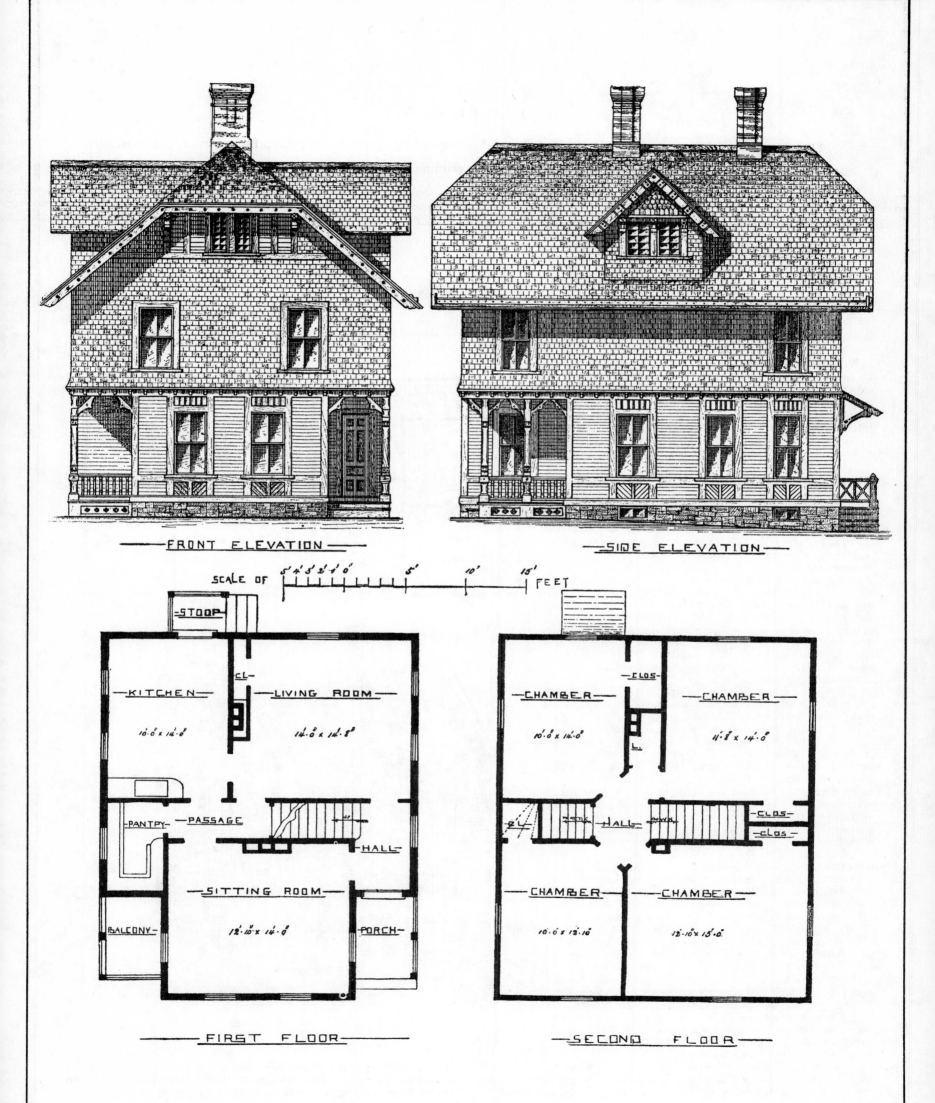

FRONT ELEVATION

SIDE ELEVATION

SCALE OF 5' 4' 3' 2' 1' 0'   5'   10'   15' FEET

STOOP

KITCHEN
10'-0" x 14'-0"

CL

LIVING ROOM
14'-0" x 14'-8"

PANTRY

PASSAGE

HALL

SITTING ROOM
12'-10" x 14'-0"

BALCONY

PORCH

FIRST FLOOR

CLOS

CHAMBER
10'-0" x 14'-0"

CHAMBER
11'-8" x 14'-0"

CL

HALL

CLOS

CLOS

CHAMBER
10'-0" x 12'-10"

CHAMBER
12'-10" x 15'-0"

SECOND FLOOR

PLATE 14.

DESIGN 24—Gives plans, elevations, details, and perspective view of a comfortable, convenient cottage home of six rooms, with tower which is designed to command a view of the surrounding country where erected.   Cost, $1,700.

We have always maintained, and shall continue to do so unto the end, that any structure, no matter how inexpensive, intended as a dwelling place for civilized people, should be designed by a skilled man, and should bear the marks of good design. Good design in architecture, as well as elsewhere, costs no more than bad in the construction.

COTTAGE FOR A MILL HAND AT CHELSEA, MASS.

This is a very attractive design, and intended to give ample accomodation at a low cost for an ordinary family.

The cellar is placed under the kitchen and hall, which was thought in this instance to be sufficient to meet all requirements, though it is generally considered, in the Eastern States at least, to be poor economy not to have a cellar under the whole house, as it only requires about one foot in depth of additional stone work to secure a cellar, it being necessary to put down the stone work in any case, so that it will be beyond the reach of frost. The kitchen is without a fire-place, the cooking to be done by a stove, which, if properly contrived, is a very effective ventilator, and preferred by many housekeepers for all kitchen purposes.

The parlor and dining-room or general living-room are provided with the healthy luxury of an open fire-place, and we know of no more elegant, cleanly and effective contrivance for this purpose than the one adopted in this instance; they are built of buff brick, with molded jambs and segment arch, and in which a basket-grate or fire-dogs can be placed for the desired fire, and in this way large rooms are kept perfectly comfortable in cold weather without heat from any other source. These fireplaces are also provided with neat mantels constructed of ash, and which are elegant compared with the marbleized slate mantel, which is a sham, and repulsive to an educated taste.

On entering nearly every house in the land we find the same turned walnut post at the bottom of the stairs with tapering walnut sticks all the way up, surmounted with a flattened walnut rail having a shepherd's crook at the top; however, in this instance, it is not so, but the staircase is surmounted with an ash rail, balusters and newel of simple, though unique design; and now that people are giving more attention to this important piece of furniture, we may look for a change in this respect.

The house is supplied with a cistern constructed with great care, the kitchen sink being supplied with water by a pump, and there is no more easy method of procuring good water for all purposes of the household.

For a compact, convenient cottage with every facility for doing the work with the least number of steps, for a low-priced elegant cottage, we do not know of anything that surpasses this. Cost, $1,200.

Mr. A. E. Jones, of Newport, Ohio, is also erecting this cottage with the necessary changes to suit points of compass. Such a house as this if tastefully furnished, and embellished with suitable surroundings, as neat and well-kept grounds, flowers, etc., will always attract more attention than the uninviting, ill-designed buildings, no matter how much money may have been expended on them.

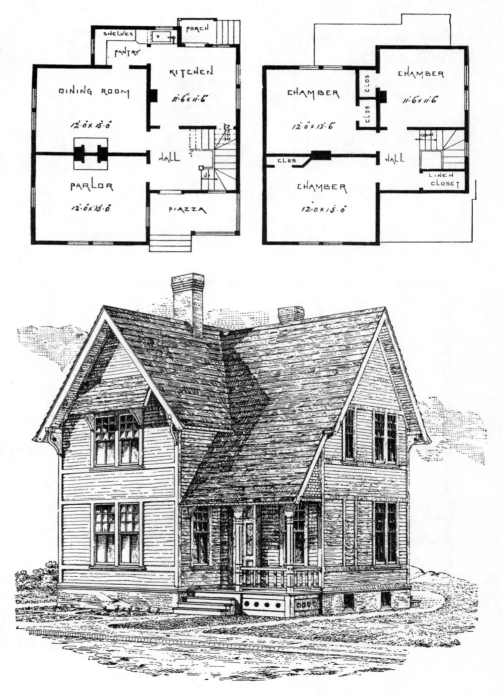

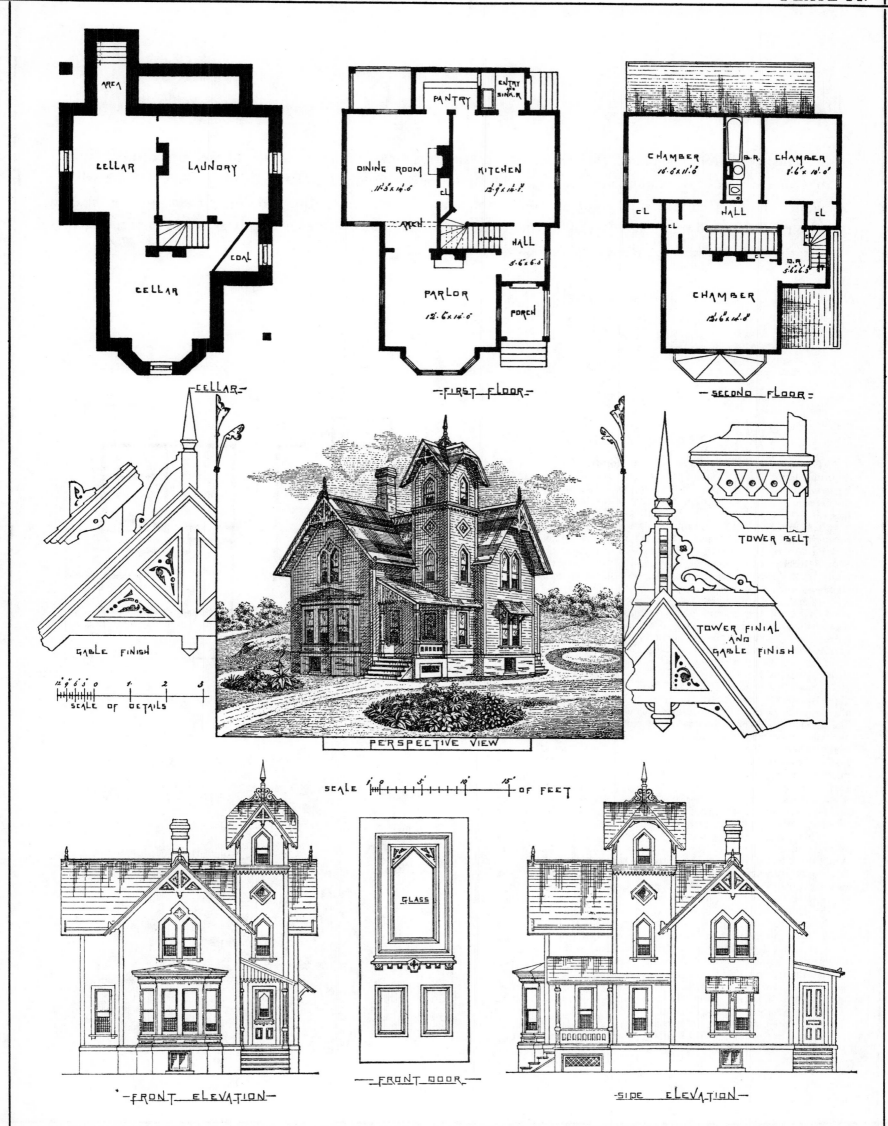

AREA

CELLAR   LAUNDRY

COAL

CELLAR

— CELLAR —

PANTRY   ENTRY and SINK R.

DINING ROOM   KITCHEN
11.6 x 14.6   14.9 x 14.9

ARCH

HALL
5.6 x 6.5

PARLOR
12.6 x 14.6   PORCH

— FIRST FLOOR —

CHAMBER   B.R   CHAMBER
16.6 x 11.6   8.6 x 10.0

CL   HALL   CL

CL   CL   B.R
5.6 x 6.5

CHAMBER
13.6 x 14.8

— SECOND FLOOR —

GABLE FINISH

12 9 6 3 0   1   2   3
SCALE OF DETAILS

PERSPECTIVE VIEW

TOWER BELT

TOWER FINIAL
AND
GABLE FINISH

SCALE   1'   0   5'   10'   15'   OF FEET

GLASS

FRONT ELEVATION

FRONT DOOR

SIDE ELEVATION

PLATE 15.

DESIGN 25—Shows plans, elevations, and perspective view of a neat cottage house, of six rooms, suitable for erection in the suburbs or country. The interior is designed to be finished in pine, in a pleasing manner and finished in natural color of wood—no paint. Mantels in parlor and dining-room to be of black walnut. The roofs to be slated; clapboards painted Venetian red; casings, cornerboards and bands, Indian red; the chamfers and cut work black. Cost, $1,600.

COTTAGE AT WEST STRATFORD, CONN.

This handsome little house is near completion for E. R. Tomlinson, and for a compact arrangement of plan cannot be beat. There is a splendid cellar under the whole house, arranged for the storage of fuel and other purposes; a well has also been put down in the cellar, which with the cistern supplies an unlimited amount of water at the kitchen sink through the aid of a pump. The attic is very spacious, and will be found very useful as a place for drying clothes, or should it be found necessary at some future time two rooms could be finished off, which would be almost as good sleeping rooms as any in the house.

There is but one chimney, which is so placed that it can be used from all the rooms on first floor; the stair-case is also placed in a position to be easy of access from all parts of the house; two doors are placed between the hall and kitchen, a feature which cannot fail to commend itself.

The windows in the hall and stair-case are filled entirely with ornamental and stained glass, as are also those in the attic; the other windows in the house have the lower sash glazed in two lights of ordinary glass, while the upper sash has a white light in center and small colored lights on each side. The interior is finished in a very pleasing, yet economical manner, the casings of doors and windows are trimmed with a back mold, though they are not mitred at the angles as is usually done, but a square block, ornamented with sunk work to be picked out in color is placed in the corner, and the molding cut square against it; this is a decided improvement on the monotonous mitred back mold which we see in nearly every house. The rooms are all of ample accommodation to meet the requirements, and each chamber is supplied with a good closet.

The exterior is very striking, the front gable is very handsome, and is a free rendering of what is known as the Queen Anne style of architecture; the front veranda and especially the hood over entrance is very pretty—in fact this is one of the prettily designed cottages which will always attract attention.

An architect designs a building with special reference to the colors to be used in painting, and as color is the life of design, his instructions in this respect should be minutely followed if the desired result is to be arrived at. This cottage is painted Venetian red, trimmed with Indian red, the chamfers, cut and sunk work being picked out in black, making it very effective and showing the detail boldly. The cost is $1,460, and we doubt if there is anyone who can show a prettier house, either in arrangement or appearance for the same price.

Blessed are they who have homes!

Let every man strive to own a home.

Mr. Tomlinson has sold this cottage to good advantage and built larger from our plans.

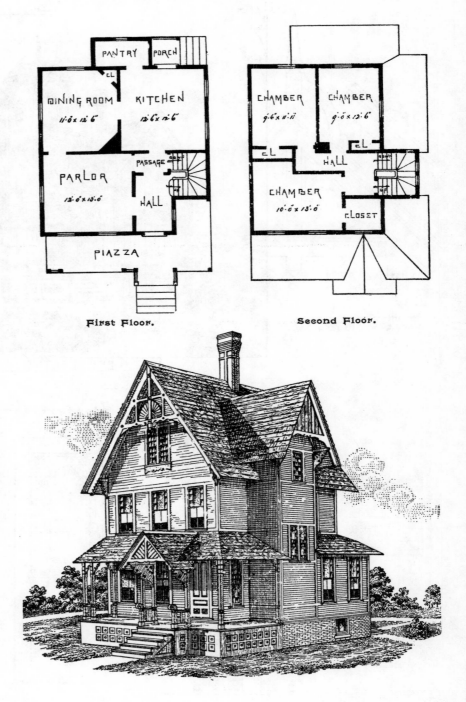

First Floor.　　　　Second Floor.

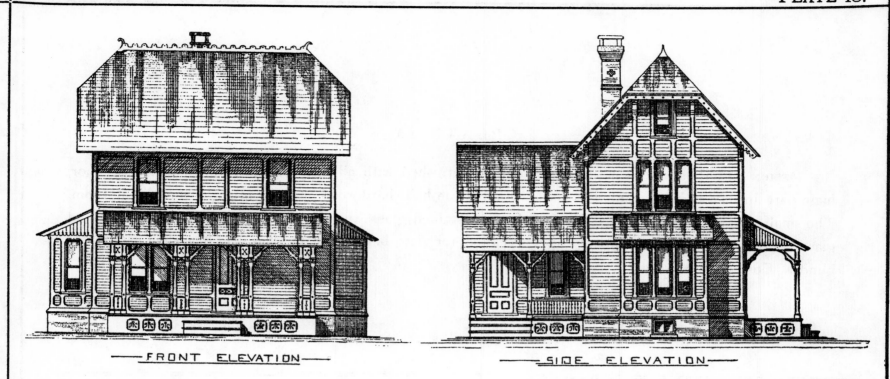

— FRONT ELEVATION —　　　　　　　　— SIDE ELEVATION —

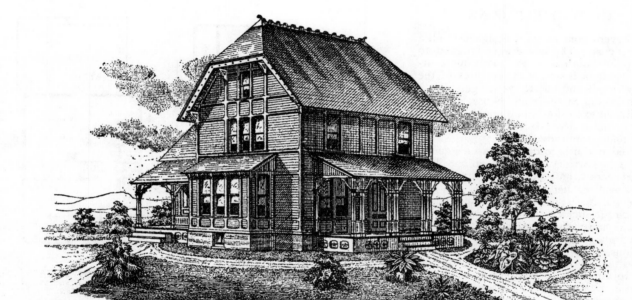

— PERSPECTIVE VIEW —
— SCALE OF — |1 2 3 4 5   10'   15'   20'   25'| — FEET —

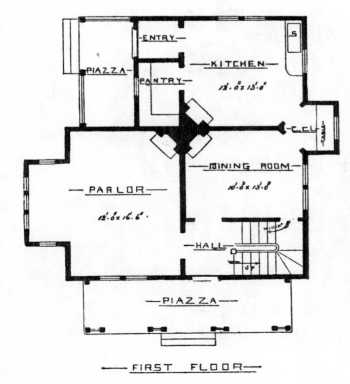

PIAZZA

ENTRY

KITCHEN
12'-0" x 13'-0"

PANTRY

DINING ROOM
10'-0" x 13'-0"

PARLOR
12'-0" x 16'-6"

HALL

PIAZZA

— FIRST FLOOR —

CLOS

BED ROOM
12'-0" x 13'-0"

CLOS

BED ROOM
12'-0" x 16'-6"

BED ROOM
7'-6" x 10'-6"

CLOS

— SECOND FLOOR —

PLATE 16.

DESIGN 26—Illustrates a seven-room house, furnished with all necessary conveniences. First floor, main part finished in hard-wood, with hard-wood floor in hall, hard-wood mantels in parlor and dining-room. The small panes in top sashes are filled with plain stained glass, the center light with ornamental ground glass; bottom sash, which is the only ones accessible for view, being of plain glass, and furnished with inside blinds. Cost, $2,000.

COTTAGE AT LITCHFIELD, CONN.

This is a neat seven-room cottage, designed to fill a narrow lot at a small cost. The house was designed to face the West, and the South side was made more attractive; the front veranda is one of the features of the exterior, and is very simple and chaste, yet elegant.

Besides the two floors in the main house, there is an attic over the kitchen extension which may be used as a stow-away. There is also a good attic over the main house, and a cellar under the whole house.

The room marked parlor is to be used as a general living-room, hence it is provided with an open fire-place and a neat hardwood mantel, and the interior throughout is finished in a plain neat manner.

The wants of people are so unequal, and their opinions so varied by the circumstances under which they are formed, that it is the most natural thing in the world for anyone to take up a plan and suggest innumerable changes and additions, always forgetting the unalterable condition of price, situation and object which restrained the architect while working it up. To prepare a design regardless of expense is an easy matter compared with that of devising one that gives the largest amount of accommodation within a fixed limit of cost, and in all our long experience we have never found a design that would meet the requirements of different individuals without some changes.

Two of these cottages are erected at Litchfield, Conn., by Messrs. Devoe and Hills. Cost, about $1,650.

The cost of a house depends in a great measure on a properly studied design, which does not consist alone in the arrangement of rooms, etc., but involves a careful study of construction; a saving can be made by a proper distribution of timbers as well as by the most economical arrangement of rooms—in fact, good or bad management produces the same results in building operations as in any other pursuit.

People will take up a work of architecture, and select a house that comes about their wants, which the book says costs $2,000, and that is just the amount they can command for building. The house is ordered, the alterations named, and put in the hauds of the best mechanic to execute it, and he goes ahead; he is not restricted except by the book, and the author of it is a man of reputation. The builder has not any specifications or details of execution to be governed by, and therefore piles on the agony, as it is not considered good policy for him to make suggestions so as to decrease the work, and when the $2,000 is expended you find the building half done, and an additional $2,000 necessary to complete it.

This is not the proper way to conduct one's building affairs, but to get the plans and details properly prepared, and then ascertain what it is to cost before going ahead—then the result will be satisfactory.

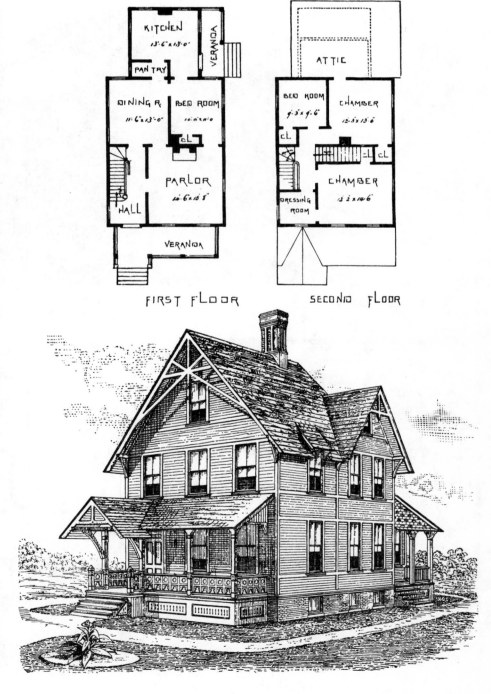

FIRST FLOOR   SECOND FLOOR

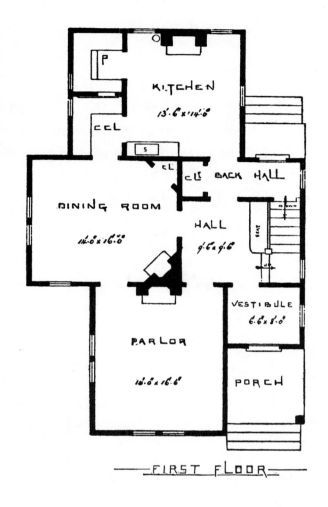

— FIRST FLOOR —

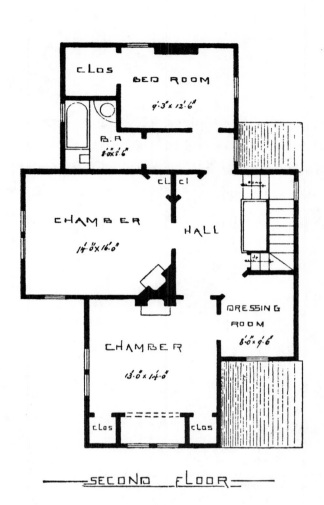

— SECOND FLOOR —

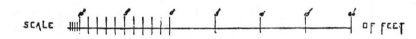

SCALE ||||||||||||||||| OF FEET

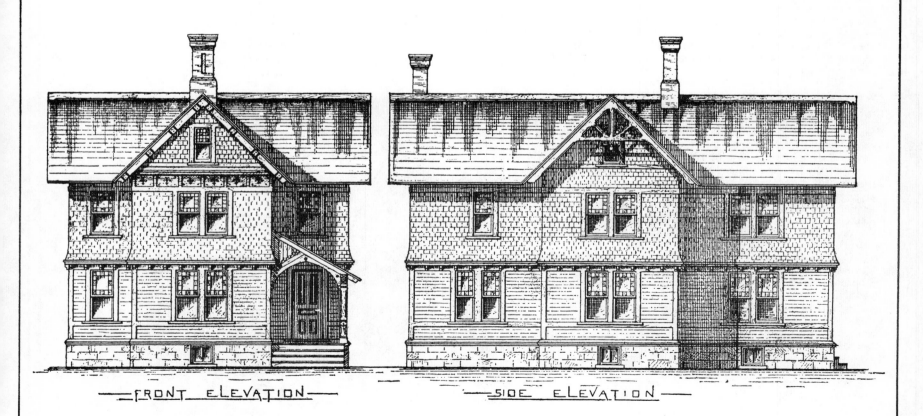

— FRONT ELEVATION —   — SIDE ELEVATION —

PLATE 17.

DESIGN 27—Shows plans, elevations, details, and perspective view of a two-story house, arranged for two families, with front and back stairs, bath-rooms, etc., and is just such a house as every mechanic of small family should own, as it will give him the required amount of room on first floor, and the second floor will rent for almost enough to pay the interest on the whole outlay.   Cost, $2,500.

RESIDENCE OF R. R. HENRY, TAZEWELL, VA.

There are many things to be taken into consideration in the designing of houses for different parts of the country. This Cottage is of a form that is compact and in every way available, the rooms are large, have high ceilings and at the same time afford every convenience in their arrangement, making them desirable for a family of refined tastes and moderate means. It is built of wood, though in favorable localities it would be better still of stone or brick, and if suitably surrounded with tasteful landscape embellishments, will make a snug, pretty, and attractive home. One can, by the exercise of appropriate taste, produce the right kind of an impression in a house of this character. It should become a part of and belong to the acres which surround it ; it should be an indispensable accessory to the place itself, and the grounds should be laid out and embellished in such a manner that the whole combination impresses one with harmonious beauty, and not, as is too often the case, seek to make up for the deficiencies in the grounds by elaborate expenditure and display about the house.

A true appreciation of a country or suburban home will not tolerate slovenly, ill-kept grounds, and no house exhibits its true value unless there is a harmony in its surroundings. If this be attended to, a high degree of effect can be produced in houses of very moderate cost ; houses that should be roomy, warm, substantial and in every way agreeable to their occupants.

The glass throughout is common sheet without color, but the dividing up of the upper sashes gives character to the whole ; the plain treatment of the exterior is more than made up by the beauty of the internal arrangements, which the plans fully explain.

Architecture is young in this country, and we have to look to the mother country for many of our ideas ; but because we do this we need not follow their custom in building our small houses, but we must meet the requirements of climate and habits ; therefore the arrangements of rooms is entirely different, and we add verandas, which are valuable appendages on account of it being pleasant to sit out of doors.

This house is substantially built and contains the modern conveniences ; there is no water closet, but an earth closet is provided in connection with bath-room, which is preferable. Cost about $1,900.

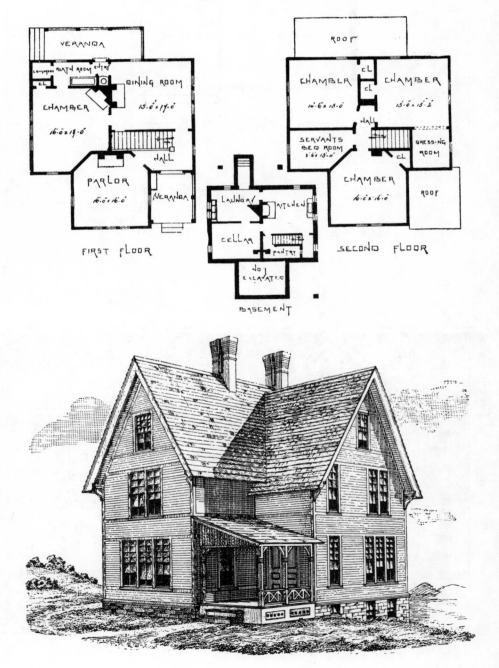

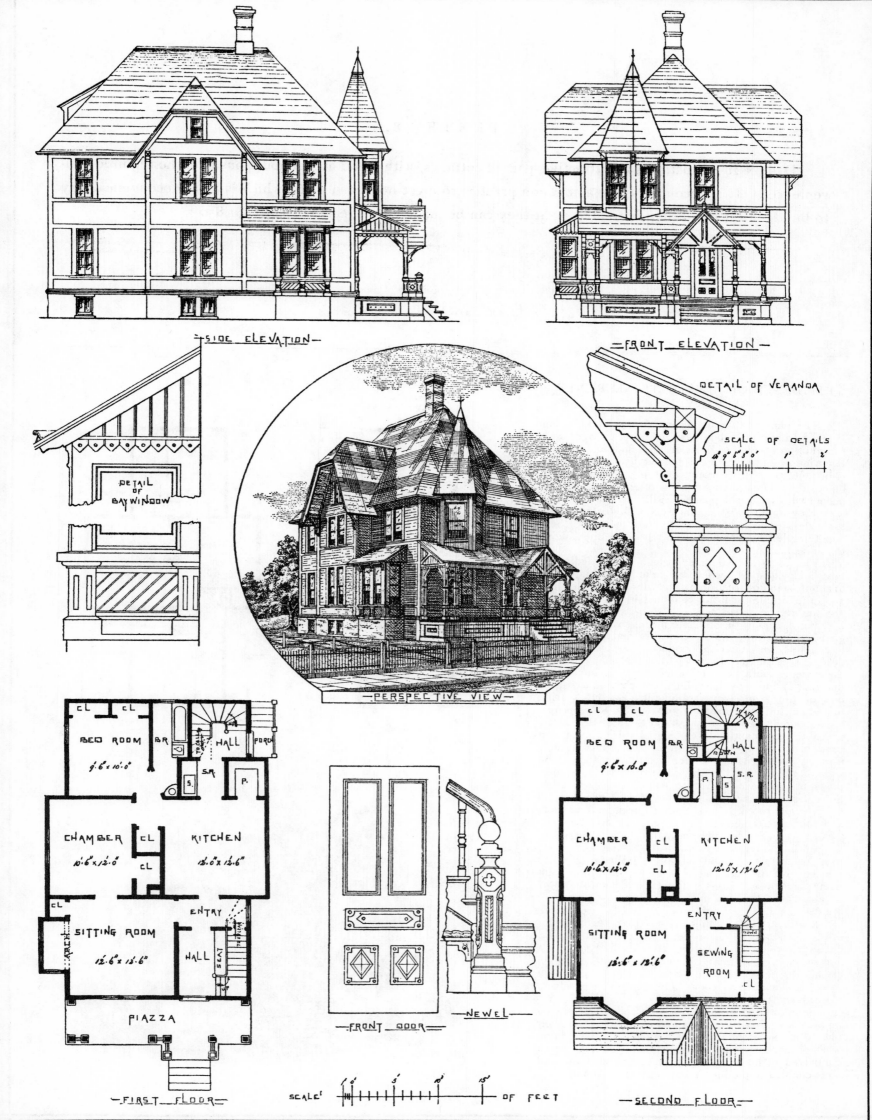

-SIDE ELEVATION-

-FRONT ELEVATION-

DETAIL OF VERANDA

DETAIL OF BAY WINDOW

SCALE OF DETAILS

-PERSPECTIVE VIEW-

FIRST FLOOR

CL   CL
BED ROOM
9'6" x 10'0"
B.R.
HALL
PORCH
S.R.
S.
P.
CHAMBER
10'6" x 12'0"
CL
CL
KITCHEN
13'0" x 12'6"
CL
SITTING ROOM
12'6" x 13'6"
ENTRY
HALL
SEAT
PIAZZA

-FRONT DOOR-

-NEWEL-

SECOND FLOOR

CL   CL
BED ROOM
9'6" x 16'8"
B.R.
HALL
DOWN
ATTIC
P.
S.
S.R.
CHAMBER
10'6" x 12'0"
CL
CL
KITCHEN
12'0" x 12'6"
SITTING ROOM
13'6" x 13'6"
ENTRY
SEWING ROOM
CL

SCALE OF FEET

PLATE 18.

DESIGN 28—Illustrates an attractive pair of cottages, with good accommodations and the required conveniences. It is becoming quite a common practice to erect houses in pairs, which is a very economical way to build, and if the design is treated right they can be made very effective. Cost, $1,850.

RESIDENCE OF ALBERT TRINLER, NEW ALBANY, IND.

The plan of this handsome cottage with tower is taken from a little book published years ago, with the addition of another room on each floor and another bay window and a change in the details on the exterior—in fact, there is scarcely anything left to remind one of the other design; and it is often the case that people will examine a plan and will say that it is just what they want, with such and such changes, and when the necessary changes are made to suit their ideas there is nothing left by which one can recognize anything of the first plan.

The roofs are all slated, which is decidedly the best and cheapest—when we take everything into account—method of roofing besides being elegant; and in favorable localities can be laid for $8.00 per 100 square feet of surface.

For a person of moderate means, wishing an elegant home with the interior comforts and convenience it contains, we can with confidence recommend this design. It is suitable for any part of the country except the extreme South, and the owner of such a house will find that its money value is far above that of a square box of the same capacity, and it costs but a trifle more than the ugly packing boxes that some people seem bound to erect in opposition to all artistic ideas, which are constantly developing in this country. In some instances we have known houses of nice design, properly managed, erected for less money than these square boxes giving but the same amount of accommodation, and which a great many people seem to think it is necessary to build if they would do so cheaply.

Usually too little attention has been paid to roofs and chimneys of houses, and they appear to have been treated as necessary evils, instead of their being made, as they should be, both useful and ornamental. A flat roof for this climate can hardly be called useful, as the action of the heat and cold on it will be more than likely to open the seams of the flat roof, and the force of a sudden shower will find its way through, sadly to the detriment of the interior decoration, as well as to the comfort and the commendable equability of temper of the inmates. In our northern climate we should have steep roofs, so as to readily shed the heavy rains and snows, and we think this cottage is well protected in this respect—the floor plans, we think, need very little explanation, as they fully explain themselves. Cost about $2,200.

Simple things become beautiful and attractive by an art inspiration. Interiors and exteriors retain their old forms substantially, but they put on new faces when touched by the real artist, who sees his work completed in his mind when he begins to plan, and so is enabled to produce a harmony throughout.

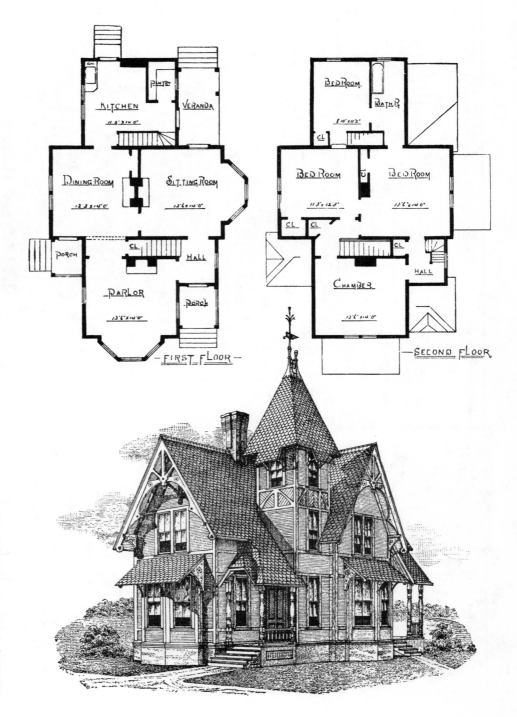

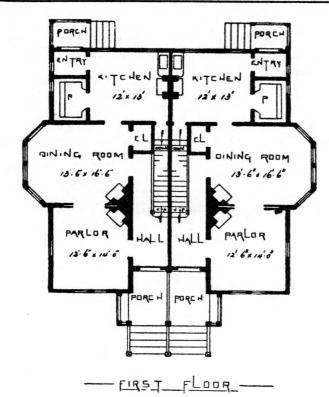

— FIRST FLOOR —

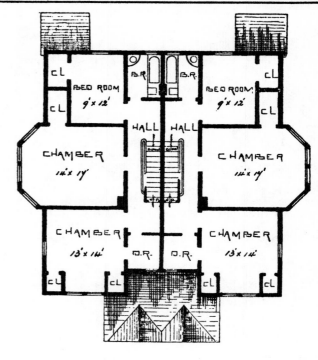

— SECOND FLOOR —

— PERSPECTIVE VIEW —

SCALE OF FEET

— FRONT ELEVATION —

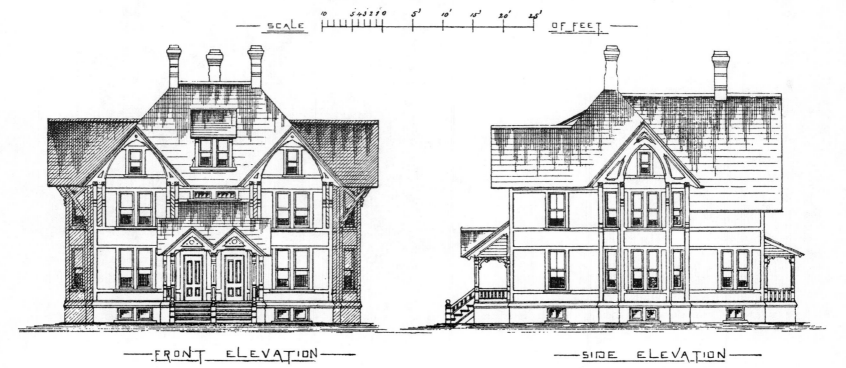

— SIDE ELEVATION —

PLATE 19.

DESIGN 29 —Shows plans, elevations and perspective view of a tasty little cottage of six rooms, with necessary conveniences to make a comfortable and attractive home. The first floor is finished in ash; mantels and side-board are executed in ash; floor in dining-room laid with yellow pine and black walnut. Second floor finished in white pine; all interior wood-work filled, and the chamfers and cut work picked out in black. Roof slated. Cost, $2,300.

RESIDENCE OF DWIGHT HOTCHKISS, SHARON, CONN.

This is a large, convenient and plain house and well adapted to the requirements of a farm residence, and yet in a farm house it would seem as though of all places this is the one where we should find large fire-places. These could have been added with very little additional expense, but instead we have what the owner desired, a single flue and the walls furred out to make a show of a breast—what we should call a sham.

Mr. Hotchkiss is undoubtedly a modest man, as when he erected his house he left off the front gable and kept the front of the building unbroken, as he was afraid his neighbors would talk if he built something different from what they had. By doing this Mr. Hotchkiss undoubtedly ruined the design and decreased the value of the building at least $500.00, spending his money to please his neighbors.

We have no doubt but what the house will be painted white, although we did not in our specifications call for it to be so, yet it is in keeping with the style of painting in the same locality, and if there is anything to mar the landscape it is this white abomination. We regret to say these things, but feel as though to be perfectly fair to our readers we should state some of the faults in our designs, and give our experiences, so that people who intend to build may avoid falling into these faults.

The veranda is a pleasant feature, and is very useful besides being ornamental; the sitting-room is the finest room in the house, both on account of its size and the view that is obtained from it; the milk room and wood shed, which are necessary appendages to a house of this kind, are located in the rear and are convenient of access from the kitchen and exterior, and are covered with a separate roof, being only one story in height. There is a cellar under the whole house built of stone found on the ground. Cost $2,900.

Some people will procure plans and specifications and then set their builder to work, being too parsimonious to furnish him with details of construction to enable him to properly carry out the design, and which is a very important matter, as what is the use of getting a good design if it is not to be carried out. Several such cases have come under our notice, and in some instances the builders have obtained details and paid for them, but it is generally the other kind of builders who get such work, and they are apt to estimate with much more liberal figures when they can carry out the designs as they please. One case of this kind in particular came under our notice, and after the building was completed it did not represent the drawings in any particular except the general form, the design being fearfully butchered and the detail all changed by the builder, who in some instances got the owner's sanction to change, persuading him that what he was going to do would be better and would cost him, the builder, more, but that he would make no charge to the owner. The house which cost him $1,800, would have been worth $500 more had the design been properly executed.

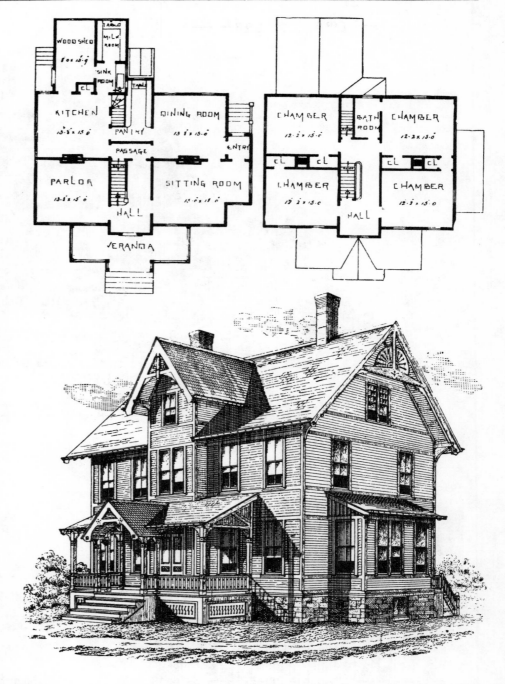

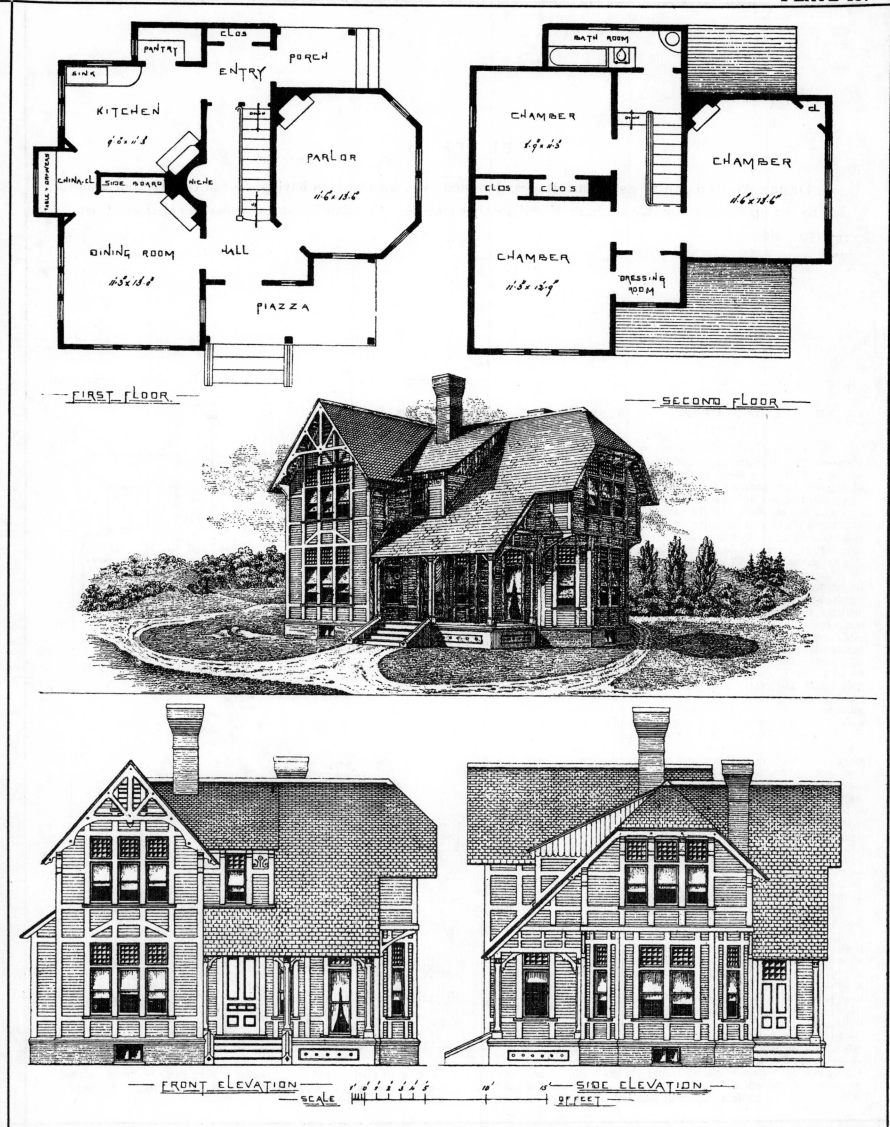

FIRST FLOOR.

SECOND FLOOR.

FRONT ELEVATION

SCALE

SIDE ELEVATION

OF FEET

PLATE 20.

DESIGN 30—Is a pair of six-room cottages, designed for a workingman having a lot in the city and wishing to put up a house suitable for himself and another member of his family, at a reasonable expense. Cost, $1,350 a side.

RESIDENCE OF N. CARPENTER, STERLING, ILL.

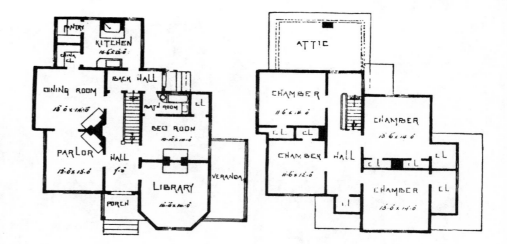

The rear extension of this house was the previous residence of Mr. Carpenter, containing but two rooms, and was put in the present position to answer the purpose of kitchen and pantries—the roof, etc., being entirely new to correspond with the new house.

The rooms on the first floor have all open fire-places, each being provided with a neat ash mantel. The library is an excellent room, with good front and side views, and the veranda is reached in an easy manner by windows from this room, making it a pleasant retreat in hot weather.

There is a variety of outline in the exterior of this house, which cannot fail to give a picturesque and pleasing appearance to the whole. The chamber above library projects slightly beyond the face of the octagon bay, and the peculiar manner in which the sides are supported is odd, but gives the appearance of stability and firmness, the construction being perfectly sound.

The upper sashes are filled with stained glass, all round the sash being very small lights of different colored glass, and the center light has the figure of a flower in white on blue ground. This manner of treating windows must be seen to be appreciated ; and no blinds are used except on the lower sash, and when the blinds are closed it gives a mellow tone to the light of the interior.

The back hall is reached by side porch, and the bathroom is placed so that anyone coming into the house can step into bath-room, and prepare their toilet before entering the main house ; the second story rooms are full height; and there is a well-lighted attic above. A laundry is provided in the cellar ; also provision is made for the storage of fuel, etc. Cost, $2,500.

There are no blinds on this house, and we should like to know of what use they are. To our mind, they are neither useful or ornamental. They are forever rattling on the outside, and always in the way of curtains on the inside, and where we have mullion windows, they must be kept closed or they are in the way; and if we use outside blinds, they are forever in the way of adding a bit of detail here, and a hood or a balcony there, which would add greatly to the effect of the whole. The only blinds that are fit for use are rolling Venetian blinds ; they slide up and down, and are out of the way, and will cover the whole or a part of the window, as required ; but these are a little more expensive, you say, than ordinary inside blinds, but we can find a substitute which is equally as good—we can make a shade of heavy cloth, to roll up by pulling a cord—or, better still, slide it with rings on a bar. These shades should fit the window, and hang flat and straight, or nearly so. The material may be cheap and coarse, and offers an excellent opportunity for embroidery, where it would show to good advantage. Rich browns are the most available colors, which might be either coarse jute cloth or burlaps. Then there is an endless variety of materials which may be used, according to taste and depth of pocket. Blinds can be better left off, and replaced by something which will be far more pleasing to the eye, and serve the same purpose.

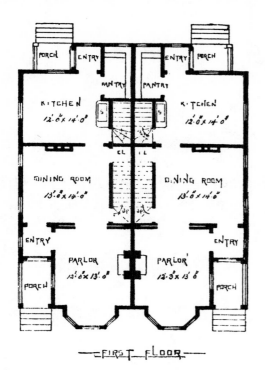

— FIRST FLOOR —

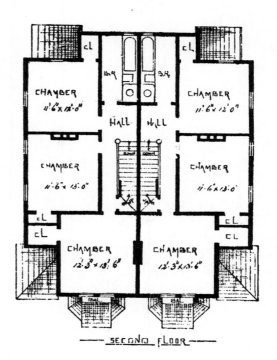

— SECOND FLOOR —

— PERSPECTIVE VIEW —

SCALE OF FEET

— FRONT ELEVATION —

— SIDE ELEVATION —

PLATE 21.

DESIGN 31—Shows plans, elevations, and perspective view of a neat, square cottage house, of eight rooms, suitable for erection in almost any location, and makes a very attractive house with a good amount of room and conveniences.   Cost, $1,950.

RESIDENCE OF W. COE, STRATFORD, CONN.

In the plans of almost every house there is more or less to commend or condemn. Some of course are much nearer perfection than others. When a plan takes such a form that it will answer in many places for exactly the same purpose, we may with truth call it a model ; and in this case we think we may be justified in calling this a model farm house. The rooms are all of good capacity and conveniently arranged, and the principal rooms have an open fire-place ; sliding doors are placed so that the parlor, sitting-room and hall can be thrown together on special occasions, a feature which is always appreciated. The dining-room is reached from kitchen through lobby, which is fitted up with press and drawers. In this way two doors are between kitchen and dining-room and hall, so that the fumes of the kitchen are kept out of the main house.

The hall is wide and spacious, and gives a stranger on entering an idea of hospitality ; the spacious veranda gives ample space for the occupants to enjoy nature, and at the same time be suitably protected from the glare of the sun.

The main house has two full and high stories, and a high attic, in which good rooms can be obtained should it be necessary. This house has the conveniences that are usually to be had in the country ; the bay window is a nice feature. In fact, it is a model home for the farmer, and a splendid house for the amount of money expended, viz., $2,406, for everything complete except cellar walls, which were built by owner with stone on the ground.

In looking over this design, it will seem hard to believe the fact that we had great difficulty in persuading our client not to alter the exterior design. He wanted a flatter roof and box cornice ; in fact, a house just after the same idea as others in his locality. We asked him to investigate, and see for himself how houses were being built, and see what they looked like ; and we requested him to examine a house recently built, no larger than his which cost nearly $10,000, which in some respects was treated similar to his. After he had examined and studied the work that was being done, he was convinced that we were right, and that his objections were the result of ignorance on the subject. It is just this want of knowledge that we have to contend with every day.

Having occasion to be in Stratford a few days ago, we observed that this house was being painted entirely different from what we specified it to be. The prevailing color was white, with dark trimmings, chamfered work in gables, etc., being white ; and, in fact, the whole effect was spoiled. The colors specified were : for clapboards, light sage ; corner-boards, bands, etc., buff ; chamfers and cut work, black ; but were entirely disregarded. That is what we call consulting a physician, and then taking our own or some one else's physic.

It requires as much judgment and taste to paint a house, so as to bring out the details, and give the desired effect, as it does to design one.

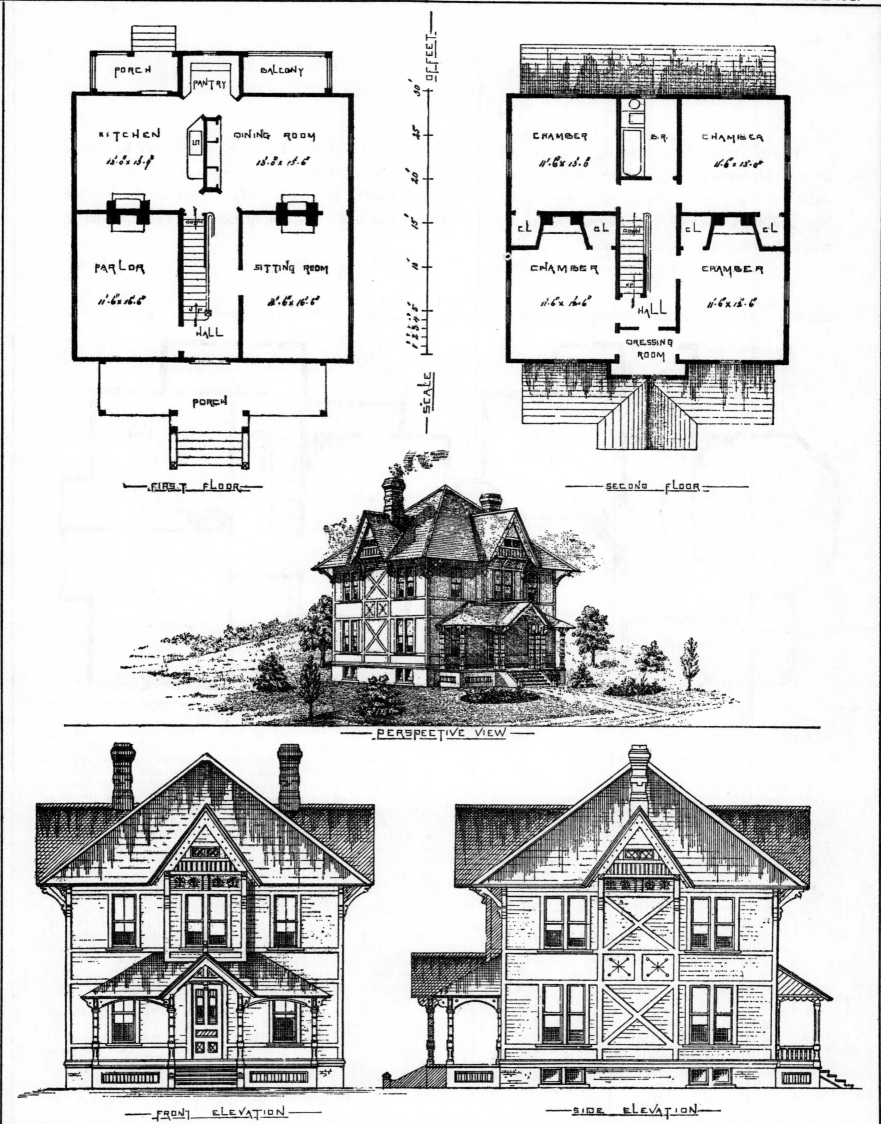

PORCH

PANTRY

BALCONY

KITCHEN
13.0 x 13.9

DINING ROOM
13.8 x 15.6

DOWN

PARLOR
11.6 x 16.6

SITTING ROOM
11.6 x 16.6

HALL

PORCH

FIRST FLOOR

CHAMBER
11.6 x 13.6

B.R.

CHAMBER
11.6 x 13.8

CL.   CL.

CL.   CL.

DOWN

CHAMBER
11.6 x 12.6

UP

CHAMBER
11.6 x 12.6

HALL

DRESSING ROOM

SECOND FLOOR

SCALE OF FEET

PERSPECTIVE VIEW

FRONT ELEVATION

SIDE ELEVATION

PLATE 22.

DESIGN 32—Is illustrated by plans, elevations, and perspective view. This design is a very handsome cottage of seven rooms, with the necessary conveniences, the interior to be finished in good style. The walls, up to first story window-sills, are of brick, faced with North Haven brick of even color, relieved with bands of black brick—the red brick laid in red mortar, and the black brick in black mortar; roofs slated, ridge of terra cotta. Cost, $2,900.

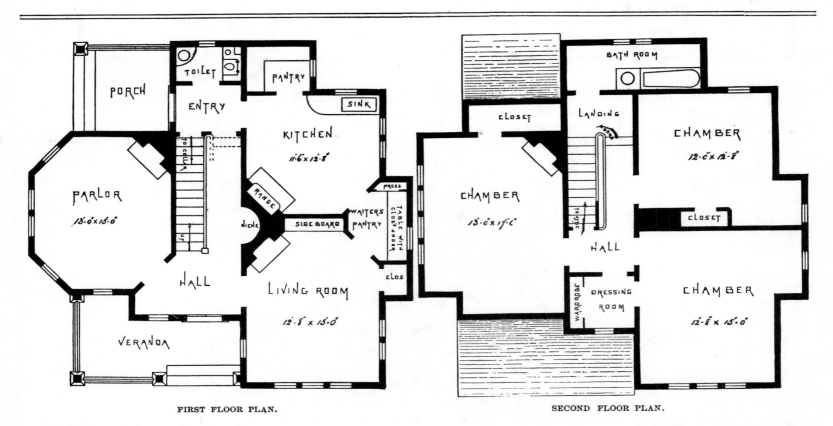

FIRST FLOOR PLAN.

SECOND FLOOR PLAN.

RESIDENCE OF F. EGGE, SEASIDE PARK, BRIDGEPORT, CONN.

This is the most charming cottage we have ever seen, and a great many people have said this; it is also our model six-room cottage. Contains all the modern improvements and conveniences, at a moderate price.

The underpinning is laid with red brick of even color, and trimmed with bands of black brick and tile. These brick are laid in red and black mortar. It will also be seen that the underpinning extends up to first story window-sill and the window-sill and water-table are one, which is thought by some to be an odd feature. The roofs are slated with the best black slate, with chipped corners, making a very handsome roof.

The interior is the main object of consideration, and is simply elegant, and it is in correct keeping with a greater refinement of taste and a higher degree of æsthetic culture, than anything we know of in this part; and while it requires a boldness to assert an honest preference for pine or ash, finished in their natural colors, over the futile attempts of imitating walnut—as the crowning boast has been all black walnut—in this case the whole of the inside work is finished in natural wood, being filled. The pine is equal to maple, and black walnut is cheap in comparison with it. There are no mouldings or paint on the interior, the doors and architraves are finished as shown in view of living-room, the chamfers, sunk work, etc., being picked out in black. The mantles are of ash, also the side-board, with black chamfers, etc, the fire-places being built of buff brick, with moulded jambs. The toilet and bath-rooms are finished in ash.

The stained-glass work introduced in all the windows above the transom is a new feature for this part, and one which is to become very popular in all domestic buildings from this time forward.

Such houses erected in the suburbs of our cities, would add very much to the value of the ground they stand on, and pay a handsome rate of interest on their cost, better than any other class of building investments, as the supply falls far short of the demand. Business men and others wishing to reside out of the city need just such a home as this, and we wonder capitalists and real estate owners do not make money for themselves and others by erecting such tasteful, yet inexpensive, suburban homes.

In former times a house like this would be painted white, but we are glad to say that much improvement has of late been made in this respect; but unfortunately this taste for white, to a certain extent, still exists. It requires a nice and cultivated eye to determine the colors most appropriate and effective for the exterior of a house, and depends entirely on its size, form, style, etc. A good design may be entirely spoiled by the colors used in painting, and the beauty of the landscape is often marred by a white house with green blinds. This cottage is painted a warm red, the trimmings being darker than the ground work, and the chamfers and sunk work are picked out in black; the sashes are painted a dark yellow, giving the whole a most striking and effective appearance.

The story of the beauty of this cottage has been noised far and wide, and hundreds of people have visited it—some who are intending to build have come a hundred miles to see it and consult us. Such cottages as this are the stimuli that is to work a revolution in domestic architecture, and sweep away everything that is ugly and pernicious to the eye of the cultivated.

A builder, who came from the country about one hundred miles, was incredulous when told the interior of the wood-work was pine,

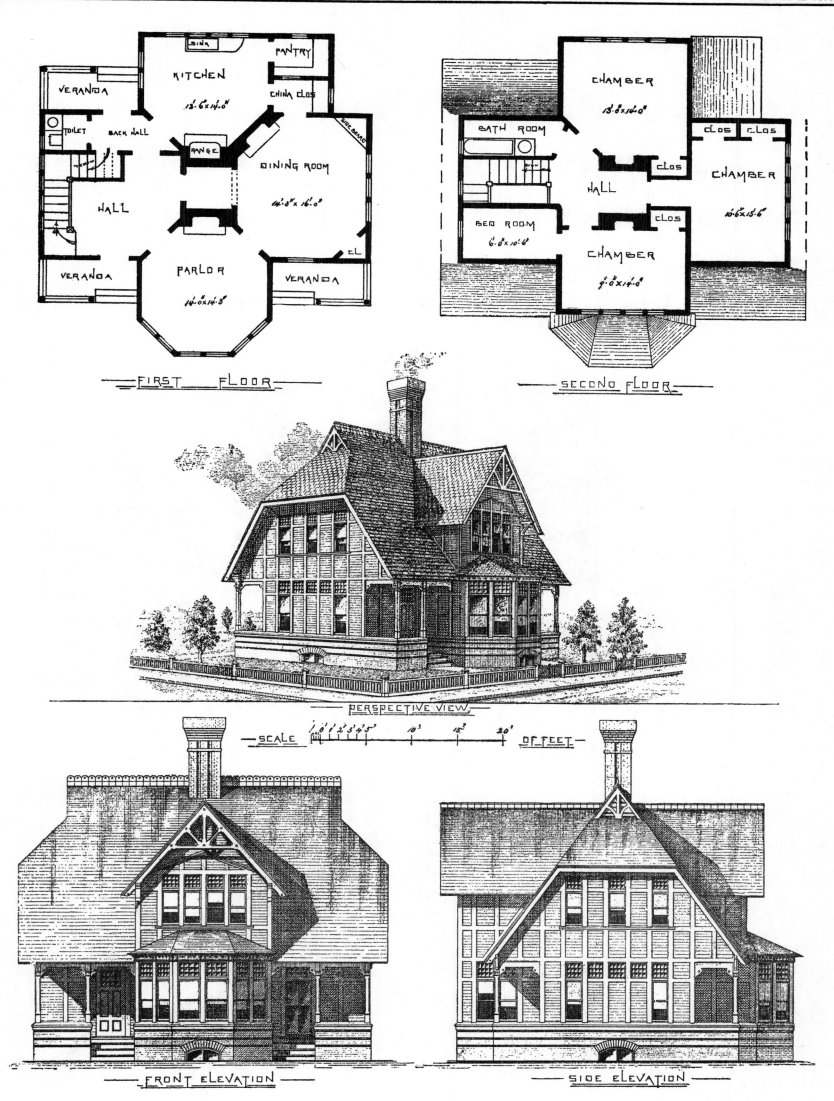

FIRST FLOOR

SECOND FLOOR

PERSPECTIVE VIEW

SCALE ——— OF FEET

FRONT ELEVATION

SIDE ELEVATION

PLATE 23.

DESIGN 33—Gives plans, elevations and perspective view of a Southern cottage of eight rooms, which, with some slight changes, is suitable for erection in almost any part of the country, and is a very attractive and convenient house at a very reasonable price. Cost, $1,500.

VIEW OF F. EGGE'S COTTAGE.

and he immediately bet a hat it was maple, and left it to us to decide, and lost.

An Englishman on first seeing it exclaimed : "It's a nice 'ouse! It would make a nice 'ome for hany man."

It is the cottage par-excellence, and possesses a beauty far beyond the houses generally seen belonging to persons much higher in the social scale, and has been coveted by those who could purchase it fifty times over.

The whole of the work and materials are first-class in every respect. Cost $2,775.

When this cottage was being designed the owner did not dictate to us how we should place the rooms, or how the exterior or interior should be, but left it entirely to us—and, therefore, he has something to his and everyone's liking.

A house of effective design and convenient and artistic interior will add, independently of its cost, to the value of the property which surrounds it, and is often what secures the purchaser. And it is the same with houses to rent. We have known houses of the same cost have a difference in rental of fifty per cent, simply because one was built without regard to taste, comfort and convenience, and the other thoroughly designed by an experienced architect.

A thing of beauty is a joy forever.

Mr. Egge sold this cottage at a very handsome profit and we have planned him a larger house which he has built on Park ave., Bridgeport, Conn.

LIVING-ROOM.

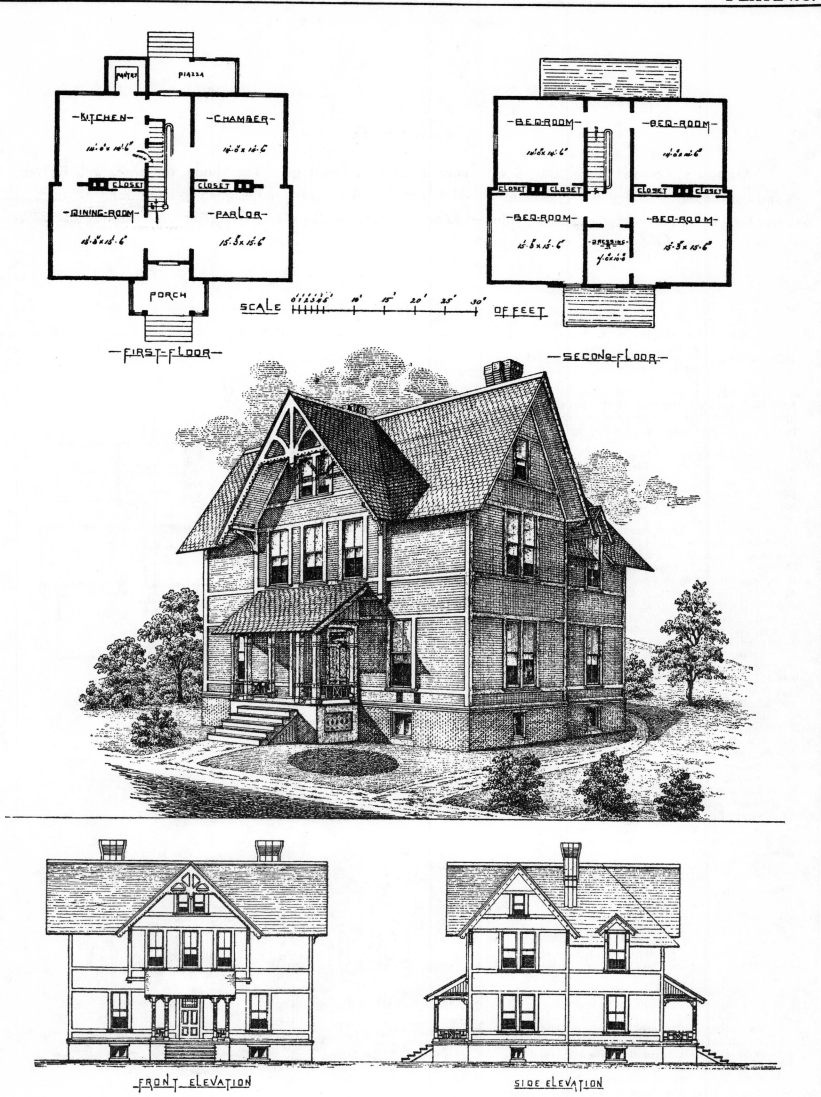

SCALE |0'1'2'3'4'5' 10'   15'   20'   25'   30'| OF FEET

—FIRST-FLOOR—   —SECOND-FLOOR—

PANTRY   PIAZZA

—KITCHEN—   —CHAMBER—

CLOSET   CLOSET

—DINING-ROOM—   —PARLOR—

PORCH

—BED-ROOM—   —BED-ROOM—

CLOSET   CLOSET   CLOSET   CLOSET

—BED-ROOM—   —BED-ROOM—

DRESSING R.

FRONT ELEVATION   SIDE ELEVATION

PLATE 24.

DESIGN 34—Shows plans and elevations of a handsome cottage. The rooms are large, well lighted, and conveniently arranged. The mantels, sideboard, and book-case are designed to be of ash; all interior finish of white pine—no mouldings—finished in natural color. The piazza is very spacious, and is an attractive feature in the design. Cost, $3,000.

RESIDENCE OF REV. DR. MARBLE, NEW-TOWN, CONN.

This house commands a particularly fine view from both sides and the front, and is situated in one of the pleasantest country towns in New England, the hotels of this town being crowded during the summer months with people from the cities.

The exterior design is plain, yet picturesque, and at once gives one an idea of ease and comfort. The roofing over the hall and sitting room is a particularly fine feature, and the elevation of the rear is very striking, the roof over porch being a part of the main roof.

The interior arrangements are very nice, the hall being spacious, and in it we have an easy and handsome staircase of plain design, constructed of Georgia pine; the newel extends up to ceiling of first floor, while the other two posts extend up to ceiling of second floor. In all country houses one of the first things to be aimed at is to secure ample staircases, and until a man can afford space for an easy ascent to a second floor he should stay below; and to-day we find in houses where there is no necessity for it, stairs that are little better than step-ladders, making a pretence of breadth at the bottom with swelled steps, and winding the steps on approaching the floor above thus making a trap for the old and for the children.

The corner fire-place between parlor and dining-room, is a feature we indulge in to a great extent in these days of economy, sliding-doors and fire-places, although we sometimes have clients who object to this, thinking it would not look as well as when placed in center of side wall; but when they are asked how this and that can be provided for with the best and most economical results, they readily give in.

There is no water-closet in the house, but an earth-closet is provided in the rear hall, which is thoroughly ventilated.

The dining-room is a very cheerful room, and the kitchen is reached through a passage also connecting with side veranda. The pantry is lighted with a window placed above press; each fire-place is furnished with a neat hard-wood mantel, and the hall is finished in Georgia pine, the floor being laid with this material, and finished in natural color.

The exterior is painted as follows: Ground, light slate; trimmings, buff; and chamfers, black. Cost, $2,925.

The sight of this house in the locality in which it is built is very refreshing, and is greatly in advance of the old styles of rural box architecture to be found there. When people see beautiful things they very naturally covet them, and they grow discontented in the possession of ugliness. Handsome houses, other things equal, are always the most valuable. They sell the quickest and for the most money. Builders who feign a blindness to beauty must come to grief.

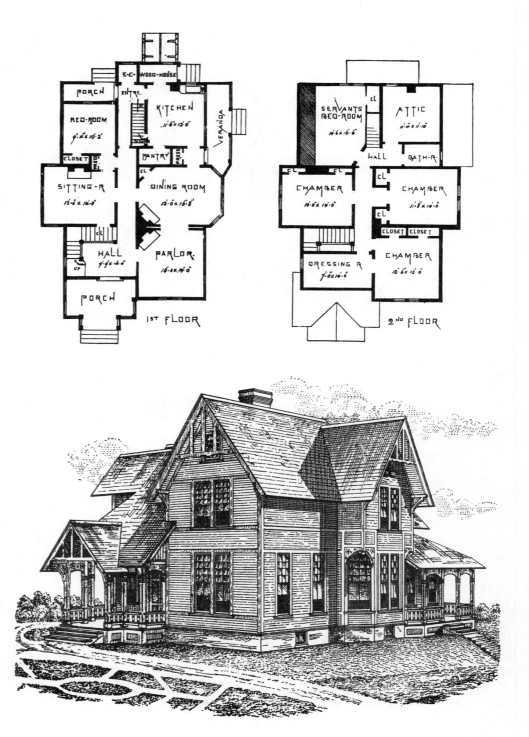

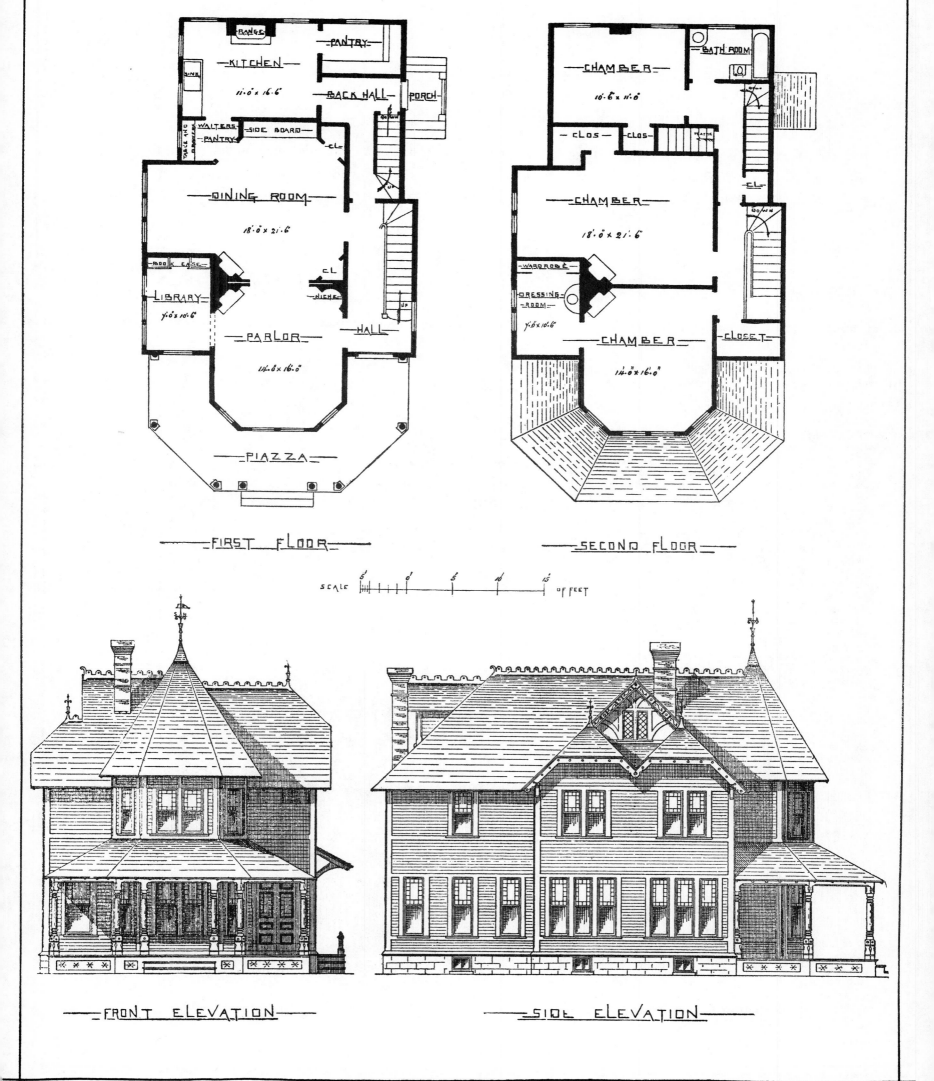

KITCHEN
11'·0 x 16'·6

RANGE
PANTRY

SINK

WALTERS PANTRY
BACK HALL
PORCH
SIDE BOARD
C.L.

DINING ROOM
18'·0 x 21'·6

BOOK CASE
C.L.
NICHE

LIBRARY
7'·0 x 10'·6

HALL

PARLOR
14'·0 x 16'·0

PIAZZA

— FIRST FLOOR —

CHAMBER
10'·6 x 11'·6
BATH ROOM

CLOS   CLOS

CHAMBER
18'·0 x 21'·6

WARDROBE

DRESSING ROOM
7'·6 x 10'·6
C.L.
DOWN

CHAMBER
14'·0 x 16'·0
CLOSET

— SECOND FLOOR —

SCALE   OF FEET

— FRONT ELEVATION —   — SIDE ELEVATION —

PLATE 25.

DESIGN 35—Is a comfortable cottage of nine rooms, with modern conveniences, and adapted to the requirements of a suburban residence. First floor to be finished in hard-wood. Cost, $2,800.

RESIDENCE OF W. W. WOODRUFF, MOUNT CARMEL, CONN.

This design was carried out by the owner, Mr. Woodruff, and is a very neat and attractive home, and as it was necessary in the arranging of this plan to obtain the required amount of room and conveniences at a given cost, the exterior had to be very plain and simple to allow it.

The front faces the west. Thus we have a south view from four rooms on first floor, and a front view from dining-room. The veranda is wide, and arranged so that a group can sit out upon it with ease; the hall is eight feet wide, with an easy flight of platform stairs leading up to floor above, the platform or landing being on a level with floor over kitchen wing, making two risers more up to floor in main house. There is a cellar under whole house, the laundry being under kitchen. The stairs to cellar are placed under main stairs, and reached directly from the kitchen. The wood-shed is a convenient feature to all country houses, and should always be connected with kitchen; the refrigerator is built in the pantry, with an opening into wood-shed, through which to put the ice into tank; the connection from kitchen to dining-room is through the large china closet, which is fitted up with shelves, press, table, etc., and makes a perfect butler's pantry. The parlor and dining-room are connected by sliding doors; the dining and sitting-rooms have open fire-places, with hard-wood mantels; the sitting-room has a hard-wood book-case built into recess to right of mantel, and the bed-room connected with sitting-room is a good room, and provided with two closets and stationary wash-bowl.

The second story contains four large chambers, with an abundance of closet room, a good servant's bed-room over kitchen, and a bath-room; hot and cold water is supplied to all wash-bowls, sink and bath. There is also a large attic over the second floor, capable of being finished off into two or three rooms if desired, and yet have enough for storage. The roof is shingled, and the exterior walls clapboarded; the interior finished in pine, which is filled with Crockett's Preservative, the cut and incised work being picked out in black. The estimated cost of this house is $3,000, and is a good example of what can be done for that sum, as the general arrangement is such as to show considerable variety on the exterior, producing an architectural effect only obtained by the natural combinations and workings of the constructive part of the structure with the least expenditure of labor and detail in design. This is one of the most attractive homes for the amount expended, and for the country is all that is desirable in every respect.

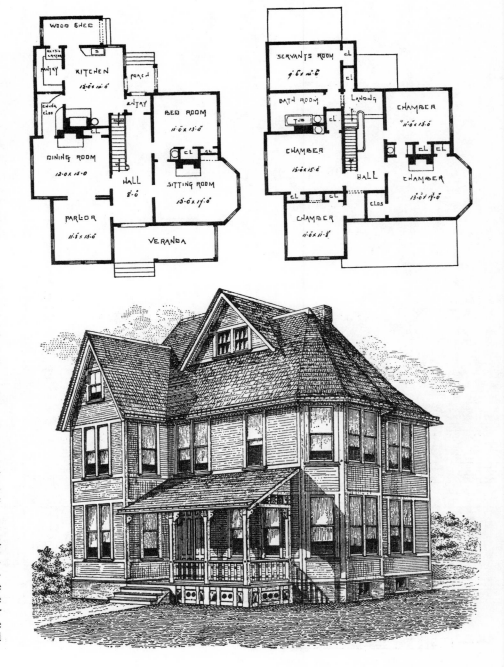

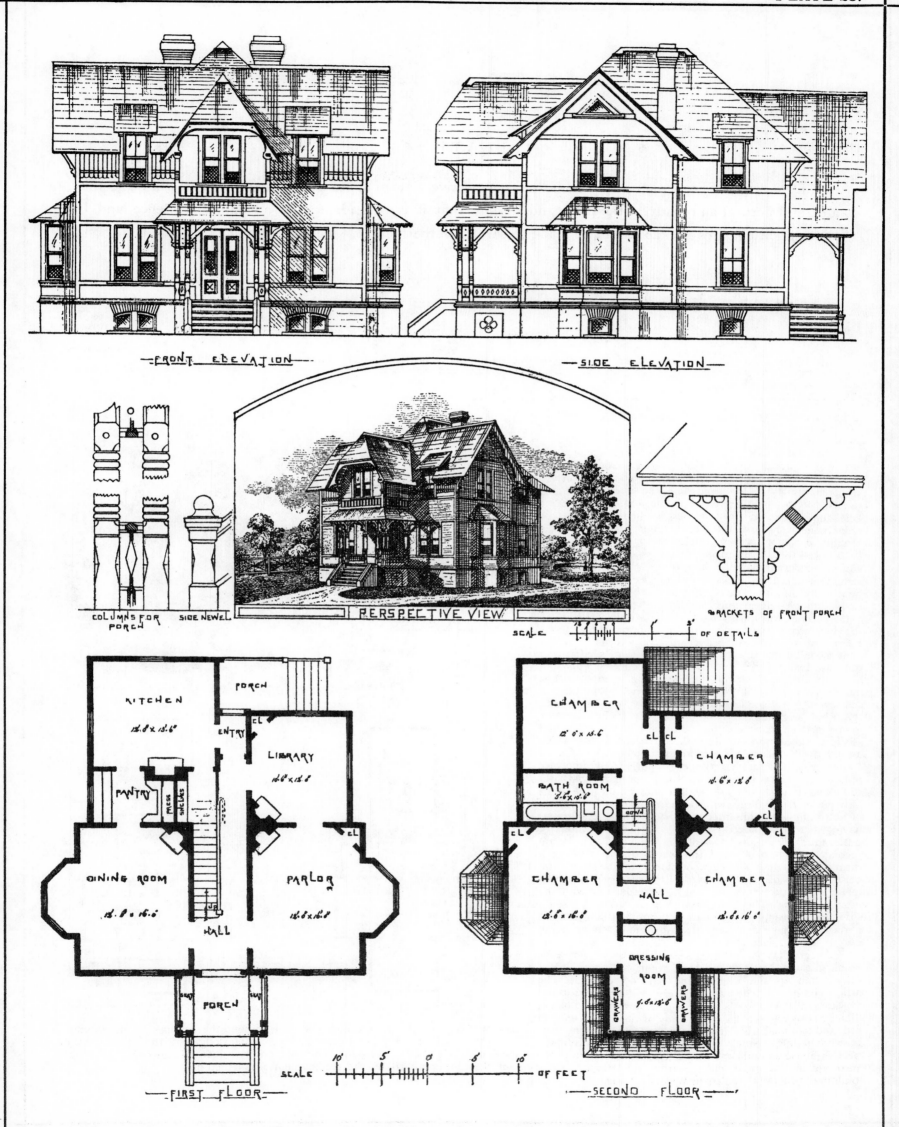

FRONT ELEVATION

SIDE ELEVATION

COLUMNS FOR PORCH

SIDE NEWEL

PERSPECTIVE VIEW

SCALE OF DETAILS

BRACKETS OF FRONT PORCH

KITCHEN
12.0 x 13.6

PORCH

ENTRY

CL

PANTRY

PRESS
SHELVES

LIBRARY
10.0 x 13.8

DINING ROOM
13.0 x 16.6

HALL

PARLOR
13.8 x 16.8

CL

PORCH

FIRST FLOOR

CHAMBER
12.0 x 13.6

CL CL

CHAMBER
10.6 x 12.8

BATH ROOM
7.6 x 13.8

DOWN

CL

CHAMBER
13.6 x 16.8

HALL

CHAMBER
13.6 x 16.0

CL

DRESSING ROOM
7.6 x 13.6

DRAWERS

DRAWERS

SECOND FLOOR

SCALE 10' 5' 0 5' 10' OF FEET

PLATE 26.

DESIGN 36—Shows plans, elevations, and perspective view of a sea-side cottage, and it will be seen by a careful perusal and study of the plans and design, that it is well adapted for a summer residence, and, by some slight changes in plan, could be made to suit a Southern clime.   Cost, $2,600

RESIDENCE OF SILAS W. GARDINER, LYONS, IOWA.

The simplicity of plan, and the simple manner in which the design expresses it, is fairly shown in the picturesque exterior here illustrated ; its constructive features are fully represented in the gables, cresting, finials, chimneys and porches.   The house stands on a brick underpinning, and is a good example of one of the half-timber and tile designs of the Jacobite period, though, unlike its prototype, shingles cut to a pattern are substituted for tiles from the second story up.   The first story shows what has the appearance of a timber construction, although it is only formed in the ordinary manner of finishing frame buildings, by continuing the belts through and connecting them with angle-boards, being clapboarded with narrow clapboards between, in the customary manner on frame buildings, the frame being first sheathed, then covered with waterproof paper. The second story is arranged so as to form a hood over the first, being furred out by a moulded cornice about eight inches, at which the shingles are curved outwards. There is also a similar cornice and curve at the head of the second story window casings, coming out flush with the window casings, which project six inches, thereby giving a deep recessed window on the inside.   The first story windows have stained glass transom lights, which are filled with foliated centers and gothic borders in leaded frames, which lend a charm to the interior not otherwise obtainable.   The floors in vestibule, conservatory, bathroom and dining-room are of ash and walnut ; the doors have pine styles and rails with butternut panels; architraves of butternut, with pine door-stops and jambs, architraves having cut-work, picked out in color ; inside blinds of butternut ; trimmings of real bronze.   The work on second story all pine ; and the whole of the wood-work throughout, including hard-wood floors, finished in natural color of the wood with Crockett's Preservative.   The mantels are of hard wood, in design corresponding with the interior finish.   The plant cabinet is placed on the south side, and connecting as it does with both sitting-room and dining-room, makes it very desirable, and renders it an easy matter to keep it warm.

The general plan suggests itself as being very economical, there being no waste of room, as everything is fully taken up and used to the best advantage.   The attic room over kitchen and scullery, will be found useful for storage.   The roofs are shingled and painted black. The exterior walls are painted—body of the work Venetian red and trimmed with Indian red, and cut-work in black ; sash cut in with yellow ; panels under veranda floors yellow.   The cost of this house as built was only $3,000, and certainly is a model of neatness, and a great change from the stereotyped style of the buildings generally erected in Western towns.

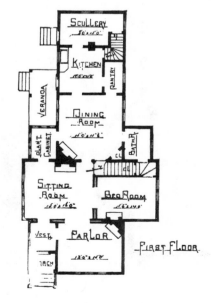

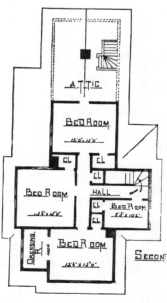

If a private house is built without the services of an architect, it is the general and candid acknowledgment afterwards, that a great mistake had been made, and how many things could have been improved by the employment of a skilled man.

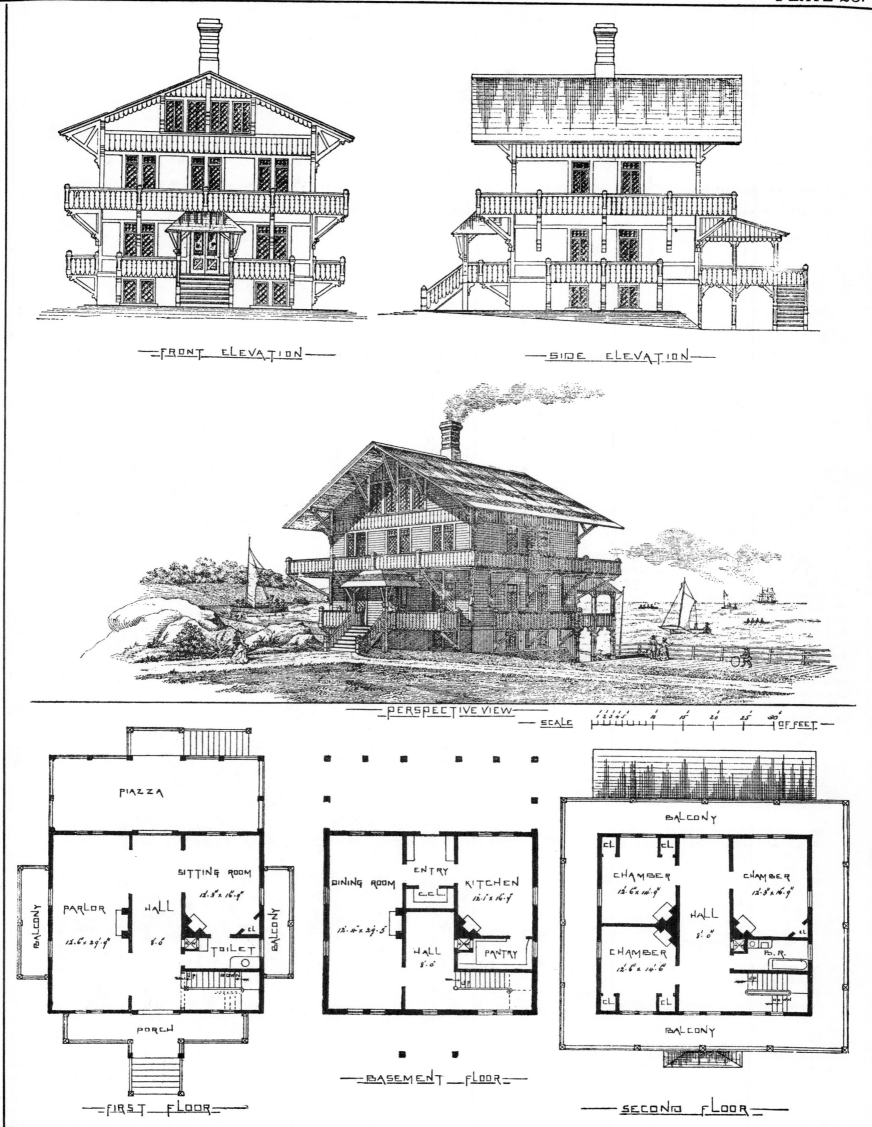

—FRONT ELEVATION—

—SIDE ELEVATION—

—PERSPECTIVE VIEW—   SCALE ⊢⊢⊢⊢⊢⊢⊢⊢⊢⊢⊢⊢⊢⊢ OF FEET.

FIRST FLOOR

PIAZZA

BALCONY

SITTING ROOM
12·5 x 16·9

PARLOR
12·6 x 29·9

HALL
8·6

TOILET

CL

BALCONY

PORCH

BASEMENT FLOOR

DINING ROOM
12·10 x 29·5

ENTRY

KITCHEN
12·1 x 16·1

C.L

HALL
8·6

PANTRY

SECOND FLOOR

BALCONY

CL   CL

CHAMBER
12·6 x 14·9

CHAMBER
12·3 x 16·9

HALL
8·0

CHAMBER
12·6 x 14·6

B. R.

CL   CL

BALCONY

PLATE 27.

DESIGN 37—Shows a barn and stable remodeled and made into a handsome residence, the parlor, toilet-room and piazzas being added. First floor is finished in yellow pine and ash; floors of hard-wood; mantels in parlor and dining-room of a neat design, executed in ash. Cost, $3,500.

PAIR OF HOUSES NEAR NEW HAVEN, CONN.

Times, places and circumstances have at all periods been found to be good governors of parties who have, or may have had, real estate that they wanted to improve, and among the many ways that have yet been devised to produce a large amount of room at a small cost, giving the necessary accommodations to separate families, the double house undoubtedly stands ahead as far as economy is concerned; one lot is thus made to do the duty of two, one chimney, one wall and one roof doing likewise; and while we have not fully made up our minds to accept the double-house system as a sure indication of the near approach of the millenium, yet we are willing to accept it as a nearer approach to the attainment of a home—even though it may seem to be only half a home—than that system, so prevalent in our country at the present day, of putting one family on a floor directly over another, the beauties of which is a theme poets never sing about; and while the double house has its many drawbacks, such as the owner of one-half painting the exterior white, and the other brown, as is frequently the case, plenty of proof of which can be seen in this locality; or one adding a bay-window and enlarging, while the other is anxious to sell out on account of his neighbor's disposition to be always making improvements, with which his pocketbook will not allow him to keep pace, and plenty of like trouble in the same spirit that we could enumerate, all of which we know from actual observation and experience. The double-house should be the property of one man, as then he can live in one-half, and either rent the other or let it stand empty to suit his pleasure; can paint, tear down and build up when it suits his fancy, or can make both sides into one should his family wants demand it, and thus eventually convert it into a home; for we must say that the half double-house never yet associated itself in our minds other than as a mere stopping place, wherein we are waiting for the home that is to be, and sometimes never comes.

The design here illustrated shows a neat and attractive front, and which cannot fail to please even the most fastidious double-house critic, and if they are as numerous all over our country as here, they are legion. The halls are in the center of the building, stairs being placed back from front doors, which gives a roomy entrance—the stairs to cellar being under main stairs, and reached from the kitchen. Each half contains six good rooms, with bath-room, dressing-room, pantry, closets, etc., with a large attic over the whole, which is divided by center wall running up to roof. The frame is a balloon, sheathed and clapboarded; roof, shingled on lath; underpinning of brick; inside blinds to bay-windows, outside blinds elsewhere, except cellar and dormer. That it is accomplishing considerable for a small equivalent is fully seen, when such a house as this is erected in a first-class manner, with all the improvements, for the sum of $3,000.

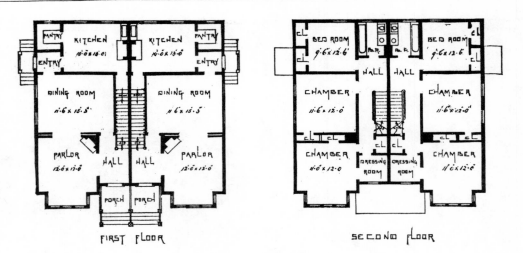

FIRST FLOOR   SECOND FLOOR

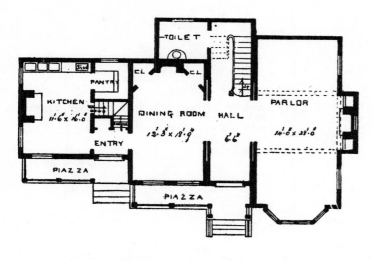

— FIRST FLOOR —

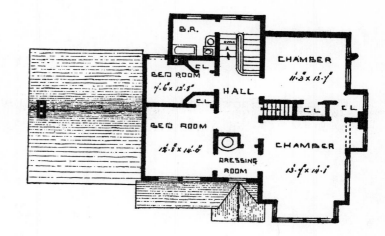

— SECOND FLOOR —

SCALE OF FEET

— FRONT ELEVATION —

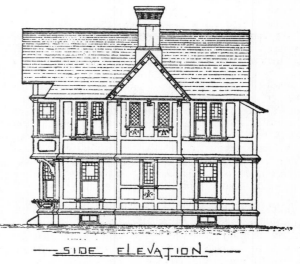

— SIDE ELEVATION —

PLATE 28.

DESIGN 38—Shows plans and view in elevation of a block of four brick and bay window houses, of nine rooms each, in Queen Anne style of architecture. Cost, $2,400 each.

RESIDENCE OF A COUNTRY PHYSICIAN.

Within a radius of fifty miles from this point, taking as a center the present position of the pen, there lives a doctor, one of those men who it is necessary to call in at stated times to help us gather our scattered roses ; or when, at certain periods, it is strictly necessary to have him to stand by as a good friend, tried and true, one who never looks into the regions of grim despair, but is ever ready to lift us up into the light of restoring hope ; in fact, one of Nature's noblemen, who we learn to look up to in our childish faith when the aches and pains are racking our weary heads. Such an one was our doctor. He owned a lot ; it was a good large one, not the city lot, 25x100—which is hardly large enough to breathe in—but a two-acre lot. This had a frontage of 150 feet on the south, thereby giving ample room for the well-kept lawn, whereon the doctor intended to take some muscular exercise during the spring and summer months in toying with the lawn mower. The doctor did not want a large house, but a good, plain, country house wherein his family could live and he could pursue his daily avocation, as far as his business went, without interfering with the privacy of his home. He must have the following rooms on first floor : parlor, sitting-room, dining-room and kitchen, with all necessary closets and other conveniences, front and back stairs, a reception-room for patients, a consultation-room and a laboratory ; a drive porch for every-day use, and a spacious front porch and front veranda if it could be done. He must be able to pass in at any door and out at the other without disturbing any part of the house. All rooms on first floor to have open fire-places, and as many on the second floor as possible ; five good bed-rooms, bath-room, plenty of closets. Cellar under the whole house and laundry under kitchen. The matter of drainage to be properly arranged, and there being a running stream in the rear of lot, the doctor congratulated himself that he would not live on sewer gas. Yet the drains must be well ventilated and a trap placed in main pipe just clear of the house. This, the doctor said, if good for nothing else, would keep the rats from entering the house by the drains. The house to be heated by steam heater placed in the cellar, the necessary provissions for which were to be made, together with store and vegetable cellars, coal and wood and a water-closet, which must be ventilated into one of the chimney flues, and also have an outside window. All the above are embodied in the design with the exception of sitting-room, which, at the specified price, could not be done, so we made the front hall into a sitting-room, which the doctor says is truly beautiful, and the best and most useful room in the house. Here is the open fire-place wherein the wood fire glows cheerfully upon the hearth, and round which it is so pleasant to gather. The mantel is built of wood, with a large hood over it and a clock built in it. The walls are wainscoted, ceiling finished in wood, giving an old-time welcome and an hospitable appearance to those coming in to visit the family, and that which should be felt on entering any house no matter how humble it may be. The staircase is of ash, and well-lighted from above through a stained-glass window in roof, which gives a mellow light to the rear of hall. The entire finish of hall, parlor and dining-room is in ash, the balance being in pine, and all finished in its natural color and beauty. The doctor said he wanted no paint, no graining, but his pine was to be pine—his ash, ash. No deception was to be put in this house and he has got none. Here our doctor

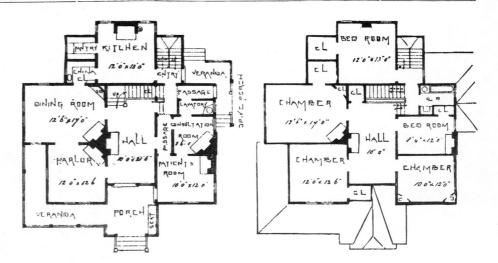

knew what he wanted. He had studied his wants for years, and when the time came for building he only had to give his problem and there was no trouble to work it out, as the plan plainly speaks for itself.

This home is not an expensive one, but a home in every sense of the word, where the homely virtues daily grow stronger, and the true, manly acts of kindness, charity and good feeling toward all men are the ruling principle. The cost of this house, without heating, is only $3,300, a proof that no country doctor can afford to be without a real live breathing place.

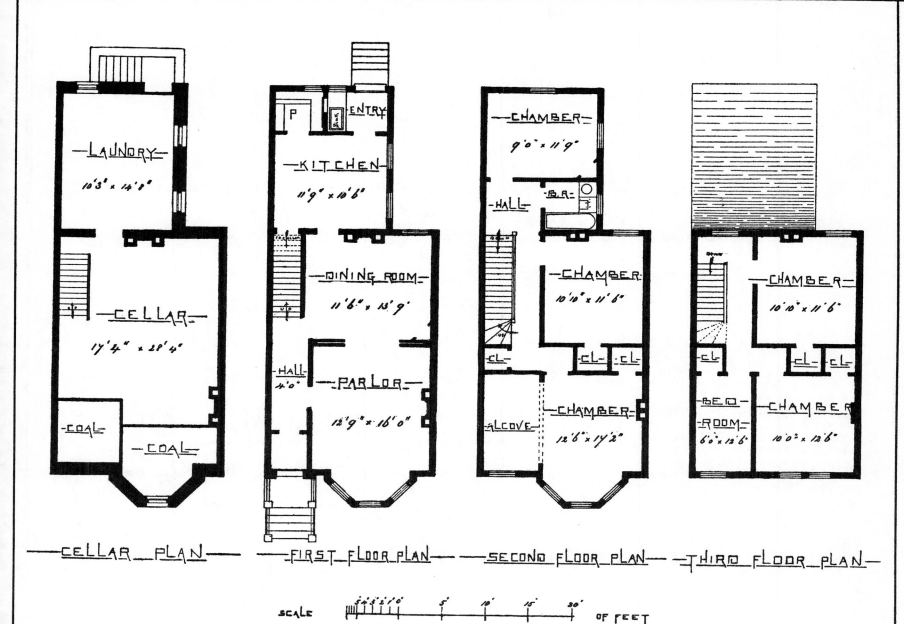

LAUNDRY
10'3" x 14'8"

CELLAR
17'4" x 28'4"

COAL

COAL

P   ENTRY

KITCHEN
11'9" x 10'6"

DINING ROOM
11'6" x 15'9"

HALL
4'0"

PARLOR
12'9" x 16'0"

CHAMBER
9'0" x 11'9"

HALL

B.R.

CHAMBER
10'10" x 11'6"

CL.   CL.   CL.

ALCOVE

CHAMBER
12'6" x 14'2"

CHAMBER
10'10" x 11'6"

CL.   CL.   CL.

BED ROOM
6'0" x 12'6"

CHAMBER
10'0" x 12'6"

CELLAR PLAN   FIRST FLOOR PLAN   SECOND FLOOR PLAN   THIRD FLOOR PLAN

SCALE   OF FEET

ELEVATION

PLATE 29.

DESIGN 39—Illustrates a pair of compact and convenient Cottages, of seven rooms each, suitable for either city or country; would make a splendid country farmhouse, for a farmer and his son to reside together, and yet have separate homes. Cost, $1,200 each.

PAIR OF HOUSES AT BRIDGEPORT, CONN.

These houses are built on an odd-shaped lot, thus giving us an opportunity to design two houses adjoining and yet independent and separate from each other. The entrances are entirely separate from each other, while they occupy the same relative position to each house. Under each front porch there is an entrance into basement, which in the rear is entirely out of ground. In this basement, on the front, is a large dining-room and on the rear a kitchen, with pantry and china closet between. There is a cellar under basement for heating purposes, fuel, etc.

By a careful study it will be seen that these houses are extremely simple in the arrangement of the rooms. In fact, it bears out this idea of simplicity all through. The rooms on the first floor are large, and arranged to make a good disposition of furniture. On the second floor the dressing-room over hall can be used as a child's bed-room in connection with the family chamber, being connected with each other by means of a sliding-door. A room is provided in attic for servant.

The interior, finished throughout, is in a plain, neat style; mantels of hard-wood; and altogether they are very desirable dwellings, which cannot fail to rent readily, and pay a good interest on the outlay.

The whole effect of the building is very happy. The shadows, which go far to produce a fine effect, in this case lend themselves to the whole in a pleasing manner. Cost $3,350.

It is astonishing what a number of people will commence building, and plan their houses as the work progresses, which is probably one of the worst ways of conducting one's building affairs; and a case came to our notice a short time ago which illustrates some of the disadvantages of building in this way. A gentleman, two thousand miles from us, went to work to build his house; got the cellar up and ready for frame, but when he came to plan the first floor, there were many things he did not know how to arrange so as to have them satisfactory. There were fire-places to get in, sliding-doors, stairs, etc., which puzzled his brain no small amount, and he finally gave it up, after spending considerable time and study on it; sent on to us for full drawings, details and specifications—sending his sketches, and informing us what he wanted. We comprehended his wants in a few moments, and by our long practice were enabled to make the desired arrangement which the amateur could not find by long study. This gentleman says if he had carried on his building without our assistance, he would have made a bungling mess of it, but now he has the most picturesque and convenient home in the town, and that he is not an architect, and never could be.

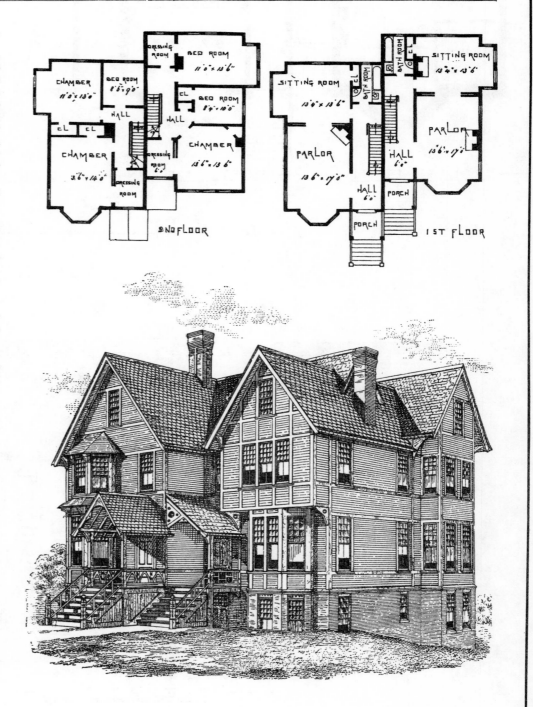

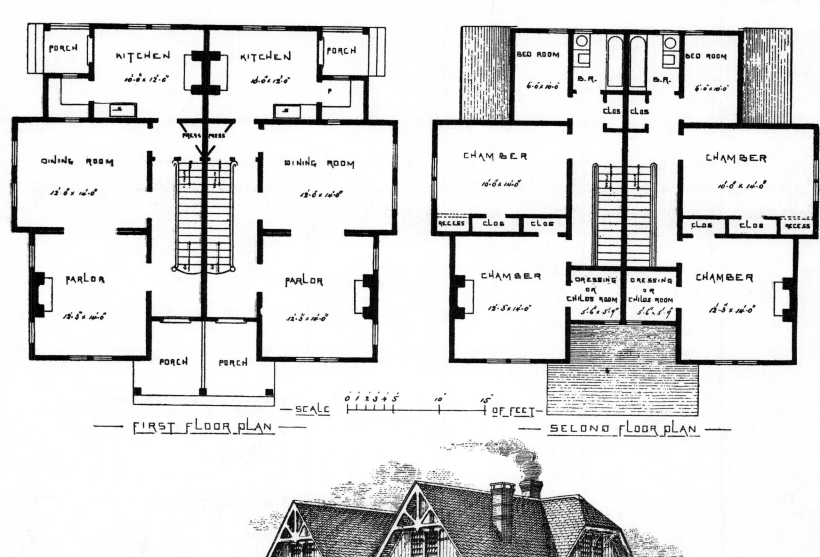

FIRST FLOOR PLAN — SCALE OF FEET — SECOND FLOOR PLAN

— PERSPECTIVE VIEW —

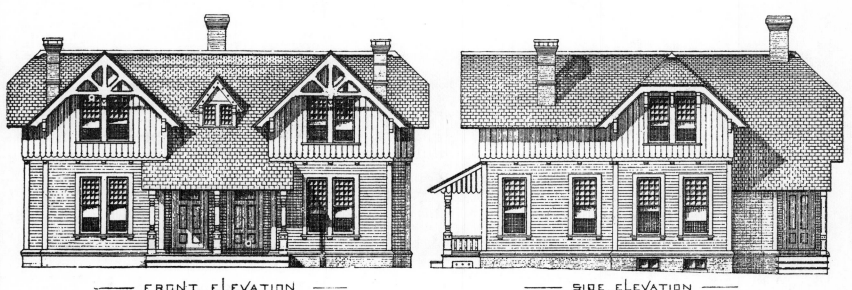

— FRONT ELEVATION —   — SIDE ELEVATION —

PLATE 30.

DESIGN 40—Shows plans, elevations and perspective view of a country House, containing eleven rooms, large attic, cellar under whole house, having laundry, etc., designed to be finished in a plain manner.   Cost, $3,200. (See specifications, latter part of book.)

RESIDENCE OF FRANK H. UNDERWOOD, TOLLAND, CONN.

This country residence embraces many novel and good features of exterior variety and interior compactness and convenience. The workmanship and material throughout have been of the best description, the materials being purchased by the owner and the work done by the day, and no pains have been spared to make it first-class in every respect.

The interior arrangement is very complete and unique, the hall being finished in oak, parlor in maple, library and dining-room in ash, all the fire-places having hard-wood mantels of handsome design. The conservatory is a pleasing feature of the first floor plan, and is accessible from the dining-room through a casement window ; access is also obtained in like manner to porch in rear of dining-room. A clothes-shute is arranged from second floor to soiled clothes-closet in laundry, an arrangement that is appreciated by every housekeeper.

Stained glass is used in all the windows above transoms. Roofs are slated and ridges covered with red terra-cotta cresting. The interior wood-work is filled with Crockett's Preservative. The heating is done by indirect radiation, steam being brought into cellar from the Underwood Belting Company's factory.   Cost about $4,500.

The cost of a house is the one thing desirable. Every one asks what this and that will cost, and a great many people who have started out to build without first ascertaining what their building would cost, have been very much deceived when all the bills have been received and the amount aggregated. We know of one instance where a gentleman, some years ago, was erecting a large residence by the day, and did not have any idea when he commenced what it was likely to cost; and long before the structure was completed he had paid out over $30,000, and was so disgusted with it that he would not keep any further account ; and to-day this house which cost so much money could be duplicated for $10,000. This is what we call bad management. However, as times are at present there is likely to be but very little of such.

It is reasonable to suppose that anyone without building experience, who undertakes the erection of a building in this way—unless there are special circumstances governing the case—will have to pay for the knowledge he will gain. A business man wants to know, after his ideas are put into a tangible form, how much all this will cost in dollars and cents, without any extras or additional charges whatsoever, and it is right and proper that everyone should look through all the links and complications that require the expenditure of a considerable sum of money. And no one who starts out with the intention of spending $4,000 in the erection of a dwelling, and winds up with three times that amount, will be likely to think they have used much judgment, and will try and shift the blame on some one else. But it is one of those things that time will place where it belongs. A building will vary in cost of construction according to locality, and will also depend greatly on the business management.

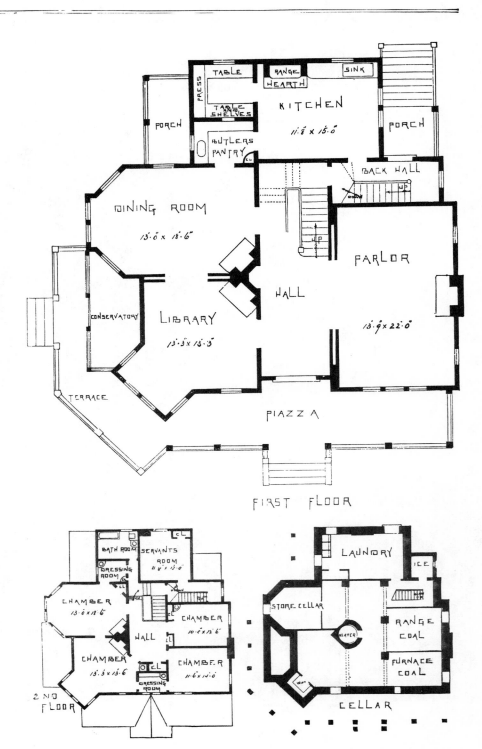

FIRST FLOOR

2ND FLOOR

CELLAR

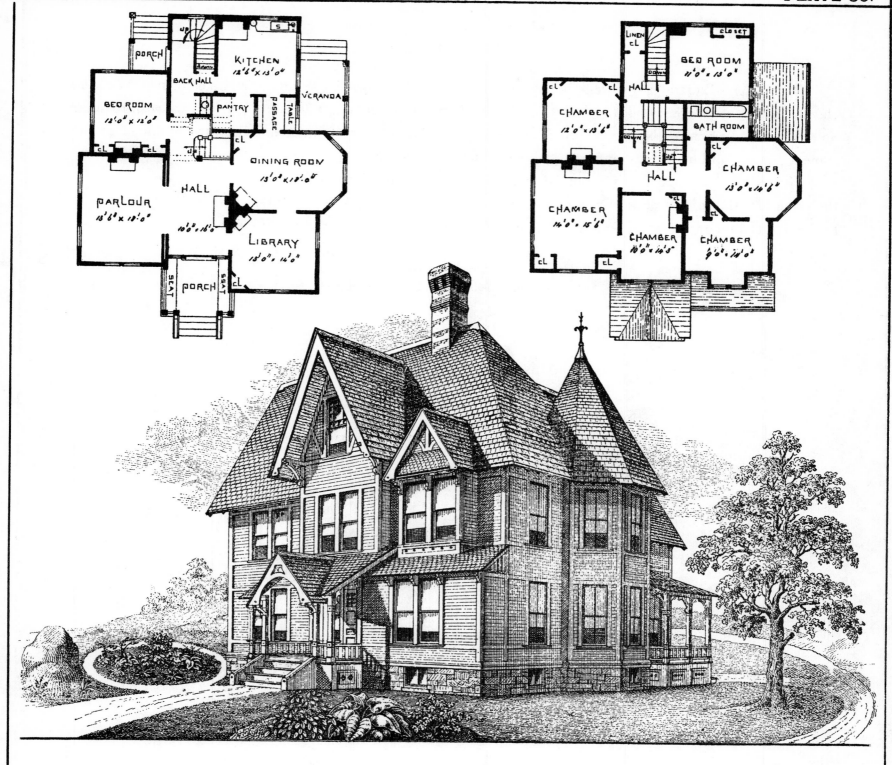

PORCH

KITCHEN
13'6" x 13'0"

BACK HALL

VERANDA

BED ROOM
12'0" x 12'0"

PANTRY

PASSAGE

TABLE

CL

CL

CL

DINING ROOM
13'0" x 18'0"

PARLOUR
13'6" x 18'0"

HALL
10'0" x 18'0"

LIBRARY
13'0" x 14'0"

SEAT

PORCH

SEAT

LINEN CL

CLOSET

BED ROOM
11'0" x 13'0"

CL

CL

HALL

DOWN

CHAMBER
12'0" x 13'6"

BATH ROOM

CL

CL

CHAMBER
13'0" x 14'6"

HALL

CHAMBER
14'0" x 15'6"

CL

CL

CHAMBER
10'0" x 14'5"

CHAMBER
9'0" x 14'0"

CL

CL

— FRONT ELEVATION —

— SIDE ELEVATION —

— SCALE —   0   5   10   15   20   — OF FEET —

PLATE 31.

DESIGN 41—Illustrates a cottage house, of seven rooms, designed for erection in the country. We give elevations in two different styles of architecture, suited to entirely different locations; in this we wish to show how different designs can be adapted to the same plan in a satisfactory manner, and they are intended to become a part of, and be in harmony with the acres that surround them.

The rooms are conveniently arranged, but could be differently disposed to suit anyone's ideas, and still the same or either of the designs carried out, as could also any of the plans given in this work, and the site has much to do with the arrangement of rooms, which we can readily adapted to different requirements. Cost, $3,100.

Where parties have their work executed by the day instead of by contract they will evidently save money, provided they are good managers, and have some one on the works to drive the men that are engaged, as it is well known by those familiar with workmen, that when they know the work is being done by the day, it is impossible to get them to do as much work unless they are drove. Some mechanics will tell you this is nonsense, but we know from experience it is not. A man may say that he will do just as big a day's work no matter which way he may be employed, but he will do the most when working by the job. Any master mechanic of experience will tell you the same, as he knows very well that if he does not keep his men to work, but allow them to do about as they please in this respect, that he will be unable to stand it and compete with others. Several of the large manufacturers contract the whole of their works in the shops, simply because they can get so much more work done for the money by contract than they can to hire the men by the day.

Some say that work is better executed when done by the day. It may and it may not. In some cases we have known it done badly, and the owner, rather than go to the expense of having it changed and made right, has said let it go; and some mechanics are liable to do things wrong, especially when they have no one to look after them, as a contractor, whose interest it is to have the work done right the first time, as otherwise he will have to be at the expense of making it right.

A first-class builder of some years ago, now retired, in a conversation recently informed us that his opinion was that half the builders of the present day did not know how to estimate on work, as when he built his residence he could not get a reasonable estimate; therefore

went to work and had it done by the day, superintending the work himself, and in this way his house cost him $4,500 less than the lowest estimate he received.

A case or two in the last few weeks came to our notice, whic convinced us that this is true to a certain extent at least. We prepared drawings, etc., for a public building for a country town, to come within a certain appropriation, but when estimates were handed in from local builders they all exceeded the amount considerable; therefore, builders from the city, a few miles distant, were allowed to estimate, and their bids all came within the amount appropriated. There being considerable art work in the design, the local builders did not know its worth and did not take the trouble to find out; and as one of these builders was on the committee, new plans were ordered and made so that the local builders could do it.

Another similar case, that of a party in a village, secured from us a design not to exceed a certain sum in execution; but his village builders did not seem to understand the design, and when they had estimated he found he would have to modify it. But the idea struck him to send to a city, one hundred miles away, and get a couple of first-class builders to estimate, men of standing, and who were known to do good work; and in less than two weeks one of them had the building under way, and the local builders were very mad at losing the work.

When estimates on a building run from $28,000 to $15,000, and the lowest does the work and makes money, somebody don't know their business, and on all work there is a vast difference between the highest and lowest bid.

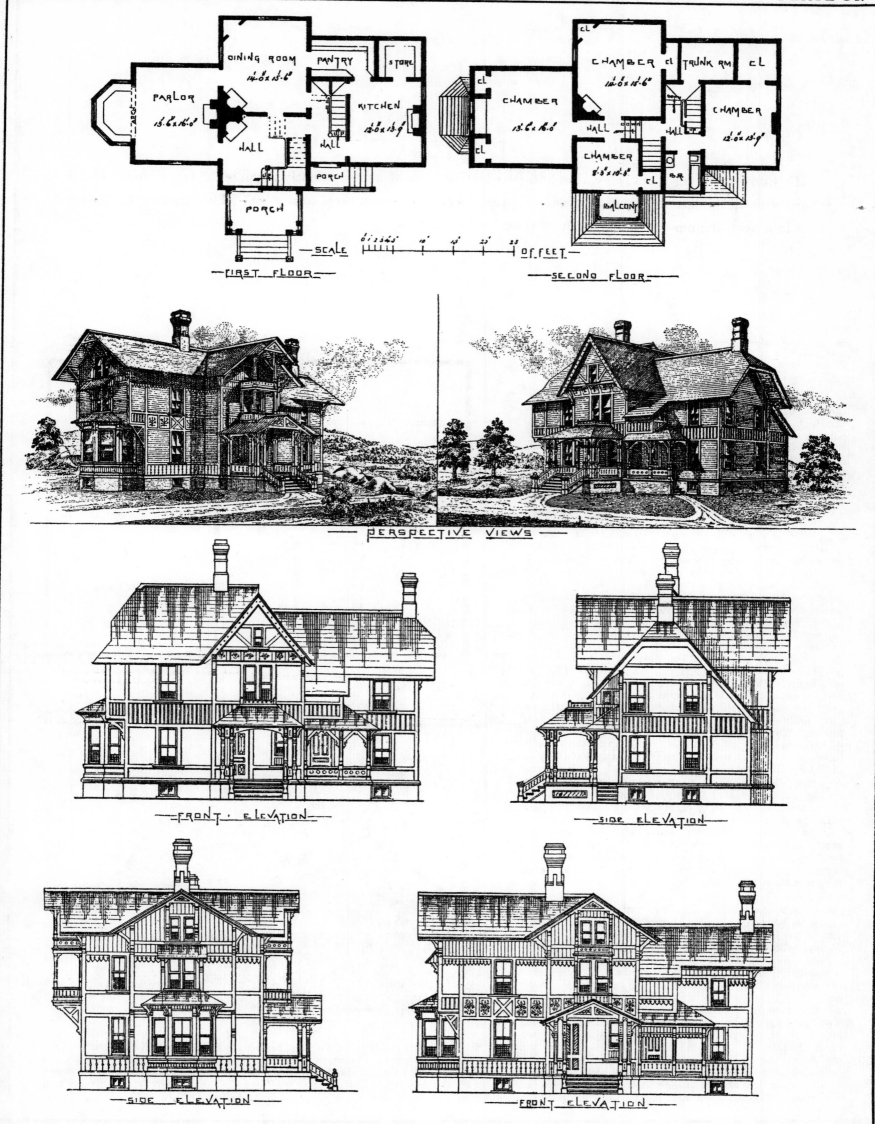

- FIRST FLOOR -

- SECOND FLOOR -

- PERSPECTIVE VIEWS -

- FRONT · ELEVATION -

- SIDE ELEVATION -

- SIDE ELEVATION -

- FRONT ELEVATION -

PLATE 32.

DESIGN 42—Gives plans, elevation and perspective view of a conveniently arranged cottage home of six rooms, with all modern conveniences, and was designed for erection on a corner lot. The interior to be finished in a neat manner first floor in hardwood. Cost, $2,500.

FARM BARN AND HENNERY.

This illustration gives a correct idea of a country farm barn, which will interest those who are agriculturally inclined. To the farmer it is one of the most important things how he shall house his stock, and provide storage for his grain, fodder, etc., and yet do it in an economical manner ; and the many farm barns that are to be seen, with their chopped up and checkered appearance, indicate that this matter has not had a proper amount of study and forethought. The farmer goes on and builds a little at a time, never thinking or looking far enough ahead to know what his wants really may be when his farm is being worked to its proper capacity. If you own a farm, and intend to be a good farmer, start out with a determination to have only suitable farm buildings, such as will look well from your neighbor's house. Let your barns look like barns, your houses like houses. We would not for anything have your barns be mistaken for houses or your houses for barns ; for such things we have seen, and it makes us feel as if there was a screw loose somewhere. Barns should not be built for show. They should, of course, be made to look well, and be pleasant spots in the landscape, and built in the most substantial manner possible—should be arranged to save as much labor as possible in the care of the animals that are to be housed and fed in them. Let them be well ventilated and lighted, properly floored ; the stonework of the foundation thoroughly built, not dry, but laid up in good cement mortar. Don't invite the rats, as they will come without.

And it has always been a mystery to us why the farmers have not, in a general way, been wide awake enough to their own interests to properly house their fowls, instead of letting them run wild over the whole place, and roost on wagons, carts and agricultural implements when not in use and stored ; to let them lay their eggs where they please, and then have the pleasure of hunting for them, and often finding them at a late day — such certainly must be the case, else why so many bad eggs amongst those "nice fresh country eggs." Chickens are one of the most profitable adjuncts to any farm, and it is a very easy matter to keep them where there is a number of cattle to feed.

The hennery here shown was carried out as an addition to barn at hill-side farm, New Milford, Conn., owned by Egbert Marsh, Esq., and shows Mr. Marsh's ideas of what a well regulated hennery should be to make it both a pleasure and a profit. As the shed below is a necessity in connection with barn, and a roof indispensable, the only additional expense is the floor, one side and ends, with the interior fittings, to make a hennery which will accommodate easily one hundred to two hundred. The floor should be tightly boarded, then covered with a coat of boiled pitch and tar, on which spread soil two to three inches in depth. This will give an elegant scratching and wallowing ground. The windows all arranged to slide sideways, the openings on outside being covered with wire netting ; the feed-bin built so as to hold several bushels, and arranged to take care of itself, by constructing the bottom so as to empty into a small trough into hen-

nery, in front of which is placed a perch ; the chicks to feed in space adjoining marked chickens, which is enclosed by pickets, open enough for them to run through. Nest boxes are arranged in tiers, one above another, and loose, so they can be taken through into nest-room and emptied, and for setting hens, turned around and fed from nest-room.

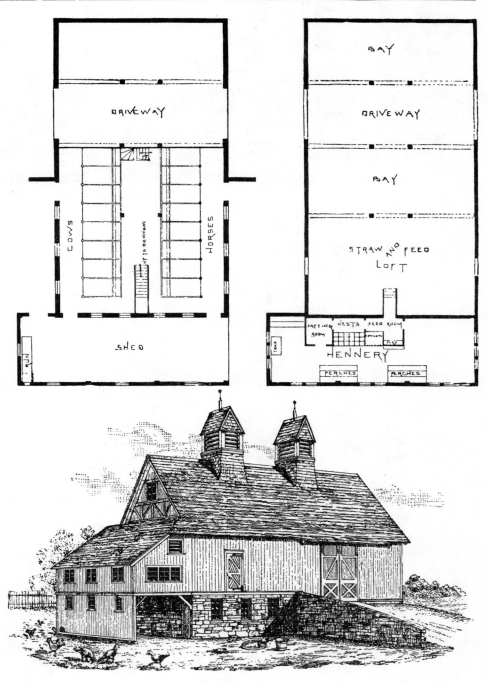

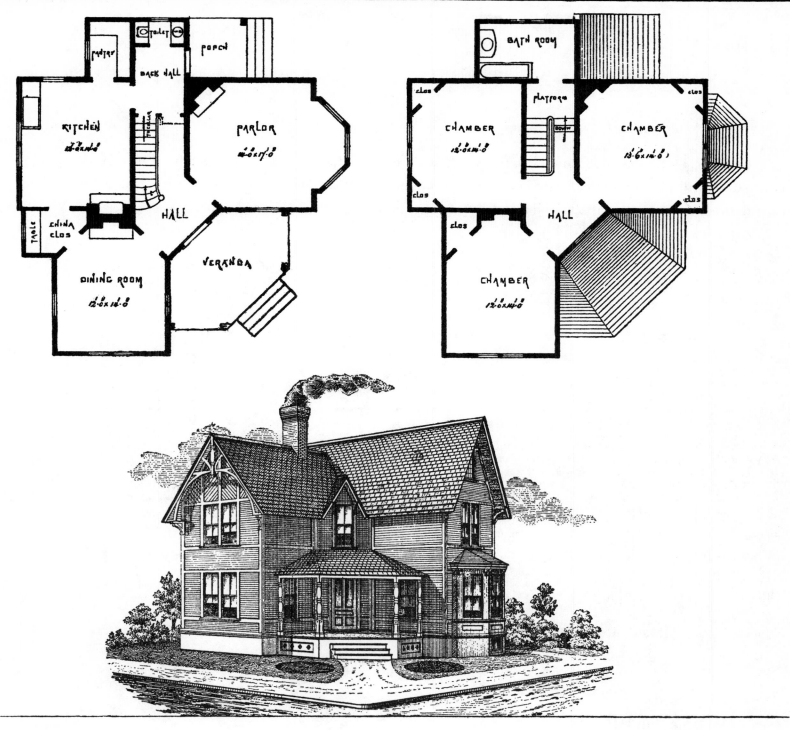

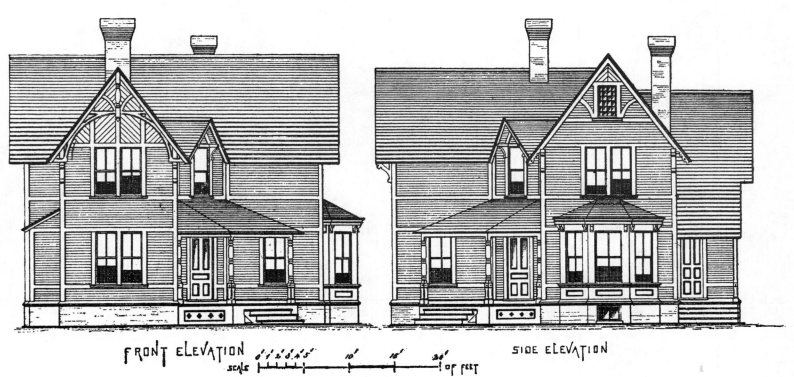

FRONT ELEVATION
SCALE

SIDE ELEVATION

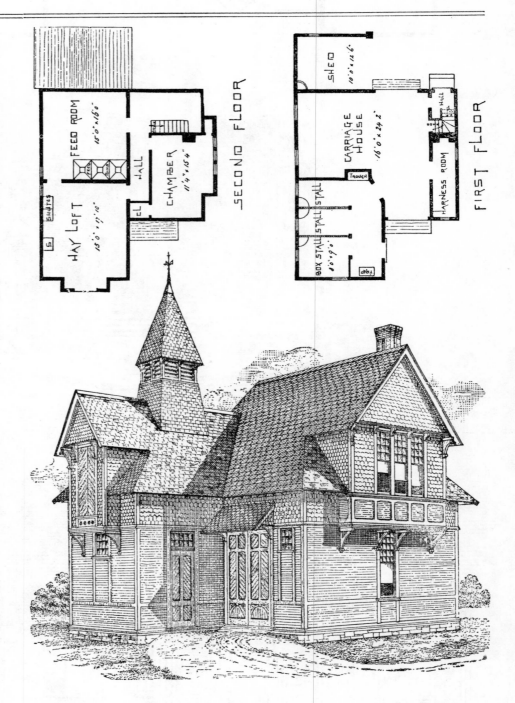

PLATE 33.

DESIGN 43—Shows plans and elevations of a plain country house, with drive porch. On examination of the plan it will be seen that a large amount of accommodation is given in a compact form and a minute description is not necessary as the plans sufficiently explain themselves. Cost, $3,300.

The fattening room is arranged so as to be darker, and will be found desirable for fattening poultry for market or home consumption. A running stream of water should be so arranged as to always supply fresh water in hennery, and which should be had in barn for cattle. This could, as in this case, be brought in a pipe from a spring in the hill-side, a short distance above the barn, and which not only supplies the barn, but the house with a never-failing supply of clear spring water. The run from hennery is so arranged that fowls can be either let into shed or directly out of doors. This run being hinged on top, and operated by weights and a cord, is controlled from feed room thus completely shutting off the hennery from floor below, when required. The arrangement of stalls, as here shown, is convenient, and cannot fail but be suggestive for those interested in such matters, while the conveniences above cannot fail to please, as the facilities for driving right in with a load from either side is what should always be had in a barn of this class. This barn is, of course, capable of many changes to suit individual wants, circumstances and locations, and is far from costly ; and there are farmers who could with very little trouble, put up their own barns, if they only wake up to the full realization of their own capabilities.

STABLE AND CARRIAGE HOUSE.

This design was prepared for erection in connection with the proposed residence of Mr. E. G. Burham, at Sea Side Park, Bridgeport, Conn., and is arranged to suit the requirements of individual wants, as well as the peculiarities of the site. There is a cellar built under carriage house, which will be found useful for storage of vegetables, roots, etc., and the carriage house being arranged to drive through, makes it very convenient for every-day use, as well as utilizing the room. The shed is designed as a shelter for horse and carriage, so that the horse can be fed noon times without unhitching—a very convenient arrangement for a business man, who has little time to spare in the middle of the day. The two stalls and box-stall give ample room for two or three horses, while there is room enough for three carriages. On second story is provided a man's chamber, hay-loft and feed room—the feed bins being built into position, and having shutes down to stable below.

The building is of wood, frame, sheathed, and lower or first story clapboarded and shingled above, roof slated. The ventilator is connected with stable below by means of wooden vent pipes, and thoroughly ventilates the whole building. Harness room has an o en fire-place, the chimney running up through man's room on second floor. The hay-racks, mangers and stable fixtures are of iron. Water is supplied on first floor, and the manure is dropped through the trap, as indicated on plan, into a pit built for that purpose, and which is accessible from exterior. The carriage house is ceiled on sides with Georgia pine ; the timbers overhead dressed and chamfered. The harness room is fitted up with necessary hooks, pins, etc., for hanging and storing harness. The whole built in a first-class manner at a cost of $850, and makes a neat building for the purpose, and one which is in harmony with its surroundings.

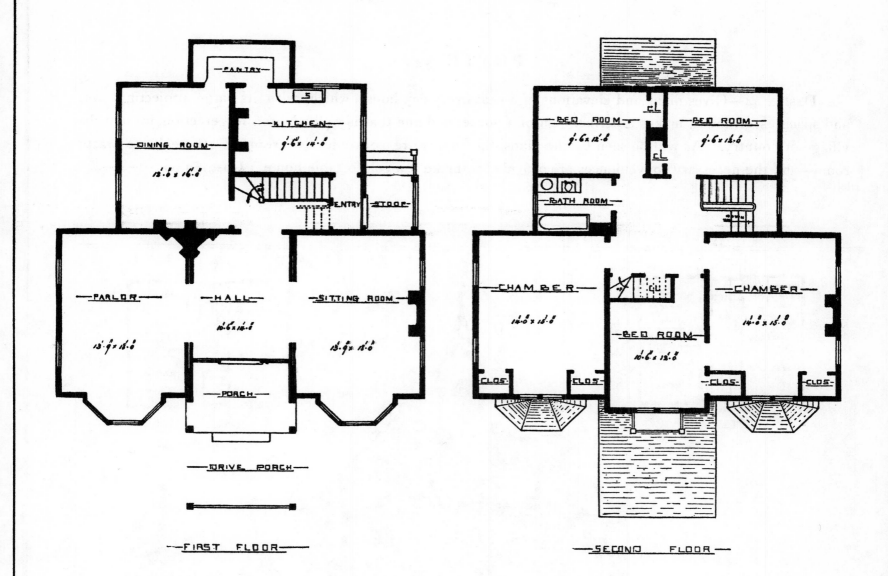

PANTRY

KITCHEN
9·6 x 14·6

DINING ROOM
12·6 x 16·6

PANTRY   STOOP

PARLOR   HALL   SITTING ROOM
13·9 x 16·6   10·6 x 14·6   13·9 x 16·6

PORCH

—DRIVE PORCH—

—FIRST FLOOR—

BED ROOM   cL   BED ROOM
9·6 x 12·6   9·6 x 12·6

cL

—BATH ROOM—

CHAMBER   CHAMBER
14·0 x 16·6   14·0 x 16·0

cL
BED ROOM
10·6 x 12·6

CLOS   CLOS   CLOS   CLOS

—SECOND   FLOOR—

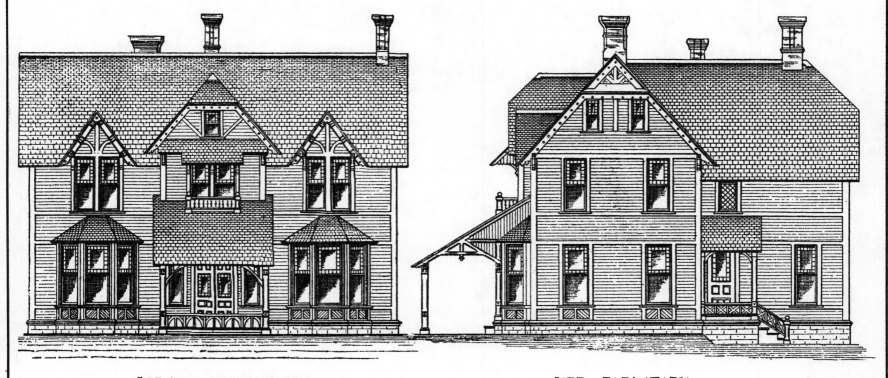

—FRONT ELEVATION—   —SIDE ELEVATION—

SCALE ⊦⊦⊦⊦⊦⊦⊦⊦⊦⊦⊦⊦ OF FEET

PLATE 34.

DESIGN 44—Gives plans and elevations of a neat every-day house, which, with its large projecting roof, and spacious verandas, makes a perfect gem of a house, and one that is well adapted for erection in suburbs village or country.   As will be seen by the plans, the rooms are conveniently arranged—there is no waste room—and the necessary conveniences are provided to make it a comfortable home.   Cost, $3,000.

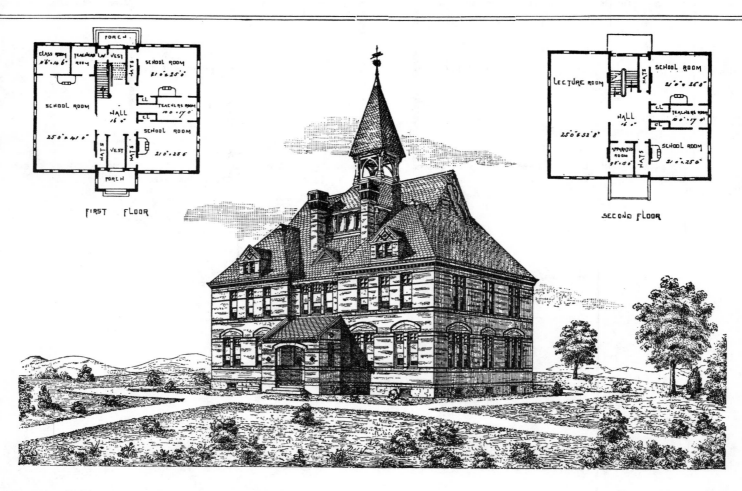

DESIGN FOR PUBLIC SCHOOL BUILDING.

The above shows a design for a good, solid, plain public school building, designed for the town of Milan, Mo. That it is somewhat out of the ordinary run of the every-day French roof architecture we are fully aware ; and in drawing the plans for this building we have had quite a difficult problem to solve.   The general dimensions are 55 by 70 feet ; first and second stories having each 14-feet ceilings, while the assembly room on third floor has a ceiling 16 feet 6 inches in height.   The materials are hard-burned brick, relieved with bands of black brick ; window-sills, lintels, water-table and underpinning of stone ; the roofs all being slated, floors all lined and deadened, walls built hollow with two inches air space.

The design is very simple, and thoroughly constructive in all its parts ; the cornices consisting of brick brackets, and surmounted with a wooden gutter, lined with metal.   The school-rooms are arranged so they have an abundance of light, are well ventilated and easy of access, and though all are in close proximity to, yet are in a measure isolated from, each other ; being divided by brick partition walls, the transmission of sound from one room to another is effectually prevented.

The entrances are placed in front and rear, and consist of spacious stone steps, with brick porch on front and slated hood on rear ; the vestibules opening into a hall 16 feet wide, which contains a wide and easy stair-case, leading up to floors above.   This hall is convenient to all rooms, and the advantages it possesses, running as it does through the building, are at once obvious, as the unequaled ventilating facilities it affords renders it one of the best features of the plan.   The basement is reached by stairs under the main stairs, and is used for heating and play-room purposes, which is well lighted, ventilated, etc.

The vestibules on front and rear are easy of access, passing through which we reach the main hall, from which the three school rooms open, also the hat and cloak rooms for each.   The sides of the school rooms are wainscoted to the height of window sills, above which are placed black-boards.   A teacher's room is placed between the two smaller school rooms, and a class room is provided in connection with the larger room, also a teacher's room, which is reached from the rear vestibule.   Ventilating flues are carried up in the four chimneys, and as these run up above the roof, superior draughts are obtained.   Ascending to the second floor by the spacious and easy stairs, we have a large lecture room, two school rooms, hat and cloak rooms, a teacher's room and apparatus room, all connected with the hall.   On third floor is a room 27x42 feet, with a ceiling 16 feet 6 inches high, well lighted and ventilated, which at times would be found indispensable for exhibition purposes, as it is admirably situated, and easy of access from all parts of the building ; and the four walls of this room being required for a support to roof, it will be seen no extra expense is added in getting this room, while the space around it serves as storage and for ventilating purposes.   The bell tower speaks for itself, and is not only useful, but gives a greater prominence to the building.   This is a common sense school building, and one that gives all that it is possible to do for the amount of money expended, as the whole of the detail is simple, everything being honest, practical and substantial.   Cost $8,000.

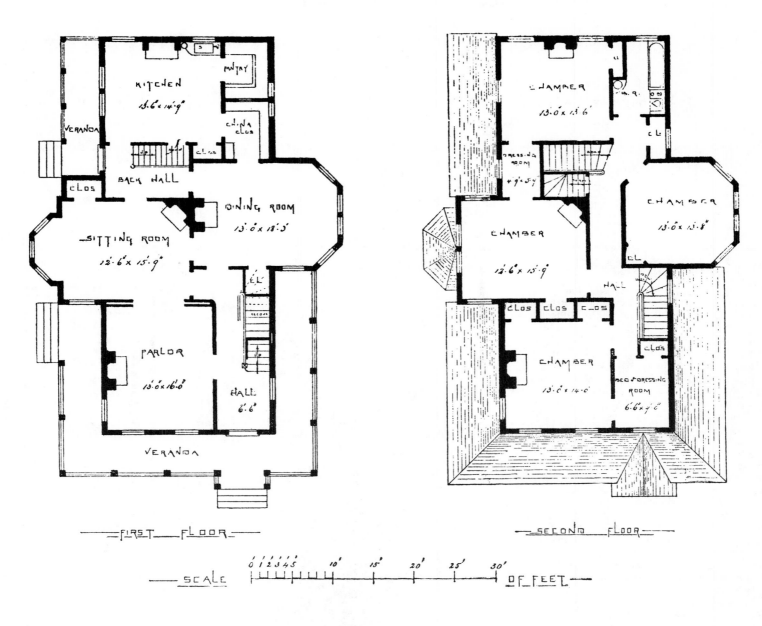

- FIRST FLOOR -
- SECOND FLOOR -

- SCALE - OF FEET -

- FRONT ELEVATION -
- SIDE ELEVATION -

PLATE 35.

DESIGN 45—Illustrates a very attractive summer residence. The design was prepared for a particular site, and gives considerable variety in outline and also an impression of solidity and breadth which should be prominent characteristics in a house of this kind. The roof presents an overshadowing, sheltering effect, which is very desirable in a summer house. Cost, $3,325.

MASONIC ASSOCIATION BUILDING.

This design was prepared for erection at Milford, Conn., for the Masonic Lodge at that town, and is a well arranged building for the purposes for which it is intended. The ground floor makes a very large and commodious store, being well lighted, ventilated, etc. The front platform and show windows are covered with a slated hood, serving as a protection to the goods displayed from the weather, as well as sheltering the entrances and show windows to the store from the heat and storm. The side front door is arranged so as to divide the store in two if required, as it was considered an excellent place in which to arrange the post-office on the right hand side of center entrance. There is a cellar under the whole building, with a stairway from store placed under main stairs, and also an outside entrance on the rear, which, as the building stands upon a corner lot, is very convenient and easy of access.

The entrance to lodge rooms is placed on the side front, and is thus isolated from the store. The entrance is protected by a cosy porch, over which the second story is extended, making the necessary recess for organ in lodge room. The lodge room, with its ante-rooms, closets, etc., will at once be seen, by those who are initiated in the mysteries of Masonry, to be all that is desirable, and arranged to suit the requirements of a regularly constituted lodge of A. F. and A. M. The east end of the lodge room is very neat and effective, the recess behind the W. M. having a circle head, with the round stained glass window placed in the upper part, in which is worked the all-seeing eye, and other appropriate emblems. The other windows have transom lights, filled with stained glass, in which is worked such designs as are emblematical of Masonry. The wood-work is all in pine, finished with Crockett's Preservative, chamfers and cut-work black. The lodge room ceiling is 16 feet high, the two sides being cut off with the slope of the roof, which forms an excellent surface for the brethren artistically inclined to show what they know about fresco work suited to such a place. The stairs leading from tiler's lobby extend up to a large room over the ante-room and preparation room, whose ceilings are 10 feet 6 inches high, arranged for storage purposes, and which will be found useful to accommodate the paraphernalia required in working the degrees of a chapter. Some of your Masonic friends may say there is something wanting, which always goes with a lodge room for a chapter. To which we would say: be not alarmed; all this has been thought about and provided for; and we would say to those requiring such plans that there is here room for everything required in working every degree known to Masonry in a manner suited to the requirements of a lodge of this kind—and we speak understandingly and from experience.

The construction throughout is of wood, built in the most thorough manner; hard pine floor in store; lodge room floors double and thoroughly deadened; frame sheathed and covered with heavy felt paper, and the roof is of black slate, with ridges of terra cotta; tower

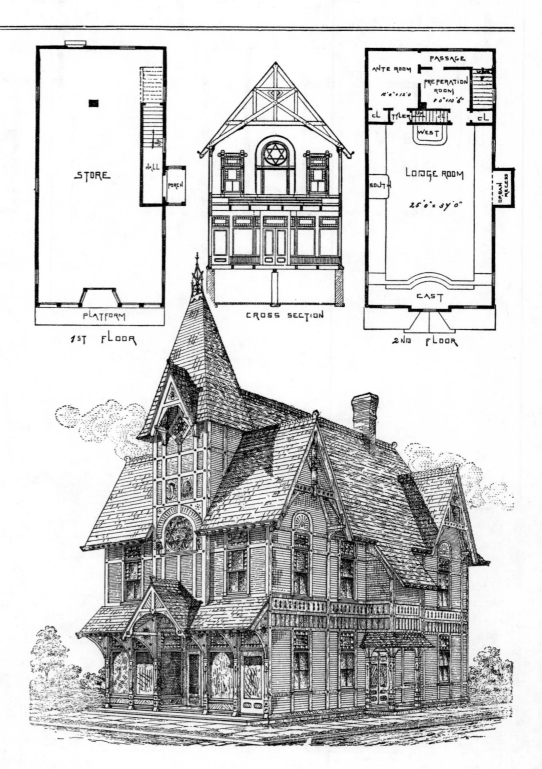

STORE · HALL · PORCH · PLATFORM

1ST FLOOR

CROSS SECTION

ANTE ROOM · PASSAGE · PREPERATION ROOM · CL · TILER · WEST · LODGE ROOM · 25'0" x 35'0" · SOUTH · ORGAN RECESS · EAST

2ND FLOOR

finial of iron. The cost of this building complete is $3,000; and we think that no country town having a lodge of Masons can afford to be without such a building as this, as by owning such a building, they are fulfilling one of the tenets of Masonry, besides being a monument of the taste, spirit and liberality of its founders.

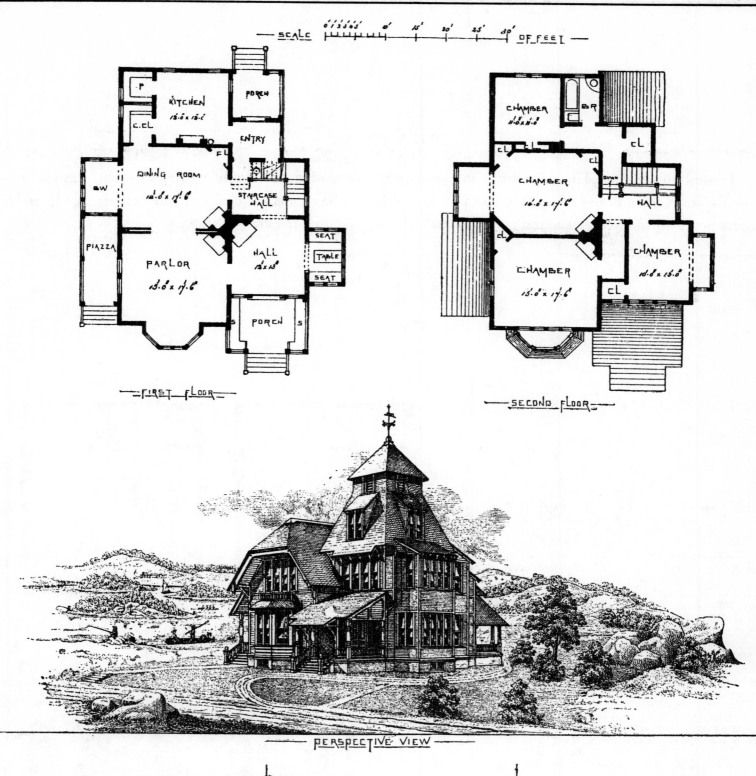

SCALE .... 0' 15' 20' 25' 30' OF FEET

FIRST FLOOR

SECOND FLOOR

PERSPECTIVE VIEW

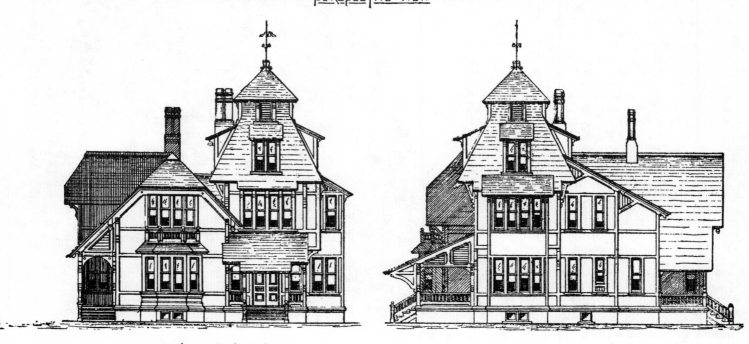

FRONT ELEVATION   SIDE ELEVATION

PLATE 36.

DESIGN 46—Shows plans, elevations and perspective view of a two-family house, with the desired conveniences to make a house of this kind what it should be. The rooms are compact and well arranged, and a large amount of room is given, and is calculated to be a good investment. Cost, $3,750.

DESIGN FOR A COUNTRY BANK AND LIBRARY.

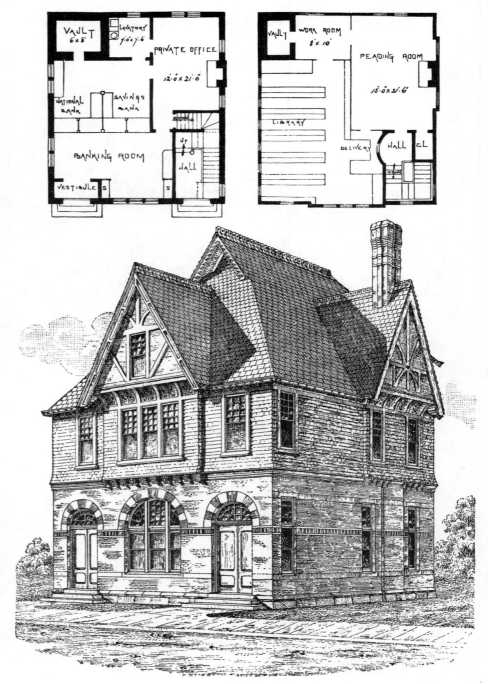

This design shows a good study for a bank and library, suited to the requirements of a small country town. The first or ground floor contains the Banking-room, which is large and spacious, and adapted to the wants and requirements of both national and savings bank. The business room is reached by a separate entrance through a tiled vestibule. The vault is very large, and should be built upon a solid granite foundation, interior lined with a steel case one inch thick, next to which should be granite stones one foot thick, doweled together with steel dowels, then outside of this one foot thick with best hard brick, laid in Portland cement; the doors to be double, with heavy iron vestibules, grouted in with Portland cement, the top covered with railroad iron, on which place a floor of granite thoroughly grouted, etc. A guard room could be here placed between the bank-vault and the library-vault. This room could be reached from lavatory and by having an opening over vault door, the guard could control the entrance.

The private office would be found very useful for directors' meetings and private business generally. The cellar contains the necessary room for heating apparatus, fuel, etc., and is reached by a stairway from directors' room, having no outside entrance. The side-wall desk, in business-room, is an indispensable feature in all banks and the settees placed each side of front windows would be found very convenient during business hours. The bank counters, fittings and finish on this floor to be of ash, filled. Floors of hard-wood with a neat border.

The second floor contains library, reading-room, etc., and is reached by a separate entrance and an easy staircase. The delivery-desk being placed in the position shown, renders it easy for those requiring books, etc., to get them without entering reading-room, and the librarian can thus see all who come and go as well as see into the reading-room. The work-room is required for unpacking, covering and labeling books, etc., while the vault makes an excellent fire-proof room in which to store valuable papers, or to be used for town records, etc. The reading-room is a pleasant room, and with its open fire-place, in which a wood fire can be burnt, would be a pleasant place to while away an evening in reading. The book-room is neatly arranged so as to store about seven thousand volumes, the alcoves containing the books being well-lighted. This floor throughout to be finished in pine in the natural color, with cut and incised work picked out in color. The stairs of hard-wood. The floor of hard-wood. The first story is brick and stone construction, the upper story being shingled; roof covered with black slate. Such a building as this is an ornament to any town, and certainly is a paying investment as it is by no means expensive, the whole of the work to be done in a substantial manner at a cost of $6,000.

— FRONT ELEVATION —

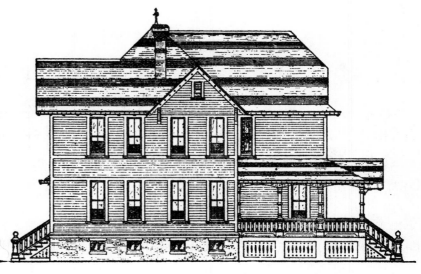

— SIDE ELEVATION —

— PERSPECTIVE VIEW —

SCALE OF | 1 2 3 4 5 | 10 | 15 | 20 | 25 | 30 | 35 | 40 | FEET —

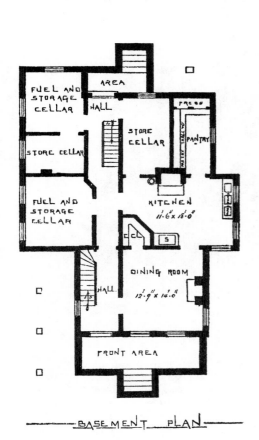

FUEL AND STORAGE CELLAR

AREA

HALL

PRESS

STORE CELLAR

PANTRY

STORE CELLAR

FUEL AND STORAGE CELLAR

KITCHEN
11'·6" x 18'·0"

DINING ROOM
12'·9" x 14'·0"

HALL

FRONT AREA

— BASEMENT PLAN —

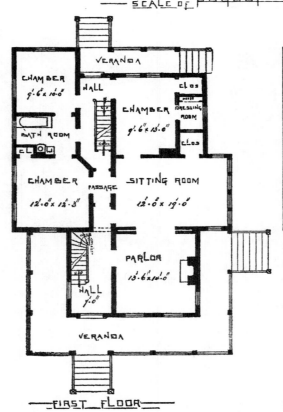

VERANDA

CHAMBER
9'·6" x 10'·0"

HALL

CLOS

CHAMBER
9'·6" x 13'·0"

DRESSING ROOM

CLOS

BATH ROOM

CLO

CHAMBER
12'·6" x 12'·3"

PASSAGE

SITTING ROOM
12'·6" x 19'·0"

PARLOR
13'·6" x 14'·0"

HALL
7'·0"

VERANDA

— FIRST FLOOR —

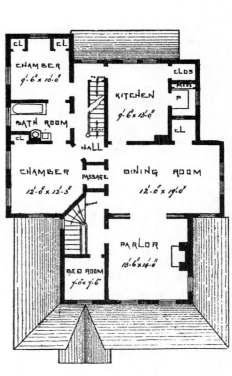

CL

CL

CHAMBER
9'·6" x 10'·0"

CLOS

KITCHEN
9'·6" x 13'·0"

PRESS

P

BATH ROOM

CL

HALL

CHAMBER
12'·6" x 12'·3"

PASSAGE

DINING ROOM
12'·6" x 19'·0"

BED ROOM
7'·0" x 7'·6"

PARLOR
13'·6" x 14'·0"

— SECOND FLOOR —

PLATE 37.

DESIGN 47—Illustrates a handsome brick and timber cottage, the plan of which is very compact and convenient. The laundry is located under kitchen. The first story is faced with select North Haven brick of even color. The second story is of timber construction, and painted a warm red color, trimmed with black. Cost, $4,000.

TOWN HALL.

Here is a study for a small town hall, suited to the requirements of a country town of from four to five thousand inhabitants. It has often seemed to us, in our professional journeys through numerous country towns in different parts of the country, that there was a lack of interest on the part of the inhabitants in those things which so often tend toward the public good—morally, intellectually and otherwise. There should be in every town the public building, in which all should take equal delight and pride. This building should not be a wooden, tumble-down, flat or mansard-roofed dry goods box, neither need it be an attic in some building, the lower part of which is used as a store-room for kerosene or any other equally combustible material, but should be a real solid, substantial brick building, which should be built in a proper manner, the floors fire-proof—not built in that slip-slop fashion that old fogies always prefer, the wooden beams and floors forming beautiful flues for the devouring flames to creep through, thereby at all times rendering such buildings perfect man-traps. The roof should be a feature of the building, and not, as many suppose, be made to appear as small as possible, as if it was something to keep out of sight. In the design here illustrated it has not been the aim to produce anything but a good, plain, honest building, suited to the requirements of a country town. The basement is reached by front entrance directly under main entrance, and the floor of porch above forms a covered porch for basement entrance. The hall is large and spacious, and communicates with court-room, heater-room and firemen's sitting-room, also hall of first floor by a flight of easy stairs. The fire-engine room is large, and has two large doors suitable for running in engine and hose wagon, and connecting as it does with sitting-room, makes a convenient arrangement. The chief's office is connected with court-room and has an outside door. Four cells are provided, in which to stow away at times the refractory individuals who insist on being in hot water. The room connected with chief's office is arranged for the reception of lady and aristocratic prisoners, as delinquent bank presidents and cashiers, insurance officers, etc. The first floor contains court-room with judges' and jury-room, town clerk's office, with a large fire-proof vault in which to stow away the town records, two good offices which should hold lawyers enough to do what legal business is necessary to be done in a town of this size. The hall is spacious and communicates directly with offices and court-room, and has a broad and easy staircase ascending to the large, high hall above, the whole of which is in one room for assembly purposes. Such a hall as this is capable of being fitted up and answering for everything required in a country town, as a caucus meeting, or theatrical performance, for private parties and public balls, church fairs or even ministers' donation parties. This hall would be a source of revenue that would almost run the entire building, and would be a source of continual enjoyment to the citizens

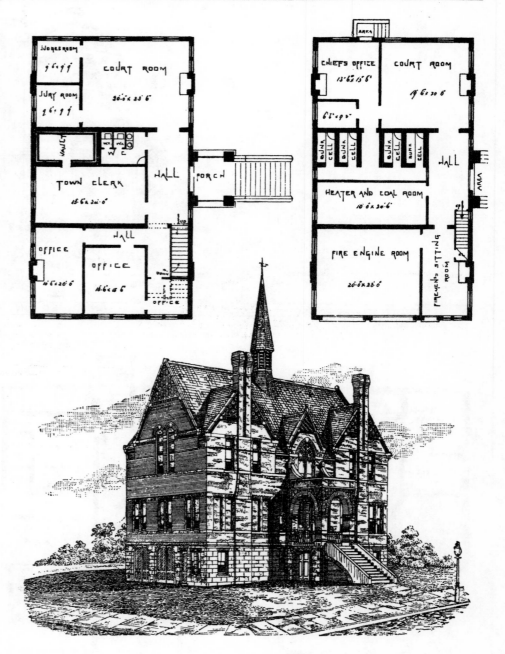

of the town. The building is thoroughly ventilated throughout. The outer walls built of good, honest red brick in colored mortar, with stone basement, water-table, sills, steps, etc. The roof slated. The first and second floors of rolled wrought iron beams and corrugated iron arches, filled in with cement concrete, on which is bedded the sleepers the hard pine floors are laid on. The interior finish to be of hard-wood, in a plain and suitable manner. Cost, $12,000.

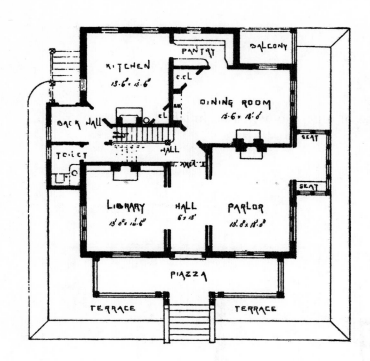

— FIRST FLOOR —

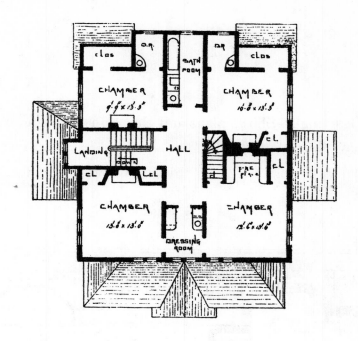

— SECOND FLOOR —

— REAR ELEVATION —

— PERSPECTIVE VIEW —

— FRONT ELEVATION —

— SIDE ELEVATION —

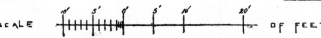

SCALE OF FEET

PLATE 38.

DESIGN 48—Shows plans and elevations of a country house of nine rooms, to be finished in a very plain manner. Cost, $2,600.

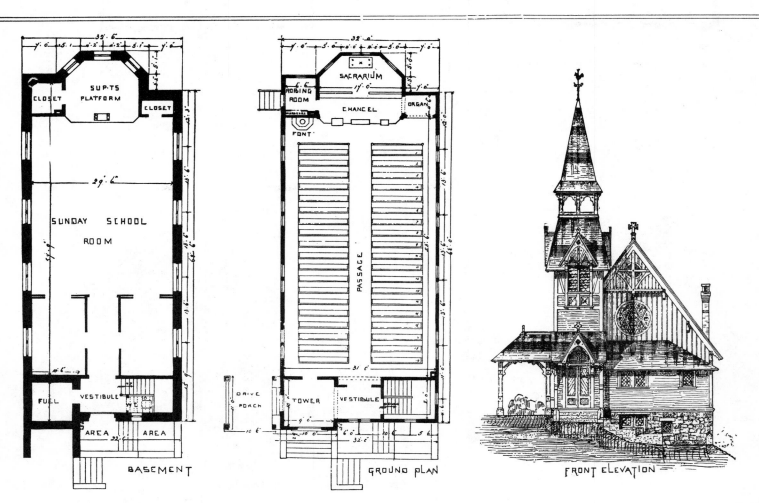

BASEMENT   GROUND PLAN   FRONT ELEVATION

EPISCOPAL CHURCH.

This church is erected at Stafford Springs, Conn., and is built on one of the most peculiar sites imaginable, being on a triangular corner lot, situated on a side of a hill, which brings the whole of one side of basement out of ground and the opposite side, where drive porch is, on a level with the church floor. The basement is built of Monson granite laid in irregular courses, with cut sills, lintels, etc., the area copings and steps being of cut granite. The basement gives good Sunday-School rooms, with a ceiling of eleven feet, and is so arranged as to be thrown into one room by means of sliding doors. The stairs from basement to floor above are convenient and easy of ascent, and gives room underneath for a water-closet, and the room under tower is used for fuel. The windows in basement are filled with diamond glass with stained borders, set in leaded frame-work. The ground floor or auditorium is 31 x 53½ feet in size, and will seat 225 comfortably. The ceiling is finished with open timber and plastered panels ; the windows are filled with rolled Scotch cathedral glass of handsome design, the chancel windows and rose window in front being very handsome. The fittings are all of pine—seats finished in natural wood and have black walnut rolls on backs. The chancel is of good size, having robing-room connected, which is reached from outside, and contains wardrobe, etc., the organ being placed on the opposite side.

The construction throughout above basement is of wood—roof slated with black slate and cut bands—and the whole exterior of wood-work is painted, the body Venetian red, and trimmings Indian red, with the cut-work, battens, etc., black. These colors, with the pic-

turesque surroundings, form a pleasing picture to the eye, and one which should be seen to be appreciated. The cross section gives an

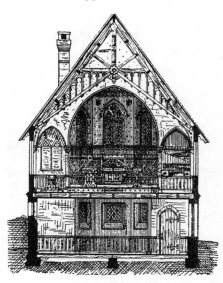

idea of the interior at chancel. This Church cost $4,500 complete, and is one of the neatest church buildings for the money that it is possible to get up.

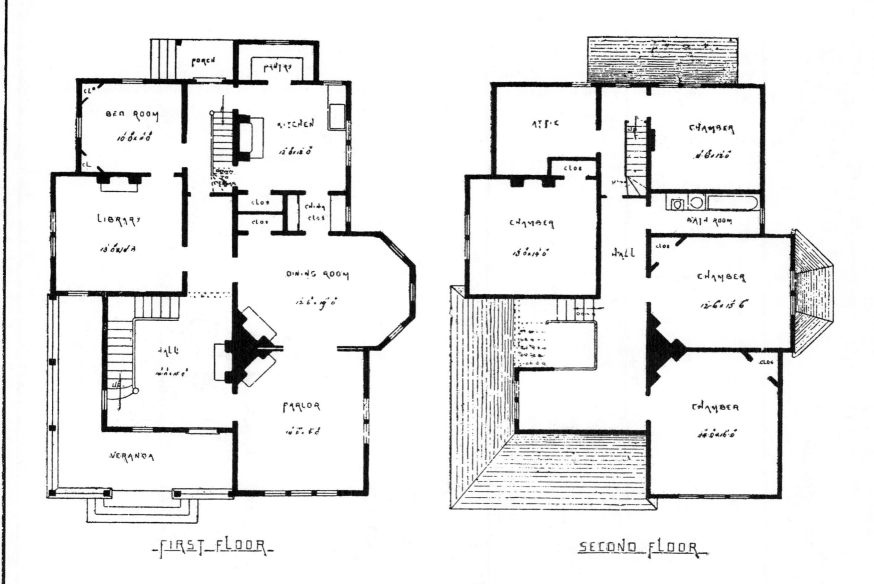

FIRST FLOOR.

SECOND FLOOR.

SCALE ——————— OF FEET

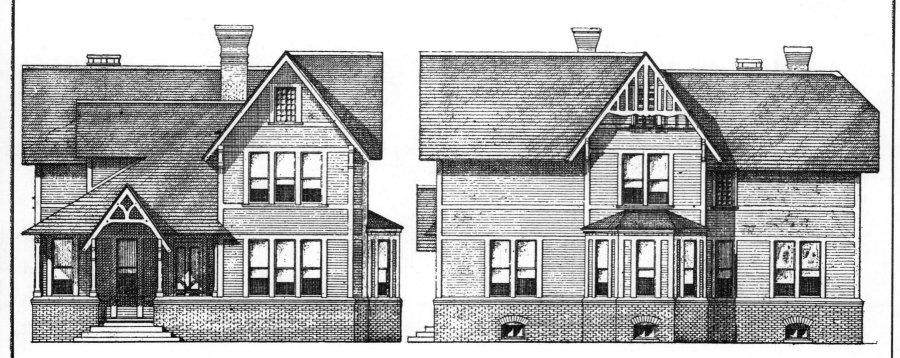

FRONT ELEVATION

SIDE ELEVATION

PLATE 39.

DESIGN 49—Illustrates a pair of brick houses, of large accommodation, with convenient and compact plan giving twelve rooms each with conveniences. The underpinning of Longmeadow brown stone, also water-table and window sills; the exterior walls faced with North Haven selected brick, of even color, laid in red mortar, and finished with a black joint; slopes of roof slated; exterior wood-work painted a warm red color and trimmed with black; interior finished in a neat manner and painted. Cost, $3,100 each.

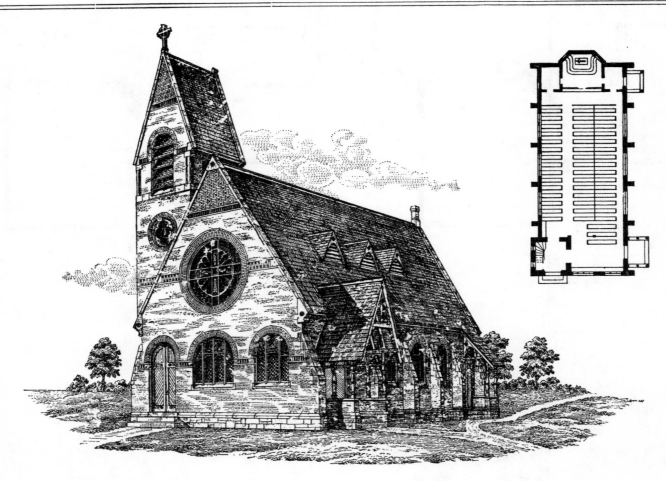

CATHOLIC CHURCH.

This design is suited to the requirements of a country parish, and is designed to accommodate 300.

In preparing this design it was necessary to produce a building which could be erected at small expense, and in a country town where only certain building materials were to be had at reasonable prices. The walls are of brick, laid up fourteen inches thick, with a two-inch air space; the stone trimmings to be of granite found in the neighborhood. The walls are kept low as possible, and are pierced with wide windows, filled with stained glass in leaded frames. The roof is open-timbered, giving plenty of height and ventilation. The gallery is placed over the front end, which is reached by means of stairs from vestibule, gives ample room for organ and choir, and is well lighted by rose window, while the tower is arranged to contain bell, or even a peal of bells if desired, which can be rung from gallery floor below.

The side porches to auditorium, also to vestry room, make these entrances desirable, as they are protected from the weather. The lower part of these porches are of stone and brick construction, while the upper portion is of wood; the roofs are all slated with Bangor, Pa., slate; the brickwork laid up with red mortar, with belts, arches, etc., in black mortar, and the joints of stone-work finished in black. The interior fittings all of pine, filled and finished in natural wood, and cut-work picked out in color; walls wainscoted four feet high, on a level with window sills, and the ceiling panels tinted an ultramarine blue, with stencilled stars in chrome yellow; the side walls a light drab, with a foliated stencil border over wainscot; the altar rail of ash; and the entire building finished in a good and first-class manner. Cost $7,000.

We are aware of the custom that is prevalent to those building Catholic churches to copy from what they have seen elsewhere, and this must be the reason for erecting so many country churches of poor design; and we would say that in preparing this design it was our aim to give something entirely different from the every-day Catholic church, yet such that would meet all the requirements of the Catholic service; and though the Catholic church to-day has the same requirements as it had five hundred years ago, it is no reason why the problem cannot be solved by the architect, and all the traditions of the great days of the church still be preserved without turning to his books and copying something to resemble its predecessors of years ago; but he must work with the materials at his command, combining them so as to form a harmonious whole, and suited to the requirements of the form of worship; and to do this, and obtain real progress, it is necessary to work out new ideas to suit each separate case, and the various materials employed should be treated without any show of deceit, but let wood be wood, brick, brick and plaster, plaster. Let the construction be visible and sound, and the decoration employed be guided by the simple desire of avoiding all shams, which will increase the beauty and effect of the edifice, and fill the souls worshipping therein with religious emotion.

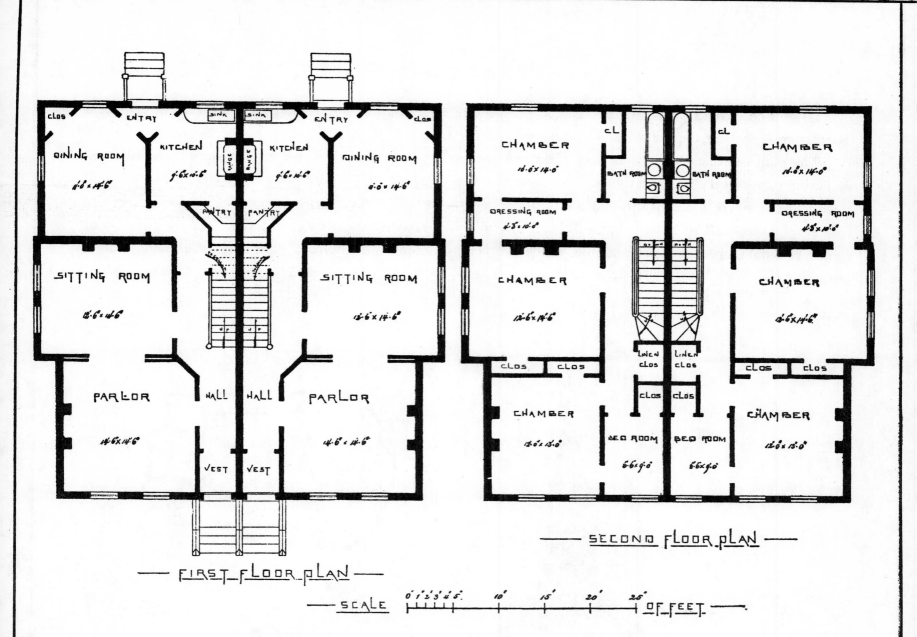

FIRST FLOOR PLAN

SECOND FLOOR PLAN

SCALE   OF FEET

FRONT ELEVATION   SIDE ELEVATION

PLATE 40.

DESIGN 50—Gives plans, elevations, and perspective view of a nine-room compact cottage, designed for a summer residence by the sea-side.   Cost, $3,500.

The plates in this work are all very plain and are intended to tell their own story, therefore but little explanation is necessary to make them so anyone can understand all their parts.   In the matter of cost, localities will have much to do with it, and the business management is a very important part and will affect the cost more or less.   The designs have all been carefully studied, with the view to get the greatest amount of room at as small an expense as possible, which is a very different matter from designing houses regardless of cost.

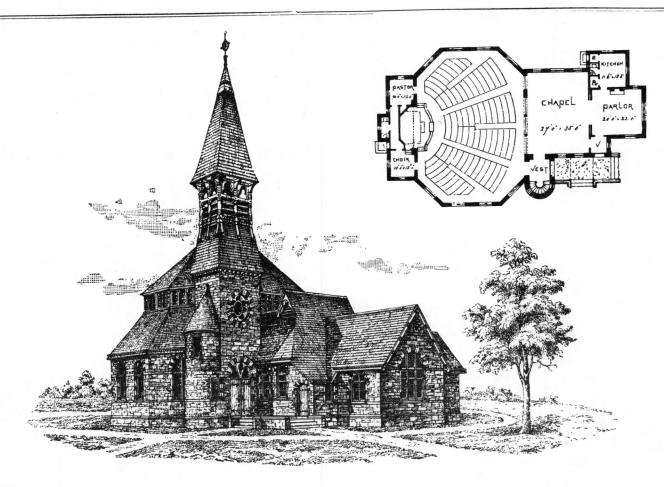

CONGREGATIONAL CHURCH.

This design was prepared with a view of erection on a peculiar site in a prosperous and growing country town, site being somewhat long and narrow, one corner of which rounded off to a sharp point on the rear portion of the church, and the peculiar lay-out of the plan was deemed necessary to carry out the problem and to suit the site.   The building is unique in design and finish, and successfully fills the demand of the modern ecclesiastical structure suited to the form of Congregational worship.   The plan is very compact, and so arranged that by rolling Venetian blinds to close the openings, the auditorium, or church proper, and the chapel can be thrown together, and the chapel and parlor, being connected with sliding doors, can be thus opened into and used as one ; and the kitchen in connection with parlor makes a desirable feature, and one which cannot fail to be appreciated by all Congregationalists.   The auditorium proper is an octagon with two long sides, the organ being placed behind the pulpit, and all seats radiating from the pulpit give each and everyone an equal opportunity to see and hear ; the doors on either side of the pulpit lead to choir and minister's room, both of which are connected

with a hallway having an outside entrance ; here also is provided a toilet-room, containing closet and bowl.   The main entrance is placed in the angle of auditorium and chapel, and connects with each, while the circular apse contains the stairway up to bell chamber above.   Over this entrance the tower rises to a height of ninety feet, and is arranged so as to hold a peal of bells, if desired.   At either flank of the octagon the walls are pierced with doors or windows, and the windows are filled with stained glass ; and as the outside walls are kept low, the principal light comes from the clerestory windows, and with the open-timber roof and stained glass the interior effect is very striking, adding much to the apparent height of the interior.   The interior finish of ash ; the walls above wainscoting to have a dark tint, and above a lighter shade.   The church body to be built out of a dark granite, found in the immediate neighborhood, laid in irregular courses, level beds and plumb joints ; the belts, sills, etc., of light granite, with drafted margins ; roofs covered with black slate.   Cost about $10,000, in favorable locality ; accommodation, 500.

The octagon must become in time both common and popular ; for when it is properly treated, it can be made to satisfy all the laws of good taste and the requirements of a Church, which will make those who worship there feel that they are really in the house of God.

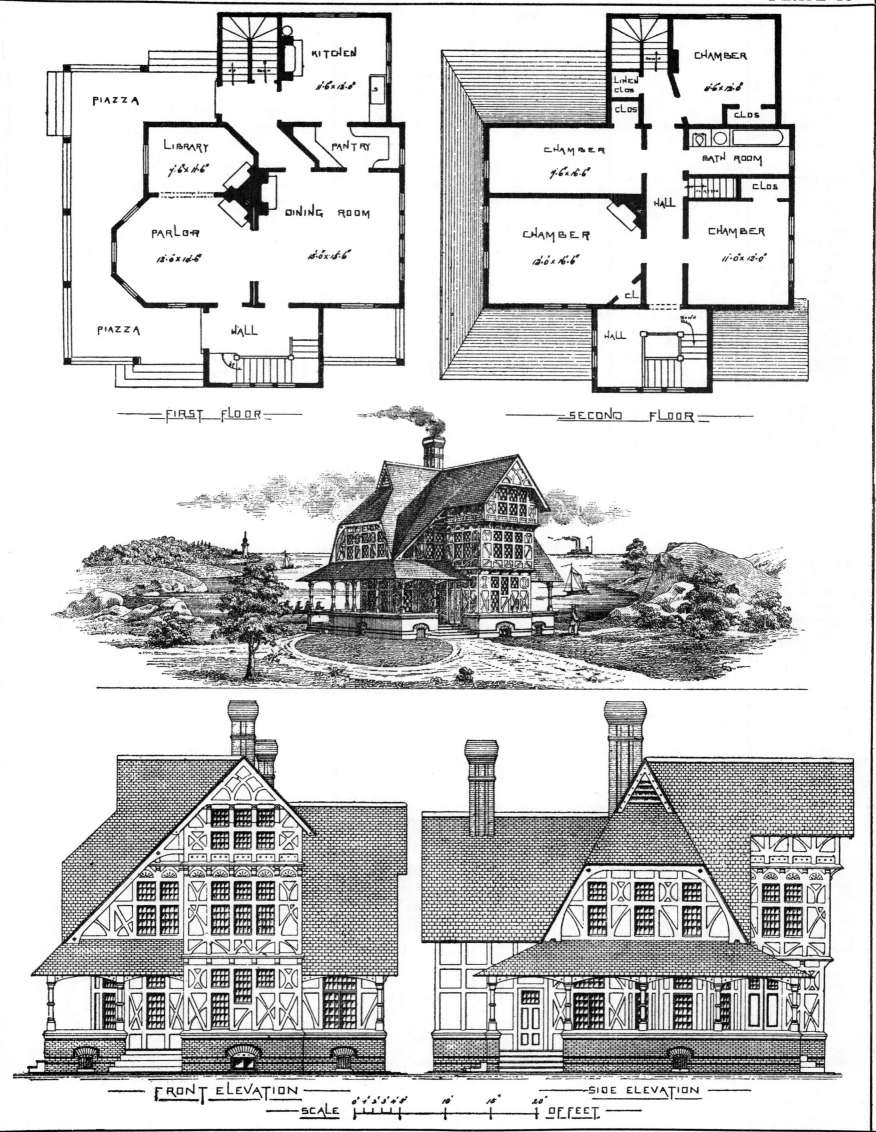

PIAZZA

KITCHEN
11·6 x 15·0

LIBRARY
7·6 x 11·6

PANTRY

PARLOR
12·6 x 14·6

DINING ROOM
15·0 x 15·6

PIAZZA

HALL

— FIRST FLOOR —

CHAMBER
11·6 x 12·6

LINEN
CLOS

CLOS

CHAMBER
7·6 x 15·6

BATH ROOM

CLOS

HALL

CLOS

CHAMBER
12·0 x 16·6

CHAMBER
11·0 x 12·0

CL

HALL

— SECOND FLOOR —

— FRONT ELEVATION —

— SIDE ELEVATION —

— SCALE   0' 1' 2' 3' 4' 5'   10'   15'   20'   OF FEET —

SPECIFICATIONS.

Of the works and materials required in the erection, construction and completion of Design No. 2, Plate 2.

DIMENSIONS.—The drawings and details must be accurately followed according to their scale, and in all cases preference must be given to figured dimensions over scale. The building to be in size as shown on plans (figured on drawings). Cellar, 6' 6''; first floor, 9' 0'' in the clear, divided, subdivided, and built in exact accordance with plans and specifications.

MASON WORK.

EXCAVATING.—Do all necessary excavating required for cellar, area and all foundations, to firm and solid ground, and all to be in depth so that foundations will be clear of frost.

STONE WORK.—Build the foundation walls of good, flat building stone, of firm bed, well bonded through the wall, laid up in clean, sharp sand, lime and cement mortar, in parts of one of cement to two of lime, laid by and full to a line on the inner face, and flushed and pointed at completion. These walls to be 1' 4'' thick. Put down in like manner foundations under all piers, chimney and exterior steps, all to be clear of frost.

DRAINS.—All drain pipes to be of the first quality cement drain pipe, in sizes as marked on the plan, and to be connected with sewer in street. These pipes to be properly graded, trapped and the joints cemented tight.

UNDERPINNING.—From the top of stone wall, at grade level, extend up two feet in height with 8'' brick wall, laid up with best hard-burned brick and clean, sharp sand lime mortar; face walls with selected brick of even color, laid in red mortar, close joints, jointed, properly cleaned down at completion, and finished with black joints. Window sills of blue stone.

PIERS —Build piers in cellar, as shown, of best hard-burned brick, laid in clean, sharp sand lime mortar, and cap off with flat stone size of piers.

CHIMNEY.—Build chimney as shown, plastered on the inside and outside, furnished with proper stove collars and ventilating covers where required; turn arch to fire place and turn trimmer arch under hearth. Hearth to be of slate properly bedded in cement. Top out the chimney above the roof, as shown, with selected brick in like manner to underpinning.

LATHING.—All stud partitions, ceilings and work that is furred off, on first and second floor, to be lathed with sound spruce laths, and joints broken every tenth lath.

PLASTERING.—All walls, partitions and ceilings, throughout first and second floors, to be plastered one good coat of brown, well haired mortar—and finish with a good coat of white hard-finish. All walls to be finished straight and plumb; all angles to be maintained sharp and regular in form, and the plastering, in all cases, to extend clear down to the floor.

CARPENTER.

TIMBER.—All timber not otherwise specified, to be of good seasoned spruce and put together in the most substantial and thoroughly workmanlike manner known to the trade.

FRAMING.—The frame to be what is known as a balloon frame, well nailed together; second floor girts to be notched into and well spiked to studs. Do all necessary framing around stairways and chimneys, properly mortised and tenoned together.

FRAME TIMBER.—Girders, 4''x6''; sills 3''x7''; posts, 4''x5''; girts of yellow pine, 1¼''x4''; plates, 2''x 4'', doubled and well spiked into ends of studding. First floor timbers, 2''x8''; second floor, 2''x 6''—16'' centres; header and trimmer beams, 3'' thick; roof rafters, 2''x 5''—2 ft. centres; door and window studs, 3''x 4''—intermediate studding, 2''x 4''—16'' centres; studdings in partitions, 2''x 3''—16'' centres. Veranda sills and cross sills, 3''x 6''; floor timbers, 2''x 6''—20'' centres; plates 4''x5''.

BRIDGING.—Bridge the floor timbers with 1''x 2'' cross-bridging, properly cut in between timbers, and nailed at each end with two 10d. nails.

FURRING.—Furr overhead on rafters, &c., for rooms on second floor, and do any other furring required; also furnish any other timber, as required by the design, of the requisite sizes and quality.

SHEATHING.—Cover all sides of frame with tongued and grooved boards, not to exceed 6'' in width, nailed through each edge to every stud with 10d. nails.

LUMBER.—The lumber to be of white pine, unless otherwise specified, free from knots, shakes and other imperfections impairing its durability and strength.

WATER TABLE to be ⅞'' thick, furred off, 1'', and capped with a beveled and rabbeted cap for clapboards to lap.

CORNER BOARDS, casings and bands to be 1¼''x 6''; bands to be rabbeted top and bottom for clapboards and beveled on top.

CLAPBOARDING.—Cover all sides with clear pine clapboards, 4½'' wide, put on with 8d. box nails, to have not less than 1¼'' lap, and underlaid with rosin-sized waterproof sheathing felt, which, also, place under all casings, water-table etc., so as to lap and make tight job.

CORNICES to be formed, as shown, on 3''x 5'' rafter feet, spiked on to rafters at plate; gutter formed on same, and lined with tin, so as to shed water to points indicated on plan; the plancier to be formed by laying narrow pine matched boards, face down on rafter feet; barge boards 2'' thick as shown, and all as per detail drawings.

WINDOW FRAMES to be made as shown; cellar frames of 2'' plank rabbeted for sash; sash hinged to top, and to have suitable fasteners to keep open or shut; all other sashes to be double hung with hemp cords and cast-iron weights, and to be glazed with best American sheet glass all sashes 1⅜'' thick, of seasoned pine, window sills 2'' thick.

BLINDS.—Outside blinds to all windows, except cellar, hung in two folds, properly secured and painted two good coats of dark green paint.

DOOR FRAMES.—Outside door frames of plank, rabbeted, and to have 2'' oak sills.

PORCHES to be constructed as shown by the detail drawings; steps 1¼'' thick, ⅞'' risers, to have cove under nosings; lay floors with 1¼''x4'' flooring, blind nailed to beams, and to have white lead joints; ceiling ceiled with narrow beaded battens of even width and molded in angles. Columns, rails, newels, panels, &c., all as per detail drawings.

ROOFING.—All roofs to be covered with 18'' sawed pine shingles, laid on 1''x 2'' strips nailed to rafters with 10d. nails; each shingle to be nailed with two white metal nails, to be well laid, joints properly broken, and made tight.

FLOORS.—Lay the floors throughout with ⅞'' flooring, not to exceed 6'' in width, to be well laid, joints broken, and well nailed to every timber; the best to be selected and laid on first floor.

PARTITIONS.—Set partitions, as marked on plans, to foot on girders, and to have 3''x3'' plates to carry second floor; all angles to be formed solid; all partitions to be bridged once in their height.

GROUNDS.—Put up all necessary grounds to skreed plaster to, to be ⅞'' thick and left on.

WAINSCOTING.—Wainscot walls of kitchen and living room 3ft. high, with beaded battens 3'' wide, and cap with molded and beveled cap.

CASINGS in front hall and living room to be cut and stop chamfered, as shown, 1¼''x6''; all doors and windows elsewhere to be cased before plastering with ⅞'' casings, and finish with a ⅞''x1¾'' band mold; put down 7'' bevelled base in front hall and bed-rooms after plastering; door jambs to be ⅞'' thick, and rabbeted for doors and beaded on edges; windows to be finished with neat stool and apron finish.

DOORS to be made in size as shown; outside doors to be sash doors, as shown; all other doors six-panel, ogee, molded solid.

SADDLES.—Put down neat hard pine saddles to all doors.

STAIRS.—Cellar stairs to be of plank, no risers; stairs to second floor as shown, 1¼'' treads, ⅞'' risers, properly put together and supported.

SINK.—Ceil up under sink with narrow beaded battens, to match wainscoting; hang door to form closet under; ceil up splash back 16'' high; also place drip board complete.

PANTRY to have counter-shelf and four shelves above; also put up one dozen pot-hooks.

CLOSETS to be fitted up with shelves and double wardrobe hooks, 9'' apart, on neat wood strips.

FURNITURE to front door Hemacite Eastlake pattern elsewhere Hemacite plain.

LOCKS to all doors to be mortise locks, brass fronts and keys; outside doors to be secured with suitable shove bolts.

STOPS.—Insert hard-wood door stops in base where requisite.

HINGING.—Hang all doors with loose joint butts of appropriate size.

MANTEL to be constructed, as shown, of ash.

CELLAR.—Partitions in cellar to be boarded with matched boards; coal bin to be boarded up 4 ft. high, to have slides complete.

FINAL.—Also do any other carpenter work as shown by and as required to carry out the design.

PAINTING.

All wood-work, both on interior and exterior, unless otherwise specified, to be painted two good coats of best white lead and raw linseed oil paint. Paint clapboards Venetian red; casings &c., Indian red, using black for all chamfers and cut work. Grain wood-work in kitchen in oak; bed-rooms paint in one color; wood-work in hall and living room to be properly filled with Wheeler's patent wood filler and finished with one coat of Crockett's Preservative No. 1, in a first class workmanlike manner; chamfers and cut work pick out in black; paint roofs dark slate color, tin work Indian red. Also, do, any other painter's work as required by the design.

TINNING AND PLUMBING.

TINNING,—Line the gutters with tin, well soldered in rosin; furnish and put up the necessary number of tin leaders to convey the water from gutters to grade level, and there connect with drains. These leaders to be firmly secured to building, and to be graded in size to suit amount of service required.

SINK to be a 20''x 30''x 6'' cast iron, supplied with water through ⅜'' lead pipe and ⅝'' brass draw cock, to have 2'' cast-iron waste, properly caulked at joints, trapped and connected closely to drain. Extend waste pipe above roof for vent.

[Written to go with Working and Detail Drawings.]

SPECIFICATIONS.

Of the works and materials required in the erection, construction, and completion of Design 40, Plate 30.

DIMENSIONS.—The drawings must be accurately followed according to their scale, and preference given to figured dimensions over scale. Detail drawings will be furnished, any work constructed without such drawings must be removed if required, and work replaced at contractor's expense. The building to be in size as shown and figured on drawings. Cellar, 6′ 9″; first floor, 9′ 0″; kitchen, 8′ 3″; second floor, 9′ 0″; over kitchen, 8′ 0″; all in the clear, divided, subdivided, and built in exact accordance with plans and specifications.

MASON WORK.

EXCAVATOR.—Excavate in depth for the cellar, area, foundations, and footings of all the walls and chimneys, also for all drains, cistern and cess-pools. Dig trenches for footings of all walls 8″ below level of cellar bottom; fill in around walls as laid; grade the excavated earth around the building as may be directed. Lay aside the top soil, at commencement, and replace over the graded surface at completion.

STONE WORK.—Build foundation walls of good building stone, of flat bed and firm build, laid in clean, sharp sand, lime and cement mortar, in parts of one of cement and two of lime. Lay down footings under all the walls of the building of flat stones, not less than 20″ long and 6″ thick, bedded crosswise of the walls on the natural, undisturbed earth; build the walls from thence to grade level, by and full to a line on the inner face, and flush and point at completion. These walls to average 1′ 6″ in thickness, the greater breadth at the base. Lay down substantial foundations under chimneys and piers in cellar; put down clear of frost, solid foundations under piers supporting porches and verandas, also under all exterior steps. Area copings and steps to be of blue stone, steps properly walled in on each end.

UNDERPINNING.—Build the underpinning walls 16″ thick from grade level, and extend up 2′ 4″ in height, with good underpinning stone, level beds, plumb joints; all angles and jambs to have chisel draft on edges, also on top to receive woodwork, and to be properly pointed and penciled with a white joint at completion. Window sills to be of blue stone; such portions of walls as are covered up with veranda to be rough work.

CESS-POOL.—Stone up cess-pool 3 feet in diameter and 8 feet deep, covered with rough flag, provided with man-hole, etc., complete; make the necessary connections with the cistern to receive the overflow through cement pipe of the required size. Also stone up, in like manner, cess-pool, to receive wastes from house, and connect with 6″ cement drain-pipe.

BRICK WORK.—To be laid up with best quality hard-burned brick and clean, sharp sand, lime mortar.

PIERS.—Build piers in cellar 16″ square, as shown, and cap with flat stone, size of piers; piers supporting porches and verandas 12″ square.

CHIMNEYS.—Build the chimneys as shown on plans; carry up the flues of uniform size, to be well plastered, furnished with proper stove collars and ventilating flues where required; turn arches to all fire-places, and turn trimmer arches under all hearths; top out above the roof, as per detail drawings, with selected brick laid in black mortar, close joints, jointed and cleaned down. Face the throat, breast and jambs of kitchen fire-place with selected brick, laid in black mortar, provided with slate shelf, to have blue stone hearth as shown on plans. Build fire-place in hall with buff brick, laid in red mortar, angles molded and as per details, also furnish the necessary brick, mortar and plaster for setting the mantels and range.

CISTERN.—Build a cistern where directed, 10 ft. diameter and 10 ft. deep, with 8″ walls laid in and smoothly coated on the inside with cement; cover man-hole in neck with flag-stone, connect to leaders with 4″ and 6″ vitrified pipe.

LATHING.—Lath all walls, ceilings, and work that is furred off, throughout first and second floors, with sound, seasoned lath, securely nailed to each stud, and joints broken every tenth lath.

PLASTERING.—All walls and ceilings throughout first and second floors, plaster with one good coat of brown, well haired mortar, and finish with one coat of white hard-finish. All angles to be sharp and regular in form, walls to be straight and plumb, and in all cases to extend clear down to floors.

CORNICES.—Run stucco cornices, as shown by the details, in hall, parlor, library and dining-room of first floor.

CENTRES.—Put up four neat and appropriate centres, of such pattern as selected by owner.

ARCHES. Finish and mold the arches in hall as shown by the detail drawings.

FINAL.—White wash walls in laundry, and do all necessary mending of walls after other craftsmen, and deliver the mason work up in thoroughly good order at completion; make the floors broom-clean from time to time as required; also remove all mason's waste materials and rubbish accumulated during the progress of the works, from off the premises and leave everything in a perfect, complete and satisfactory state.

CARPENTER.

TIMBER.—The whole of the timber used in and throughout tihs building to be the best of their several kinds, well seasoned and free from sap, shakes and other imperfections impairing its durability and strength.

FRAMING.—The frame to be what is known as half balloon, the studs to be tenoned into sills and plates, to be braced with long angle braces cut in barefoot and well spiked. The girts to be of yellow pine, notched into and well spiked to studs. Do all necessary framing around stairways and chimneys, all properly mortised and tenoned together and all to be done in a thoroughly workmanlike and substantial manner.

FRAME TIMBER.—Sills and girders, 6″x6″; posts, 6″x6″ with inside angle cut out to make them 4″ from faces. Girts 1¼″x4″; plates, 4″x5″; first floor timbers, 2″x10″; second floor, 2″x8″; attic 2″x6″—all 16″ centres; header and trimmer beams, 3″ thick, all floor timbers under partitions running same way to be 4″ thick, roof rafters, 2″x6″—2 ft. centres; hip and valley rafters, 3″x8″. Door and window studs, 3″x4″ intermediate studding, 2″x4″—16″ centres; long braces, 2″x4″. All main partitions to be set with 2″x4″ studding—16″ centres, to be set as the frame is raised, and foot on girders, to have 3″x4″ plates on which to foot second story partitions and carry floor timbers; other partitions set with 2″x3″ studs—16″ centres, and all partitions that are directly over each other to be set in like manner to above, all to be well braced and spiked; all angles to be formed solid, and all partitions to be bridged once in their height. Porch and veranda sills, 4″x6″; floor timbers, 2″x6″—16″ centres; plates, 4″x5″; rafters, 3″x5″—2 ft. centres.

BRIDGING.—All the floor timbers to be bridged through centres with 2″x2″ cross-bridging, properly cut in between timbers and nailed with two 10d. nails at each end, also furnish any other timber of the required size and necessary to fully complete the works.

FURRING.—Properly support and furr under stairs, furr for arches, and do any other furring required by the design.

SHEATHING.—Cover the entire frame with tongued and grooved boards, not to exceed 6″ in width, nailed through each edge to every stud with 10d. nails; this includes all roofs.

LUMBER.—The lumber to be of white pine, unless otherwise specified, well seasoned and dry, and free from shakes, loose knots and other imperfections. Sashes and panel work to be perfectly clear lumber.

CLAPBOARDING.—Cover all sides with clear pine clapboards, put on with 8d. box nails, with not less than 1¼″ lap. These boards to be underlaid with beaver-brand, rosin-sized, waterproof sheathing felt, which also place under corner boards, casings, etc., so as to lap and make a tight job.

CORNER BOARDS, casings, and bands, 1¼″x 7″; bands to be rabbeted top and bottom for clapboards.

WATER TABLE.—To be furred off from frame, and to have beveled cap 1½″ thick.

CORNICES.—To be formed on 3″x 5″ rafter feet, cut as shown, and spiked on to rafters at plate; the plancier to be formed by laying narrow pine matched boards, face down on rafter feet; barge boards and gable staffs to be 2½″ thick and as shown. Brackets, as shown, and all as per details. Gutters to be of galvanized iron, graded to shed water to points indicated on plan.

LEADERS.—Furnish all the required leaders of sufficient size to convey the water from the gutters to the cistern and the tank in attic; said leaders to be firmly secured to building.

FINIAL.—To be of wrought iron, as per details, to have galvanized iron cover to base.

WINDOW FRAMES.—To be made in the ordinary manner; cellar frames to be made out of 2″ plank, rabbeted for sash; sash hinged to top and to have suitable fasteners to keep open or shut: all sash to be of seasoned pine, 1½″ thick, and double hung with best hemp cords, iron weights, and 1¾″ sham axle pulleys, and to be glazed with English sheet glass, all to be well bedded, bradded and puttied; window in dining-room, on to veranda, to be hinged; window sills 2¼″ thick.

BLINDS.—Outside blinds to all windows, except cellar, hung in two folds, with the best kind of hinges, and secured with best style fasteners, and painted three coats of paint, invisible green.

DOOR FRAMES.—Outside door frames to be of plank, rabbeted, and to have 2½″ oak sills.

VERANDAS.—Construct veranda and porches, as shown, and as per detail drawings; steps, 1¼″ thick, risers 1″, to have cove under nosings; lay the floors with 1⅛″x 3¼″ flooring, blind nailed to beams, and to have paint joints; rafters to be dressed and chamfered; lay on rafters, face down narrow beaded ceiling of even widths. Columns, rails and brackets to be as shown; cornices formed with beaded ceiling on rafter feet in like manner to main roof; rafter feet to be cut as shown; panels formed under floor as shown.

FLOORS.—Lay the kitchen floor with yellow pine, ⅞″x3″, blind nailed to every beam; all other floors lay with white pine, not to exceed 5″ in width, to be well laid, joints broken, and blind nailed in a thorough manner. Lay front hall floor with yellow pine and black walnut in alternate strips, to have neat border.

WAINSCOTING.—Walls of kitchen to be wainscoted 3 ft. high with beaded battens ⅞″ x 3″, and to have neat bevelled molded cap.

CASINGS.—Case all doors and windows throughout, before plastering with ⅞″ casings, and trim hall, parlor, dining-room and library with a 1¼″ x 3″ band-mold; elsewhere trim with 1″x 1¾″ band-mold; windows in above rooms to be finished down to floor with framed and molded panel-backs to match doors; other windows to have neat stool and apron finish; door-jambs to be 1″, beaded on edges, and rabbeted for doors; no moldings in closets.

BASE.—Put down after plastering, 8″ molded base in principal rooms first floor; 7″ plain beveled elsewhere.

DOORS.—To be made in size and thickness as marked on plans; front doors as per details; top panels glazed with colored glass; all other doors to be six-panel ogee molded solid.

SADDLES.—Put down molded hard-wood saddles to all doors.

STAIRS.—Stairs to cellar to be of plank, no risers, to have flat rail on side; main stairs as shown 1″ risers, 1¼″ treads, with returned molded nosings, to be well supported and rough bracketed, steps housed into strings; newel posts, rails and balusters to be of black walnut, as per details. Back stairs, and stairs to attic to be box stairs.

WASH TUBS.—To be constructed out of 2″ plank, rabbeted and put together with white lead joints, and to have hinged lids—these tubs to be 14″ deep.

SINK.—Ceil up under sink with narrow beaded battens; to have door properly hung; ceil up splash back 16″ high, and cap same as wainscoting also place drip board complete.

WASH BOWLS.—Ceil up under with narrow beaded ash battens, and hang door to form a closet under.

BATH-ROOMS.—Wainscot walls of bath-room, 3 ft. high, with narrow beaded ash battens, and cap with neat cap; water closet to be fitted up with seat, riser and mitre-clamp flap, hung with brass butts.

BATH-TUB to be cased in most approved manner, all of ash.

TANK.—Construct out of 2″ plank, a tank in attic, over bath-room 7 ft. long, 5′ 6″ wide and 3 ft. deep, framed, braced and supported in a substantial manner; the bottom of tank to be furred and plastered in bath room, and finish 7′ 6″ in the clear.

PANTRY.—To have counter-shelf and four shelves above; closet for barrel of flour, with lid in counter-shelf; also put in two dove-tailed drawers, and put up one dozen pot-hooks.

PASSAGE.—To have table with closet under, and three dove-tailed drawers; also shelves as shown.

CLOSETS.—To have shelves on neat strips, and double wardrobe hooks 8″ apart, on neat molded strips.

FURNITURE.—To front doors to be Tucker bronze; other doors, first, floor, principal rooms, Hemacite Eastlake pattern; other doors, mineral japanned, sash fasteners to correspond; all small closets to have suitable catches; all drawers to have suitable pulls, locks, etc., complete.

LOCKS.—All doors throughout to be secured with mortise locks, of best city make, brass fronts, bolts and keys; outside doors to have suitable shove bolts.

STOPS.—Put rubber-tipped door-stops in base where required.

HINGING.—Hang all doors with loose joint butts, of appropriate sizes; all doors over 7′ 6″ high to have three butts each. Sliding doors to run on brass track and patent slot sheaves.

BELL.—Front door to have bell connected with kitchen, with pull, etc., complete.

NIGHT-LATCH to front door, combined with lock, and supplied with two keys.

COAL BINS, and partitions in cellar, to be boarded up with matched boards, as shown; doors in cellar to be batten doors.

MANTELS. Construct mantel in hall of ash, as per details; furnish and put up four slate mantels; all hearths of slate, to have summer fronts, etc., complete, and to cost $ 100 and be selected by owner; mantels in bed-room on first floor, and two chambers, to be neat wooden mantels.

FINAL.—Any other work that is shown by the drawings, and necessary to fully complete the work, to fully complete the same to the true intent and meaning of these particulars, is to be done without extra charge.

SLATER.

Cover all roofs with best Bangor, Pa., black slate, of small size, laid with a lap of at least 3″ of the third over the first; each slate to be nailed with two galvanized iron nails; lay under slate heavy tarred felt paper; cover the ridges with zinc, also flash valleys and chimneys with heavy zinc, and secure with slater's cement. To be a first class job, and warranted tight for two years.

PLUMBER.

IRON SOIL-PIPE.—Furnish, and connect with drain, a 4″ cast iron soil-pipe, extend up and connect with water closet in bath-room through 6lb. lead trap; soil-pipe to be properly secured and the joints caulked tight with lead, and extend up above roof and cap with ventilator. All traps in plumbing to have 1″ vent pipes of lead run up to attic and connected with soil or outlet pipe up above roof.

SUPPLY-PIPE.—Furnish a ¾″ B lead pipe, connect with the attic tank, and run to and connect with boiler in kitchen; tank to be lined with 4lb. lead, and to have 2″ overflow run through outside wall.

BOILER.—To be a 35-gallon, galvanized iron, of the best construction, connected to water back of range, through double A lead pipe and brass couplings; these pipes to be left ready for connection.

SINK.—To be 20″ x 30″ x 6″ cast iron, galvanized, supplied with hot and cold water through ⅝″ B lead pipe, ⅝″ brass draw cocks, to have 2″ waste, properly trapped and connected.

PUMP.—Put in a combination lift and force pump, to cost $12: connect the same with cistern and well through 1¼″B. lead pipes, provided with stop cocks, one on each pipe, placed beneath the pump, connect with tank in attic through 1″ B lead pipe and run tell-tale back from tank to sink.

WASH TUBS.—Supply the two wash tubs in laundry with hot and cold water, through ⅝″ B lead pipe and brass thimble tray draw cocks, to have 2″ main waste and 1½″ branch wastes, properly trapped and connected.

WASH BOWLS.—To be of Wedgewood ware, and to have marble counter sunk tops and surbases, supplied with hot and cold water through ½″ B lead pipe and compression double nickel plated draw cocks, and plated plug and chain; to have 1″ lead wastes, properly trapped and connected: lead pans to each with ½″ lead waste run down to underside cellar ceiling.

WATER-CLOSET to be a Harrison best closet, with patent drip tray; also patent shut-off cock to regulate flow of water to bowl; to be set and fit up in a perfect, tight and complete manner.

BATH TUB.—To be a 12oz. sheet-copper tub, well tinned and planished, supplied with hot and cold water through ⅝″ B lead pipe and nickle-plated draw-cocks; also to have plated plug and chain; also rubber hose shower-bath attachment; waste, 1½″ lead, properly trapped and connected.

COCKS.—Put in the necessary stop-cocks over the boiler to shut the water off from the upper part of the house; also put in a lead branch connected with drain with stop-cock for emptying the boiler; also put in one draw-cock in cellar and all other stop and draw-cocks necessary to make a complete and first-class job; all pipes to be graded, so that if the water is shut off they will drain dry, and the whole of the work to be done in the very best and workmanlike manner, and delivered up in a complete and perfect state at completion.

PAINTER.

Properly stop and otherwise prepare for and paint all wood work that is customary and usual to paint, both on the interior and exterior, two good coats of the best white lead and raw linseed oil paint.

Paint finial invisible green, and gild the tips with gold leaf.

Grain the wood work in kitchen and back hall light oak; grain dining-room and liarary walnut and maple; paint parlor and hall in tints: elsewhere paint in one color.

All hard wood to be properly filled with Wheeler's patent filler and finished with two coats of Crockett's Preservative No. 1. properly applied and rubbed down smooth; all grained work to be varnished. Fill the front doors with Wheeler's filler and finish with two coats of Crockett's Spar Composition and rub down.

Paint clapboards light olive drab; paint corner boards, casings, etc., Indian Red; pick out all chamfers and cut work in black, paint sash Venetian red; Veranda ceilings ultramarine blue, with rafters Indian red; and do any other painting as required by the design, and necessary to fully complete the same.

FORM OF CONTRACT.

𝕬rticles of 𝕬greement, MADE and entered into this_____day of_____
in the year One Thousand Eight Hundred and_____, BY AND BETWEEN_____
_____, of the_____of_____, County of_____
and State of_____, as the part____of the First Part, and_____,
of the_____of_____, County of_____, and State of_____,
as the part____of the Second Part,

Witnesseth: First—The said part____of the first part do____hereby, for_____
heirs, executors, administrators or assigns, covenant, promise and agree to and with the said part____of the second
part,_____heirs, executors, administrators or assigns, that_____, the said part____of the first part,_____
heirs, executors, administrators or assigns, shall and will for the consideration hereinafter mentioned, on or before the
_____day of_____, in the year One Thousand Eight Hundred and_____
well and sufficiently erect, finish and deliver, in a true, perfect and thoroughly workmanlike manner, the
_____
_____
for the part____of the second part, on ground situated_____
_____, in the_____of_____, County of_____, and State
of_____, agreeably to the plans, drawings and specifications prepared for the said works by
_____, Architect, to the satisfaction and under the direction and personal supervision of
_____, Architect, and will find and provide such good, proper and sufficient materials, of
all kinds whatsoever as shall be proper and sufficient for the completing and finishing all the_____
_____and other works of the said building mentioned in the
_____specifications, and signed by the said parties, within the time aforesaid, for the sum of_____
_____Dollars.

Second—The said part____of the second part do____hereby for_____heirs, executors,
administrators or assigns, covenant, promise and agree to and with the said part____of the first part,_____
heirs, executors, administrators or assigns, that_____, the said part____of the second part_____heirs, executors,
administrators or assigns, will and shall in consideration of the covenants and agreements being strictly executed,
kept and performed by the said part____of the first part as specified, will well and truly pay or cause to be
paid, unto the part____of the first part, or unto_____heirs, executors, administrators or assigns, the sum of
_____Dollars, lawful money of the
United States of America, in manner following :

First payment of $_____

Second payment of $_____

Third payment of $_____

Fourth payment of $_____

Fifth payment of $_____

when the building is all complete, and after the expiration of_____days, being the number of days allowed by law
to lien a building for work done and material furnished, and when all the drawings and specifications have been returned
to_____, Architect ;

Provided, that in each case of the said payments a certificate shall be obtained from and signed by
_____, Architect, to the effect that the work is done in strict accordance with
drawings and specifications, and that he considers the payment properly due ; said certificate, however, in no way
lessening the total and final responsibility of the part____of the first part ; and, Provided further that in each
case a certificate shall be obtained by the part____of the first part, from the clerk of the office where liens are recorded,

and signed and sealed by said clerk, that he has carefully examined the records and finds no liens or claims recorded against said works, or on account of the said part____of the first part.

And it is hereby further Agreed by and between the said Parties:

Third.—That the specifications and the drawings are intended to co-operate, so that any works exhibited in the drawings and not mentioned in the specifications, or *vice versa*, are to be executed the same as if they were mentioned in the specifications and set forth in the drawings, to the true intent and meaning of the said drawings and specifications, without extra charge.

Fourth.—The Contractor, at his own proper costs and charges, is to provide all manner of labor, materials, apparatus, scaffolding, utensils and cartage of every description needful for the due performance of the several works ; and render all due and sufficient facilities to the Architect for the inspection of the work and materials.

Fifth.—Should the Owner, at any time during the progress of the said works require any alterations of, deviations from additions to, or omissions from the said Contract, he shall have the right and power to make such change or changes, and the same shall in no way injuriously affect or make void the Contract ; but the difference shall be added to or deducted from the amount of the Contract, as the case may be, by a fair and reasonable valuation.

Sixth.—Should the Contractor, at any time during the progress of the said works, refuse or neglect to supply a sufficiency of material or of workmen, or cause any unreasonable neglect or suspension of work, or fail or refuse to comply with any of the Articles of Agreement, the Owner or his agent shall have the right and power to enter upon and take possession of the premises and provide materials and workmen sufficient to finish the said works, after giving forty-eight hours notice in writing, directed and delivered personally to the part____of the first part ; and the expense of the notice and the finishing of the various works will be deducted from the amount of Contract.

Seventh.—Should any dispute arise respecting the true construction or meaning of the drawings or specifications, the same shall be decided by_____, Architect, and his decision shall be final and conclusive ; but should any dispute arise respecting the true value of any extra work, or of works omitted by the Contractor, the same shall be valued by two competent persons—one employed by the Owner and the other by the Contractor—and these two shall have the power to name an Umpire, whose decision shall be binding on all parties.

Eighth.—No work shall be considered as extra, unless a separate estimate in writing, for the same, shall have been submitted by the Contractor to the Architect and the Owner and their signatures obtained thereto.

Ninth.—The Owner will not in any manner, be answerable or accountable for any loss or damage that shall or may happen to the said works, or any part or parts thereof respectively, or for any of the materials or other things used and employed in finishing and completing the said works.

Tenth.—The Contractor will insure the building before each payment, for the amount of the payment to be made ; and the policy will not expire until after the building is completed and accepted by the Architect and Owner. The Contractor will also assign the policy to the Owner before the payment will be made.

Eleventh,—Each artisan and laborer will receipt the Architect's certificate, that he has been paid in full, and the Contractor will make oath according to the Architect's certificate, that all bills have been paid and that there are no unpaid accounts against the works.

Twelfth.—Should the Contractor fail to finish the work at or before the time agreed upon,_____shall pay to the part____of the second part, the sum of_____ dollars per diem, for each and every day thereafter the said works shall remain unfinished, as and for liquidated damages.

𝔍𝔫 𝔚𝔦𝔱𝔫𝔢𝔰𝔰 𝔚𝔥𝔢𝔯𝔢𝔬𝔣, The said parties to these presents have hereunto set their hands and seals, the day and year above written.

Witnesses, {_____ *Part____of the First Part* {_____[SEAL.]
{_____   {_____[SEAL.]

Witnesses, {_____ *Part____of the Second Part* {_____[SEAL.]
{_____   {_____[SEAL.]

MODERN COTTAGE

With four rooms on each floor, also showing how it can be built with only three rooms on a floor and with or without tower.

SPECIFICATIONS

Of the works and materials required in the erection, construction and completion of the accompanying design, as shown by the different drawings and as herein specified.

Dimensions.—The drawings must be accurately followed according to their scale, and in all cases preference given to figures over scale. The building to be in size as shown and figured on drawings, divided, subdivided and built in exact accordance with plans and specifications, and the work executed in the best, most substantial and workmanlike manner and according to the true meaning and intent of these particulars and the drawings referred to, and which are intended to include everything requisite and necessary to the proper and entire finishing of the work, even though every item involved by the work is not particularly mentioned, and the work to be delivered up when finished in a perfect and undamaged state without exception, and at completion all rubbish, surplus and waste materials shall be removed from the premises, scrub the floors, wash the windows, and leave the building fit and ready for occupation.

MASON WORK.

Excavation.—Excavate in depth for all cellar and foundations, and for footings of all walls and chimneys, also for drains, cistern, and cess-pools; dig trenches for footings of walls 4 inches below finished level of cellar bottom, fill in and pack around walls when mortar is dry; grade the excavated earth around the premises as may be required and directed, lay aside the top soil at commencement and replace over the graded surface at completion.

Stone Work.—Build foundation walls of good flat building stone, of flat bed and firm build, laid in clean, sharp sand, lime and cement mortar, in equal parts lime and cement; lay both sides by and full to a line and point the inner face at completion. Lay down substantial foundations under chimney and piers in cellar; put down, clear of frost, foundations under piers supporting veranda, also under all exterior steps; area steps and coping to be of good blue stone properly walled in, etc.

Underpinning.—Build the underpinning walls 16 inches thick from grade level, with good quality quarry stone, laid (rock face) level beds and plumb joints on such portions as show, and neatly pointed and penciled at completion, parts under verandas to be good stone walls, same as cellar walls. Window sills to be of blue stone. Leave all openings in stone work as required for drains and other pipes.

Cistern.—To be built as shown, the walls of brick laid in cement and smoothly coated on the inside with cement, and the bottom paved with brick and coated same as sides.

Cess-pools.—Stone up one cess-pool for overflow from cistern as shown, one for wash-tray waste as shown, also main cess-pool placed 50 ft. from house and to be 5 ft. diameter, and 7 ft. deep in the clear, stoned up in good shape, drawn in on top, and to have manhole 18 inches under ground covered over with flagstone.

Drains.—To be laid as shown, and to be of best quality Akron sewer pipe salt-glazed and laid on a proper grade, joints made tight with cement, and to be trapped as shown.

Brick Work.—To be laid up with best quality hard-burned brick and clean, sharp sand and lime mortar.

Piers.—Build all piers as shown in cellar, and cap same with a flat stone size of piers, also build piers supporting verandas as shown.

Chimneys.—Build the chimneys as shown on plans. Carry up the flues of uniform size, well pargeted, and to have the required stove collars and ventilating covers inserted where required; turn arches to all fire-places and trimmer arches under hearths. Top out above the roof with selected brick, trimmed, etc., as shown by the drawings, laid up in red mortar and cap with a stone 5 inches to 8 inches thick. The chimney tops above roof to be laid up with 8 inch walls for exterior and 4 inch partitions between flues. Arrange ash-pit in cellar as shown and place a small iron door in bottom, and dumps in hearths of parlor and dining-room fire-places. Face the throat, breast and jambs of kitchen fire place with good selected red brick in red mortar, and place a 5x10 inch cut-stone lintel or shelf over same. Face the other fire-places with good quality buff brick laid in mortar colored to match, and pave backs of fire-places with fire brick, the hearths to be of slate, in style, etc., as shown, and firmly bedded on mortar, and laid about 3-16 of an inch above finished floor adjoining.

Lathing.—Lath all walls and ceilings of first and second floors, also tower room, with sound, well-seasoned lath, joints broken every tenth course, securely nailed to studs.

Plastering.—All walls and ceilings that are lathed on 1st, 2d, and 3d floors to be plastered with one good coat of brown, well-haired mortar, and finish with one good coat of white sand or hard finish. All angles to be maintained sharp and regular in form, walls finished straight and plumb, and in all cases plastering to extend clear down to the floor.

Centers.—Furnish and put up three neat and appropriate center pieces of such pattern as selected by owner.

Arches.—The arch beams to be molded on angles with rule joint molding and to be finished at ends with suitable and appropriate corbels.

Cellar.—Level off and settle the cellar bottom and cover it flush and smooth throughout with cement concrete in 3 parts of clean, coarse gravel and one of cement, 2 inches deep and finished with a true and even surface.

Final.—Whitewash twice the walls in cellar and laundry, also all brickwork in same, and joist overhead. Do all necessary patching and mending of walls after other workmen, and leave the whole in a complete and perfect state of completion.

CARPENTER WORK.

Timber.—The whole of the timber used in and throughout the work to be the best of their several kinds, well seasoned and free from sap, shakes or other imperfections impairing its durability or strength: timber not exposed to be of spruce, pine or clean hemlock, and where exposed to view to be of good quality pine.

Framing.—The frame to be a balloon frame, properly halved and spiked together, the girts to be notched into and well spiked to studs. Do all the necessary framing around stairways and chimneys, all properly mortised and tenoned together, all to be done in a workmanlike and substantial manner.

Frame Timber.—Girders, 6x8 inches; sills, 4x6 inches; posts, 4x6 inches; girts, 1x4 inches; plates, 2x4 inches, double and well spiked together and on to studs: first and second floor joists 2x9 inches—16-inch centers; attic, 2x7 inches—16-inch centers; header and trimmer beams double; roof rafters, 2x6 inches—2 ft. centers; hip and valley rafters, 2x8 inches. Door and window studs, 3x4 inches; intermediate studding, 2x4 inches—16 in. centers; main partitions to be set as the frame is rased, and to foot on the girders below, having 3x4 inch plates on which to foot second story partitions and carry floor joists. All angles to be formed solid and all partitions to be bridged once in their height; veranda sills, 4x7 inches; floor joist, 2x7 inches—20 inch centers; rafters, 2x5 inches; plates, columns, balusters, etc., as shown by the design; also furnish any other timber as required by the design.

Bridging.—All floor timbers to be bridged every five feet with 1x2 inch cross bridging well nailed.

Furring.—Do all necessary furring as required for stairs, closets, arch beams, etc.

Sheathing.—Cover the entire frame on exterior with tongued and grooved boards not to exceed 8 inches in width, placed diagonally and well nailed with 10d. nails.

Lumber.—The lumber to be of white pine unless otherwise specified, well seasoned and dry; the clapboards to be perfectly clear, as also the sashes and panel work throughout.

Corner Boards.—Casings, bands, etc., to be one and a quarter inches thick, 6 inches face; bands rabbeted top and bottom for clapboarding, etc., water-table to be formed as shown, furred off from frame and to have rabbeted beveling cap to receive clapboards.

Clapboarding.—The sides of first story and rear wing, as shown, to be covered with 5 inch clapboards having one and a quarter inch lap and nailed with 8d. box nails; these, as also all other exterior finish, to be underlaid with ...... brand rosin-sized waterproof sheathing felt, properly stretched, lapped and nailed on so as to make a tight job.

Shingle Work.—Side walls of second story, tower, etc., as shown, to be covered with shingles 6 inches wide and 6 inches to weather, laid in style as per drawing, and properly flashed at all corners and connections so as to insure a perfectly tight job.

Cornices.—The cornice to eaves to be formed with 2x5 inch dressed rafter feet and plancier of narrow matched boards face down on rafter feet. The raking eaves and cornices to be formed as shown, with 2 inch barge boards, soffits, etc., as per plans, and all other cornices, caps and exterior finish to be executed in accordance with the drawings for same.

Roofing.—The whole of the main and veranda roofs to be covered with best quality 18 inch pine shingle, laid on one and one-eighth by two inch strips and five and one-half inch to the weather, put on in best manner, properly laid, joints broken and each shingle nailed with two 4d. nails, the valleys to be properly lined with tin 20 inches wide; also do the necessary tin work behind tower as required to throw the water out to the front, as shown by plan. Balcony over front bay to be covered with tin in the ordinary manner.

Gutters.—To be lined with tin throughout, and to have galvanized iron .... conductor pipes from same to convey the water from gutters to cistern or drain, as shown by the drawings; these conductors to be secured with galvanized iron hold fasts and to have proper curves and bends as required.

Finial.—On tower, as shown, to be of wrought iron, vane to work on a pivot, to have galvanized iron cover for top of roof at base, and to be properly secured inside in the best manner possible, finial to be painted, gilded and finished up in a complete manner.

Windows.—Cellar frames to be of 2x6 inch plank rabbeted to receive sash; sash hinged to top and to have suitable fasteners to keep either open or shut—other frames to be made for double hung sash as shown; 1 inch pulley styles, 2 inch sills, and seven-eighth inch counter sills; sash to be one and one-half inch thick hung with .... sash cord; one and three-quarter inch enameled face pulleys and cast iron weights, secured with .... sash locks placed on the meeting rails; glazed with second quality 21 oz. sheet glass (except staircase and toilet room window, which are to be glazed with Scotch cathedral glass in different tints). Window from dining room to rear veranda to be a French window with sliding head. Bay windows to be finished, built, etc., in strict accordance with the drawings for same.

Blinds.—All the windows in parlor, sitting room and dining room of

MODERN COTTAGE

With four rooms on each floor, also showing how it can be built with only **three rooms on a** floor and with or without tower.

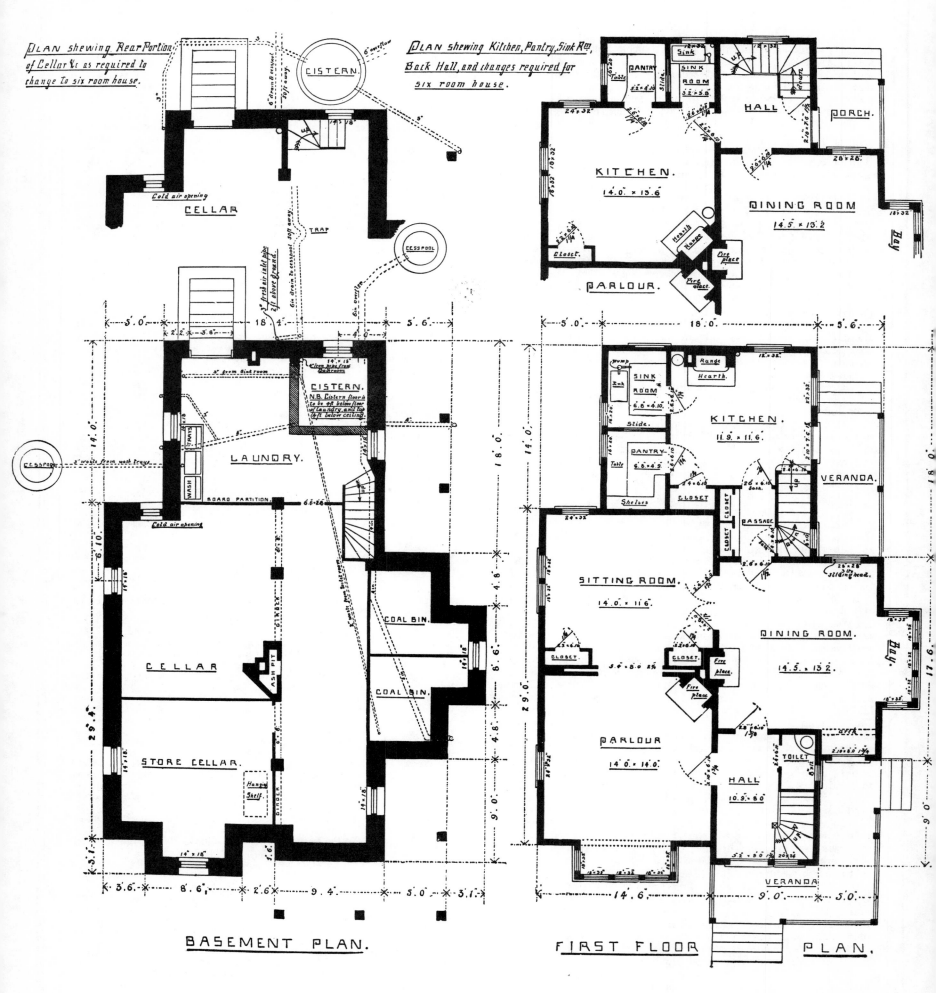

BASEMENT PLAN.

FIRST FLOOR PLAN.

first floor, and the second floor, to have .... patent inside window blinds, maple slats with red trimmings, etc., and fit up complete ready for use.

Door Frames.—Outside door frames to have plank jambs rabbeted for doors ; casings as before specified and hardwood door sills.

Verandas.—To be constructed as shown ; floors laid with one and one-eighth by four inch pine plank, paint joints and well nailed to bearings ; steps, one and one-quarter inches thick, risers seven-eighth inches with coves under nosings and enclosed below floor to grade level with panels, facia, etc., as shown. Columns, plates, rails, balusters, etc., to be as shown, the ceiling to be formed by laying narrow matched and beaded boards face down on the dressed and chamfered rafters similar to main roof eave finish, and the cornices, gutters, etc., formed as shown by the drawings.

Floors.—Lay the kitchen, pantry, sink room and passage or back hall floors with yellow pine flooring not to exceed 3 inches wide, and blind nailed, All other floors lay with seven-eighth by five and one-half inch matched flooring well nailed, and selecting the best for first and second floors, and using only sound flooring in attic ; all spaces to be closed up completely around outer walls and partitions.

Casing.—The three main rooms and front hall of first floor to have doors and windows cased with seven-eighth by five inch casings, the windows to be cased to floor, having finish of narrow matched ceiling under sill and base board continued across same as on plastered walls, and the sill finished to match casings. Door jambs to be rabbeted to receive doors and beaded on the edges ; the above work all to be finished up in a neat manner for natural wood finish, all inside work to be hand-smoothed and properly sandpapered with the grain of the wood. All other parts to be cased with four and one-half inch casings and finished with two and one-quarter inch back mold, the windows having rabbeted nosing stools and neat molded aprons.

Saddles.—All doors to have hardwood saddles one-half inch thick, and in width to be on a line with base boards both sides of partitions.

Base.—Base on first floor to be seven-eighths by eight inches, with one and three-quarter inch mold on top, and e sewhere eight inch plain beveled.

Wainscot.—Walls of kitchen to be wainscoted 3 feet high with one-half inch narrow beaded battens and cap with a neat rabbeted and molded cap.

Doors.—To be in size, etc., as marked on plans. Those on first floor main rooms and halls to be two panels wide and three high, with molded rails and chamfered styles and muntins. Front doors make as shown by drawings. All other doors to be good stock molded, doors of size and thickness as marked on plans ; sliding doors to be hung overhead with ....patent adjustable hangers on hardwood tracks securely bolted to timber work, and to have the necessary guides as required, to have astragal joint up center, and flush bronze furniture.

Hinges.—Doors on first floor main to be hung with three and one-half by three and one-half inch black japanned loose pin butts, and elsewhere with three and one-half inch plain loose pin butts. All doors over 7 feet high to have three butts to each.

Locks.—Secure all doors with a three and one-half inch brass front mortise lock, except front door, which is to have a 5 inch lock with night-latch combined. (All locks to be of .... Company's make throughout.)

Knobs.—Front outside door to have bronze knob and escutcheons. First floor main rooms, etc,, to have .... knobs of Eastlake pattern, elsewhere .... plain, and suitable escutcheons to all.

Bolts.—The double doors to have brass face flush bolts of suitable size ; also put six ...... patent door bolts on rear outside and dining room front door, and on such other doors as directed.

Stops.—Put rubber-tipped door stops in base boards where required.

Stairs.—Cellar stairs to be plank stairs (no risers), and slat rail down one side. Back and attic stairs to be box stairs, as shown, put up in good style and a rail placed up one side of each, and rail around the top of attic stairs at floor level, as required. Build main staircase as shown, one and one-eighth inch tread and strings, seven-eighth inch risers, molded nosings, and the whole put together and supported in the best manner ; to have 7 inch turned newel at start, 4x4 inch posts with turned caps, two and one-quarter by three inch molded rail and one and three-quarter inch turned balusters. Rail, newels, posts and balusters to be of ash.

Bath Room.—To be fit up in good style, the water-closet seats and lid and bath tub top to be of hard wood, other fittings of pine. The walls over tub to be ceiled up 2 feet high with one-half inch beaded battens and neatly capped ; fit up drawers as shown at head of bath tub, and enclose under washbowls and doors properly hung and secured. Put up one dozen hooks in bath and toilet rooms as directed.

Closets.—All closets to be properly fit up with shelves and wardrobe hooks, 8 inches apart, passed all around on neat molded strips. Linen closet to have shelves placed in same 11 inches apart up to ceiling ; other closets fit up as directed.

Passage.—Fit up presses in passage way from dining room to kitchen as shown ; to have hinged doors, six drawers under counter shelf and small closets, all fit up in complete order with pulls, catches, locks, etc., as required.

Sink Room.—To be fit up in good style, the counter-shelf at sink level to go on three sides as shown, and two sides to be enclosed under with narrow beaded lumber and to have doors properly hung and secured. Fit up shelves above the sink on one side up to ceiling and 16 inches apart, and put up one dozen hooks on neat strips as directed.

Pantry.—To have counter shelf and four shelves above ; closet under counter shelf for barrel of flour, with lid to take out flour, and three drawers properly fitted, etc.

Bell.—Front door to have bell-pull, etc., to match other finish, and swing bell in kitchen properly connected with same.

Wash Tubs.—Construct wash tubs in laundry as shown, to be constructed out of 2 inch plank and to be 14 inches deep, having hinged plank lids on top, to be properly set up and finished complete.

Tank.—Construct a tank in attic as shown, 3 feet deep, made out of 2 inch plank, properly supported, braced, etc., and to have a hinged cover over same to keep out dust, etc. The floor under tank arranged as a tray, with drip and pipe running outside upon roof, properly tinned and arranged to carry away any leakage that might occur.

Cellar Partitions.—To be constructed with matched and dressed boards, secured to the requisite frame-work, and the doors to be good battened doors, properly hung and secured. Place outside slanting doors

over the outside cellar steps, and put up a double swing shelf as shown in store cellar, and 30 feet of other shelving, as directed.

Coal Bins.—To be built up in good manner, as shown, to be boarded up 5 feet high with matched boards, and to have the necessary slides, etc., as required for taking out coal.

Cold Air Inlet.—Frame to be put in as shown, to have wire netting over outside, and a sash hinged on inside, same as the other cellar windows.

Mantels.—Construct and set two ash mantel pieces in parlor and dining room, as shown by the design for same, the tile in frieze of mantels to be fables for parlor and rural scenes for dining room ; the mantel in room of second floor to be of pine, as shown by drawings, and the whole to be secured and put together in best manner possible.

PLUMBER'S WORK.

Iron Soil Pipe.—Furnish and put up, properly connecting with drain at outside cellar walls, a 4 inch cast iron soil pipe, extend up and connect with water closet in bath room with 6 lb. lead Strap soil pipe to extend up through roof and be there capped with a .... ventilator ; soil pipe to be properly secured, tar-coated both inside and out, and joints caulked with lead. Run a 2-inch cast-iron waste pipe, properly hung from cellar ceiling and connected to 4-inch pipe, for waste of washbowl in toilet room, and run lines of 1-inch or iron pipe from top of all traps in the building, and carry up and connect into the 4-inch soil vent at a point not less than 2 feet above highest waste connection. Put in a 3 inch fresh air inlet pipe, as shown, on outside, with opening 2 feet above ground, and with a screen over to exclude dirt and filling up.

Supply from boiler to be a five-eighth inch A pipe connected with tank in attic and boiler in kitchen, and to such other parts as required.

Boiler to be a 35-gallon .... patent copper boiler, set on a single legged cast iron stand, connected to water-back of range through double A pipe and brass couplings.

Range to be a .... single oven No. 0, set up with all the connections complete ready for use.

Pump.—Put in a brass lift and combination force pump, connect with cistern through one and one-quarter inch B lead pipe, and connect with tank in attic through one inch B lead pipe. Place a stop-cock on pipe, so cold water can be drawn direct at sink, and run a one-half inch tell-tale pipe back to sink from tank.

Sink to be of cast iron, 20 inches by 34 inches by 6 inches in size, galvanized, and to have hot water through five-eighth inch A pipe, five-eighth inch brass draw-cock, 2 inch lead waste, properly trapped and connected to main 4 inch soil, as required.

Wash Tubs to have hot and cold water through five-eighth inch A pipe and brass thimble-tray draw-cocks ; 2 inch main waste and one and one-half inches branch wastes from each tray, properly trapped and connected with drain to cess-pool at outside cellar wall, to have brass plugs, chain, etc., complete to tubs.

Wash Bowls to be of .... ware, to have marble countersink tops, surbases 10 inches high, to be supplied with hot and cold water through one-half inch A lead pipe and compression nicke plated cocks, plated plugs and chains ; ½ inch heavy lead wastes, properly trapped and connected. Place lead pans under each with three-fourth inch drip pipe connected and running to cellar ceiling and there left open. Overflow pipes from basins and bath to be branched into dips of traps to each.

Water Closet.—To be a .... Sanitary Closet, all earthenware, supplied with water through five-eighth inch A pipe, and having a stop-cock to regulate the flow of water to bowl, and to be fit up in a complete and perfect manner without exception ; lead pan to be placed under water closet same as wash bowls.

Bath Tub.—To be 14 oz. sheet copper well tinned and planished ; supplied with hot and cold water through five-eighth inch A pipe, five-eighth inch double hot and cold bath bibb, plated plug and chain, rubber hose shower attachment ; waste, one and one-half inch, with running trap properly connected to Y branch of iron soil pipe.

Tank.—To be lined with 4 lb. sheet lead ; wipe the seams, dot the sides and leave lead smooth all around, only copper nails to be used ; place a stop-cock on supply under tank to shut water off from house ; provide overflow near top of tank, run to outside of house or into gutter. All lead waste connections to iron to be made through brass ferrules soldered to lead and caulked into the iron.

Circulation.—A one-half inch AA lead pipe to be connected to hot water pipes at highest points, and to run down and connect to sediment pipe below boiler inside sediment cock, to keep up a continued circulation of hot water, and a one-half inch pipe run from top of hot water pipe and up 3 inches above tank, turned over i to same for steam escape, having end left open.

Cocks.—Put in the necessary stop-cocks over the boiler, to shut the water off from upper part of the house, also put a branch and stop-cock connected with drain for emptying the boiler, and all other stop or draw-cocks as may be necessary to make a complete and first-class job. All cocks to be of the best quality of .... make. All pipes to be so graded that they drain dry when water is shut off, and the whole of the work delivered up in a complete and perfect state without exception.

PAINTER'S WORK.

Properly stop and otherwise prepare for and paint all wood work that is customary and usual to paint, both interior and exterior, two good coats of the best lead and oil paint, the exterior work in the following colors, which are taken from.................card of pure tinted gloss paints, ... Body of the work, as clapboards, No. .... ; trimming colors, as casings, water table, corner boards, belts, veranda columns, frame work, barges, etc , No. .... Shingle work of second story side walls, No. .... ; veranda ceilings, planciers, panels of gables, etc., No. .... ; sash, No. .... ; exterior doors trimmed with Nos. ... and ... ; veranda floors, No. ... ; finial to be painted with No. ... and glided with gold leaf, etc. The inside work of three main rooms and front hall, first floor, mantels and main stairs and door saddles to be filled with .... filler, properly applied and finished with one good coat of............ preservative. The balance of inside work to be painted in tints as may be directed, except kitchen part, which is to be grained oak and varnished. Hard pine floors to have two good coats linseed oil, rubbed in.

MODERN COTTAGE

With four rooms on each floor, also showing how it can be built with only three rooms on a floor and with or without tower.

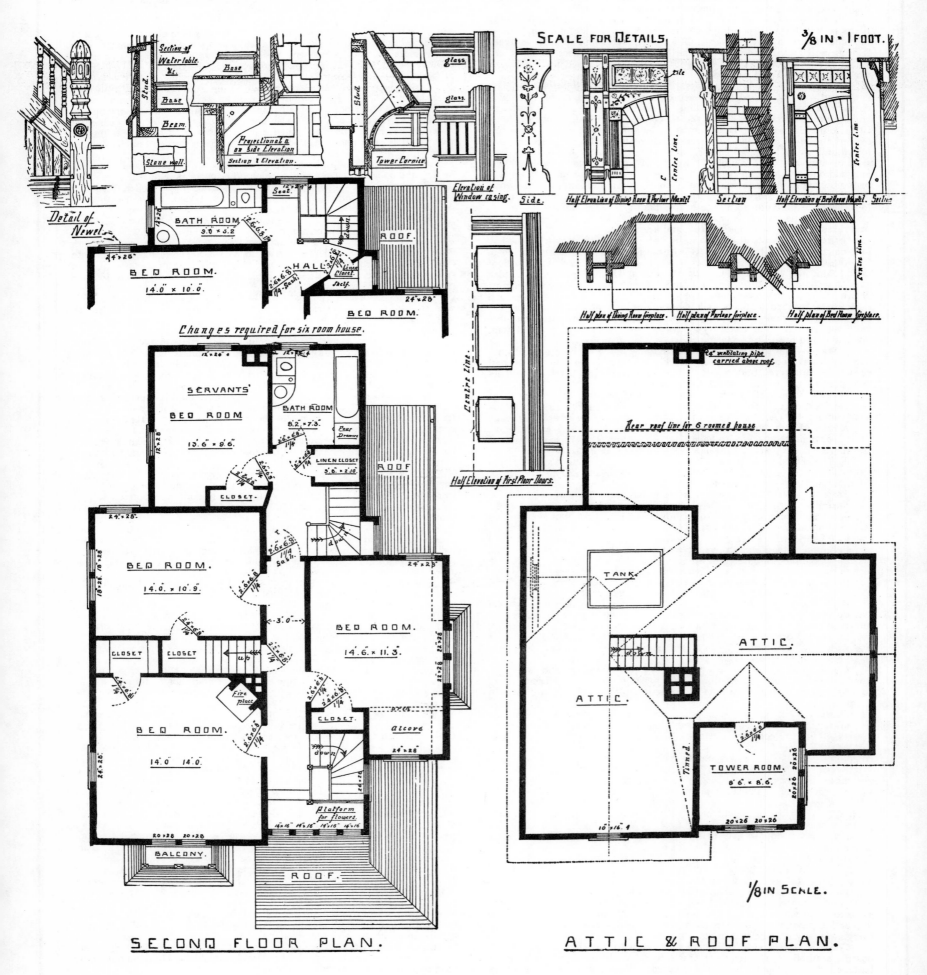

SECOND FLOOR PLAN.

ATTIC & ROOF PLAN.

MODERN COTTAGE

With four rooms on each floor, also showing how it can be built with only three rooms on a

floor and with or without tower.

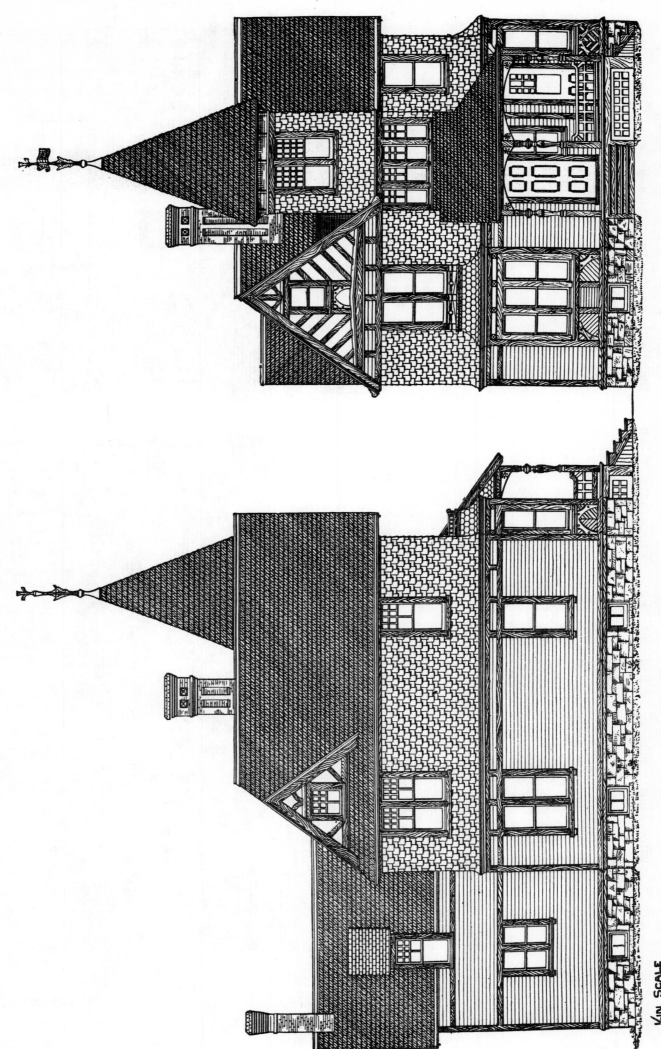

FRONT ELEVATION

SIDE ELEVATION

⅛ IN. SCALE

MODERN COTTAGE.

With four rooms on each floor, also showing how it can be built with only three rooms on a floor and with or without tower.

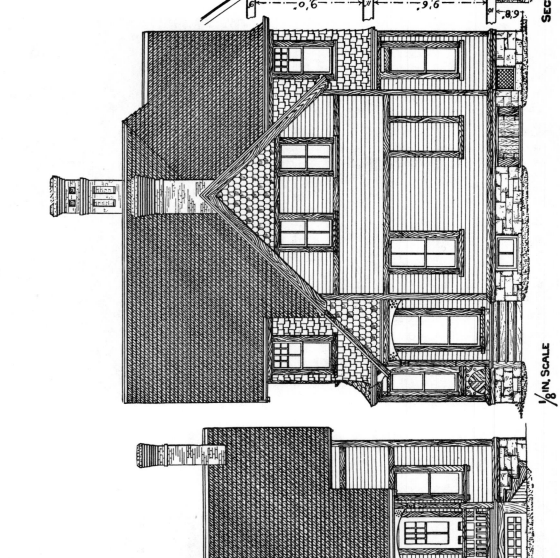

SECTION

REAR ELEVATION

⅛ IN. SCALE

SIDE ELEVATION

Palliser's New Cottage Homes

"Ah, to build to build!
That is the noblest art of all the arts.
Painting and Sculpture are but images,
Are merely shadows, cast by outward things.
On stone or canvas, having in themselves
No separate existence.   Architecture,
Existing in itself, and not in seeming
A something it is not, surpasses them
As substance shadow."

Longfellow.

Palliser, Palliser & Co., Arch.

SKETCH OF A HOUSE ERECTED AT WATERBURY, CONN.

PALLISER, PALLISER & CO., ARCHITECTS, 24 E. 42D ST., N. Y.

FRONTISPIECE.

PALLISER'S
NEW COTTAGE HOMES

AND

DETAILS,

CONTAINING

Nearly Two Hundred & Fifty New & Original Designs in all the Modern Popular Styles,

SHOWING

Plans, Elevations, Perspective Views and Details of low-priced, medium and first-class

Cottages, Villas, Farm Houses, Town and Country Places, Houses for the Seashore, the South, and for Summer and Winter Resorts, etc., etc.

CITY BRICK BLOCK HOUSES,

Farm Barn, Stables and Carriage Houses,

AND

1500 DETAIL DRAWINGS,

Descriptive and Instructive Letter Press, also Specifications and Form of Contract.

Elevations and Plans to Scale of 1-16 inch to the Foot.

Details to Scale of 3-8 inch to the Foot.

Making in all a most practical book for Architects, Builders, Carpenters, and all who are interested in the subject of Building, and those who contemplate building, or the improvement of Wood, Stone or Brick Buildings.

NEW YORK:

PALLISER, PALLISER & CO.,

DEDICATED

To those, who happy homes have always known,
To those, who plan and work such homes to own;
To all, who building homes would bless mankind,
To all, who in their homes a refuge find.

To youth, whom wedded life will soon employ,
To children dear, each day their parents' joy;
To all who favor honor, truth and love,
To all whose virtues promise homes above.

"Architecture is delightful in itself, and valuable to society, in proportion to its power of exalting the soul and refining the intellect."
—SIR S. FERGUSON.

PREFATORY.

Some years ago when there was but one building journal in existence in the United States and that published but once a month, and when Architectural books were comparatively scarce and sold at $10 to $15 each and a circulation of 700 to 1,000 copies was considered a big thing, the authors of this work published "Palliser's American Cottage Homes," "Palliser's Model Homes" and "Palliser's Useful Details," at prices bringing them within the reach of everyone, which, as soon as they were presented to the Building community of the country, met with a rapid sale, and judging from the number of editions through which they have passed, and the immense circulation reached—50,000 copies of "Palliser's Useful Details" alone having been issued—they have, without doubt, met the approval of those most interested in practical Architectural works, and must have filled, in a measure, a want before unsupplied.

As a result of their popular teachings we find in the rural districts among the buildings erected at the present day almost an entire absence of the vulgar, meaningless, square-box like or barnesque style of Architecture, sometimes pretentious and therefore jig-sawed and ginger-breaded to the death, which years ago was the rule rather than the exception with white lead for exterior painting and the regulation green blinds. It is also worthy of note that the idea is no longer prevalent that good taste in Architectural design should be exercised only in regard to the erection of the more costly structures built for people of means, but on the contrary, more thought and attention is now paid to the design and erection of the smallest Cottages and Villas than has been given in the past to the more ornate and costly dwellings.

The success achieved by the above mentioned books—brought about by their own merit and their reasonable price, together with the help of our many friends, and the friends of Architectural taste and its development, to whom we tender our many thanks not forgetting that most potent power in the land, The Public Press, which has been most liberal in praising and extending our efforts—has induced the authors to publish another to take their place, and which is now presented to the public, and in its pages will be found a more extensive collection of designs of modern domestic Architecture of low and medium cost than ever appeared in a single volume before, all fully drawn out and explained, and with Detail Drawings illustrating the features which go to make up structures such as are needed to meet the wants of the American people, and the materials at hand for construction in this country, which are principally of wood.

All the designs given are new and original, and have never before been produced in any Architectural work, and what is aimed at in this instance is to present a mass of practical Architectural designs and details, easy of construction, pleasing in form, and generally of an inexpensive though artistic and tasteful character, which cannot fail to interest and help all who are in any way connected with improvement in building, and there are thousands of cities, towns and villages in all the States of the Union in which the wants of the people continually demand the erection of buildings such as are represented in this book, which we trust will prove more than suggestive to them by assisting their judgment and decision as to their plans and character of the buildings they will erect so as to obtain the best results, as it should not be forgotten that there is a commercial value to be attached to a well arranged plan and carefully studied grouping of the exterior of a house, for it is evident that a dwelling built on these principles require no more material or labor, but is simply a scientific rendering to produce harmony and convenience, and the difference between a house of this kind and one of ordinary construction when placed in the market is at once apparent. Then again, in the matter of constructing the work material is economized in these days of modern ideas and progress, the old principles, which were to use large timbers and cut them all to pieces by morticing and notching down to levels, being discarded and smaller timbers used, but so put together and constructed as to give greater strength without wasting material and labor.

To attempt to give here a table of contents or list of illustrations and all the details contained in this book would require considerable room and—in our opinion—entail a waste of space, therefore it is omitted.

We have felt some hesitation in giving the actual cost of building the different dwellings described, as many people forget to consider that time, site, fluctuations in prices, various localities, style of finish, and business management will affect the cost very materially. We can give but one cost of the construction and finishing of a house exactly as it has been built from our plans, etc., and that is the sum total of the actual amount of money expended, but as to what is the best method to adopt in building so as to have it done in a good manner, and with the least expenditure of money and saving of time and trouble, can only be settled on after a careful consideration of all the circumstances connected with each individual case. It would be manifestly absurd for us to make the statement that it is cheapest and best in every instance for an owner to buy materials and have the work done by the day, dispensing with a contractor, as it is certainly not true and by far the greater number of buildings are erected by contract, sometimes under one general contract, or sub-divided amongst the different trades. Another method is that of the owner buying the materials and giving out the labor to the various mechanics for lump sums. All these several modes of doing work have been employed by our many clients, and ourselves too, on buildings of our own, and as a general rule building by contract in one form or another has the preference, although we know instances where good management in building by day's work has proved advantageous. The designs here presented have been carefully selected from a very large number in our office with a view of giving the best results at as small an expense as possible.

We also desire to state here that we do not publish these designs in any other form, giving costs of constructing each on an increased scale, or separate from the designs for the use of builders only, as we understand has been done in other quarters. The costs given on the one hand stated to be in the interest of the public to protect them against the demands of dishonest builders, and to be the actual cost of structures, not the cost and a contractor's profit added, which was alleged might be all the way from the honest ten to fifteen per cent. to the dishonest forty, fifty or a hundred per cent., which they assert some builders try to get, while on the other hand printing the designs on single sheets for builders to show parties intending to build, giving no costs, that information being reserved for the builder, and so that if it were possible he might monopolize his customer and get an exorbitant price. We beg to say most emphatically that we resort to no such means to try and serve our customers, and in connection with our work have but one side to present to the entire public, whether Architects, Carpenters and Builders, or people intending to build, and we believe that all may find many valuable hints, while at the same time we are confident of its kind reception and success in all that it aims to accomplish.

THE AUTHORS.

24 East 42nd Street, New York.

INTRODUCTORY.

We present on the following pages American Homes of to-day, not, however, of any well defined style of Architecture, except what may be termed our National style, for it would be folly for us, who live in the nineteenth century, a nation noted for its inventive genius, to undertake to transplant to this new country any foreign style which was perfected centuries ago, and which, though eminently fitted for the age in which it flourished, is not adapted to our wants and times. There has been enough attempts and failures in this direction the past half century, and the evidences are to be plainly seen in many directions even to-day in existing classical tubs, the Italian villas and Mansard roofed boxes of all grades and sizes, to say nothing of numerous nondescript extravagances, all of which have been found wanting for this people, and instead there is springing up a National style which is becoming more distinctive in character and unlike that of any other nation, as the American climate, life, economy of time and labor, requiring greater facility and conveniences, with snug and comfortable quarters for Winter and shady porches and verandas for Summer. This style of design in building is usually stamped by the genius and individuality of its author, the conditions he has to meet, and the materials used. Some time in the future it is probable that there will be a multitude of styles adapted from the Classic, each possessing more or less merit.

The designs illustrated in this book are of a varied character, some of them indicate work of an expensive kind, but the greater number are for that of a cheap kind, or of a moderate cost, and all are such as may be readily executed.

The ornament used in nearly every design is of a plain, but at the same time effective order, and easy of execution. Very little carved ornament is introduced, and that may be readily produced by any ordinary mechanic.

The scale on which the detail drawings are made is large enough to render them perfectly plain to enable any good mechanic to put the same into execution without the least difficulty, and full-size detail drawings can be made for the work very easily. The plans and elevations, or designs, are drawn to a scale of $\frac{1}{16}$ inch to the foot, and the details to a scale of $\frac{3}{8}$ inch to a foot. Where any other scale is used the fact is mentioned on the plates.

Since the issue of our first book on building homes, some 10 years ago, in addition to a large local practice we may be said to have been the first to organize a system by correspondence for furnishing people everywhere about to build with working plans, specifications, &c., &c., to meet all their requirements, and more especially people in the country where Architects had done but little business and the people had been obliged to plan their own houses, or copy from their neighbors, and it seems to have gotten into the minds of many people that we sell ready-made plans to suit all the different ideas of persons who intend building, the amount of money to be expended, or their depth of pocket, their families, climate, soil, views, winds and storms, seasons the house will be occupied, water supply, drainage, and all the other numerous and varied details connected with building. This, of course, is impossible, if it is to be done correctly, and we must treat each individual case separately, as Architects should.

Another thing, as we anticipated, there has sprung up during the past five or six years in many directions several persons and firms imitating that part of our business referred to above. Most of them, however, put out designs that are very crude, and offer services that would apparently be of a very inferior order and clap-trap generally. Their methods are of the worst order of quackery, making deliberate calculations to mislead the public by issuing pictures, sketches of the imagination, never built, and with impossible costs of construction, given to catch the ignorant, only to prove disappointing to them when tried. Rumor has it that one of these quacks has been scheming to close up all the Architects' offices in the country so as to have a monopoly of the plan business himself, though he is not an Architect, but claims to know more than them all.

An Architectural journal, which has been supported by Architects furnishing for it, free of cost, designs, &c., for publication, wishes to draw plans, and inserts the following: "Should any of our readers desire to procure plans and specifications for building, whether churches, schools, dwellings, stores, carriage houses, homes, &c., or if they desire plans made for alterations, enlargements or additions of any kind to existing buildings, erection of porches, bay windows, extensions, wings, &c., they are reminded that all business of the kind will receive prompt attention at this office on very moderate terms. Address ———." A well known building monthly commenting on this says: Doubtless the very "moderate terms" prove quite effective, and while the regular skilled practitioner may by these terms be enabled to "take a rest" young draftsmen and would-be Architects will have excellent opportunities to pick up a few ideas at the expense of the persons caught by the moderate terms.

Others in the field issue catalogues of plans, giving a few dimensions, and the same matter on every page, about furnishing plans and urging people to pay from $25 to $250 for a set of ready-made plans of the design they may select, although that would probably never be what could be used to meet their wants. These venders of ready-made plans will tell you that it is much the best for you to order plans, &c., of designs in the catalogue that suit you, or nearly so, without having alterations made in the plans, as all changes can be indicated to the Builder when the plans are turned over to him. Now, anyone with common sense would ask in such cases what can be the good of these plans but to make trouble between owners and builders, changes and extras followed by a law suit, which is frequently the result of half prepared plans, specifications and contracts.

We were once shown by a client plans and specifications for an 18 room house, for which he paid $15. It was all contained on a sheet of paper two feet square, specifications and everything, but this plan being useless to the owner he employed us as Architects to draw up proper plans, details, &c., and have the works executed, which cost $3,800, and cheerfully paid us properly for our services.

If one writes these venders of plans, asking if a design can be executed for the amount asked they will answer yes, it can be done if our plans and specifications are followed. If so much can be done why don't they complete the thing and deliver the house itself at any point for a stated price? But their great object is to sell you plans, etc. The costs given in the catalogue are stated to be the actual cost of the structures just such as will be secured by buying the materials and hiring the labor performed by day's work. And it is further stated that the plans are practical, having stood the test of construction, many of them under their own superintendence; and in another place that the cost is figured from prices of material and labor in the neighborhood of ———— on such a date just one month before the catalogue is issued. Therefore it would appear that a great deal of building is done in that locality by the day, and awful cheap and quick, which, however, is a delusion and a snare. A builder once remarked: "Why, at such prices the material must all be stolen. How can it be accomplished otherwise, I cannot understand?"

These venders advertise that they alone inform owners fully and accurately about actual costs and all other things that should be known, instead of being like others giving information to Architects, or plainly in the interest of builders, and they conjure the public that the way to avoid trouble in building is to have plans and specifications, and advise them not to trust untried plans made by amateurs, but be sure and get theirs, that they make no mistakes, and sell them for a quarter what an Architect charges. They state that in all their specifications good materials are called for, that it is poorest economy to expend the labor in working up inferior materials, and yet, look at the costs given for completed buildings—often less than the best materials can be bought for that is required in the building. Beware of persons offering to do more than they or anyone can possibly accomplish.

We know of a gentleman, thinking of building him a Cottage Home, saw in a newspaper a cut and advertisement of a handsome house, cost $1,500, giving a glowing description of the interior finish, its beauties in the way of Qneen Anne stairs, mantels, &c. He wrote and asked the advertisers if it had ever been built for the money, and if so where and for whom. In reply he was referred to two parties in the same State, but at different towns, and he communicated with them and received replies, stating that they cost very much more, and then were not built according to the description in the advertisement. One of the parties had received a letter from the advertisers saying that the house should certainly be built for $2,000, but finding they were cornered, they finally had to acknowledge to him that no builder would build it for less than $2,800 to $3,000, and this they stated after some of their own builders had figured it up, and this in view of the fact that the advertised cost is $1,500, figured according to material and labor in that locality in which the two parties had built, whose names were given as reference. The advertised $1,200 house by same parties has cost in like manner to build in a cheap way $2,100. Many more such instances could be recited, but we think enough has been given to enable anyone to form their own opinion as to the adoption of such methods and their certain results, and there are many victims, some of whom, rather than acknowledge they were taken in, allow their names to be printed as references, but if closely questioned will generally admit the truth. The moral is a common one and as old as history: "Fear the Greeks bearing gifts."

Please bear in mind that we are not in the ready-made plan business, and in all our experience, serving as we have upwards of two thousand clients all over the United States by correspondence, we have not found two persons wanting to build just the same house; in fact, every person's location and wants differ, and their ideas and everything connected with the subject must be considered and taken into account, and this we do to arrive at a proper and practical solution of each problem presented.

In Architecture there is a method to follow in all cases presenting themselves, but no receipts or procedures. This method is none other than the application of one's reasoning power to each special case; for what is good in one case is not available in another. It is then on the observation of these circumstances, facts, habits, climate and sanitary conditions that one's reasoning will rest before conceiving the design and drawing out the plan.

So little does the public appreciate the difference in the skill and labor of one Architect and another, that they often allow a paltry difference in charges of one-half per cent. of cost—a difference which he would think trivial in comparing the merits of two existing buildings if he were purchasing—determine the choice between Architects, without regard to the qualification on which the whole success or failure of the building will depend. It should be borne in mind that it requires from seven to ten years of study and close application to be reasonably admissible to practice, and for this time and cost of preparation the Architect is entitled to as fair a return as any investment of time and money can be. If you get cinders in your iron, it is because there are cinders in the pay; there is always good iron to be had.

It is the legitimate claim of an Architect that his skill enables him not only to contribute his own ideas of comfort and beauty, but to satisfy the special wants of his client—to carry out his wishes, and even whims, if need be, more successfully than another, provided he is made fully acquainted with these wants and wishes; and the Architect's claim is pretty generally acknowledged now-a-days wherever his profession is well established.

That the American people are taking up with great vigor the question of home building for themselves goes without saying, and each one should be stamped with more or less individuality so as to fit into and harmonize with the lives to be spent under its roof, and this may be readily accomplished by calling in the services of a skilled Architect and making him your confidential and responsible adviser, and a single suggestion from him is often worth his fees. Not a single building, no matter how inexpensive, should be attempted without having first a properly studied and prepared set of plans and specifications setting forth the work to be done so that after regrets may be avoided. Any one who cannot afford this certainly cannot afford to build.

Speaking of Home, what tender associations and infinite meanings cluster around that blessed word! Home—the temple of love, the nursery of virtue, the circle of loving hearts, the play-ground of children, the dwelling of manhood, and the retreat of old age. It is the place on earth where health can best enjoy its pleasures, wealth revel in its luxuries, poverty bear its sharp thorn, sorrow nurse its grief, and dissolving nature expire.

PALLISER, PALLISER & CO., ARCHITECTS.

24 EAST 42ND STREET, NEW YORK.

PLATE I.

The large house represented on title page by first floor, second floor and roof plans, together with general perspective view, is a fair sample of the American country house, devoid of all nonsensical features tending to belittle the character of the general design, and illustrates one of the most sensible homes it has been our lot to plan. This house is built of red croton brick, with trimmings of buff brick, terra cotta and brown stone. The face of gables are tiled, roofs slated and ridges covered with terra cotta. It was recently built at Peekskill, N. Y., at a cost of about $9,000, and is said to be the most attractive house yet built in the place although several erected there have cost many times what it did. The entrance hall is eleven feet wide, and contains fireplace, stair case, seat, closet, alcove, etc., is very finely finished in oak, a rich dark color, giving an impression that is sure to be pleasing to the incomer. The parlor, to left, and sitting room, at right of hall, are connected by wide sliding doors, as are also the library and sitting room. Thus the three rooms and front entrance hall can be opened up as one room—a most desirable feature in a house of this class. The angle bay in sitting room, and location of fireplaces, are especially happy in their relation to each other. The library connects with a spacious toilet room, which in turn opens into back hall, a large closet being provided in each of these, as will be seen by a careful study of the plan. The back hall is very conveniently arranged for free and easy access to all parts of the house, and the Porte Cochere, in connection with the side veranda or porch, is a feature that cannot well be dispensed with in a country home. The dining room is a fine one, replete with conveniences, having fireplace on one side and a sideboard built in opposite ; also a spacious china closet is here provided, in which to lock up rare and costly china, and the passage way, or butler's pantry, from dining room to kitchen, is fitted up with tables, presses, drawers, etc., and is well lighted from the pantry by means of a glass slide in the partition, which is also convenient for passing dishes through. There is also a door from this passage way to cellar stairs—as well as one from kitchen—a feature essential to all first-class houses, as it often occurs that it is necessary for members of the family to pass to cellar-way, and they dislike to go through kitchen to get there. The laundry is placed on the first floor, and contains the wash tubs and refrigerator ; also a clothes closet for dirty clothes, with shute from floor above.

The second floor contains six fine chambers, a sewing room over front hall, bath room, and well lighted halls, closets in abundance, and the rooms are so connected together as to be very desirable for family use in suite as may be required.

The attic contains two finished rooms and a large amount of storage accommodation. There is a cellar under the whole house, containing storerooms, partitioned off, and the house throughout is warmed by a large portable hot air furnace, fed with cold air taken from a point about ten feet above grade level, the cold air duct or inlet being built in with the brick work behind parlor chimney. This is considered an excellent arrangement when the construction is such that it can be adopted, as it takes the cold air supply from a point where the air is more pure than is usually the case at the ground level.

The first story of the house is finished in hard woods, principally cherry and oak, the kitchen and back hall parts of yellow pine ; second story rooms all of white pine, the whole of the woods being filled and then finished with two coats of superior varnish, rubbed down to a true, even, dead finish. The transom lights to first story windows are of art glass, as are also the top panels in front entrance and vestibule doors. The staircase windows are also of art glass.

Such a house as this requires a large lot on which to build it, so as to show it up to the best advantage, and is a good sample of what the homes of many successful business men ought to be who appreciate their spare moments and desire to spend them in enjoyment and social intercourse with the family, free from the cares and restraints of the business world. Such homes as this are wanted all over our country, and it is the business men of fair means who can live in them, and who, by so doing, will educate the public taste to appreciate the sensible and artistic treatment that is so satisfying and pleasing to the mind through the eye, cultivating the taste for something honest and simple in construction, and leading the desire away from that which is pernicious and in and taste, made only to gratify the whims and caprices of the ignorant and uneducated, as is too often the case where houses of considerable pretension are sometimes executed and built by impracticable and selfish builders, whose great boast is generally that they planned this and that, and it was awful expensive ; in fact, costing in many instances double what a carefully studied design in harmony with the requirements would have done had the parties building exercised the same care and judgment in so doing that they would in any other business matter involving a like outlay.

The style of this house would be termed by many an adaptation of the so-called Queen Anne, with all the eccentricities and nonsensical features of the same entirely dispensed with, being free from all objectionable features and absurdities that have become so common in such styled houses the last two or three years. The exterior wood work is painted Indian red and bronze green, giving very happy contrasts with the buff and red brick, and they are probably the best colors that could be adopted.

The small perspective sketch on upper left corner of title page is a general view of design No. 3, plate No. 2.

The centre perspective on margin is a view of design No. 2, plate No. 2, and the lower one is a general perspective view of design No. 4, plate No. 2, to which the reader is referred for full particulars.

Palliser's New Cottage Homes

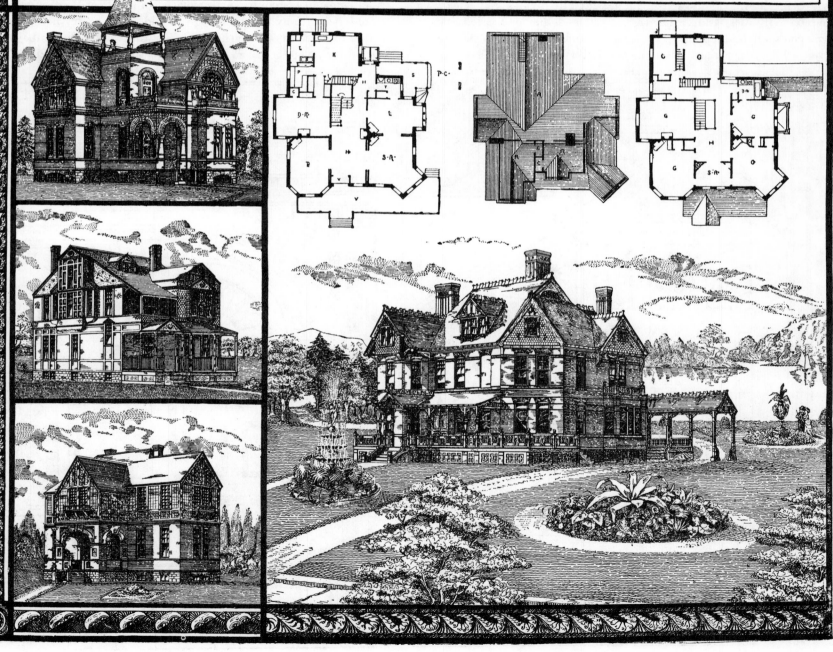

PLATE 2.

Design 2 represents an attractive two story cottage in wood, containing eight rooms and bath room, there being two very nice rooms on third or attic floor, where there is ample space for same; the front hall is large and roomy, answering nicely for a reception room, the seat by stairs and closet under stairs being very useful accessions; the back stairs are very handily arranged and the kitchen is nicely isolated from the main part of the house; the front porch and piazza are very spacious, giving ample room for two groups to gather without interfering with each other, and the second-floor balcony opening from the hall is a very nice feature, affording a cool and secluded nook in which to sit and read or sew. The style of this house, with first-story clapboarded, second story shingled and gables finished in plaster with stencil work stamped into same and picked out in color, may be termed unique. Such a house painted on body of first story a green drab, shingles of second story old gold, the gable work buff, and general trimmings of sage green, with the mouldings, etc., picked out with Indian red, makes a very attractive appearance, very pleasing to the eye, and a bright spot in the landscape. Cost, $3,200.

Design 3 is a pleasant little brick cottage, suitable for a small family, and is one of those pleasant little buildings that are always agreeable to the eye in almost any position. The plan is a very compact and convenient one, and the design is suitable for a gate lodge to a brick mansion, which might be in harmony with the style here shown. This house, built with an even-colored, clean, common red brick, trimmed with pressed and moulded brick and terra cotta, all laid up in red mortar and oiled, the roofs tiled or slated with red or black slate, makes it very effective. The open

balconies on second and third stories over hall are nice features of the design which give a character to the whole not otherwise obtained. The sliding doors between parlor and dining room are a great help to sociability, and the fire places as arranged together in the corners of the rooms, come prettily into one chimney above the roof; the inside woodwork in natural white or Georgia pine filled and varnished. Range in the kitchen, brick set, and the whole house heated by a small furnace placed in the cellar at less cost than if heated by two stoves, and the latter could only heat about one-third of the house at best. Cost, $3,800.

Design 4 is an example of brick, timber and tile, which makes an excellent combination when rightly handled. The first story is brick on a stone underpinning of irregular ashlar in rock faced range. The front porch is particularly handsome and spacious. The first floor plan is conveniently arranged and well suited to the needs of a small family of refined tastes; the dining room has a recess for sideboard, and the conservatory connecting with parlor and dining room is a nice feature and a source of enjoyment to the lover of nature in plant life; the second floor has four fine chambers with good closets, and there is space in attic to finish off a servant's room. Cost, $4,100.

Design 5 is a neat frame cottage well adapted for a gardener's or a coachman's residence. Could be built with or without cellar, as circumstances require, and if placed in a proper location where it would be partially hid by foliage, would make a very necessary addition to a country seat, where the servant would always be within easy call and under the master's eye. Cost complete, $1,200.

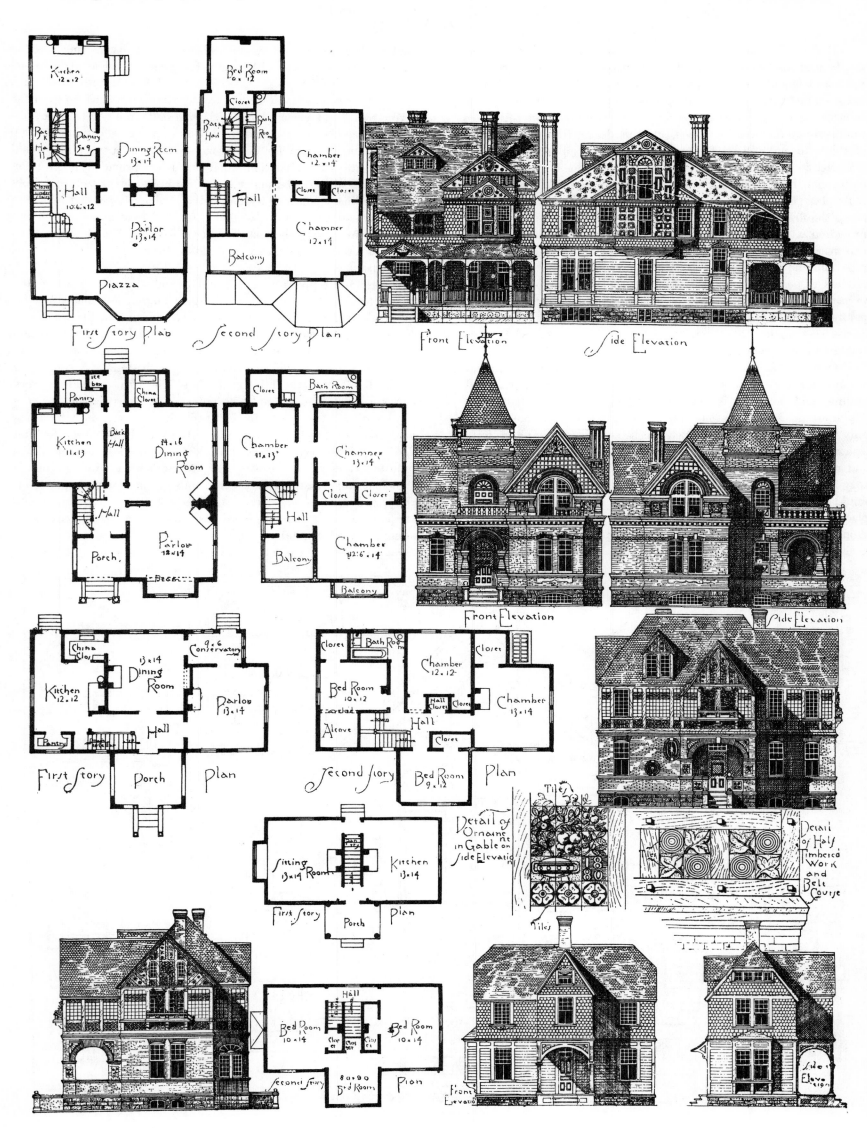

Kitchen 12 x 12
Bed Room 10 x 12
Back Hall
Pantry 5 x 9
Dining Room 13 x 14
Closets
Chamber 12 x 14
Closet Closet
Hall 10.6 x 12
Hall
Bath Room
Parlor 13 x 14
Chamber 12 x 14
Balcony

Piazza

First Story Plan   Second Story Plan   Front Elevation   Side Elevation

China Closet
Pantry
Kitchen 11 x 13
Back Hall
Dining Room 14 x 16
Closet   Bath Room
Chamber 11 x 13
Chamber 13 x 14
Closet Closet
Hall
Hall
Parlor 12 x 14
Chamber 11.6 x 14
Porch
Balcony
Balcony

Front Elevation   Side Elevation

China Clos.
Dining Room 13 x 14
9 x 6 Conservatory
Kitchen 12 x 12
Parlor 13 x 14
Hall
Pantry

Closets   Bath Room
Bed Room 10 x 12
Chamber 12 x 12
Closet
Alcove
Hall Closet Closet
Chamber 13 x 14
Hall
Closet
Bed Room 9 x 12

First Story   Porch   Plan   Second Story   Bed Room   Plan

Detail of Ornament in Gable on Side Elevation

Tiles
Tiles

Detail of Half Timbered Work and Belt Course

Sitting Room 13 x 14   Kitchen 13 x 14

First Story   Porch   Plan

Hall
Bed Room 10 x 14   Bed Room 10 x 14
Closet Closet
80 x 90 Bed Room

Second Story   Plan

Front Elevation   Side Elevation

Design 6 comes somewhere near the requirements of the thrifty mechanic who, by dint of steady perseverance and self-denial, has saved enough money to buy a suburban lot where it is not too far out for him to walk to and from his daily toil. Such lots in the suburbs of a large city are nearly always laid out twenty-five feet wide and one hundred feet deep, and this design is adapted to a lot of this size and still leaves ample room to get all around it. By reference to plans it will be seen that it contains six good rooms, bath-room, front and back stairs and plenty of good closet room. A fireplace is provided in the parlor which would serve for ventilating the first floor. The front porch has seats on each side, thus providing a ready and convenient sitting-down place. The side-rear veranda is a nice, cozy spot to sit evenings and enjoy a quiet pipe and the daily paper. The sash-door from the dining-room renders it possible for anyone to pass out without disturbing the privacy of the kitchen. Such houses as this, neatly finished, painted in tints, with bath-room fixtures and cellar under whole house, cost about $2,000, and on a lot in value about $500 more would be a reasonable rent to live under.

Design 7 is another cottage suited to a narrow lot, and gives seven rooms on two floors. This house is very simple in plan and outline, and is, what is generally called, a one-and-a-half-story. There are no back-stairs, no bath room and no waste room. The only water fixture is a sink which can be supplied with water from cistern in rear, so arranged as to collect all the water from the roofs and supply it at kitchen sink through a pump. This would make a cozy home for quite a large family, and nicely built and finished, would make a home that no one need be ashamed of. The fire-places on first floor can easily be left out if economy demanded it; though they would be better in, as they help to furnish the rooms,

and are both useful and ornamental. Such a house as this is not so costly as No. 6 by some $300, and yet it gives as much available room.

Design 8 illustrates a small cottage of four large rooms, which can be placed on a lot twenty feet wide; the stairs start up from the living-room, and cellar is reached from hall; the general character of the design is pleasing, and would paint up very effectively in deep tones; there is room for one or more rooms in attic which would help out the accommodation; good closets are provided, porch-room ample, and with a cellar under the whole house, gives sufficient room for an ordinary family at a small outlay, being simple and free from expensive features. Cost, $1,600. In good localities where lumber and labor are plenty, the cost would be much less. This design is capable of several changes that would add or diminish the cost as parties might need.

Design 9 represents a very roomy and attractive house suited to an ordinary city lot and would give ample accommodation for quite a large family, there being space enough in attic for two rooms, if needed; the entrance hall is large and makes a nice reception room and with a simple staircase of pine with ash rails, newel and balusters, and the hall windows stepping up with stairs and containing border lights of cathedral tinted glass, the effect would be very cheerful and enlivening to those entering. The space under stairs can be utilized for closets for hall and dining-room, and the three main rooms connecting as they do with front hall makes the first floor very desirable. A private back stair is arranged up and down from the kitchen and the back entry to kitchen and dining-room is a good arrangement. Four good chambers, each with large closet, are provided on second floor. A slate roof would be appropriate and add to the appearance more than the difference in cost over shingle. Cost, $2,800.

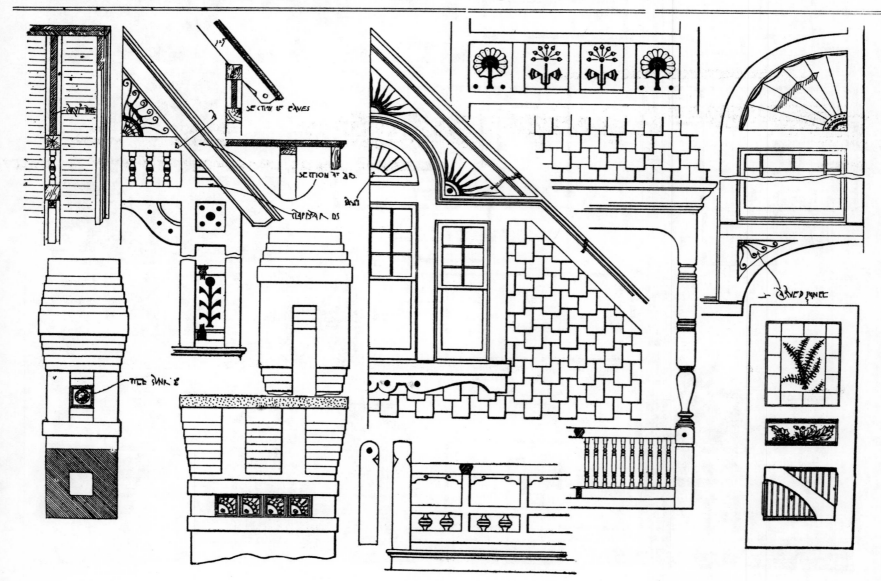

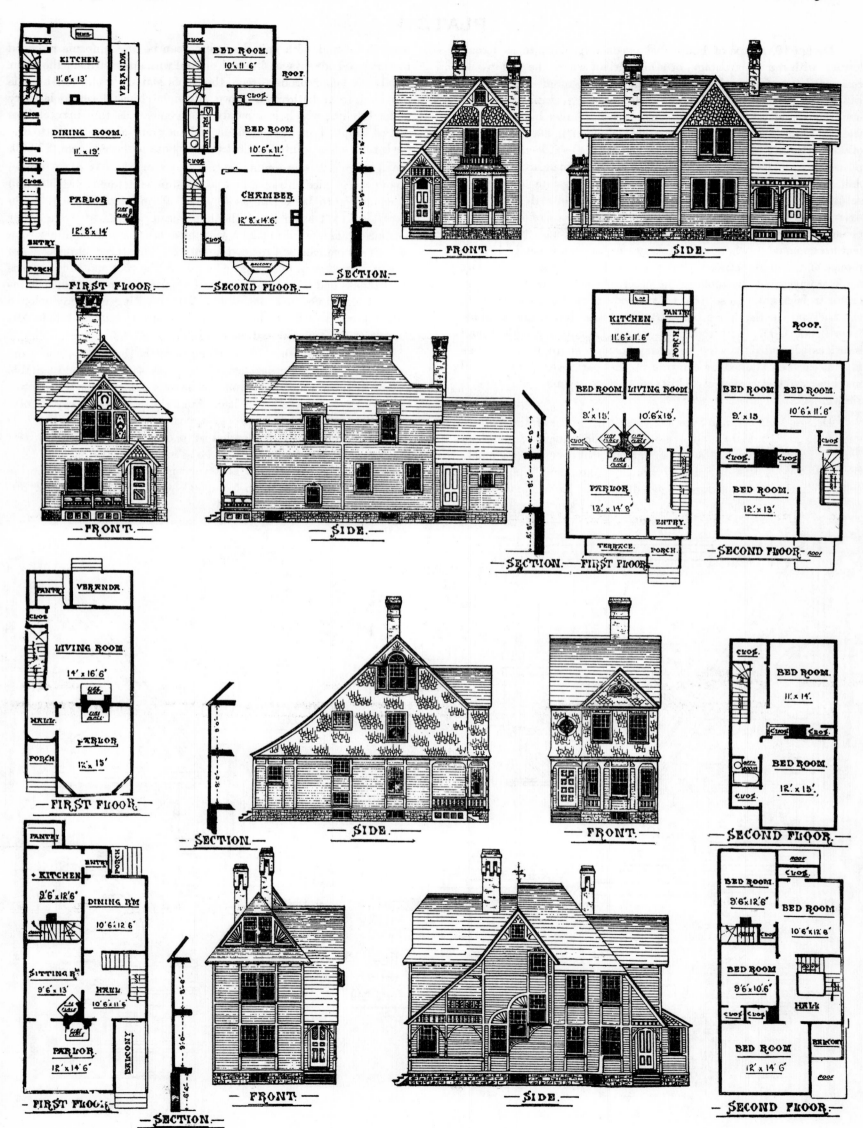

PLATE 4.

Design 10, a type of house that needs a special site, as a shallow lot with a good frontage, or a hillside lot where the rear would come well out of ground. The arrangement of rooms is good, and will suit a large number of people who want a very nice home of few rooms, and yet need the conveniences of a larger house. With the two rooms and front hall on first floor finished in hard wood, and other parts in pine, filled and polished, the effect would be very pleasing. The sideboard built in recess with a small art glass window through centre of same, with glass worked into an appropriate subject; the corner fireplace to have a neat mantel with shelves or overmantel above, on which to display a few pieces of china; the china closet forms the communication to kitchen, and is a convenient arrangement, as here the crockery can be stored handy to both rooms and a slide between pantry and china closet will save many steps around from one room to the other. The ice closet or refrigerator in back entry is so fixed that ice can be put into same from the back porch, the door from entry being used for access to same from inside. The bath room on second floor is convenient and well located, and if it were necessary to have more room on this floor it can be obtained by carrying up the part over pantries, and making two bed rooms over kitchen part where now only one is shown. Cost of erection, $2,500.

Design 11 is another type of house with some of the features similar to No. 10, and contains about the same amount of room and general conveniences, but with an entirely different exterior mold; the first story of this design is of brick on a stone underpinning or cellar wall, the whole having a decidedly classic feeling in the ornamentation of same; the main body of the second story over the brick

work is covered with shingles, which can be of California redwood to very good advantage, finished natural with spar varnish, the other woodwork being bronze green, the roofs slated; a clothes shute is provided from bath room down through china closet to laundry under kitchen, which is a handy arrangement, as the dirty clothes can be dropped in at each floor, and they are always ready to the wash tubs when wanted. Cost to carry out as here shown, $2,800.

Design 12 represents another type of the six room house, giving a very nice entrance hall, containing stairs and fireplace and so connected to back hall as to shut off and isolate the kitchen nicely, and yet any part of the house can be reached from either entrance. This would make a very nice suburban home and a good servant's room can be provided in attic. The three chimneys are brought together in one large stack above the roof and thus reduces the expense and adds to the general appearance, as too much chimney is sometimes not desirable. The painting is—body color, a light sea green buff; trimmings of olive drab; outside blinds and shingle work, Venetian red, sash white. Cost, $2,700.

Design 13, another six room house with about the same room as the three preceding designs, is a very pleasant home and suitable for erection on a fifty feet front lot having a nice lawn and flower beds in front, to stand well back from the street line, say twenty-five feet, so as to make a proper appearance. It is often the case that attractive houses are spoiled by people locating them too near the street line; thus they cannot be seen to any advantage.

The angle bay window is a very nice feature, as are also the large piazza and balcony on front. Cost, complete with small furnace to heat whole house, $2,700.

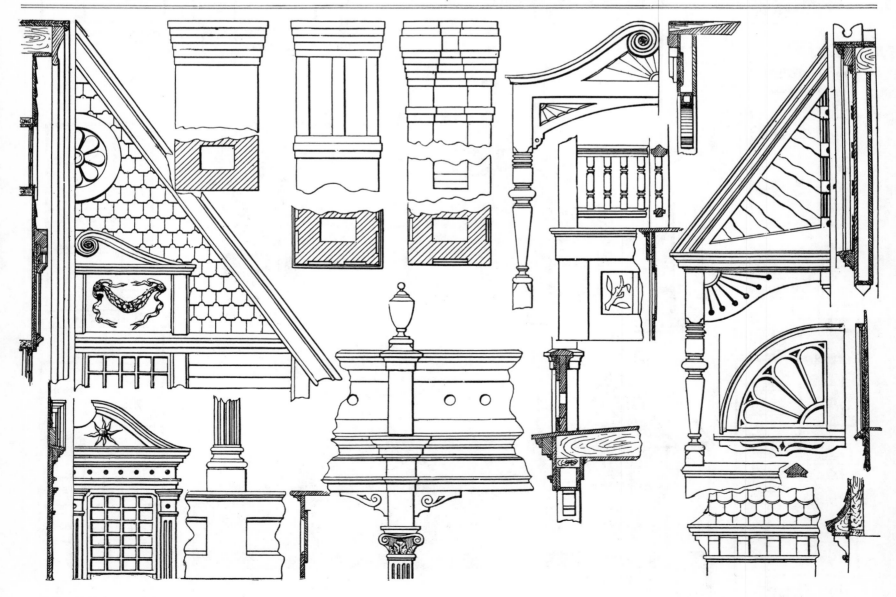

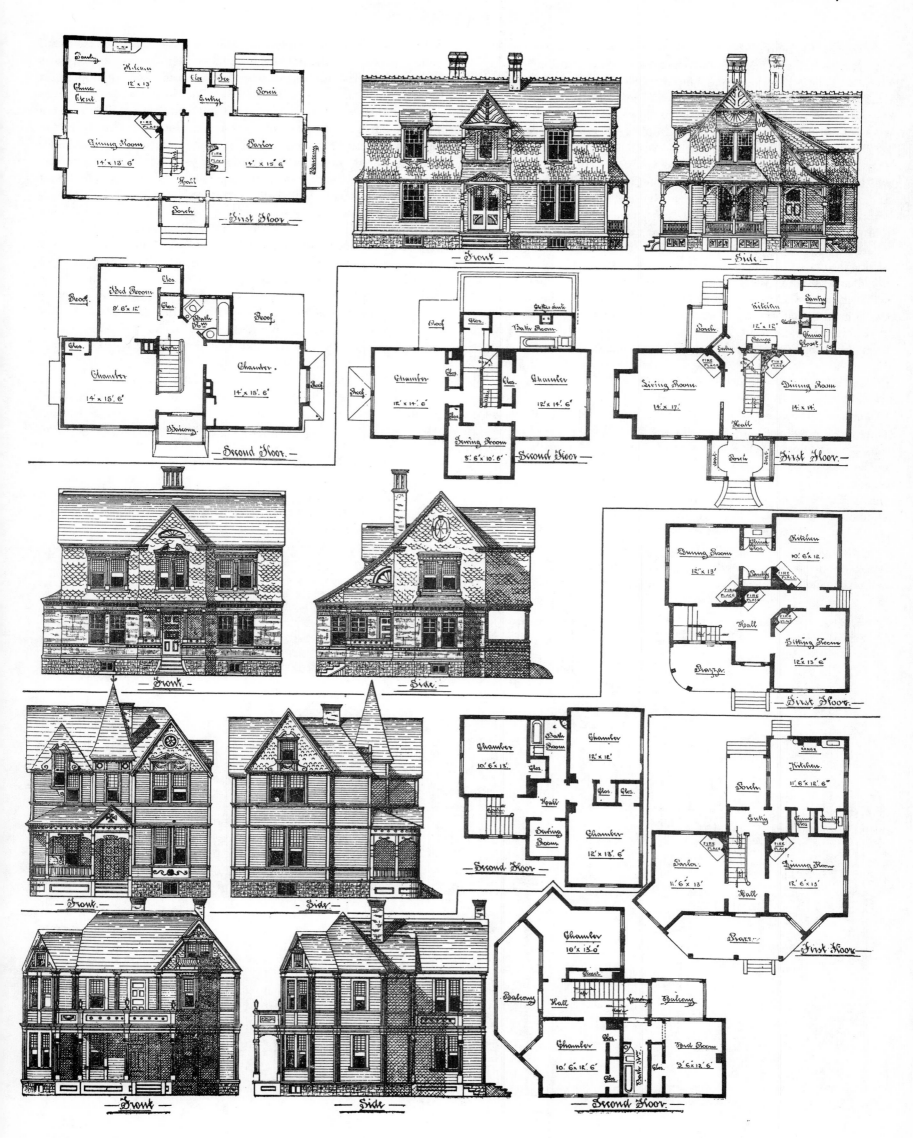

PALLISER'S NEW COTTAGE HOMES AND DETAILS.

PLATE 5.

Design 14 represents an excellent plan for a country house, with good porch and veranda conveniences, the recessed front porch gives a secluded entrance and ample space for a good bed-room over. The stairs are well arranged, and are lighted by the large stained glass window; there is a large closet in the front hall, and a wash-bowl in the junction between front hall and kitchen and cellar stairs. Library and parlor are thrown together by sliding doors. The fire-places are placed where the two come in one chimney, which is built to show on the outside, and is quite a feature of the design, the square panel containing sun dial is designed to be of terra cotta and the belt below with the inscription "Tempus Fugit" is there to remind us of the flight of time and in the right position where it can be seen to good advantage. The general arrangement of this design will commend itself to those needing a plain, roomy home, and is one of those designs that will give as large amount of satisfaction for the money expended as it is possible to obtain, and the interior comforts are such that they can be enlarged upon or contracted to suit individual wants. The roofs are slated and have terra cotta ridge crest; the cellar of stone, with underpinning of irregular ashlar, rock faced work, laid with level beds and plumb joints, the chimneys built with good quality red brick laid in black mortar, clapboards painted Venetian red and vermillion, in equal parts, trimmings of bronze-green, shingles, old gold. The small panels between first and second story being of buff color, sash and chamfers, etc., in chrome yellow, all of which colors can be easily found in the many ready mixed paints now so popular in the market and which so greatly assist in the selection of combination of colors that will look best together and be in harmony with all the requirements. Cost, $4,000.

Design 15 is a plan well suited to many sites where the peculiar shape or circumstances dictate something radically different from the every-day plan so common to houses of this size. The arrangement is well adapted to quite a large family of taste, and would probably suit the ideas of more people needing eight or nine rooms, with the conveniences here shown than any other design of same size herein illustrated. The Entrance Hall is large, roomy and well lighted, the large window being susceptible to a fine heraldic effect in art glass of appropriate design. This hall communicates with the three principal rooms of first floor, and connecting, as it does, with parlor by sliding doors, it makes a very roomy and open arrangement, giving ample room and opportunity for hall furniture, which goes so far towards making a good impression on the visitor when entering. The staircase hall is well placed, being nicely isolated from main entrance and yet in close proximity and where it can be seen sufficiently to just give a charm to the general effect, the glimpse of stairs being far more desirable in entering a house than to see the whole stairs open before you; and it is by far the nicest for the ladies of the house, as they are not compelled to walk down the whole flight of stairs in front of their visitor, which is too frequently the case. The toilet-room under stairs contains bowl and water-closet, and provides ample room for hanging wet or damp clothing, the stair hall giving ample room for the hat-rack and stand for general use of the household. The dining and sitting-room, connecting together as they do, make a desirable living part, the sitting-room having a corner cheffonier, built in opposite fire-place. The conservatory opening to dining-room by means of portiere is a very nice feature, and by means of door from same to terrace, an outside entrance to rear garden is obtained. The pantry, laundry and kitchen offices are excellent; back stairs just right, and the general plan and conveniences on second floor unexcelled. The servants' rooms in attic are reached direct from back stairs, and the privacy of second floor is entirely preserved. Such a house, with all improvements and hard-wood finish on first floor, costs to build it about $4,800.

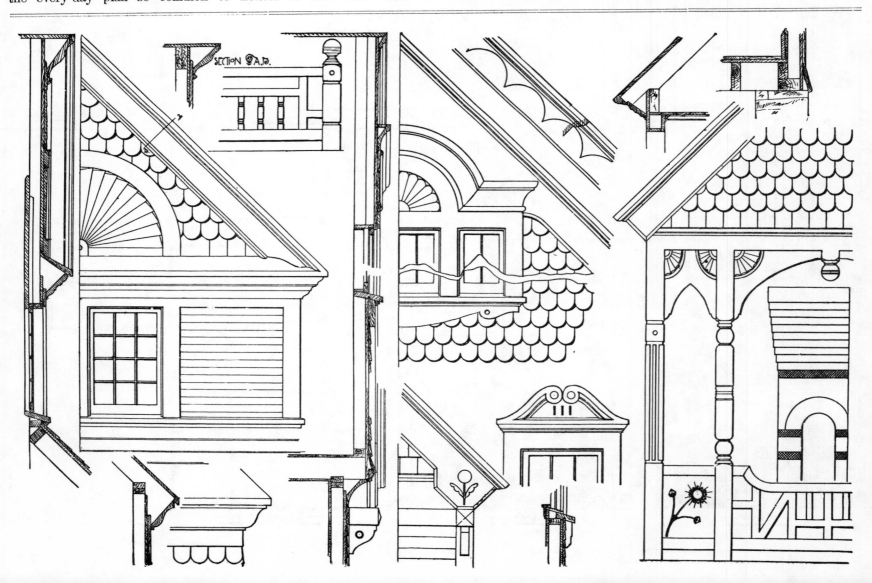

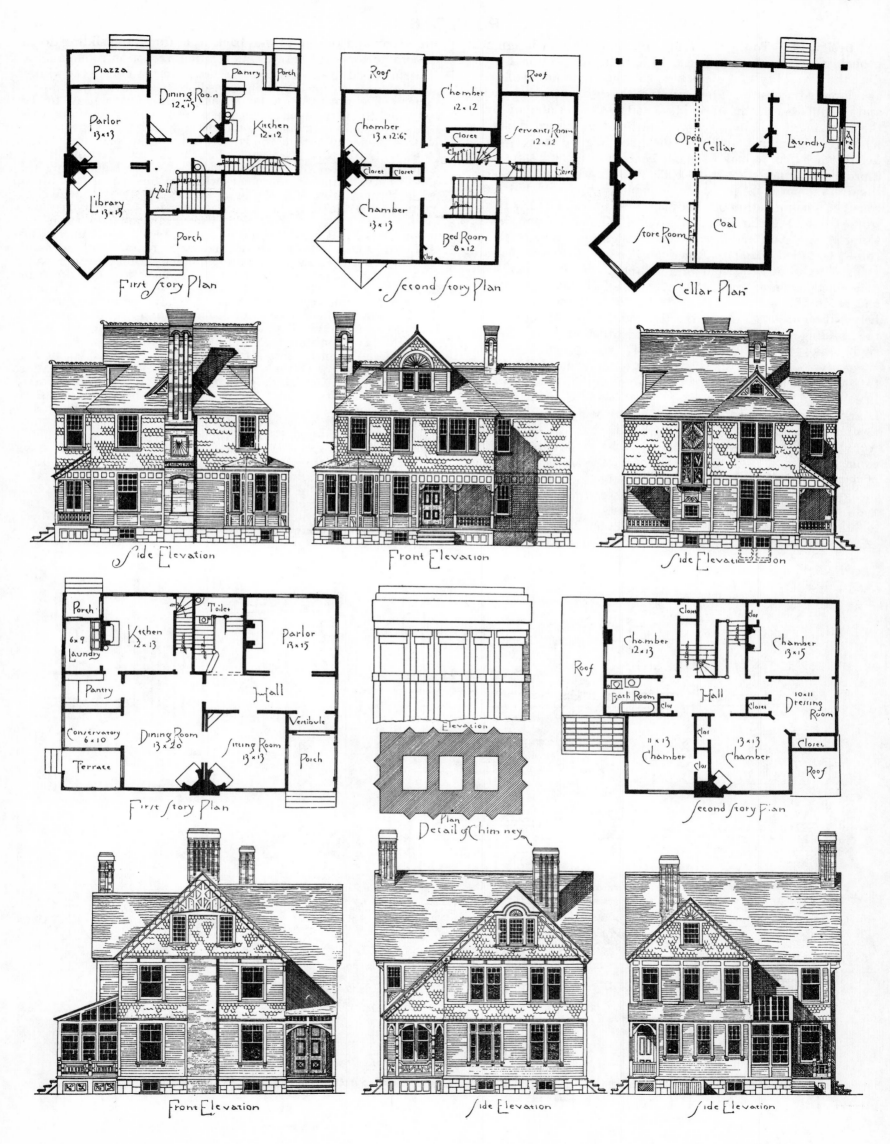

First Story Plan

Second Story Plan

Cellar Plan

Side Elevation

Front Elevation

Side Elevation

First Story Plan

Elevation

Plan

Detail of Chimney

Second Story Plan

Front Elevation

Side Elevation

Side Elevation

PALLISER'S NEW COTTAGE HOMES AND DETAILS.

PLATE 6.

Design 16. — To the observing and studious this design will probably lend itself more, and help to indicate a national style, than the generality of designs here shown. In building of wood, as is largely the custom of our country, the great object is variety ; and the difference in peoples' ideas and necessities of plan to suit them creates an infinite, variety of outline that in wood can be made very attractive, and when designed in good taste, with no desire other than to make a good, honest and artistic thing, with a proper clothing to cover the body, the exterior being simply the dress to cover the plan, the outcome cannot help but be a sensible consummation of the difficulties encountered. To the trained mind the plan is the first object of consideration, the exterior being subordinate to it. This design may very justly, we think, be called "Modern American Renaissance," the features being of a decided classic mould, adapted to the general style and construction of wood, the external effect when completed and painted in suitable tints of drabs, toned in together, cannot help but be pleasing and instructive ; and as to the outlines of the building and the proportions of the different parts, the design speaks for itself, and we believe it will prove more than suggestive to many who are looking after models and designs, that they feel they can safely build after and make no mistake in so doing. The general plan of this house commends itself to a large majority of people who require a roomy house ; and for a suburban residence, with good grounds and shrubbery, etc., it would make as pleasant and artistic a home as the most fastidious could desire, and the large number of houses we have planned of the size and general shape of this for erection in all parts of the country, convinces us that this will become a popular design and be universally liked by a large number of those who are looking for permanent homes. The entrance hall with a large fire-place, and the stairs well back from front, and sliding doors to both parlor and library, makes a fine reception-room, and, a cheerful wood fire blazing on the hearth in the hall in the winter time, gives a welcome that only needs to be seen to be appreciated. The fire-place in the hall is a feature that ought to be extended to every house, even when not near as large as this one. The main staircase is somewhat odd in plan, yet very sensible and easy of ascent, the large window over platform being filled with art glass, giving good light to the rear part of hall for first floor and also for hall of second floor. The back stairs are nicely located, and communicate with servants' room and attic, without interfering with the main house. A slight change converting the dressing room on second floor into bath-room, and present bath-room into bed-room, would give another room on second floor, making five good chambers in place of four. The attic will give room for two or three good rooms and general storage room. The windows are intended to have lower sash glazed with clear plate, and the upper sash with plain glass in leaded frames, having a small square piece of cathedral tinted glass in the intersection of lights (see details) ; the windows to have inside blinds of cherry, or other suitable hardwood ; the clapboards to show 3 inches wide, and be moulded on the bottom edge ; shingles on side walls of California redwood, which could be oiled and stained ; roof if of shingle, to be painted red, or red slate would be good, if not too expensive. Added cost of latter would be about $300. Chimneys built of good brick ; fire-places of buff pressed brick, and showing the same open (see details.) The interior first floor ought to be finished in hardwoods— ash, oak, birch, cherry and maple all being suitable, and could all be used to good advantage ; the kitchen part in Georgia pine, and the second story in white pine, all filled and polished so as to show up the natural grain of the wood. The cornices, centre-pieces and picture mouldings to be of wood, so as to match the general finish, mantel pieces of wood with over-mantels and mirrors, side-board built into the recess in dining-room, the whole of the improvements adapted to such a house to be first-class and with laundry under kitchen. Cost, $7,500.

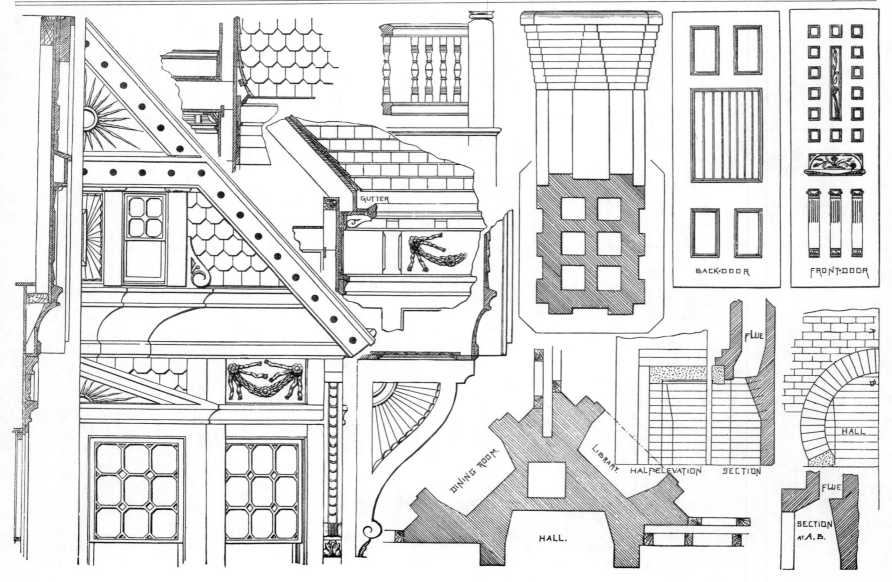

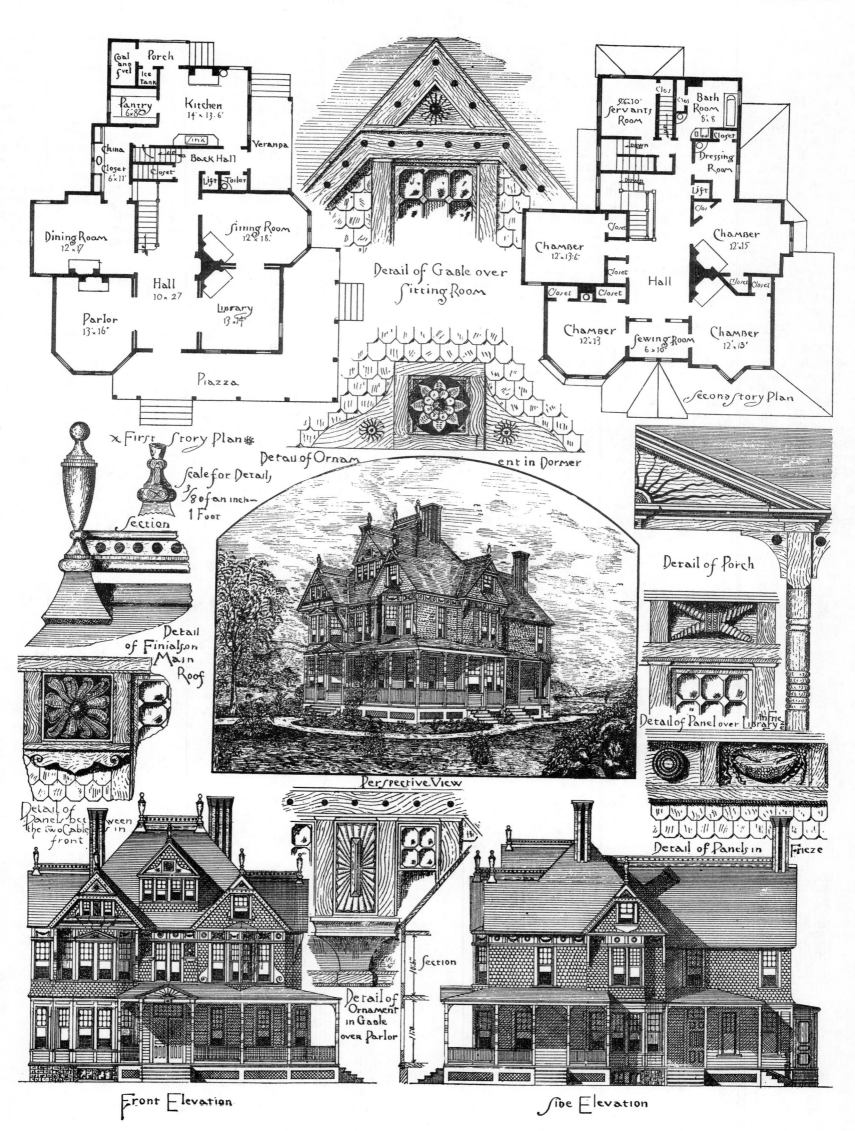

Coal and Fuel — **Porch** — Ice Tank

Pantry 6'×8' — **Kitchen** 14'×13'6' — Veranda

China Closet 6'×11' — Sink — Back Hall — Closet — Lift — Toilet

Dining Room 12'×17' — **Sitting Room** 12'×18'

Hall 10'×27' — **Library** 13'×24'

Parlor 13'×16'

Piazza

x First Story Plan ✳

Detail of Gable over Sitting Room

Scale for Detail,
⅜ of an inch =
1 Foot

Section

Detail of Ornament in Dormer

Detail of Finials on Main Roof

Detail of Panel between the two Gables in front.

9'6"×10' Servants Room — Clos — Clos — **Bath Room** 8'×8'

Down — Closet — Dressing Room

Lift — Clos

Chamber 12'×13'6' — **Chamber** 12'×15'

Closet — Closet — Hall — Closet Closet

Chamber 12'×13' — **Sewing Room** 6'×10' — **Chamber** 12'×13'

Second Story Plan

Perspective View

Detail of Porch

Detail of Panel over Library

Detail of Panels in Frieze

Detail of Ornament in Gable over Parlor

Section

Front Elevation

Side Elevation

PALLISER'S NEW COTTAGE HOMES AND DETAILS.

PLATE 7.

Design 17, shows floor plan, front and side elevation of a one story cottage which might be termed the settler's cottage; this and the next design being very nicely adapted for that purpose. This and the next design being very nicely adapted for that purpose. This cottage has three nice rooms, good pantry and closet and quite a spacious porch and is a capital plan for a small family of limited means. Such a house can be built on posts set in ground and tightly boarded up under sill to grade level and the interior can be finished by planing the timbers, the one thickness of sheeting forming both inside and outside covering (which often has to be done for economy's sake,) and the interior can be plastered at any time the owner might be able to do so; the roof is shingled and chimney built of brick. Such a house nicely built as above described, painted a lively red and trimmed with white would look well and cost in ordinary locations about $200. to build.

Design 18 represents floor plan, front and side of a two-room cottage built in a similar manner to No. 17 previously described, the side boarding being 8 feet high, making height of ceiling 7 ft. 8 in. as shown. The cost of such a house as this unplastered would be in the vicinity of $75 to $100.

Design 19 shows a small cottage of more pretensions, and containing two rooms down and three up stairs, the second floor being reached from back entry. The conveniences in this house are very ample and in external appearance it is all that is desirable for a house of this class. The exterior of first story is clapboarded, or might be covered with novelty siding, the second story and roof being shingled, the whole would paint up very nicely, always look attractive and homelike and make an exellent home for quite a large family or for a farmer having a small family of his own and a larger farm where he has to keep and house two or three men. Cost, $450.

Design 20 shows a four-room house with two rooms on each floor, and is a very attractive little cottage; the front entry gives access to both rooms. The back porch and door to kitchen keeps the front entrance more private; the stairs from kitchen communicate to second floor and are conveniently located for the best use of the room above. One of the advantages this house has over the three preceding designs is the front room which makes a best room and into which the visitors can be shown, although our observation has been that parlors are not of much use out in the west on farms where everything has to be turned to good account, and more especially in new homes. Cost, $400.

Design 21 is a type of house not at all uncommon in the New England States, built sixty to one hundred years ago, many of which are still in a good state of preservation, thanks to the honesty and good material used in their construction. The plan is square and gives a large amount of room and would meet the needs of quite a large family; with a good cellar under the whole house walls of which might be of stone in many cases picked up from the ground and could be built by the owner. Such a house can be built at cost not exceed $900, if rightly managed.

Design 22 illustrates a six-room cottage, the style and type of which is very popular. This would make a gate lodge or gardener's cottage and would be well adapted to any nice place requiring such a building. The rooms are well arranged, and for a design capable of being built economically, we can commend this plan. Cost, $850.

Design 23 has about the same room and conveniences as No. 22, with some slight changes in plan and a radical difference in external appearance. The gambril roof makes a low, roomy house, and utilizes the entire space almost up to the very ridge tree. The cost of this is about $40 to $50 less than the preceding design.

Design 24 gives a nice roomy cottage of six rooms, good conveniences and provides a small bath-room on second floor; a very desirable feature in many locations where water is conveniently had, and it is necessary to get the water-closet in-doors. This house would suit a small hillside lot and make a cozy home for a small family. Cost, $1,050.

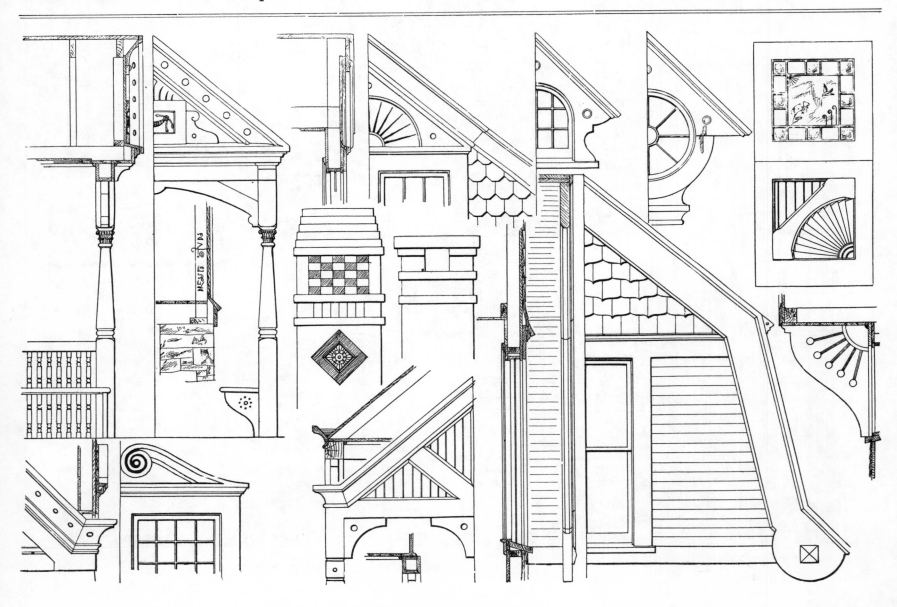

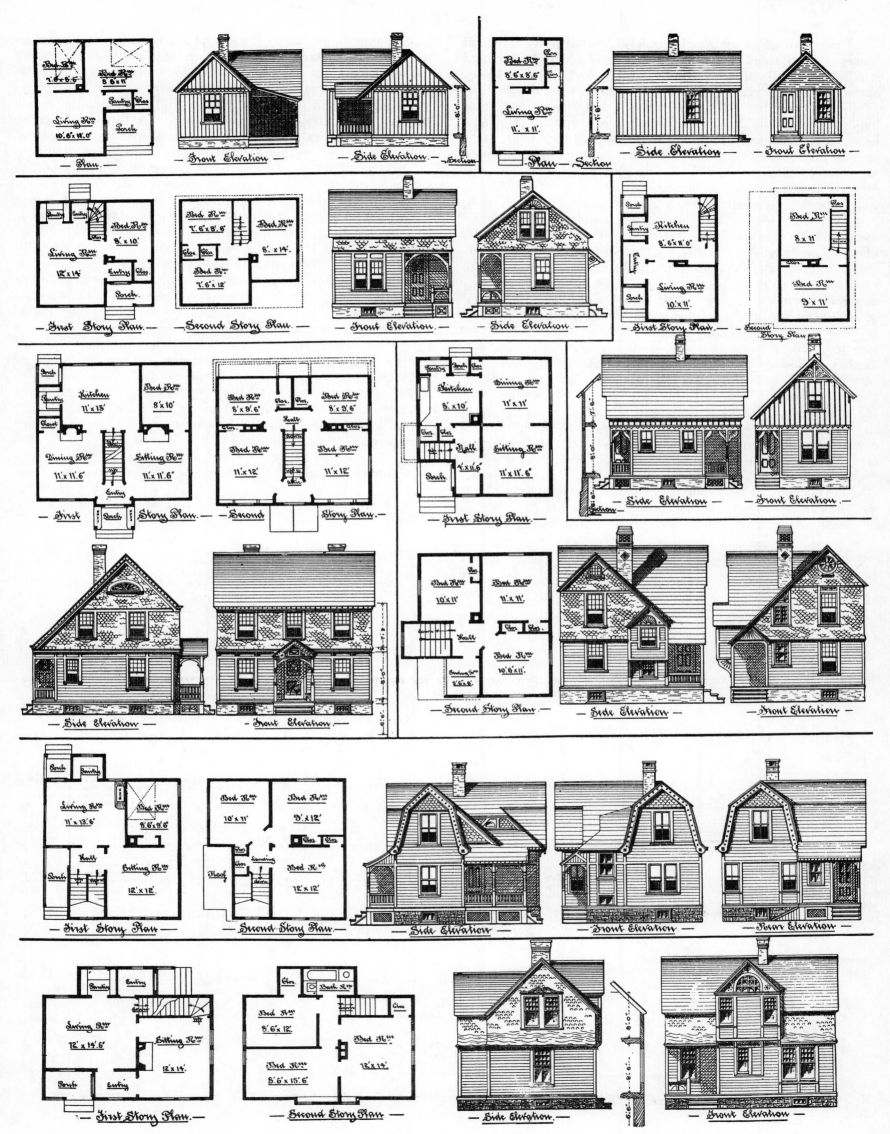

PALLISER'S NEW COTTAGE HOMES AND DETAILS.

PLATE 8.

Design No. 25 presents a plan of a very roomy and convenient house well adapted to the requirements of a large family, and would be equally a good house for the mountains or the sea shore. The large veranda on three sides gives ample room for a promenade and the balcony over front entrance makes a nice lookout from second floor. There is a cellar under the whole house, giving ample room for storage, heating apparatus, fuel; laundry under kitchen part containing stationary tubs, servants' water-closet, drying room and the general conveniences to be found in a first-class residence; the arrangement of first floor is well adapted to a summer residence where any of the family being old or infirm, can use the first floor chamber and have the use of the bath-room there provided, the small toilet room on first floor being convenient for use by the whole family from hall as well as forming the communication and private way from hall to chamber, which at times might be very desirable. The sliding doors between the sitting room, hall, parlor and dining room, make a very open house and one that would be well adapted to social events and parties. The dining room is a large room, an excellent shape for the purpose and the communication to kitchen through butler's pantry, having a sink in same, and thus placing two doors between the kitchen and dining room, makes it more private for both and keeps the fumes from back part of the house away from the main rooms. The kitchen is convenient in its appointments. The back hall is large and contains stairs to the second floor and to the cellar; the second story containing as it does five good chambers with good closets and dressing rooms, together with a large and commodious bath-room is all that can be desired; the stairs to attic are located from front hall, and in the attic there are three very nice rooms, finished in an inexpensive manner and still leaves a large open garret for general storage purposes; the fire-places come in the corners on the first floor, and the chimneys are brought into one stack under the roof so that they come out in the centre of main ridge; the roofs are covered with good shingles dipped in oil or shingle stain and finished a warm dull red; the side walls of frame sheathed diagonally on studs and covered with all wool sheathing felt before the exterior finish is put in place; this plan of protection against heat and cold is now accepted as preferable to the old method of filling in between the studding with brick, as the brick rots the timbers around the base quickly in many cases and when the timber shrinks it is apt to leave cracks between the brick and studding that the wind will blow through; while with the diagonal sheathing and the whole covered with paper, a wind-tight job is assured and the frame work is thoroughly protected and kept free from moisture of outside and will consequently last much longer. The siding on exterior is ordinary beveled and lapped and should in all cases be only the best of selected lumber perfectly clear and free from all imperfections whatever and with such properly fixed and secured it will last with good care in painting an indefinite length of time. A good treatment for the colors of this house would be a dark buff for body and bronze green for trimming color, with roofs red as before named, sash white and outside blinds in maroon. A third color of Indian red to be used on incised work, chamfers, etc., which would blend the whole together and make a very harmonious effect; the interior finishing can be mostly on the wood, pine or whitewood, if nicely stained, being very good and economical and could be made very effective and pleasing. Cost, $6,000.

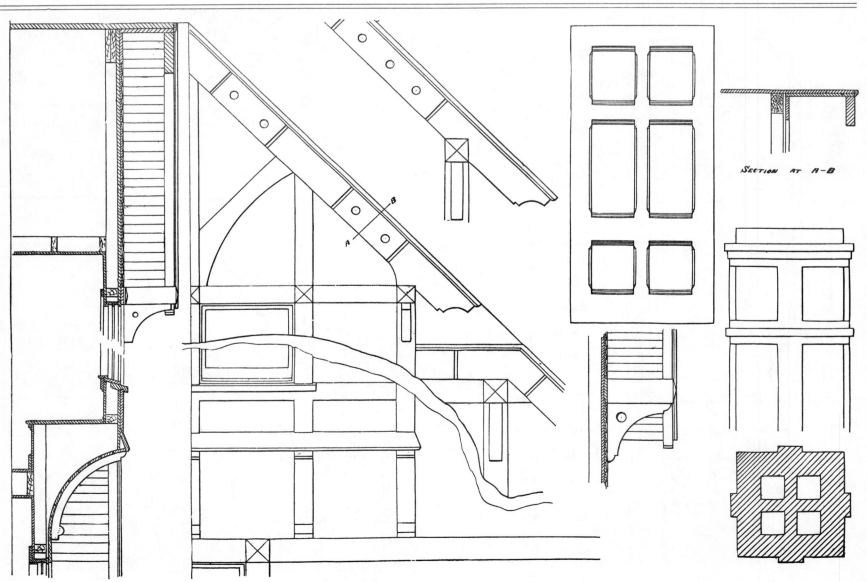

SECTION AT A-B

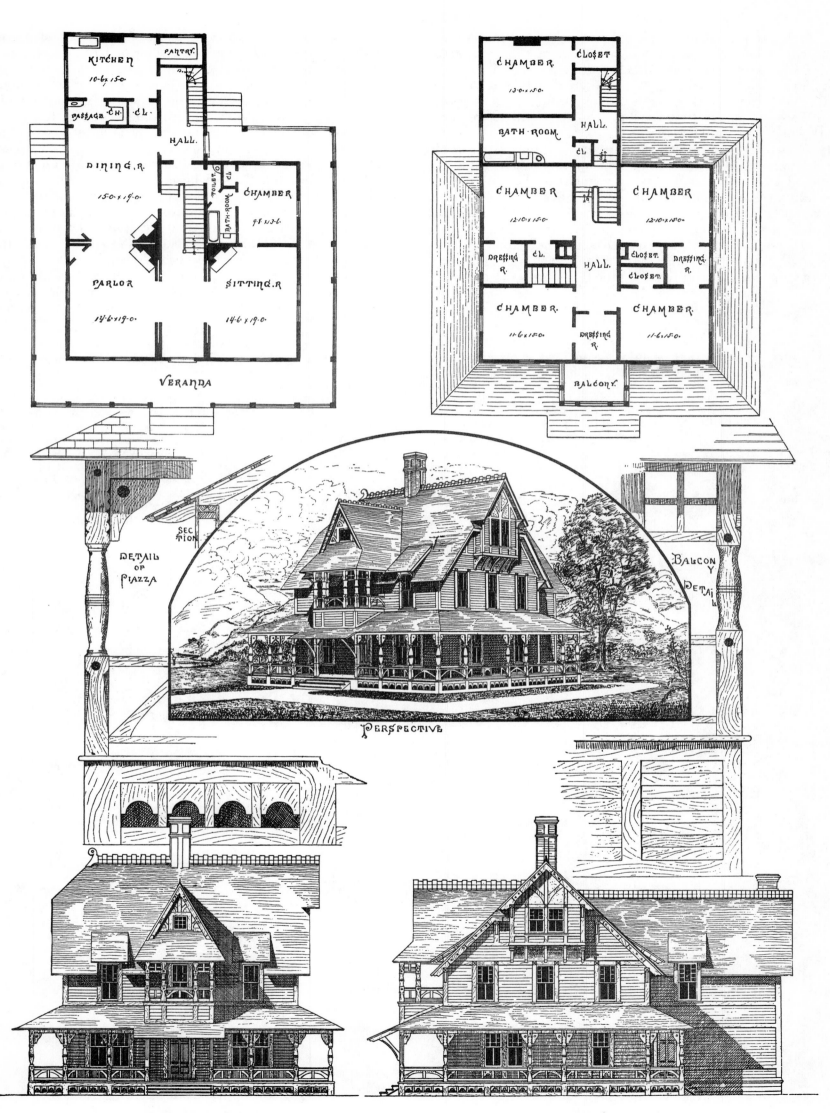

KITCHEN
10·6 x 15·0

PANTRY.

CHAMBER.
13·0 x 15·0

CLOSET

PASSAGE CH. CL.

BATH·ROOM.

HALL.

CL.

HALL.

DINING·R.
15·0 x 19·0

TOILET CL.

BATH·ROOM

CHAMBER
9·6 x 13·6

CHAMBER
12·10 x 15·0

CHAMBER
12·10 x 15·0

DRESSING
R. CL.

HALL.

CLOSET. DRESSING
CLOSET. R.

PARLOR
14·6 x 19·0

SITTING·R
14·6 x 19·0

CHAMBER.
11·6 x 15·0

DRESSING
R.

CHAMBER.
11·6 x 15·0

VERANDA

BALCONY.

DETAIL OF PIAZZA

SECTION

PERSPECTIVE

BALCONY DETAIL

FRONT ELEVATION.

SIDE ELEVATION.

PALLISER'S NEW COTTAGE HOMES AND DETAILS.

PLATE 9.

Design 26 represents a type of the suburban or country home that will come near to the wants of a large class who need a good home, with such conveniences as are here shown. There are a very large class of business men who need such homes as this, and to take New York City as a guide, it might safely be said that there are not less than 5,000 people who need such a home as this and who could live in the country, within 25 miles of the city, in such a home at one-half the expense they are under in occupying a brick or brownstone front and being hemmed in and crowded by their neighbors, very much to their discomfort generally. Such a house as this ought to have a lot about 100 ft. by 200. This would give ample room for a barn, garden and ground enough to keep the family in full supply, and, with the care of horse, etc., would just give one man all he could reasonably do to take care of the place and keep it looking as it should. Every man has his ideal and, at times, pictures and dreams of what his house must be when built. Some dream too long, others too large, and how many end in dreams, by trying and striving after that which is too far away from their reach, when by circumscribing their desires to the circumference of their means and ability to pay, they would be enabled to own their own homes, and avoid paying high rents for poor quarters in a crowded atmosphere. Another thing that few people think of is, it is certainly as cheap, and very generally a little more so, to own a place than to hire one, and that money is very plentiful, and in most of cases one-half to two-thirds of what a place would cost can be borrowed at a low rate of interest ; and to the man who pays his bills, where is the difference between paying rent and interest ? It is clearly every man's duty to himself and those dependent upon him to provide a home that will be permanent in the family, and to do this it is necessary to run into debt some ; and how many of the rich and successful men of to-day would have been as they are if they had never run into debt at the outset of their business career. Such homes as this, built at an expense of $5,000, on plots worth about $2,000, would, no doubt, pay both to rent and to sell, if built in the right section, and to those who are seeking a home or investment we cheerfuly recommend a careful study of this design. The general plan of first floor gives a spacious hall, communicating with and opening the parlor and sitting-room together by means of sliding doors. The front and back hall also connect together, so that it is possible to go to and from any part of the house without interfering with the privacy of any of the rooms. The dining room is conveniently arranged ; is private and well isolated from front entrance, and is all that is desirable. As to kitchen connections and appointments the laundry being placed on the first floor, economizes fuel, and the expense of a stove for special laundry use is avoided, as the kitchen range answers both purposes. A toilet room is provided under stairs, and contains a water-closet and bowl. The second floor contains five good rooms, bath and sewing-room, together with good closets, and there is ample room on the third floor for four nice rooms, the attic stairs being placed over the back stairs, so that there is free access to attic from first floor, without troubling main part of the house. The store cellar, divided with brick walls from the main cellar, is a good feature, being placed where it is always cool and well lighted and being shelved makes a convenience very necessary in houses of any pretension. The shingled exterior and general character of exterior finish, gives a cozy and old-time appearance to the design, and takes away the general stiffness that goes with anything new. The main roofs could be of slate, veranda roofs being shingled same as the sides of house. The shingles on sides to be olive green, and other work painted red. Panels on front gable buff, and sash white. Whole house heated by furnace, and to have brick-set range in kitchen fireplace.

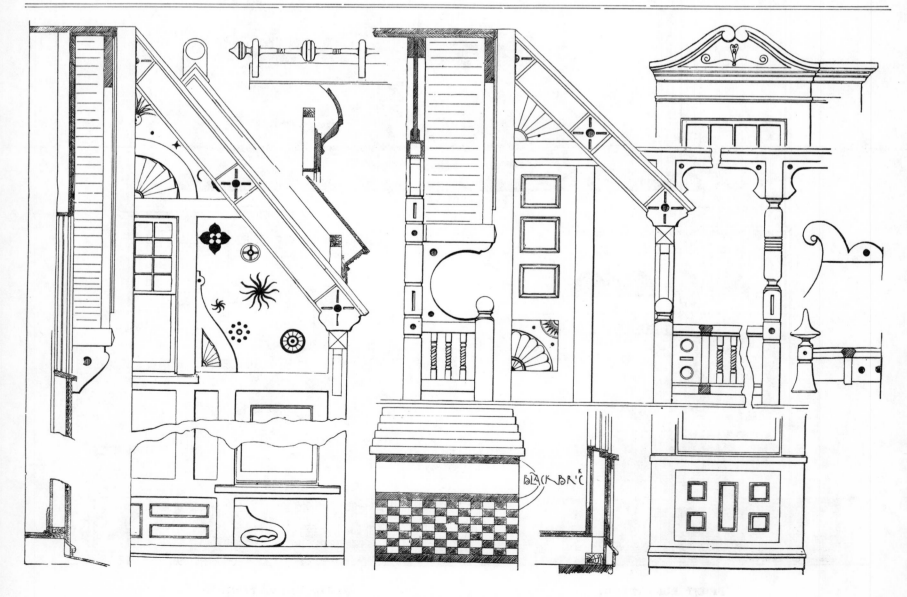

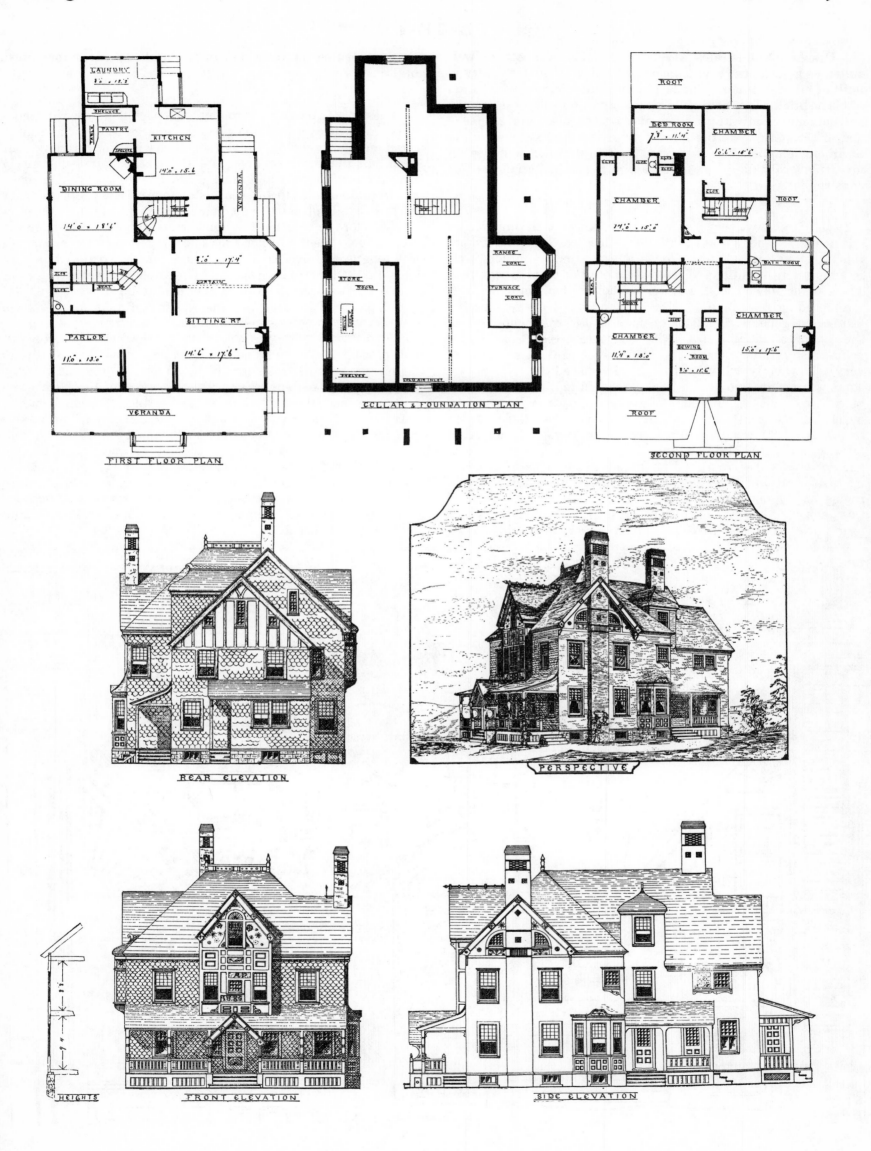

FIRST FLOOR PLAN

CELLAR & FOUNDATION PLAN

SECOND FLOOR PLAN

REAR ELEVATION

PERSPECTIVE

HEIGHTS   FRONT ELEVATION

SIDE ELEVATION

Design 27 illustrates a very nice four-room cottage, well suited as a gardener's cottage or gate lodge. The first story is built of brick on a stone underpinning and trimmed with bands of black brick. This cottage is very simple and plain, yet would present an exellent appearance if placed in just the right place and in harmony with the surroundings, the first story could be of frame, clapboarded if desired ; cost of such a house in favorable locality is $700 to $900, according to materials used in construction.

Design 28 shows a very pretty six-room house, with three rooms on each floor and a bath-room nicely located on second floor ; this is quite a roomy, small house, and one that would look well in almost any position where that amount of room is required. The general finish of this design, although in a similar vein to the preceding one, is more elaborate and has some very pretty features in general detail that cannot fail to commend itself to the lovers of architecture. The star and crescent in the side gable finish is quite a simple and effective feature and would look very well properly painted, with a good granite base wall, brown stone watertable, red croton brick, laid in red mortar and the black brick in black mortar, the woodwork properly painted in harmonious tints, this little cottage would make as artistic a home as the most fastidious would require and built well in a favorable locality, for $1,400. It is undoubtedly a good plan to study from and no doubt will serve a good purpose in assisting many to make up their ideas and ascertain what their wants are in the way of rooms and general conveniences, as one of the chief objects of this book is to help the inexperienced in putting their ideas into form ; the examples here illustrated being good guides more

than otherwise as to what can or ought to be done for a given outlay.

Design 29 gives a very roomy and spacious house with modern conveniences ; first floor has three large rooms, the dining-room and parlor being thrown together with sliding doors ; the front hall and staircase are quite happy, the stairs being nicely placed out of the way and arranged to very good advantage from the front door so as to be seen just enough for a proper display of the detail of stairs and just enough out of the way to be pleasant for the ladies of the house when they are called down to meet a book agent who has succeeded in gaining entrance by his glib tongue well used on Biddy, whose business really is to keep such out rather than let them in. The kitchen is well placed, one chimney answering for both kitchen and dining-room fire-places ; the china closet is large and gives plenty of room for storage of all necessary crocks, the butler's sink in china closet being convenient and will save many steps ; the large store-room in rear of kitchen will be found handy for general work and answers for passage way to back door and is the mugby junction between the kitchen and outside rear porch ; as play-room for the children and reception-room for the butcher, baker and candlestick maker, this room will play an important part and be found serviceable and just the thing in many ways ; the open balcony on second floor makes a quiet nook in which to sit and read or smoke. There is room for two good finished rooms on attic floor, which would make eight good rooms in all. The general appearance of this house is in a classic vein and works up well both for economy and good looks ; and costs to build, with heater and range nicely finished, $3,500.

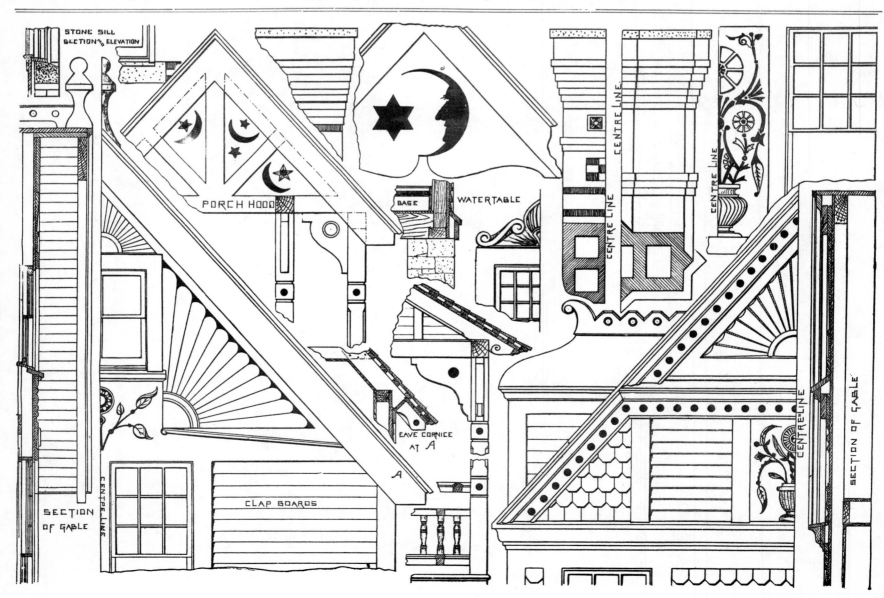

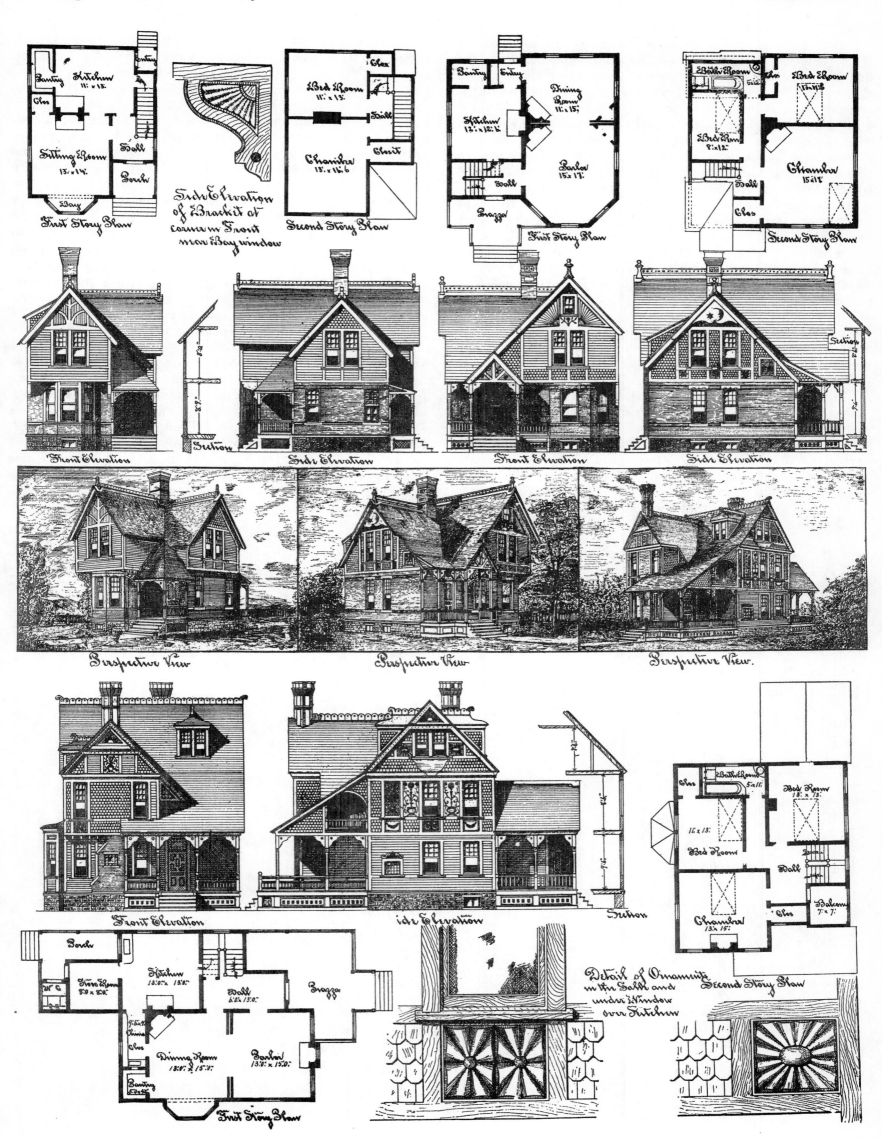

First Story Plan

Side Elevation of Bracket at corner in Front near Bay window

Second Story Plan

First Story Plan

Second Story Plan

Front Elevation

Section

Side Elevation

Front Elevation

Side Elevation

Perspective View

Perspective View

Perspective View.

Front Elevation

Side Elevation

Section

Second Story Plan

First Story Plan

Detail of Ornament in the Gable and under Window over Kitchen

Design 30. — In this design we have three rooms besides a large reception hall, store-room, entry and china closet on the first floor, and three good chambers, servants' room and good closets on the second floor. This is what is termed usually a one-and-a-half-story house ; is nearly square in plan and gives good rooms throughout. The first story walls are faced or venered with brick, which is becoming quite a common way to procure a brick finish for one story, and still have the frame house inside ; this is done by building the cellar walls larger than the frame by about 6 inches, the frame is then put up and sheathed in the ordinary manner, and the brickfacing built only 4 inches in thickness on the outside of frame and is anchored to same every two feet in height, by irons laid in and turned up at right angles against the sheathing and well secured to same with screws. We have had a number of houses carried out this way the last two or three years and they have been satisfactory in all cases. This method of construction commends itself to any one wanting a house of brick which can be built very economically and be warm, dry and strong, and requires very little material in the mason work to accomplish good results. This design would look well with a tile roof ; the frame work of second story filled in with shingles of California redwood which, finished in red and the other portions of wood work painted a bronze green trimmed with old gold would present a very handsome appearance, and certainly would be a great contrast to the ordinary style of houses of this size that are so common in the smaller towns and villages of the country, and it is to be hoped in the course of time, the ideas and suggestions contained in architectural works will be more followed by those building in such places than has been the case in the past, and that both the owners and those putting up the building will have more pride in their work and try and do something artistic as well as economical, and we think such books as this, and the general knowledge and information contained therein will greatly assist those who are willing to learn and study, and add to the features of the country largely by having more sightly buildings to look at, and give ones minds and eyes greater satisfaction as well as help to cultivate a love for the beautiful which inspires the soul to do more and more until we reach as great a degree of perfection as may be possible in the short stay allowed here, and after our departure leave such foot prints in the sands of time, as will be pleasing to and help educate those that follow, having to start where we leave off. Cost, $3,350.

Design 31 shows a very nice cottage, somewhat of an ordinary type as to general shape and plan ; yet with some features that are far more suggestive than is usual in such plans. The large piazza is good for many locations and is susceptible of many changes to suit individual wants ; the location of front stairs and the balcony from platform of same, is a very pretty feature. The general arrangement of main rooms on first floor could easily be changed and have sliding doors, so as to throw the three rooms and hall into one which would suit many people perhaps better than as here shown. The attic is roomy and there could be two rooms finished there to good advantage with furnace and range and improvements, and a nice finish in pine throughout, roofs slated ; this house costs $4,000. There is, however, a vast difference, in locations as to cost, sometimes a distance of fifteen or twenty miles, making a great change. As an instance ; we have found the same work in New Haven, Conn., only seventeen miles from Bridgeport, to cost fully twenty per cent. more than in Bridgeport, a difference we could never explain, but which our experience has shown us existed.

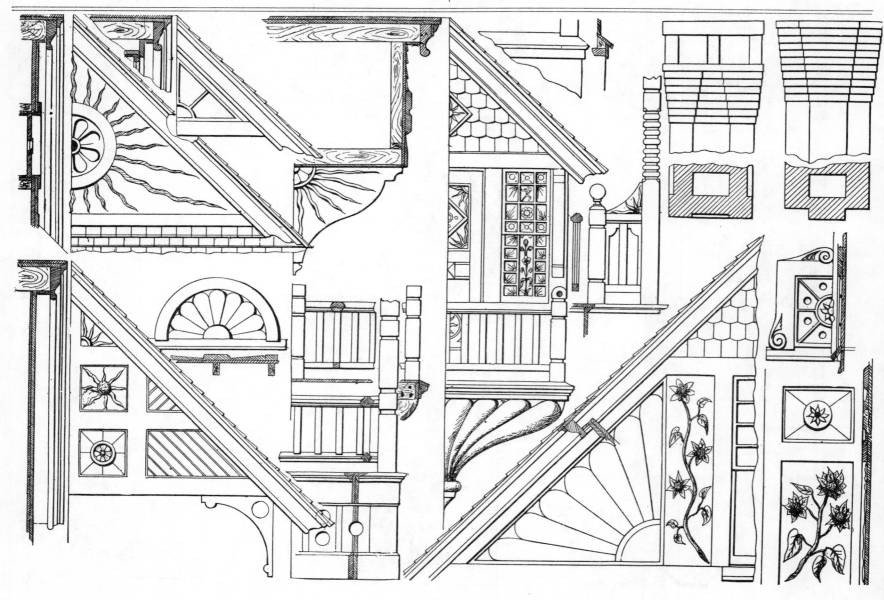

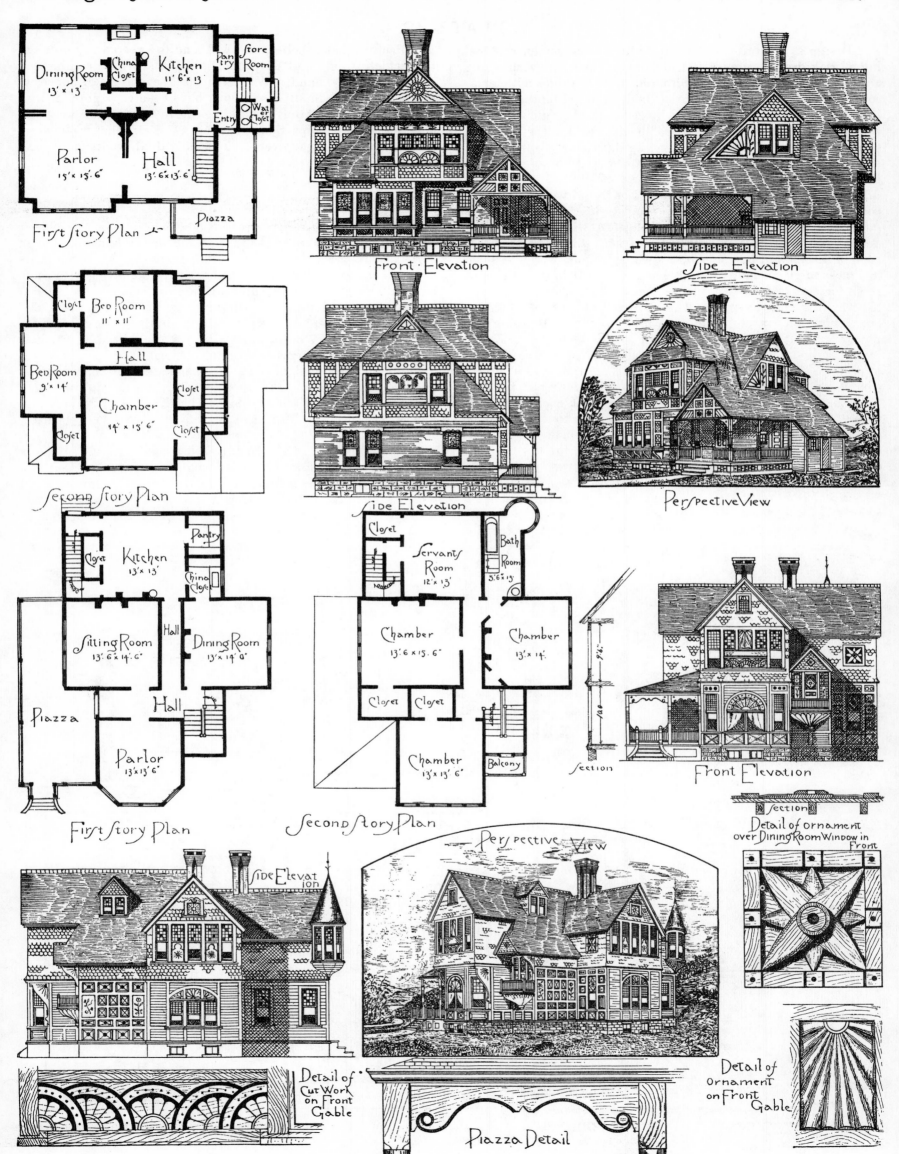

First Story Plan

Dining Room 13' x 13'
China Closet
Kitchen 11' 6" x 13'
Pantry
Store Room
Entry
Water Closet
Parlor 15' x 15' 6"
Hall 13' 6" x 13' 6"
Piazza

Second Story Plan

Closet
Bed Room 11' x 11'
Hall
Bed Room 9' x 14'
Chamber 14' x 15' 6"
Closet
Closet
Closet

First Story Plan

Closet
Kitchen 13' x 13'
Pantry
China Closet
Sitting Room 13' 6" x 14' 6"
Hall
Dining Room 13' x 14' 0"
Piazza
Hall
Parlor 13' x 13' 6"

Second Story Plan

Closet
Servants Room 12' x 13'
Bath Room 5' 6" x 13'
Chamber 13' 6" x 15' 6"
Chamber 13' x 14'
Closet
Closet
Chamber 13' x 13' 6"
Balcony

Front Elevation

Side Elevation

Side Elevation

Perspective View

Section

Front Elevation

Section
Detail of Ornament over Dining Room Window in Front

Side Elevation

Perspective View

Detail of Cut Work on Front Gable

Piazza Detail

Detail of Ornament on Front Gable

PLATE 12.

Design 32 illustrates a very happy little villa residence, showing a brick first story with tile or shingle covering overhanging above ; the roofs are covered with red tile and ridges with terra-cotta. The first story, of red brick laid up in red mortar, would look best, the lower part of sash glazed with clear glass and the upper sash with cathedral glass in neutral tints set in small squares and leaded frame work. The stairs start up from back end of front hall, which gives a platform and landing over the front door ; this leaves ample room for a nice alcove under same directly in front of door, which will be found very ample and convenient for hall stand. The second floor front balcony is large and roomy, and in some localities will be found very desirable. The rear part over kitchen by narrowing up the bathroom a little might be made into two bedrooms, which in some instances might be more desirable as it would then give an extra room for servants' use on the second floor in place of going up to attic for this purpose. The first and net cost of a furnace large enough to warm this house would be about $50, piping and registers about as much more. Net cost of a suitable brick-set range about $17, which with cartage and setting would cost inside $20 ; this includes the water-back and couplings for boiler connection ; plumbing and heating work, including all fixtures for same, would cost about $350, painting $150, carpenter work $1,800, mason $1,250, tile work on roofs $280 ; to which add 2½ per cent. for plans amounting to about $100—makes the whole cost about $3,930. In some locations where brick, etc., are convenient and cheap it might be done for less, probably by $500, and would make a very satisfactory house at that price and one that would be a good improvement in any neighborhood even where large houses were the rule, as such houses as these are the ones that help so largely to educate the public taste to that in architecture that is better, and will tend to sweep away much of that which is ugly and ill proportioned, and which can be seen on almost every hand. We have built several small houses of this stamp, and in all cases they have been very popular and pointed to as models that it would be safe to follow ; and we could cite one house in particular of about this size that we have re-planned and changed over to suit individual, wants more than twenty times.

Design 33 is a very handsome and roomy house similar in style as the preceding design. This house has kitchen and its conveniences in the basement, the back hall connecting with same and butler's pantry, with dumb-waiter from below nicely placed for use in connection with dining-room and back stairs. The general arrangement of this plan will no doubt commend itself to any large family of culture requiring a substantial and artistic home. The back staircase communicates with the attic, in which are provided servants' sleeping rooms, there being space for four good rooms if desired. The general interior wood finish in such a house should be of cabinet finish in hard woods on the first floor and pine elsewhere, all finished on the wood ; to have cornices, picture mouldings and centre pieces of wood to match the finish ; floors of hard wood filled and polished and with neat borders worked in same. The modern conveniences and comforts in the line of improvements incident and requisie to such a house, all of which would cost $6,000 ; and is a house that looks twice what its actual cost is, when placed in the right position as to site, location, etc.

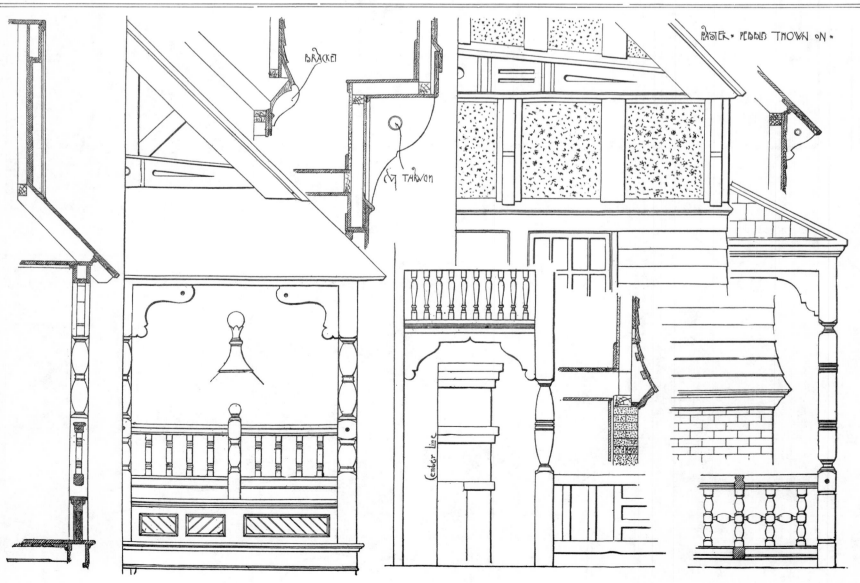

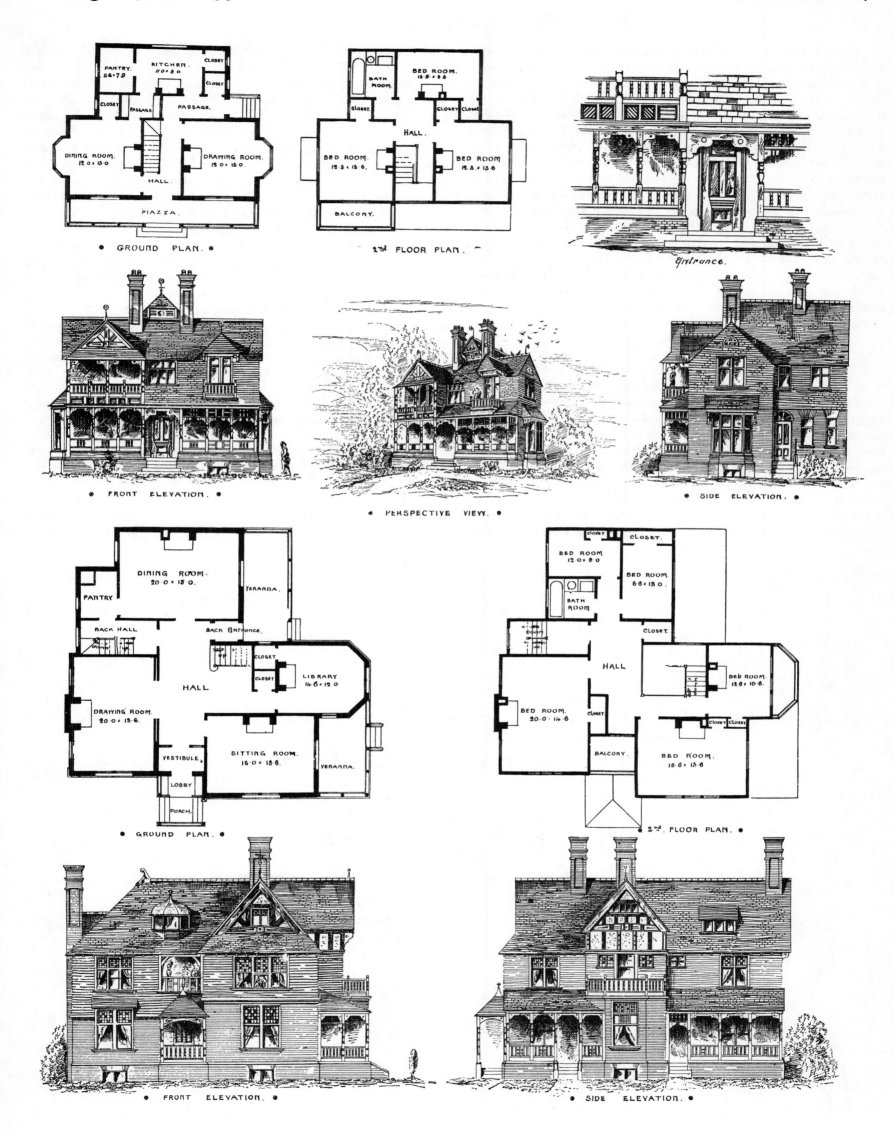

PANTRY. 5·6·7·9
KITCHEN. 11·0·8·0
CLOSET
CLOSET
CLOSET
PASSAGE
PASSAGE
DINING ROOM. 12·0·13·0
DRAWING ROOM. 12·0·13·0
HALL
PIAZZA.
· GROUND PLAN. ·

BATH ROOM
BED ROOM. 12·8·8·8
CLOSET
CLOSET CLOSET
HALL.
BED ROOM 12·8·13·6
BED ROOM 12·8·13·6
BALCONY.
2ⁿᵈ FLOOR PLAN.

Entrance.

· FRONT ELEVATION. ·

· PERSPECTIVE VIEW. ·

· SIDE ELEVATION. ·

DINING ROOM. 20·0·15·0
VERANDA.
PANTRY
BACK HALL
BACK ENTRANCE.
CLOSET
CLOSET
LIBRARY 14·6·12·0
HALL
DRAWING ROOM. 20·0·13·6
VESTIBULE.
SITTING ROOM. 18·0·13·6
VERANDA.
LOBBY
PORCH.
· GROUND PLAN. ·

CLOSET
CLOSET.
BED ROOM 12·0·8·0
BED ROOM 8·6·13·0
BATH ROOM
CLOSET.
HALL
BED ROOM 12·6·10·6
BED ROOM 20·0·14·6
CLOSET
BALCONY.
CLOSET CLOSET
BED ROOM. 18·6·13·6
2ⁿᵈ FLOOR PLAN.

· FRONT ELEVATION. ·

· SIDE ELEVATION. ·

PLATE 13.

Design 34 illustrates the first and second floor plan and front and side elevations of a type of house often built in the suburbs of cities where the rule of laying out the ground in regulation sized lots of 25x100 feet. In building on such sites it is generally the custom to place the house about one foot or so from the line on the least prominent side of the lot and build the house such width as will leave a suitable pass-way to the rear on the other side ; hence houses from twenty to twenty-two feet in width by about forty to fifty deep are of the size required. This design gives four rooms on the first floor and four and a bath-room on the second, and provides room for two or three in the attic. Such houses as these are generally built on the same stereotyped plan, and, any one who has lived in a city where such houses prevail cannot have helped but notice the monotonous appearance that the hundreds of gable ends facing the street, where the houses are all after one plan, presents. Such houses as this vary in cost from $2,800 to $3,500, according to location and improvements contained therein.

Design 35 shows the front and side elevation, first and second floor plans of another house suited to the narrow lot, the first floor being nicely laid out for a fair sized family. The porch and veranda both come under the second story, that part being run out and built over so as to increase the rooms above. The general plan, though somewhat odd, has some good features, and would make a good house for any one who does not care to keep a servant, as the rooms are all very nicely situated for the least labor in living therein. The stairs to attic are over the front or main stairs, and if necessary there could be two rooms finished on the third floor. To build this house would not require as

large an outlay as the preceding design by about $400, calling the finish in them both about equal.

Design 36 gives us first floor plan, side elevation, front view and second floor plan of a very economical house for a narrow lot, and suited to the needs and requirements of two families. There are many young people who have saved a little money, perhaps just enough to buy them a building lot, and who are determined to own their own home, and who are known to be steady and industrious, hence can borrow enough money on mortgage to erect the house. To this class of readers this design is specially interesting for the following reasons : — First, the ground floor gives a good home for the owner himself to live in, the large living room being the kitchen and general dining-room, the front room or parlor making a nice room for the reception of visitors and for general best room. The two bedrooms are roomy and well placed ; pantry large and convenient, and the front and back stairs accessible to both floors, and rear stairs to attic. One stove will in a general way warm the entire rooms, and the second reason is that the upper floor will rent at from $12 to $16 a month, paying the entire interest on amount borrowed, and thus enable the owner to live, as it were, rent free, in his own house, and enable him to save enough in time to pay off the entire indebtedness. It is well for many to consider this way of being their own landlords. Cost to build, $2,200.

Design 37 gives a small house, but only arranged for one family, and is a roomy, small house. The stairs go up from parlor, and to cellar from living room ; a good pantry and china closet are provided, and the china closet answers a connecting link between the living room and kitchen. A house of this general design looks very well when built and costs about $2,000.

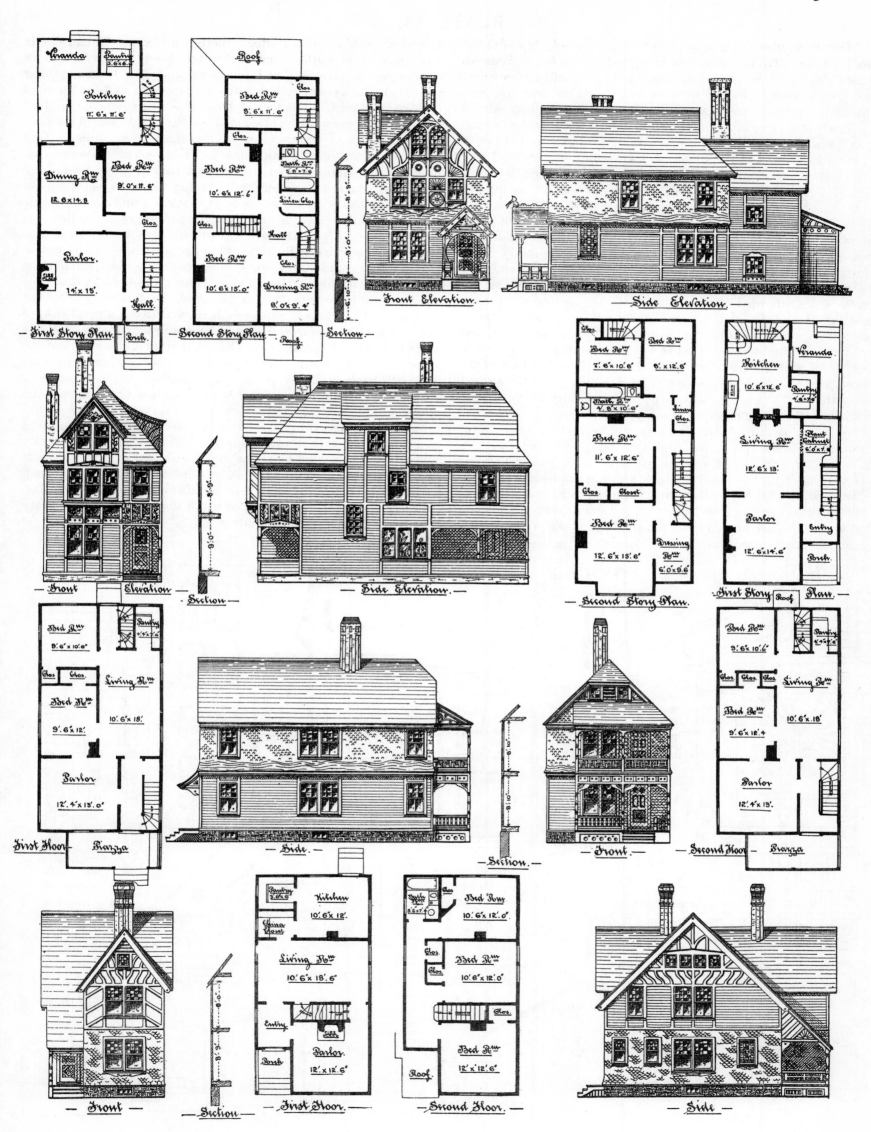

PALLISER'S NEW COTTAGE HOMES AND DETAILS.

PLATE 14.

Design 38 gives us a most excellent plan admirably adapted to a lot about fifty feet wide and is a good design for a suburban home. This plan is well adapted to a large class of house-owners who need a cosey and comfortable home for their own use, and who take a pride in seeing their families comfortably housed and provided for. Probably it would be a very hard matter to find such houses as this to rent as it is seldom they are built with that end in view, and such can only be rented in a general way when being vacated by owner for good reasons, and then they very seldom rent for enough to pay more than about five or six per cent. on the investment, having to be rented to compete with smaller plans of less cost and value, but which may give about the same amount of room. The arrangement of plan is clearly shown by the drawings, and it requires very little study to see and take in the good features illustrated. The hall and staircase are very nicely arranged, the fireplace being on opposite side of stairs, is well lighted, and the general perspective effect upon entering at the front doors could not fail but please the most exacting, for the first impressions obtained upon entering a house are always valuable and tend to help the mind of a visitor to a solution of what he may expect to find in the other part of the house, and also as giving some characteristics of the lives spent under the roof. A hall of this kind will generally be furnished and trimmed with as much skill and taste as most any part of the house. The toilet-room under stairs will be found a very useful arrangement both for toilet and general closet purposes and, although not quite so privately situated as is the case generally, it is only used by the family itself, who can appreciate the convenience thus afforded by its location enough to excuse any little unpleasantness arising from the same ; and since the improvements that are now in use in water-closets, and the excellent system and means of ventilation they afford, there is no excuse for bad smells any more from bath-rooms and water-closets ; but such places can be keep as sweet and as clean and free from anything objectionable as any other part of the house, and we know of bath-rooms that have had these vent pipe arrangements applied where the room could be filled with smoke and it would all pass out through the water-closet in less than five minutes. It is needless to add that with such facilities for ventilation as this no smell can emanate from a water-closet at any time. The time has surely come when everybody having to put in water closets and using them will make this their first care, and certainly it is the duty of all architects who have the welfare of their clients at heart to be diligent in their efforts to give them of the best appliances and to see that the same are properly set and put in place. The laundry, in some cases, could be placed under the kitchen, but in this instance it is well located and is very desirable as a saver of help as it enables the domestic to attend to all the duties in the kitchen on wash days, and saves a great deal of running up and down stairs ; and there are locations where it is inconvenient and bad to place the laundry in a lower part of the house than here shown. The second floor contains five nice rooms and bath-room, and the back stairs continue up to the attic in which there is ample room for servants and storage rooms, etc. The veranda, porches and balconies are very generous and give opportunities for groups to sit and converse without hearing each other, and also to take advantage of the breeze and cool or shady places. To those requiring a home at a cost of from $5,000 to $6,000, this design will have special interest and will, we trust, assist many in making up their minds on a plan and serve as a guide to the practical solution of what, to many, is a very knotty problem—the planning of a home.

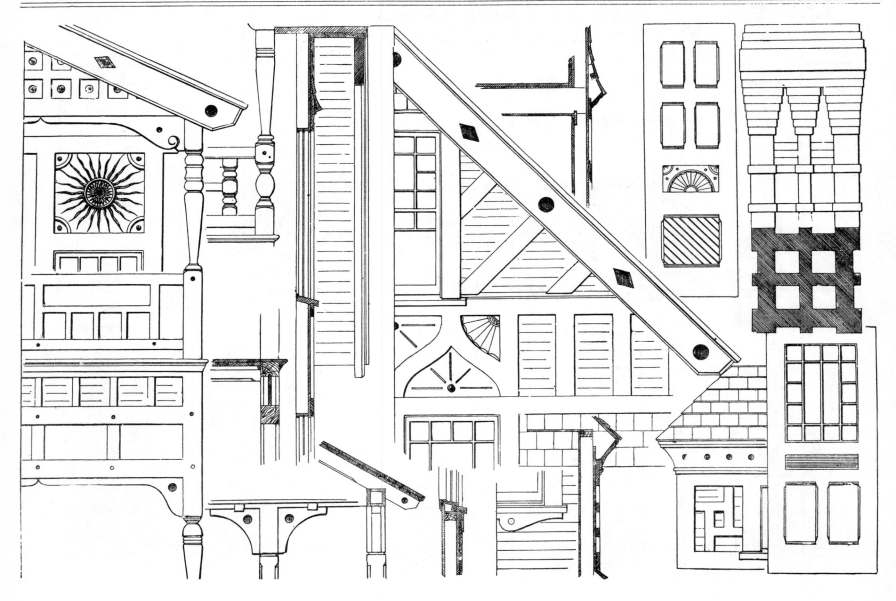

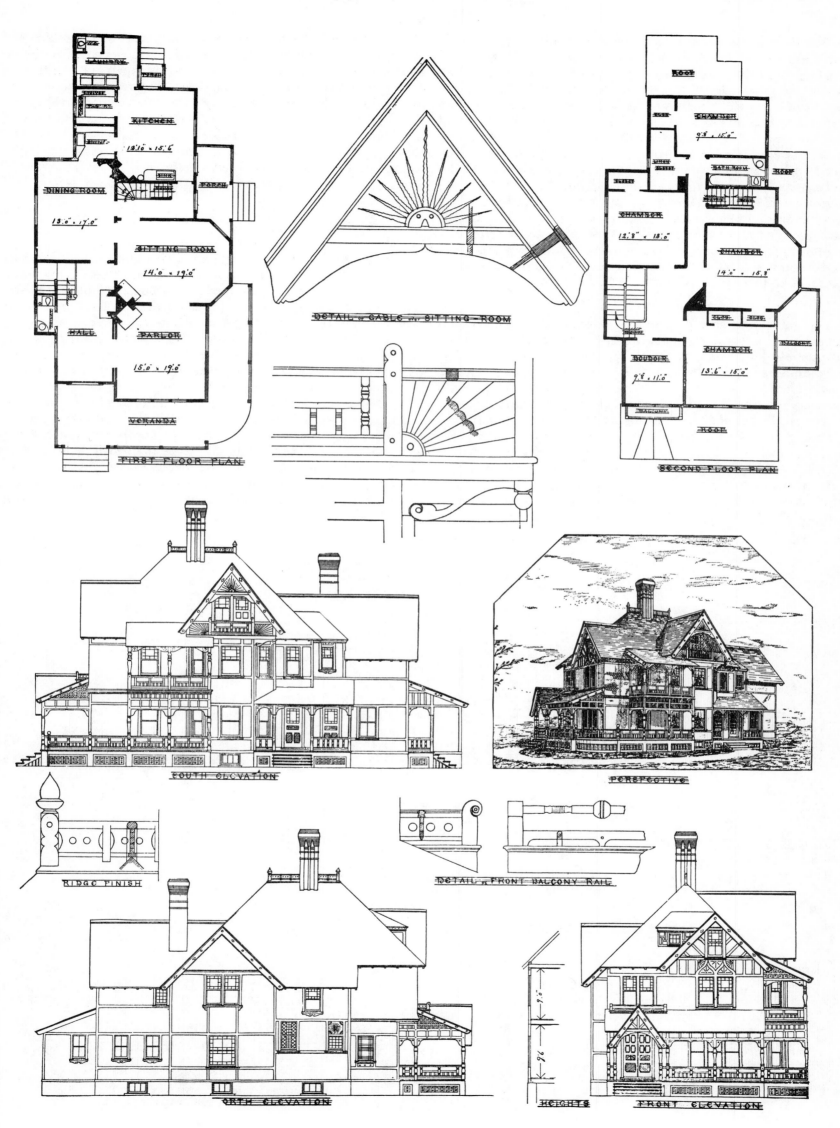

FIRST FLOOR PLAN

DETAIL of GABLE over SITTING ROOM

SECOND FLOOR PLAN

SOUTH ELEVATION

PERSPECTIVE

RIDGE FINISH

DETAIL of FRONT BALCONY RAIL

NORTH ELEVATION

HEIGHTS

FRONT ELEVATION

PLATE 15.

Design 39 gives us a neat design for a small cottage which would make a very comfortable home for a small family and give them largely of the comforts and conveniences of a larger house. The first story is designed for red brick, outer walls laid up one brick thick or eight inches, and furred inside for lathing and plastering which makes a warm and dry house ; second story of frame and covered with shingle or tile covering, the shingle being cut to pattern as shown, secured to sheeting which should be placed horizontally across the framework well nailed and the sheeting covered with heavy rosin-sized felt paper before the shingles are nailed in place ; roofs slated. The bath-room on second floor might be without the fixtures, and this room used as a bed-room, a water-closet being provided for in cellar or outside as circumstances required ; such a house would look well in many situations and add largely to the harmony of the landscape, make a pleasant and cosey home, and cost from $1,200 to $1,400.

Design 40 gives us a design of a house built of brick, tile and terra cotta. This is really a plain, square house, with the exception of conservatory and pantry, which are one story high. The first floor plan is susceptible of some changes which would tend to improve it in some respects as to kitchen arrangements, which could be accomplished by the dining room and kitchen changing places. The second floor is good in its appointments and gives four very satisfactory rooms, with good closets and a bath-room well placed. There is probably no material used in the erection of buildings that will lend itself so freely to the hands of the designer as will brick and terra cotta, and the many buildings erected in these materials the last two or three years indicate that they have been taken advantage of and good results obtained in many instances.

The use of terra cotta for ridge crests on a slate or tile roof is one of the best things in the world, as when it is once on and properly set it is there for all time, and never needs repairs or painting as would almost everything else used for the purpose. This results in a saving in the first place many times, and avoids breakage of slate, not having to climb over same to paint or make repairs at the ridge, the quoins and brick work around openings would look well laid in buff brick and balance in red brick, the gable copings and chimney tops of terra cotta, window frames painted bronze green, and sash white. Cost of such a house, $4,500.

Design 41 illustrates a very attractive house which contains many excellent features in its composition. The chimneys are located in outer walls, and made very conspicuous, are nicely arranged for utility and effect, the date panels in terra cotta being very appropriate in their situation. The first story is of red brick, second story shingled or tiled, roofs tile or slate ; painting would be similar to that described for No. 40. Interior wood work ought to be in natural woods ; glass in upper part of windows in cathedral tints and other part plain glass. Such houses need no blinds, unless it be Venetian inside blinds to windows on such portions as may be subject to the glare of the sun in the middle of the day or afternoon. Almost any house will look much better and more cheerful when without blinds than with them, and far easier to keep clean and free from dirt and dust. Any one who doubts this only need to try it for a year without and they will never want them again. Cost about the same price to build it as No. 40.

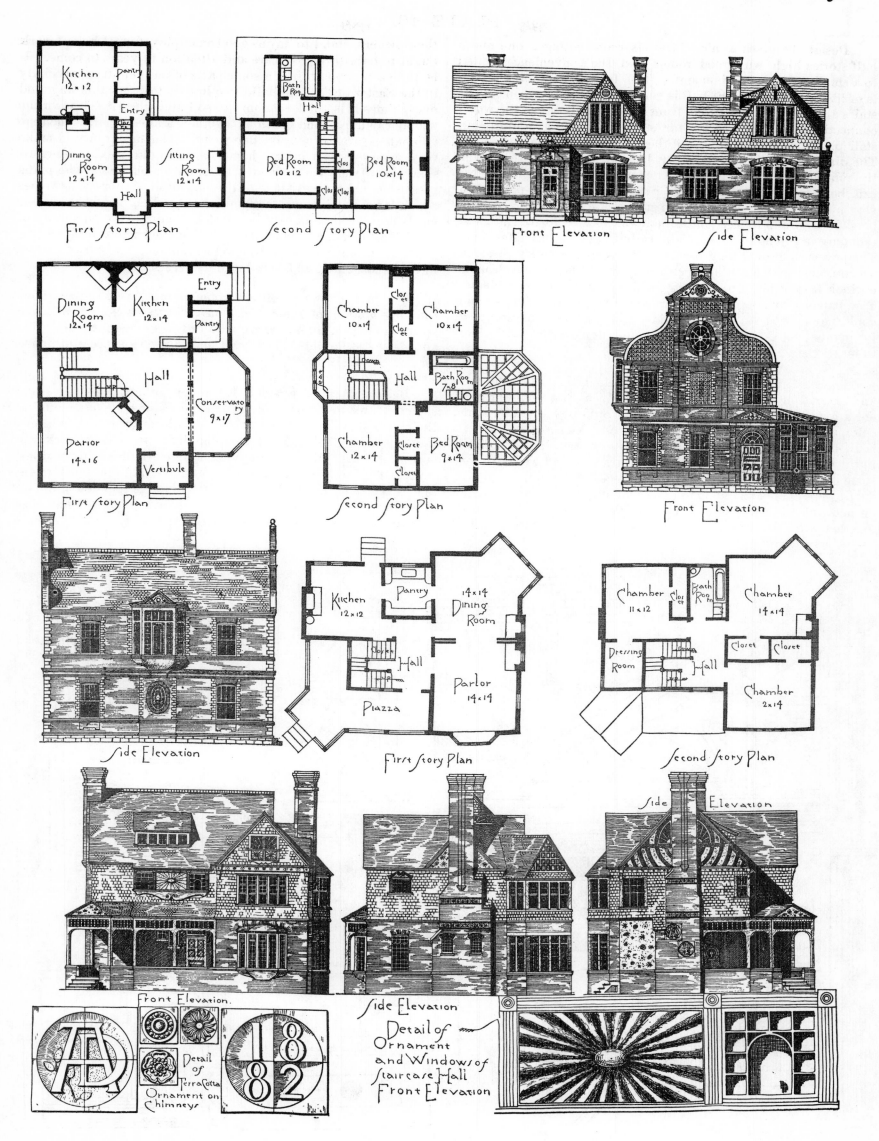

First Story Plan

Kitchen 12 x 12
Pantry
Entry
Dining Room 12 x 14
Sitting Room 12 x 14
Hall

Second Story Plan

Bath Room
Hall
Bed Room 10 x 12
Bed Room 10 x 14
clos
closet closet

Front Elevation

Side Elevation

First Story Plan

Dining Room 12 x 14
Kitchen 12 x 14
Entry
Pantry
Hall
Conservatory 9 x 17
Parlor 14 x 16
Vestibule

Second Story Plan

Chamber 10 x 14
Closet
Chamber 10 x 14
Closet
Down
Hall
Bath Room 7 x 8
Chamber 12 x 14
Closet
Bed Room 9 x 14
Closet

Front Elevation

Side Elevation

First Story Plan

Kitchen 12 x 12
Pantry
Dining Room 14 x 14
Closet
Hall
Parlor 14 x 14
Piazza

Second Story Plan

Chamber 11 x 12
Closet
Bath Room
Chamber 14 x 14
Dressing Room
Hall
Closet
Closet
Chamber 2 x 14

Side Elevation

Front Elevation.

Detail of Terra Cotta Ornament on Chimneys

A C

1882

Side Elevation

Detail of Ornament and Windows of Staircase Hall Front Elevation

PALLISER'S NEW COTTAGE HOMES AND DETAILS.

PLATE 16.

Design 42 gives a nice little six-room cottage, one and a half stories high, with good rooms and the conveniences suited to a small family of refinement. The front porch, or veranda, is of liberal size and front hall is very nice and convenient. The stairs are placed back from front and are well out of the way; connections to kitchen and cellar stairway are made under main stair platform, which shuts off the kitchen part from main hall. The dining-room is conveniently located, the pantry serving as the connecting junction between kitchen and it, so the china, etc.; can be reached from either room as required. The parlor is a very nice room and well suited to such a house. The three chambers are large and roomy; bath-room well located for warmth and economy in piping and non-liability to freeze up in winter time. The flower shelf on dining-room windows makes a very pleasing feature, and with a southern exposure would be a very pleasing outlook from dining-room when the flowers, etc., were in bloom. The balcony on second story is also a very pretty feature and could be enclosed with sash in winter and used as a conservatory for plants, etc. Cost $2,600, which would vary full $500 according to location and finish.

Design 43 illustrates a pair of semi-detached houses, the first and second floor plan of which are given, and front and side elevation of two styles, the first of which would be termed by some colonial and the other a free adaptation of Queen Anne; the first is about the general style and character of work which prevailed in this country seventy-five to eighty years ago, and we have seen some of these old houses which for execution and minutenes of detail were exellent models to copy and study from, and which, on account of their exellent materials and good workmanship together with the great care exercised in their preservation by their owners, stand to-day as good examples of what honest work ought to be with proper care and attention in years to come. It is quite a common thing in some parts of our country, especially in the Eastern States, to build two houses together this way, and many times it is good economy to so build when it is known the people can agree and get along together, and especially when the two halves are owned by one party. This design would make very appropriate country homes and would need an elevated shady site well back from the road to look well. The plans present some features that would be very desirable for use as homes near a large hotel where the families could dine out or have their meals brought in, and as this is fast becoming a popular way of spending the summer months, we think the suggestion might be acted upon in some cases to good advantage. A pair of houses like this cost about $6,500 to build as here shown.

Design 44 shows a neat six-room cottage, which gives about the same amount of room and conveniences as No. 42, with the addition of attic room where two or three nice rooms might be added; cost to build $3,000, and makes a very successful house for that expenditure.

Design 45 gives a small five-room cottage, which contains some features in exterior design that may suit some on account of their oddity. The second story is built out over and is larger than the first. This is a feature often shown in modern work and is simply a repetition of many existing examples of work done from one to two hundred years ago in certain parts of Europe that is very familiar to the tourist and which is so much admired by the traveling public. Chester, England, presents some nice features of this kind that are worth study. Cost $2,300.

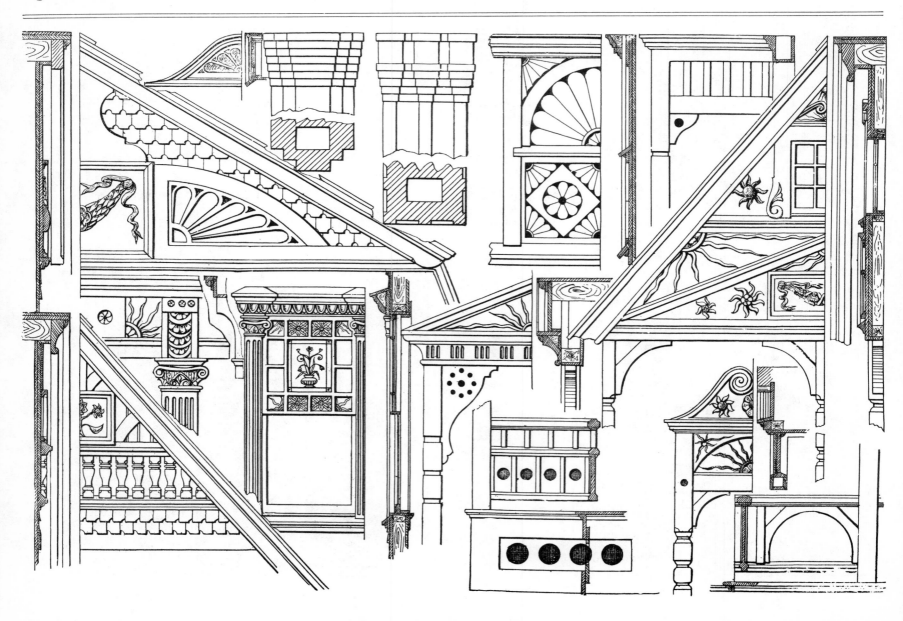

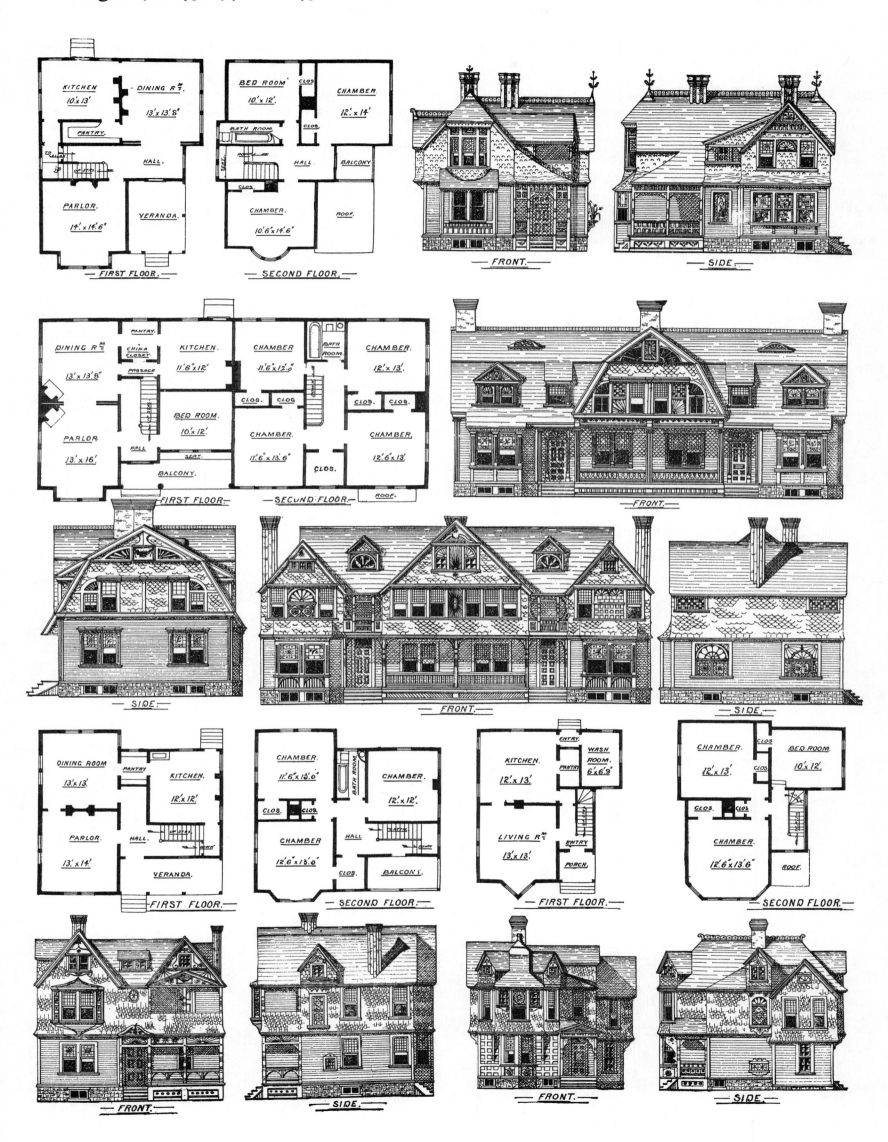

KITCHEN 10' x 13'   DINING R⁴ 13' x 13' 8"

PANTRY.

HALL.

PARLOR. 14' x 14' 6"   VERANDA.

— FIRST FLOOR. —

BED ROOM 10' x 12'   CLOS   CHAMBER. 12' x 14'

CLOS

BATH ROOM.   HALL   BALCONY

CLOS.

CHAMBER. 10' 6" x 14' 6"   ROOF.

— SECOND FLOOR. —

— FRONT. —

— SIDE. —

DINING R⁴ 13' x 13' 8"   PANTRY   CHINA CLOSET   KITCHEN. 11' 6" x 12'   CHAMBER. 11' 6" x 12'   BATH ROOM.   CHAMBER. 12' x 13'

PASSAGE

BED ROOM 10' x 12'   CLOS.   CLOS

CLOS.   CLOS.

PARLOR. 13' x 16'   HALL   CHAMBER. 11' 6" x 13' 6"   CLOS.   CHAMBER. 12' 6" x 13'

SEAT

BALCONY.

— FIRST FLOOR.—   — SECOND FLOOR.—   ROOF.

— FRONT. —

— SIDE. —

— FRONT. —

— SIDE. —

DINING ROOM 13' x 13'   PANTRY   KITCHEN. 12' x 12'

PARLOR. 13' x 14'   HALL.

VERANDA.

— FIRST FLOOR. —

CHAMBER. 11' 6" x 13' 0"   BATH ROOM   CHAMBER. 12' x 12'

CLOS.   CLOS.

CHAMBER 12' 6" x 13' 0"   HALL

CLOS.   BALCONY.

— SECOND FLOOR. —

ENTRY

KITCHEN. 12' x 13'   PANTRY   WASH ROOM. 6' x 6' 9"

LIVING R⁴ 13' x 13'   ENTRY

PORCH.

— FIRST FLOOR. —

CHAMBER. 12' x 13'   CLOS   BED ROOM 10' x 12'

CLOS

CLOS.   CLOS

CHAMBER. 12' 6" x 13' 6"   ROOF.

— SECOND FLOOR. —

— FRONT. —

— SIDE. —

— FRONT. —

— SIDE. —

PLATE 17.

Designs 46 to 56 illustrate eleven different front elevations for a twenty-two-foot front city house, adapted to the floor plan shown, with such changes in front as may be required to suit the individualities of the front chosen. In the erection of city houses it has always been a mystery to us why those building them should persist in making the fronts all alike; in many cases they are so for whole streets, and look like a lot of bakers' loaves set on end; there is no sky outline, no visible appearance of any artistic conception in the make-up and the general perspective effect is about as bad as it is possible to conceive. This is all wrong, and ought to be changed, and the only way to change it is by educating the people who buy and occupy such houses as these to that point where they can discriminate and know the good from the bad, and thus will insist upon getting the good, certainly as far as it is practicable to do so. Those who build such houses will try and cater to the public wants and demands by building in such improved ways as they think will enable them to sell or rent to the best advantage; and as soon as it is found that by going to a little trouble and expense and the pains to produce something more attractive and artistic, that will sell or rent more readily than the usual stereotyped styles, there will be no lack of energy put forth among builders, who are generally the most prominent men in such speculations, to vie with each other as to who shall take the lead and build the best and most artistic houses. And already in some portions of New York City this influence has been largely felt, and the improvement is becoming quite marked; while other parts, which are controlled by the worst and most greedy speculators, who are so parsimonious as to take nothing into account except how little of their own money and how small an amount of materials they can get along with and give a big show for an amount of money that will appear small to a purchaser,

but still be enough to give about one-third profit to the seller. Just how many cases there have been that a buyer has bought such houses, and has found too late that his house was only half built, and the repairs would start with his ownership of the premises, it would be hard to say. The many improvements in building, both as to materials and workmanship, have played an important part in the erection of city homes, and architects have worked hard in shaping and forming their designs to conform to the improved possibilities of such materials, and have worked for good more than can be told or ever known by an unthinking public, who see only with their eyes, and care not to go beyond that point on account of the trouble and uninterestedness of the subject to them. These designs will, we trust, be suggestive in many cases and help mould the minds of those interested in what may be, and we think may tend to show it is a very easy task to build a block of houses similar in plan, but entirely different to outward appearances, and yet preserve a harmony throughout, and give to each house some individual characteristics not to be found in its neighbor. Variety of design and a unity of materials will accomplish this, if properly handled. The floor plans are such that they can be changed to suit any needs, made deeper or shorter, although the plan here shown is very good for ordinary places and purposes, and is such as can be carried out for from $6,000 to $7,000, according to location and style of finish, and we think is such that meets ordinary needs very generally.

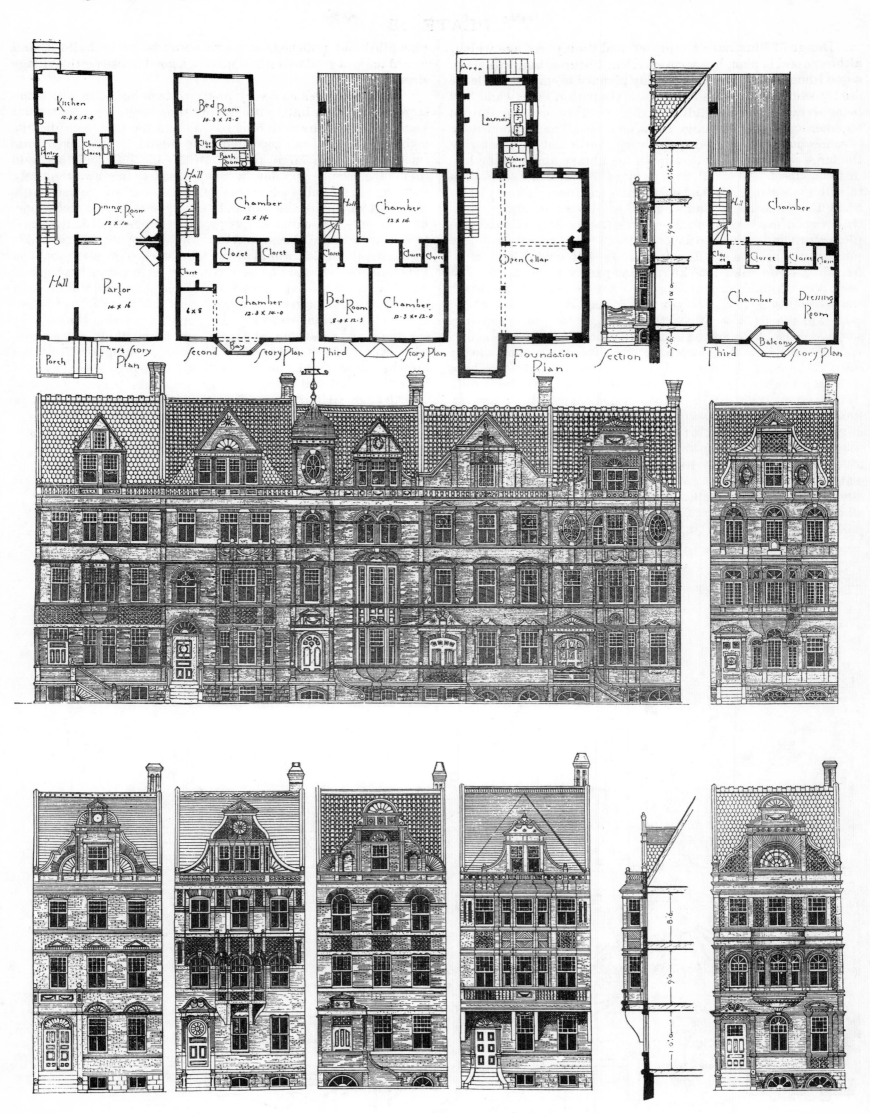

Kitchen
10.3 x 12.0

Pantry

China Closet

Dining Room
12 x 14

Hall

Parlor
14 x 16

Porch

First Story Plan

Bed Room
10.3 x 12.0

Closet

Bath Room

Hall

Chamber
12 x 14

Closet   Closet

Chamber
12.3 x 14.0

6 x 8

Closet

Second Story Plan

Bay

Hall

Chamber
12 x 14

Closet

Bed Room
8.0 x 12.3

Closet   Closet

Chamber
12.3 x 12.0

Third Story Plan

Area

Laundry

Water Closet

Open Cellar

Foundation Plan

Section

Hall

Chamber

Closet

Closet   Closet

Chamber

Dressing Room

Balcony

Third Story Plan

PALLISER'S NEW COTTAGE HOMES AND DETAILS.

PLATE 18.

Design 57 illustrates a compact and roomy cottage which, although odd in plan, has some excellent features, and will make a good house to live in, being nicely planned to suit quite a large family who may be socially inclined, the parlor, library and hall being so connected by sliding doors that they can be thrown together and made one large room, as it were. The front entrance is somewhat oddly placed, yet is very convenient, and entering the large vestibule, from this opens the library and also the hall or toilet closet. The hall, with its large fire-place and settee built in with the stairs, makes an excellent living room ; is finely lighted by the three large stained-glass windows over stairs, and, with a good fire blazing on the hearth, would be a welcome and pleasant room in which to usher a guest. Library and parlor are pleasant rooms, and the dining-room is well placed, both as to front hall communication, kitchen and pantry connections. The back porch from dining-room gives a garden entrance and saves the possibility of having to pass out to rear through the kitchen ; and, if in the right location, this dining-room porch can, at a small expense, be arranged so as to be enclosed with glass, and made into a conservatory for winter time. This can be done and the sash, etc., removed in summer, and as it is desirable to have some place to winter the plants other than in the house, this would be convenient, as it can be easily warmed same as the room adjoining. The rooms on second floor are large and roomy, well closeted and very desirable ; there is space in attic for two or three rooms, and stairs to same are directly over the front stairs. Such a house, with good cemented cellar, drains run and connected, water in, and all plumbing of good quality, and thoroughly ventilated traps and waste-pipes, furnace large enough to heat the whole, and a suitable brick-set range in kitchen fire-place ; hall, parlor and library finished in ash or birch, and balance in white pine filled and polished, is worth about $4,300 to build it, and would make a good suburban home or a good house for the village street.

Design 58 gives us a very pretty cottage home, in which the large sitting-room hall, with its old-time fire-place containing seats, and the stairs with oriel bay on platform, constitutes the main features. It has become quite common to build even quite small houses with large reception-room and hall combined, and they have become popular, in many cases doing away entirely with the parlor and such rooms as are in so many houses little used and which are shut up and only opened on state occasions. In this case one chimney answers all purposes ; it is designed to heat by furnace placed in cellar ; there is space for two nice rooms in attic which would answer for storage or servants' use. This house is designed to be covered on exterior with shingles, and, if of red wood, in about four different patterns would look well, there being a great many different cuts that can be applied to the butts of shingles which bring out the pecular character of the detail and presents a very varied and harmonious appearance when completed ; for the possibilities of what shingles will do and accomplish we think the general detail drawings of the designs here illustrated will tell a story that cannot help but be suggestive and agreeable if studied from the right stand-point. Cost of such a cottage as this, $2,600, with any good management.

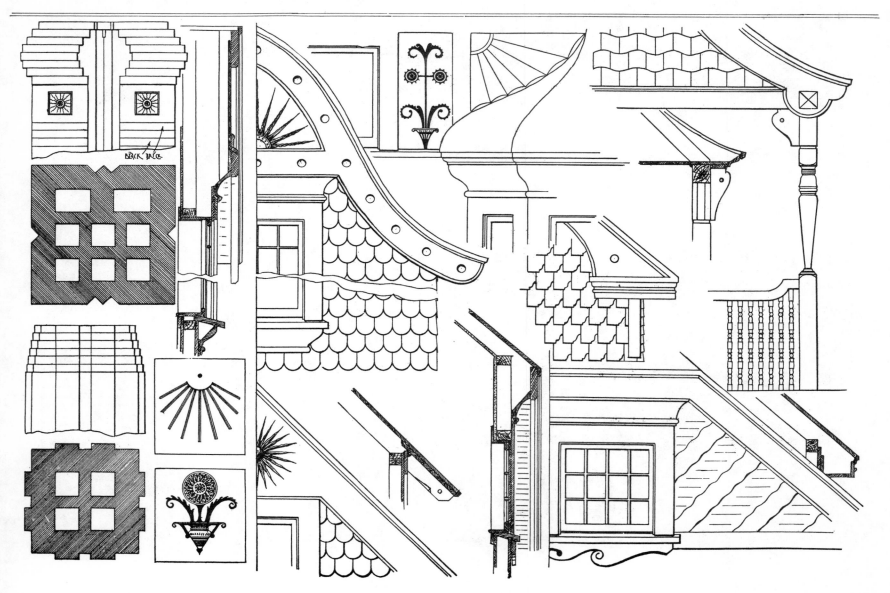

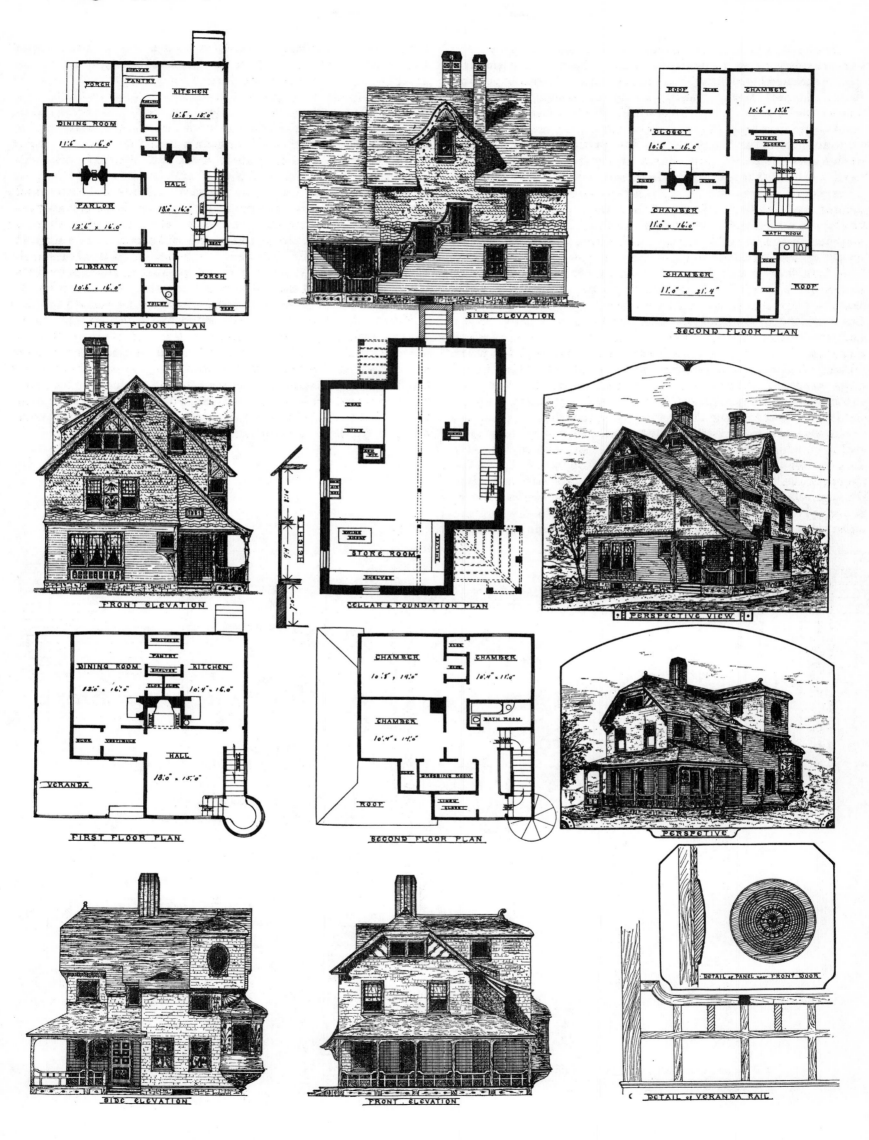

FIRST FLOOR PLAN

SIDE ELEVATION

SECOND FLOOR PLAN

FRONT ELEVATION

HEIGHTS

CELLAR & FOUNDATION PLAN

PERSPECTIVE VIEW

FIRST FLOOR PLAN

SECOND FLOOR PLAN

PERSPECTIVE

SIDE ELEVATION

FRONT ELEVATION

DETAIL OF PANEL NEAR FRONT DOOR

DETAIL OF VERANDA RAIL

Design 59 gives us a good plan suited in its general lay-out and accommodations to a family of means, either as a permanent or as a summer home, space has been economized as far as possible in the internal arrangements, and the necessary conveniences placed where least outlay involved in their construction, and least liable to get out of order. The large and roomy veranda on four sides of the house gives a fine promenade as well as a choice of position and ample shade at any time from the sun's rays, a feature that is desirable in country houses, it being almost a necessity to have room enough on the exterior so as to move around and take advantage of the shady places. The Porte Cochere is a nice and convenient shelter for the occupants when stepping in and out of a carriage, and which has almost become an indispensible feature of all country houses of any pretension. The first floor is well laid out, the main rooms and hall being so connected by sliding doors that they can be thrown together and the whole house brought into one large room as it were. Entering the front door we find ourselves in a fine, roomy hall, twelve feet wide and thirty-two feet deep, the end of which terminates in a large, old fashioned alcove recessed fire-place, which, with its large, upholstered seats, wood mantel and stained glass windows, terminates the vista that meets the view upon entering; the stairs are placed in a side-hall, starting in the main or front hall and turning the corner by quarter-circle platform, continues up to large platform three steps below second floor level and from which opens a nice, cosey balcony, entered by a sash door in the centre of a stained glass window which lights the stairs; the back hall connects this side stair-case hall and gives through communication to any part of the house; the toilet-room is here provided and is in a very retired location and where the water works of the house are all placed. The dining-room is a fine one, having large fire-places at the end and a recessed sideboard on the side. The parlor and sitting-room are so arranged as to make one fine, large room, or yet be in two, the corner fire-place being nicely placed for effect and utility. The kitchen offices, laundry, pantries, etc., are well arranged for the best and easiest doing of the work for a large family, and as arranged we consider this floor plan a model that can be safely followed by those needing such room and conveniences. The second floor has seven good rooms, bath-room and halls, good closets, and the balconies give pleasant outlooks of the surrounding country and make the rooms more desirable for summer use. The back stairs continue on up to attic, in which there is space for five or six nice rooms, which will accommodate servants and part of the family if desired. A house of this kind should have painted shingle roofs, and be painted in about four tints, nicely trimmed and shaded to blend together; the interior to be finished throughout in white pine, which can be stained to give variety to the finish; the mantels, sideboard, cornices, etc., being of same woods as general finish and floor of birch, yellow or norway pine and such woods as will avoid the necessity of using any carpet; such a home as this would be very suitable for and fill the wants of a large class of people who are looking for country homes and it will no doubt be suggestive to many as to wnat they ought to do for a given amount of room at a certain cost, which is $7,500 in a favorable location.

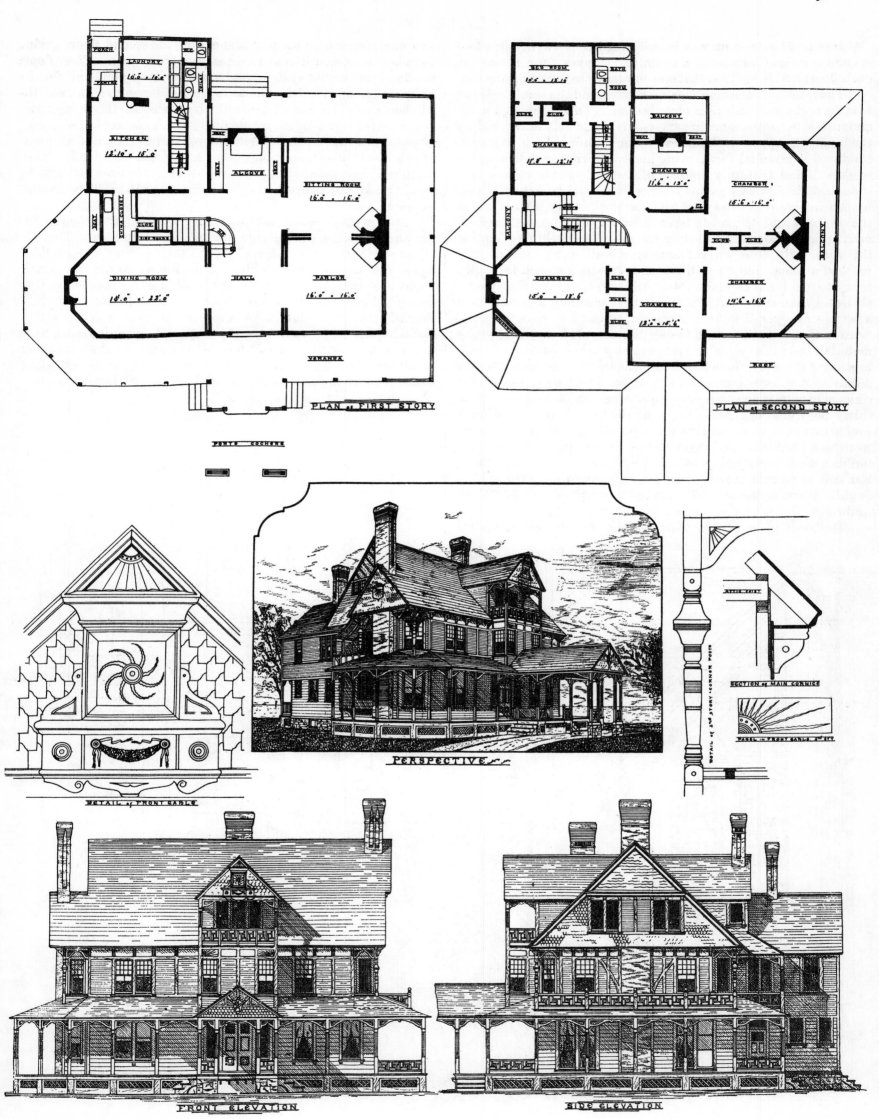

PLAN of FIRST STORY

PLAN of SECOND STORY

PORTE COCHERE

DETAIL of FRONT GABLE

PERSPECTIVE

SECTION of MAIN CORNICE

DETAIL of 2ND STORY CORNER POSTS

PANEL IN FRONT GABLE 2ND STY

FRONT ELEVATION

SIDE ELEVATION

PALLISER'S NEW COTTAGE HOMES AND DETAILS.

PLATE 20.

Design 60 gives a narrow house suited to a twenty-five foot lot and arranged for one family only. It gives four rooms on each floor, and is so fixed that one chimney answers all purposes.

The front and side verandas are roomy, and the small balcony over front door would be a nice feature. The front and back and also attic stairs come in very handy when only to be used by the family occupying the house. Such a house built in a neat, solid and substantial form, using good materials and having the work well and faithfully done, could not help but be satisfactory if done at the lowest possible cost, which could be defined either by contracting it out to one of four responsible men, any of whom the owner would be glad to have build it, and who in their estimating figure honestly as low as they dare with a hope of getting the work. By this way of figuring, a bottom price is generally reached at once, and when the bottom is once touched it is folly to try to get it at less than cost, or below the market value. Or better than this would be the plan of engaging a good man at a certain rate per diem for his services, and let him have the entire control of the work ; to make all bargains and contracts, buy materials, and take such measures as may seem best in the premises to get the work done in the best manner at the least possible outlay. We have had several jobs done this way, and with a right man to manage, we have found a saving of from twenty to thirty per cent. and better work as the result, and we always prefer this plan of operations when practical, and we can name work executed this way at prices that, to the ordinary practical builder, would be laughed at and doubted as to its truthfulness ; but still we cannot change the facts, and would not wish to if we could. Such a house as Design 60 is worth about $2,200 to build it.

Design 61 gives a house which is laid out to accommodate two families, one on the first and one on the second floor, giving to each five rooms with the neccessary conveniences. These floors are fixed on the flat system, and are very nicely laid out for the purpose intended. One flue answers for the entire house, the kitchen stove and one which could be placed in the living-room being ample to warm the whole floor. This class of house is very popular in many suburbs, both to own and to rent, and is generally a good investment that pays handsome dividends. Cost $2,700, which, with lot at $800 and other incidentals inside $200, would make $3,700 in all, and would rent for $18 to $20 per month for each floor.

Design 62 gives another plan, a little larger than the preceding one, having one more bedroom and two chimneys. There is also a side veranda on second floor, thus giving to each floor equal conveniences in this line. This house would be worth about $300 more than the last design, and to some people needing the added room this would be cheap. The back stairs go up to the attic, in which might be finished two neat rooms, which could be used for servants' use if so required and still leave ample room in the attic for general storage purposes and clothes drying in winter time. The details of this plate present some excellent features which are well worth the study of the practical mechanic.

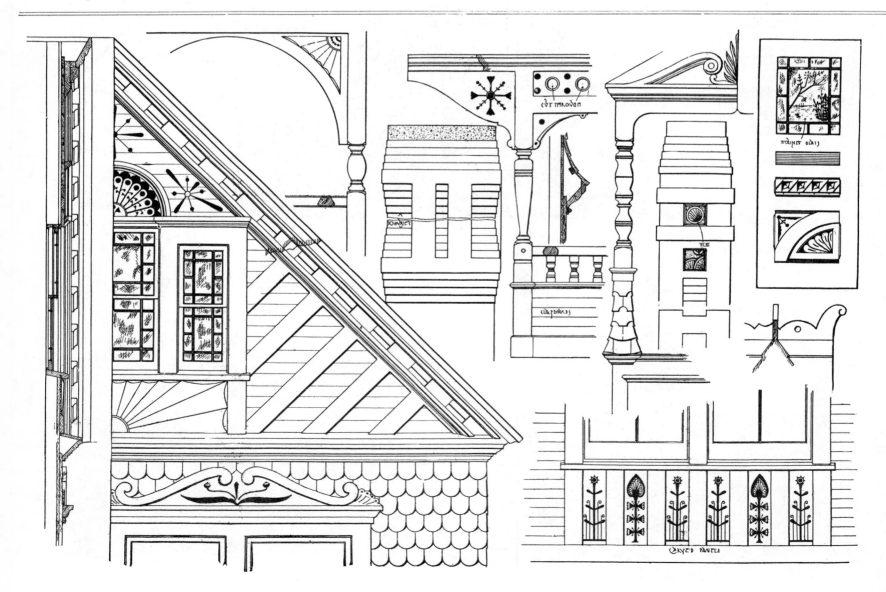

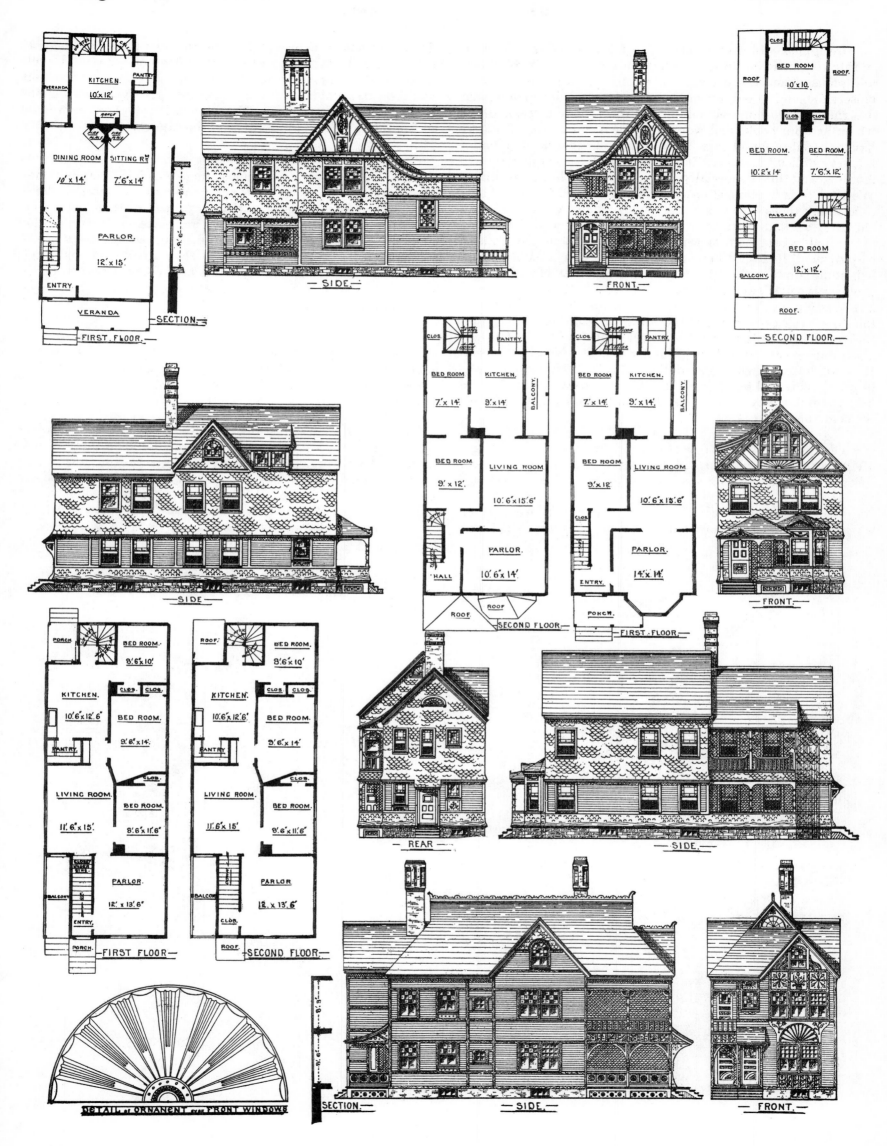

KITCHEN. 10'x12'

PANTRY

VERANDA

DINING ROOM 10'x14'

SITTING R'M. 7'6"x14'

PARLOR. 12'x15'

ENTRY

VERANDA

FIRST FLOOR.

SECTION.

— SIDE. —

— FRONT. —

ROOF.

BED ROOM 10'x10.

ROOF.

CLOS. CLOS.

BED ROOM. 10'2"x14'

BED ROOM. 7'6"x12'

PASSAGE

CLOS.

BED ROOM 12'x12.

BALCONY

ROOF.

— SECOND FLOOR. —

— SIDE. —

CLOS.

PANTRY

BED ROOM 7'x14'

KITCHEN 9'x14'

BALCONY

BED ROOM 9'x12'

LIVING ROOM 10'6"x15'6"

PARLOR. 10'6"x14'

HALL

ROOF

ROOF

SECOND FLOOR.

CLOS.

PANTRY

BED ROOM 7'x14'

KITCHEN 9'x14'

BALCONY

BED ROOM 9'x12'

LIVING ROOM 10'6"x15'6"

CLOS.

PARLOR. 14'x14'

ENTRY

PORCH.

FIRST FLOOR.

— FRONT. —

PORCH.

BED ROOM. 8'6"x10'

KITCHEN. 10'6"x12'6"

CLOS. CLOS.

BED ROOM. 9'6"x14'

PANTRY

CLOS.

LIVING ROOM. 11'6"x15'

BED ROOM. 8'6"x11'6"

BALCONY

PARLOR. 12'x13'6"

ENTRY

PORCH. FIRST FLOOR.

ROOF.

BED ROOM. 8'6"x10'

KITCHEN. 10'6"x12'6"

CLOS. CLOS.

BED ROOM. 9'6"x14'

PANTRY

CLOS.

LIVING ROOM. 11'6"x15'

BED ROOM. 8'6"x11'6"

BALCONY

PARLOR. 12'x13'6"

CLOS.

ROOF. SECOND FLOOR.

— REAR. —

— SIDE. —

DETAIL OF ORNAMENT OVER FRONT WINDOWS.

SECTION.

— SIDE. —

— FRONT. —

Design 63.—In such a varied lot of designs as are presented in this volume it would seem as if those who are looking for ideas and plans of something near their wants, would be able to come closely to beiug suited, yet our large experience in planning and designing houses for erection in all parts of the country, many of whom had our books and worked up their ideas therefrom, we have invariably found there were always changes desired, and it is a very difficult matter to find one house that is suited to two families, and this is especially the case when locations differ. We have thus re-planned some houses illustrated in our publications many times over to suit different locations, wants, and individual ideas, and we suppose it will continue to be the case that individual wants and tastes will differ, and thus give added employment to architects and those interested in building that will stimulate them to strive for something new and fresh, as each problem is solved, and thus lead eventually to the highest degree of perfection possible in the art, and it is needless to add that if the same progress is made in the future as in the past ten years the present generation will live to enjoy much of the good felt, and future posterity will only wonder at that which has passed. In small houses, where the outlay is of limited amount, the improvements will be of great benefit, as anything tending to help the rich always has a like effect on the poor, and works for the common good.

The Design 63 tells its own story, and is a nice, roomy cottage, giving six good rooms and the necessary conveniences, which cost not to exceed $1,400.

Design 64 shows a small double or semi-detached cottage which gives four good rooms on each side, and for which one chimney is made to answer. The entrances are placed as far apart as can be, and are thus private from each other. To build such houses as these requires for the two an outlay of $2,250, and would be cheap homes for the price, and give good accommodations for a gardner and coachman on a large place as well as add to the value and appearance of the same.

Design 65 shows a six-room cottage which in plan is somewhat ordinary in arrangement, yet presents a very attractive and picturesque exterior, and one that by proper treatment would be very agreeable to the eye and form a pleasing feature in the landscape ; such homes as these are sadly in need for use of working people who desire to give play to their good sense and good taste, and who would rather live in a pretty house than a poor-looking one ; such homes are generally occupied and are always appreciated. Cost about $1,650.

Design 66 gives a very simple double cottage which would not be expensive to build, such a home being plain and with few corners and little detail. Erected for $1,600.

Design 67 gives a picturesque cottage which contains some nice features, and will also give rooms in attic in addition to the six on first and second floor. This plan gives front and back stairs, and might be used by two families did occasion require, as it is often the case that small families need but three rooms or so and for some people this design may present a pecnliar interest on this account Such a cottage costs $1,900.

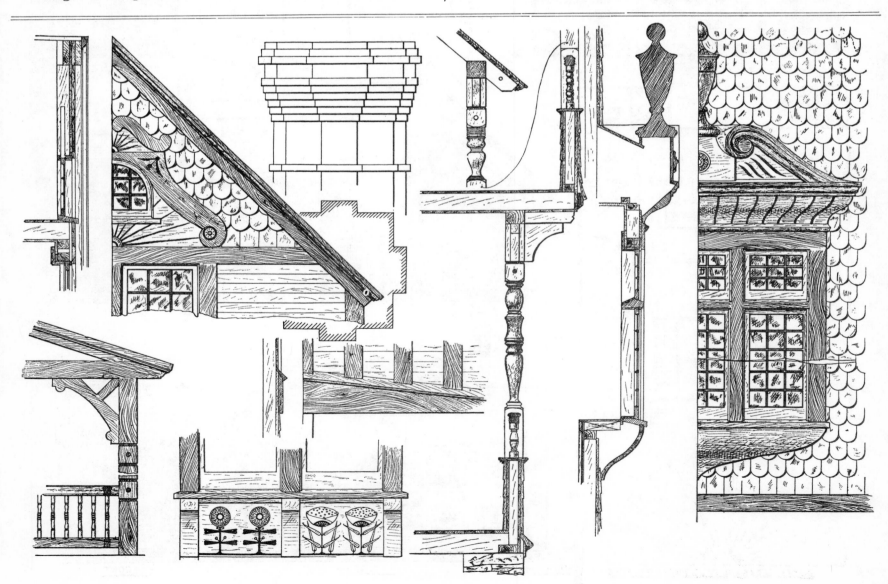

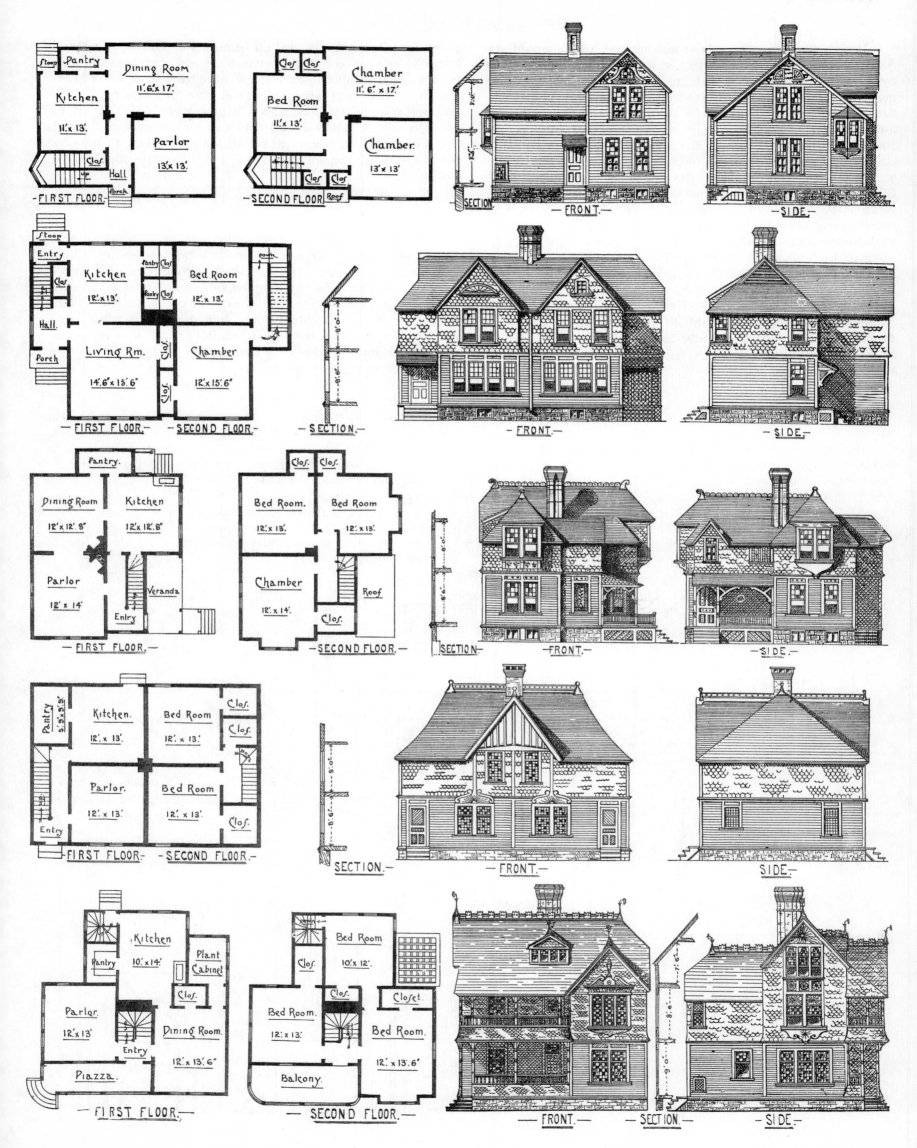

Design 63

FIRST FLOOR.
- Stoop
- Pantry
- Kitchen 11'.x 13'.
- Dining Room 11'.6".x 17'.
- Parlor 13'.x 13'.
- Clos.
- Hall up
- Porch

SECOND FLOOR.
- Clos. Clos.
- Bed Room 11'.x 13'.
- Chamber 11'.6".x 17'.
- Chamber 13'x 13'.
- Clos. Clos.
- Roof

SECTION. — FRONT. — SIDE.

Design 64

FIRST FLOOR. — SECOND FLOOR.
- Stoop
- Entry
- Clos.
- Kitchen 12'.x 13'.
- Pantry Clos.
- Pantry Clos.
- Bed Room 12'.x 13'.
- down
- Hall
- Porch
- Living Rm. 14'.6"x 15'.6"
- Clos.
- Chamber 12'.x 15'.6"
- Clos.

SECTION. — FRONT. — SIDE.

Design 65

FIRST FLOOR. — SECOND FLOOR.
- Pantry.
- Dining Room 12'x 12'.8"
- Kitchen 12'.x 18'.8"
- Bed Room 12'.x 13'.
- Bed Room 12'.x 13'.
- Clos. Clos.
- Parlor 12'.x 14'
- Veranda
- Entry
- Chamber 12'.x 14'
- Roof
- Clos.

SECTION. — FRONT. — SIDE.

Design 66

FIRST FLOOR. — SECOND FLOOR.
- Pantry 5'.9"x 9'.9"
- Kitchen 12'.x 13'.
- Bed Room 12'.x 13'.
- Clos.
- Clos.
- Parlor 12'.x 13'.
- Bed Room 12'.x 13'.
- Clos.
- Entry

SECTION. — FRONT. — SIDE.

Design 67

FIRST FLOOR. — SECOND FLOOR.
- Kitchen 10'x 14'.
- Plant Cabinet
- Pantry
- Clos.
- Bed Room 10'x 12'.
- Clos.
- Closet.
- Parlor 12'x 13'
- Dining Room 12'.x 13'.6"
- Entry
- Bed Room 12'.x 13'.
- Bed Room 12'.x 13'.6'
- Clos.
- Piazza.
- Balcony.

FRONT. — SECTION. — SIDE.

PLATE 22.

Design 68 shows a neat five-room cottage which would give nice accommodations for a workingman and his family, and which by its plan is well adapted to the needs of a large class who are generally house owners to the extent of their own homes; the first floor being planned with only two rooms, and closets, pantry and entries, etc., as shown, may strike some as wanting the third room. In this case, however, the large kitchen is intended to cover the needs of a dining-room and kitchen, and to be used as a general living room; the front room being used as a sitting-room, the back entry is large and contains a water-closet, or this might be an earth-closet, if the house is built where there are no water conveniences other than cistern, as is frequently the case where such houses as this are built; with proper care and attention the earth-closet is a very desirable convenience, and can safely be placed in connection with the house and under the same roof in a lean-to or shed, and when proper fixtures are put in and a system of ventilation arranged for, which can be done in connection with chimney flue, they are preferable to any outside fixture, and in many cases to the ordinary water-closet, as there is in the earth-closet, no complicated plumbing work to get out of order or freeze up in winter and no bills to pay for use of water, etc. The second floor gives three good rooms. Cost, $1,050.

Design 69 illustrates a nice plan for a cottage that is well adapted for a mountain home, and which would give good room and suitable conveniences for quite a large family; the hall running as it does through the house gives a good draught of air through, and placing the stairs on one side they are more private and it gives nice room for china closet under platform. The rear

porch for kitchen use is shut off from main part by a screen of lattice work; the second floor gives four good chambers and closet room; each chamber opens out upon the balcony or veranda over first floor veranda; this is also a good plan for a Southern house, and well adapted to Florida for a winter home, our experience being that the house well suited to a summer mountain home in the Adirondacks, is also good for winter in Florida. Cost $2,500, with right management and in a good locality for obtaining materials.

Design 70 illustrates another popular plan for a mountain or Southern cottage, giving good rooms and conveniences and plenty of veranda room; there is room for three bed-rooms on second floor, and leave the hall open to the veranda over front entrance, this house is in finish, etc., about same as the preceding design. Cost, about $1,700; this does not include any foundation other than the necessary posts set firmly in the ground to support all work above, and the necessary foundations for chimneys.

Design 71 gives a style of house suitable for summer use, the living hall being the main room, and communicating as it does with the two chambers on second floor, it is very desirable; the dining-room is retired and very well arranged for privacy, the portiere between it and the hall being all that is necessary to close it during meal times or when needed. The cottage-like appearance of this house makes it appropriate for many places, and the cost of erection at $1,400 makes it a desirable plan generally.

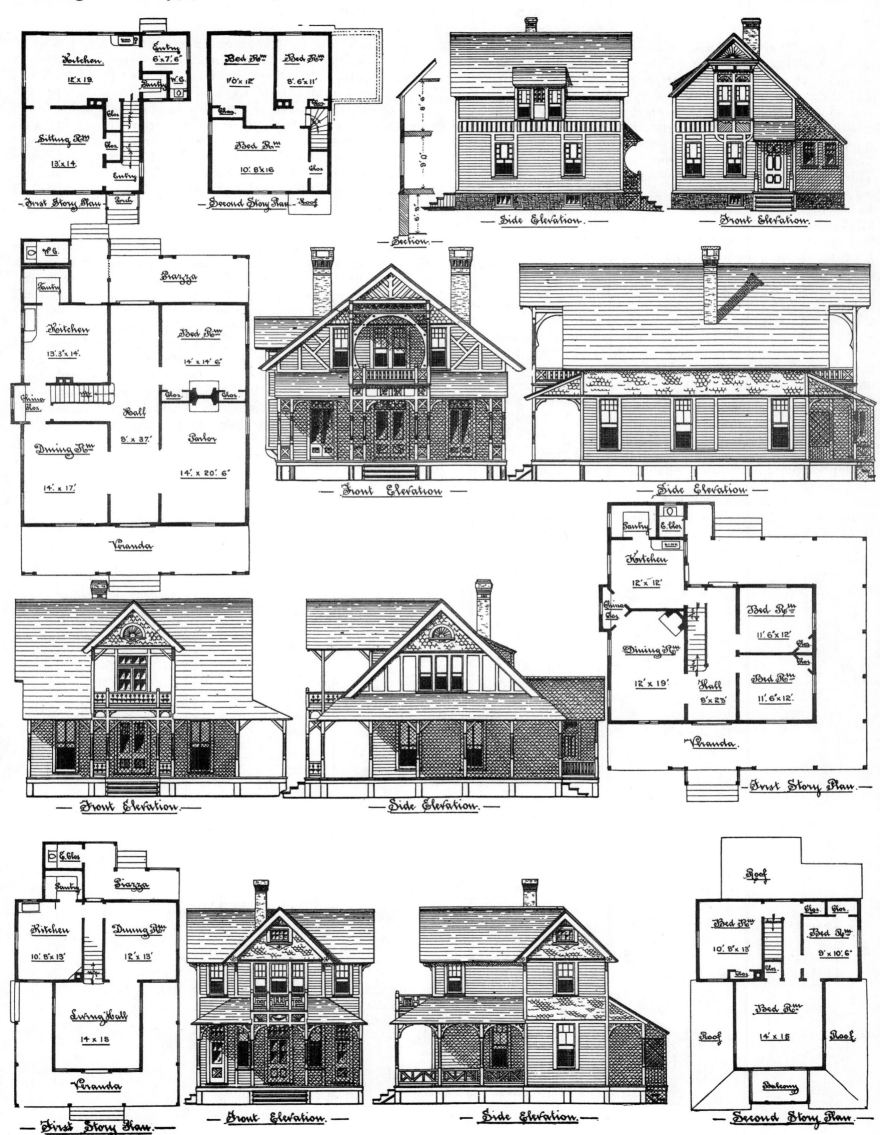

Design 68:
— First Story Plan —   — Second Story Plan —   — Section —   — Side Elevation —   — Front Elevation —

Kitchen 12'x19.   Entry 6'x7'6.   Pantry   W.C.   Sitting Rm 13'x14.   Entry   Porch

Bed Rm 17'x12'   Bed Rm 8'6 x11'   Bed Rm 10'8 x16   Roof

Design 69:
W.C.   Pantry   Piazza   Kitchen 13'3"x14'.   Bed Rm 14'x14'6'.   China Clos.   Hall 8'x37'.   Dining Rm 14'x17'.   Parlor 14'x20'6'.   Veranda

— Front Elevation —   — Side Elevation —

— Front Elevation —   — Side Elevation —

Design 70:
Pantry   C. Clos.   Kitchen 12'x12'   China Clos.   Dining Rm 12'x19'   Hall 8'x23'   Bed Rm 11'6"x12'   Bed Rm 11'6"x12'.   Veranda   — First Story Plan —

Design 71:
C. Clos.   Pantry   Piazza   Kitchen 10'8"x13'   Dining Rm 12'x13'   Living Hall 14'x18   Veranda   — First Story Plan —

— Front Elevation —   — Side Elevation —

Roof   Bed Rm 10'8"x13'   Clos.   Clos.   Bed Rm 9'x10'6'   Bed Rm 14'x18   Roof   Roof   Balcony   — Second Story Plan —

PALLISER'S NEW COTTAGE HOMES AND DETAILS.

PLATE 23.

Design 72 gives us an illustration of a semi-detatched pair of cottages, giving four rooms on the first floor and three on the second. The first-story walls are designed to be faced with brick, and the second of frame, shingled, with the exception of part of the sides, which is of frame and finished with a paneled face, the panels being formed with plaster and painted, which has become a popular way of doing some pieces of work, and which gives a good contrast with the adjoining work when properly treated. This is a repetition of old methods of construction, specimens of which are very plentiful in England, many of which are two hundred years old, the frame-work there being mostly of oak, filled in with brick and plastered between, showing the face of the timbers, the common method of treatment being to whitewash the plaster and paint the woodwork black, which is very effective and looks well from a distance. Still the combination of black and white is not what we would advise for such work, preferring buff and bronze-green or buff and red, or several other combinations which would be acceptable, in good taste, and in harmony with the general design. Unless where the immediate surroundings are such that it is necessary to build in this way, it is rarely the case that a semi-detached house would be built of materials other than wood; still it is policy to build well and good in all cases, and at times to gratify even a little pride and strive for something a little better than usual and different from that of the neighbors. Such pride means progress and improvement at all turns, and results in the cultivation of public taste which cannot help but be felt in the long run. Cost $4,500.

Design 73 gives us a delightful and convenient cottage in stone for first story and timber and plaster for second story, with tile or shingle-hanging for gables. The stone walls are intended to be laid up with rock-face stone in irregular Ashlar work, the joints being tucked in with colored mortar to match the stone or give a suitable contrast with same. The roofs would look best if of red tile ; they might be of red slate, or even good shingle painted or stained red ; interior wood-work in natural woods. Such houses always look well built on grounds appropriately laid out, and with suitable background and trees surrounding same would be a very agreeable home to live in, and is a good house for a young couple to start houskeeping in, and one that it would not be expensive to furnish. Cost $3,600.

Design 74 illustrates a very nice brick and wood cottage, the principal feature of which is "ye hall" on first floor, which makes a general living-room, it being parlor, library, sitting-room and hall combined ; the large fire-place by the stairs, with seat built in, makes a cosy nook ; the sliding doors between hall and dining-room gives a fine lengthy room, and opens up the whole house to good advantage. The back stairs are well located and convenient from either kitchen or dining-room, and the cellar is reached by stairs under same by either of two last rooms mentioned. Second floor has three good rooms, bath-room and two good balconies, the front one of which could be enclosed and another bed-room obtained. Such a house as this costs $3,500.

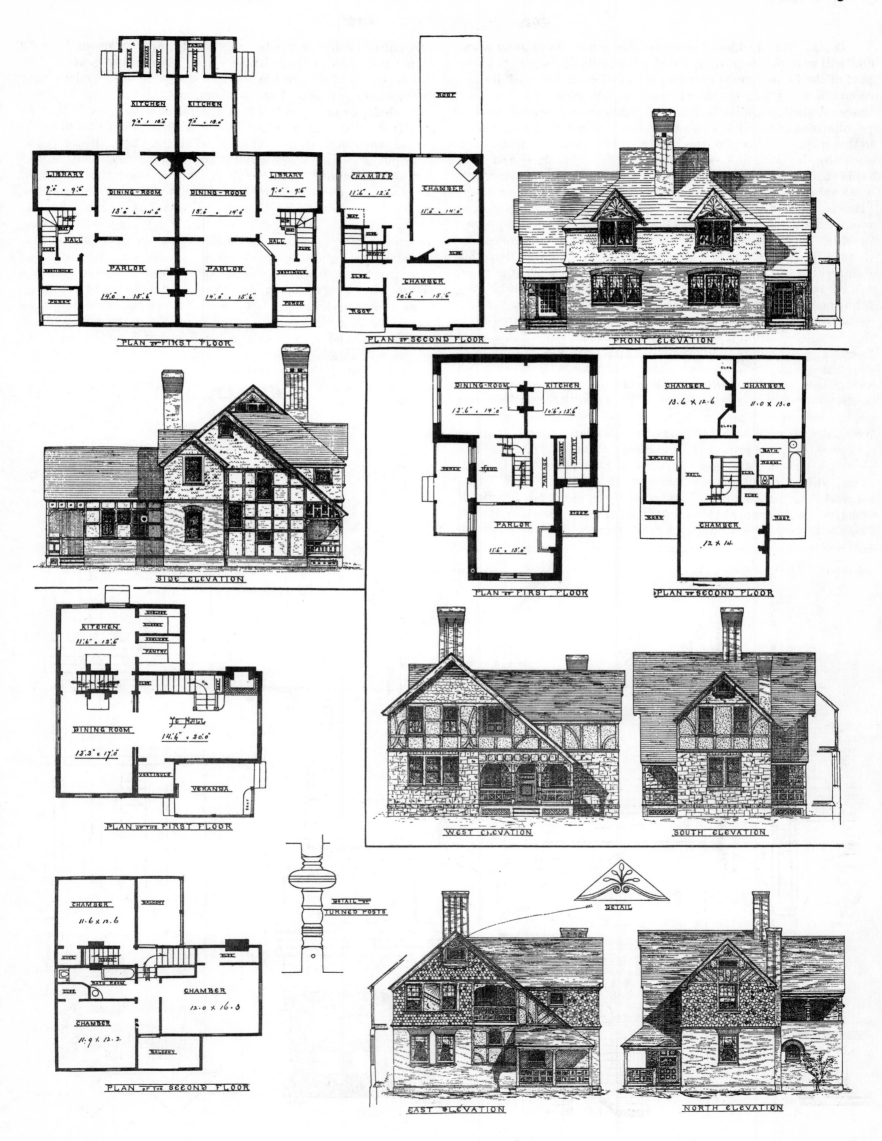

PLAN OF FIRST FLOOR

PLAN OF SECOND FLOOR

FRONT ELEVATION

SIDE ELEVATION

PLAN OF FIRST FLOOR

PLAN OF SECOND FLOOR

PLAN OF THE FIRST FLOOR

WEST ELEVATION

SOUTH ELEVATION

DETAIL OF TURNED POSTS

PLAN OF THE SECOND FLOOR

DETAIL

EAST ELEVATION

NORTH ELEVATION

PLATE 24.

Design 75 is decidedly a house for some one of good taste, and will suit the requirements of a hill-side lot where the rear part of the house would give ample room for kitchen and dining-room offices on the basement floor, which, although not at all times desirable under certain circumstances, owing to the peculiarities of site it is almost necessary to utilize the basement in this way. In this plan the basement is reached from the floor above by the back hall, which contains the back-stairs and connects to all parts of the house. The kitchen contains the sink and wash-tubs. The range is intended for brick set, the jambs and fire-place being built to suit the same. The dining-room is a generous room, with good connections to the kitchen through passage-way in which is placed two good closets for general use in connection therewith. There is also a separate door from the hall to this room which is a great convenience, as the two doors to the room can be used without interfering with each other, as might happen if but one door were used. The other parts of the basement give ample room for fuel, furnace and general storage. The first-floor hall is entered from the front porch, and is a large room well lighted, and contains the main stairs and a fire-place, and communicates with the three rooms and back hall on this floor. The two main rooms are large, and when thrown together make very desirable parlors. A toilet room is placed in the back hall and contains closet and bowl, and the bed-room on this floor, connecting as it does with both halls, makes a desirable room for use as a library, or other uses than as marked. The second floor has three large rooms, and there is room in the attic for two or three more, which would answer for servants' use, the attic being reached from back stairs. The first story is designed for brick construction, and would look best in good red pressed brick with stone sills, etc. The upper part is of frame with plaster panels.

The entire design is treated vigorously, and is strong in good points and features that will wear well. And in the general style and make-up of this design we trust many of our readers may find something that will please them, and if it happens to please as a whole, or even with slight alterations, we hope it may be strictly carried out, as when it is, it will be a credit to all concerned when built right. This is what may be called a good example of modern work without any of the nonsensical features and gew-gaws so often met with in the so-called houses of Queen Anne style, many of which are as foreign to their pretensions of style as it is possible for them to be. And as it has been the custom lately for some architects to call everything Queen Anne, for want of a better name, we must excuse many mistakes that have been made, as it really would be impossible to give any name to a large number of the designs made unless they were honestly called, what they are in reality, "American Vernacular," as they come nearer to what might be termed an American style than anything else, being the results of the needs of each case and the materials at hand with which to combine and form the construction as well as the cost or amount to be expended, which has to be largely taken into account and has had great effect upon the formation of a style for general use. Cost about $5,500.

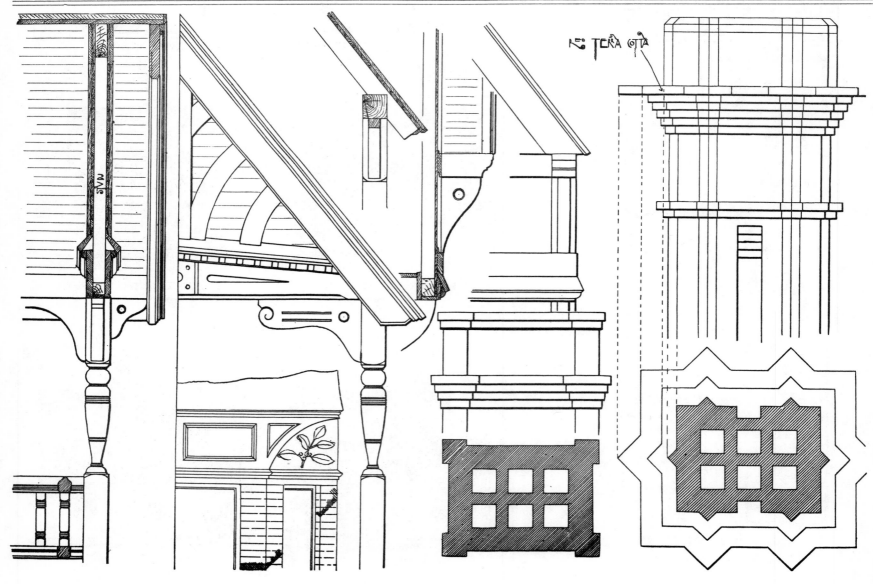

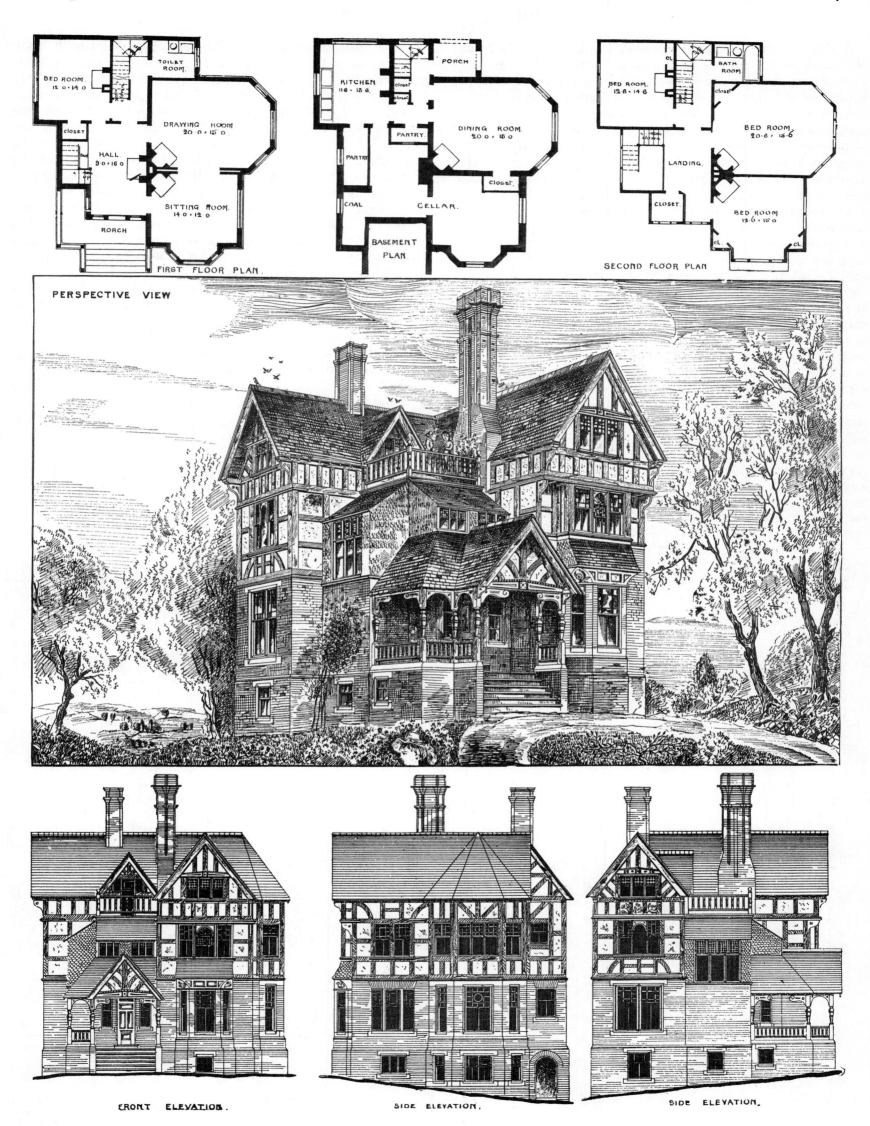

BED ROOM
12 0 · 14 0

TOILET
ROOM.

closet

DRAWING ROOM
20 0 · 15 0

HALL
9 0 · 16 0

SITTING ROOM.
14 0 · 12 0

PORCH

FIRST FLOOR PLAN.

KITCHEN
11 6 · 13 6

closet

PORCH

PANTRY.

DINING ROOM.
20 0 · 15 0

PANTRY

CLOSET

COAL

CELLAR.

BASEMENT
PLAN.

cl

BATH
ROOM

BED ROOM.
12 6 · 14 6

closet

UP

DOWN

LANDING.

BED ROOM
20 6 · 15 6

CLOSET

BED ROOM
12 6 · 15 0

cl.

cl.

SECOND FLOOR PLAN

PERSPECTIVE VIEW

FRONT ELEVATION.

SIDE ELEVATION.

SIDE ELEVATION.

Design 76.—Invariably the house that in plan gives the broadest front view and most number of rooms looking to the street will present a better appearance than if of the same number of rooms so planned as to give only one room and front door to the street; hence a broad house is preferable to a deep one when the size of the site will allow of same, and it is generally the case that a broad house will work up in nicer shape and proportion than a narrow one, and look much larger than it really is; and for country homes we like to get the main entrance on the broad side when possible on the above account; also another feature, which is no small one to be considered in the erection of a small house, is the advantages to be derived from its general shape and adaptability to increased needs and enlargement in the future when the purse or family is increased in accordance with same. We have met with a great many cases where, having planned and built houses just to suit present needs and funds, not taking into account the fact that any more room would ever be needed, it has, in such cases, been a hard study to know just how and where to build on, to do it in any way for convenience in internal arrangement and external appearance, and this especially on a narrow house, while on a wide house additions can be made that will always harmonize with the general design and with less outlay by reason of the advantages derived from the shape and ease of adding thereto, and it is well in most cases to look a little to the future in building homes, especially when building to suit young people. The design here shown is a good house for a small family, and is capable of being added to at some future time so as to make quite a large house. The first story is of brick, second story shingled or tiled, roofs slated or tiled; erected in a nice manner with all conveniences at a cost of $3,350.

Design 77 gives us a very nice plan of a cottage with about same room and cost as the last one, and which is nicely adapted to the needs of a small family with a view to future enlargement. The conservatory is a very pretty feature, and being large and roomy, gives as it were almost another room on the first floor. This house is only one and a half story high, yet is very well proportioned and looks very well when executed. One of the principal parts of a building, and which have much to do with the successful appearance thereof are the chimneys, and there is certainly a great deal of character given to a house by the chimneys. Many good designs are spoilt by their being too low, small, or not in proportion to the general size and shape of the whole mass, it being too often the case that chimneys are simply treated as necessary evils, and anything that answers to carry away and get rid of smoke is considered ample, and no further thought given to the matter. Again, many who are planning houses have one peculiar style of chimney; and we know of cases where a certain style chimney has been made to answer for a $25,000 mansion, a school house, stable, cottage, and several buildings, all totally different from each other in use, style and cost, that common sense would say needed chimneys as different as possible from each other, and which it was the duty of the designer to study and obtain, had a plain duty been done.

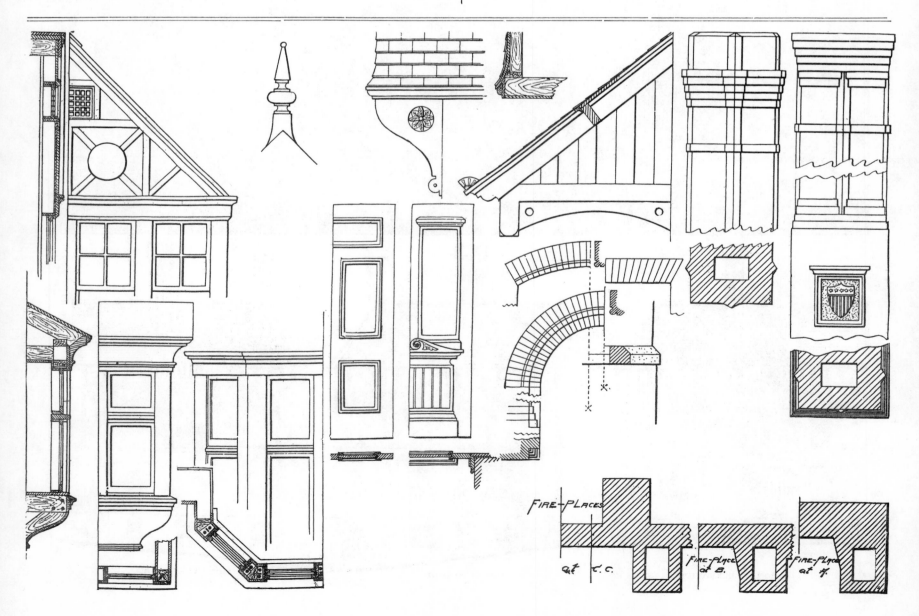

FIRE-PLACES

at C. C.   FIRE-PLACE at B.   FIRE-PLACE at A.

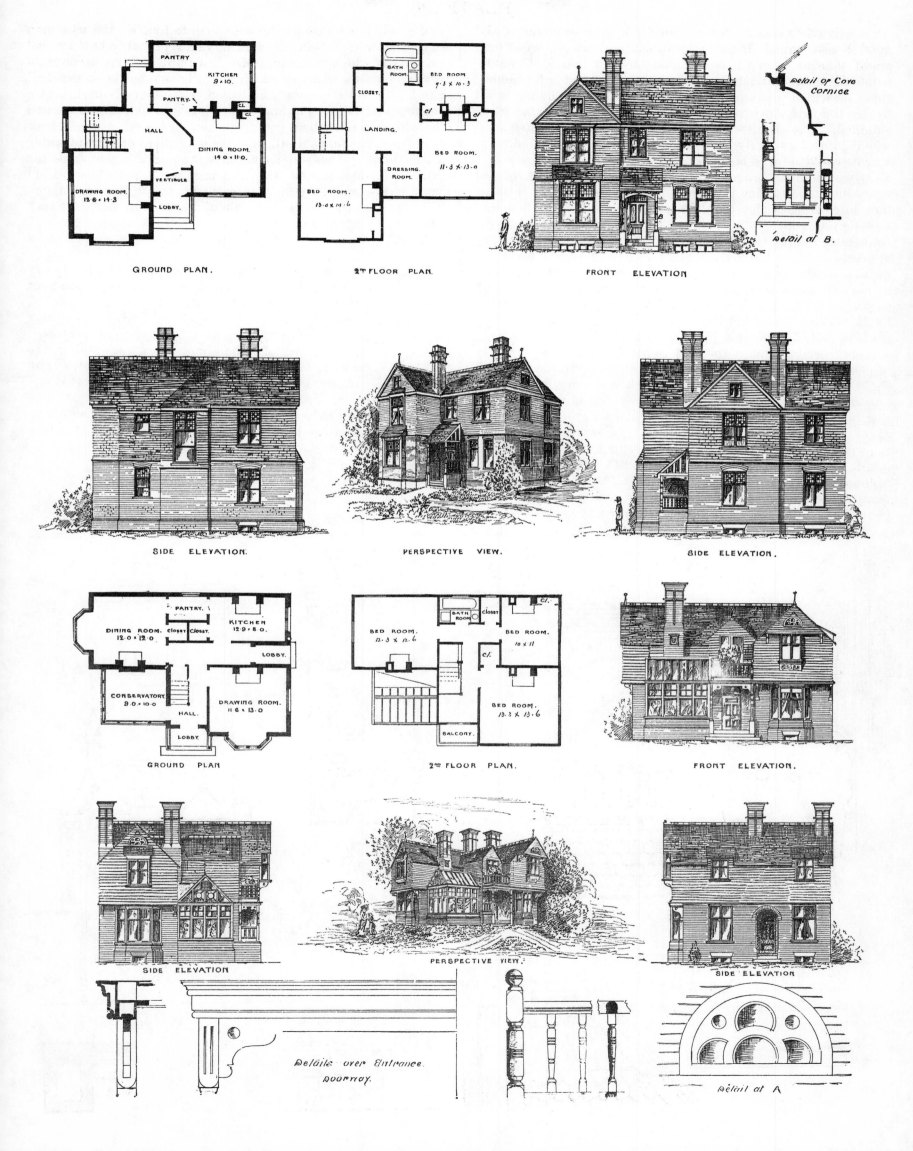

GROUND PLAN.　　　2ᴺᴰ FLOOR PLAN.　　　FRONT ELEVATION

Detail of Cove Cornice

Detail at B.

SIDE ELEVATION.　　　PERSPECTIVE VIEW.　　　SIDE ELEVATION.

GROUND PLAN　　　2ᴺᴰ FLOOR PLAN.　　　FRONT ELEVATION.

SIDE ELEVATION　　　PERSPECTIVE VIEW.　　　SIDE ELEVATION

Details over Entrance Doorway.

Detail at A

Design **78** gives a roomy plan for a very economical and good house, suited to many locations, and which, with such slight changes as might be necessary to suit individual wants, would fill the requirements of many who are longing for homes, some of which perhaps will never come. This house is all frame, the first story being clapboarded and the second story shingled. The details are very simple and expressive, and when painted properly give character to the general design, which would always be interesting to study, there being constantly something new or overlooked before that is of interest every time the building is passed. And it is simply astonishing how interesting a nice building is to the studious public, and how they will stop, talk, look and become intensely bent on the features contained thereon almost every time they pass by. To appreciate this it is only necessary to live in such a house for awhile, as the writer has done, and watch from the windows inside the different expressions of the passers-by, as they would see the house for the first time or find new things to wonder at. Such houses as these are also always marketable and will sell readily, where a common-place design will hardly be noticed; and it is certainly policy to build something that will be likely to please others as well as be suitable for the wants and necessities of the party building, even though necessary to go a little outside the strict requirements of the case. 'Tis an old saying, that fools build houses and wise men live in them. This may apply in some few cases, but in a general way it is wrong, as the wise man will invariably build his own house, and live in it too, it being far more interesting to live in a house that has been planned and built after the owner's ideas and that has grown from castles in the air to a castle in reality than in other people's cast-off ideas or failures, as is often the case when the fool builds the house for the wise man to live in; the wise man in the latter case being he who buys for probably half its real value that which some one else has built and on account of various reasons, many of which might have often been avoided, has failed to carry out that which was planned for his own comfort and enjoyment, and hence it is sacrificed and sold, and the wise man (so-called) gets the benefit of the other man's loss. It is few who cannot recall such cases as this; and in planning a new house, it may be sometimes a good thing to have the fable of the foolish and wise men in mind to help keep within your means and to help you profit by the failures of others. This design costs somewhere about $4,400 and makes a very pleasant country home.

Design **79** illustrates a simple cottage, one and a half story high, with front and back stairs, and four rooms on each floor and bath-room, and is a very neat suburban house, well suited to a fifty-foot lot, and can be built at a cost of $2,500, or it may be made to cost $3,000, according to finish, it being a very easy matter to vary the cost of a building, by a variation in the general character of the detail and quality of materials used, by fully twenty per cent., and in some cases the management will vary as much more. So it can safely be said in many cases that in some hands prices may vary as much as forty per cent. from what could actually be done if taken hold of right, and the bottom price reached and adhered to.

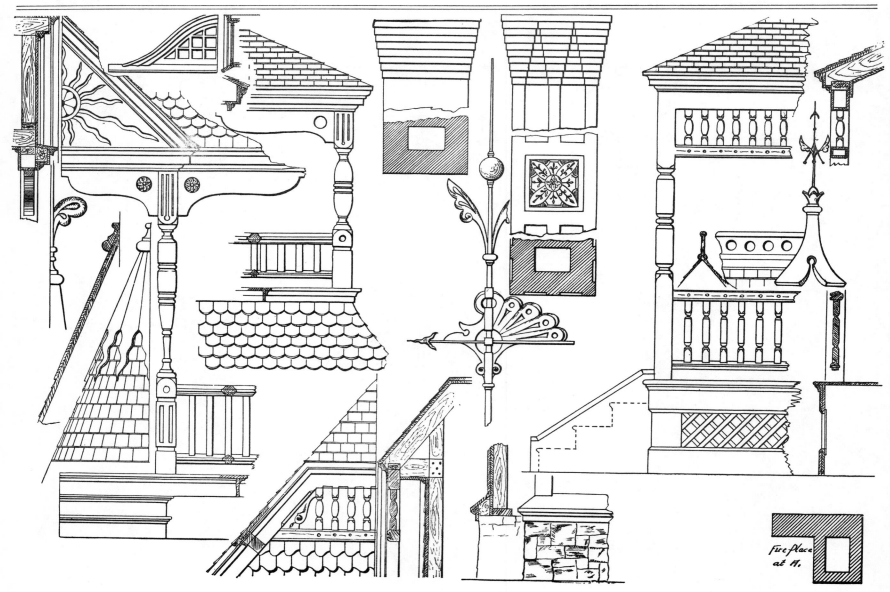

Fire Place at A.

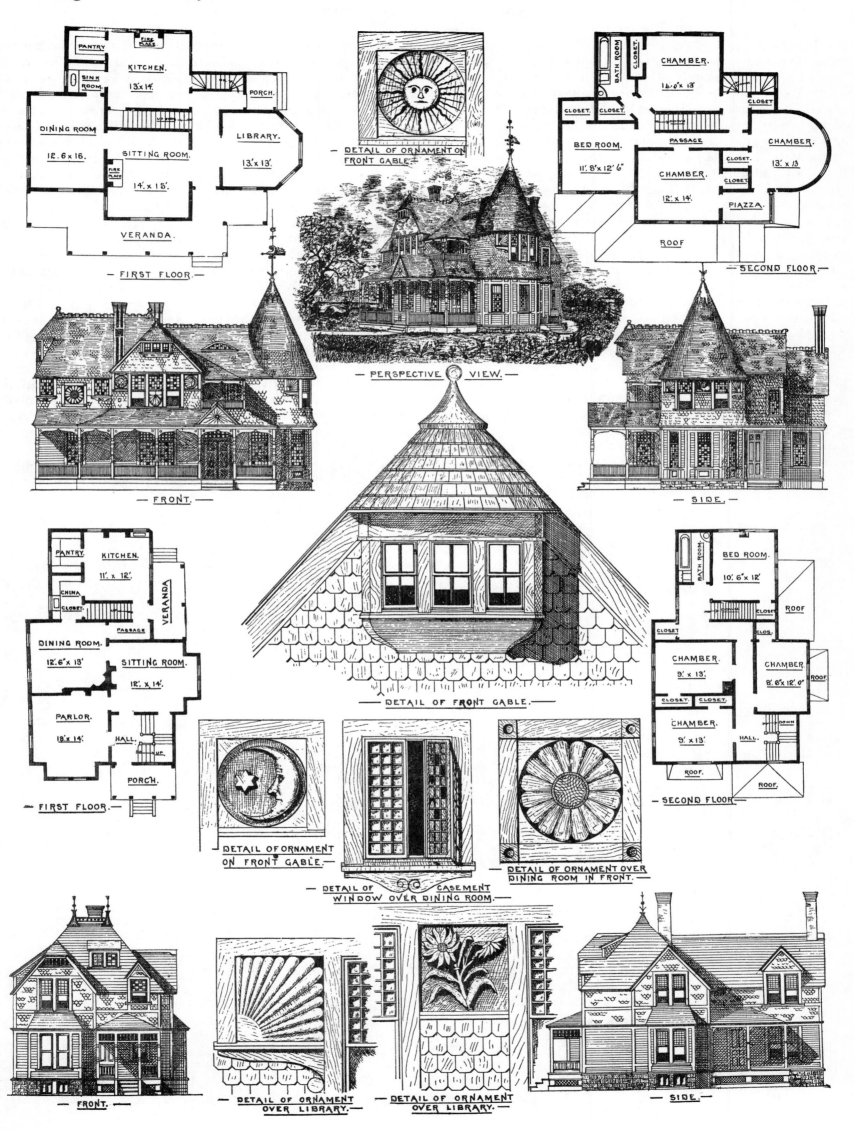

PANTRY

SINK ROOM.

FIRE PLACE

KITCHEN.
13'x 14'

PORCH.

DINING ROOM
12.6 x 16.

SITTING ROOM.
14'. x 15'.

FIRE PLACE

LIBRARY.
13'. x 13'.

VERANDA.

— FIRST FLOOR. —

— DETAIL OF ORNAMENT ON FRONT GABLE.

BATH ROOM

CLOSET

CHAMBER.
14.'0"x 13'.

CLOSET.

CLOSET.   CLOSET.

CLOSET.

BED ROOM.
11'. 8'x 12' 6"

PASSAGE

CHAMBER.
13'. x 13

CHAMBER.
12'. x 14'.

CLOSET.

CLOSET.

PIAZZA.

ROOF.

— SECOND FLOOR. —

— PERSPECTIVE VIEW. —

— FRONT. —

— SIDE. —

PANTRY.

KITCHEN.
11'. x 12'.

CHINA CLOSET.

PASSAGE

DINING ROOM.
12.'6"x 13'

SITTING ROOM.
12'. x 14'.

VERANDA

PARLOR.
18'. x 14'.

HALL.

UP.

PORCH.

— FIRST FLOOR. —

BATH ROOM

BED ROOM.
10'. 6'x 12'

ROOF

CLOSET

CLOS.

CHAMBER.
9'. x 13'.

CHAMBER.
8'. 6'x 12'. 0".

ROOF

CLOSET.   CLOSET.

DOWN

CHAMBER.
9'. x 13'.

HALL.

ROOF.

ROOF.

— SECOND FLOOR. —

— DETAIL OF FRONT GABLE. —

— DETAIL OF ORNAMENT ON FRONT GABLE. —

— DETAIL OF CASEMENT WINDOW OVER DINING ROOM. —

— DETAIL OF ORNAMENT OVER DINING ROOM IN FRONT. —

— FRONT. —

— DETAIL OF ORNAMENT OVER LIBRARY. —

— DETAIL OF ORNAMENT OVER LIBRARY. —

— SIDE. —

PALLISER'S NEW COTTAGE HOMES AND DETAILS.

PLATE 27.

Design 80 gives us a two story frame house, with good rooms and the necessary conveniences in connection therewith, and which gives some good points and features that may be studied with profit. The first floor is nicely arranged, having the two largest rooms connected by sliding doors. The absence of any large veranda on front is marked, the porch being arranged to give the necessary covering and shelter to the entrance, and the large vestibule, with its hard-wood or tile floor, with an ample mat at the front door, would presage a comfort and welcome within; while the glass partition and door to conservatory on left and the art glass on each side of the inner door between main hall and vestibule will lend a charm in which nature and art combine to vie with each other in giving a welcome and render the vestibule light, cheerful and mellow with the grace and freedom of nature, the conservatory being really a part of the vestibule. The main hall is large and roomy, and so arranged that it communicates to all parts of the house. The stairs ascend by easy stages to the floor above and are lighted by a large stained-glass window, which does duty for both first and second-floor halls and gives a desirable light; and the many-tinted hues of the cathedral glass in this window impart a tone that pervades the whole and shows that good taste is as much within the reach of modest as of those of more liberal incomes, it being possible to obtain the effect in glass by a proper combination of colors at very little expense. A hard-wood floor in the main hall and two principal rooms, with a nice, plain finish of oak, ash or cherry, would be the appropriate thing, and with nice rugs and a border worked in around the floors of cherry and oak would be a fine contrast and make a finish to the wall sides where the rugs do not cover. Even a plain floor is preferable to the ordinary carpet covering of the whole floor. The room on first floor marked bed-room will do for library or office-room as well as for sleeping-room, and makes a nice one for many purposes. Back hall and stairs are well located, and the back stairs can be carried up into the attic floor, where the necessary rooms can be finished for servants' use. This is an ordinary frame-house, with diagonal sheathing placed on frame and covered with rosin-sized sheathing-felt under clap-boards and all exterior finish. The greatest of care ought at all times to be exercised in the putting on of this paper, so as to be sure and have it cover all parts, and especially to come under the joints of all work, so as to insure tightness at the most important places. We have seen many houses built where they made out to paper it, but failed to put any strips under the casings, corner-boards or other constructive parts; hence the paper, being only put on under clap-boards, did not lap at corners, and when the wood shrinks, as it very often does, there is a crack up the full length of the casing, where the wind and rain can find entrance through and between the joints of sheathing, and the result is cold drafts and a cold house generally, and the most critical parts of a house are left exposed; this may be termed one of the reasons why in driving storms so many leaks occur around the edges of window-frames and such places. The simplicity of this design commends itself, and to those needing a house of this size we trust it may be more than suggestive, and that it may meet with the approval of many who are looking for a home. Such a house, nicely carried out, costs in the vicinity of $4,800, which includes furnace, range, laundry under the kitchen, and all necessary improvements.

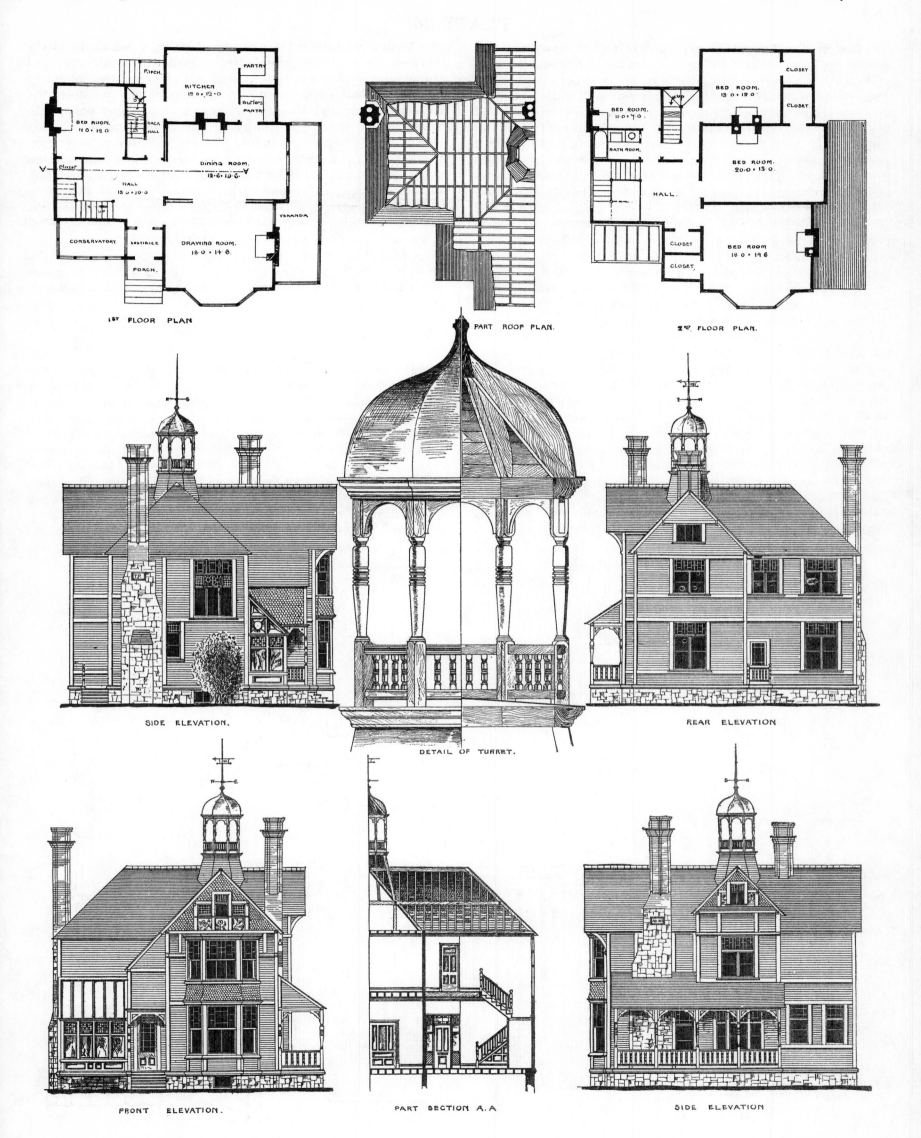

1ST FLOOR PLAN

PART ROOF PLAN.

2ND FLOOR PLAN.

SIDE ELEVATION.

DETAIL OF TURRET.

REAR ELEVATION

FRONT ELEVATION.

PART SECTION A.A

SIDE ELEVATION

Design 81.—Among the general wants of those owning and occupying houses there is a large class whose first need is room, and all other requirements have to be made subordinate to this great need, to accomplish which the question of halls and large open staircases have in a great measure to be dispensed with, and the maximum of room obtained with the minimum of outlay in construction ; and as it is desirable at all times to make the best possible appearance and to work in such features as will enhance the value and architectural beauty of a design, care and judgment has to be used in putting the parts together to secure the most satisfactory results as above. Such a design as this is well adapted to the country and would not be a bad plan for a farm house, there being good room below for general storage purposes, milk room, etc., the cellar being reached very conveniently from either the kitchen or dining-room under the main stairs. The parlor and dining-room being connected together makes these two rooms very desirable, as either of them can be entered from the front entry ; the latter being large and roomy and well lighted, and the front porch coming, as it does, within the main building and the roof of the same covering the whole, makes a picturesque finish and simplified the construction, leaving the roofs less liable to leakage than would be the case did one roof come in below the other, as is usually the way. The room over the porch can also be floored over and is useful for storage, there being no attic room above the second story. The stairs going up from the dining-room are convenient, this being the living room of the house and will be the most used of any. The four good bed-rooms and closets on the second floor give good accommodations for a large family. This design, with a shingle roof and the work faithfully and honestly executed, costs about $2,000 ; in some locations a little less.

Design 82 illustrates a six-room cottage, which is nicely adapted for use as a gate lodge or gardener's residence, and would be an ornament to any well kept place. One chimney answers for all rooms, and it consisting of but one flue, the expense is light and the greatest degree of economy possible in mason work practised. Many people think that a chimney consisting of one flue 8x8 in size will only do for one stove connection ; this is a mistaken idea, as we have known cases where as many as six stoves, all connected with their pipes into a flue of this size, and all worked well. In building such flues provision ought always to be made at the bottom for cleaning out the dust and dirt, else it may stop up in time by filling up solid above the lowest connection and make trouble. Usually too little care is taken in arranging the cleaning-out holes at the base of tight flues, such matters being generally left to guess work and the mason building the chimneys. Such a house as this costs $1,475.

Design 83 represents a nice little cottage, only one story high sensible and simple in plan and in outline, easy to construct, and would fit many locations where the amount of room here shown is needed and the house must be kept down low. Such houses as these are needed on almost every place of two or three acres where the accommodations provided in the stable for the use of coachman are not sufficient for the gardener's use as well. This design would be good to build in any out-of-the-way corner, would never be noticeable, and when it was seen would always suggest comfort and happiness by its general shape and surroundings. Cost of this cottage is $900.

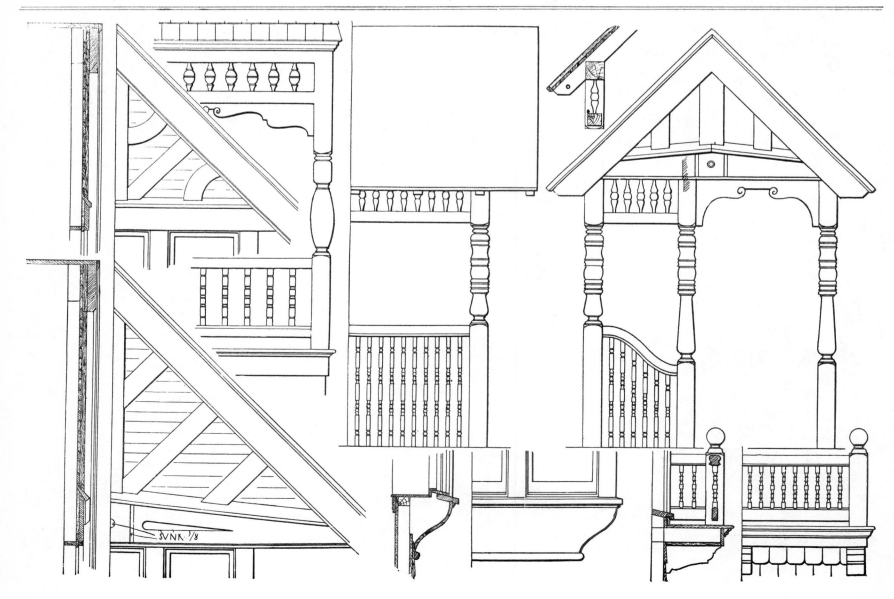

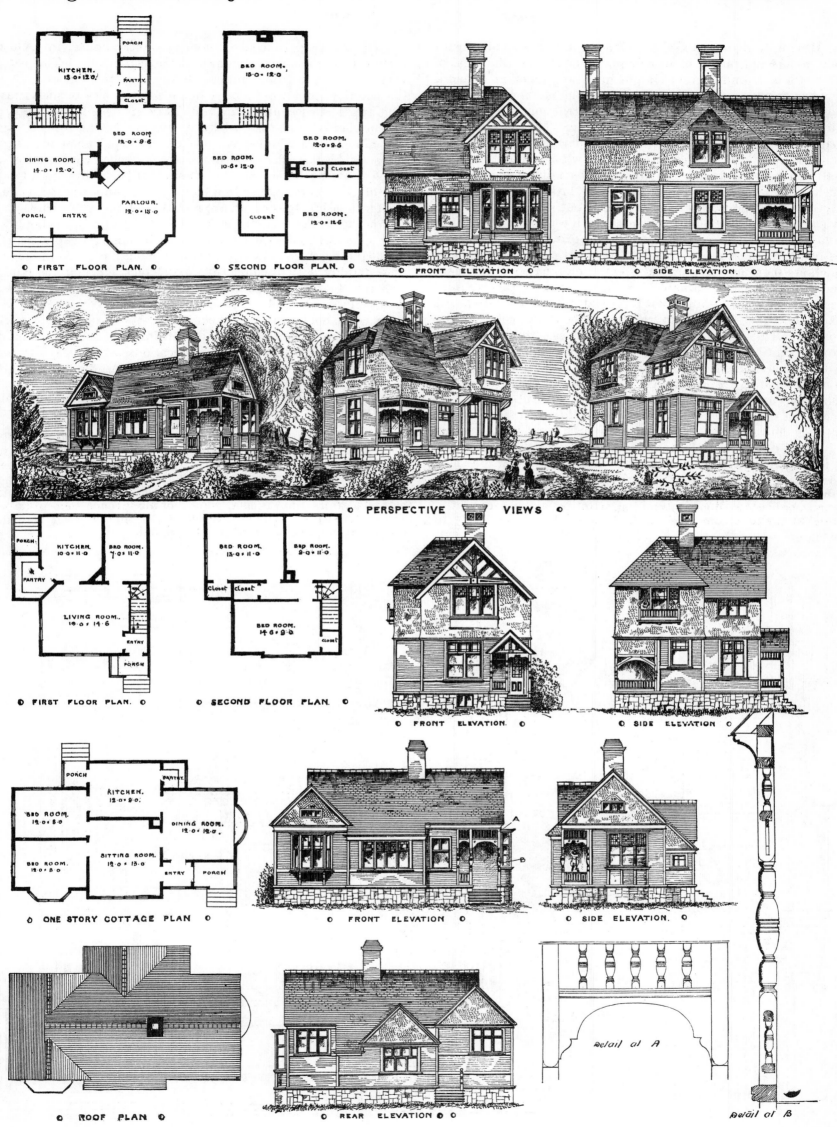

○ FIRST FLOOR PLAN. ○

KITCHEN.
13·0 × 12·0.
PORCH
PANTRY
Closet
BED ROOM.
12·0 × 9·6
DINING ROOM.
14·0 × 12·0.
PARLOUR.
12·0 × 15·0
PORCH. ENTRY.

○ SECOND FLOOR PLAN. ○

BED ROOM.
13·0 × 12·0
BED ROOM.
10·6 × 12·0
BED ROOM.
12·0 × 9·6
Closet Closet
Closet
BED ROOM.
12·0 × 12·6

○ FRONT ELEVATION ○

○ SIDE ELEVATION. ○

○ PERSPECTIVE VIEWS ○

○ FIRST FLOOR PLAN. ○

PORCH.
KITCHEN.
10·0 × 11·0
BED ROOM.
7·0 × 11·0
PANTRY
LIVING ROOM.
19·0 × 14·6
ENTRY.
PORCH.

○ SECOND FLOOR PLAN. ○

BED ROOM.
13·0 × 11·0
BED ROOM.
9·0 × 11·0
Closet Closet
BED ROOM.
14·6 × 9·0
Closet

○ FRONT ELEVATION. ○

○ SIDE ELEVATION ○

○ ONE STORY COTTAGE PLAN ○

PORCH
KITCHEN.
12·0 × 9·0.
PANTRY
BED ROOM.
12·0 × 8·0.
DINING ROOM.
12·0 × 12·0.
BED ROOM.
12·0 × 8·0
SITTING ROOM.
12·0 × 13·0
ENTRY PORCH

○ FRONT ELEVATION ○

A
B

○ SIDE ELEVATION. ○

Detail at A

Detail at B

○ ROOF PLAN ○

○ REAR ELEVATION ○ ○

PALLISER'S NEW COTTAGE HOMES AND DETAILS.

PLATE 29

Design 84 gives an excellent plan for a country house with good rooms and plenty of attic room. The style is after that of 100 years ago, and is very simple in arrangement and detail. This has become a very popular style in the last few years, and is capable of the most economical construction, giving good solid results for the least outlay possible. The first story is clap-boarded, and the walls of upper part are shingled, the finish being placed on sheathing boards which are put on diagonally on frame and with felt paper between these and exterior finish, thus, making a warm and wind proof house in every respect. Such houses as this, with the front door in the centre, give a better appearance than a plan with the same amount of room, having the entrance on one corner, or to side of front, and are better adapted to general country use than narrow houses which are more for city and suburban use on narrow lots where the ground is more valuable. Such houses as this require plenty of room, and should not be crowded together into small spaces, but have large plots and stand about the centre of the grounds. This then allows for nice drives, walks, and the proper planting of trees, which latter should never be so close to the house as to throw a shadow on the same before 2 P. M. Many fine places are spoilt just by this, and we have known of instances where property has been sold cheap, and at a loss, on account of the dampness and gloominess of the situation, which has been entirely cured by the new owner having sense enough to just cut down the trees and bushes too near the house, and let in the genial sunshine. There is space for three or four nice bedrooms in the attic, which can be finished in an inexpensive manner, making a good ten-room house, which, with a suitable furnace, to heat two floors, plumbing, painting, and other requirements to make a complete and first class job. Costs $4,300 to $4,500.

Design 85 gives a nice, roomy, country house, in style of architecture, somewhat similar to the preceding one. The plan is very well arranged and adapted to the requirements of a life in the country, and would be a home for the city business man who appreciates country life enough to give his family the full benefit thereof, and take whatever comfort he can from it himself, after hours of business. With the rapid growth of such cities as New York, and the enormous rents charged for as much room as herein shown, whether it be in the high-toned flat, or the poorer house in a block there cannot help but be a change tending toward an appreciation of the suburbs, as it is cheaper to live twenty-five miles from the city, pay about $100 a year commutation fares to and from business, keep a man, a horse and carriage, and have ground enough to keep the man's time employed in raising fruit, vegetables, etc., for the family use, and the time is certainly coming when the careful business man will avail himself of the benefits that can be had from having a permanent home in the country. Such homes as this will help play an important part in settling the question, and no doubt there are many convenient locations within easy distance of the city where a number of such houses would rent readily and for fully 10 per cent. on the investment. A careful inspection of the plan is all that is needed to explain the good points. The attic will supply about four good sleeping rooms, making a good 12-room house, the appearance of which no one desiring a quiet dignified and pleasant home need be ashamed to live in. Such a house ought to be painted a warm chocolate color for body, trimmed with bronze green, sash white, blinds red, roofs painted red, the chimneys being laid up with red brick. Such a house finished inside in white pine, natural wood, nice mantels, stairs, etc., of ash, good hot air furnace well plumbed and water supply, will cost about $5,000 under good management and in an economical neighborhood.

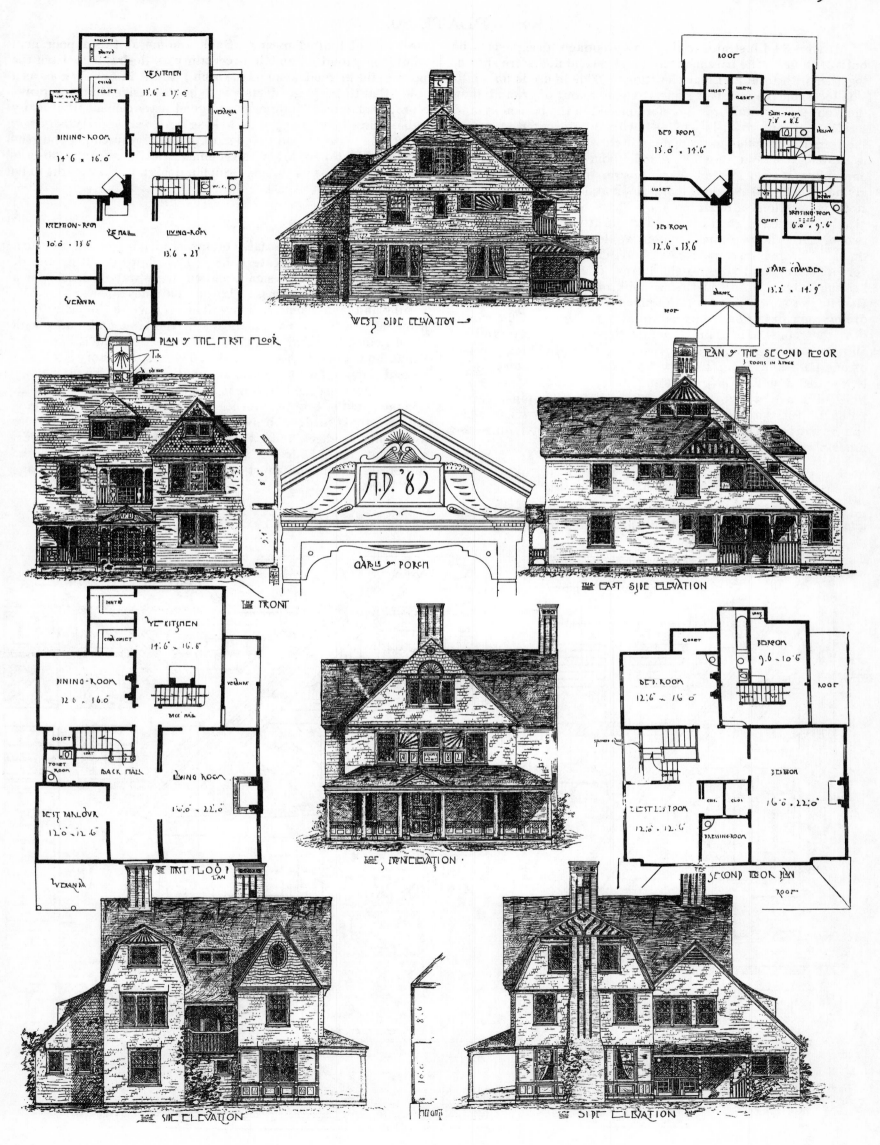

PLAN OF THE FIRST FLOOR

WEST SIDE ELEVATION

PLAN OF THE SECOND FLOOR
3 ROOMS IN ATTIC

THE FRONT

GABLE OF PORCH
A.D. '82

THE EAST SIDE ELEVATION

FIRST FLOOR PLAN

FRONT ELEVATION

SECOND FLOOR PLAN

SIDE ELEVATION

SIDE ELEVATION

Design 86 illustrates a very cosey cottage, designed to be built of stone. The basement, first and second floors are shown, together with front and rear elevations. This house is for a hillside location, the rear being one story more out of ground than the front. The kitchen is therefore placed in the basement, and service to dining-room is obtained with dumb-waiter placed in the corner of kitchen, and opens into closet on first floor, which is well lighted and provides ample room for china, etc. The one chimney is so located that it answers for the entire house, giving two fire-places on the first floor and ample facilities for stove connections at other points. The second floor gives four nice bedrooms and good closets, and the attic provides room for two or three more rooms, which would be very desirable at times. The general appearance of this design when executed is very effective, and adds to the beauty of the landscape. For heating such a house as this a Jackson grate, a Fire on the Hearth heater, or Boynton fire-place heater, set in either the dining-room or parlor fire-place would be the thing. This would heat the rooms above and the first floor very nicely, and an abundance of pure warm air be insured. The plumbing consists of one sink and pump to draw the water from a cistern which is supplied from the roof gutters and leaders. The first floor to be finished in ash, with neat mantels; the balance in pine, plainly painted. Such a house costs, in a neighborhood where stone can be had cheaply and where the same does not require too much labor in working, about $2,800.

Design 87 illustrates a convenient six room cottage, nicely adapted for a variety of situations, and suited to the wants of a mechanic of limited means. Such a home as this a poor man would be proud of, and it is certainly as desirable to have the poor build in good taste as the rich; and it in nowise goes as a rule—that to be in good taste is to be expensive, but it requires a proper amount of judgment and good management (that many ladies know how to apply in making up a neat and stylish dress at little expense) to lead to the most practical result and obtain the best combination of art with economy, and in all ways observe the proper fitness of things. Such a design as this ought to be executed at about $2,200.

Design 88 gives a small cottage, well adapted for use as a gardener's cottage or gate lodge. The plan is well arranged, and is roomy, though small, and in every way desirable for a large variety of locations. The one chimney answers for all; pantry and sink-room are convenient. Down to the cellar from kitchen, to attic over the main stairs, the sink and pump with cistern constitute that part of the service. A cellar is under the whole house, the cellar being 6 feet 6 inches, first story 8 feet and second story 7 feet 6 inches, all in the clear. The first story (body color) painted a bright red; second story, old gold, trimmed with bronze green. Paint the sash white, blinds maroon, roofs medium brown; and this combination produces a very happy effect, and gives a harmonious and artistic appearance that would be lost if not properly painted, as color is the life of all design and must not be lost sight of. This cottage cost $1,200.

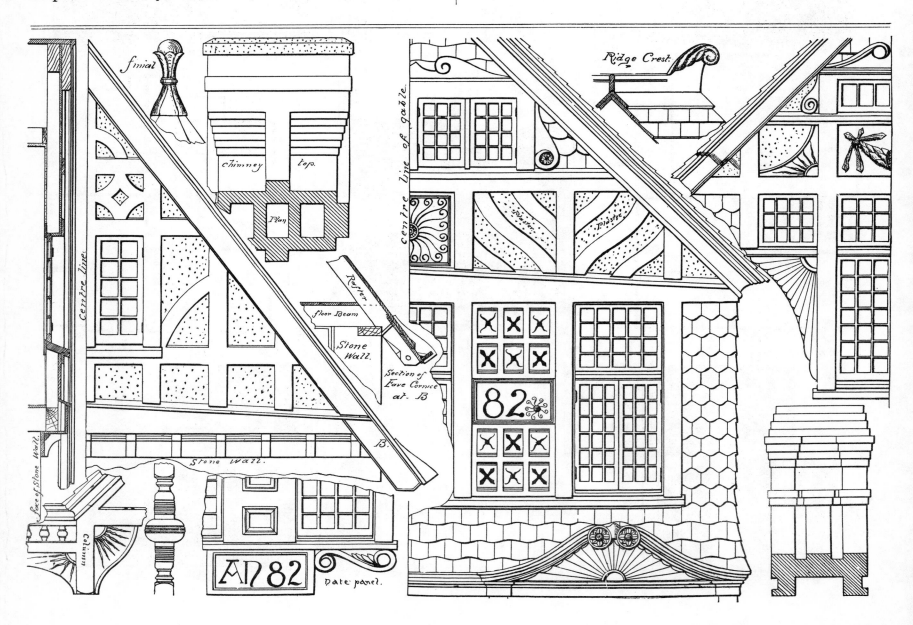

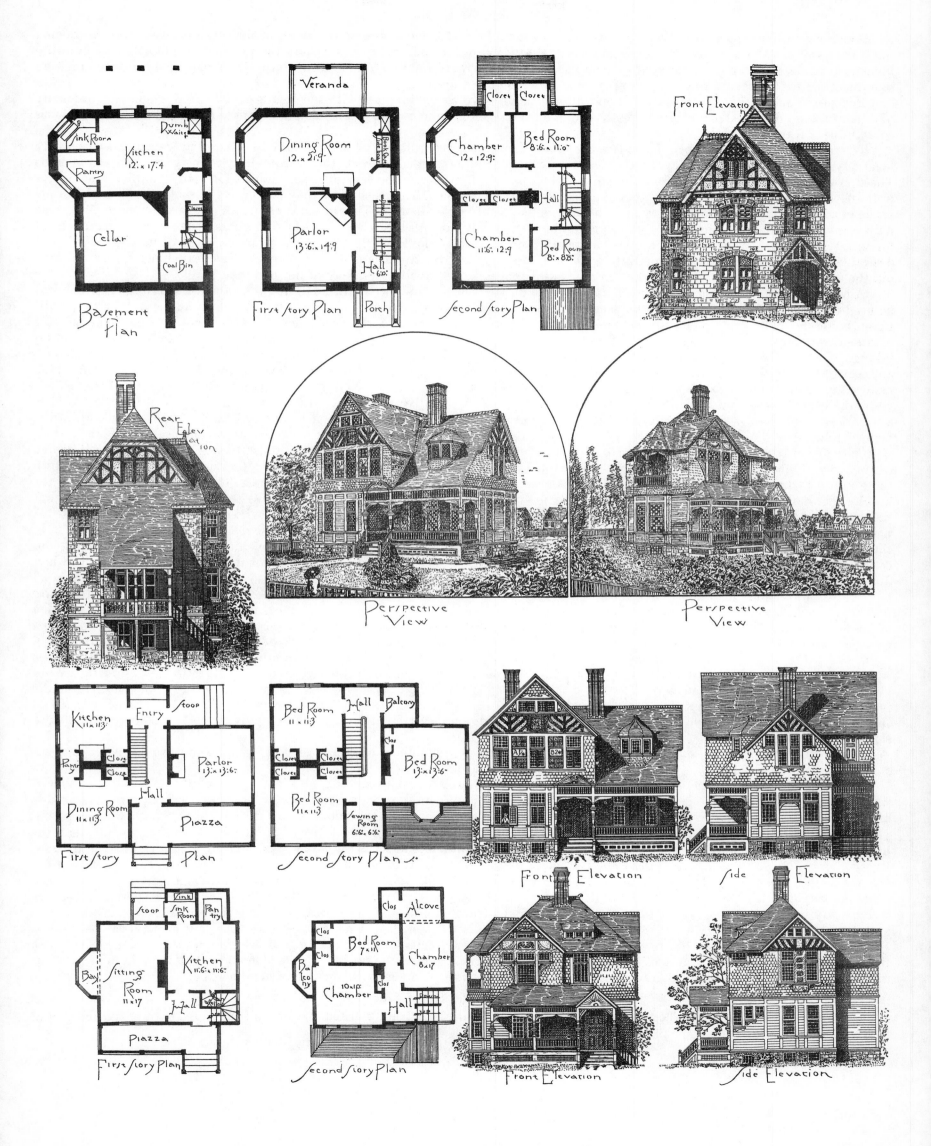

Sink Room
Dumb Waiter
Kitchen 12 x 17:4
Pantry
Closet
Cellar
Coal Bin
Basement Plan

Veranda
Dining Room 12 x 21:9
Book Case
Parlor 13:6 x 14:9
Hall 6:0
First Story Plan
Porch

Closet Closet
Chamber 12 x 12:9
Closet Closet
Hall
Chamber 11:6 x 12:9
Bed Room 8:6 x 11:0
Bed Room 8 x 8:3
Second Story Plan

Front Elevation

Rear Elevation

Perspective View

Perspective View

Kitchen 11 x 11:3
Entry
Stoop
Pantry
Clos Clos
Parlor 13 x 13:6
Hall
Dining Room 11 x 11:3
Piazza
First Story Plan

Bed Room 11 x 11:3
Hall
Balcony
Closet Closet Closet
Bed Room 11 x 11:3
Bed Room 13 x 13:6
Sewing Room 6:6 x 6:6
Second Story Plan

Front Elevation

Side Elevation

Stoop
Sink Room
Pantry
Bay
Sitting Room 11 x 17
Kitchen 11:6 x 11:6
Hall
Piazza
First Story Plan

Clos Alcove
Clos
Balcony
Bed Room 7 x 11
Chamber 8 x 17
Chamber 10 x 10
Clos
Hall
Second Story Plan

Front Elevation

Side Elevation

PALLISER'S NEW COTTAGE HOMES AND DETAILS.

PLATE 31 AND 32.

American business men and others possessing considerable wealth have been in the habit of making the city house the home ; but during the past ten or twelve years the tide has again turned to the country, and it is now the proper thing to make the country house the home, and for the family to occupy it, if not all the year round—from Spring until Christmas, and for three or four months of the indoor season to live in an apartment or hotel in the city.

Designs 89 and 90 give the floor plans, elevations, perspective views, together with the details of the exterior points of interest, of a pair of semi-detached country houses, having a driveway built in common ; practically these are two distinct houses, and each contain the features of a single house.

To build two such houses together as are here shown, a location peculiarly adapted would be necessary to insure success. A level plateau overlooking a valley, or the ocean, and commanding a good view of the surrounding country, would be the best. These are houses that would suit many people for summer use, and would be very desirable homes for many families who might well afford to own their own summer homes, and could keep house at less cost than they could live in a hotel. There is ample space in attics to finish six or eight rooms, in each, which would give plenty of servant's rooms, trunk or spare rooms. The large halls answer for general living-rooms, and communicating as they do with the other rooms of first floors, make a good arrangement for social gatherings. The verandas are also large, and supply room enough to live out-doors as much as may be needed—a very desirable feature in houses for summer use. These houses are not by any means what can be called cheap houses, and to carry out the design as here shown, in a good and first-class manner, would involve an outlay of not less than $15,000.

A careful study of the plans with the details for the outside work, as shown, will, no doubt, give a great many ideas which can be used to good advantage, sometimes on smaller houses. The terraces in front of the verandas are a nice and novel feature, built up on boulders in the wall, and with the rail containing seat on one side and the flower shelf on the other, an excellent effect is obtained, which ever way it is seen. Sometimes the building of a country house in an artistic manner proves to be quite an undertaking. One case we have in mind where a party having bought a piece of shore property on which he started out to build a house and barn by days work, under a noted City Architect, expecting to spend about $6,000 on former, and $600 on the latter, which resulted in changes and alterations that brought the final cost of the house up to $30,000, just five times the cost originally intended, while the barn followed suit, and the $600 wound up with an outlay of $10,000. This result certainly shows that it is policy to have a well-developed plan before the job is started ; many useless expenditures would then be avoided, and in the end a more satisfactory solution of the question be arrived at. Many people start to build when the fit takes them, never taking time to study their wants or find out what a given amount will do or how much of a house can be had for a stipulated sum. The most satisfactory ending of building operations is that which is conducted and carried out without any changes or alterations, as at the final wind-up there are no fights about extras and overcharges for doing this and that, and which, in many cases, do not fairly compensate the builder for what he has done. When changes are made in contract work, the price should always be agreed upon on the spot, and paid for as soon as it is done, so as not to interfere and get mixed in with other work. If people who are building would adopt this plan, about one-half the changes usually made would be dispensed with. Another source of changes often arises from the desire of those who are having the work done to change simply because they do not like this or that when the work is in an unfinished condition, and we have often known changes made at this stage of the work which have resulted in great additional expense, and when done, the work has neither looked as well or been as good as first designed. Such houses as these should be finished in hard wood on first floors and pine for other parts, the whole being filled and finished in natural woods, the mantel-pieces. stairs and general finish designed with a special fitness for their places The general detail of the exterior work on an enlarged scale gives a good idea of the finish on the different parts of the building, and a study of the same and comparison with the design cannot but prove interesting to those who are engaged in building or thinking of doing so. The general appearance of these houses give an impression of solid, every-day comfort and an abundance of the good things required to make life pass pleasantly. When we look back and see what has been accomplished the last fifteen years in this line and anticipate by contrast what the future will bring forth, we are obliged to give up the problem and leave it for the future to decide when and how these things shall come about, and leave the future to take care of itself, busying ourselves with the present and struggling to do whatever we can towards elevating our art to the highest plain attainable with the times and means at hand, so that when future races run they may see our footprints on the sands of time.

In selecting a spot for the erection of a country house great care should be exercised to avoid plague spots or their making ; as a careless step, or one of inattention, may lead to the most disastrous results.

Early last spring the elegant mansion of one of New York's wealthiest capitalists, situated on a beautiful hill in New Jersey, was turned into a house of mourning. It had been constructed on the most approved sanitary and scientific principles. Thousands of dollars had been expended in the drainage, plumbing and ventilation. The surroundings were healthful, the air was pure, and yet an epidemic of diphtheria swept away a family of young and beautiful children. It was the theory of the physicians that the house was filled with malaria, which always invites diphtheria, and, skeptical as the father was, he instituted a rigid examination. Every closet, pipe and drain, was found to be perfect, and they were about to give up, baffled, when by accident they examined the furnace fresh-air box, and a few feet from its opening, in a neighbor's lot, they discovered a mass of putrifying garbage ! The mystery was explained. The malaria had found an entrance through the "fresh" air flue, and three loved ones perished because "somebody had blundered !" The same result was seen at Princeton College, seven students losing their lives by the faulty drainage of the college grounds. These occurrences were not "dispensations of Providence," they were the result of plain carelessness.

Life is a constant struggle for existence, and as the fittest always survives, it is the duty of every man to acquaint himself with the methods of prevention and cure of influences which would hurry him to the grave. There is much doubt nowadays as to what, for instance, causes malaria, but there is no doubt that it is the basis of the most obstinate chronic disorders.

Eratta on First Story Plan.

On the right-hand side, first-floor plan, the dining-room should have been marked **parlor**, and the room marked **parlor** should be dining-room.

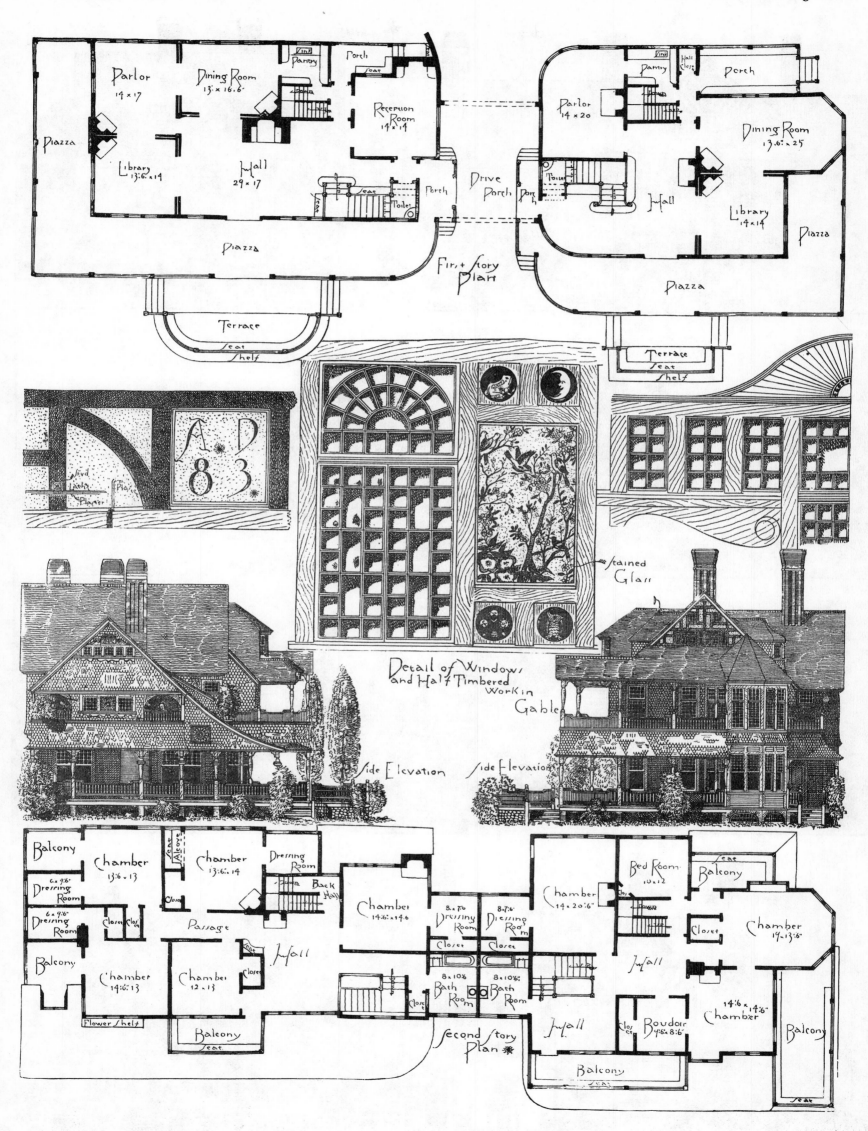

First Story Plan

Parlor 14 × 17
Dining Room 13 × 16.6
Link Pantry
Porch
Piazza
Library 13.6 × 14
Hall 29 × 17
Reception Room 14 × 14
Seat
Toilet
Porch
Terrace
Seat shelf
Drive Porch

Parlor 14 × 20
Pantry
Hall Closet
Porch
Dining Room 13.6 × 25
Toilet
Hall
Library 14 × 14
Piazza
Terrace
Seat Shelf
Piazza

A D 83

Stained Glass

Detail of Windows and Half Timbered Work in Gable

Side Elevation   Side Elevation

Second Story Plan

Balcony
Chamber 13.6 × 13
Dressing Room 6 × 9.6
Dressing Room 6 × 9.6
Closet
Alcove
Chamber 13.6 × 14
Dressing Room
Back Hall
Closet
Passage
Balcony
Chamber 14.6 × 13
Hall
Chamber 12 × 13
Closet
Seat
Flower Shelf
Balcony Seat

Chamber 14.6 × 14.6
Dressing Room 8 × 7.6
Dressing Room 8 × 7.6
Closet
Closet
Bath Room 8 × 10.6
Bath Room 8 × 10.6
Closet

Bed Room 10 × 12
Seat Balcony
Chamber 14 × 20.6
Closet
Hall
Chamber 19 × 13.6
Hall
Closet
Boudoir 4.6 × 8.6
Chamber 14.6 × 14.6
Balcony
Balcony
Seat

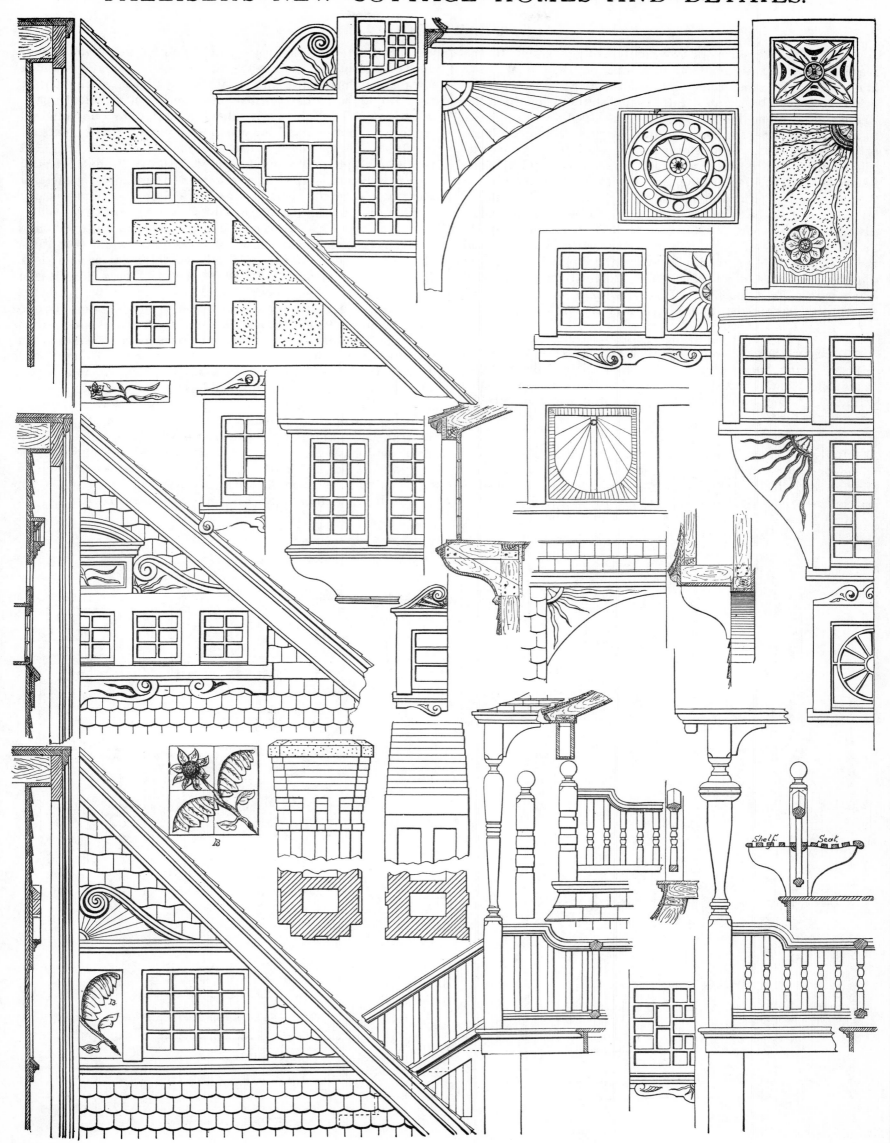

PALLISER'S NEW COTTAGE HOMES AND DETAILS.

PLATE 33.

Design 91 represents a two-family cottage suited to the requirements of two small families, one on each floor, each family using the same front door, and the rear side doors also being fixed that both can use the back stairs up to the attic. There will be room there to finish two nice rooms, thus giving to each family an extra room on third story with an abundance of attic room for general storage purposes. Such houses as these are needed in the outskirts of large towns and cities as homes for the working people, and would rent for about $16 a floor, in the New England cities. This house would require a lot not less than 35 to 40 feet front, roofs to be shingled, cellar divided into two parts. Such a house with drainage properly applied and the water run in and connected to two sinks, and the work finished in a good, plain way, and painted throughout ought to be built at a cost of $2,200. This, with land, ought to come within an expenditure of $3,000, thus making a good investment, paying about ten per cent. on the outlay.

Design 92 shows a more simple and less expensive two-family cottage, giving four rooms on each floor with ample room for two finished ones in attic. The cost of this cottage is estimated at $1,900, and ought to be built in a very complete and substantial manner for that sum.

Design 93 shows a more elaborate plan which gives ample accommodation for quite a large family on each floor and which, if built near the city of New York, would be called a French flat in preference to the more unpretentious name, "a tenement." That it might not be quite so high-toned to live in a house of this kind in a quite refined rural neighborhood con-venient of access to the city where the full benefits and enjoyments of plenty of room, pure air, genial surroundings and a few pleasant neighbors who would always be on visiting terms, as it would be to be crowded into one of the so-called apartment-houses in New York where from ten to one hundred families are housed, and for which they pay enormous rents for miserable, dark, unventilated and in many cases unlighted rooms, looking down upon squalid back yards and rears of tenement blocks. We know of some of these high-toned tenement houses in the heart of New York City that house nearly one hundred families under one roof running up ten, eleven or twelve stories high, giving groups of rooms in suites of from three to eight each, some of which do not have more than three exterior windows, and nearly all contain more or less dark rooms that rent from $800 to $3,000 a year. That this class of people are paying enormously for the privilege of living in what they no doubt think a fashionable house in a location close to their business cannot be denied, and no doubt the same people if offered double the room and conveniences in a suburban location at one-third the rent would think they were being robbed to pay such. Still, for fashion sake, they will do much, pay cheerfully and get along with all kinds of inconveniences and murmur not. We predict for these lofty tenements a large fall in rents and shall find them given up to an entire different class than at the present in a few years time, while the present incumbents will have taken up a suburban residence and will be appreciating a house by themselves. Such a design as 93 should be carried out for about $2,550 and would rent for about $20 per month for each floor, a good return on the investment.

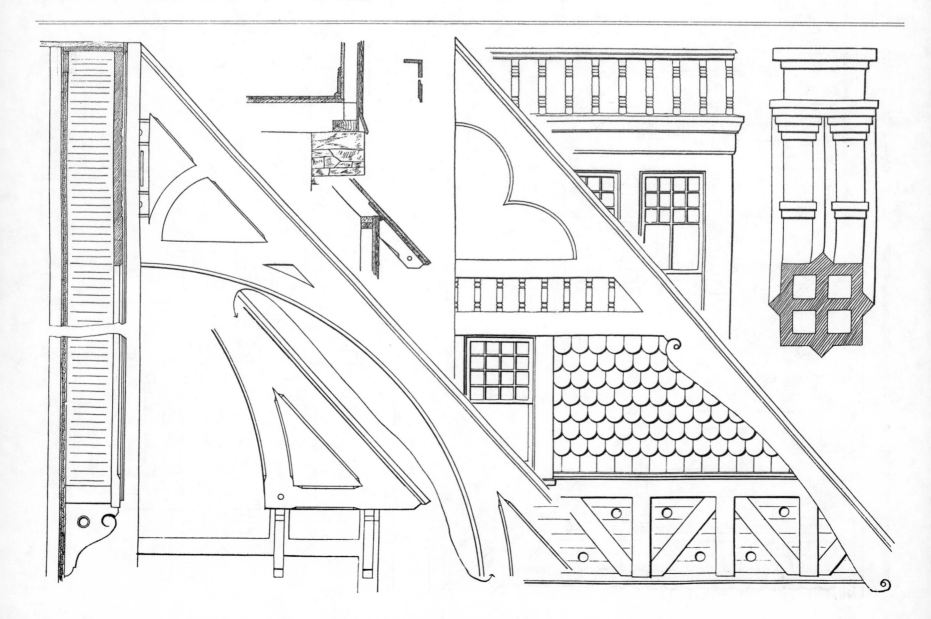

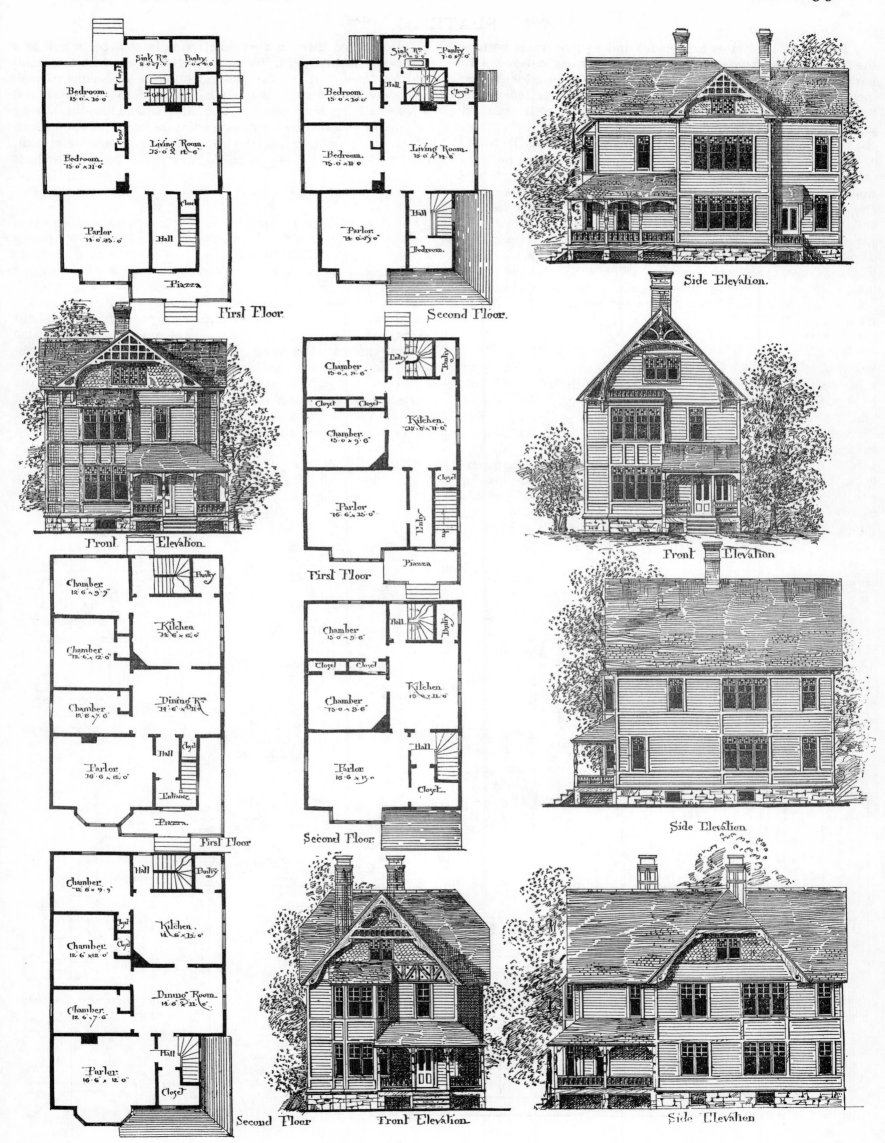

Bedroom. 15·0 × 10·0

Bedroom. 15·0 × 11·0

Sink Rm 8·0 × 7·0   Pantry 7·0 × 4·6

Living Room. 15·0 × 14·6

Parlor 14·0 × 15·0   Hall   Closet

Piazza

First Floor.

Bedroom. 15·0 × 10·0

Bedroom. 15·0 × 11·0

Sink Rm 7·0 × 6·0   Pantry 7·6 × 7·0   Hall   Closet

Living Room. 15·0 × 14·6

Parlor 14·0 × 9·0   Hall

Bedroom.

Second Floor.

Side Elevation.

Front   Elevation.

Chamber 12·6 × 9·9   Pantry

Chamber 12·6 × 12·0   Kitchen 14·6 × 12·0

Chamber 12·6 × 7·6   Dining Rm 14·6 × 11·0

Parlor 16·6 × 12·0   Hall   Clgl

Entrance

Piazza.

First Floor

Chamber 15·0 × 9·6   Entry   Pantry

Closet   Closet

Chamber 15·0 × 9·6   Kitchen 15·0 × 11·0

Closet

Parlor 16·6 × 15·0   Entry

Piazza

First Floor

Front   Elevation

Chamber 15·0 × 9·6   Hall   Pantry

Closet   Closet

Chamber 15·0 × 9·6   Kitchen 15·0 × 11·0

Parlor 16·6 × 15·0   Hall   Closet

Second Floor.

Side Elevation

Chamber 12·6 × 9·9   Hall   Pantry

Chamber 12·6 × 12·0   Clgl   Clgl   Kitchen 14·6 × 12·0

Chamber 12·6 × 7·6   Dining Room 14·6 × 11·0

Parlor 16·6 × 12·0   Hall   Closet

Second Floor

Front Elevation

Side Elevation

PALLISER'S NEW COTTAGE HOMES AND DETAILS.

PLATE 34.

Design 94 illustrates a compact and square frame cottage the frame of which is sheathed, and lower story covered with narrow clapboards, while the second story is covered with ten-inch matched and grooved boards, and the joints battened with flat three-inch battens. The plan is simple and well arranged giving the greatest amount of room for the least possible outlay. No room is here wasted in useless halls or passages, the whole arrangement is close, compact and cosey—one chimney answers for all and gives facilities for at least three stove-pipe connections—a sink, pump and cistern constitutes the improvements and conveniences in the kitchen part. For water closet, if suitable drainage and water service were convenient, it might be placed in the cellar; if not, it is better to have it at a respectful distance from the house, and then arrange it as an earth-closet which is much preferable to an ordinary privy vault; this makes a very good cottage for quite a large family and is a nice little village home, of which no one need be ashamed to live in for a cost of $1,375.

Design 95 shows a very well arranged and roomy cottage of eight rooms giving a good large living or dining-room, with back kitchen conveniences, the pantry is large, well arranged and lighted, and the stairs so placed that they are accessible from either living-room or parlor; the exterior finish is similar to the preceding design, and having a more broken surface and gable finish, would present for some localities a better appearance than that one; there being two chimneys in the design, and the exterior being more cut up and complicated, the cost is $150.00 higher than last design, or rather there is about that difference between the two plans, finish being equal.

Design 96 gives a very small simple cottage, which is a mansion compared with the ordinary New York City tenement, and for those needing the amount of room and conveniences here shown it is a study that can be looked into with profit and some small degree of pleasure. A little cottage like this is very easy to furnish and does not need a fortune in carpets and furniture, with a cellar under the whole house, a suitable cistern, pump, sink and proper drainage, this house costs to build it about $850.

Design 97 shows a study of a very tasty and neat six-room cottage presenting a very picturesque and pleasing appearance as to exterior. The front entrance hall is very roomy and is lighted by a stained-glass window; the rooms are all of good size and are desirable as to their relations to each other, and with a plain neat interior finish, water, drainage and cellar, such a home can be built under favorable circumstances for about $1,400. All the cottages shown on the plate are of the same general character and design, with variations as to size and general plan, and would all look well painted in the same style. The lower stories look best with a red body, the body of upper parts and gables having an orange buff, and the whole trimmed with bronze green, the sash to be white, and the shingle work of roofs red. These colors are very striking and appropriate in every way.

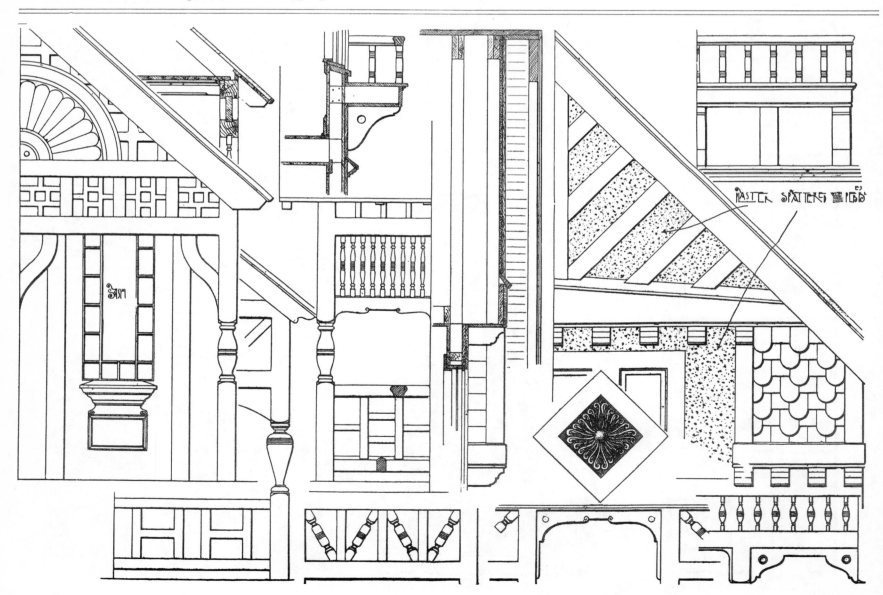

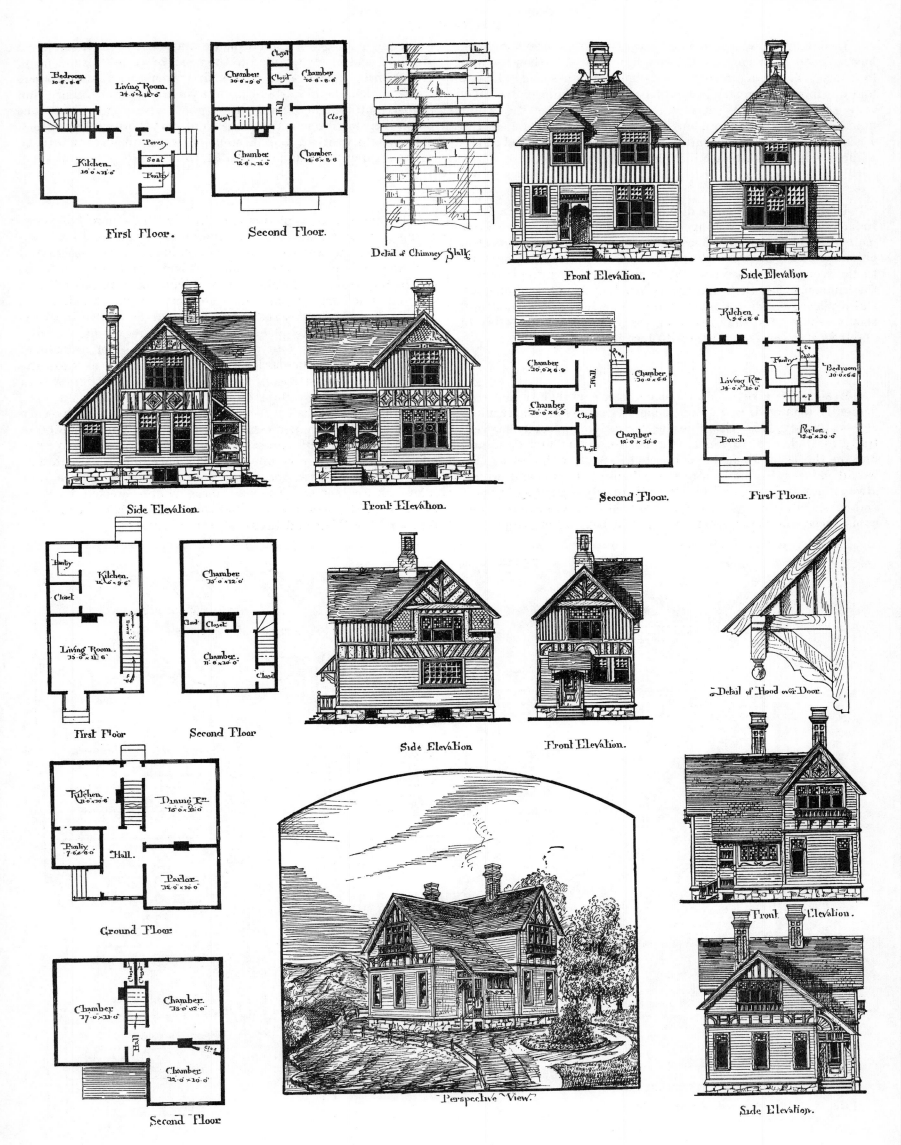

First Floor.

Second Floor.

Detail of Chimney Stalk.

Front Elevation.

Side Elevation.

Side Elevation.

Front Elevation.

Second Floor.

First Floor.

First Floor

Second Floor

Side Elevation

Front Elevation.

Detail of Hood over Door.

Ground Floor

Front Elevation.

Perspective View.

Second Floor

Side Elevation.

PALLISER'S NEW COTTAGE HOMES AND DETAILS.

PLATE 35.

Design 98 shows a rather ordinary type of six-room cottage, having good rooms and being well suited for suburban use and location. The space over the kitchen part on second floor is laid out in one room still it would be large enough for two, if it were so required. With a suitable cellar under the whole house, cistern, sink, pump and drainage, the interior finished in a neat, plain and substantial manner in pine and painted; such a house would cost about $1,200 in its erection.

D. sign 99 gives a very nice and economical plan of a seven room house which is arranged in very compact form, the three main rooms on the first floor being grouped around a central chimney which answers for all parts of the house. The stairs to the second story are reached from either the sitting-room or the kitchen, while the cellar can be reached from the kitchen by stairs placed under the main stairs. The house has good and roomy closets, and makes a very cosey home for an outlay of about $1,400, varying a little with location.

Design 100 gives a six-room cottage, very handy and conveniently arranged, with good, generous rooms and convenient closets, pantry, etc. One flue answers all purposes being centrally located, and to which two stoves on the first floor and one on the second can be connected. Such a house as this would be very suitable for a mechanic's home, and would always look welcome and inviting if properly treated as to paint and colors, and can be built for about $1,300, according to cir. cumstances, the management brought to bear upon it, etc.

Design 101 gives a good plan for a seven-room house, well arranged and nicely adapted to the needs of quite a large family, giving three good rooms on the first floor and four chambers above. There is no waste or useless room here everything being properly utilized and used up to good advantage. The front porch is a closed one making the front part thoroughly comfortable in cold weather, and in summer, when opened up will be equal to an open veranda. Cost $1,475.

Design 102 is a picturesque little cottage home of seven rooms suitable for the residence of almost any of America's citizens desiring to keep up with modern ideas in the design and building of homes. Cost $1,600. This design can be reversed, can be improved by the addition of a bath room on second floor without much trouble, and in other ways its value enhanced; and, in fact, all the designs in this book can be treated in different ways to suit people's various ideas, requirements, site, depth of pocket, etc., etc. And to make a correct estimate of cost to suit any particular location it is necessary to know the exact circumstances, cost of materials, labor, etc., together with the complete specifications as to improvements, finishes, etc., to be included, as it is a fact that the cost of a house can very easily be varied fifty per cent. or more, according to method of construction, cost of materials finishes adopted and improvements applied, and very often the difference in cost of materials and labor between two localities varies one hundred per cent. or more—as for instance, some of these houses erected in Nova Scotia for $600, would cost in Massachusetts $1,500 and in other States of the West and South $1,000 to $1,200.

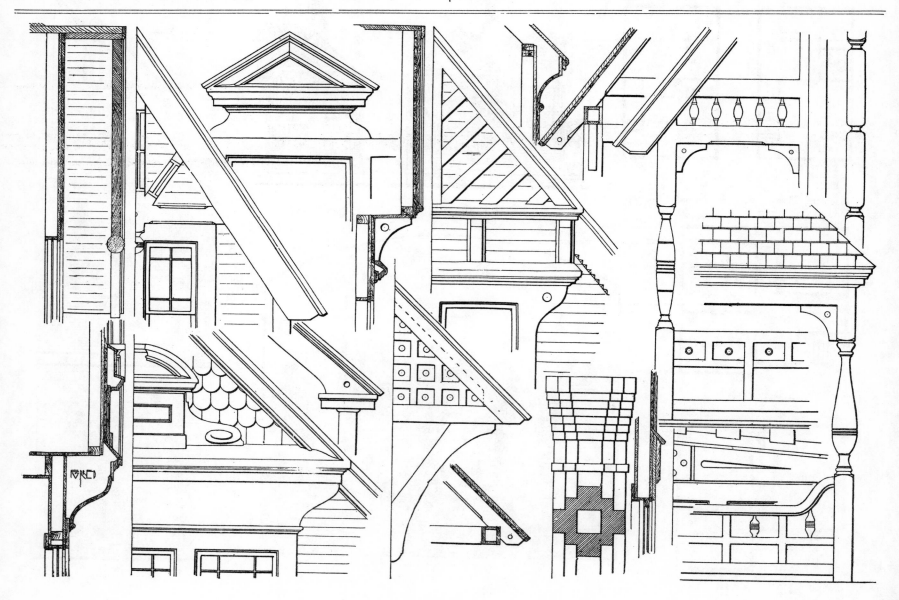

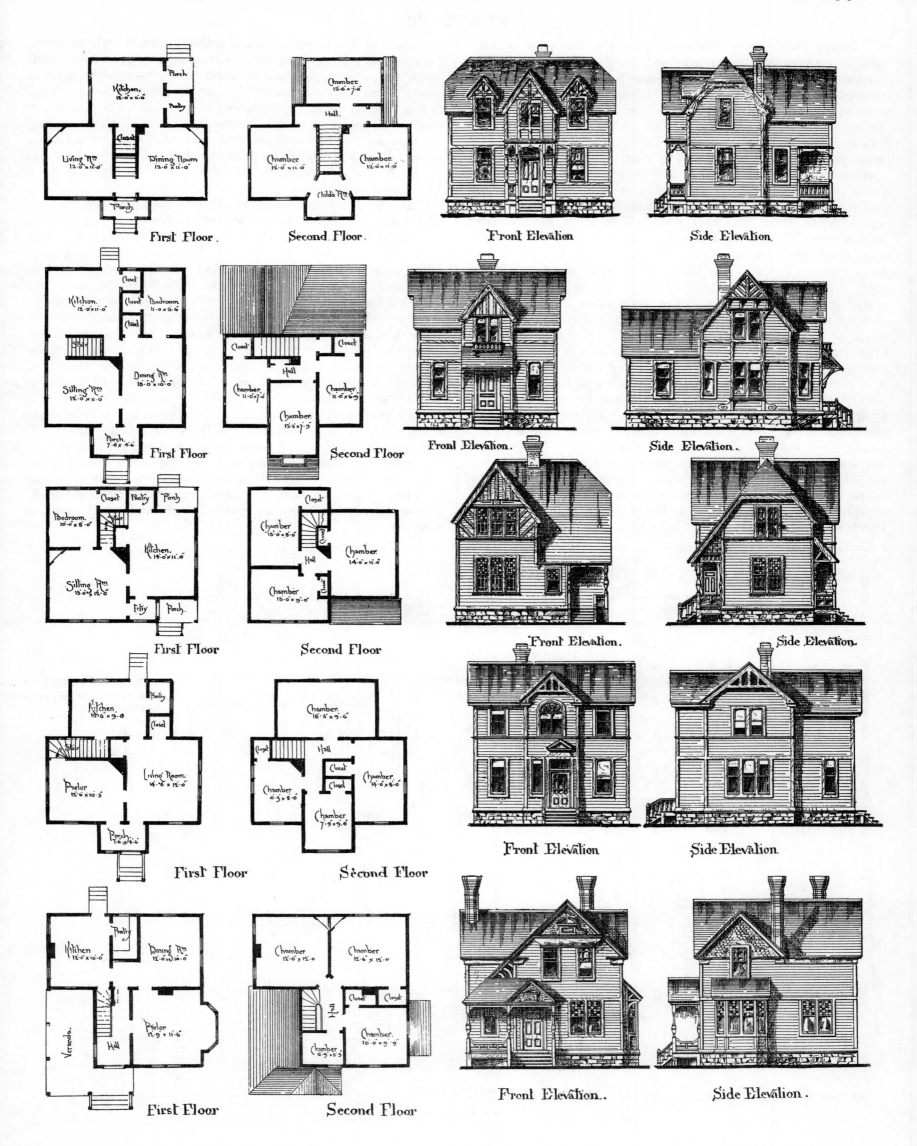

First Floor.

Second Floor.

Front Elevation

Side Elevation.

First Floor

Second Floor

Front Elevation.

Side Elevation.

First Floor

Second Floor

Front Elevation.

Side Elevation.

First Floor

Second Floor

Front Elevation

Side Elevation.

First Floor

Second Floor

Front Elevation.

Side Elevation.

Design 103 shows two floor plans, two elevations and general perspective view of a picturesque and cosey one-and-a-half-story cottage in wood, which presents some features in the general composition that cannot fail but be suggestive, both from an economical and artistic point of view. One chimney answers for the whole house, starting from cellar bottom gives an ample flue for connection to heater in cellar, and the kitchen stove or range on first floor. It is economy in such houses as this where there is bath-room and three or four rooms to be warmed to put in the cellar a portable hot air furnace, with the necessary pipes and registers to heat the two main rooms and hall of first floor, and the two main chambers and bath-room of second floor. Such a furnace, with the necessary piping, would not be much more costly than two self-feeding parlor stoves; the actual net cost of such a furnace for a house of this kind only being about $100, and the dirt and dust arising from their heating and warming is thus kept down in the cellar where it can be easily cleaned up and taken care of, much to the comfort and cleanliness of the upper part of the house. The first floor is nicely arranged, and the large entrance hall will furnish up very good and present an appearance that could not fail but impress the new comer very favorably, the small sash and top half of the hall window being in Cathedral glass of many tints, would lend a very harmonious coloring to the whole; same in top lights of the windows of parlor and dining-room. The four bed-rooms are all good and serviceable, easily reached, and in close proximity to each other although not directly connected. The bathroom is very nicely situated in a good warm place, not likely to freeze up and make trouble in winter time (a very important trouble that it is always well to avoid as far as possible, and which when avoided, results in both pleasure and profit to the

occupant of the house); with a cellar under the whole house, furnace and hot and cold water, cistern and tank, and the whole work properly carried out in good and workmanlike style as here shown, such a house as this can be built, under ordinary favorable circumstances, for about $2,450. The exterior painting of such a house as this has much to do with the success of the design, and we would suggest red for the body of the lower part, golden bronze for the sides that are shingled, and bronze green for the trimming color. The roof if painted, to be a brown of medium color.

Design 104 gives a very roomy and attractive little home, which to many will embody the wants and needs of a permanent and social residence. The first floor arrangements are on a scale well suited to quite a family, and the parlor and dining-room being closely connected by means of the sliding doors can be made available as one large room on social occasions, or on any occasion for that matter; the bed-room on this floor will make for many who are used to living in the country an indispensable feature, closets and pantry arrangements are well provided for. This house, built in like manner to the preceding design, less the bath-room and the fixtures and expense attending the same, ought to be carried out at a cost of about $2,300. In the painting, such colors as are specified for last design are very suitable for this, and would make a very nice appearance. This style of cottage always looks well when built among suitable surroundings, and to the lovers of nature might be pictured as a perfect paradise when almost enveloped in running vines, rose bushes, lilacs and flowering shrubbery so common to all parts of our country. That such homes are greatly needed cannot be denied, and we trust that these designs may stimulate their erection somewhat.

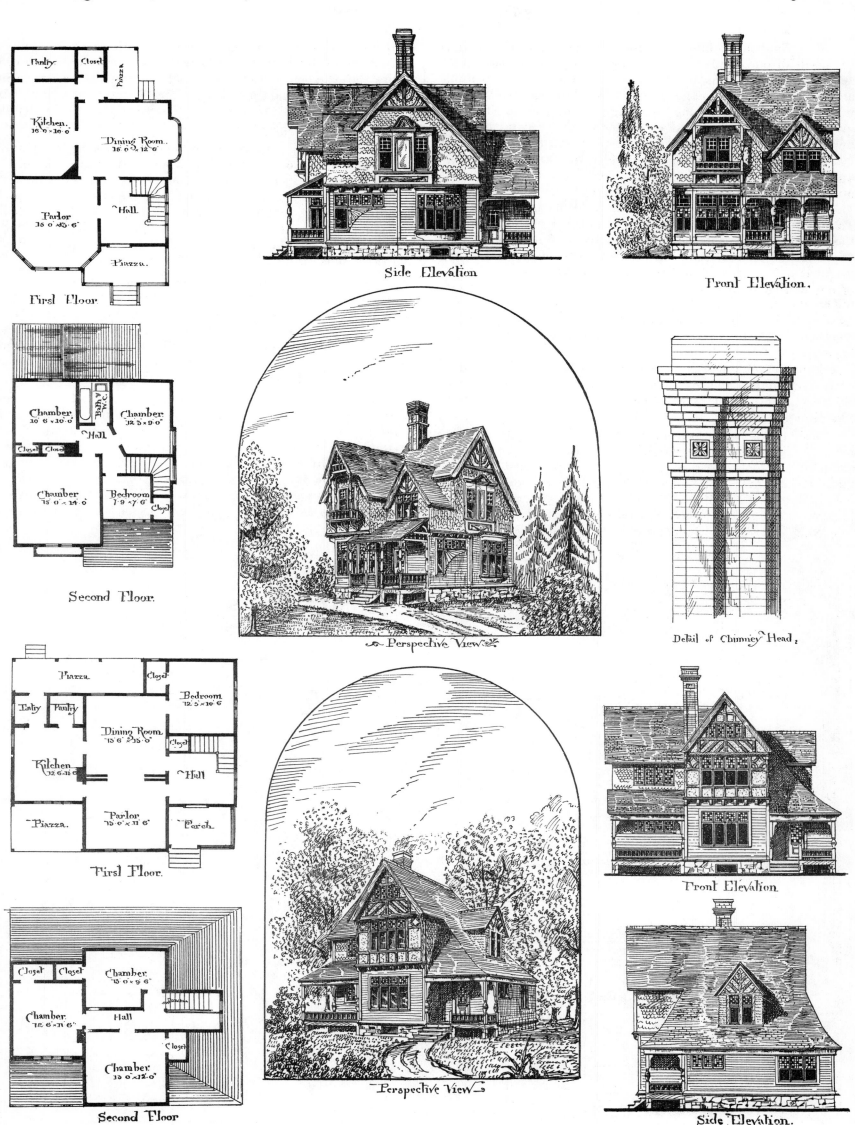

First Floor.

Second Floor.

Side Elevation

Front Elevation.

Perspective View

Detail of Chimney Head.

First Floor.

Second Floor

Perspective View

Front Elevation

Side Elevation.

Pantry · Closet · Piazza

Kitchen · 16'0"×10'0"

Dining Room · 16'0"×12'6"

Parlor · 15'0"×13'6"

Hall

Piazza.

Chamber · 10'6"×10'0"

Bath · W.C.

Chamber · 12'5"×9'0"

Hall

Closet · Closet

Chamber · 15'0"×14'0"

Bedroom · 7'9"×7'6" · Closet

Piazza · Closet

Entry · Pantry

Bedroom · 12'5"×10'6"

Dining Room · 15'6"×13'6"

Closet

Kitchen · 12'6"×11'6"

Hall

Piazza · Parlor · 13'0"×11'6" · Porch

Closet · Closet · Chamber · 13'0"×9'6"

Chamber · 12'6"×11'6" · Hall

Chamber · 13'0"×12'0"

Closet

This plate shows four plans for two-family houses suited to the needs of one family for each floor. All are designed with a special fitness for using up the least amount of ground possible and are well suited to narrow lots. The designs are all simple in outline, the detail being of a very economical construction giving a suitable finish and character to the general external appearance. In such houses as these room and economy are the watchwords, and when we have provided the first with the most approved conveniences and arrangement of rooms at the minimum of cost, we have accomplished that which thousands are looking for and which many who have built have failed to find. To build well and yet on an economical basis is probably one of the hardest problems in the world to solve, and it requires some experience as well as good business management, as it is a very frequent occurrence to find that in two men estimating, the figures of one will be double that of the other, and still it will be possible for the lowest to do the work at a fair profit. To those not used to these things it may look peculiar; yet to the architect, who is used to this sort of thing, and who has it coming up in his daily experience, it does not appear strange, as he is able to discriminate and judge upon the accuracy of a bid by his general knowledge of the cost of like structures by his past experience gained by actual cost of parallel buildings erected under like circumstances.

Design 105 shows a very convenient plan, both families using the same front and rear entrance doors. This is desirable at times, as it does not give so much the appearance of a two-family house, and, in a general way, it is owned by the party who lives on the first floor and he has his own choice of a tenant for the second, and naturally chooses one that he does not object to mixing with. The kitchen, dining-room and parlor, with the two bed-rooms, make a good tenement, while there is room on attic floor to finish each family two nice small rooms in each gable, the attic being reached by front stairway over main stairs. The two-story veranda gives equal privileges to the family up stairs, and does not interfere with the privacy of the family on first floor. Cost $2,500 to build in ordinary locality.

Design 106 gives a very general type of house as to outward show, each family having a private front entrance and both using back door and stairs in common. One large living-room answers for general kitchen and dining-room, and the other rooms opening into this renders it an easy house to warm, the kitchen stove being ample to heat the whole house, except in very cold weather. We have had such houses as this built for about $2,200, including two rooms in the attic.

Design 107 is a square, compact cottage, very much in use in the New England States, renting for from 12 to 16 dollars per month each floor. Two rooms can be finished in attic, each family use the same front door and have separate back entrances. Such houses as this seldom stand empty, and are always a good investment on the outlay if built in the right locality. Cost of this design does not exceed $2,000.

Design 108 gives a very roomy plan with sliding doors between two main rooms. Each have their own front hall and entrance, and the attic is controlled by the second floor. Such may at times be found best as the owner can live on the top floors and have additional finished rooms in the attic for sleeping purposes. This house is built at a cost of about $2,600. All these designs can be enlarged or in many ways changed to suit individual wants, as those using them may see fit or the case may demand.

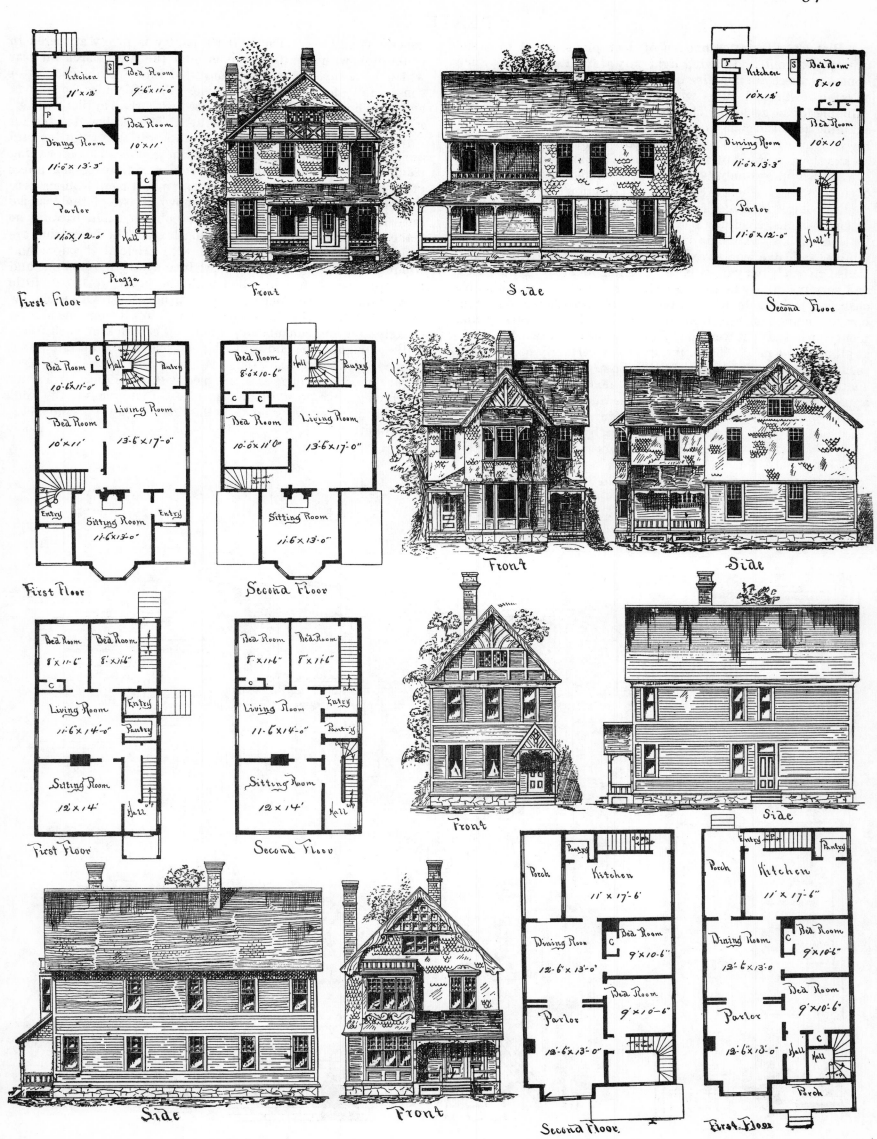

Design 105

Kitchen 11'x12'
Bed Room 9'-6"x11'-0"
Dining Room 11'-0"x13'-3"
Bed Room 10'x11'
Parlor 11'-0"x12'-0"
Hall
Piazza

First Floor

Front

Side

Kitchen 10'x12'
Bed Room 8'x10
Dining Room 11'-0"x13'-3"
Bed Room 10'x10'
Parlor 11'-0"x12'-0"
Hall

Second Floor

Design 106

Bed Room 10'-6"x11'-0"
Hall
Pantry
Bed Room 10'x11'
Living Room 13'-6"x17'-0"
Entry
Sitting Room 11'-6"x13'-0"
Entry

First Floor

Bed Room 8'-6"x10'-6"
Hall
Pantry
Bed Room 10'-0"x11'-0"
Living Room 13'-6"x17'-0"
Sitting Room 11'-6"x13'-0"

Second Floor

Front

Side

Design 107

Bed Room 8'x11'-6"
Bed Room 8'x11'-6"
Living Room 11'-6"x14'-0"
Entry
Pantry
Sitting Room 12'x14'
Hall

First Floor

Bed Room 8'x11'-6"
Bed Room 8'x11'-6"
Living Room 11'-6"x14'-0"
Entry
Pantry
Sitting Room 12'x14'
Hall

Second Floor

Front

Side

Design 108

Side

Front

Porch
Pantry
Kitchen 11'x17'-6"
Dining Room 12'-6"x13'-0"
Bed Room 9'x10'-6"
Bed Room 9'x10'-6"
Parlor 12'-6"x13'-0"

Second Floor

Porch
Entry
Pantry
Kitchen 11'x17'-6"
Dining Room 12'-6"x13'-0"
Bed Room 9'x10'-6"
Bed Room 9'x10'-6"
Parlor 12'-6"x13'-0"
Hall
Porch

First Floor

PALLISER'S NEW COTTAGE HOMES AND DETAILS.

PLATE 38.

Plate 38 illustrates one set of floor plans suited to a site twenty feet front, and having light only at front and rear. Such houses as these are in active demand in suburbs or new portions of large towns and cities where ground will soon become too valuable for large lots. The city of Philadelphia is a very fair example as to the general needs of some improvement in its long rows of narrow fronts, all just alike. Almost anything that breaks the monotony of the line would be very agreeable to the eye and would no doubt be largely appreciated by the occupants of such a street. There is certainly no objection to making a long continuous row of house fronts all different in design or of three or four designs, erecting them in alternate blocks of from two to four in each style. This is possible and yet a harmony be retained, and the whole vastly improved in general appearance. It also gives a better variety both for selling and renting purposes, and very materially helps to give a more decided and distinctive character to a man's home, whereby it is possible for his neighbor to distinguish him from the others. Give us variety and plenty of it and if it were possible to never build two buildings at all alike, so much the better, and it is certainly best to vary them as much as circumstances will allow, there may justly be a similarity in the general plan, but it is inexcusable as to outward appearances; even nature will teach us this lesson, and those of the world who will think and study nature as they pass along, may soon see and learn the lesson thereby taught. The plan gives a house 20 x 42 feet, with four floors, containing ten rooms and bath-room. Such a plan would give very good accommodations for quite a large family and would be a very convenient home to live in generally; the parlor on the first floor would answer as general reception-room, while the drawing-room on the floor above would give a more retired and pleasant room for

general family use. The butler's pantry is nicely arranged in connection with the dining-room, and the little porch on rear which is recessed, could be converted into a plant cabinet or conservatory for use in winter-time. The balconies on second and third floors could also be enclosed with glass in like manner, which would make a warmer house. The twelve designs for front elevations, as given, show quite a variety of outline and are all capable of being carried out in good construction, and could be so arranged that all would look well, even in a block of twelve houses. In some cities there might be objections as to the use of wooden construction, as shown in two of the designs, but with brick backing this would be obviated and it could be made to pass the most rigid building laws. The fronts that are of stone ashlar could be trimmed with brick at the door and window openings which would produce a very harmonious and nice appearance in connection with the brick work. A little terra cotta and nice stone carving, sparingly used with some few bands of moulded brick properly worked in will combine to form an agreeable and consummate whole. The brick of such fronts as these ought to be laid up with good materials, and the best of pressed brick should be used. White or buff brick can be used to very good advantage and trimmed with red brick, terra cotta and brown stone, would look very nice. Plate glass in the front windows also lend very much to the richness of the whole and a few dollars here spent is money well invested. Cost of such houses are $3,000 to $3,500.

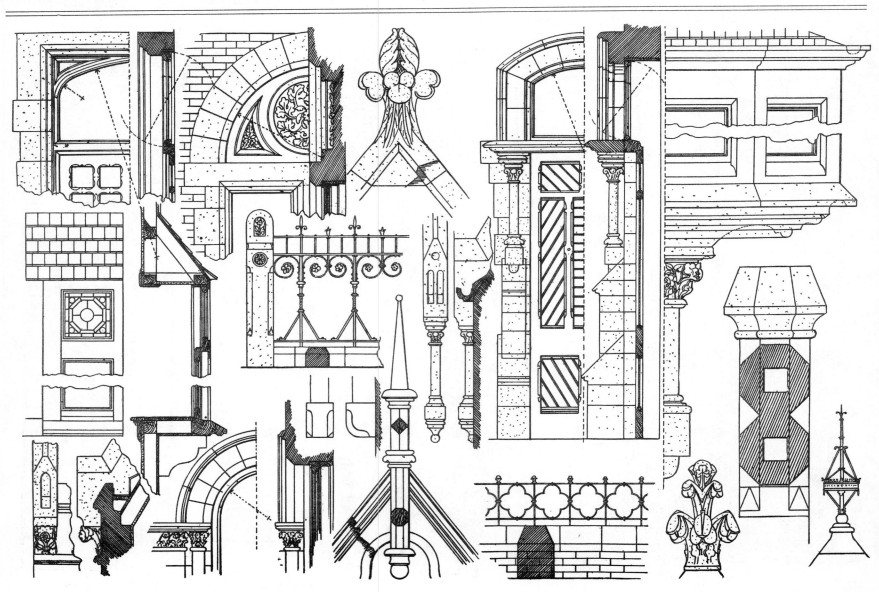

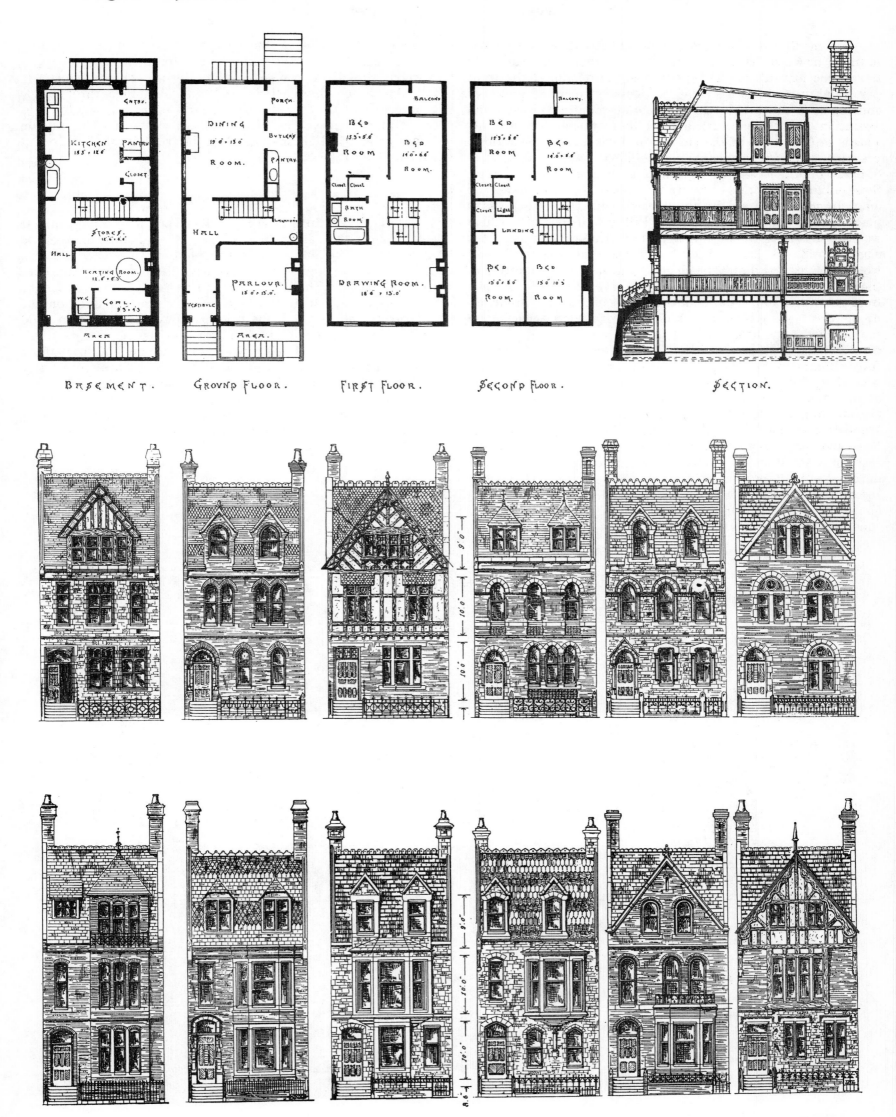

BASEMENT.   GROUND FLOOR.   FIRST FLOOR.   SECOND FLOOR.   SECTION.

PALLISER'S NEW COTTAGE HOMES AND DETAILS.

PLATE 39.

Design 121 represents a very solid and artistic-looking house in frame or wood, having a very strong tendency or leaning to the classic features of the renaissance, the details of the front porch and the main gables being particularly good and pleasing, and are such as to be capable of a transplanting process and execution on a house worth several times the cost of this one. This is probably one of the most radical changes of the style so prevalent some few years ago, yet retaining many of the features of that date which can well be utilized even in what we may term these enlightened times. Anything that is good will never die out. It may be passed by and thrown aside for a time to give place to some new innovation which will have its day after which we have time to again look upon and admire the beauties of the classic world. So it is and has been for all time past and to-day we are obliged to admire the elegant and massive proportion of the works executed by the ancients, and which are handed down from generation to generation as examples of the art of architecture never yet surpassed and which are copied and accepted by the best artists as being beyond their improvement in many of their details and fine proportions. The design here shown is fully illustrated by the plans, elevations and details together with the perspective view giving the finished and general effect of the whole when completed and in harmony with its general surroundings. The cellar plan gives a good open cellar and laundry in the part under the kitchen. The first-floor rooms are large and very cosey, well arranged for the comfort and convenience of a small family. The four rooms on second floor give ample sleeping accommodations. The first story is clapboarded, second story shingled with square butt shingles, the panels in gables being finished in plaster and wood; the whole frame is sheathed and covered with paper; the roofs can be either shingle or slate, the latter being somewhat more expensive. The colors we suggest for painting exterior are for first-story, body, a maroon; shingle work of second story, terra cotta red; the panels in gables, etc., orange red; and the trimmings throughout, bronze green; the carved work on cornices, etc., being brought out with chrome yellow; window sash white and the outside blinds green of a lighter shade than the trimmings. The cost of such a house is $3,000.

Design 122 brings us very forcibly back to the days of our great grandfathers and at once puts us in mind of the times of the revolution. The plan is very conveniently arranged and is a very desirable layout, and would provide ample room for a large family, the style of architecture here illustrated is termed by many, "Old Colonial," with the large stone chimneys built on the exterior walls, up which the ivy vine could be trained to good advantage; and the other quaint features here shown we think the aesthetically inclined will in this design find something worth studying. Such a house as this will harmonize finely with nature and properly placed on a suitable site with rocks, trees, and perhaps a running brook to blend in with it, and about two or three acres of nice ground of an uneven nature, nicely undulating, is a home fit for a prince to live in, and the cost is $5,000.

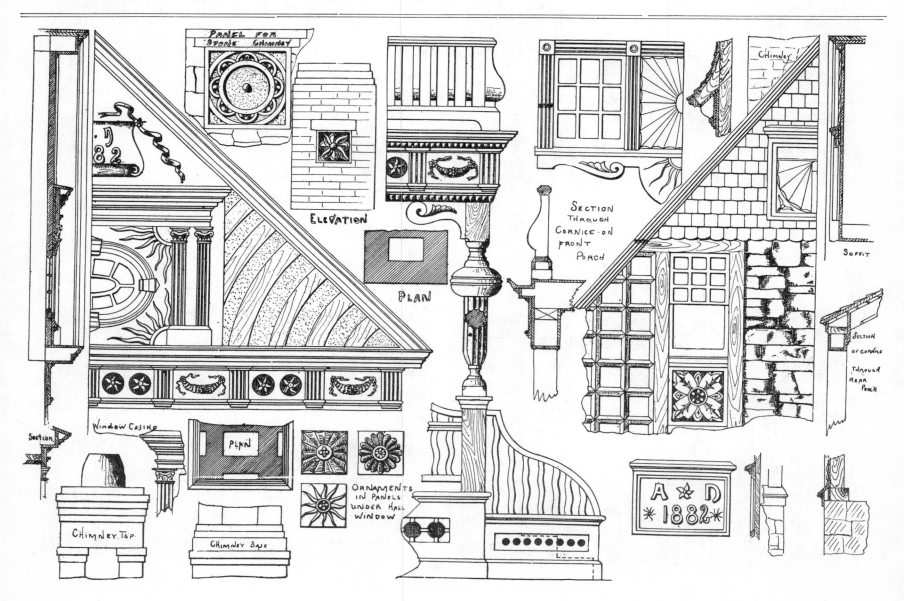

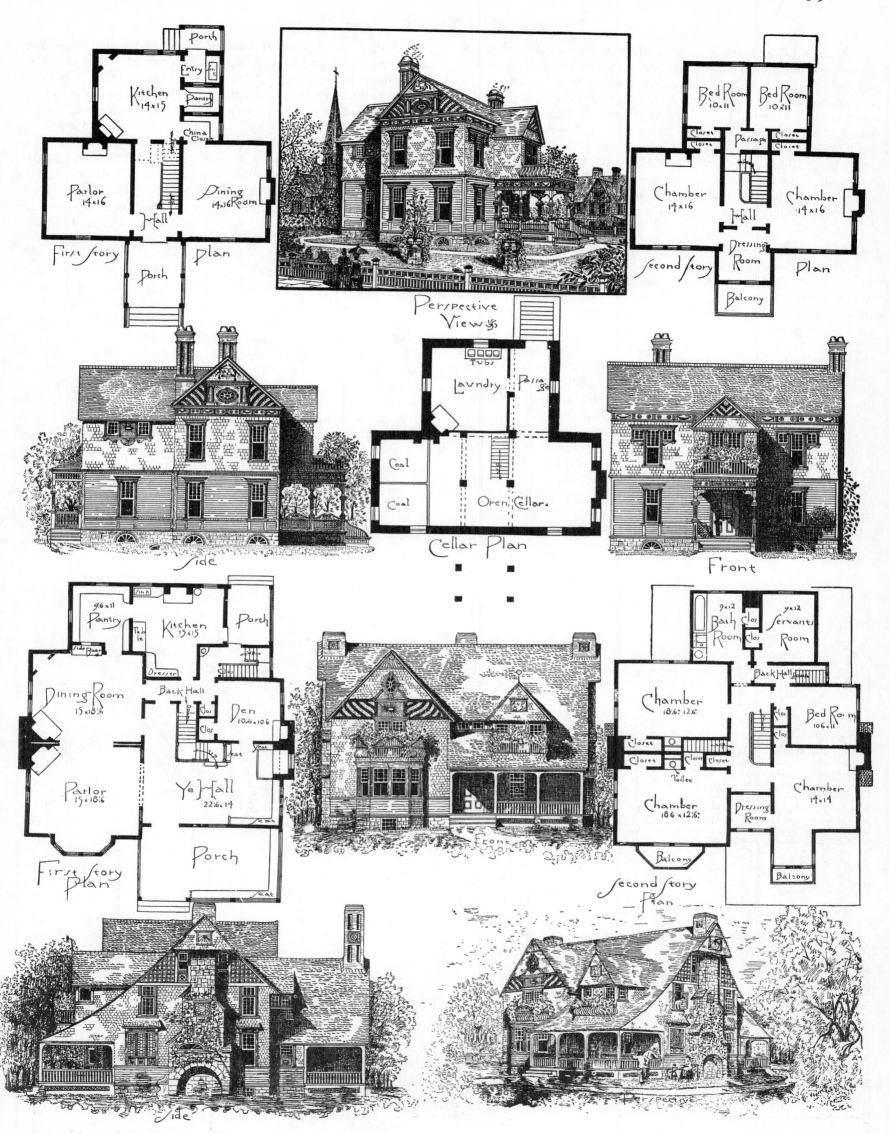

Porch
Entry Sink
Kitchen 14x15
Pantry
China Closet
Parlor 14x16
Dining Room 14x16
Hall
First Story Plan
Porch

Perspective View

Bed Room 10x11
Bed Room 10x11
Closet Closet Passage Closet Closet
Chamber 14x16
Hall
Chamber 14x16
Second Story
Dressing Room
Plan
Balcony

Side

Tubs
Laundry Passage
Coal
Coal
Open Cellar.
Cellar Plan

Front

96x11 Sink
Pantry
Kitchen 15x15
Porch
Side Board
Table
Dresser
Dining Room 15x18:6
Back Hall
Den 10:6x10:6
Parlor 15x18:6
Ye Hall 22:6x14
Seat
Seat
First Story Plan
Porch

9x12 Bath Room Clos Clos 9x12 Servants Room
Back Hall
Chamber 18:6:12:6:
Closet Closet Closet Closet
Bed Room 10:6x11
Toilet
Chamber 186x12:6:
Dressing Room
Chamber 14x14
Second Story Plan
Balcony
Balcony

Front

Side

Perspective

PALLISER'S NEW COTTAGE HOMES AND DETAILS.

PLATE 40.

Design 123 shows a very pleasant and nicely planned house of seven rooms—four on the first and three on the second floor—all well laid out and as convenient as can be considering the amount of money it costs to build. The external appearance is very tasty and desirable. This design is well adapted to a suburban lot 50 feet front, and is well suited to a family of taste and refinement. A bath room can be easily worked in on the second story at an added cost of about $250. With a neat painted finish internally and the cellar under the whole house, we have had such houses built for inside $2,100, still there are localities in our knowledge where it would require as much as $2,800 to build.

Design 124 gives a first-floor plan and front elevation of a very nice little one-story cottage, giving four nice rooms well adapted to the wants of a small family. Such a home as this is worth about $550 to build it, and would fill the wants of a large class of people who want to own their own home, no matter how small it may be.

Design 125 shows a very roomy plan which is well suited to the wants of a large and growing family. The dining-room is large and would be the general living part of the house, the whole arrangement of rooms and conveniences in connection therewith being specially happy in their relation to each other and the exterior giving a suitable covering to the whole; this house should have a cellar under with a stone wall well laid in mortar and neatly pointed. On exposed surfaces a well-sheathed frame papered before the finish is applied, and a good shingle roof. It will make a warm, comfortable house at a cost of about $2,800.

Design 126 is a one-and-a-half story six-room cottage, very simple and economical in its appointments and yet of considerable pretension to artistic effect which is obtained in a very legitimate way and not by any expensive means. The layout of the rooms is good and in every way suited to the house and its style. No waste room; but every inch of room counts towards the strictest economy and comfort of the family to be sheltered. The cost of such a cottage as this does not exceed $900 to $1,000, including cellar, cistern, pump, sink and proper drainage. As to what constitutes the latter a large book might be written and then justice not be done to the subject. The circumstances vary so much with different locations and sites that a special treatment is very necessary to suit each individual case. On some grounds where not built up thickly and with a gravelly bottom, a leaching cesspool placed fifty to seventy-five feet from the house might safely be used with a four or six-inch pipe running from the house to it. All pipes in the house ought to be of iron and to a distance of three to six feet outside where the iron pipe connects to the earthen tile in the ground. A running trap and fresh-air inlet on the house side of the trap ought to be connected and the iron waste pipe run up through the house and out two or three feet above the roof, and be there capped with a neat galvanized iron ventilator. All the plumbing fixtures should be trapped with the most approved anti-siphon traps, or if ordinary traps are used they should be ventilated from top of same and connection made from the vent pipes into the iron wastes, care being taken to make them well above the highest waste connection. This would prevent all bad effects from the traps, and if the work was properly done with good materials would make a first-class sanitary job and be practically safe.

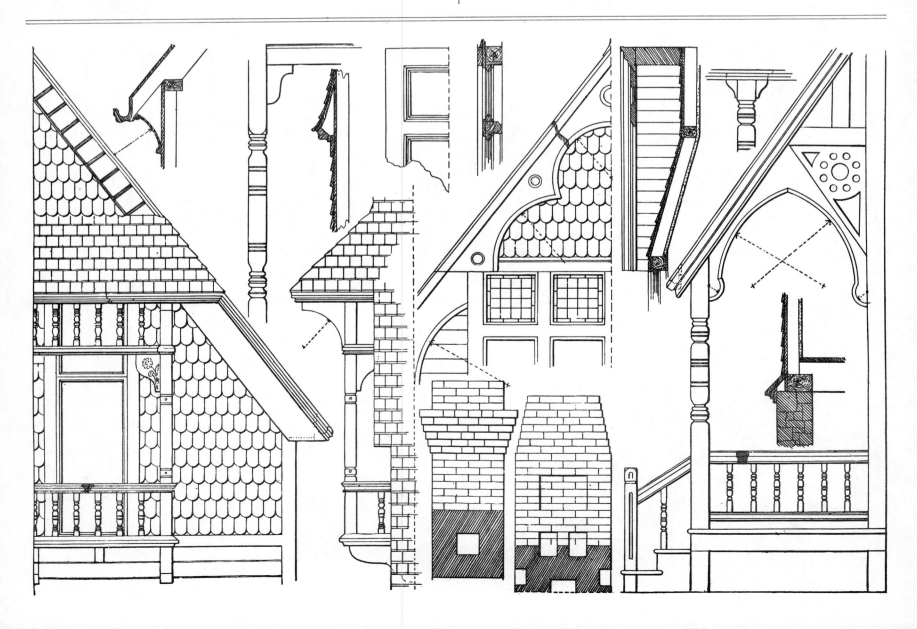

First Floor

Second Floor

Front Elevation.

Side Elevation.

Ground Floor

Front Elevation.

Perspective View.

Ground Floor

Second Floor.

Front Elevation

Side Elevation.

First Floor

Perspective View.

Front Elevation

Second Floor.

Perspective View.

Side Elevation

PALLISER'S NEW COTTAGE HOMES AND DETAILS.

PLATE 41.

Design 127 shows plans and elevations of a well-arranged eight-room two-story cottage, which is designed in the popular style often called Queen Anne. This house is very suggestive for a country home where fair sized rooms and comfort are looked for more than style in the largeness of halls and general internal beauties that are so largely made for show. The perspective view here shown gives a very good idea of the external appearance of the house when erected, and shows the advantage of having a view of this kind, in connection with the plans and elevations, as it enables those who are not at all versed in plans, and who cannot tell what a geometrical elevation will look like when built, to know and study the appearance to their full benefit and satisfaction. The house here shown, in cost, is about $3,000, varying somewhat as to location and general management displayed.

Design 128 illustrates a square one-and-a-half story cottage, with quite a picturesque exterior, giving four good rooms on a floor and very simple and economical in plan. To many people needing a home, room is the first consideration, and the second item the cost; and to accomplish the one within the compass of the other is often a very hard and difficult problem to solve, and although it is often apparently an impossibility for the architect to bring the two extremes together, and make the minimum of cost cover the maximum of room, still the only way to do is to persevere and not aim too high, nor be too particular about the building of a monument to one's own skill, but to produce one based on the ability of the client to pay, and the room needed. If this is safely done the result is invariably satisfactory, and the client made happy; and when the architect has so far succeeded as to do this his own peace of mind, cannot help but prove right as a duty faithfully done and conscientiously exe-

cuted to the satisfaction of all concerned, is one of the most agreeable things that can be worked for, and makes life pass pleasantly and smooth. 'Tis, alas, only too true that often the architect is hampered to a great extent by the unreasonableness of his client, in which case it is far better to quarrel outright and get through with each other as soon as the trouble is found out, unless the client can be brought to a realization of his error. We have known many of these cases, and have had one or two instances in our own practice in one case we were plain, and told the client we were positive we would not be able to suit him, and we preferred him to settle for what we had done, and get some one else. He did so, much to our great relief; and, as he found out afterwards, much to his great disappointment. It so happening that we had two clients who built one on each side of him; the one house we designed in stone and brick for first story and wood above, which was built at a cost of $9,000; the other was all frame, a very fine house in every respect, and was built at a cost of $5,000. Both of these houses were large and roomy, and had the front door in the centre of fronts, had each five rooms on the first story, with halls 9 feet wide (between) and elegantly finished inside, while the house built by our former client had a narrow front, only one room to the street, not as much room in it or nearly so well arranged as the less expensive one planned by us; back stairs dark and no light on them; bath-room built over a porch so as to freeze up every winter, which has not failed to happen, we have been informed, and the whole house is pointed out as one of the most expensive houses of its size, and the most illy-contrived possible, and looks like an ordinary $4,000 house, while in reality it cost the most of the three, and is to-day a standing advertisement of the difference in the abilities of the architects employed, and the way the clients co-operated with them. A unity of purpose between architect and client is necessary to success in such cases.

Front Door

Water Table

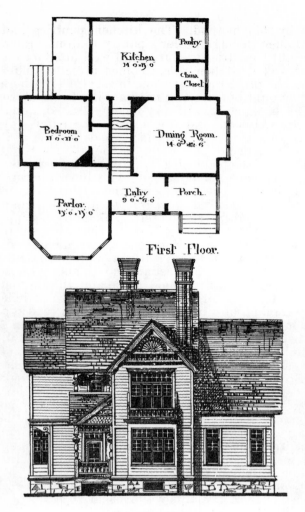

First Floor.

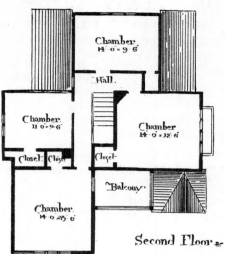

Second Floor.

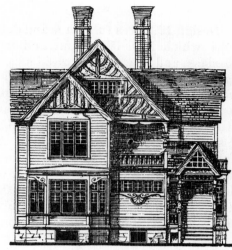

Front Elevation.

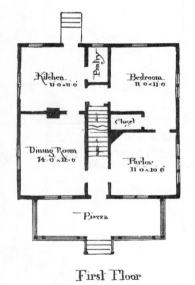

Side Elevation.

Perspective View.

First Floor

Perspective View

Front Elevation.

Second Floor.

Side Elevation

Design 129 gives full plans and details of a very good country house, which is well laid-out and in every way suitable for a first-class and permanent residence. The main hall is very large and the stairs being placed well back from the front door, makes a very spacious inner-room, from which the other rooms open. This is well lighted by the stained-glass windows on the stairs, which shed a mellow and subdued light throughout the halls of first and second floors. A very good vestibule is arranged, also well lighted by stained-glass windows on sides and transoms over the doors. This would give ample room on one side for an umbrella stand and a seat on the other. The hall is also a good shape for furnishing both economically and artistically. The sitting-room and parlor at left of hall are well arranged. The alcove in sitting-room is a very pretty feature, giving a nice opportunity in furnishing as well as helping the outlook from the room. The portiere across the partition between the two rooms is, in this case, undoubtedly preferable to the ordinary sliding doors—saves room and is more economical and convenient, as the two rooms will be largely used as one or together. The dining-room is nice in shape and size; fireplace being in the corner, is entirely out of the way, and the sideboard is placed to good advantage, being recessed in the front wall and having a small window filled with art glass through the centre, makes a very effective as well as a useful article of furniture in the room. To build a sideboard in the dining-room of a first-class house is the proper thing to do, and in scores of cases we have done this within the last few years, always designing the sideboards with a special reference to the requirements of the room and in harmony with the mantel pieces, and other trimmings showing in connection therewith. A sideboard recessed into the wall does not interfere with the room, and frequently two feet can be saved in the width or length of a room by this method. The kitchen pantries and connection from kitchen through butler's pantry to dining-room are admirably laid out; pantries are large and well fitted for the purposes intended. The kitchen range comes directly under the bath-room, and the pipes to latter come in very nicely where there are the least amount of them and not liable to freeze up or cause trouble. The back stairs are very nicely situated, going up directly from the kitchen and down from the entry-way between front hall and kitchen. This is a good feature, as it enables anyone in the house to pass down to the cellar without disturbing the privacy of the kitchen, a feature that is very often appreciated by the members of a household who have the welfare of the family at heart. The washbowl under the stairs in main hall is convenient for general toilet purposes. The second story gives four good chambers, six closets, bath and dressing-rooms, and the front stairway runs on up to the attic, where there is ample room to finish four or five good rooms, if required. The cellar would contain laundry with stationary washtubs, furnace and fuel room, store and cold cellar, and is about seven and a half feet high, walls built of good stone and the bottom well cemented; the furnace large enough to heat the whole house without any forcing, as a large furnace run with ease at a slow-going fire is much more effective and economical than a smaller one, that has to be forced to do the work required of it. For the internal finish of this design we suggest, oak for front hall, stairs, etc.; ash or birch for dining-room; cherry for sitting-room and parlor; the floors of hall and dining-room of oak with a neat cherry strip for border; the kitchen part of yellow pine, and other parts of white pine, all filled and finished on the wood. For the exterior finish the design shows clearly what is best—chimneys of good red brick in red mortar (fire-places laid up in pressed brick and trimmed with tile and brass on facings), first story painted maroon for body, second story red and third story orange yellow, trimmed throughout with bronze green; the roofs brown, window sash white and blinds green is a very happy combination. The cost of this we place at $6,500, varying with location, etc.

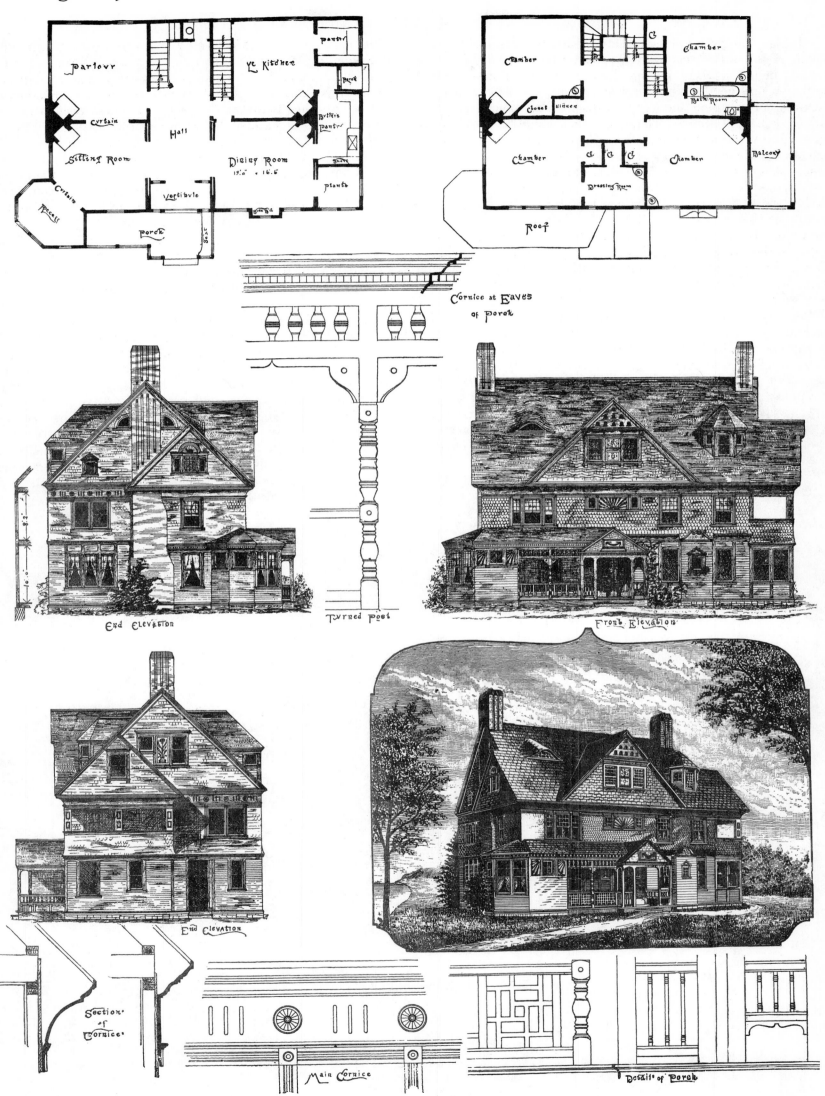

Plate 42.

Parlour

Ye Kitchen

Pantry

Curtain

Butler's Pantry

Sitting Room

Hall

Dining Room
15.0 × 16.6

Recess

Vestibule

Curtain

Porch

Seat

Chamber

Chamber

Closet Kitchen

Bath Room

Chamber

Chamber

Balcony

Dressing Room

Roof

Cornice at Eaves of Porch

End Elevation

Turned Post

Front Elevation

End Elevation

Section of Cornice

Main Cornice

Details of Porch

PLATE 43.

Design 130 gives a plan of a very roomy, well arranged house, which would suit a great many people living in the country who are not in the habit of having their work, etc., done by hired help. A very good plan for a farm house, and has some good features both in plan and exterior design that cannot help but fall into play at times. That there is very great diversity of opinion on the question of house planning, and what suits one man and is his meat is very apt to be poison to the next one who comes along cannot be denied; that our aim has been to meet this diversified opinion, and that we have fairly succeeded we shall leave to the reader to judge, hoping that said reader will be one of the many who will profit by our endeavors to meet the wants of such a large class as the designs and ideas as illustrated in this work are intended for. The plan here shown has no waste room, every part being well utilized for the rooms; the stairs are simple box stairs about 3 feet, 4 inches wide, and are very well located so as to get upstairs from the kitchen and dining-room as well as from the entry at their foot from outside, while the cellar is reached from the passageway which answers as a press or Butler's pantry between the dining-room and kitchen. The kitchen pantry is large and nicely located, well away from the heat of the range. This is an important feature in a house of this kind, a large cool room for the proper storage of the kitchen crockery, eatables and such articles as must always be kept within reach of the careful housekeeper, the sliding sash connection from pantry to passageway is so fixed as to save many steps, a feature that every housewife will appreciate. The plan of the three rooms on first floor being such as to throw them into one room by opening the sliding doors, gives ample room for the social element of the household, and furnishes the necessary space for any entertainment the young folks may have on hand; a provision very much overlooked in the planning of many country houses, although one that tends in no small extent to the general pleasure and great enjoyment in many farming districts where it is the custom to have pleasant social times amongst themselves at their residences. Certainly this is a feature that can be cultivated in all country neighborhoods to the mutual advantage of all concerned. Such a house is capable of many changes, and will no doubt serve as a key note to many as to what are their needs, and thus assist them by the many suggestions gleaned from it. Such a house ought to have a cellar under the whole of it, and be built at a cost of about $2,750 in any favorable locality.

Design 131 illustrates a very cosey and comfortable cottage, very good in its appointments, and withal very suitable for erection as a neat and attractive country home. The elevations are low; still the rooms on second floor are desirable, being cut on external sides only about one third the height of walls. The large hall and main stairs therein, also the addition of a fireplace, makes this a fine sitting room, and connecting as it does with parlor and dining-room, and the latter joining together with sliding doors, is very desirable. The drive-porch is a feature that in many houses of this size would not be necessary, still there are many instances where it could be utilized to very good advantage, the location and the family wants of those occupying being the guide. This house costs, to erect complete, with neat finish and shingle roof, $2,300. The details of this plate are very suggestive as to chimney-tops, gable porch and balcony finish.

Blessed is the man who owns a home.

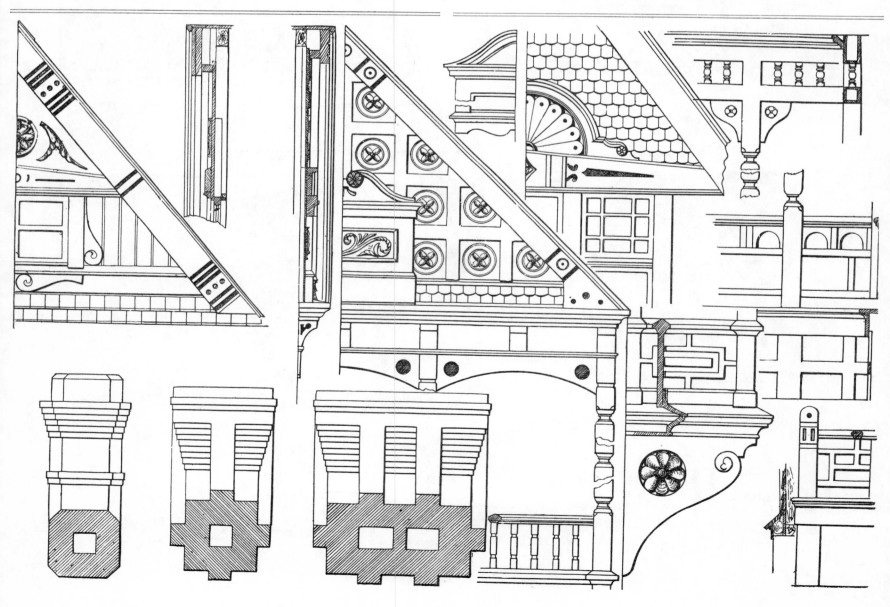

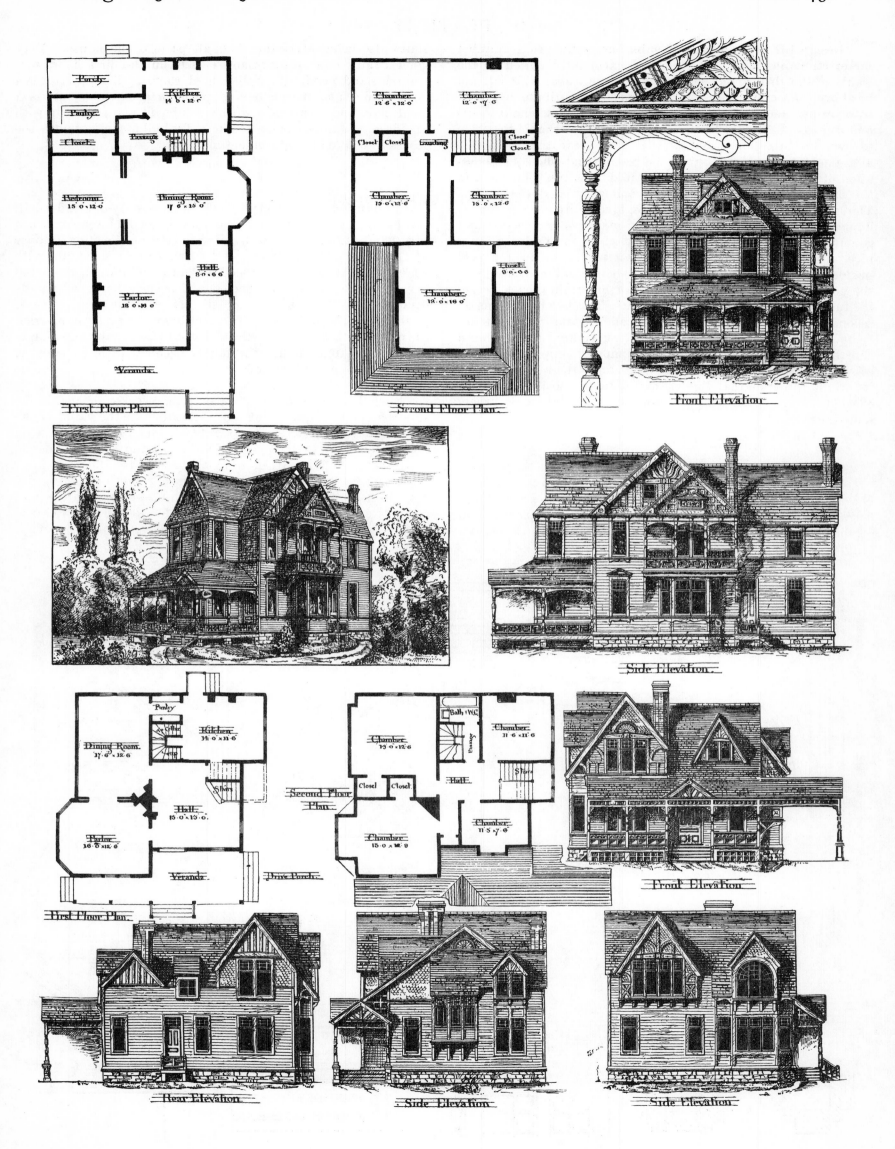

First Floor Plan

Second Floor Plan

Front Elevation

Side Elevation

First Floor Plan

Second Floor Plan

Front Elevation

Rear Elevation

Side Elevation

Side Elevation

PALLISER'S NEW COTTAGE HOMES AND DETAILS.

PLATE 44.

Design 132 gives a type of suburban cottage well adapted for erection on a fifty foot lot and excellently suited to the wants of the thrifty and sensible mechanic whose wife will not be above the point where she is willing to contribute her help by a proper and economical care of her own household wants and duties. It should be the duty of every mechanic to strive to own his own home, and undoubtedly a great help to this attainment can be meted out by the prompt and efficient co-operation of the better-half, whose duty it is to help her husband in the saving of his earnings for the common weal of the family. The large kitchen 13x15 feet in size, gives ample room for all domestic living purposes, the dining-room being a better and general sitting-room for family uses, while the parlor gives a nice, cosey room in which the modest parlor organ and neat parlor suite will help smile a sweet welcome to the company of the young folks and in which they can entertain themselves to the full enjoyment and mutual benefit. The five bed-rooms on second story gives ample sleeping accommodations with a sufficient supply of closet-room. A sink, pump and cistern would constitute the full complement of the modern improvements so essential to family wants, and a cellar under the whole house is the right thing in that line. Such a house cost to build it, $2,475.00. The small bedroom could be made into a Bathroom if so desired.

Design 133 gives a large amount of room on first and second floors, with a sensible lay-out, well adapted to the needs of a large family. This cottage has a number of good features to commend it—first, an absence of waste room in hallways, the stairs also being accessible from all parts of the house. Very good pantry conveniences and closets on the first floor, nice verandas and good, airy well-lighted rooms. The exterior is a good model, and makes a very pleasing perspective. It is a good plan, and as a whole will no doubt, fit and groove in with the ideas of a great many people. To build such a house the cost is $2,850 in any convenient locality.

Design 134 shows a very pretty cottage, only one-and-a-half stories high, containing six fine rooms, good closets, and is a very handy little home, well suited to any one needing a house of this size. This cottage, as to quantity of materials with which to construct it, is reduced down to a minimum, the detail is very simple, easily constructed and is such that good results emanate from it, both in an artistic and sensible point of view. Such a house would make a pleasant home for a young married couple just starting out in life, and would be capable of enlargement at any time should the family needs require it. Cost of this design to execute, $1,560.

Such houses as are illustrated in this work if erected in the suburbs of our cities would add very much to the value of the ground they stand on and pay a handsome rate of interest on their cost, better than any other class of building investments, as the supply falls far short of the demand. Business men, clerks, mechanics and others wishing to reside out of the city need just such homes as this, and we wonder capitalists and real estate owners do not make money for themselves and others by erecting such tasteful, yet inexpensive, suburban homes.

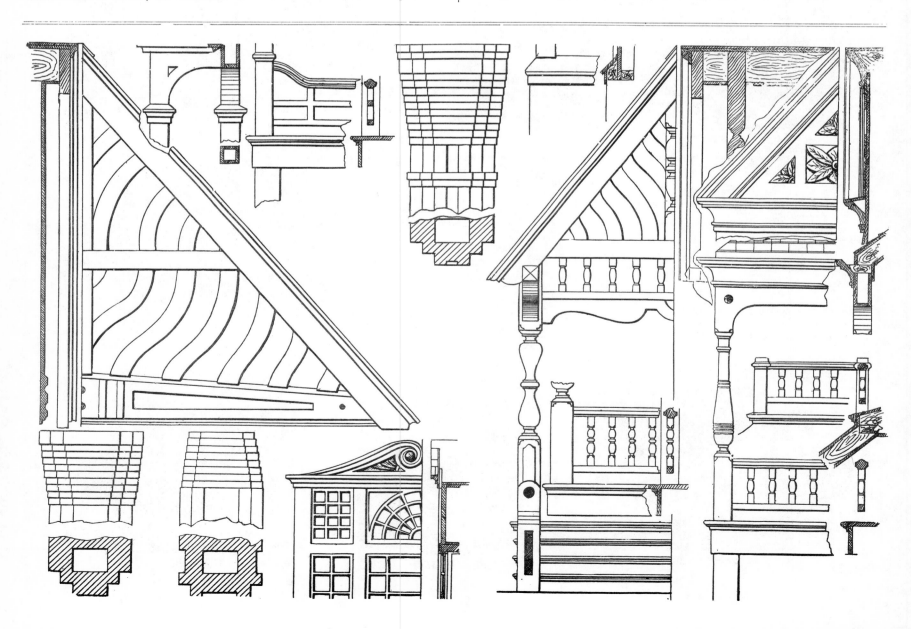

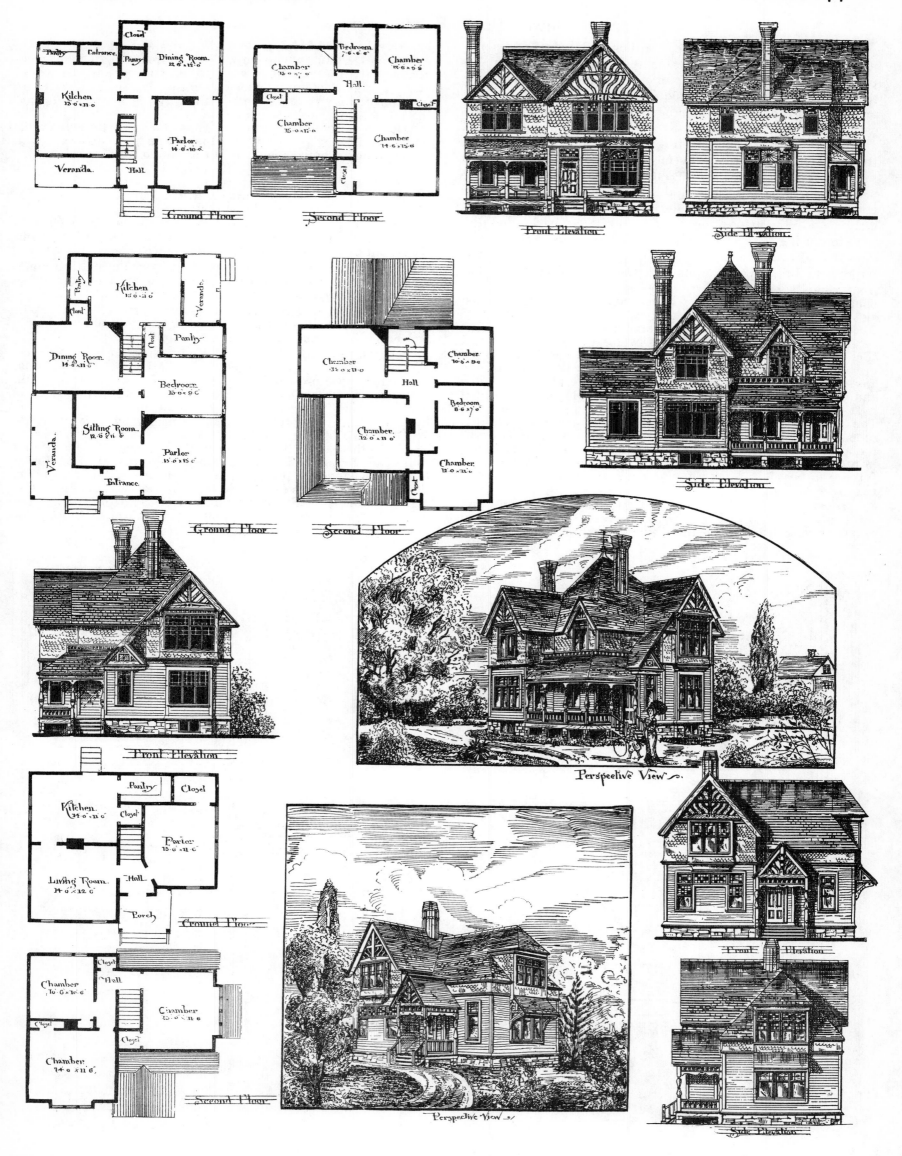

Ground Floor

Second Floor

Front Elevation

Side Elevation

Ground Floor

Second Floor

Side Elevation

Front Elevation

Perspective View

Front Elevation

Ground Floor

Second Floor

Perspective View

Side Elevation

Design 135 gives us a house, although in plan of a somewhat ordinary type, and in its many arrangements a commonplace character, yet presenting an exterior and general make-up that is quite artistic and unique in its varied detail. The arrangement of the parlor chimney, placing the same on the outside of the wall and facing the exterior work up with rough stone, makes a very good feature and one that will commend itself as being good in its convenience, thus leaving the parlor a square room without the addition of a large chimney breast to use up a large part of the available space, as is usually the case in houses of this class. The first floor arrangement is particularly good in the disposition of the rooms. The parlor and dining-room being connected with sliding doors makes a roomy and open house and one that would be pleasing and give a fine impression to the visitor upon entering the parlor door. The front veranda is very wide; much more so than the same is usually on ordinary houses. The library is pleasantly situated and is such that it could be used as a bedroom, should it be desirable. The rear hall and stairway gives access to the second floor and cellar as well as provides a closet—a very great convenience—in which to hang wet wraps, leave one's overshoes, umbrella, etc., and which might be provided in every house of any pretension to very good advantage. The kitchen, pantry and closet arrangements are good and desirable and well suited to the domestic family wants of the inmates to be sheltered. The second story gives four roomy bed-rooms, two dressing-rooms, bath-room, large linen closet and a good closet in every room. There is also ample room to finish three or four rooms in attic which would be desirable. This house should have a furnace to heat it, a brick set range in kitchen and ought not to cost over $4,300.

During the past ten years, P. T. Barnum, the greatest and most successful showman on earth, has erected large numbers of cottage homes from our plans. In this respect he has done a great deal toward helping along the improvement of the town of Bridgeport, Conn., where he makes his home. His ideas were always carried out with a view to making money, he would acquire large tracts of land at low figures, lay the same out into lots and displayed originality of mind by the method of bringing his lots into market. Some of the lots were thought to be inferior in value to the rest. On these he caused houses to be built, relying on an old idea which some men entertain who prefer to buy a house ready built than build for themselves.

> "He who builds a house
> Pays for every pin;
> He who buys one ready built
> Gets the pins thrown in."

He sold part of his grounds to such buyers as wished to become immediate owners of house and lot. Other lots found ready purchasers at constantly advancing prices.

P. T. Barnum has become a wealthy man, making much money out of his real estate and building operations, and at the same time has benefited hundreds of other people.

Every town and city of consequence presents like opportunities for the land speculator to put up tasty, well-built homes and bring his ground into market at a handsome profit.

Design 136 is an admirable design for a suburban residence, with a sensible plan, well suited for a small family. In external finish this house presents a very quaint and old-time look; still, with a new, fresh and inspiring temper. Old-time houses of fifty or seventy years ago were built far better than many of their more modern prototypes, as evidenced by their ability to stand the test of time. Still, it is possible to do as good work to day as then, as we have better facilities now to do it and do it well; the difference in cost between a good and poor job is never over five to ten per cent., and frequently at the same price, the difference lying very often in the selection of a builder. Get a good builder, by all means, pay a reasonable price, and then you get a good job. Such a house as this can be erected for about $2,000.

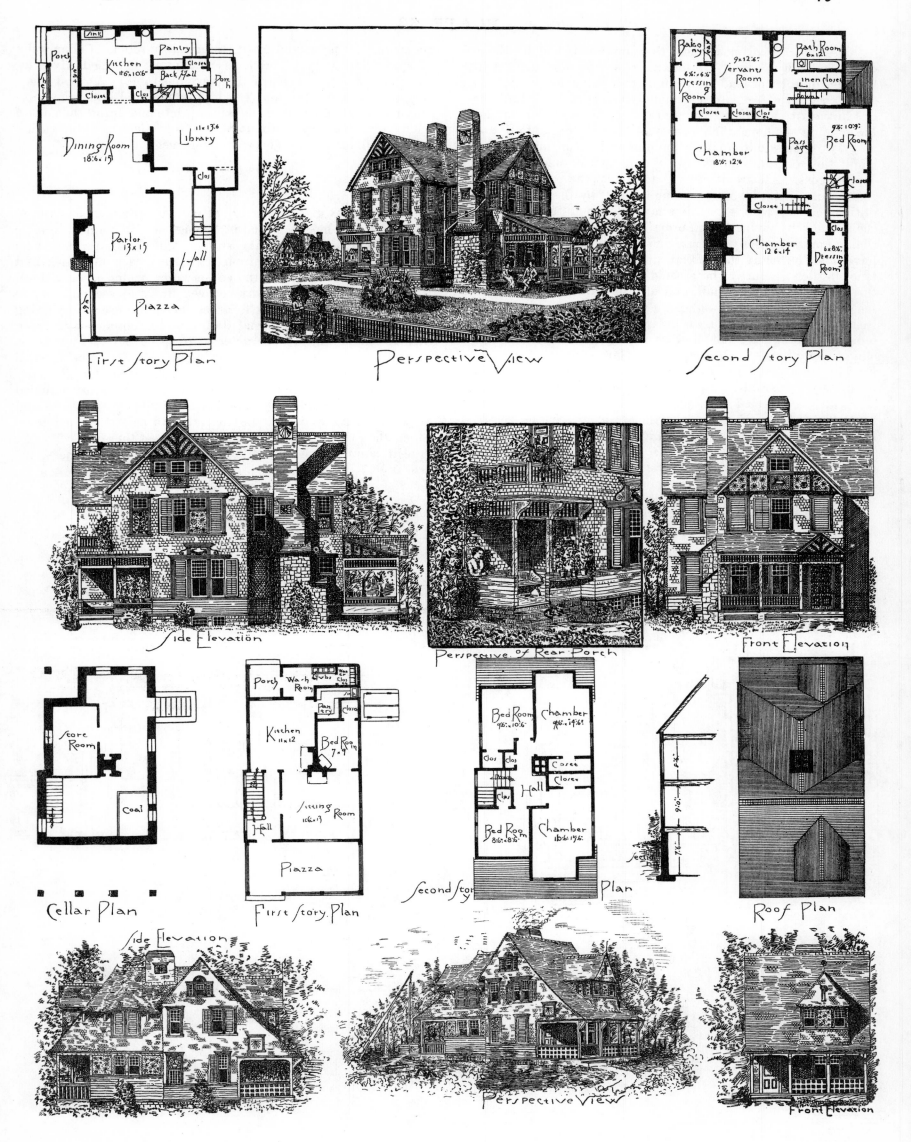

First Story Plan

Perspective View

Second Story Plan

Side Elevation

Perspective of Rear Porch

Front Elevation

Cellar Plan

First Story Plan

Second Story Plan

Roof Plan

Side Elevation

Perspective View

Front Elevation

PALLISER'S NEW COTTAGE HOMES AND DETAILS.

PLATE 46.

Design 137 gives us a house that, no doubt, will fill the eye of a great many people. In looking over a book of designs like this, no doubt the reader will find something he would like; but the reader will please remember that it is easier to build castles in the air than in reality, and to the man who contemplates the erection of a home there is some sensible thinking to be done, and it does not do to theorize too much; but he must carefully count the cost, and then count the room to come within this limit of cost. All architects will agree that the greatest bane of their professional labors is brought about by the adverse wills of their clients, who, after they have delivered themselves and their minds by giving the information as to their limit of cost, then go on and specify the size and number of rooms they must have, and the many things that are indispensable to their existence in the structure to be erected, until they have gone two or three times over their limit, and still they won't cut down, but insist the architect must and can give them what they ask for at their price. Verily it is no wonder architects seldom live to be old. This design is a model of its class and in every way a sensible, roomy house, well adapted to a large family who may be happily enough fixed to live in luxury and such ease as a house of this style warrants. The rooms on first floor are of a nice size and so connected together as to open up practically into one. The entrance hall is very nicely arranged, the recessed fire-place under stairs, fully illustrated in section, through hall being a pleasant feature, giving an air of warmth and welcome to those entering which could not fail but be cheerful. The roomy conservatory on the rear connecting the sitting-room or parlor, is a good and pleasing arrangement. Second floor is well planned for good chambers, closets and bath-room. The back stairs extending to attic gives access to four or five good

rooms on that floor, and good storage attic-room. Cellar walls of stone, first story of brick—second story shingled, gives an external variety of construction very desirable. A good heating apparatus, a slate roof, good plumbing and hard wood finish on the first floor would be appropriate and bring the cost of such a structure up to about $7,500, this amount being varied by finish, location and general management.

Design 138 gives us a very attractive cottage of one-and-a-half stories in height, which in arrangement of plan is capable of furnishing many good suggestions. The children's play-room on ground level, reached from back hall, is a nice idea and utilizes this space under the conservatory which is on a level with stair platform, half way between first and second story to very good advantage, this location for the conservatory being very desirable. The external design of this cottage is pleasing and of such a unique character as to meet the ideas of those wanting a small house of an artistic order, the style being such that will wear and grow upon those seeing it most. The sides of first story are paneled and clapboarded, second story shingled and the roofs could be covered with shingles painted red and very effective. Should it be desirable to enlarge or get more room, the plan is capable of changes to meet this end. To execute it about as shown, with the necessary conveniences, the cost is $3,750.

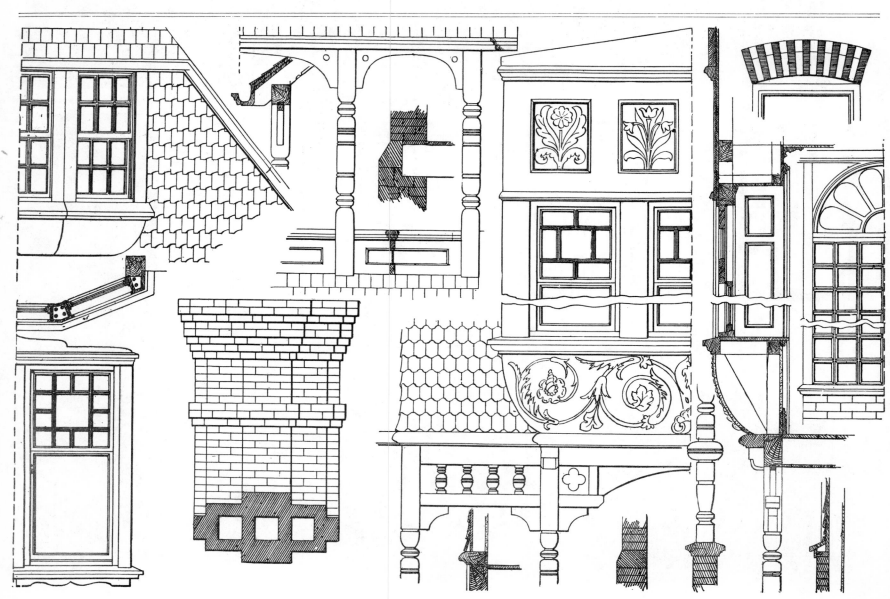

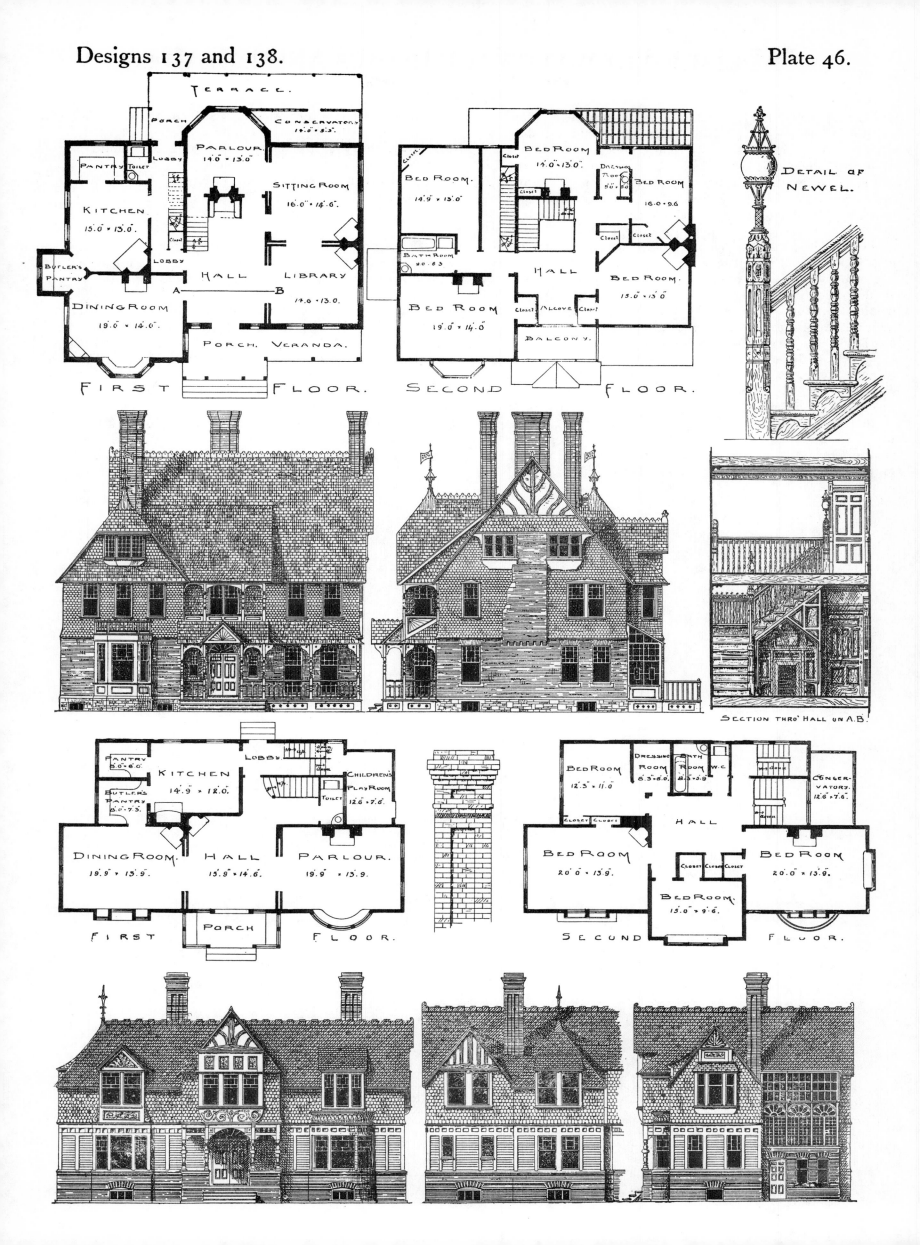

PLATE 47.

Design 139 is a type of house well adapted to suburban erection. The lower story is of brick, and could well be done with four inches of brick work laid up on the outside of the frame work and anchored to same. This method of construction is known as brick veneering, and is a good way of giving a brick appearance with very little material and at little cost, compared with having to build a twelve-inch wall, which would be the ordinary way of doing it. The frame work of second story is covered with shingles. This exterior is very plain and simple, both in detail and construction, yet gives a sensible and pleasing structure, which, when complete and properly painted, would present to the view of the passer-by an appearance that would strike the beholder as being what common sense would naturally apply in the erection of a house of that size. Some one has said you can always know a man by the house he lives in. Still, we do not think this applicable in all cases, though to a very large extent it may be true, as a tasty and artistic mind will generally try and keep his home surroundings in keeping with his artistic ideas, and have it, at least, present a clean and tidy appearance; and nothing embellishes a house at little cost more than a well arranged front yard and garden. A few flowers and flowering shrubs, and occasionally a group of evergreens, if the grounds are large enough to admit of it, judiciously distributed, and so planted with a view to their best effect from the windows, as well as from the street—these always come in and help out the artistic effect and add to the personal enjoyment and contentment of the inmates of any home. Nature is a great satisfier, and flowers and plants always lead the mind into bright and pleasant channels, no matter how worried or tired one may be. We cannot help but love nature, as displayed in these beautiful things, that come for the season and brighten and cheer our way through life. Such a house as this, with creeping vines climbing and running over the brick work of the first story, always looks well, and is a thing that should be more encouraged and done. We commend this house for its simplicity, and trust that it will be honored for the good there is in it. Cost, $4,800.

Design 140 is a house well adapted for a residence by the seashore or elsewhere, for summer use; gives a liberal amount of piazza accommodation, for living outdoors; and the arrangement of hall through centre of house, with doors from piazza at both ends, and its general arrangement, with the principal rooms all connecting with it, makes the whole living portion of the house, for the purposes it is intended, "a model," and one that any person will be perfectly safe in following after. The locating of the kitchen and its entrance have been carefully studied, so as to make the communication to the other portions of the house perfectly convenient and desirable in every respect and at the same time keep that portion of the house isolated to as great an extent as possible. There is a cellar under the whole house. The rooms are large. Five bed rooms and bath room, with a liberal closet to every room, are provided on second floor, with a linen closet in hall, and the attic gives four sleeping rooms and trunk room. Perfect earth closets, properly ventilated and furnished with simple, mechanical dust-sprinklers, make a perfect sanitary system. A good storage closet on rear piazza is found to be a great convenience for keeping together all the implements connected with the sports of the lawn and field. Cost of construction is $3,000.

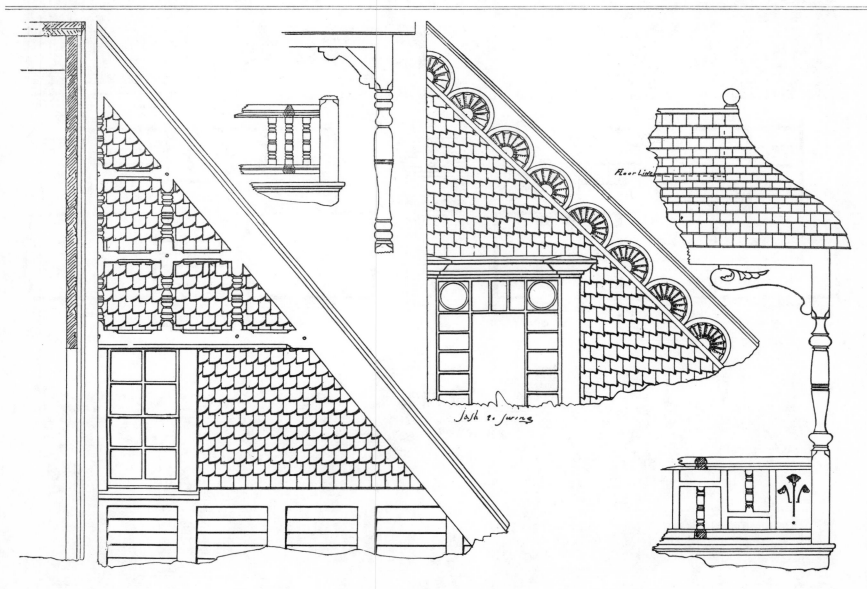

Sash & Swing

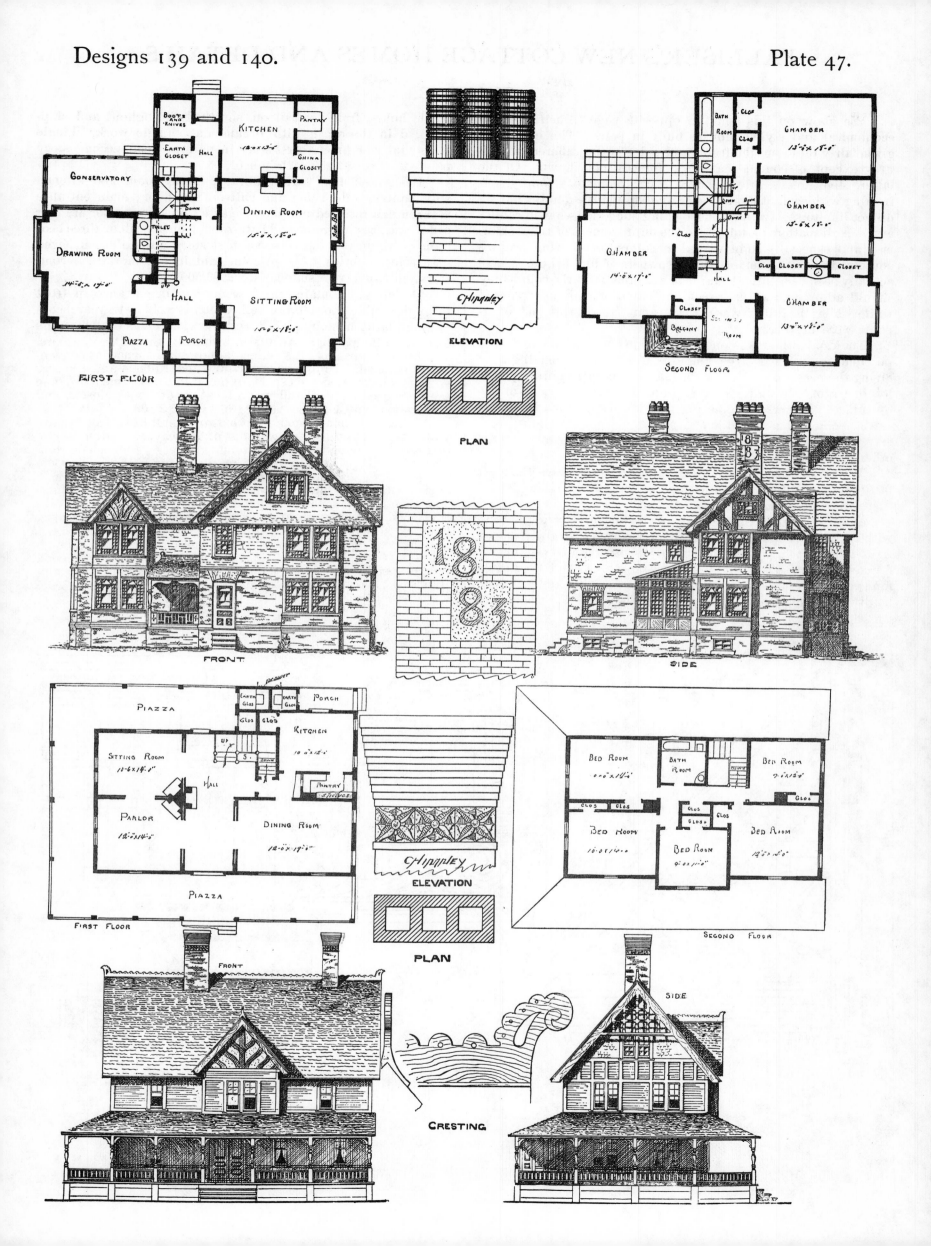

FIRST FLOOR

Conservatory

Drawing Room
14'-6" x 19'-0"

Hall

Piazza   Porch

Boots and Knives

Earth Closet

Hall

Kitchen
13'-0" x 13'-6"

Pantry

China Closet

Toilet

Dining Room
15'-0" x 15'-0"

Down

Sitting Room
15'-0" x 18'-0"

ELEVATION

C. Hippley

PLAN

FRONT

1883

SECOND FLOOR

Bath Room   Clos   Clos

Chamber
15'-6" x 18'-0"

Chamber
14'-0" x 17'-0"

Clos

Chamber
13'-6" x 18'-0"

Hall

Clos   Closet   Closet

Down   Down

Chamber
13'-0" x 17'-0"

Closet   Sewing Room   Balcony

SIDE

FIRST FLOOR

Piazza

Earth Clos   Earth Clos   Porch

Clos   Clos

Sitting Room
10'-6" x 14'-0"

Hall

Parlor
12'-0" x 14'-5"

Up   S

Down

Kitchen
10'-0" x 12'-0"

Pantry
shelves

Dining Room
12'-0" x 19'-0"

Piazza

ELEVATION

C. Hippley

PLAN

SECOND FLOOR

Bed Room
10'-0" x 14'-0"

Bath Room

Bed Room
9'-0" x 15'-0"

Clos   Clos   Clos

Bed Room
10'-0" x 14'-0"

Clos   Clos

Bed Room
9'-0" x 11'-0"

Bed Room
13'-0" x 15'-0"

FRONT

CRESTING

SIDE

PALLISER'S NEW COTTAGE HOMES AND DETAILS.

PLATE 48.

We show on this and the opposite page, illustrations of economical and stylish houses built in pairs. The elevations given fairly represent the fronts and sides of the different structures, except, of course, that the colors are not shown. Of the latter, olive greens, grays and reds predominate, strongly contrasting with each other, and clearly defining the detail; but we do not like to see two persons owning such houses who cannot agree in all matters pertaining to the improvement of their premises, and especially so in regard to colors for painting, and we could name several instances where owners of double houses have actually been very bitter towards one another as to the colors they should adopt, and we have seen one half of such houses painted white while the other was brown, and the owners and occupants were brothers at that.

The double house is one of the many ways by which it is possible to obtain a large amount of room at a small outlay giving the necessary accommodation for separate families. One lot, one roof, one wall, etc., etc., is made to do the duty of two but unless two persons come together in owning such houses as can agree in all matters, it is better that they should be the property of one man, as then he can live in one-half and rent the other, and do as he pleases with the whole.

We think that these designs cannot fail to please the most fastidious double-house critics and in the New England States there are many of them.

Design 141 gives each family a two-story and attic dwelling with three good liberal rooms and hall, with nice staircase, well lighted on first floor; a pantry and rear entry is also well placed for convenience and economy on this floor. Second floor gives four good bed-rooms, with closets and bath room, and the attic has two bed-rooms and space for storage. Cellar under the

whole house, frame is balloon, sheathed throughout and clapboarded in the main with ornamental shingle work, shingle roofs; interior finish—first story in natural wood, second story painted. Cost $2,250 each house.

Design 142 has parlor, library, dining-room and kitchen with pantry, toilet-room and hall on first floor; main entrance is through a recessed porch at the side; on second floor are four bed-rooms, sewing-room and bath-room; on attic floor three bed-rooms. Underpinning of stone, first story walls of brick, faced with selected brick of even color laid in red mortar; second story, shingled, roof slated. Cost, $3,500.

Design 143 contains on first floor main entrance in front through double doors to the hall, which is 8x16 feet square, containing platform stairs placed well back, and has double doors leading to the parlor; passage to kitchen is through two doors, and from this passage the cellar, laundry and furnace is conveniently reached. Dining-room, pantry and kitchen and the rear entrances as located are especially good in arrangement. There are four good-sized chambers and bath-room, with closets, and also rooms in attic for servants, etc. Cost $3 100.

Design 144 has a good front entrance hall 8x11 feet square, with a flight of box-stairs, well out of the way, ascending to second floor. Parlor and dining-room are large rooms and connected to hall. Cellar stairs are reached from both dining-room and kitchen; a side piazza at end of dining-room which can be closed with glass for conservatory if desired is quite a feature. The second floor gives three good bed-rooms with closets, bathroom and sewing-room and the attic floor has two bed-rooms. Cost, $2,300.

For the suburbs of large towns and cities there can be no better style of houses built than these that will give as good returns on the investment; business men in moderate circumstances need just such homes and they will rent for $30 to $50 a month easily.

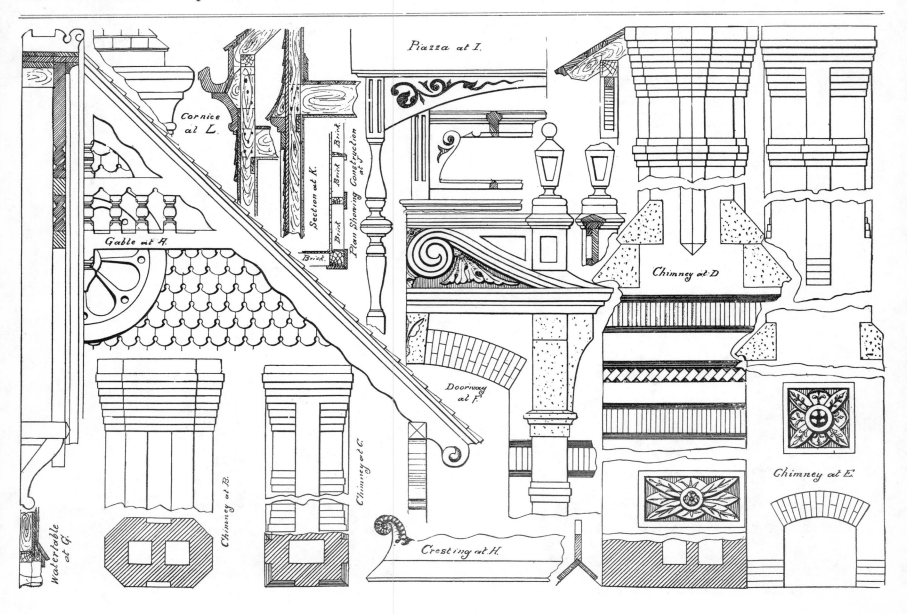

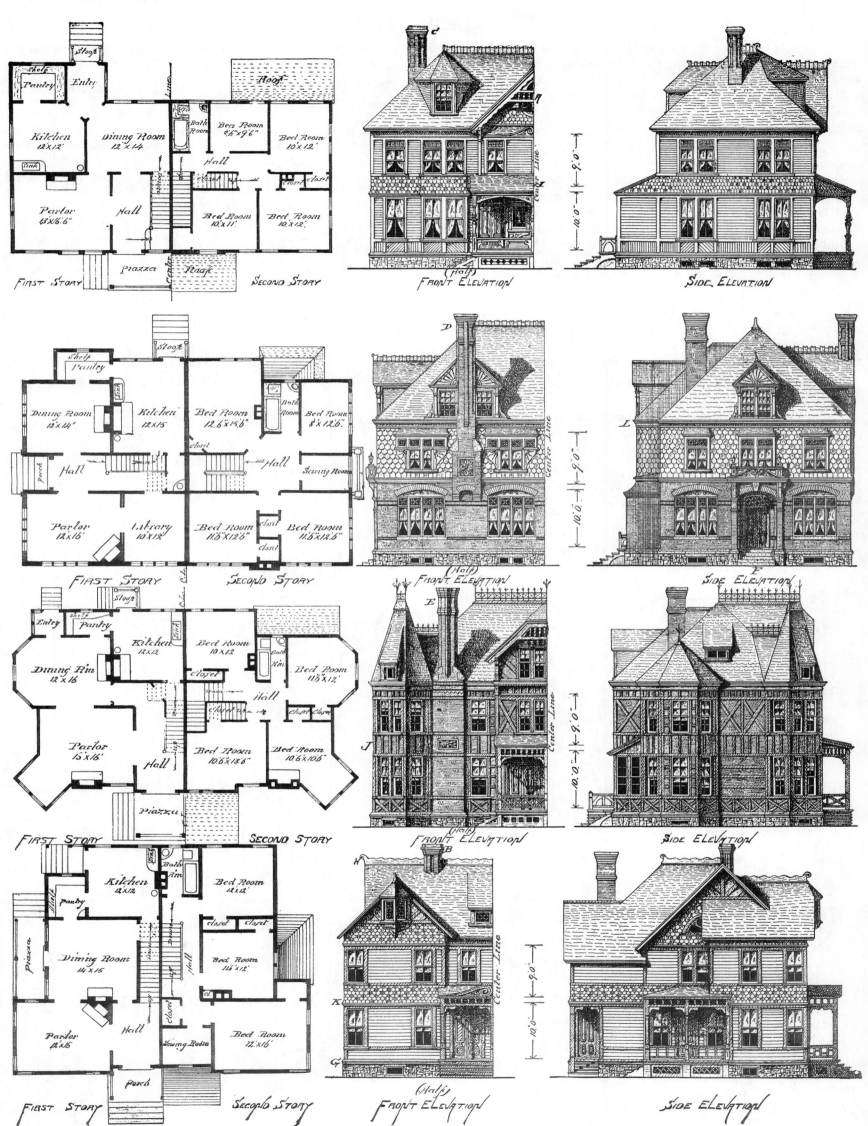

FIRST STORY   SECOND STORY   FRONT ELEVATION   SIDE ELEVATION

Kitchen 12'x12'   Dining Room 12'x14'   Bed Room 8.6'x9.6'   Bed Room 10'x12'
Shelf Pantry Entry Stoop
Sink
Parlor 13'x16.6'   Hall   Bath Room   Closet   Closet
                   Bed Room 10'x11'   Bed Room 10'x12'
Piazza   Roof   Roof
(Half)

Dining Room 12'x14'   Kitchen 12'x15'   Bed Room 12.6'x13.6'   Bed Room 8'x12.6'
Shelf Pantry Stoop Sink Bath Room
Porch   Hall   Hall   Sewing Room
Parlor 12'x16'   Library 10'x12'   Bed Room 11.6'x12.6'   Bed Room 11.6'x12.6'   closet
FIRST STORY   SECOND STORY   FRONT ELEVATION   SIDE ELEVATION
(Half)

Entry shelf Pantry Stoop Sink
Kitchen 12'x12'   Bed Room 10'x12'   Bed Room 11.6'x12'   Bath Rm
Dining Rm 12'x16'   closet   Hall   closet   closet
Parlor 15'x16'   Hall   Bed Room 10.6'x13.6'   Bed Room 10.6'x10.6'
Piazza
FIRST STORY   SECOND STORY   FRONT ELEVATION   SIDE ELEVATION
(Half)

Kitchen 12'x12'   Bed Room 12'x12'   Bath Rm
Shelf Pantry Entry
closet   closet
Piazza   Dining Room 14'x15'   Hall   Bed Room 11.6'x12'
Parlor 12'x16'   Hall   Sewing Room   Bed Room 12'x16'
Porch
FIRST STORY   SECOND STORY   FRONT ELEVATION   SIDE ELEVATION
(Half)

10'0"   9'0"
10'0"   9'0"
10'0"   9'0"
10'0"   9'0"
Center Line

PLATE 49.

Design 145. We here present the reader with a substantial, plain, yet very good appearing brick and shingle country house, with accommodation for a family of a dozen or more persons, and its style is thoroughly in keeping with the character of a rural neighborhood and is suggestive of comfort and cheerfulness.

The outlines of each elevation, the materials of the different stories and the window and door openings are arranged to be dissimilar in form; strong and decided contrasts of color are applied to different parts and tinted glass of various shades are used for the smaller lights of the sash. There is an absence of large verandas with their roofs so generally found on houses of this class and which are so apt to shut out the genial sunshine, so much wanted in homes in the cold season, and to effectually shut out the same must result in weakness and death to the occupants.

The liberal front porch connecting with the large main hall makes a cool retreat for summer, and in winter the porch is arranged to be effectually closed up by the aid of sashes and a storm door so that the cold can be excluded from the house.

The floor plans explain themselves; kitchen has a dresser built into recess. Dining room has a sideboard in recess and a hall stand is built in recess in the main hall and all in a thoroughly convenient and practical manner. The arrangement of the office or business room, with its outside private entrance, and the conservatory located above on a level with platform of stairs will, we are sure, commend itself to many persons who wish for both these in a country house; and there are many reasons why a special room for business should be provided not only for the large farmer, politician or medical man, but also for those who,

doing business in the city, make their family home in the suburb or adjacent rural neighborhood.

The third story supplies necessary accommodation for the hired help. Cost of erection $7,000.

Design 146. This is perhaps in style a more ambitious house than the preceding, although smaller in plan, and may be adapted to a similar domain.

The materials of which it is built is brick for the first story, which could be of stone, and for second story, timber construction, with plastered filling of cement between the timbers which requires careful work to make a good and perfect job; and this rough casting of panel work is coming more and more into favor, and mechanics will therefore become more familiar with the modes of carrying out the same in a workmanlike manner, although it is a fact that nearly all mechanics working at masonry trades discourage and condemn the adoption of anything out of their ordinary routine of brick and mortar, and we have known cases where the downright pigheadedness of a mason has spoiled many a good piece of work that he might have otherwise made a reputation on, if he only had had the sense to see his own interests.

A veranda on the south side of this house is a pleasant feature, and at the same time does not shut out the sun from living and dining rooms, both of which are well exposed and are large and elegant for living apartments.

The porch shields the front hall in winter by enclosing the same; and for an elegant convenient house to live in this house can be recommended to the reader. Cost, $4,000.

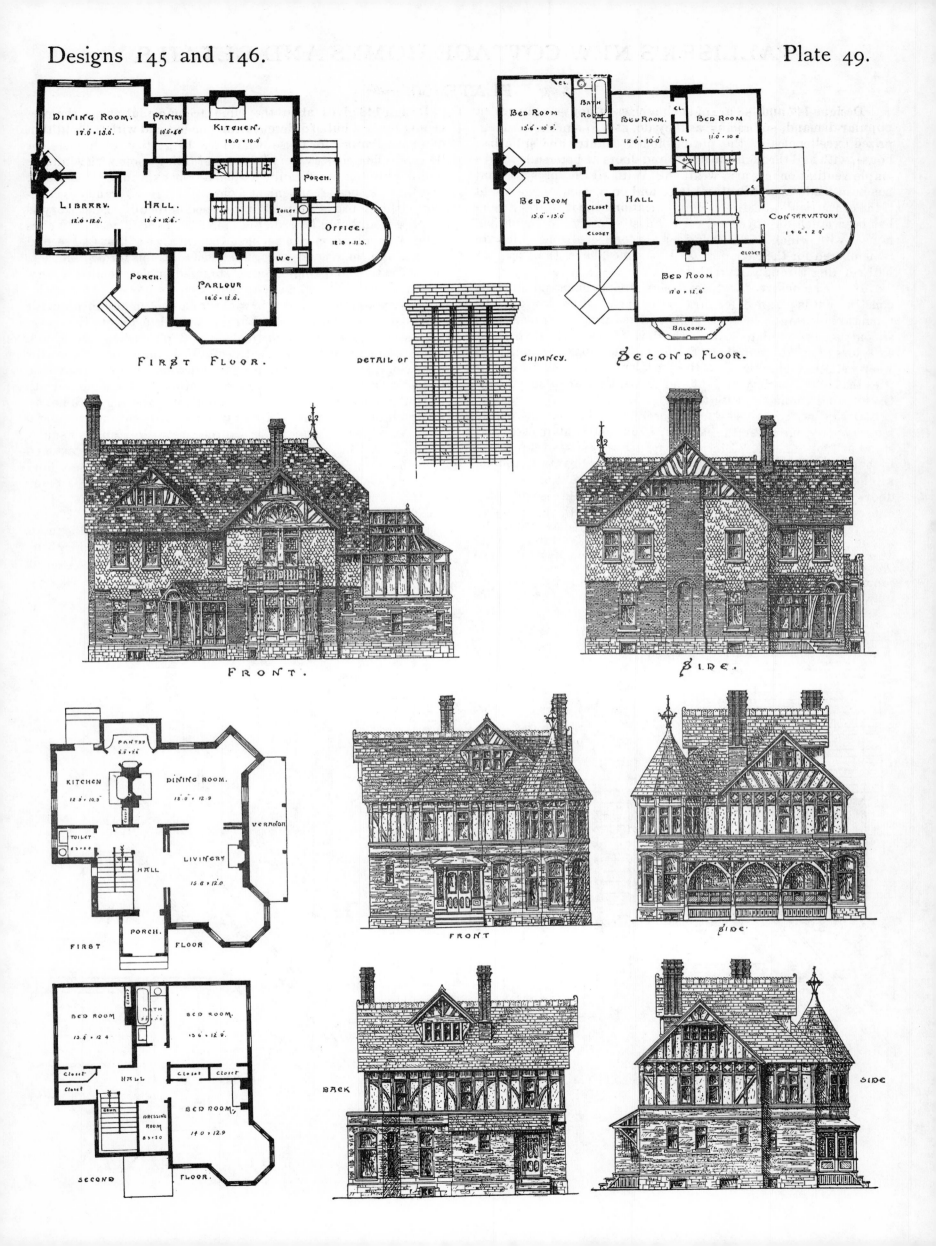

Designs 145 and 146.

Plate 49.

PLATE 50.

Designs 147 and 148 are of snch a class of houses as answer a popular demand, embracing, as they do, at a low price the long-prized excellencies of the old-fashioned country and suburban house, with hall through the centre and doors at both ends to give ample ventilation in warm weather. With all the progress that has been made in architectural taste and conveniences, we doubt if the central hall and direct communication from it to every room has been much improved on. The finest country and surburban houses with which our associations are connected, and which are remembered for their comfort and elegance, have the spacious hall running through the middle.

It will be observed in these designs that as far as possible the construction is planned for straightforward, square work. The rooms are pleasantly located, easily reached and, for economy, are as compact as any plans that may be devised of similar area. The exteriors are plain, but at the same time they look well and will wear well, and while without the prevalent numerous irregularities that afford variety of light and shade, they are also without the expense connected with them.

Design 147 contains on first floor four good rooms and all the requisite conveniences ; the hall is spacious and contains seat and stand at foot of stairs. Dining-room has a recessed fire-place with seats on each side. A passage through china pantry, between kitchen and dining-room, cuts off the smell of cooking, and the doors through this passage are hung with spring hinges and without locks or other fastenings ; they are opened with the foot and close immediately after passing. The domestic can pass from the kitchen to dining-room with the service of the table, while flies and the aroma of cooking have little chance of getting into the main part of the house. On second floor there are five rooms, bath-room and plenty of closets, and on third floor are four rooms. Exterior is clapboarded throughout. Cost $3,600.

Design 148 gives about the same accommodation as the preceding design, but of different arrangement, and with the addition of a conservatory for those who love to gratify their taste for flowers. This conservatory is in rear of dining-room with windows looking into same, forming a splendid background and effect, and the entrance is convenient from hall via rear veranda. Exterior of this house is simple but yet good in detail. First story is clapboarded, being mitred at corners. A band 2 feet, 6 inches deep of shingles comes in between the windows of first and second stories, and the second story is ceiled and panels formed on face, which with the panelled and shingled gables, makes a very effective finish. Cost, $4,000.

To make houses warm in winter and cool in summer, an air chamber for confined or dead air is formed between the outer sheathing on the frame and the lath and plaster of the inside. The old method of filling in with soft brick laid on edge in mortar has been discarded some time ago, and where special provision is made, on account of an exposed situation, for securing warmth in winter, in addition to the sheathing and papering of the exterior of frame, a system of filling in with sawdust, or of mineral wool, or of back plastering or lathing between studs is usually adopted—nailing of rough pieces or of lath against strips fastened to each side of the studs and covering with coarse mortar, and this has been found very serviceable, but this also is being rapidly superceded by sheathing up the inside of the frame, before plastering, with a patent sheathing lath, a combination of sheathing and lath, which makes a perfect and tight job, and is made ready for plastering by the operation ; and the Byrkit Sheathing Lath is something that will be shortly used in the construction of all buildings, and is already highly recommended by architects and builders.

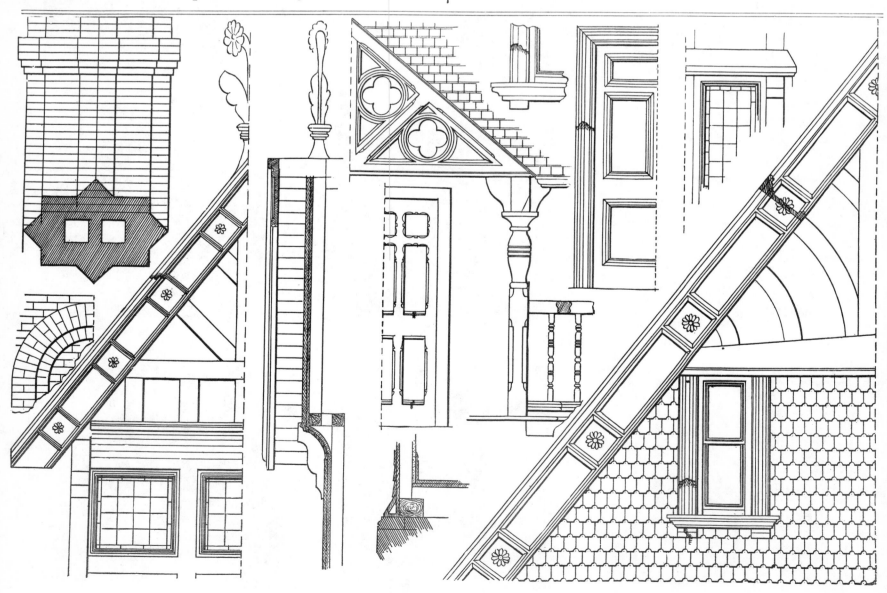

Designs 147 and 148.

Plate 50.

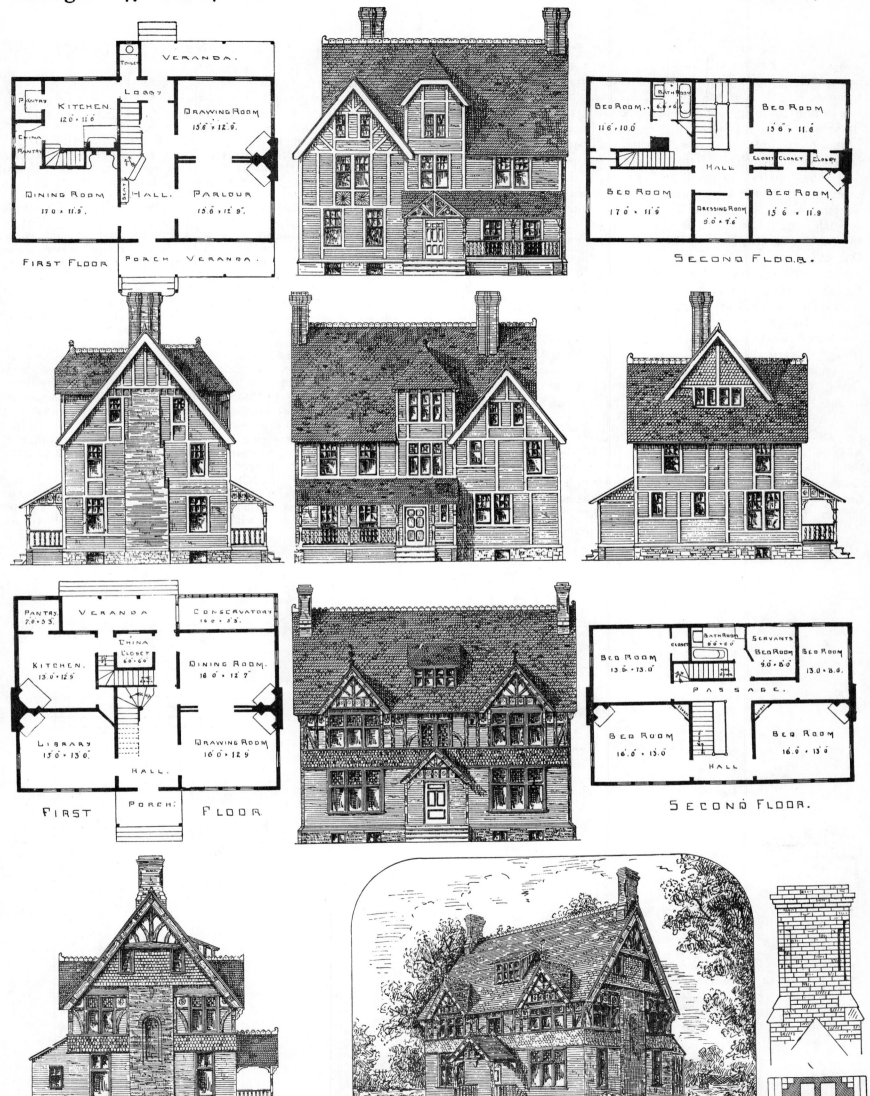

FIRST FLOOR

PORCH VERANDA.

SECOND FLOOR.

FIRST FLOOR

PORCH

SECOND FLOOR.

PALLISER'S NEW COTTAGE HOMES AND DETAILS.

PLATE 51.

The designs given on this plate are for houses specially adapted for erection in Florida, or by the sea shore, for summer occupancy, and we have designed, from time to time, a large number of such houses for permanent and winter residence at the South and summer residence at the North; they have no cellars under them; no mason work is required in the walling of under-pinning, etc., but they are supported on posts set in the ground, and admit of a free circulation of air. The post holes should be dug about one foot larger than the post, and the space around filled in with water-lime concrete, being careful to bring the concrete above the level of the finished grade, and to slope it off in such a manner as to form a water shed around the post on the surface of the ground; this will prevent the post from rotting at the ground line and will insure its preservation for many years. The ground under the house should be rounded up to the centre and graded from that and sloped down on all sides, then a substance of coarse gravel, ashes and water-lime mixed so as to form a concrete should be spread over the surface under the house, thus preventing damp and malarious vapors from rising up into the house. A little foresight will render such houses healthful and wholesome, but as a rule such matters are never thought of and are carelessly neglected, and, as a consequence, sickness and other distress follow which could easily have been prevented.

Design 149 has a large hall, parlor and dining-room, with kitchen properly isolated from the other rooms, though easily reached from dining-room; piazza and porch room is liberal, and there is every opportunity of getting through the house all the breeze there may be about; five bed-rooms and closets, also a balcony are obtained on second floor. Cost $1,000.00.

Design 150 contains a like amount of room as the former, but distributed a little differently, yet meeting all the requirements of climate and wants of the people. Cost $800.00.

Design 151 gives a somewhat different plan from the other two, though very convenient, and, as will be seen by careful study, is well adapted to the purposes for which it is intended. Cost, $900.

Balloon framing is technically as well as sarcastically applied to a system of putting together frame buildings, that had its origin in the early settlement of our prairies, where it was impossible to obtain heavy timbers and skillful mechanics, and its simple, effective and economical manner of construction has been of great benefit in building up of new territory and sections of this country, and being stronger than any other method of framing has led to its universal adoption for buildings of every class throughout the United States. In olden times, before the portable saw mill, or easy transportation by railroad of timber and lumber usurped the functions of the broad-axe, the skillful framing of a building required no inconsiderable talent and practice. He indeed was considered a boss carpenter who could "in his mind," with magic scratch awl, indiscriminately "lay out" mortices and tenons in cabalistic characters upon a confused accumulation of dimension sticks, which on "raising day" without hinderance of mismatched jointing, assorted and assembled themselves into a harmonious whole, from sill to roof-tree. Such was the building practiced forty years ago. Now, in these days of cheap things, substantial frames are, as it were, knocked together, and men who appear to indifferently wield hammer and saw, are employed in the carpentering.

The balloon frame is a characteristic American invention, and like all successful improvements, has thrived on its own merits, the balloon frame has passed through and survived the theory, ridicule and abuse of all who have seen fit to attack it, and may be reckoned among the prominent inventions of the present generation, an invention neither fostered nor developed by any hope of great rewards, but which plainly acknowledges its origin in necessity.

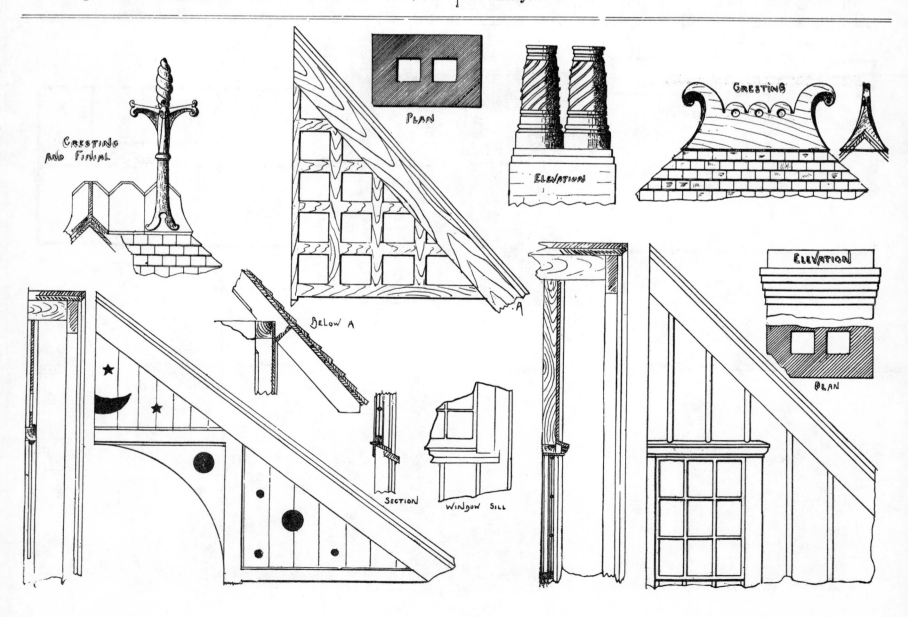

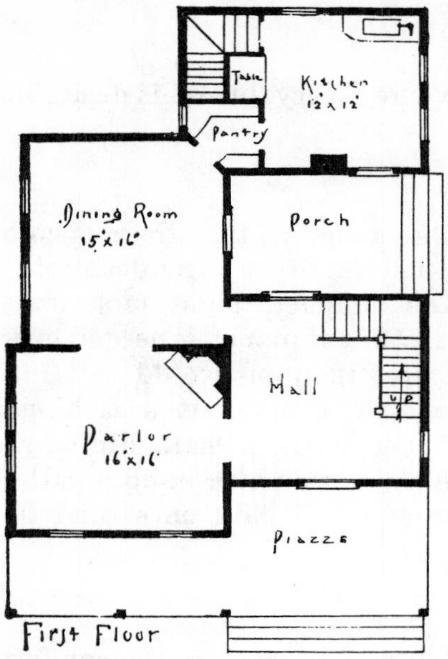

First Floor

Kitchen 12 x 12

Pantry

Dining Room 15 x 16'

Porch

Parlor 16' x 16'

Hall

Piazza

Second Floor

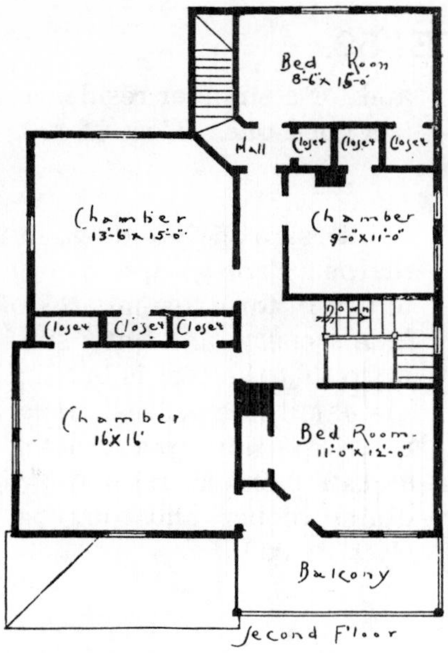

Bed Room 8'-6" x 15'-0"

Hall

Closet Closet Closet

Chamber 13'-6" x 15'-6"

Chamber 9'-0" x 11'-0"

Closet Closet Closet

Chamber 16' x 16'

Bed Room 11'-0" x 12'-0"

Balcony

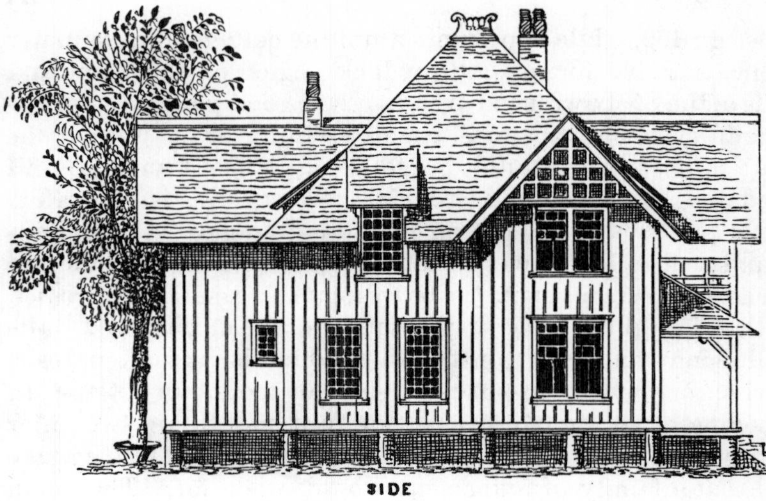

SIDE

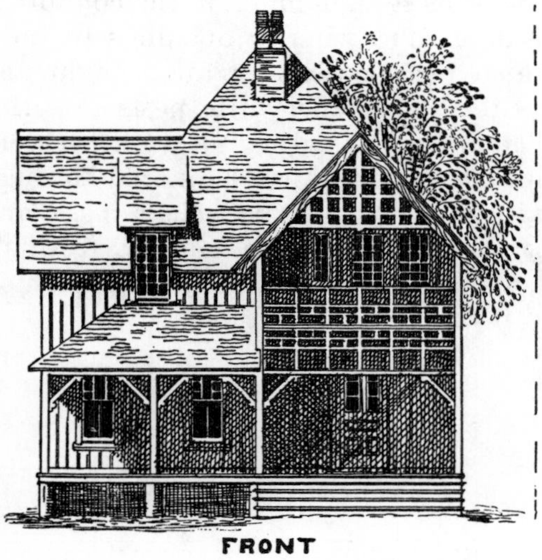

FRONT

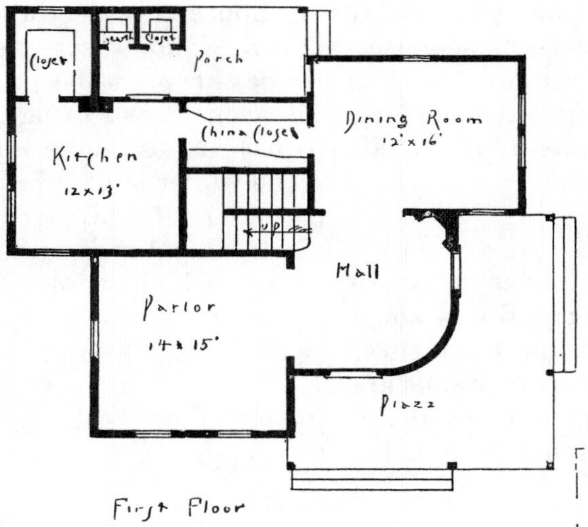

First Floor

Closet

Porch

Kitchen 12 x 13'

China Closet

Dining Room 12' x 16'

Parlor 14' x 15'

Hall

Piazza

Second Floor

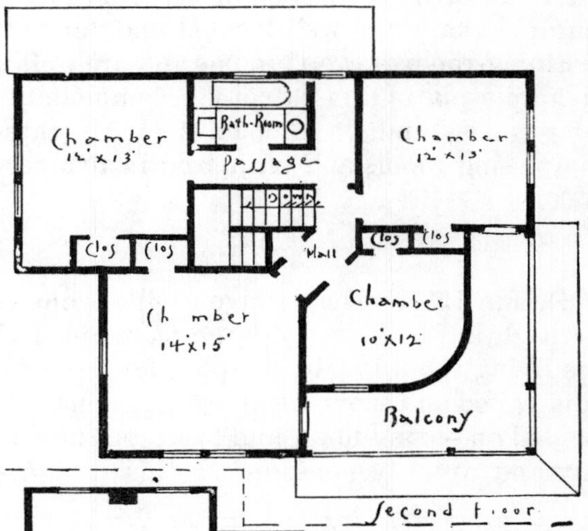

Chamber 12' x 13'

Bath-Room

Passage

Chamber 12' x 13'

Clos. Clos.

Hall

Clos. Clos.

Chamber 14' x 15'

Chamber 10' x 12'

Balcony

First Floor

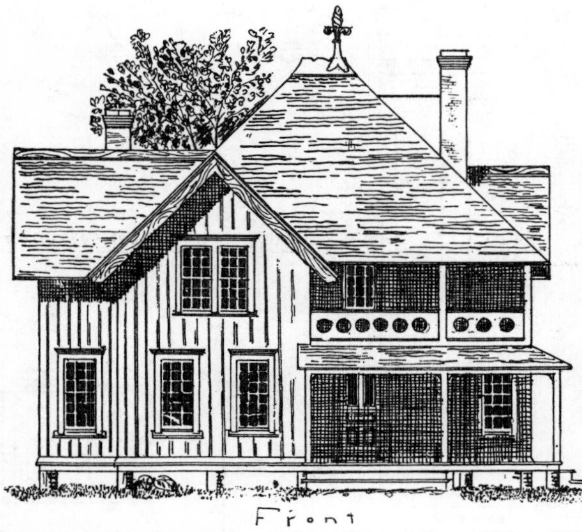

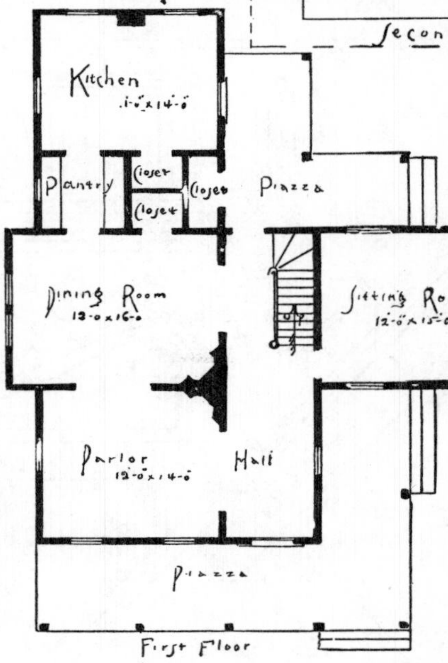

Kitchen 11'-0" x 14'-0"

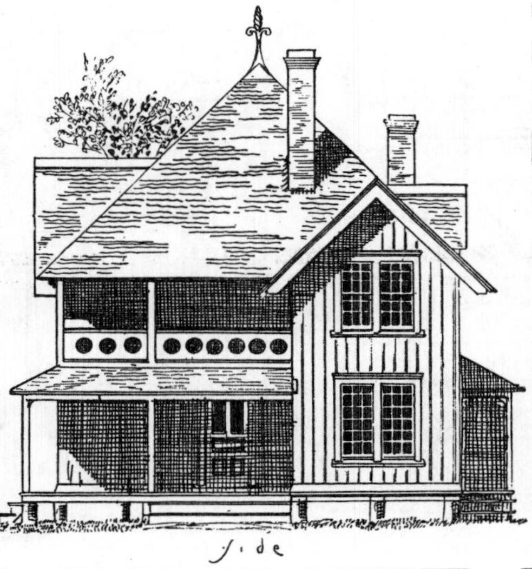

Pantry

Closet

Closet

Closet

Piazza

Dining Room 13'-0" x 16'-0"

Sitting Room 12'-6" x 15'-0"

Parlor 13'-0" x 14'-0"

Hall

Piazza

Front

Side

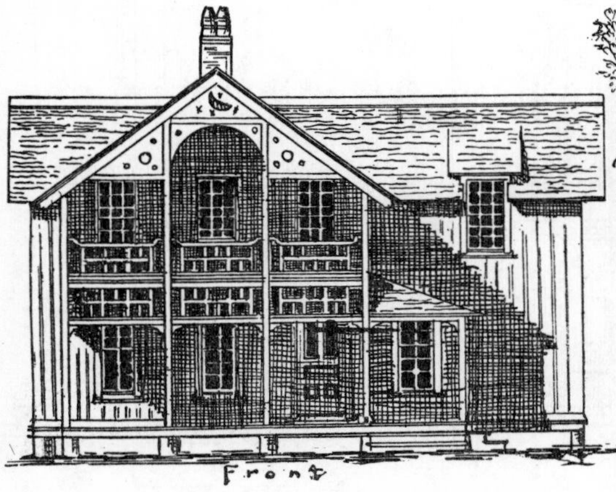

Front

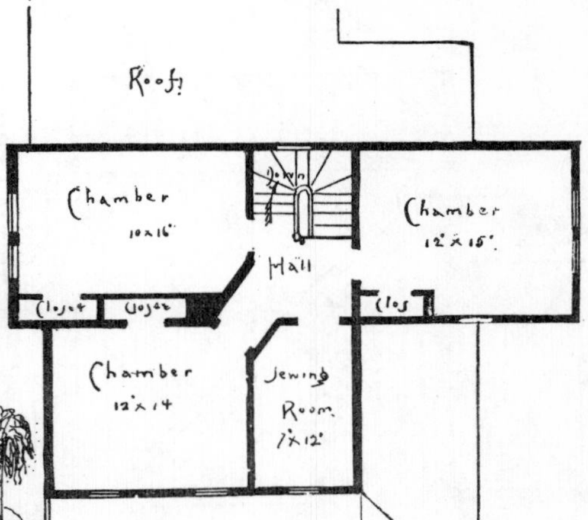

Perspective View

Roof

Chamber 10' x 16'

Chamber 12' x 16'

Hall

Closet Closet

Clos.

Chamber 12' x 14'

Sewing Room 7' x 12'

Porch

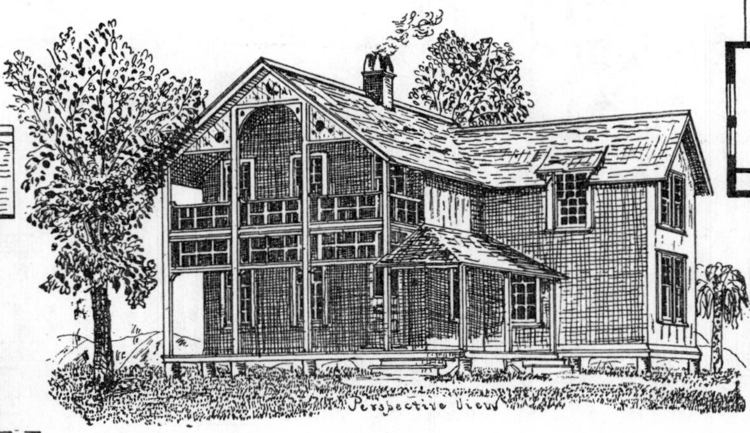

Second Floor

Design 152, while it presents a unique cottage for a summer residence suitable for the Adirondack region or the Thousand Islands of the St. Lawrence River, is also a good plan for a permanent country or suburban residence. If built for the former, the design here shown should be followed. The framing is all dressed and is exposed in the rooms. The covering is of narrow, matched pine boarding, put on outside of frame, laid horizontally and well nailed to every stud. The floors and partitions are constructed in like manner, the boarding in all cases being dressed on both sides, thus doing away with the use of plastered walls and allowing of a quick construction, which is very often desirable when one wishes to put up a shore or mountain cottage, at the opening of spring, for occupancy in a month or two after deciding to build it. The interior arrangements of this cottage are all that a family of refinement would wish for. The main hall is liberal in size, has a floor of narrow hardwood, with neat border; an open fire-place, in which to burn wood when the air is damp. Stairs are well located and out of the way; the parlor and dining-room are good rooms and are well placed and connected; ample piazza and balcony accommodation are provided, for cool retreats, and on second floor are three good chambers, two dressing rooms and bath, and in attic servants' room. Cost, $1,500.

Design 153 gives a cottage of like construction as the above described, and has a very large piazza for living outdoors, and a large living room inside, adapted for general use of the family, and is a good and economical arrangement. Four bed rooms are provided on second floor, and to anyone needing a simple cottage, easily and quickly constructed, this design should be a help,

and for a summer residence, where every breeze is desirable, it is a good one. Cost $1,000.

Design 154 provides, in like manner as the others, a cottage that is a little gem, and for a small family a very desirable one to live in for a few months of the summer, amid mountains or lake scenery, and but a small amount of money is needed to erect it, so that the cost is but little more than one would pay out for his family expenses for a season's sojourn at a fashionable resort, putting up at a hotel. It gives large hall, dining-room and kitchen on first floor, with open fire-place in both hall and dining-rooms, and four bed rooms and bath on second floor. Cost, $1,000.

During the summer months it adds much to the comfort of a house to protect all the doors and window openings by neat wire window screens, which do not obstruct air or sight and does keep out flies, mosquitoes and other little pests that this season of year brings. The method of adjusting these screens to their position is very simple, and they can be stored through the winter in a closet or attic, and by their use cleanliness and comfort of an open country-house can thus be enjoyed, fresh air can be had in abundance, and a feeling of comfort insured which those who have once tried it will never be without.

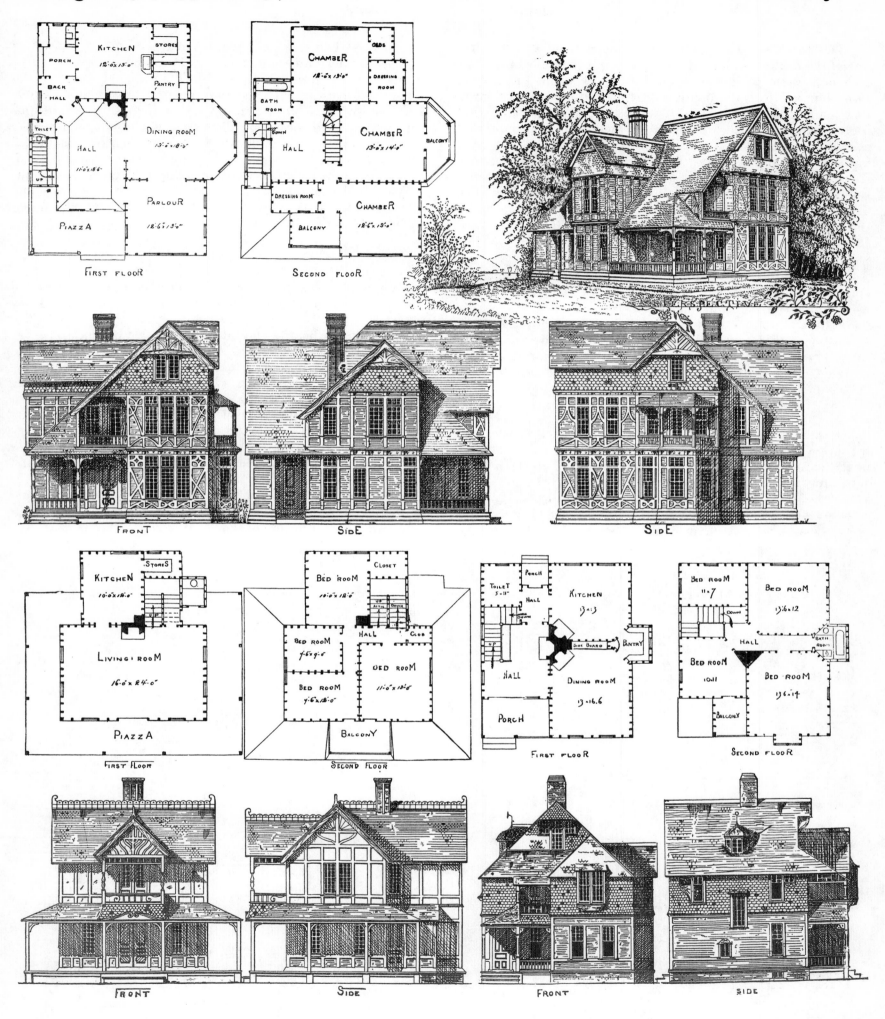

FIRST FLOOR

KITCHEN 12·0 x 13·0
STORES
PORCH
BACK HALL
PANTRY
TOILET
HALL 11·0 x 18·6
DINING ROOM 13·0 x 18·0
UP
PIAZZA
PARLOUR 12·6 x 15·0

SECOND FLOOR

CHAMBER 18·6 x 13·0
CLOS.
DRESSING ROOM
BATH ROOM
DOWN
HALL
CHAMBER 13·0 x 14·0
BALCONY
DRESSING ROOM
CHAMBER 18·6 x 13·0
BALCONY

PERSPECTIVE

FRONT   SIDE   SIDE

FIRST FLOOR

STORES
KITCHEN 10·0 x 18·0
LIVING ROOM 16·0 x 24·0
PIAZZA

SECOND FLOOR

BED ROOM 10·0 x 18·0
CLOSET
ATTIC
DOWN
BED ROOM 7·6 x 9·5
HALL
CLOS.
BED ROOM 7·6 x 13·0
BED ROOM 11·0 x 13·0
BALCONY

FIRST FLOOR

TOILET 5·11
PORCH
HALL
UP
DOWN
KITCHEN 13 x 13
HALL
PORCH
SIDE BOARD
DINING ROOM 13 x 16·6
PANTRY

SECOND FLOOR

BED ROOM 11·7
BED ROOM 13·6 x 12
DOWN
BATH ROOM
HALL
BED ROOM 10·11
BED ROOM 13·6 x 14
BALCONY

FRONT   SIDE   FRONT   SIDE

PALLISER'S NEW COTTAGE HOMES AND DETAILS.

PLATE 53.

Design 155.—This design is quite compact and works up into one of the neatest and prettiest houses it is possible to get up and there are many good reasons for it. The front entrance or reception hall with its unique staircase, its toilet conveniences, its open fire-place, etc., is all that can be desired. The parlor, dining-room and conservatory arrangements and connections are attractive and good. The library is in a quiet and easy corner of the house, and the rear portion of house, of the kitchen, back stairs and hall are especially good. The second floor gives five bed rooms, dressing room, bath room and necessary closets. The front bed room could be made six feet larger by leaving out the dressing room. Two rooms are also provided on third floor. Cost, $4,600.

On the exterior we give by way of variety the hipped or truncated gable, a style of finish which needs to be carefully used, but answers well in some places, and where there is not a disposition to do too much of it. We remember a place where it was introduced on a building some years ago, and the fashion thus set was persistently followed in all manners until it became quite a disagreeable feature there abouts. Better make ordinary gables pointed.

Design 156 is for a cosey, suburban house, such as is wanted by an employee of a bank, office or store, with a considerable family, who desire all the comforts and conveniences of a home suited to people in moderate circumstances of life, yet possessing a degree of taste which could be shown up by them in such a cottage residence as this one, being very good, both in interior arrangement and exterior design. The roofs are covered with

California redwood shingles stained to give them the appearance of English tile, thus obtaining a unique and picturesque roof which is very agreeable to the eye; the second story is also covered with these shingles and the first story clapboarded. The interior wood-work throughout is also of this California mahogany or redwood, which is a beautiful wood when rightly finished up and costs less in the New York market than good, clear, white pine, and it is a wonder that more of it is not used, and we presume it will now come rapidly into favor, and much of it is capable of taking the place of mahogany in color and grain, and at one-third the cost. Cost of building this house $3,500.

Every frame erected for a habitation should be well protected and braced by sheathing it either horizontally or diagonally on same. The latter is the strongest and best method. Each edge of the sheathing boards should be well nailed through to every timber of the frame; yet with all these modern ideas we find many houses put up for rent or sale, and some for occupancy by the owners and builders that are actually with no outer sheathing on frame, without papering or any other protection except a covering of clapboards or novelty siding, and a common lathing and plastering on the inside, thus giving both wind and rain every chance to penetrate, while a few rough boards and some paper laid all over the boarding and well lapped under all casings and corner boards would afford at a cost of a few dollars means of protection that would save fuel and doctors' bills, exceeding the amount in one year, to say nothing about the promotion of both comfort and health of the occupants.

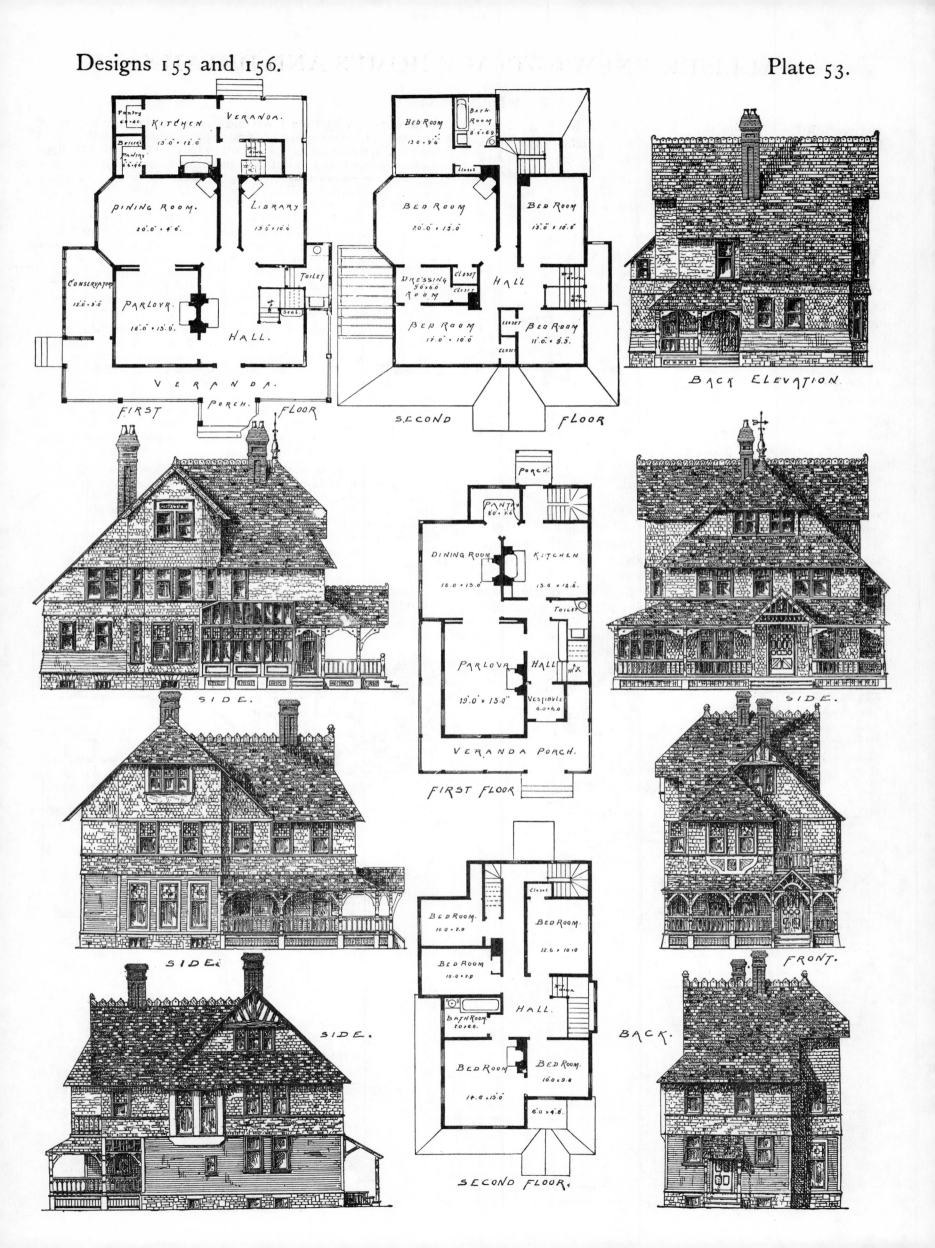

Pantry 6'0x4'0

KITCHEN
13'0 x 13'0

VERANDA.

Butler's
Pantry
6'6x4'6

DINING ROOM.
20'0 x 14'0

LIBRARY
15'0 x 10'6

CONSERVATORY
15'0 x 5'0

PARLOUR.
16'0 x 13'9

TOILET

HALL.

Seat

FIRST

PORCH.

FLOOR

VERANDA.

BED ROOM
13'0 x 9'6

BATH
ROOM
8'6x6'6

Closet

BED ROOM
20'0 x 15'0

BED ROOM
15'0 x 10'6

DRESSING
ROOM
9'0 x 6'0

CLOSET

Closet

HALL

BED ROOM
17'0 x 10'0

Closet

BED ROOM
11'0 x 9'3

Closet

SECOND

FLOOR

BACK ELEVATION.

SIDE.

PORCH.

PANTRY
8'0 x 3'6

DINING ROOM
18'0 x 13'0

KITCHEN
13'6 x 12'6

TOILET

PARLOUR
19'0 x 13'0

HALL

W.X

VESTIBULE
6'0 x 6'0

VERANDA PORCH.

FIRST FLOOR

SIDE.

SIDE.

BED ROOM
10'0 x 7'9

Closet

BED ROOM
12'6 x 10'10

BED ROOM
10'0 x 7'9

X Room

BATH ROOM
7'0 x 6'6

HALL.

BED ROOM
14'6 x 13'0

BED ROOM
10'0 x 9'6

6'0 x 4'6

SECOND FLOOR.

FRONT.

BACK.

PALLISER'S NEW COTTAGE HOMES AND DETAILS.

PLATE 54.

Design 157.—We here show a design for a brick residence adapted for erection in the suburbs of a city, which always seems to require more ornate styles than are suited to the broad and open country. The evidences of the position and taste of the occupants of such houses and their proximity to the city seem to justify a special treatment and elaboration in their design, which, however, is not necessarily to be of an expensive character, and in this case effective treatment has been obtained by the broken front, its veranda and the expressive chimney-stacks, together with a little color in the brickwork carefully worked in so as to avoid a shoddy or cheap appearance, and, of course, it is no more costly to lay a brick of one color than it is of another. Such effects are worthy of careful study by all who are engaged in building. The environs of London, particularly Bedford Park and St. John's Wood, are studded with handsome places and pretty cottages, well arranged for the purposes of the life for which they were built. In fact, Europe is full of them, while in this country the suburban villa is too often dragged right into the heart of the city, with a house too large for the small grounds and to whimsical for contrast with the forms around, and wanting a large, cheerful lawn and a background of trees to set it off to advantage ; and in turn the city house is frequently taken out into the suburbs or country and set up with its bare straight sides, sloping roof to rear, nearly flat, and three windows in front. And we contend that a man has no right to disfigure some grand scene by an inharmonious dwelling. How often this has been done, those who have rambled on the banks of the Hudson and in the vicinity of all large cities can testify.

The villa or suburban residence should always be built on a lot of good width and with a depth of 150 feet, so that it can stand well back from the street and have a retired appearance, and an opportunity for a lawn and shrubs, which are necessary adjuncts. The arrangement of first floor provides veranda in front which is the southern exposure, and a hall in the centre of house, with staircase, having a platform rendering the ceilings of the front portion of the house two steps higher than the rear or kitchen part, an arrangement which is often very desirable when one wishes to keep the roof at the rear lower down than that of the main part. The dining-room or living-room of the house is of large size and shapely, has passage through entry to kitchen, and conveniently arranged, while on the other side of the hall are parlor and bed-room, the latter being placed on this floor by special request, together with bath room. The kitchen and pantry occupy the northern exposure. The second story contains four bed-rooms, with good closets, and two rooms are provided in attic. Cost, $4,500.

The cost of houses, according to circumstances, will range all the way from 50 to 100 per cent., and this difference exists in nearly all classes of buildings, according to the section of country in which they are built, the facility of getting materials and the business management brought to bear. As prices constantly change, a good way is to show the nearest good mechanic the style of house you have decided on to adopt. Tell him, as near as possible, your wishes, and he can generally give you an approximate estimate of the amount of money you will need to carry out your wants and wishes.

Design 158 is a somewhat plain structure, though, with sufficient character in outline to give it some distinction among the class of house to which it belongs—viz., the residence of a working man who believes in owning his own comfortable home, containing all the necessary rooms and suited to his family wants, and of such arrangement as to be convenient and avoid unnecessary steps in the carrying out of the household duties attended to by his wife and family, and the bath room, so often left out on the score of economy, is not lost sight of in this instance, but is constructed into the building at the outset ; and the whole cost is $2,050.

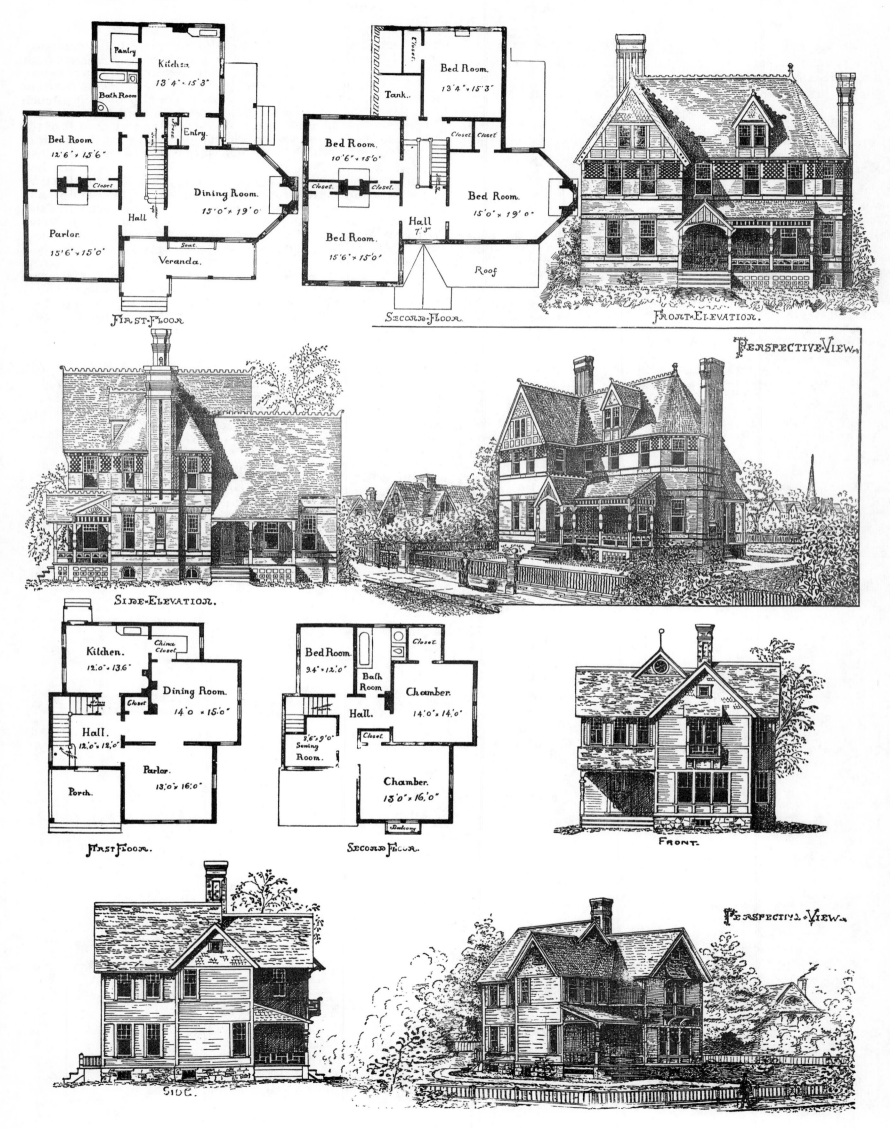

FIRST FLOOR

Pantry

Kitchen
13'4" x 15'3"

Bath Room

Bed Room
12'6" x 15'6"

Closet

Entry

Hall

Dining Room
15'0" x 19'0"

Parlor
15'6" x 15'0"

Seat

Veranda

SECOND FLOOR

Bed Room
13'4" x 15'3"

Tank

Closet Closet

Bed Room
10'6" x 15'0"

Closet Closet

Bed Room
15'0" x 19'0"

Hall
7'3"

Bed Room
15'6" x 15'0"

Roof

FRONT ELEVATION.

PERSPECTIVE VIEW.

SIDE ELEVATION.

FIRST FLOOR.

Kitchen
12'0" x 13'6"

China Closet

Dining Room
14'0" x 15'0"

Closet

Hall
12'0" x 12'0"

Parlor
13'0" x 16'0"

Porch.

SECOND FLOOR.

Bed Room
9'4" x 12'0"

Closet

Bath Room

Chamber
14'0" x 14'0"

Hall

Sewing Room
8'6" x 9'0"

Closet

Chamber
13'0" x 16'0"

Balcony

FRONT.

SIDE.

PERSPECTIVE VIEW.

PALLISER'S NEW COTTAGE HOMES AND DETAILS.

PLATE 55.

Design 159, which is for a pair of dwellings will answer well for a country gentleman; or two of them, for a farmer and his son to live in, or for two city business men to occupy for their families in summer as their country home; it presents good variety and is considered attractive, home-like and picturesque in exterior effect and well suited to almost any surroundings of a rural nature. It is worthy of careful study and we will here state that the principles upon which architectural beauty was obtained in the village and country houses built fifty or sixty years ago, and which are now so much admired, principles which apply equally well to buildings of to-day were simplicity, reality and intention. Their importance cannot be too strongly insisted on and so impressed therewith should architects be that in devising any plan they should mentally train themselves to reply to a question that should be the query of the present age,—is it honest? In a few years, how beautiful may this country be made by its rural architecture. No country in the world is so favored by nature, and by reason of the unfettered freedom for expression of individual taste, the lack of restraint by any well defined style or precedent, and the presence of a common sense which will teach us to judge of a thing only by its intrinsic merits. No land on the face of the earth has such opportunities for the advancement of art. The interior arrangements are well worth a close examination by any one who needs about the room that either side of this house provides, whether they wish to build jointly with some one else, or all alone by themselves. The hall makes a good living-room, and as all houses have their luxuries, we may safely say that this is indeed that portion of the house which is elegant; and the rooms opening from it are so placed as to help its utility as well as assist its elegance. Piazzas and porches are liberal for out-door living, and the whole arrangement for its purposes are good. Six bed-rooms and bath room with good closets are provided on each side on the floors above. Cost, $4,500 a side. Though, an ingenious farmer who can supply from his farm a considerable portion of the materials, do his own

hauling, and with the aid of a skillful mechanic and one or two handy laborers, if the work is not to be pushed too fast to completion, could execute this and similar designs by the use of very little money and discount the cost above by considerable, and we have assisted many all over the country to build at extremely low figures either by getting material furnished from the proper markets at first cost or in some other way to get what they could not furnish reasonable, and by lumping out the labor to say two or three men to do the various mechanical work requiring skilled labor.

A great many conflagrations throughout country districts are caused through carelessness in construction around fire-places and chimneys, and the common expression is "it was caused by a defective flue." The timbering and wood-work should be kept well away from any fire-place or flue, and should be carefully framed around them and protected by the proper use of incombustible material, and too much careful inspection of such work cannot be given to even the very best mechanics doing such work as this. Great care should also be taken in constructing chimneys, and their flues, as fuel gases will disintegrate the mortar joints of the best constructed brick flues, and if a spark escapes through either, the fuel is ready and waiting the conflagation in all dwelling houses—our homes—whether the occupants are asleep or awake. Think of this.

While nothing adds more to the outward appearance of a dwelling than the style of its chimneys, they should be built solid above the roof, and where exposed to the elements so as to avoid the falling to pieces in two or three years, and therefore they should be more than one brick thick and aside from the architectural beauty obtained by the use of good bold chimney stacks properly studied and in keeping with the general effect they denote good cheer, social firesides and a generous hospitality within, features which should always mark the country dwelling, and more particularly that of the farmer or country gentleman. Our illustrations throughout this work show them of very many kinds, generally cheap in construction, yet expressive in their treatment.

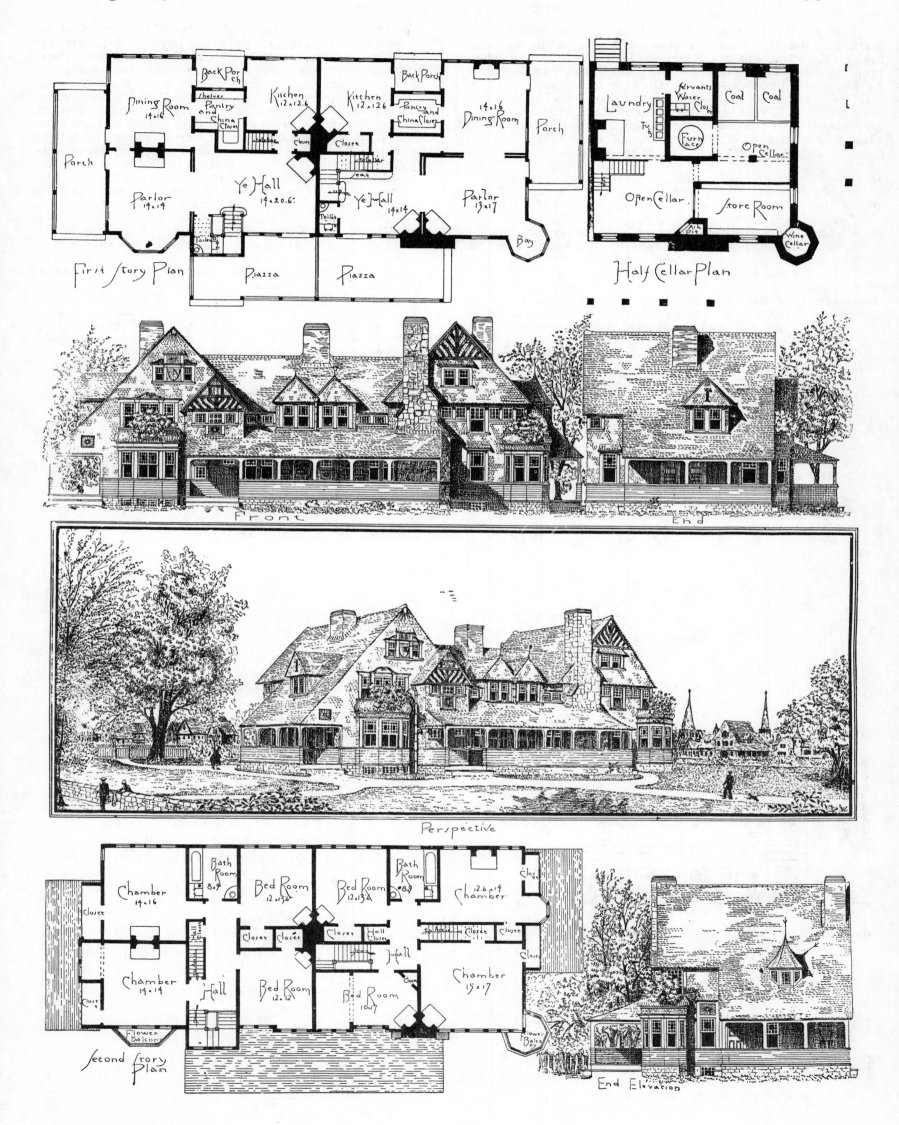

First Story Plan

Porch

Dining Room 14x16

Back Porch

Shelves Pantry and China Closet

Kitchen 12x12.6

Kitchen 12x12.6

Back Porch

Pantry and China Closet

14x16 Dining Room

Porch

Parlor 14x14

Ye Hall 14x20.6

Closet

Closet

Seat

Toilet

Ye Hall 14x14

Parlor 13x17

Bay

Toilet

Piazza

Piazza

Half Cellar Plan

Laundry

Servants Water Closet

Coal

Coal

Tubs

Furnace

Open Cellar

Open Cellar

Store Room

Ash Pit

Wine Cellar

Front

End

Perspective

Second Story Plan

Chamber 14x16

Closet

Bath Room 8x9

Bed Room 12x13.6

Bed Room 12x13.6

Bath Room 8x9

12.6x14 Chamber

Closet

Chamber 14x14

Hall

Closet

Closet

Closet

Hall Closet

To Attic

Closet

Closet

Chamber 15x17

Closet

Hall

Bed Room 12x12

Bed Room 10x7

Hall

Flower Balcony

Flower Balcony

End Elevation

PALLISER'S NEW COTTAGE HOMES AND DETAILS.

PLATE 56.

Design 160 is of a house built of good common, hard-burned brick, selecting the best and even-colored ones for the facing of the outside walls, which are laid up in red mortar, and when properly cleaned down with a correct solution and stain, makes work equal in appearance and certainly less harsh than is usually obtained by the use of pressed brick. The trimming-bands of brick are of a different or darker color, and the whole exterior is very pleasing with wood-work painted bronze green and red, with white for sashes. The arrangement of rooms throughout the first and second floors is excellent, as will be seen by a study of the plans, and servants' rooms are obtained in attic. The halls are especially deserving of attention, and the conservatory is a feature of this house that is both a pleasing and useful addition appreciated by very many people nowadays. Cost, $6,600.

Design 161 presents a house having good features in its outlines, which are just sufficiently broken to give it the requsite character without making it expensive or whimsical; in fact, it is of the good, common-sense order of architecture, adapted to the wants of many people requiring the amount of room that it gives; the hall in the centre, with parlor and dining-room on either side, connecting all together by means of sliding-doors, is the features of this house. The dining-room and kitchen arrangement is good; and with back stairs and the liberal veranda adds much to the whole house.

The arrangement of second floor, giving five good bed-rooms, is all that can be desired. Cost, $3,650.

Every cellar under a dwelling-house should be sweet and clean at all times, and no excuse allowed for its being foul. Ventilate and purify it always. Decaying vegetation should not be tolerated in it. The floor should be well grouted in cement, walls and ceilings should be whitewashed, and ceiling, if possible, plastered; and one flue of the chimney should start from and open into the cellar for ventilation. In fact, pure air and enough of it is the cheapest blessing one can enjoy, and to deny ones self so necessary an element of good health is the sheerest folly, if not criminal. Yet thousands who build at much expense to protect their health and that of their families, as they allege and sometimes suppose, by neglecting the simplest of all contrivances in the work of ventilation, invite disease and infirmity from the very pains they so unwittingly take to ward off such afflictions. Their memory carries them back to their boyhood days, prehaps, and the old homestead with its fire-places, scarcely throwing off sufficient heat to warm one side of a person at a time, withplenty of good air coming in at ill-fitting doors, windows, etc., which they did not regard as much of a luxury, but which, however, made them healthy and vigorous, and they say to themselves that their children shall be made comfortable, so that in their house building they take extra pains and expense to make a tight, warm house. They discard the open fire-place, perhaps, entirely, and put in an air-tight furnace or air-tight stoves in the various rooms, and provide no means of carrying off the bad air, and the rooms, as a rule, become overheated; windows and doors are sometimes opened to cool a room, and as a result all sorts of bodily afflictions follow in the family, and they wonder what is the matter, but never dream that day after day they are breathing decomposed air, which cannot escape, because there is no means for it to do so, and go where you may into houses that are without fire-places, and you will invariably find the subject of ventilation entirely overlooked.

Health and comfort depend on proper ventilation, which ought always to be considered carefully. In connection with the heating, the air in the room must be kept in constant circulation, and there is no better ventilator than an open fire-place with a fire; this will carry off the chilled, foul air as it falls to the floor, and keep the purer air circulating, and the fire-place even without a fire will aid in this way to equalize the temperature.

In all rooms that have no fire-places there should be a vent opening with register in the inner wall near the floor. Another vent opening and register near the ceiling is also desirable, that the room may be cooled when too hot and avoid draughts and also for the purpose of summer ventilation. These openings should be connected with tin pipe carried up to attic and to a hot, tight flue in chimney. Closets, pantries and bath-rooms are seldom ventilated even in houses of considerable pretention, yet it can be done at a very small cost by a tin pipe with an area of four inches square with an opening near the ceiling carried up to the ventilating flue.

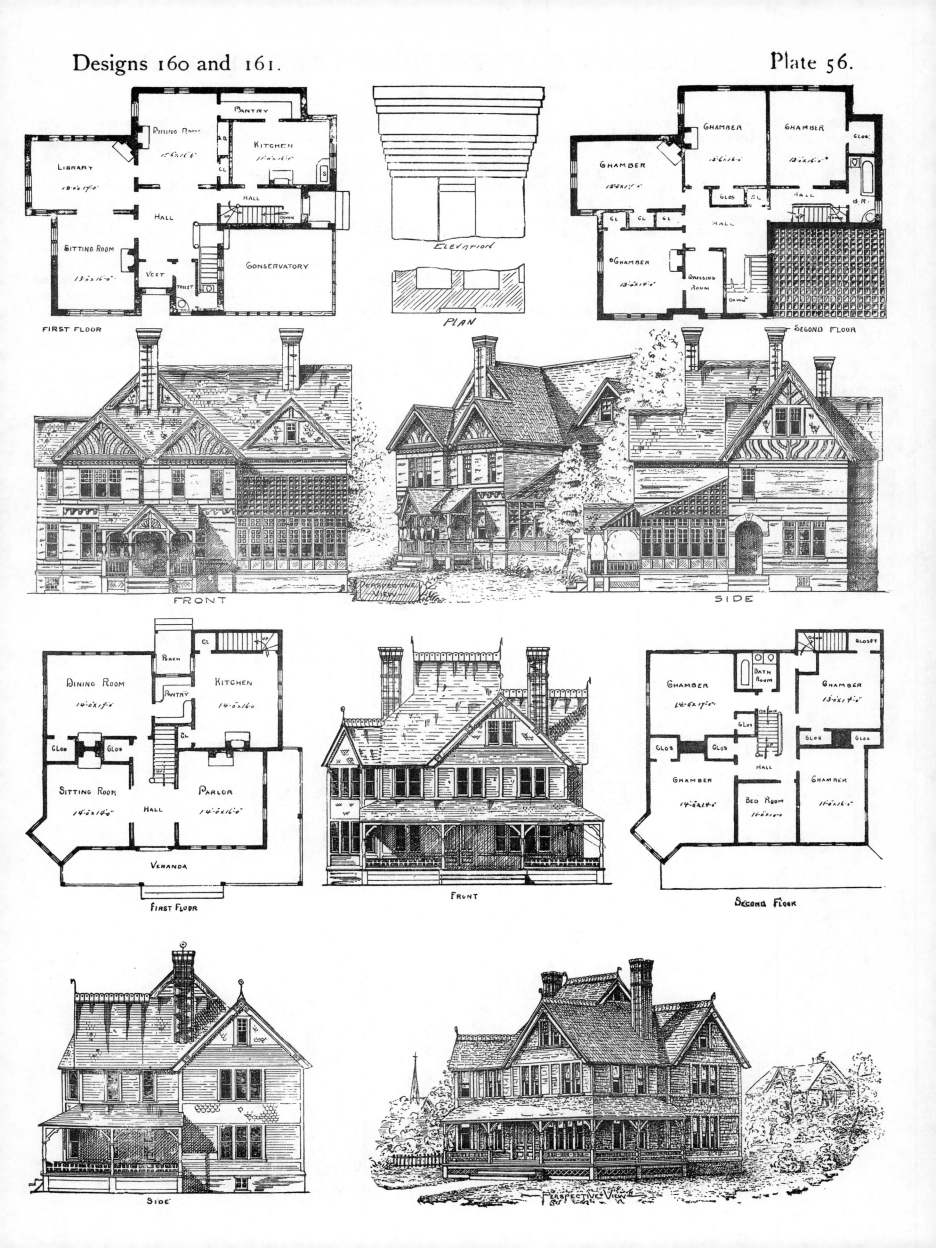

FIRST FLOOR

PLAN

ELEVATION

SECOND FLOOR

FRONT

PERSPECTIVE VIEW

SIDE

FIRST FLOOR

FRONT

SECOND FLOOR

SIDE

PERSPECTIVE VIEW

PALLISER'S NEW COTTAGE HOMES AND DETAILS.

PLATE 57.

Design 162 shows a double house adapted for two families to live on each side, the owner of his side could occupy basement and first floor and rent the upper floors, thus helping him in his investment. The style of exterior is like many we have designed for erection by mechanics in New England towns and cities, and embody all that can be wished for. Large numbers of such houses are built throughout New England by people of means for purposes of investment and give probably as good returns as any real estate will do.

The main front entrances on each side are used by both families, while the family on second floor has its own back porch and back stairs and separate cellar entrance at rear, and the family on first floor has its back door from basement, where they have dining-room, kitchen, pantry and cellar. The plan explains fully the arrangement. Cost, $2,800 a side.

Design 163 gives a pair of houses, each for a single family, giving them the same amount of room, but not of the same arrangement, and avoiding in a measure that appearance of the double house so common, and which some genteel people like to get rid of as far as possible when building and intending to occupy one themselves. Such houses as these are good property to own, and bring in a rental in New England cities of $25 to $30 a month, and in the suburbs of New York a considerable advance on this, if located where they can be reached inside of an hour by railroad. Cost, $2,250.00.

Chimneys are an important feature of the exterior design of a dwelling, and we like to see them treated boldly, and of sufficient height above the roof as to overlook all other obstructions, and thus insure a good draught.

Design 164 gives an inexpensive double cottage, adapted for a farm or other country estate, for the housing of workmen connected therewith, or wherever ground can be obtained cheaply. This plan could be adopted by mechanics who wish to get a home of their own at a small outlay of money, and secure to themselves the blessings of home comfort and the privileges of being their own landlords, which is a desirable thing to be, and the American mechanic is not slow in this matter, but is making rapid strides in that direction, and no other country in the world can show a like advancement and helpful condition in this direction as the United States.

A parlor, dining-room and kitchen with pantry, nice hall and staircase, with convenient access from kitchen to cellar and two doors between hall and kitchen and between kitchen and dining-room; china closet in the dining-room; front and back porch are given on first floor, and on second floor three bed-rooms with good closets, a sewing-room or child's bed-room, make this a cosey and desirable residence at a cost of $1,200 a side. The rooms as shown on the plan would probably be better if increased in size, though if one undertakes to build low-priced houses we must adhere firmly to the plan—a little here and a little there, will, when all bills are paid, be found to double the cost.

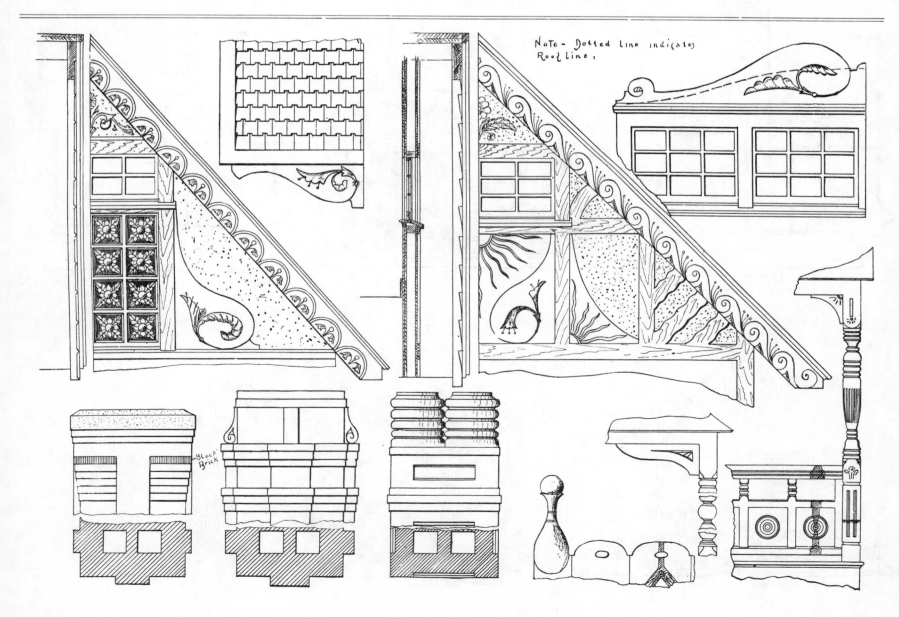

Note—Dotted line indicates Roof Line.

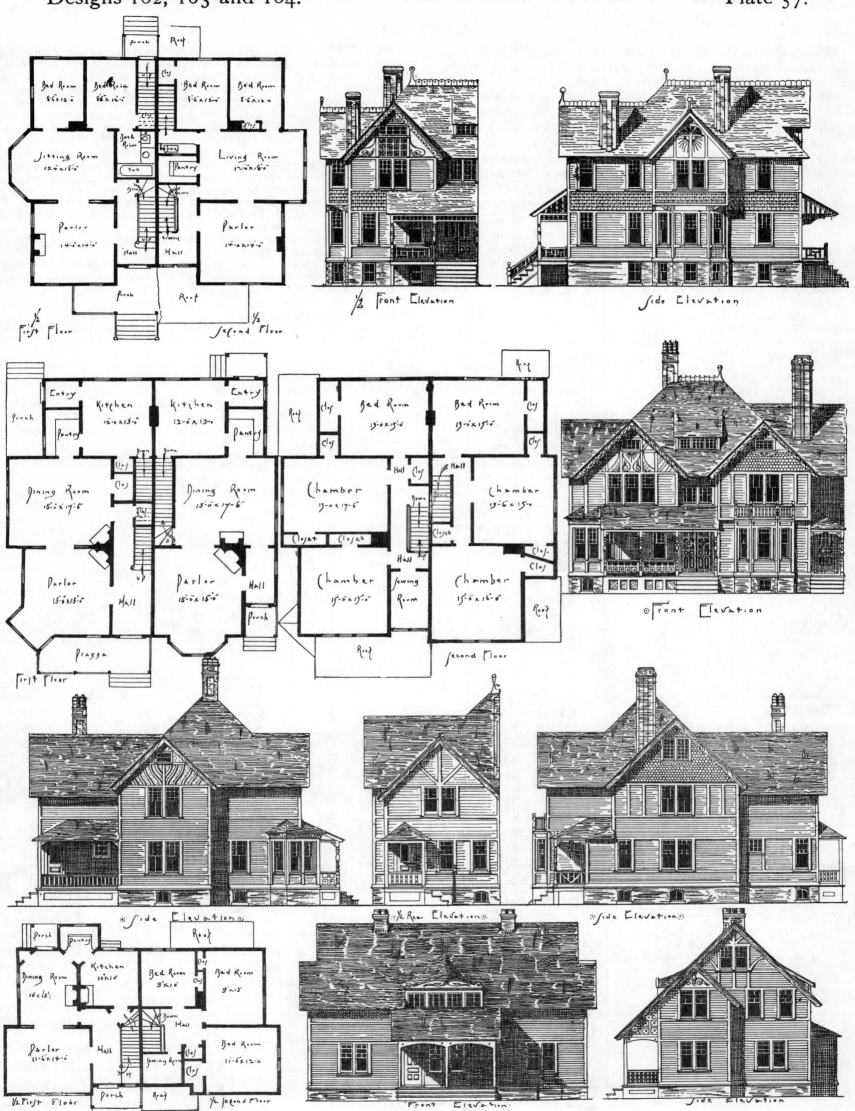

½ First Floor   ½ Second Floor

½ Front Elevation   Side Elevation

First Floor   Second Floor

Front Elevation

Side Elevation   ½ Rear Elevation   Side Elevation

½ First Floor   ½ Second Floor   Front Elevation   Side Elevation

PALLISER'S NEW COTTAGE HOMES AND DETAILS.

PLATE 58.

The designs on this plate are for city brick houses for a block of three, and are such as give variety of outline to the fronts and at the same time preserving a quiet dignity in their make-up.

The first design shows but one house, viz.: The left hand one, the one on the right hand to be the same reversed, and the centre house is intended to finish up with a tower having an ogeé-shaped roof.

The second design shows the three houses just as they appear in the block, giving a very solid and massive appearance, and one that would strike the observer in the street of almost any ordinary town or city.

The third design shows the centre, and right hand house, the left hand house to be the same as on the right side but reversed, and makes a very elegant and attractive block of houses.

These houses are built on twenty feet of ground each, underpinning of basement story is laid up with dark blue granite, rock-faced ashlar, laid in irregular courses, level beds and plumb joints, and this kind of work is by far the handsomest of any and far ahead of the smooth cut faced stone work that one sees so much of in the larger cities. The water table, sill courses, etc., are of red stone, and the main walling of brick; fronts faced with pressed brick, with a little effect from terra cotta, very sparingly used; the steps and platforms are of hard red stone.

The plans of the several floors explain themselves fully and provide cellar, dining-room, kitchen, laundry, parlor, sitting-room, six bed-rooms and bath-room, with closets and other requisites. Cost, $5,000 to $7,000 each.

"In wall and roof and pavement scattered are full many a pearl, full many a costly stone."—*Artosto.*

A gentleman writing us for advice with regard to plans for a dwelling-house, says: "I have heard that it is possible to build without employing an architect; what would you advise?" Our reply was to the effect that a well-developed and matured set of building plans, with details and specifications drawn in such a manner as to get the best, most practical and generally pleasing results, by a competent and practical architect, is usually money saved to the client. By means of such plans he knows just what he is going to get, and just what it will cost him, and should he require any changes in the plans, or should the estimates on the work run higher than he contemplates, he can easily make the changes or modify his plans before putting the work under contract.

On the other hand, if he attempts to build a house or other building without well-matured plans, and without having first counted the cost, he is almost sure to become involved in a greater expense than he intended; and he has no redress, but is likely to get deeper and deeper in the bog, the more he struggles to get out. It goes without saying that a systematized method of doing business is preferable to a haphazard, "rule of thumb" way. The fact that it pays to employ an architect is becoming more and more appreciated by the general public, and we find that owners who have employed an architect once, do not hesitate about it when they build a second time. Where several years ago it was necessary to spend a great deal of time in argument in order to convince the owner that the services of the architect would be profitable to him, and would save him much trouble and annoyance, now no such importunity seems to be needed. The public is becoming educated in matters of art and architecture. We knew, some ten or fifteen years ago a young architect, just starting in business for himself, who solicited a commission of a gentleman of his acquaintance who contemplated building a house. Now the said gentleman had never built before, and although an intelligent man and well informed on many other subjects, had never interested himself in architecture, and consequently knew very little about the methods employed by architects in the development of working-plans, specifications, etc., nor the amount of mental labor therein involved. On accosting this gentleman, the architect said: "I understand Mr. ————, that you intend to build a house. Cannot I make arrangements with you to prepare your plans?" "No!" replied the gentleman very decidedly; "I have no use for your kind of work; I don't want any pictures"—contemptuously; for he was a very plain practical sort of man, with little respect for art. "I have my plans all in my head, and I expect to employ men by the day, and tell them just what I want as we come to it." About an hour's conversation between Mr. ———— and the architect, however, resulted in securing the commission for the latter. The plans were made, the building erected, and after its completion the gentleman came to the architect and made the following statement: "I have now learned what an architect's business is; my house has not cost me a dollar more than I intended when I started out, and I am converted to the custom of employing an architect. And I want to say that if I ever have occasion to build again, even if it should be nothing more than a chicken-coop, I shall have all my plans, specifications, etc., drawn and prepared before starting out with the work."

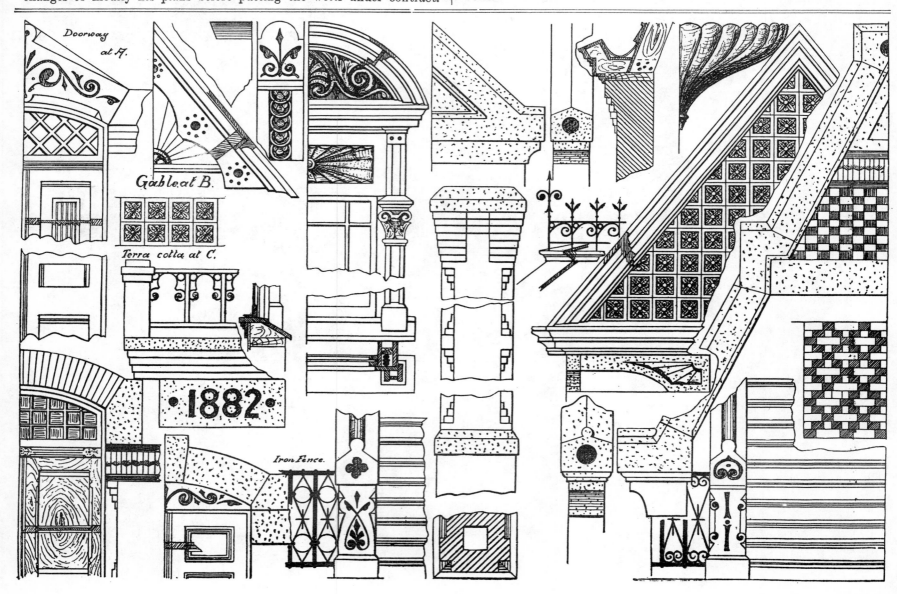

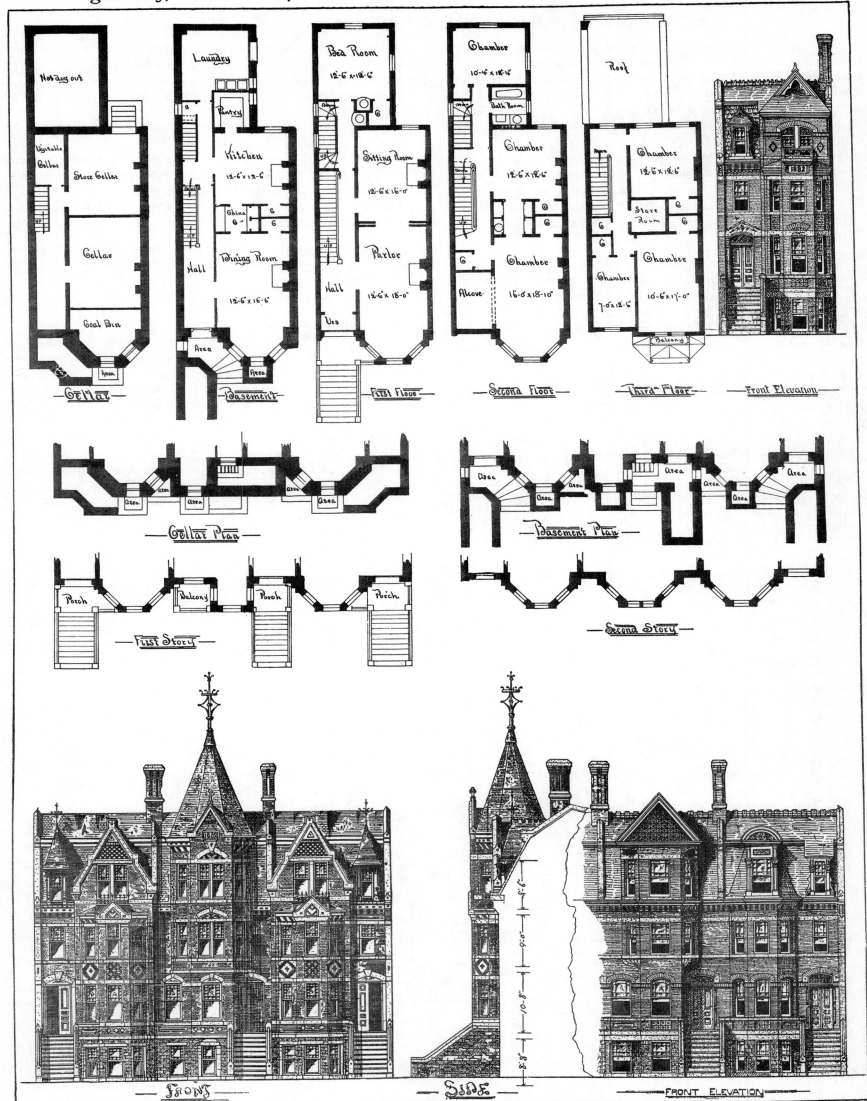

Not dug out

Vegetable Cellar

Store Cellar

Cellar

Coal Bin

Area

Cellar

Laundry

Pantry

Kitchen
12-6 x 12-6

China
6-0

Hall

Dining Room
12-6 x 16-6

Area

Basement

Bed Room
12-6 x 12-6

Sitting Room
12-6 x 16-0

Hall

Parlor
12-6 x 18-0

Ves

First Floor

Chamber
10-4 x 12-6

Bath Room

Chamber
12-6 x 12-6

Chamber
16-6 x 18-10

Alcove

Second Floor

Roof

Chamber
12-6 x 12-6

Store Room

Chamber
7-0 x 12-6

Chamber
10-6 x 17-0

Balcony

Third Floor

1882

Front Elevation

Cellar Plan

Basement Plan

Porch

Balcony

Porch

Porch

First Story

Second Story

9-3

10-0

8-0

3-3

FRONT

SIDE

FRONT ELEVATION

Design 168 is a cottage that gives a good deal of room for a small amount of money ; is compact and well arranged ; it gives parlor and library connected together by sliding doors, while the dining-room is on the other side of hall and communicates only with hall and through china closet to kitchen, being away from the other rooms ; this arrangement of the dining-room, it is contended by many, is the proper one for many reasons, and is frequently insisted on by many people in building as the only one that is satisfactory to them. The second floor contains four bed-rooms, closets and bath-room, and the exterior, which is shingled throughout, makes a perfect picture with its colors of orange, red and green, and is both simple and picturesque. Cost, $2,300.

Design 169.—Stone for building purposes is the most durable in the long run, the cheapest, and, as a consequence, the best material which can be furnished for the walls of a dwelling, and especially so if the walls are low, as the expense of erecting high and strong scaffolding, and of raising the stone up to a great height is often too great to allow of its use in dwellings for more than one story, and in this way houses are made from necessity far more picturesque than would be the case if the walls were built entirely of stone up to the roof. Rock faced rubble masonry without dressing or working beyond what is necessary in fitting, which can be done with a stone hammer, is the best for country houses of small expense, and over this work vines may be trained and add further to the effect.

This design is of a farm cottage built of stone for first story and shingled above, is plain but neat and a veranda can be added across the front at any time the owner sees fit or is able to have it done.

The arrangement of plan is of a kind that will please many people and contains no waste room and the stairway is reached directly from hall and porch at rear, and four good bed-rooms are provided on second floor. Cost, $2,250.

Design 170 is a good one for the country or sea shore, and the living hall and dining-room, with all the necessary conveniences, tell their own story, and will be found unique. There is plenty of porch room and on second floor are three large bed rooms and balcony, while the exterior is as good as possible to get up, all things considered ; first story clapboarded and second story shingled. Cost, $2,000.

Design 171 gives a unique octagon hall, a nice, easy stairs, parlor, dining-room, conservatory, kitchen, pantry and china closet on first floor, and on second floor three bed-rooms with closets. The exterior is plain but attractive and in every way suitable for the country.

It is difficult to persuade people who live in the country to place their dwellings on the best and most sightly part of their grounds ; they will invariably keep in a close proximity to the road, the passing vehicle or traveller being a very acceptable sight for those who see but few people in their vicinity, but it should ever be remembered that the great charm of a country home in pleasant weather is its surroundings, and the dwelling should be so placed as to make the most of them, but if one must build near the road, as a matter of taste, it is best to have a broad and roomy foreground between the house and road. It gives a finer effect to the house and an opportunity for enhancing its value and appearance when properly taken care of, and it should not be allowed to exist under any other circumstances.

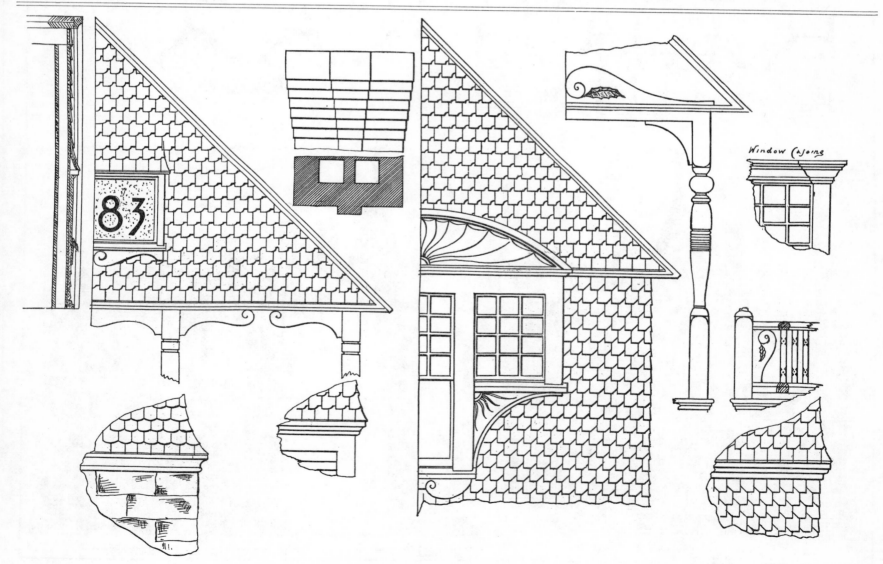

Window (adjoins)

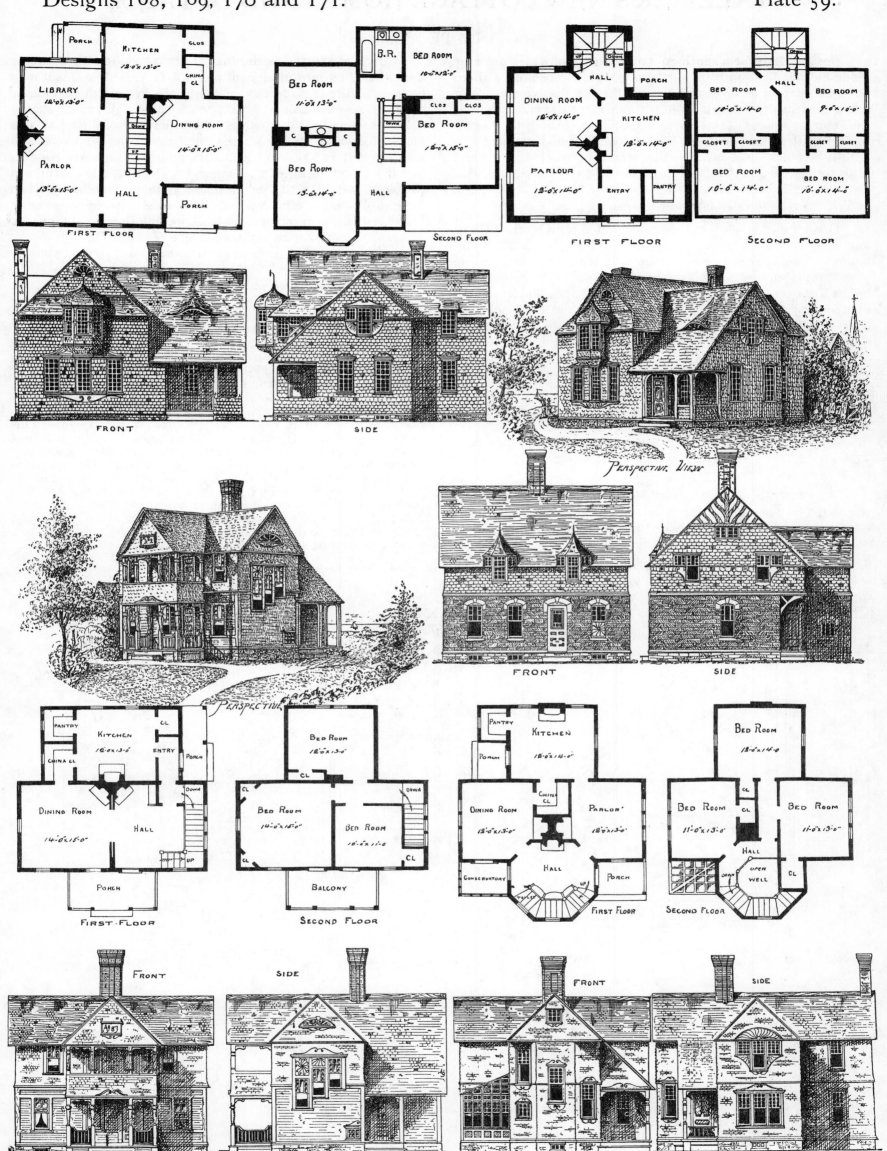

FIRST FLOOR   SECOND FLOOR   FIRST FLOOR   SECOND FLOOR

LIBRARY 12·0"x13·0"
PORCH
KITCHEN 12·0"x13·0"
CLOS
CHINA CL
DINING ROOM 14·0"x15·0"
PARLOR 13·0"x15·0"
HALL
DOWN
UP
PORCH

B.R.
BED ROOM 10·5"x12·0"
BED ROOM 11·0"x13·0"
CLOS CLOS
C C
BED ROOM 15·0"x15·0"
BED ROOM 13·0"x14·0"
HALL
DOWN

UP DOWN
HALL PORCH
DINING ROOM 12·0"x14·0"
KITCHEN 13·6"x14·0"
PARLOUR 12·0"x14·0"
ENTRY
PANTRY

DOWN
BED ROOM 10·0"x14·0"
HALL
BED ROOM 9·0"x10·0"
CLOSET CLOSET
CLOSET CLOSET
BED ROOM 10·6"x14·0"
BED ROOM 10·0"x14·0"

FRONT   SIDE   PERSPECTIVE VIEW

PERSPECTIVE   FRONT   SIDE

FIRST FLOOR   SECOND FLOOR   FIRST FLOOR   SECOND FLOOR

PANTRY
KITCHEN 12·0"x13·6"
CL
ENTRY
PORCH
CHINA CL
DINING ROOM 14·0"x15·0"
HALL
DOWN
PORCH

BED ROOM 12·0"x13·0"
CL
CL
BED ROOM 14·0"x15·0"
BED ROOM 10·6"x11·0"
CL
DOWN
CL
BALCONY

PANTRY
KITCHEN 18·0"x14·0"
PORCH
CHINA CL
DINING ROOM 13·0"x13·0"
PARLOR 12·0"x13·0"
HALL
CONSERVATORY
UP DOWN
PORCH

BED ROOM 12·6"x14·0"
CL
BED ROOM 11·0"x13·0"
CL
BED ROOM 11·0"x13·0"
HALL
DOWN OPEN WELL
CL

FRONT   SIDE   FRONT   SIDE

PLATE 60.

Design 172 is for a southern house, many of which are now being built at the South by northern people for residence there so as to escape the severe winter weather at the North during a few months of the year; similar houses can also be used at the summer resorts of the North for residence during the heated term, and thus one might be like the bird of migration, and be able to avoid almost wholly the worst of any weather and take things comparatively comfortable all the year round; this can be and is carried out to a considerable extent by invalids and others who have leisure and wealth.

This kind of house is however more often built by the planter and people who are going South to build up the country and make for themselves permanent homes; the design is therefore plain, unpretending, devoid of ornamentation, but such as can be readily executed out of the materials at hand, and therefore inexpensive in construction and the arrangement of rooms with door and window openings at both ends, plenty of piazza on both floors, kitchen away from the living rooms, etc., are all calculated to give as cool a house as possible, and this plan fills the wants of the people and meets their case as to climate, etc. Cost, $700.

Design 173 provides three living-rooms on first floor and a large amount of piazza. The kitchen is not shown as it is intended to be located in a separate shed at rear of the piazza. The second floor gives three bed-rooms and a large porch. Cost, $800.

Design 174 contains on first floor a large living-room with recessed fire-place and seats, kitchen and pantry at the rear, a good piazza, and on second floor two bed-rooms and large balconies, making in all a desirable southern home. Cost, $600.

It may strike the reader that the two last described houses have a lavish appropriation of piazza. In regard to this it may be remarked that no feature of the house in a southern climate can be more expressive of easy, comfortable enjoyment, than a spacious veranda. The habits of southern life demand it as a place of exercise in wet weather, and the cooler seasons of the year, as well as a place of recreation and social intercourse during the fervid heats of the summer. Indeed, many southern people almost live under the shade of their verandas. It is a delightful place to take their meals, to receive their visitors and friends; and the veranda gives to a dwelling the very expression of hospitality, so far as any one feature of a dwelling can do it. No equal amount of accommodation can be provided for the same cost. It adds infinitely to the room of the house itself, and is, in fact, indispensable to the full enjoyment of a southern home.

As to the use of materials in the construction of such houses, it is generally simply a matter of calculation with him who needs them to figure the first cost of any material he has at hand and adapted for the buildings he wishes to erect, and adopt the cheapest he can find is not by any means the result of a pinched pocket, but it is purely business considerations which control the people who need the buildings and study up all matters connected therewith to the spending of as little money as possible, which in its results is the most advantageous to his interests, provided the main points are attained and the time being provided for and taken care of, and, therefore, wood may be said to be the best material to use, as it is usually abundant and easily obtained at the South, is worked with greater facility than brick, and on many accounts is the cheapest material, for the time, of which a building can be constructed, but, of course, it is perishable and requires every few years a coat of paint, and is associated with the idea of decay, but then everything is, to a greater or lesser degree.

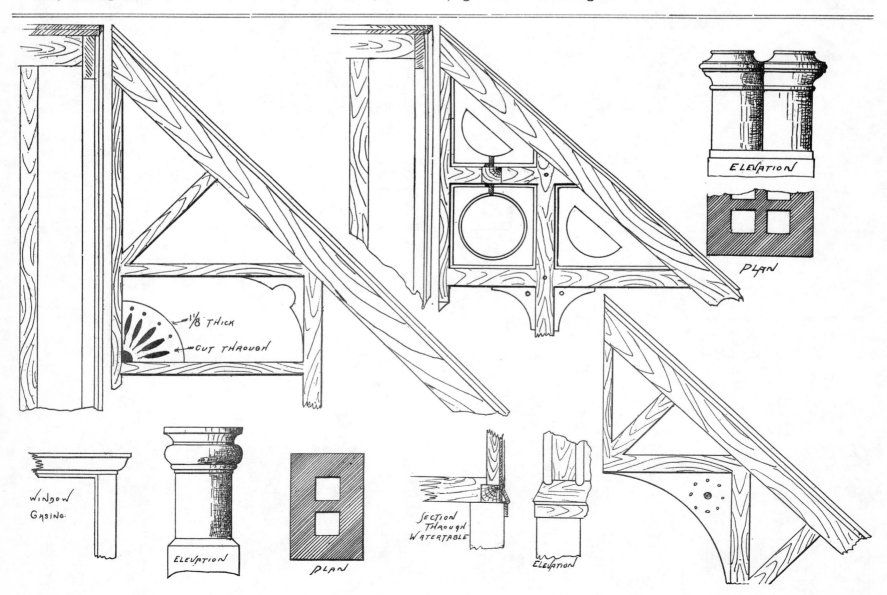

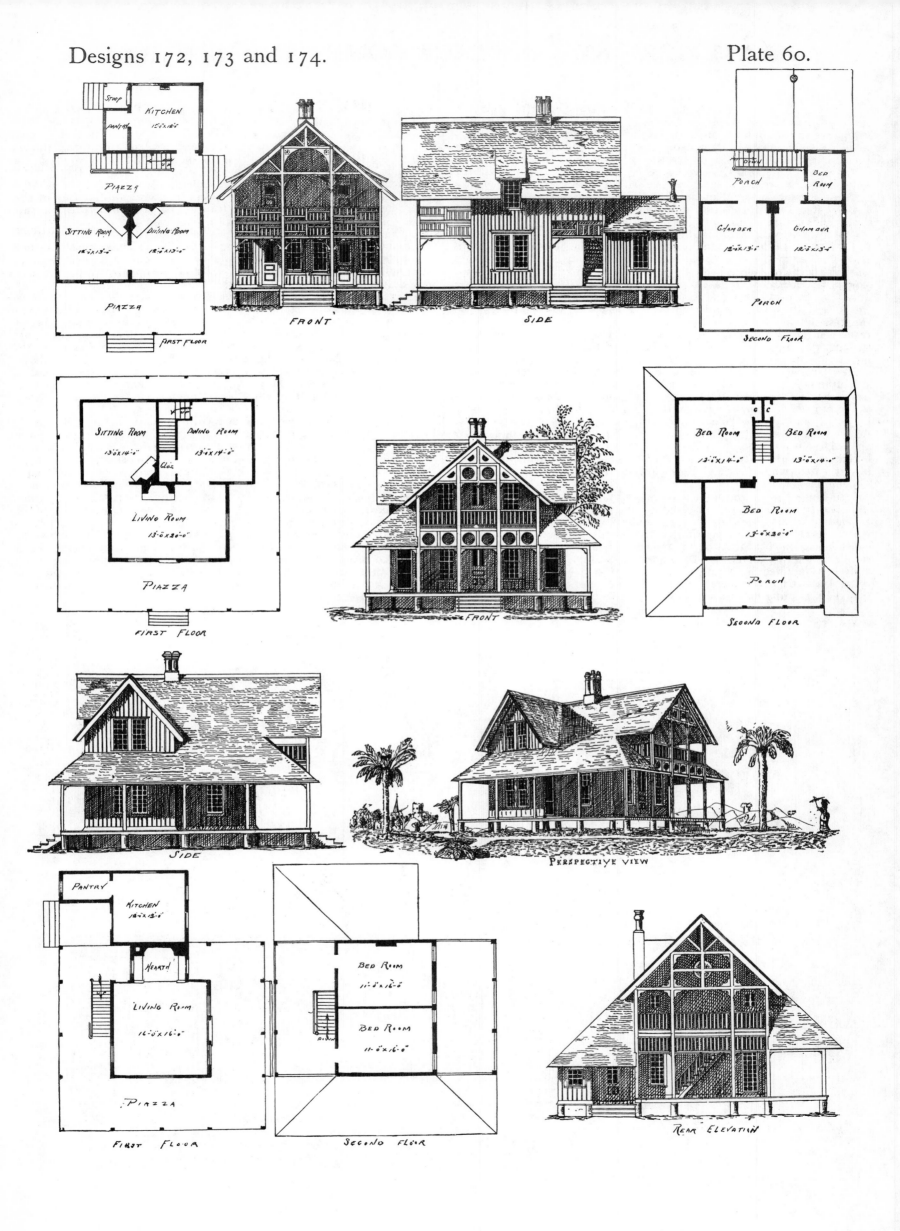

FIRST FLOOR

FRONT

SIDE

SECOND FLOOR

FIRST FLOOR

FRONT

SECOND FLOOR

SIDE

PERSPECTIVE VIEW

FIRST FLOOR

SECOND FLOOR

REAR ELEVATION

Design 175 provides, on account of the situation, a broad front in a locality where there is plenty of ground, and can be set off to the best advantage in the country, answering well for a farmer or country gentleman, the room marked "Den" being the master's business or smoking room, but if the house was otherwise used, would do for a sewing-room or for any purpose that the occupants might see fit. The hall with its handsome staircase at the end gives one a hospitable welcome on coming within the front doors. The dining-room is a very pleasant room, and the kitchen offices are all that can be desired. On the second floor, four bed-rooms and bath-room are provided. Cost, $2,800.

We have always maintained and advised that the two principal fronts of a house should face east and south, and where the ground is laid off in narrow plots, the front is best to be towards the east, but it is said that Carl Vogt, the eminent scientist of Geneva, Switzerland, by experiment, established the fact that, leaving the north side of a building out of the question, the south side is found during the summer months to be always the coolest, the east side following next in degree of temperature, while the west side he found to be the warmest. The direct effect of the solar rays upon the eastern and western walls of a house he found to be greatly stronger than upon the southern walls, this difference being accounted for by the different angles of incidence of the solar rays falling upon the walls. On the east and west sides, the said angle reaches its maximum size of ninety degrees, while the south walls are struck at an acute angle, hence the effect is much slighter. Vogt for the first time called attention to the problem of computing scientifically how our dwelling houses should be placed to insure for them a sufficient quantity of solar heat and light. Although the idea would not seem to be of much practical value when applied to our customary city dwellings, surrounded, as they are, by other buildings, it must be conceded that in its application to detached dwellings it is deserving of careful consideration at the hands of the professional architect.

As long as nineteen hundred years ago, Vitruvius, the Roman architect, laid stress on the principle that in planning cities the streets must not be laid parallel with the direction of the prevailing atmospherical currents. In Germany, the prevailing currents are northeast and southwest; hence her towns, if laid out on the rectangular plan, should have streets running from east to west and from north to south. This plan has actually been followed in a number of cases, for instance, the cities of Mannheim, Darmstadt and others. Supposing a house so placed, it is evident that the prevailing northeast winds must strike the sides of the house at angles of incidence averaging forty-five degrees. Other winds striking the walls squarely, or nearly so, are usually of short duration, blowing only for a few hours at one time.

It will be observed that if we locate our homes on the principle advocated by Vitruvius, we are, at the same time, fulfilling the requirements demanded by Professor Vogt. During the summer months, the sun rising in the northeast and setting in the northwest, the east and west walls of a house will be heated to a greater, and the south wall to a lesser degree since the rays of the sun then being at its greater declination, fall more obliquely upon the latter than they do upon the former. On the other hand, during the winter months, the sun rising in the southeast and setting in the southwest, it is the south wall which is exposed to rays thrown upon it almost at right angles by the sun, which then is at its minimum declination, whilst both east and west walls receive oblique rays only only. Hence, if your house is so planned that one side greatly exceeds in length the other, place its long side on a line running from east to west to insure for the same greater warmth in winter and less heat in summer, whilst the short side can better afford to be the cooler side in winter and the hotter one in summer, just because it is the shorter side.

Design 176 is suited to a suburban lot of fifty or more feet in width, or might be adapted to the open country or seaside, having a large amount of piazza room, and a compact and economical arrangement of rooms that is taking, and fully explained by the plans. In addition to the bed-rooms on first floor, there is also one provided in the attic. Cost, $2,400.

Design 177 gives a good plan adapted for a farm house, with liberal hall and connections to parlor and dining-room, making a grand house for the open country, and we know of no reason why a farmer, because he is a farmer, should occupy only an uncouth, outlandish house, as many of them do, any more than a professional man, a merchant or a mechanic. Is it because his occupation in life is degrading, his intellect ignorant or his position low? Surely not. Yet, in many of the plans and designs got up for his accommodation, all due convenience, to say nothing of the respectability or the elegance of domestic life, is as entirely disregarded as if such qualities had no connection with the farmer or his occupation.

This plan and the many others submitted in this work for the farmer are intended to be of the most practical kind: plain, substantial and applicable throughout, to the purpose intended, and such as are within the reach, each in their kind, of every farmer in our country. Cost of erecting this house, $3,100.

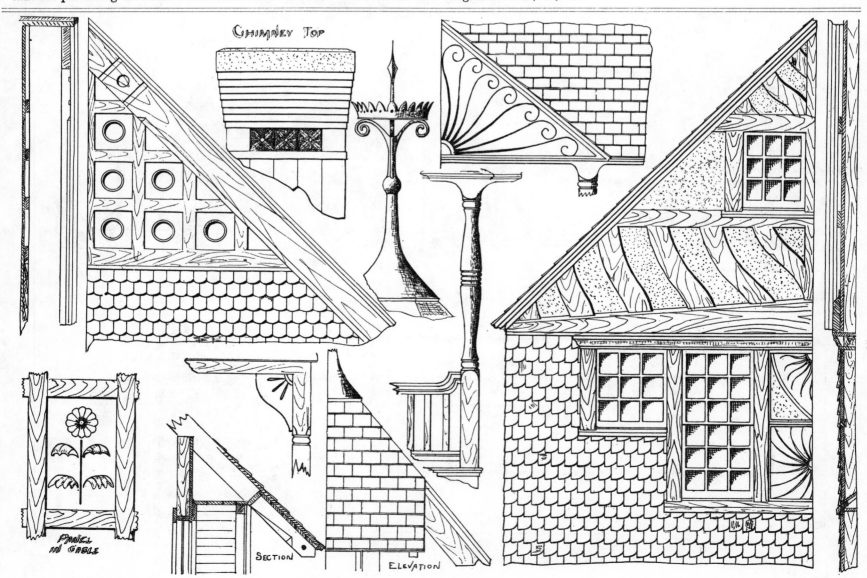

CHIMNEY TOP

PANEL IN GABLE   SECTION   ELEVATION

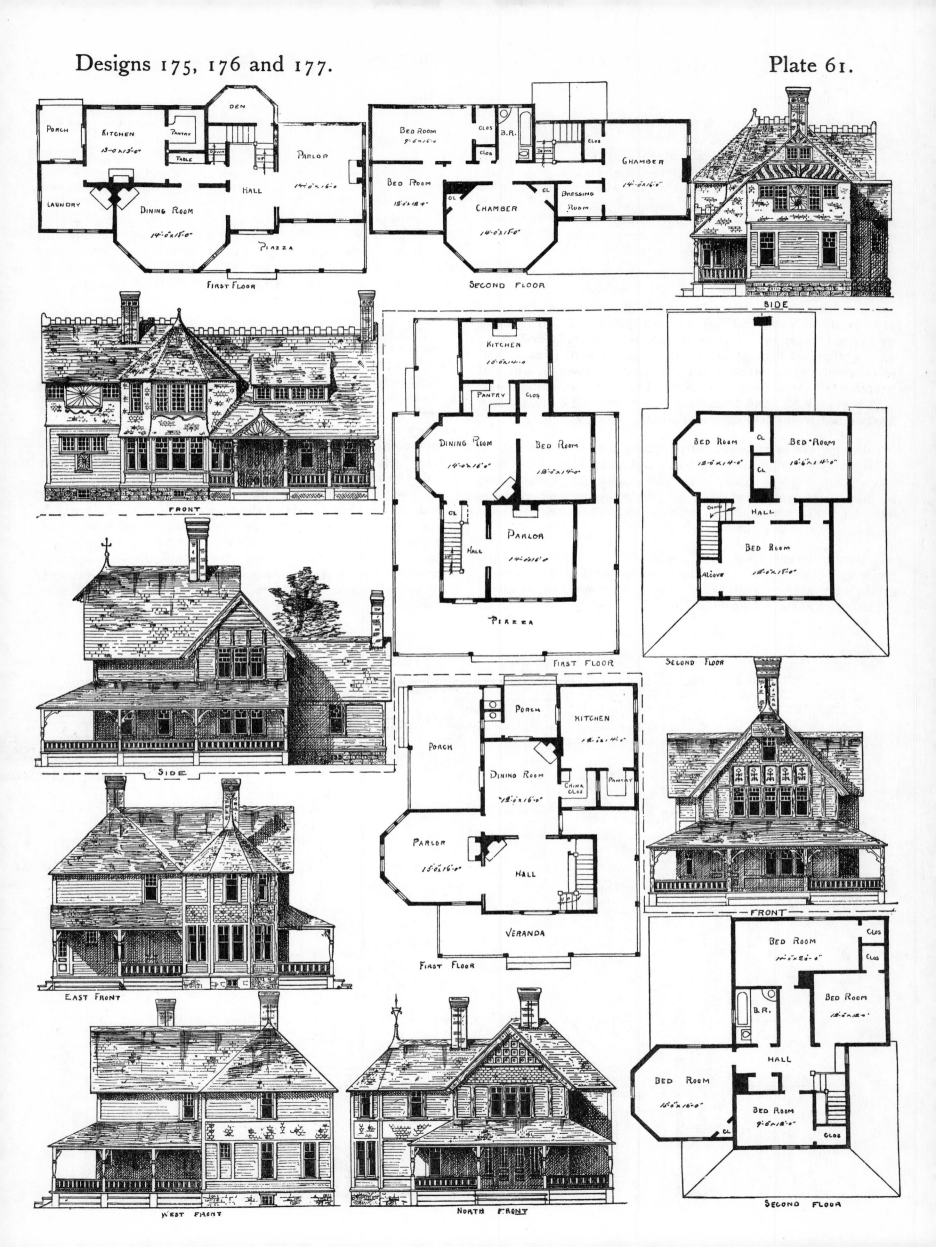

PORCH

KITCHEN
13'-0"x15'-0"

PANTRY

DEN

TABLE

DOWN   UP

PARLOR
14'-0"x16'-0"

LAUNDRY

DINING ROOM
14'-0"x18'-0"

HALL

PIAZZA

FIRST FLOOR

BED ROOM
9'-6"x16'-0"

CLOS   B.R.

CLOS

CLOS

BED ROOM
12'-6"x18'-0"

CL.

CHAMBER
14'-0"x16'-0"

CL   DRESSING
ROOM

CHAMBER
14'-0"x16'-0"

SECOND FLOOR

SIDE

FRONT

KITCHEN
10'-6"x14'-0"

PANTRY   CLOS

DINING ROOM
14'-0"x16'-0"

BED ROOM
13'-0"x14'-0"

CL.

PARLOR
14'-0"x16'-0"

HALL

UP

PIAZZA

FIRST FLOOR

BED ROOM
12'-6"x14'-0"

CL

CL

BED ROOM
13'-6"x14'-0"

DOWN

HALL

BED ROOM
13'-0"x18'-0"

ALCOVE

SECOND FLOOR

SIDE

EAST FRONT

PORCH

PORCH

KITCHEN
13'-0"x14'-0"

DINING ROOM
13'-0"x16'-0"

CHINA
CLOS

PANTRY

PARLOR
15'-0"x16'-0"

HALL

VERANDA

FIRST FLOOR

FRONT

BED ROOM
11'-0"x24'-0"

CLOS

CLOS

B.R.

BED ROOM
13'-6"x14'-0"

BED ROOM
15'-0"x16'-0"

HALL

BED ROOM
9'-6"x13'-0"

CL

CLOS

SECOND FLOOR

WEST FRONT   NORTH FRONT

PALLISER'S NEW COTTAGE HOMES AND DETAILS.

PLATE 62.

Design 178 is for a suburban dwelling constructed of brick with the window sills of first story windows on a level with the floor; a feature that is seldom carried out in the planning of dwellings in this country. The exterior design is of a plain, substantial kind and well calculated to wear well and give no trouble by way of repairs or expense in the way of painting, and is such as will attract the attention of those who like to possess a house combining such desirable features as they will find this one does, after a careful study of the same.

The interior gives a unique hall, which is entered through a vestibule; an attractive and easy stairs to second floor, toilet-room under stairs, a parlor, drawing-room and dining-room, all of large dimensions and very pleasantly situated and opening up in a most hospitable and useful manner. A study or library, an easy flight of back stairs, a large kitchen with pantries and store-room, and an entrance that will shut out the cold winds of winter. On the second floor is five bed-rooms, dressing-room, bath-room, W. C., and abundance of closets, and on third floor are two bed-rooms and large store-room. Cost, $7,500.

Design 179 is of a perfectly square house, the first story veneered with brick outside of frame and sheathing. First floor has a good arrangement in large hall, parlor, dining-room and kitchen, conservatory at rear of dining-room and veranda extending nearly around the entire house. There are four bed-rooms and bath on second floor.

You will very often hear people talking about a square house and that is the kind they mean to build, and we would say to such here is a model to study and work after without offending good taste. Cost, $2,800.

Objections may be made to some of the plans we have submitted because there is no bed-room marked on first floor and then again some may object to the bed-room on first floor and prefer it upstairs and so on with other arrangements which may be objected to. The answer to these may be, that the bed-room when it is wanted on first floor can be, as a rule, easily obtained there, although not marked and where it is not wanted and is marked, it may be used for other purposes equally as well, and that people's wants, with utility and convenience, are the main objects to be attained in any well ordered dwelling. These requisites attained, the principal one—comfort—is secured.

Cellar kitchens—the most abominable nuisances that ever crept into a country dwelling—might have been adopted, no doubt, to the especial delight of some who know nothing of the experimental duties of housekeeping, but the recommendation of these is an offence which we have no stomach to answer for hereafter. In the country where there is room, it should always be the aim of the intending builder to select a plan that spreads over rather than goes down into the ground and high up in the air. Steep, winding and complicated staircases have been avoided as far as possible, dark closets, intricate passages, cubby holes and all sorts of gimcrackery might have amused our pencil; but we have avoided them as well as everything which would stand in the way of the simplest, cheapest and most direct mode of reaching the object in view; a convenient, comfortably arranged dwelling within, having a respectable dignified appearance without to meet the wants of the people intended for, and such we have endeavored to gather together for presentation in this work.

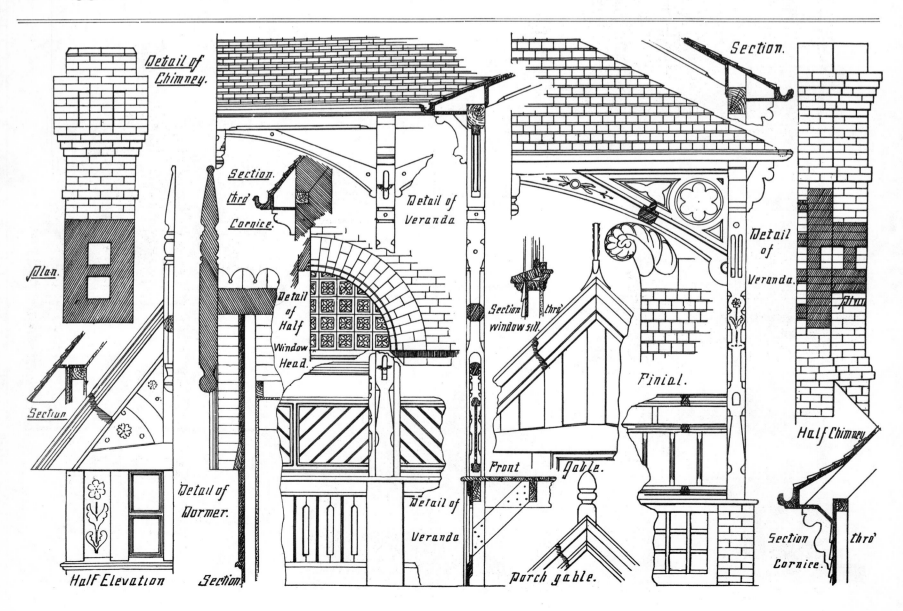

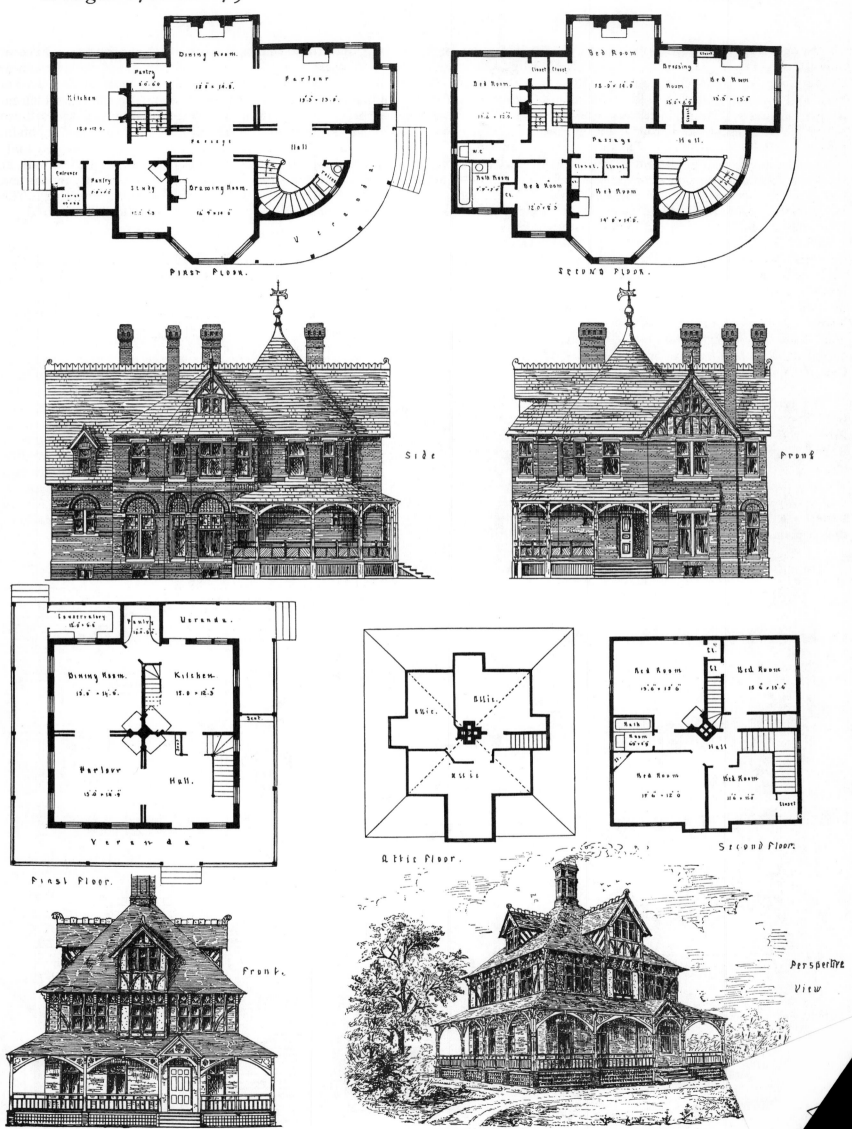

FIRST FLOOR.

SECOND FLOOR.

Side

Front

First Floor.

Attic Floor.

Second Floor.

Front.

Perspective View

PALLISER'S NEW COTTAGE HOMES AND DETAILS.

PLATE 63.

Design 180 represents a perfect gem of a suburban or country house, giving a wide hall through the centre, with fire-place and sliding-doors to sitting-room from hall; a piazza at both front and rear, with an entry-way at rear to main hall, away from the kitchen entrance. Main staircase is well back out of the way, yet can be seen sufficiently from main entrance. A toilet room is located under these stairs. The rear stairs are convenient to the domestic offices and continue right up to the attic, and can be shut off from the second floor at pleasure. The dining-room is of good dimensions and good shape for its uses. Some people insist on having a dining-room made 16 or 17 feet wide, which we regard as foolish in an ordinary house, as 12 or 13 feet for the width is all that is necessary or desirable. The second floor gives five bed-rooms, bath-room and closets, all finished up in a very plain, neat manner, painted, with very simple and small mouldings, and the finish of first floor, main rooms and hall is in natural wood, without paint, thus bringing out the natural beauty of the grain of the wood. The exterior is simple, but in good taste; first story of clapboarded finish, and second story shingled with California redwood shingles, all butts rounded. Cost, $4,800.

Design 181 gives a good style, solid and substantial house, built of stone for outside of first story, which is laid around a frame, put up in about the ordinary manner before the stone work is begun to be laid, which is put up in a simple and rough manner, letting the stones run in between the studs inside and working to a face line only on the outside, and then sheathing on the inside of studs with Byrkitt's sheathing lath, making a perfectly substantial, tight and dry job. The second story is of the clapboarded finish, with a roof covered with California red-wood shingle, finished so as to give it the appearance of English tile. The first-floor plan is especially interesting in the arrangement of its hall and the rooms around it, while the second floor contains four chambers, dressing-room and bath-room, with plenty of closets, the woodwork throughout being of California mahogany or redwood. Cost, $7,500.

Among the many objects used for adornment in connection with a dwelling, there is a very pretty one which we would like to see more frequently employed, and which, when properly placed in a gable or on the panel of a brick chimney, with "Tempus fugit," in terra cotta below it, or placed on a summer house by the side of some walk or retired spot, is in itself highly suggestive. It is the sun-dial we refer to. What thoughts this monitor suggests to the mind? How silent, yet how eloquent. His must be a vacant mind who can pass such a teacher without finding in memories of the past something to dwell upon and also hopes of pleasant things for the future. A shadow reminds us of the flight of time, and we learn in the end that we have pursued but shadows. In the words of the poet:

> "This shadow on the dial's face,
> That steals from day to day,
> With slow, unseen, unceasing pace,
> Moments and months and years away;
> This shadow which, in every clime,
> Since light and motion first began,
> Hath held its course sublime—
> What is it? Mortal man!
> It is the scythe of Time—
> A shadow only to the eye;
> Yet in its calm career
> It levels all beneath the sky;
> And still, through each succeeding year,
> Right onward, with resistless power,
> Its stroke shall darken every hour,
> Till nature's race be run,
> And time's last shadow shall eclipse the sun."

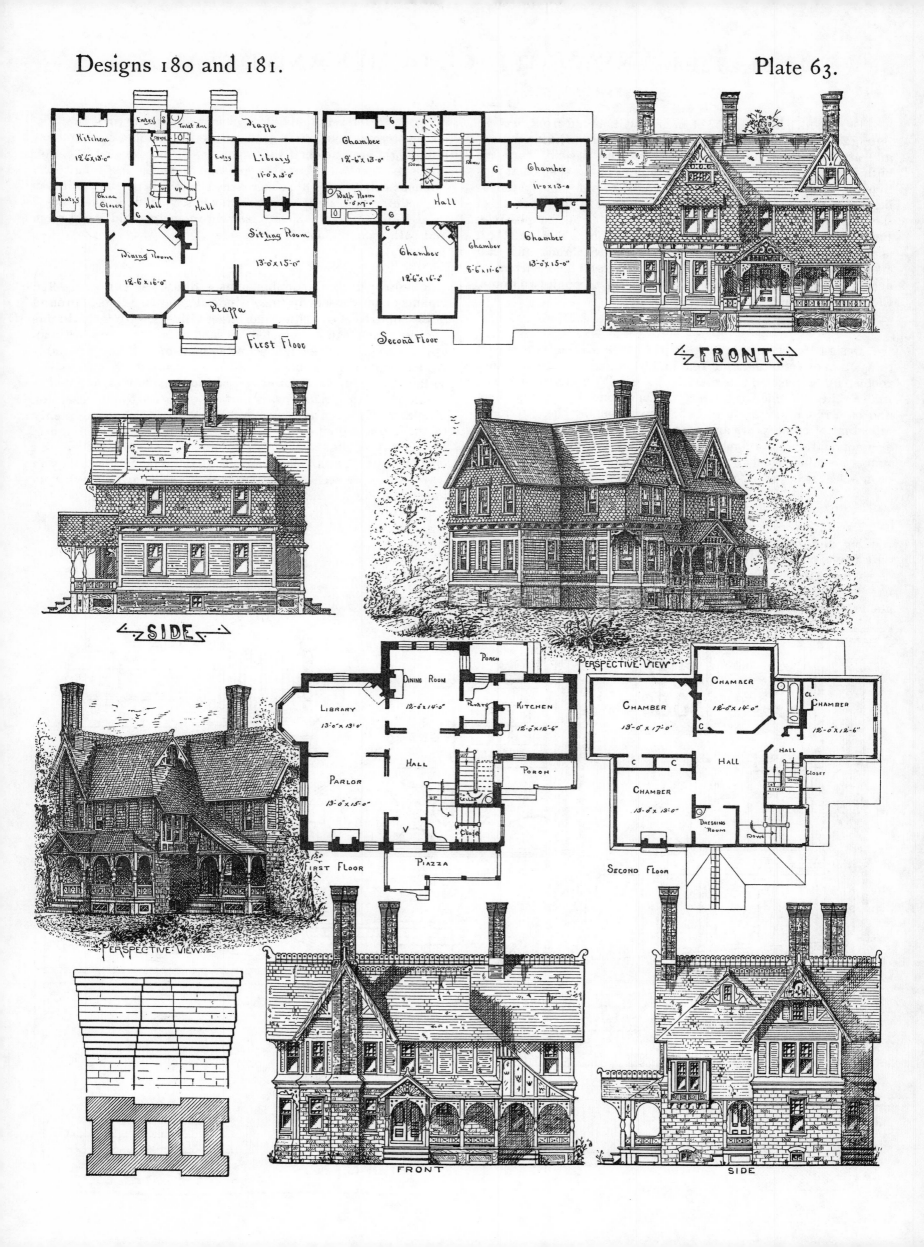

Kitchen
12·6×13·0

Pantry's

China Closet

Hall

Dining Room
12·6×16·0

Entry

Toilet Am

Hall

Library
11·0×13·0

Sitting Room
13·0×15·0

Piazza

Piazza

First Floor

Chamber
12·6×13·0

Bath Room
6·0×7·0

Hall

Chamber
12·6×16·0

Chamber
8·6×11·6

Chamber
11·0×13·0

Chamber
13·0×15·0

Second Floor

FRONT

SIDE

PERSPECTIVE VIEW

PERSPECTIVE VIEW

Dining Room
12·6×14·0

Library
13·0×13·0

Parlor
13·0×15·0

Hall

Pantry

Kitchen
12·6×12·6

Porch

Porch

Closet

First Floor

Piazza

Chamber
13·6×17·0

Chamber
13·6×13·0

Hall

Chamber
12·6×14·0

Chamber
12·0×12·6

Hall

Closet

Dressing Room

Second Floor

FRONT

SIDE

Design 182 shows a pair of houses with broad front, having four gables on main roof, which is very simple in construction, and at the same time attractive. First and second story are both of shingle finish, and the gables have about them that old-time look which is now coming into vogue so much in the finishing up of the exterior of country houses even to the staining of the shingle to give them that appearance as far as possible. Each house gives 7 good rooms and bath-room. The main hall is just large enough to get an easy stairs with rack and hall stand, door to both parlor and dining-room, and also convenient access to cellar and kitchen, the latter being through two doors, therefore well shut off. Cost, $2,000.

Design 183 gives another pair of houses with entrances well away from one another, and front and back stairs; 3 good living-rooms, all connected on first floor; good dining-room closet under stairs; kitchen and pantry. On second floor, 4 chambers and bath-room, and on third floor 3 bed-rooms. The exterior is after that of some years ago with its gambrel roof, giving good accommodation for rooms on third floor; in fact, these bed-rooms are almost as good as any and are obtained in a very economical manner. Cost, $2,800 a side.

Design 184 gives a house of different type from the two preceeding designs, the halls and entrances being brought together with front piazza in the centre of the house front. This house gives about the same accommodation as the last-mentioned, and can be built on a much narrower piece of ground. Cost, $3,000 a side.

Design 185 is a double house, each side being for a family of six or more persons, gives an immense living-room on first floor, a fine light entrance hall with open fire-place, and seat in corner opposite it, a wash-bowl in passage between front hall and kitchen; cellar stairs are also reached from this passage; kitchen has pantry and large closet, and on second floor there are 3 good bed-rooms with closets, sewing-room or child's bed-room and bath room. Cost, $1,700 a side.

Those who build double houses like these can easily find tenants or purchasers for them; indeed good large lots of ground in the suburbs of our cities and larger villages, with tasty double houses which can be erected at moderate cost, and with an appropriate amount of landscape embellishment, and a suitable garden, would not remain uncalled for many days. There is a certain steady demand for cosey, comfortable homes, adapted to the means of the great masses that should attract more attention from capitalists. Any convenient locality; and there are plenty of them near all cities where a store, a church, a school-house, etc., can be established, and a number of houses built up and made into an attractive community, that would induce many to leave the crowded town and city tenements, generally so unhealthy, for a home in the open country.

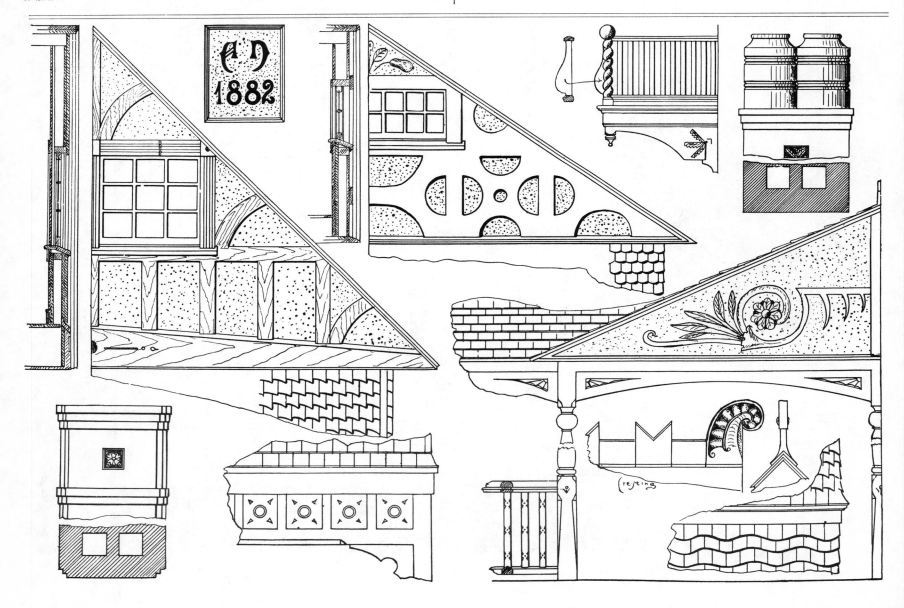

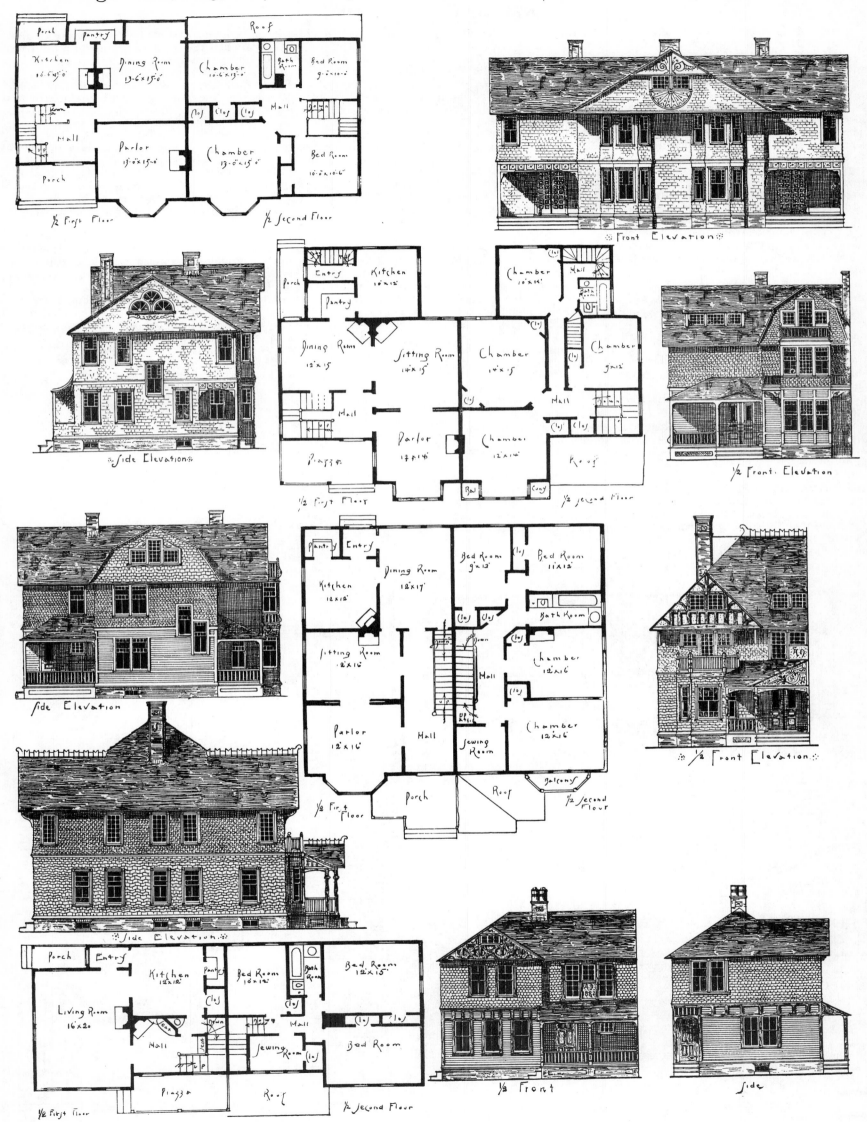

½ First Floor   ½ Second Floor

❊ Front Elevation ❊

❊ Side Elevation ❊

½ Front. Elevation

½ First Floor   ½ Second Floor

Side Elevation

½ Front Elevation

Side Elevation

½ First Floor   ½ Second Floor

½ First Floor   ½ Second Floor

½ Front   Side

PALLISER'S NEW COTTAGE HOMES AND DETAILS.

PLATE 65.

Such designs for fronts of town and city brick street architecture here given if carried out more frequently in the erection of the smaller kind of such houses as they are applicable to, would assist the owner or investor to meet more readily with customers looking for rents or for the purpose of purchasing a snug and attractive home for themselves, but instead of striving to produce something really good and artistic that will be taking with whoever sees them, the builder of blocks of brick houses of moderate cost usually follows a monotonous and unpicturesque, if not an ugly method of building a perfectly straight level top or cornice and an unbroken skyline, and frequently an entirely plain, unbroken front; in fact it has simply the appearance of a lot of brick boxes all joined together with holes for windows cut symmetrically in them and a flat roof sloping a little to the rear and if one will but take the trouble to watch the life of such houses it will invariably be found that they meet with many trials at the hands of a great army of tenants, and that in the course of eight or ten years they are entirely run down, and the owner has kept reducing the rent and is reducing it still to try and get tenants to occupy the premises, which have gone entirely by the board until they are the dirtiest and meanest of tenements so that no one cares to live in them.

Such houses as these are usually built by investors and speculators, and it is a rare occurrence to find a single individual, building a small brick house in line with a lot of others, and it would be a great deal better for all the parties who are to live in these houses if they could each have their own built to meet their own wants and ideas, and if so, how much more pleasing would be the result of street architecture, as each would vie with the other to put some artistic feature on his front, and therefore, if a box did occasionally creep in, it would only tend to make the others—who had put in a few more dollars for beauty—more prominent, and show that they were wise in doing so, and would therefore teach others a lesson.

Very little, however, can be done with such houses in the city of New York where lots are so costly, run up in price because people have drifted into the manner and custom of living in stuffy tenement houses, four families on a floor of a house of 25 feet in width, with only light to one room in each tenement and in this way a large number of families are squeezed into a single house on a small ground area, and consequently the ground is thus made to yield a fair interest on a large valuation, and as the demand creates the supply, and in this it is for tenements in the city more than for small suburban houses, and we are sorry to see such a state of things, but hope for a movement in the right direction and some one to start the erection of such houses a few miles out of the city where ground is cheap and plenty, and where people could be very easily induced to come out and live, as there are many who would be glad to go out into the suburbs and live in a house by themselves, and this subject is of vital interest to persons having any consideration for their personal comfort and the preservation of the health of their families. As an investment there cannot be any better one than the building of such houses as these, and we know whereof we speak, as we have superintended the erection of several blocks of such, having from five to eight houses in a block, in some of the smaller cities, and which are rented to mechanics at reasonable rents, and pay the owners over ten per cent. on the investment.

On this plate we give six different styles of fronts sixteen feet in width; four of double fronts of twenty-five feet; two of three houses on fifty-foot fronts, and ten fronts of fourteen feet each, all of different design, making in all a grand field for selection, and from which the intending builder can adapt features to meet his case. Cost of such small houses range from $1,500 to $2,500 each.

No pains or expense have been spared in making this work reliable. All designs are of a practical character, can be added to, enlarged reduced and worked from in various ways, and all are well worthy of careful study and attention of the building community, the general public and especially of any one who contemplates building. We mean that it shall supply a want for modern designs of convenient and attractive homes for the million.

We trust that its study will help many a one who does not yet possess a home to strive to own one.

BLESSED ARE THEY WHO HAVE HOMES.

I want to be home when the night comes down—
　When the night comes down and the sun is hid—
And the pale, cold moon lights the glimmering town,
　And is heard the shrill cricket and the katy-did,
Ah me! "There's no place like home."

I want to be home when the night comes down,
　When the storm-king raves and the billows roar,
And the sign-boards creak in the rickety town,
　And the mad waves dash strong ships on shore,
Ah me! what a snug place is home.

With my books, my papers, and my glowing hearth,
　With my wife and children around me there;
With health and love and innocent mirth,
　With a heart content and free from care,—
Ah me! what a heaven is home.

What need I care for the storm-king's wrath?
　What to me is the rain or the lightning's glare?
Though the hurricane sweeps over the doomed ship's path,
　And men lie bleeding, and mangled and bare,
Ah me! what a heaven is home.

Ah! my heart does go out to the homeless band—
　To the homeless and wretched o'er all the earth—
To the wanderer by sea and the wanderer by land,
　And I wish them God-speed from my humble heart;
Ah me! Would that all had a home.

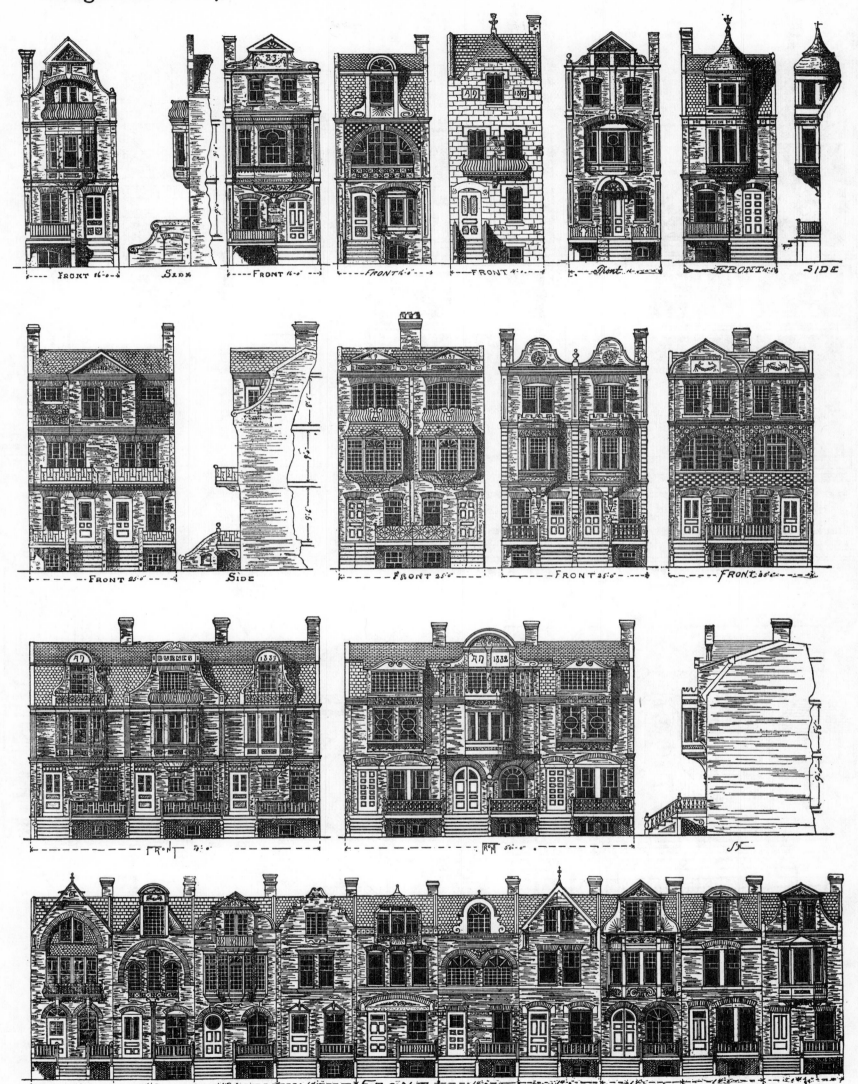

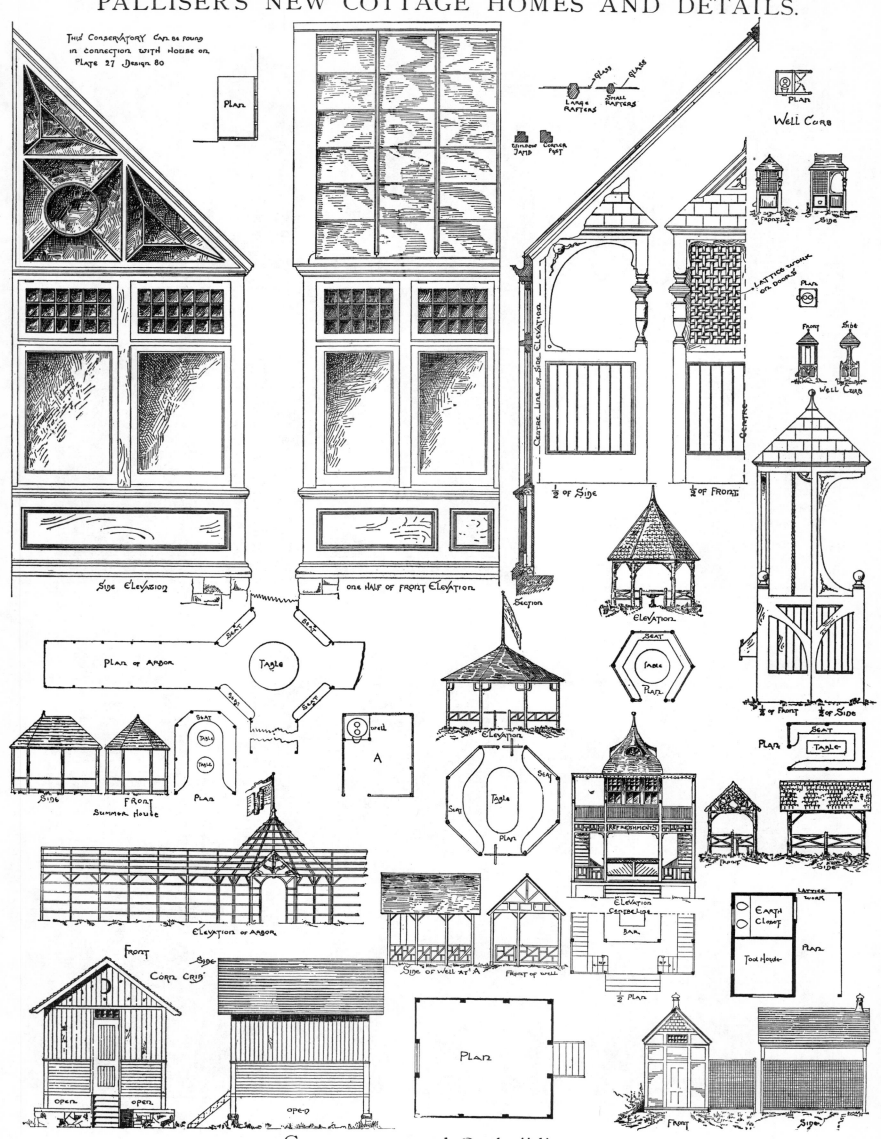

This Conservatory can be found in connection with House on Plate 27 Design 80

Conservatory and Outbuildings.

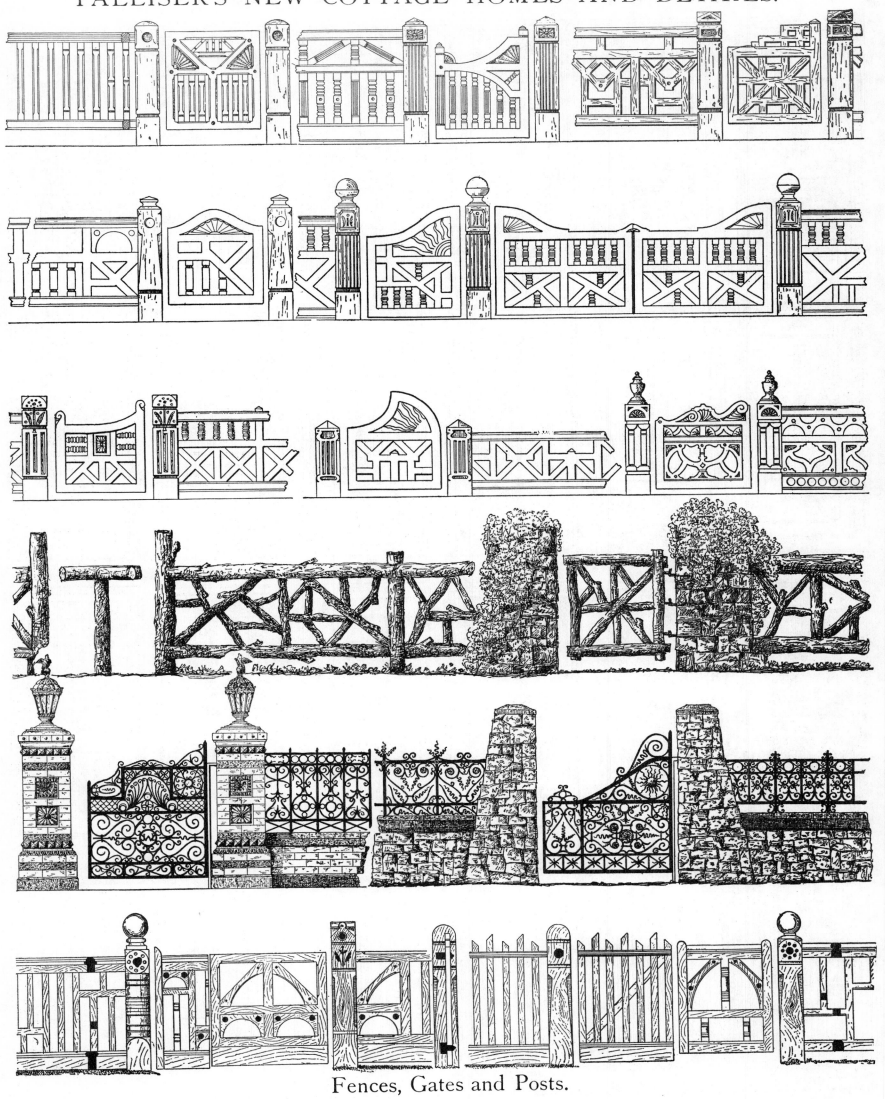

Fences, Gates and Posts.

Doors and Casings.

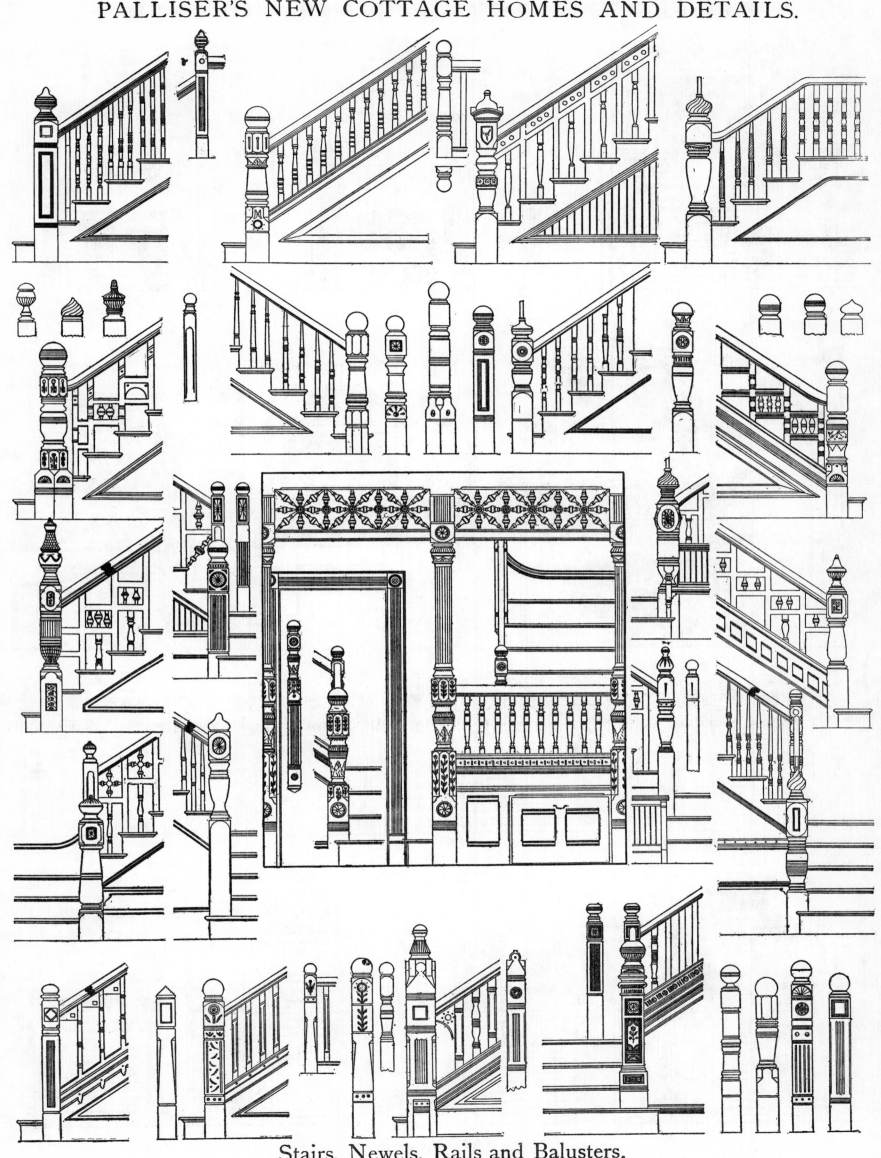

Stairs, Newels, Rails and Balusters.

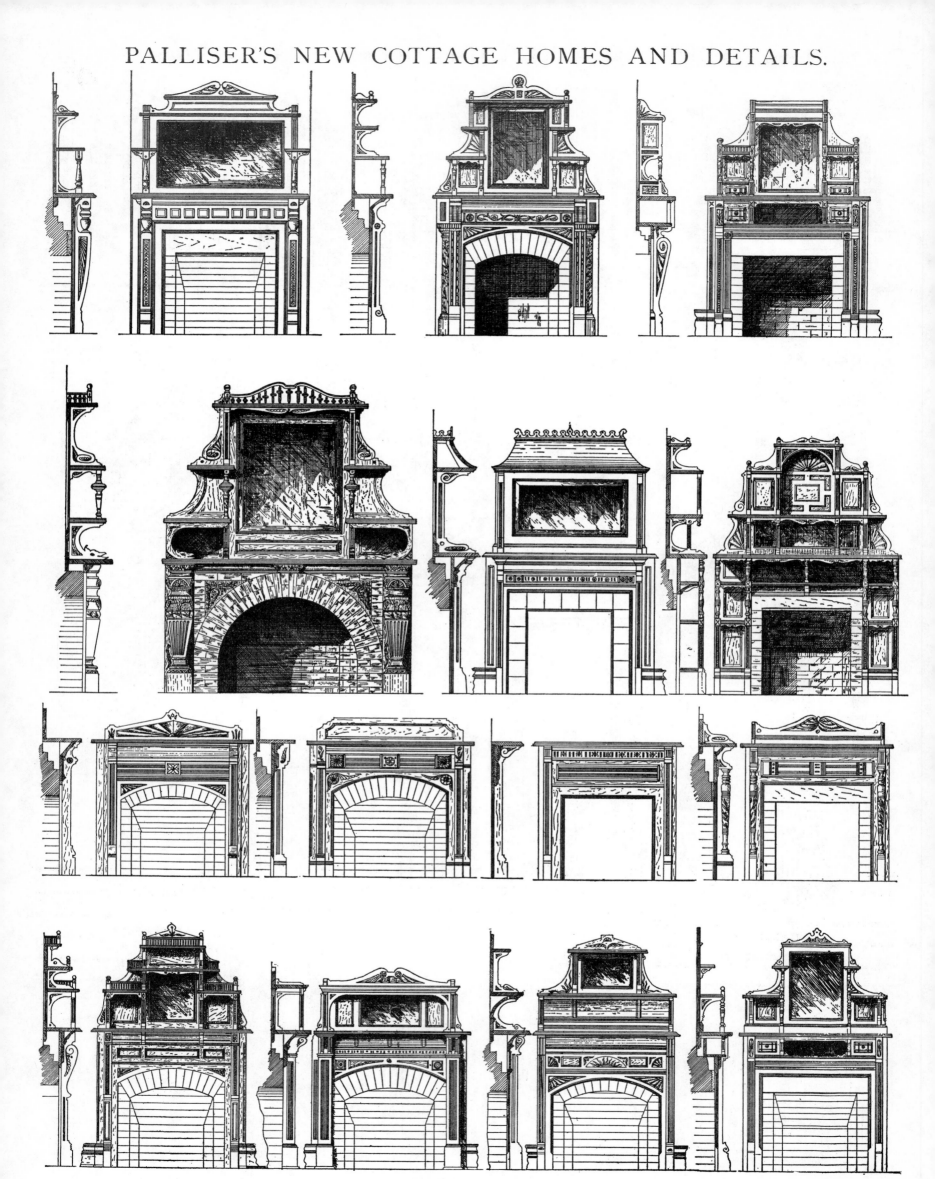

Mantels.

SCALE OF CENTRE PIECES SECTIONS
AND
CASINGS

ONE AND HALF INCHES—ONE FOOT

Window-Trim, Wainscots, Panelled Ceilings and Centrepieces.

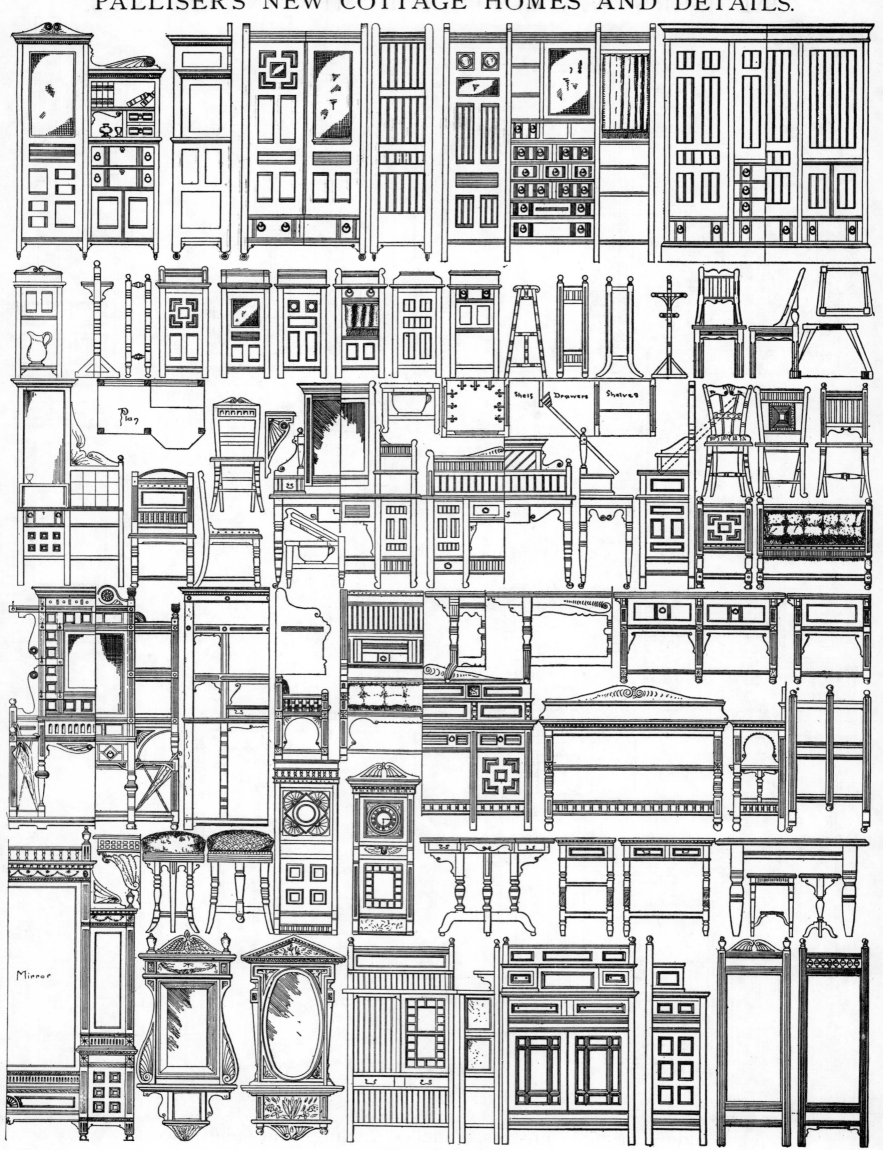

Furniture.

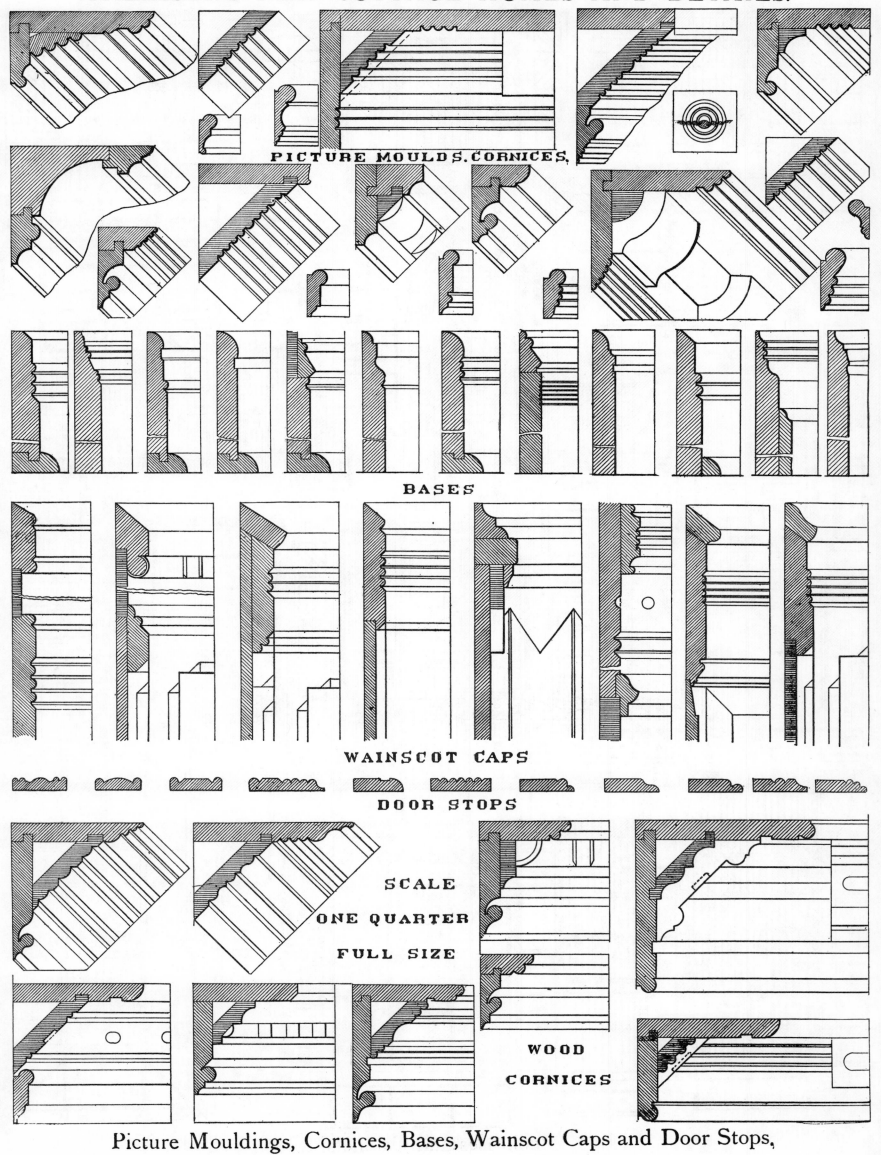

PICTURE MOULDS. CORNICES.

BASES

WAINSCOT CAPS

DOOR STOPS

SCALE
ONE QUARTER
FULL SIZE

WOOD
CORNICES

Picture Mouldings, Cornices, Bases, Wainscot Caps and Door Stops.

PALLISER'S NEW COTTAGE HOMES AND DETAILS.

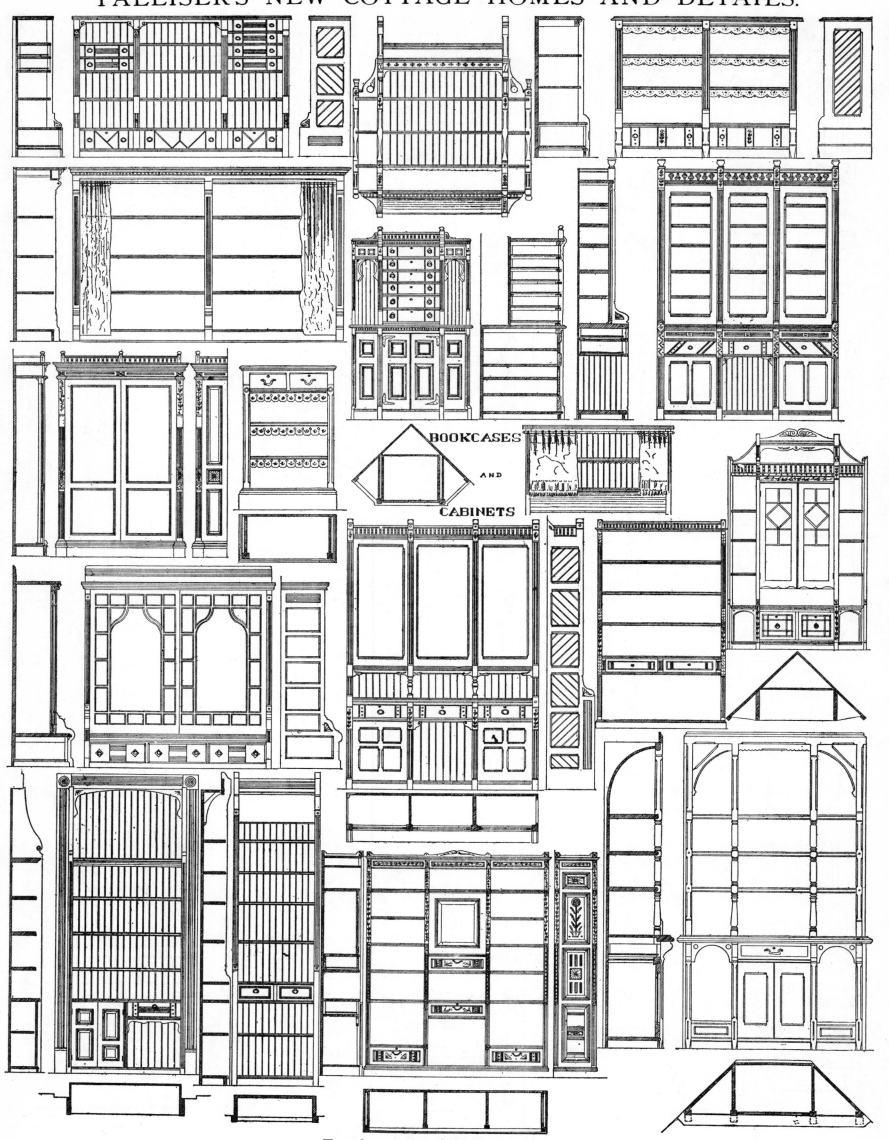

BOOKCASES AND CABINETS

Bookcases and Cabinets.

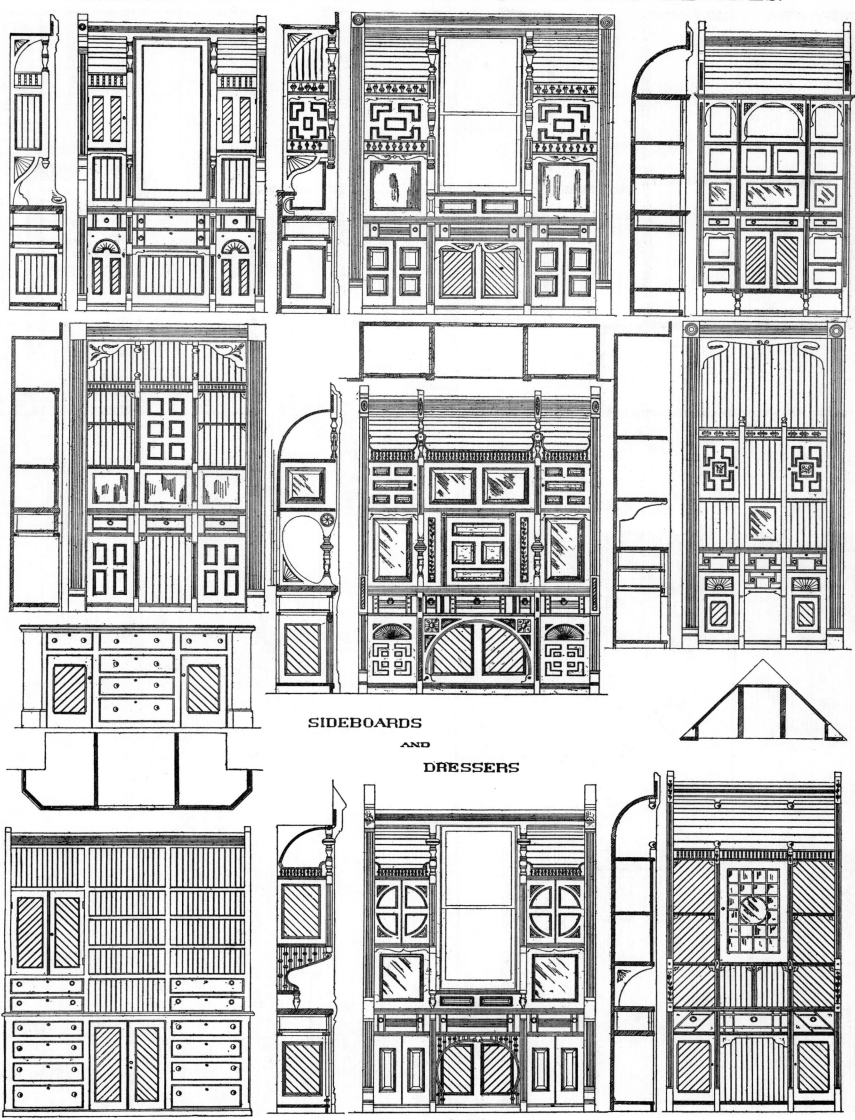

SIDEBOARDS

AND

DRESSERS

Sideboards and Dressers.

PALLISER'S NEW COTTAGE HOMES AND DETAILS.

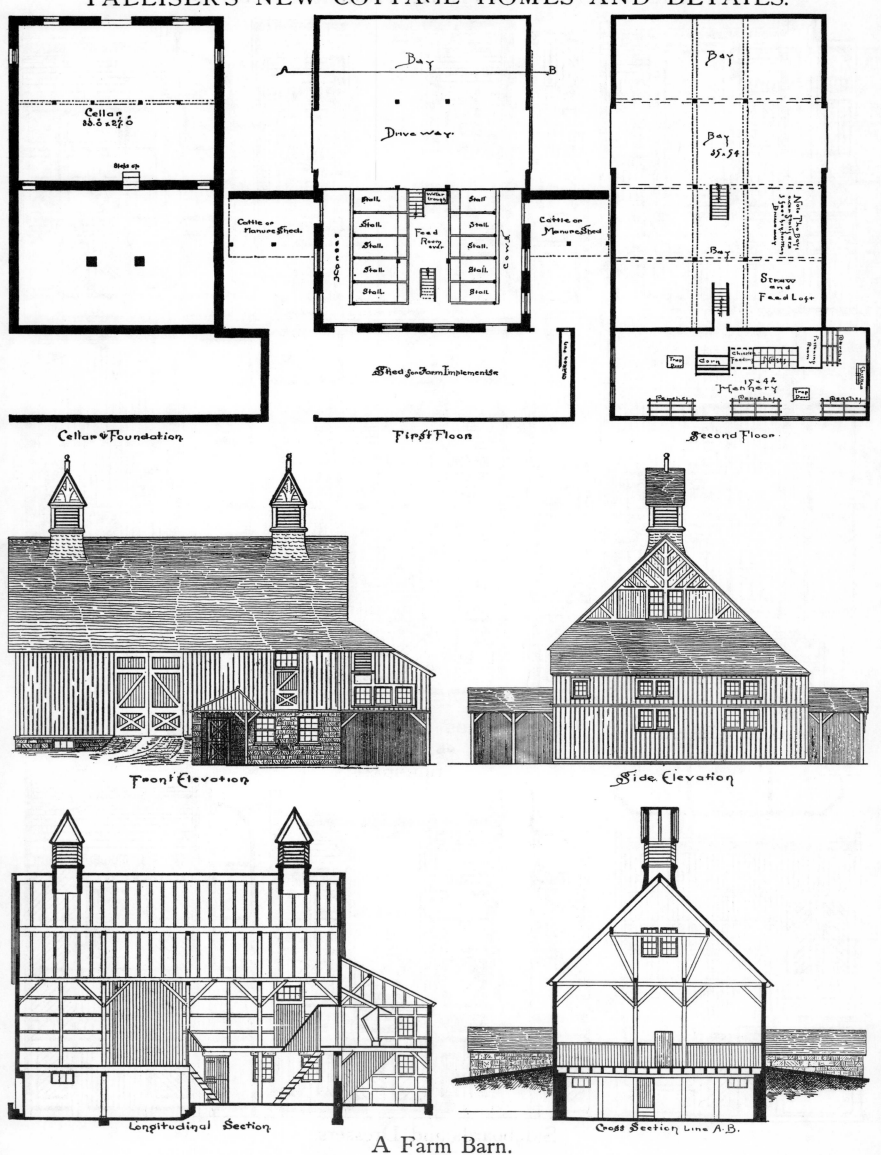

Cellar & Foundation.

First Floor.

Second Floor.

Front Elevation.

Side Elevation.

Longitudinal Section.

Cross Section Line A·B·

A Farm Barn.

PALLISER'S NEW COTTAGE HOMES AND DETAILS.

Plans

Front. Side

Plan Elevation Section Rear

Stable

Stall Stall Stall Stall

Harness

Carriage Room 17. 0. 23. 0

First Floor

Mixing Trough

Seed Bin

Hay Loft

Second Floor

Front Elevation. Side Elevation.

Stall Stall Stall Stall Stall Box Stall. 9. 0. 10. 0

Water Harness

Carriage Room 15. 0. 20. 0

Porch

First Floor

Granary

Hay Loft

Man's Room

Second Floor

Front Elevation. Side Elevation.

Stall Stable W.C.

Stall

Shed Carriage Room 15. 0. 19. 0

First Floor

Seed Room Hall

Hay Loft Man's Room 10. 0. 12. 0

Trap Door in Floor

Second Floor

Front Elevation. Side Elevation.

Shed Shed

Stall

Bin

First Floor

Side Elevation

Loft

Second Floor

Box Stall 9. 0. 10. 0

Closet

Stall

Stall Harness

Stall

Carriage Room 16. 0. 24. 0

First Floor

Feed Room Bin Man's Room 9. 0. 12. 6

Closet

Hay Loft

Second Floor

Elevation

Summer House, Garden Seat and Stables and Carriage Houses.

PALLISER'S NEW COTTAGE HOMES AND DETAILS.

Cow Stall | Stall | Stall | Carriage Room 15.0 x 17.0

Porch

First Floor

Food Bin | Hay Loft

Second Floor

Front Elevation.

Side Elevation.

Box Stall. 9.0 x 10.0

Seed Bins

Feed Room.

Stalls | Stall | Stall | Stall

Harness Room

Porch

Earth Closet

Carriage Room 15.0 x 17.6 | Shed.

Man's Room.

First Floor | **Second Floor**

Front Elevation | **Side Elevation.**

Cow Stall.

Box Stall. 9.0 x 10.0

Stall.

Stall.

Cl.

Cl.

Carriage Room 15.0 x 18.6

Hay. | Man's Room. 11.0 x 13.0

First Floor | **Second Floor** | **Front Elevation.** | **Side Elevation.**

Front Elevation.

Stall | Bin | Stable | Stall | Harn cl. | Carriage Room 16.0 x 26.0

First Floor

Hay Loft.

Second Floor.

Side Elevation.

Stall. | Stall. | Stall. | Carriage Room

Seed Room | Harness Room

W.C. | Ice Room

Feed Room. | Hay Loft.

Oat Bin

Man's Room.

Cl. | Ice Room

Stables and Carriage Houses.

PALLISER'S NEW COTTAGE HOMES AND DETAILS.

SPECIFICATIONS

(Written to go with Working and Detail Drawings).

Of the works and materials required in the erection, construction and completion of Design No. 10, Plate 4.

DIMENSIONS.—The drawings and details must be accurately followed according to their scale, and in all cases preference must be given to figured dimensions over scale. The building to be in size as shown on plans (figured on drawings). Cellar, 6ft. 6in.; first floor, 9ft. 0in.; second floor, 8ft. 6in. in the clear, divided, subdivided, and built in exact accordance with plans and specifications.

MASON WORK.

Excavations.—Do all necessary excavating required for cellar, area and all foundations, to firm and solid ground, and all to be in depth so that foundations will be clear of frost, also excavate for cesspools and dig out space where shown three feet deeper than cellar bottom for cistern. Fill in around all walls and grade off the ground at completion, and remove any surplus earth.

Foundation Work.—Build the foundation walls of good flat building stone, of firm bed, well bonded through the wall, laid up in clean, sharp sand lime and cement mortar, in parts of one of cement to two of lime, laid by and full to a line on the inner face, and flushed and pointed at completion. These walls to be 1ft. 4 in. thick. Put down in like manner foundations under all piers, chimneys and exterior steps, all to be clear of frost.

Underpinning.—From the top of foundation wall, at grade level, extend up 2 ft. 4 in. in height, with stone wall 1 ft. 4 in. thick, laid up with good even colored gray underpinning stone, rock faced, beds and joints worked off with stone hammer to level and plumb and cleaned down and pointed at completion—window sills of blue stone.

Piers.—Build piers in cellar also for support of Porches, as shown, of best hard-burned brick.

Chimneys and Fire Places.—Build the chimneys as shown, using hard-burned brick, the flues to have all mortar joints flushed up close and smooth, and plaster over the brick work in rooms before studding or furring is done—with one good coat. Open fire places to be faced up with buff brick laid in buff mortar. Turn trimmer arches to fire places under hearths, hearths to be of smooth slate properly bedded. Top out the chimneys above the roof, as shown, with selected brick of even color.

Hatchway.—Build the hatchway to cellar as shown on plan, treads of stone walled in, on each end, risers of hard brick, jambs to be of same material as cellar walls and coped with stone on which to secure frame and doors.

Lathing.—All stud partitions, ceilings and work that is furred off, on first and second floors, to be lathed with sound spruce lath and joints broken every tenth lath.

Plastering.—All walls, partitions and ceilings, throughout first and second floors, to be plastered one good coat of brown well-haired mortar, and finish with a coat of soapstone finish. All walls to be finished straight and plumb; all angles to be maintained sharp and regular in form, and the plastering, in all cases, to extend clear down to the floor.

Whitewashing.—Stop, point and lime whiten twice the whole of mason work in cellar, also whitewash floor joist and timber work overhead.

Cellar Bottom.—Level off the cellar bottom, settle it thoroughly and cover it flush and smooth throughout with cement concrete, three parts of clean, coarse gravel, and one of good cement 2 in. deep and finish with an even surface.

Drains.—To carry off wastes from plumbing, to be of vitrified pipe, size; as marked, and to run 60 ft. to rear of house and there connect with cesspools to be properly graded and all joints made tight.

Cistern.—Build a cistern as shown under pantry 6 ft. deep, 8 ft. long and 5 ft. wide, inside measurement, lay the walls of hard brick, 8 in. thick, bottom to be laid in two courses of brick laid flat, the whole laid in and smoothly coated on the inside with cement. Connect the cistern with house leaders through 6 in. vitrified pipe. Lay a 6 in. drain overflow connected closely with the cistern near its top, trap it and connect with drain to cesspool.

Cesspools.—Construct a cesspool 5 ft. in diameter and 7 ft. deep in the clear, draw in on top in a substantial manner, leave manhole with cover of flag stone. Build a separate cesspool for overflow from cistern—with stone walls laid dry and 3 ft. in diameter and 5 ft. deep. Cesspools to be located 60 ft. from house.

CARPENTER.

Timber.—All timber not otherwise specified, to be of good seasoned spruce and put together in the most substantial and thoroughly workmanlike manner known to the trade.

Framing.—The frame to be what is known as a balloon frame, well nailed together; second floor girts to be notched into and well spiked to studs. Do all necessary framing around stairways and chimneys properly mortised and tenoned together.

Frame Timber.—Girders, 6x6 in.; sills, 3x7 in.; posts, 4x5 in.; girts of yellow pine, 1x4 in.; plates, 2x4 in., double and well spiked into ends of studding. First floor timbers, 2x9 in.; second floor, 2x8 in.—16 in. centres; header and trimmer beams, 3 in. thick; roof rafters, 2x5 in.—2 ft. centres; door and window studs, 3x4 in. intermediate studding, 2x4 in.—16 in. centres; studding in partitions, 2x4 in.—16 in. centres. Porch sills and cross sills, 3x6 in.; floor timbers, 2x6 in.—20 in. centres.

Bridging.—Bridge the floor timbers through centres with 1x2 in. cross-bridging, properly cut in between timbers, and nailed at each end with two 10d. nails.

Furring.—Furr overhead on rafters, using 2x3 in. stuff for ceilings of rooms on second floor, and do any other furring required; also furnish any other timber, as required by the design, of the requisite sizes and quality.

Sheathing.—Cover all sides of frame with tongued and grooved boards, not to exceed 8 in. in width, nailed through each edge to every stud with 10d. nails.

Lumber.—The lumber to be of white pine, unless otherwise specified, free from knots, shakes and other imperfections impairing its durability and strength.

Water Table to be $\frac{7}{8}$ in. thick, beveled and rabbeted for clapboards.

Corner Boards, casings and bands to be $1\frac{1}{4}$x6 in.; bands to be rabbeted top and bottom for clapboards and beveled on top.

Shingling on sides of second story to be as shown, using shingle 6 in. wide and laid 6 in. to the weather and all laid close and made tight at angles and corners, each shingle nailed with two nails.

Clapboarding.—Cover first story with clear pine clapboards $4\frac{1}{2}$ in. wide, put on with 8d. box nails, to have not less than $1\frac{1}{4}$ in. lap and underlaid with rosin-sized, waterproof sheathing felt, which, also, place under all covering, casings, watertable, etc., so as to lap and make tight job.

Cornices to be formed as shown, gutter formed on same and lined with tin, so as to shed water to points indicated on plan; all as per detail drawings.

Window Frames to be made as shown; cellar frames of 2 in. plank rabbeted for sash; sash hinged to top, and to have suitable fasteners to keep open or shut; all other sashes to be double hung with braided cotton cord and cast-iron weights, and to be glazed with best American sheet glass all sashes $1\frac{3}{8}$ in. thick, of seasoned pine, window sills 2 in. thick.

Blinds.—Outside blinds to all windows, except cellar, hung in two folds, properly secured.

Door Frames.—Outside door frames of plank, rabbeted, with 2 in. oak sills.

Porches to be constructed as shown by the detail drawings; steps $1\frac{1}{8}$ in. thick, $\frac{7}{8}$ in. risers, to have cove under nosings; lay floors with $1\frac{1}{8}$x4 in. flooring, blind nailed to beams, and to have white lead joints; ceiling ceiled with narrow beaded battens of even width and molded in angles. Columns, rails, newels, panels, etc., all as per detail drawings.

Roofing.—All roofs to be covered with 18 in. sawed pine shingles, laid on 1 x 2 in. strips, nailed to rafters with 10d. nails; each shingle to be nailed with two 4d. nails, to be well laid, joints properly broken and made tight; valleys to be lined with tin 20 inches wide and well painted both sides. Put small scuttle in roof and step ladder to same.

Floors.—Lay the floors throughout with $\frac{7}{8}$ in. flooring, not to exceed 6 in. in width, to be well laid, joints broken, and well nailed to every timber; the best to be selected and laid on first floor.

Partitions.—Set partitions as marked on plans, to foot on girders, and to have 3x4 in. plates to carry second floor; all angles to be formed solid; all partitions to be bridged once in their height.

Grounds.—Put up all necessary grounds to skreed plaster to, to be $\frac{7}{8}$ in. thick and left on.

Wainscoting.—Wainscot walls of kitchen 3 ft. high, with beaded battens 3 in wide, and cap with molded and beveled cap.

Casings in front hall, parlor and dining-room to be moulded on face as shown, 1x6in.; all doors and windows elsewhere to be cased with $\frac{7}{8}$ in. casings, and finish with a $\frac{7}{8}$x$1\frac{3}{4}$in, mold; put down 8 in. beveled and moulded base after plastering; door jambs to be $\frac{7}{8}$in. thick, and rabbeted for doors and beaded on edges: windows to be finished with neat stool and apron finish.

Doors to be made in size as shown; outside doors to be sash doors, as shown; all other doors six-panel, ogee moulded solid.

Finish of first story hall, parlor and dining room to be of ash, elsewhere clean pine for natural wood finish.

Saddles.—Put down neat hard pine saddles to all doors.

Stairs.—Cellar stairs to be of plank, no risers; stairs to second floor as shown, $1\frac{1}{4}$ in. treads, $\frac{7}{8}$ in. risers, properly put together and supported. Newel to be 6 inches square with turned top, rail $2\frac{1}{2}$ x $3\frac{1}{2}$ in. worked as shown, balusters 2 in. turned and all of ash.

Sink.—Ceil up under sink with narrow beaded battens, to match wainscoting; hang door to form closet under; ceil up splash back 16 in. high; also place drip board complete.

Pantry to have counter-shelf and four shelves above, also put up one dozen pot-hooks.

China Closet to have counter-shelf with closet under and three drawers and press with doors and shelves.

Clothes Presses to be fitted up with shelves and double wardrobe hooks, 9 in. apart, on neat molded strips.

Knobs and Escutcheons on front door and main part of first floor to be of ash and elsewhere mineral.

Locks to all doors to be mortise locks, brass fronts and keys; outside doors to be secured with suitable shove bolts. All sash to have a burglar-proof sash lock to match other furniture.

Stops.—Insert hard-wood door stops in base, where requisite.

Hinging.—Hang all doors with loose joint butts of appropriate size; those on first floor to have acorn-drops and japanned.

Hatchway Doors to Cellar to have a frame well secured and doors made out of 1x6 in. stuff well battened and secured.

Side Board to be constructed of ash as per details.

Mantels to be constructed, as shown, of ash as per details.

Cellar.—Partitions in cellar to be boarded with matched boards; coal bin to be boarded up 5 ft. high, to have slides complete; put up two swing shelves in cellar.

Door Bell.—Put a good gong bell on front door with suitable pull, etc., to match other furniture.

Ice Closet.—Line inside with two thicknesses of spruce matched ceiling with air space and paper between and fill in between studs with mineral wool, prepare tank for lining by plumber, fit up shelves and drawers, etc., as directed.

Bath Room.—Fit up with ash, wainscot walls 3 ft. high, ceil up over bath and closet 20 in. high. Case up bath-tub and wash bowl and finish with neat capping. Hang seat and cover to W. C. in most approved manner.

Tank.—Construct of plank and support in a substantial manner, a tank 3x4x3 ft. inside measurement.

Final.—Also do any other carpenter work as shown by and as required to carry out the design.

PAINTING.

All wood-work on exterior, to be painted two good coats of Lucas & Co.'s pure tinted gloss paints in the following colors:

Body of the work, 1st story, No. 241. Body of the work, 2d story, No. 244, Corner boards and casings, No. 258. Sash, No. 240. Blinds, No. 234. Roof. No. 240.

Paint tin work two coats, leaders two coats to match other work. Finish the front door and all interior wood work by filling with Wheeler's filler, and give two good coats of varnish and rub down.

TINNING AND PLUMBING.

Tinning.—Line the gutters with tin, well soldered in rosin; furnish and put up the necessary number of tin leaders to convey the water from gutters to grade level, and there connect with drains. These leaders to be firmly secured to building, and to be graded in size to suit amount of service required.

Sink to be a 20x30x6 in. steel, supplied with water through $\frac{5}{8}$ in. lead pipe and $\frac{5}{8}$ in. brass drawcock, to have 2 in. cast iron waste, properly caulked at joints, trapped and connected closely to drain. Extend waste pipe above roof.

Pump to be lift and force, and connected to cistern and well, and supply to tank in attic, with tell tale return—line tank in attic with lead.

Boiler to be 35 gallon galvanized iron set on stand and connected to water back of range, and fitted up complete.

Bath Room to have W. C. selected by owner net cost not to exceed $12, to have drip tray and set open. Bath-tub 12 oz. sheet copper planished, and to have combination bibb for hot and cold water. Washbowl of best ware marble top, counter sunk, hot and cold water—all properly supplied with water and wastes to go into 4 in. cast-iron soil down to drain, and this pipe to extend up above roof—put safe wastes under W. C. and bowl. All fixtures to be properly trapped and vented, and the whole to be a first class sanitary job. Faucets to be nickel plated. Stop-cocks to be provided wherever requisite. Ice tank to be lined with zinc.

PALLISER'S NEW COTTAGE HOMES AND DETAILS.

SPECIFICATIONS

(Written to go with Working and Detail Drawings.)

Of the works and materials required in the erection, construction and completion of Design No. 22, Plate 7.

DIMENSIONS.—The drawings and details must be accurately followed according to their scale, and in all cases preference must be given to figured dimensions over scale. The building to be in size as shown on plans (figured on drawings). Cellar, 6ft. 6in.; first floor, 8ft. 6in., and second floor, 8ft. 0in. in the clear, divided, subdivided, and built in exact accordance with plans and specifications.

MASON WORK.

Excavating.—Do all necessary excavating required for cellar, area and all foundations, to firm and solid ground, and all to be in depth so that foundations will be clear of frost; grade off the ground as directed at completion.

Stone Work.—Build the foundation walls of good, flat building stone, of firm bed, well bonded through the wall, laid up in clean, sharp sand lime and cement mortar, in parts of one of cement to two of lime, laid by and full to a line on the inner face, and flushed and pointed at completion. These walls to be 1 ft. 4 in. thick. Put down in like manner foundations under all piers, chimney and exterior steps, all to be clear of frost.

Drains.—All drain pipes to be of the first quality cement drain pipe, in sizes as marked on plan and to be connected with sewer in street. These pipes to be properly graded, trapped and the joints cemented tight.

Underpinning.—From the top of stone wall, at grade level, extend up two feet in height with 8 in. brick wall, laid up with best hard-burned brick and clean sharp sand lime mortar; face walls with selected brick of even color, laid in red mortar, close joints, jointed, properly cleaned down at completion, and finished with black joints. Window sills of blue stone.

Piers.—Build piers in cellar, as shown, of best hard-burned brick, laid in clean, sharp sand lime mortar.

Hatchway.—Build the hatchway to cellar as shown, treads of blue stone 3 in. thick, risers of hard brick, jambs to be of stone same as foundation walls and leveled up on top just above grade.

Chimney.—Build chimney as shown, plastered on the inside and outside, furnished with proper stove collars and ventilating covers where required. Top out the chimney above the roof, as shown, with selected brick in like manner to underpinning.

Lathing.—All stud partitions, ceilings and work that is furred off, on first and second floors, to be lathed with sound spruce lath and joints broken every tenth lath.

Plastering.—All walls, partitions and ceilings, throughout first and second floors, to be plastered one good coat of brown well haired mortar and finish with a good coat of white hard-finish. All walls to be finished straight and plumb; all angles to be maintained sharp and regular in form, and the plastering, in all cases, to extend clear down to the floor.

Cellar Bottom.—Clean out all rubbish, level off cellar-bottom and settle it thoroughly.

Whitewashing.—Give all brick, stone and timber work in cellar one good coat of whitewash.

Privy Vault.—Excavate for and stone up a privy vault 3x5 ft. and 5 ft. deep and level up on top to receive framework.

CARPENTER.

Timber.—All timber not otherwise specified, to be of good seasoned hemlock and put together in the most substantial and thoroughly workmanlike manner known to the trade.

Framing.—The frame to be what is known as a balloon frame, well nailed together, second floor girts to be notched into and well spiked to studs. Do all necessary framing around stairways and chimneys, properly mortised and tenoned together.

Frame Timber.—Girders, 4x6 in.; sills, 3x5 in.; posts, 4x5 in.; girts of yellow pine, 1x4 in.; plates, 2x4 in., doubled and well spiked into ends of studding. First floor timbers, 2x8 in.; second floor, 2x7 in.—16 in. centres; header and trimmer beams, 3 in. thick; roof rafters, 2x5 in.—2 ft. centres; door and window studs, 3x4 in. intermediate studding, 2x4 in.—16 in. centres; studding in partitions, 2x3 in.—16 in. centres; also furnish any other timber, as required by the design, of the requisite sizes and quality.

Bridging.—Bridge the floor timbers with 1x2 in. cross bridging, properly cut in between timbers, and nailed at each end with two 10d. nails.

Sheathing.—Cover all sides of frame with tongued and grooved boards, not to exceed 10 in. in width, nailed through each edge to every stud with 10d. nails.

Lumber.—The lumber to be of White pine, unless otherwise specified, free from knots, shakes and other imperfections impairing its durability and strength.

Water Table to be ⅞ in. thick, furred off, 1 in., and capped with a beveled and rabbeted cap for clapboards to lap.

Corner Boards, casings and bands to be 1⅛x5 in.; bands to be rabbeted top and bottom for clapboards and beveled on top.

Clapboarding.—Cover sides of first story with clear pine clapboards, 4½ in. wide, put on with 8d. box nails, to have not less than 1¼ in. lap, and underlaid with rosin-sized waterproof sheathing felt, which, also, place under shingling and all casings, water-table, etc., so as to lap and make tight job.

Shingling.—The side walls of second story and gables to be covered with California redwood shingle 6 in. wide with rounded butts and laid 6 in. to weather, to be put close at all angles, well nailed and made perfectly tight.

Cornices to be formed, as shown, gutter formed on same, and lined with tin, so as to shed water to points indicated on plan; and all as per detail drawings.

Window Frames to be made as shown; cellar frames of 2 in. plank rabbeted for sash; sash hinged to top, and to have suitable fasteners to

keep open or shut; all other sashes to be double hung with hemp cords and cast iron weights, and to be glazed with best American sheet glass, all sashes 1⅜ in. thick, of seasoned pine, window sills 1½ in. thick.

Blinds.—Outside blinds to all windows, except cellar, hung in two folds, properly secured and painted two good coats of invisible green.

Door Frames.—Outside door frames of plank, rabbeted, and to have 1½ in. oak sills.

Porches to be constructed as shown by the detail drawings; steps 1⅛ in. thick, ⅞ in. risers, to have cove under nosings; lay floors with 1⅛ x4 in. flooring, blind nailed to beams, and to have white lead joints; ceiling ceiled with narrow beaded battens of even width and molded in angles. Columns, rails, newels, panels, etc., all as per detail drawings.

Roofing.—All roofs to be covered with 18 in. sawed pine shingles, laid on 1x2 in., strips, nailed to rafters with 10d. nails; each shingle to be nailed with two 4d nails, to be well laid, joints properly broken, and made tight. Valleys to be lined with tin 20 in. wide. Put small scuttle in roof and step ladder up to same in closet.

Floors.—Lay the floors throughout with ⅞ in. flooring, not to exceed 6 in. in width, to be well laid, joints broken, and well nailed to every timber; the best to be selected and laid on first floor.

Partitions.—Set partitions, as marked on plans, to foot on girders, and to have 3x3 in. plates to carry second floor; all angles to be formed solid; all partitions to be bridged once in their height.

Wainscoting.—Wainscot walls of kitchen and dining-room 3 ft. high, with beaded battens 3 in. wide, and cap with molded and bevelled cap.

Casings in front hall and sitting-room to be beaded on face, as shown, ⅞x5 in.; all doors and windows elsewhere to be cased before plastering with ⅞ in. casings, and finish with a ⅞x1¾ in. band mold; put down 7 in. bevelled base in front hall, sitting-room and bed-rooms after plastering; door jambs to be ⅞ in. thick, and rabbeted for doors and beaded on edges; windows to be finished with neat stool and apron finish.

Doors to be made in size as shown; to be six-panel, ogee molded solid.

Saddles.—Put down neat hard pine saddles to all doors.

Stairs.—Cellar stairs, to be of plank, no risers; stairs to second floor as shown, 1¼ in. treads, ⅞ in. risers, properly put together and supported; 2x3 in. rail on side.

Sink.—Ceil up under sink with narrow beaded battens, to match wainscoting; hang door to form closet under; ceil up splash back 16 in. high; also place drip board complete.

Pantry to have counter-shelf and four shelves above, also put up one dozen pot-hooks.

China Closet—In dining-room, to be fitted up with two drawers and four shelves above.

Closets to be fitted up with shelves and double wardrobe hooks, 9in. apart, on neat molded strips.

Furniture to front door to be jet pattern, elsewhere mineral, plain.

Locks to all doors to be mortise locks, brass fronts and keys; outside doors to be secured with suitable shove bolts. Sash to be secured with burglar proof sash locks.

Stops.—Insert hard-wood door stops in base, where requisite.

Hinging.—Hang all doors with loose joint butts of appropriate size.

Mantel in sitting-room to be constructed, as shown, of ash.

Cellar.—Partitions in cellar to be formed with matched boards; coal bin to be boarded up 4 ft. high, to have slides complete.

Privy.—Build a privy 4 ft. 6 in. x5 ft. 0 in. inside, board it with tight matched boards, hang batten door properly secured, small sliding sash in one end, shingle roof.

Hatchway doors to Cellar.—To be constructed out of 1x5 in. stuff, battened and to be properly hinged and secured.

Final.—Also do any other carpenter work as shown by and as required to carry out the design.

PAINTING.

Furnish all materials and perform all labor for the proper painting of the building.

Cover all sap and knots with shellac, putty up all wood-work smoothly and use New Jersey ochre in oil for priming exterior work as put up, and finish with one good coat of Lucas' pure tinted gloss paints in the following colors.

Body of the work, No. 258.
Corner boards and casings, No. 205.
Shingling of sides, stain and oil.
Sash, white.
Front door, grain walnut.
Paint tin work two coats, leaders two coats to match other work.
Paint privy two coats to match house.
Paint all wood work of interior that it is customary and usual to paint two good coats such tints as directed; grain wood work of kitchen and dining-room oak and varnish same and leave all work in a complete state.

TINNING AND PLUMBING.

Tinning.—Line the gutters with tin, well soldered in rosin; furnish and put up the necessary number of tin leaders to convey the water from gutters to grade level, and there connect with drains. These leaders to be firmly secured to building, and to be graded in size to suit amount of service required.

Sink to be a 20x30x6 in. cast iron, supplied with water through ⅝ in. lead pipe and ⅝ in. brass draw cock, to have 2 in. cast-iron waste, properly caulked at joints, trapped and connected closely to drain. Extend waste pipe above roof for vent.

It is desirable for parties who contemplate building to obtain the greatest amount of room, with the best architectural effect for the amount of money expended, and to accomplish this they should secure the services of a competent architect, one who has made such things a study and pursuit for years, and has used every means to become familiar with it in all its detail. The parties for whom the building is to be erected should carefully study their wants, and give their ideas to the architect to be worked out by him; he can then prepare a complete set of drawings, details and specifications. The proprietor knows just what he is going to have before the building is commenced, and he feels the assurance that there can be no misunderstanding with his contractor, as the architect's drawings and specifications serve as a mediator between the owner and contractor, to remind the former what to require, and the latter what his agreement is to perform.

Care should be taken by clients not to place too many restrictions on the architect —how he shall do this or that, and make a mere draughtsman of him; but after stating the price, it would be well to say what room is required, and give him your ideas on the matter; and you may be sure that everything will be added to the building which can be, internally and externally, that will enhance its beauty and usefulness.

When parties communicate with us with a view to obtain our services in preparing plans, etc., they will please give the following particulars and any and all the ideas they have on the subject which they may deem of importance.

1. The amount you will expend on the building to make it complete in every particular. Do not state an amount less than you really intend to spend as by so doing you may be disappointed, as some of our clients have been heretofore on account of their understating the amount they were willing to expend with the idea that it was sure to run up above the amount they named. A lady client of ours instructed us that her house and barn must not exceed $10,000 in cost, and the actual cost by contract was $9,500, and she was disappointed and would have been glad to have had it better finished and more elaborate work and would willingly have paid $15,000 and believed at the start that it would run up to that figure before it was finished, her friends having informed her that architects' estimates were always increased in actual execution by about one half.

2. Prices of labor and materials in your locality for cash; also state how you intend to have your work done, by contract or how, or would you give it proper, personal attention yourself, and sharp business management in buying the material and getting the work done according to advice and suggestions that we could give as to purchase of some of the materials and doing the work; give character and ability of contractors in your locality that you are likely to employ; are they mechanics and workers, thorough, pushing, wide-awake business men and close buyers for cash or are they bound to buy in the local market and pay whatever some one chooses to ask, who gives them credit, and are unable to buy elsewhere.

3. Nature of ground, size and shape of lot, grade of ground and in which direction the building will front, also principal side. The best way is to send a rough draft of the lot, with points of compass, and indicate roughly where building is to be placed, something like this:

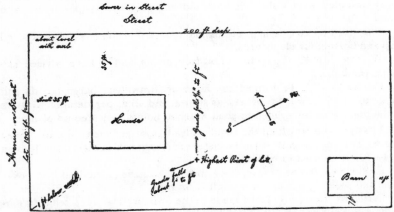

4. What material will be used in construction? Wood, brick or stone? Give full particulars where material can be obtained, and state which can be had most conveniently and economically for the several purposes. What is your preference for foundations and also for underpinning.

5. Particulars of other buildings near it, if any.

6. Number and what rooms are required on each floor; heights of ceilings and number of floors; also give particulars of any special disposition to be made of any of the rooms on account of scenery, views, or otherwise.

7. What the building and rooms are to be used for.

8. From which direction are your most severe winds and storms.

9. Give particulars of locality and character of the grounds and surroundings, and any special circumstances to be considered in the design, and in the location and arrangement of rooms.

10. What improvements are required, such as heating, hot and cold water, bath, gas, water-closets, etc.

11. Out-side finish—Porches, Tower, Bay-window, Verandas, etc., etc.

12. Have you any public water works? Do you require Cisterns to receive water from roof, or what provision must be made for water service? Also give full particulars of drainage. Can yours connect with a sewer in the street or must a cesspool be provided and state whether the ground has a bottom of sand, gravel, hard-pan or clay.

13. What fence and out-buildings are required?

14. Name any work and materials you wish to do or supply, so that they may be mentioned in specifications.

Write your name and address legibly, giving your post-office, county and state, and write your own name at the bottom of your letters.

After receiving particulars, anything that will interfere with the proper arrangement of the rooms, and the carrying out of a suitable design, will be brought to your notice, and we shall correspond with you until everything will harmonize. We do not wish to send out designs when we think they will not give satisfaction.

Correspondence invited from those who contemplate building, which will always receive our prompt and careful attention.

When we are employed by parties at a distance, we make preliminary sketches of floor plans, and usually with this we send a small free hand-sketch of the Elevations. These we send to the client and they are returned, with whatever alterations, corrections and suggestions he makes. Then we make the changes suggested as far as proper and send again to the client for final approval if necessary and when our sketches show just what is wanted by our client to meet his necessities and desires, we make the working plans, detail drawings and specifications, etc, as required for the builders to work from. Parties who wish to employ us, should not wait until the last moment, but should open correspondence with us two or three months, or even more, before they wish to commence building.

Our charges for services, are for full working plans, all detail drawings for exterior and interior work and fittings, specifications and forms of contract, two and a half per cent. on cost of erecting and completing building, and where parties are unknown to us, one-quarter of said charges usually accompanying the order for preliminary sketches, and as a guarantee of good faith.

In addition to above rates, one per cent. is charged when elaborated sketches and perspective in line or color are required to be made previous to making full working plans; also one per cent. additional when there is a large amount and variety of elaborate interior wood work and fittings to design in detail for first-class dwellings, mansions, etc.

For preparing complete bills of quantities of materials, a charge of three-quarter per cent. is made.

For superintendence, one and one half to three per cent., according to the requirements or by the visit by special agreement for inspecting the work to see whether contractor's payments are due or not, and that he is fulfilling the conditions of the contract.

When required, we furnish our client with a competent and reliable Clerk of Works to be constantly on the ground superintending the construction, and which is very necessary in case of large or intricate buildings.

For designs in detail of Furniture and Interior Decorations, ten per cent. on cost.

For buying material and appliances required in building and furnishing, such goods in all cases being bought at the best wholesale trade rates, a charge of five per cent. is made.

For appraising and valuing, charges are made according to time occupied and circumstances.

Traveling expenses and surveying in all cases are charged in addition to above rates.

Charges are based on the total cost of actual execution and payment of full value, but previous to ability to arrive at the proper and full cost, the approximated intended cost is used as the base on which to reckon charges.

It is our constant aim to please our clients, and we usually succeed. Our long practice has convinced us that it is quite as easy to satisfy parties with our designs when we never see them, as in any other way. When parties correspond with us in regard to procuring designs, we are always prompt in answering their inquiries; but oft-times people have written us simply to get our ideas and not pay for them. To all such we would say that our time is valuable, and we sincerely wish they would not trouble us. We mention this fact, because we have received scores of letters, and answered them, when the parties really never intended to employ us, but simply steal our ideas. Now our ideas are for sale, and by this means we live, and it is a pleasure as well as a livelihood, to assist people to build artistic, convenient and comfortable homes. Perhaps if architects were rich—they seldom are—it would be sufficient compensation to them to assist people as far as possible with ideas; but as they are not, they are obliged to combine pleasure and profit in a way it is seldom done, except in architecture.

When you want a lawyer do you ask all the attorneys you know to make a "bid" and then employ the cheapest? Do you not rather look for the attorney whose skill, knowledge of the law, and personal character insure thorough and honest effort in your interest? Level-headed business men seek the best legal talent; in their judgment the best is the cheapest and it should be just the same in regard to the employment of architects, yet many think that the least they can get a design for is so much made. This is a great mistake and is admitted by all intelligent men. It is impossible to get anything for less than its value, and at the same time have it prove satisfactory. It is but a very small design that will occupy a week's time in its study, and the proper preparation of the drawings and specifications.

We shall be very glad to hear from all persons who intend to build, and wish our services, and we will serve them faithfully.

Our aim is to please our clients and to give just as much for their money as possible.

It may seem a curious fact, but to design a small cottage, and get the most for a limited cost, is a much harder study than to design a house to contain so many rooms, and have this and that, where we are not limited to cost.

Our drawings are made on vellum, so that they will stand wear and tear; are thoroughly lettered, figured, and made plain as daylight. Also, any one can understand our full-size working drawings. The specifications are always made complete in every particular, and are furnished in duplicate, for builder and proprietor, as are also our forms of contract; and all instructions are given our clients in the most complete way to enable them to have the design properly executed, and their building affairs satisfactorily conducted.

To those who need our services, we would say that our aim at all times is to produce what will in every way give satisfaction, and our services, advice, etc., are rendered in full confidence that they will do so.

You will do us a favor by showing this book, or speaking of it to your friends and any one in your locality who intends to build or is otherwise interested.

We have the honor to be yours most respectfully,

PALLISER, PALLISER & CO.,
ARCHITECTS.

[Written to go with Working and Detail Drawings.]

SPECIFICATIONS.

Of the works and materials required in the erection, construction, and completion of Design 16, Plate 6.

DIMENSIONS.—The drawings must be accurately followed according to their scale, and preference given to figured dimensions over scale. Detail Drawings will be furnished; any work constructed without such drawings must be removed if required, and work replaced at contractor's expense. The building to be in size as shown and figured on drawings. Cellar, 7 ft. 0 in.; first floor, 10 ft. 0 in.; second floor, 9 ft. 0 in.; all in the clear, divided, subdivided, and built in exact accordance with plans and specifications.

MASON WORK.

EXCAVATOR.—Excavate in depth for the cellar, area, foundations, and footings of all the walls and chimneys, also for all drains, cistern and cess-pools. Dig trenches for footings of all walls 8 in. below level of cellar bottom; fill in around walls as laid; grade the excavated earth around the building as may be directed. Lay aside the top soil at commencement, and replace over the graded surface at completion.

STONE WORK.—Build foundation walls of good building stone, of flat bed and firm build, laid in clean, sharp sand, lime and cement mortar, in parts of one of cement and two of lime. Lay down footings under all the walls of the building of flat stones, not less than 20 in. long and 6 in. thick, bedded crosswise of the walls on the natural, undisturbed earth; build the walls from thence to grade level, by and full to a line on the inner face, and flush and point at completion. These walls to average 1 ft. 6 in. in thickness, the greater breadth at the base. Lay down substantial foundations under chimneys and piers in cellar; put down clear of frost, solid foundations under piers supporting porches and verandas, also under all exterior steps. Area copings and steps to be of blue stone, steps properly walled in on each end.

UNDERPINNING.—Build the underpinning walls 16 in. thick from grade level, and extend up 2 ft. 4 in. in height, with good underpinning stone, level beds, plumb joints; all angles and jambs to have chisel draft, and to be properly pointed and penciled with a red joint at completion. Window sills to be of blue stone; such portions of walls as are covered up with veranda to be rough work.

CESS-POOL.—Stone up cess-pool 3 feet in diameter and 8 feet deep, covered with rough flag, provided with man-hole, etc., complete; make the necessary connections with the cistern to receive the overflow through vitrified pipe of the required size. Also stone up, in like manner, cess-pool, to receive wastes from house, and connect with 6 in. vitrified drain-pipe.

BRICK WORK.—To be laid up with best quality hard-burned brick and clean, sharp sand, lime mortar.

PIERS.—Build piers in cellar 16 in. square, as shown, and cap with flat stone, size of piers; piers supporting porches and verandas 12 in. square.

CHIMNEYS.—Build the chimneys as shown on plans; carry up the flues of uniform size, to be well plastered, furnished with proper stove collars and ventilating flues where required; turn arches to all fire-places, and turn trimmer arches under all hearths; top out above the roof, as per detail drawings, with selected brick laid in red mortar, close joints, jointed and cleaned down, stained and oiled. Face the throat, breast and jambs of kitchen fire-place with selected brick, laid in red mortar, provide with cut stone shelf, to have blue stone hearth as shown on plans. Build fire-places with buff brick, laid in buff mortar, as per details, also furnish the necessary brick, mortar and plaster for setting the range. Clean out all flues and test the draught of flues and fire-places, hearths to fire-places of slate.

CISTERN.—Build a cistern where directed, 10 ft. diameter and 10 ft. deep, with 8 in. walls laid in and smoothly coated on the inside with cement; cover man-hole in neck with flag-stone, connect to leaders with 4 in. and 6 in. vitrified pipe.

LATHING.—Lath all walls, ceilings, and work that is furred off, throughout first and second floors, and three rooms in attic, with sound, seasoned lath, securely nailed to each stud, and joints broken every tenth lath.

PLASTERING.—All walls and ceilings throughout to be plastered with one good coat of brown, well haired mortar, and finished with one coat of white hard-finish. All angles to be sharp and regular in form, walls to be straight and plumb, and in all cases to extend clear down to floors.

FINAL.—Whitewash walls in cellar and do all necessary mending of walls after other craftsmen, and deliver the mason work up in thoroughly good order at completion; make the floors broom-clean from time to time as required; also remove all mason's waste materials and rubbish accumulated during the progress of the works, from off the premises and leave everything in a perfect, complete and satisfactory state.

CARPENTER.

TIMBER.—The whole of the timber used in and throughout this building to be the best of their several kinds, well seasoned and free from sap, shakes and other imperfections impairing its durability and strength.

FRAMING.—The frame to be what is known as half balloon, the studs to be tenoned into sills and plates, to be braced with long angle braces cut in barefoot and well spiked. The girts to be of yellow pine, notched into and well spiked to studs. Do all necessary framing around stairways and chimneys, all properly mortised and tenoned together, and all to be done in a thoroughly workmanlike and substantial manner.

FRAME TIMBER.—Sills and girders, 6 in. x 6 in.; posts, 6 in. x 6 in., with inside angle cut out to make them 4 in. from faces. Girts, 1¼ in. x 4 in.; plates, 4 in. x 5 in.; first-floor timbers, 2 in. x 10 in.; second-floor, 2 in. x 8 in.; attic, 2 in. x 6 in.—all 16 in. centres; header and trimmer beams, 3 in. thick, all floor timbers under partitions running same way to be 4 in. thick, roof rafters, 2 in. x 6 in.—2 ft. centres; hip and valley rafters, 3 in. x 8 in. Door and window studs, 3 in. x 4 in. intermediate studding, 2 in. x 4 in.—16 in. centres; long braces, 2 in. x 4 in. All main partitions to be set with 2 in. x 4 in. studding—16 in. centres, to be set as the frame is raised, and foot on girders, to have 3 in. x 4 in. plates on which to foot second-story partitions and carry floor timbers; other partitions set with 2 in. x 3 in. studs—16 in. centres, and all partitions that are directly over each other, to be set in like manner to above, all to be well braced and spiked; all angles to be formed solid, and all partitions to be bridged once in their height. Porch and veranda sills, 4 in. x 6 in.; floor timbers, 2 in. x 6 in.—16 in. centres; plates, 4 in. x 5 in.; rafters, 3 in. x 5 in.—2 ft. centres.

BRIDGING.—All the floor timbers to be bridged through centres with 2 in. x 2 in. cross-bridging, properly cut in between timbers and nailed with two 10d. nails at each end; also furnish any other timber of the required size and necessary to fully complete the works.

FURRING.—Studd off 3 rooms in attic, properly support and furr under stairs, furr for arches, and do any other furring required by the design, as grounds, etc., etc.

SHEATHING.—Cover the entire frame with tongued and grooved boards, not to exceed 10 in. in width, nailed through each edge to every stud with 10d. nails; this includes all roofs.

LUMBER.—The lumber to be of white pine, unless otherwise specified, well seasoned and dry, and free from shakes, loose knots and other imperfections. Sashes, panel work and inside casings to be perfectly clear lumber.

CLAPBOARDING.—Cover first story with clear pine clapboards, put on with 8d. box-nails, with not less than 1¼ in. lap. These boards to be underlaid with rosin-sized, waterproof sheathing felt, which also place under corner boards, casings, etc., so as to lap and make a tight job. Second story shingled with California redwood shingles, with paper under, and made tight.

CORNER BOARDS, casings and bands, 1¼ in. x 6 in.; bands to be rabbeted top and bottom for clapboards.

WATER TABLE.—To be furred off from frame, and to have beveled cap 1⅛ in. thick.

CORNICES.—To be formed as shown by drawings; barge boards and gable to be as shown. Brackets, as shown, and all as per details. Gutters to be lined with tin, graded to shed water to points indicated on plan.

LEADERS.—Furnish all the required leaders of sufficient size to convey the water from the gutters to the cistern and the tank in attic; said leaders to be firmly secured to building.

CRESTING.—To be of iron, as per details, to have galvanized iron cover base and securely put up on wrought-iron rods.

WINDOW FRAMES.—To be made in the ordinary manner; cellar frames to be made out of 2 in. plank, rabbeted for sash; sash hinged to top and to have suitable fasteners to keep open or shut; all sash to be of seasoned pine, 1⅜ in. thick, and double hung with best cotton cord, iron weights, and 1¾ in. sham axle pulleys, and to be glazed with Chances English sheet-glass, all to be well bedded, bradded and puttied; top sash leaded and diamonds of Cathedral glass; stair-case sash filled with art glass, cost $2 a sq. foot; window sills 2 in. thick.

BLINDS.—Inside blinds of cherry to all windows on first and second floors hung in folds about 7 in. wide, with bronze hinges, and secured with best style fasteners and filled with Pratt & Lambert's filler, and finished with two coats Pratt & Lambert's No. 110 Cabinet varnish.

DOOR FRAMES.—Outside door frames to be of plank, rabbeted, and to have 2 in. oak sills.

VERANDAS.—Construct veranda and porches, as shown, and as per detail drawings; steps, 1¼ in. thick, risers 1 in., to have cove under nosings;

lay the floors with 1⅛ in. x 3½ in. flooring, blind nailed to beams, and to have paint joints; narrow beaded ceiling of even widths. Columns, rails and brackets, to be as shown; cornices formed as shown; panels formed under floor as shown. Roofs to be covered with tin.

DEAFENING.—Deaden the floors throughout the first and second stories by laying diagonally a rough floor, surfaced and ⅞ in. thick, well nailed through top edges to each bearing; on this lay all-wool heavy deadening felt properly lapped, then place ½ x 2 in. strips over each joist, and well nailed through, on which to nail flooring.

FLOORS.—Lay the floors of kitchen part with yellow pine, ⅞ in. x 3 in., blind nailed to every beam; all other floors lay with white pine, not to exceed 5 in. in width, to be well laid, joints broken, and blind nailed in a thorough manner. Lay front hall floor with oak, to have neat border of oak and cherry strips.

WAINSCOTING.—Walls of kitchen to be wainscoted 3 ft. high, with beaded battens ⅜ in. x 3 in., and to have neat beveled molded cap.

CASINGS.—Case all doors and windows throughout with ⅞ in. casings, hall, parlor, dining-room and library finish of oak and cherry, elsewhere finish of ash and white pine; windows in main rooms to be finished down to floor with framed and molded panel-backs to match doors; other windows to have neat stool and apron finish; door-jambs to be 1 in., beaded on edges, and stop for doors.

BASE.—Put down 9 in. molded base in principal rooms, first floor; 9 in. plain beveled elsewhere.

DOORS.—To be made in size and thickness as marked on plans, and all as per details.

SADDLES.—Put down molded hard-wood saddles to all doors.

STAIRS.—Stairs to cellar to be of plank, no risers, to have slat rail on side; main stairs as shown, 1 in. risers, 1¼ in. treads, to be well supported and rough bracketed, steps housed into strings; newel, posts, rails and balusters to be of oak, as per details. Back stairs, and stairs to attic to be box stairs.

WASH TUBS.—To be constructed out of 2 in. plank, rabbeted and put together with white lead joints, and to have hinged lids—these tubs to be 14 in. deep.

SINK.—Ceil up under sink with narrow beaded battens; to have door properly hung; ceil up splash-back 16 in. high, and cap same as wainscoting; also place drip board complete.

WASH BOWLS.—Ceil up under with narrow beaded ash battens, and hang door to form a closet under.

BATH-ROOM.—Wainscot walls of bath-room, 3 ft. high, with narrow beaded ash battens, and cap with neat cap; water-closet to be fitted up with seat, riser and mitre-clamp flap, hung with brass butts.

BATH-TUB to be cased in most approved manner, all of ash.

TANK.—Construct out of 2 in. plank, a tank in attic, 7 ft. long, 5 ft. 6 in. wide and 3 ft. deep, framed, braced and supported in a substantial manner.

PANTRY.—To have counter-shelf and four shelves above, closet for barrel of flour, with lid in counter-shelf; also put in two dove-tailed drawers, and put up one dozen pot-hooks.

PASSAGE OR CHINA CLOSET.—To have table with closet under, and three dove-tailed drawers; also shelves in closets as shown.

CLOSETS.—To have shelves on neat strips, and double wardrobe hooks, 8 in. apart, on neat molded strips.

FURNITURE.—To front doors and main rooms 1st floor to be bronze; other doors jet, sash fasteners to correspond; all small closets to have suitable catches; all drawers to have suitable pulls, locks, etc., complete.

LOCKS.—All doors throughout to be secured with mortise locks, of best make, bolts and keys; outside doors to have suitable shove bolts.

STOPS.—Put rubber-tipped door-stops in base where required.

HINGING.—Hang all doors with loose joint butts, of appropriate sizes; all doors over 7 ft. 6 in. high to have three butts each. Sliding doors to run on track overhead and adjustable hangers.

BELLS.—Front door to have bell connected with kitchen and annunciator with four other connections.

NIGHT-LATCH to front door, combined with lock, and supplied with four keys.

COAL BINS, and partitions in cellar, to be boarded up with matched boards, as shown; doors in cellar to be batten doors.

MANTELS.—Construct mantels of oak, cherry and pine, as per details furnish of best cabinet work and finish and set complete.

SIDE BOARD.—To be of oak as per details, best cabinet work furnished and finished into recess as shown.

CORNICES AND CENTRE PIECES.—To be as per details, and corresponding with other wood.

FINAL.—Any other work that is shown by the drawings, and necessary to fully complete the work, to fully complete the same to the true intent and meaning of these particulars, is to be done without extra charge.

SLATER.

Cover all roofs with best Franklin Tunnel black slate, of small size, laid with a lap of at least 3 in. of the third over the first; each slate to be nailed with two galvanized iron nails; lay under slate heavy tarred felt paper; cover the ridges with zinc, also flash valleys and chimneys with heavy zinc and secure with slater's cement. To be a first-class job, and warranted tight for two years.

PLUMBER.

IRON SOIL-PIPE.—Furnish and connect with drain, a 4 in. cast iron soil-pipe, extend up and connect with water-closet in bath-room through 6 lb. lead trap; soil-pipe to be properly secured and the joints calked tight with lead, and extend up above roof and cap with ventilator. All traps to be anti-siphon.

SUPPLY-PIPE.—Furnish a ¾ in. B lead pipe, connect with the attic tank, and run to and connect with boiler in kitchen; tank to be lined with 4 lb. lead, and to have 2 in. overflow run through outside wall.

BOILER.—To be a 35-gallon, copper, of the best construction, connected to water back of range, through double A lead pipe and brass couplings; these pipes to be left ready for connection.

SINK.—To be 20 in. x 30 in. x 6 in. steel, supplied with hot and cold water through ⅝ in. B lead pipe, ⅝ in. brass draw cocks, to have 2 in. waste, properly trapped and connected.

PUMP.—Put in a combination lift and force pump, to cost $12; connect the same with cistern and well through 1¼ in. B lead pipes, provided with stop cocks, one on each pipe, placed beneath the pump, connect with tank in attic through 1 in. B lead pipe and run tell-tale back from tank to sink.

WASH TUBS.—Supply the two wash tubs in laundry with hot and cold water, through ⅝ in. B lead pipe and brass thimble tray draw cocks, to have 2 in. main waste and 1½ in. branch wastes, properly trapped and connected.

WASH BOWLS.—To be of best ware, and to have marble counter sunk tops and surbases, supplied with hot and cold water through ½ in. B lead pipe and compression double nickel-plated draw cocks, and plated plug and chain; to have 1 in. lead wastes, properly trapped and connected; lead pans to each with ½ in. lead waste run down to underside cellar ceiling.

WATER-CLOSET to be a Sanitas closet, with cistern, to be set and fit up in a perfect, tight and complete manner.

BATH TUB.—To be 14 oz. sheet-copper tub, well tinned and planished, supplied with hot and cold water through ⅝ in. B lead pipe and nickel-plated draw cocks; also to have plated plug and chain; also rubber hose shower-bath attachment; waste, 1½ in. lead, properly trapped and connected.

COCKS.—Put in the necessary stop-cocks over the boiler to shut the water off from the upper part of the house; also put in a lead branch connected with drain with stop-cock for emptying the boiler; also put in one draw-cock in cellar and all other stop and draw-cocks necessary to make a complete and first-class job; all pipes to be graded, so that if the water is shut off they will drain dry, and the whole of the work to be done in the very best and workmanlike manner, and delivered up in a complete and perfect state at completion.

PAINTER.

Properly stop and otherwise prepare for and paint all wood-work that is customary and usual to paint, on the exterior.

Paint finials and crest green, and gild the tips with gold leaf.

All interior wood-work to be properly filled with Pratt and Lambert's filler and finished with two coats of Pratt and Lambert's No. 110 cabinet varnish, properly applied and rubbed down smooth.

Stain and oil the shingles.

Paint clapboards No. 244; paint corner boards, casings, etc., No. 246; pick out all sunk and cut work in red, paint sash, No. 245; Veranda ceilings, No. 217; and do any other painting as required by the design, and necessary to fully complete the same. Tin work two coats metallic paint.

HEATER.

FURNACE.—Furnish and set complete a No. hot-air furnace in cellar, as indicated on plan, to be properly enclosed in galvanized iron, and to be connected with cold-air duct; to have the required man-hole door, and evaporating pan to hold 5 gallons, supplied with ⅜ in. pipe and ball-cock; to have all required mason work in setting, and for ash pit, etc.; all necessary fire tools, and smoke flue connection, ready to start fire.

Hot-air pipes to be connected to top of heater as shown, and in size as marked on plans, and extend up to registers with pipes 8 and 10 inches in size, made of XX. bright tin, joints soldered, and all properly connected, and wood-work to be protected by tin linings, and where plastering will be over face of heater pipes to be lathed with iron lath. The registers to have boxes, to be fixed properly, those in floors to be black japanned, and in side walls convex enameled, and to be in sizes as marked on plans.

All cutting for the pipes will be done by the Carpenter; any beams, etc., cut by the Heater man will be replaced at his expense.

HEAT REGULATOR.—The draughts on the heating apparatus to be automatically controlled by the Johnson Heat Regulating Apparatus, from a thermostat placed in the main hall, said thermostat to be adjustable to any temperature desired, and to control both the door over and the door under the fire; closing the lower and opening the upper door when the house warms to point at which the thermostat is set, and reversing them when the house cools one degree.

FORM OF CONTRACT.

In some States, according to law, it is important that within 48 hours after a Contract is made for Building, it be put on file or record at the Town Clerk's Office by the party of the second part, for his proper and legal protection. Several cases might be quoted where Proprietors have had to pay money twice over, to the amount of several hundred dollars, on account of omission to put on record the Contract.

AGREEMENT FOR BUILDING.
Copyright the property of PALLISER, PALLISER & Co., New York.

Articles of Agreement, MADE and entered into this_____ day of_____

_____ in the year One Thousand Eight Hundred and_____

By and Between_____ of the _____

of_____ County of_____ and State of_____

as the part_____ of the first part, hereinafter called the Contractor :

And_____

of the_____ of _____ County of_____

and State of_____ as the part_____ of the second part, hereinafter called the Proprietor :

Witnesseth, first.—The said part_____ of the first part do____ hereby, for_____ heirs, executors, administrators or assigns, covenant, promise and agree to and with the said part_____ of the second part,_____ heirs, executors, administrators or assigns, that_____the said part_____ of the first part,_____ heirs, executors, administrators or assigns, shall and will, for the consideration hereinafter mentioned, on or before the_____ day of_____, in the year One Thousand, Eight Hundred and_____ well and sufficiently erect, finish and deliver in a true, perfect and thoroughly workmanlike manner, the_____

_____work

required in the erection and completion of_____

_____

or the part_____ of the second part, on ground situated_____ in the_____ of_____

_____ County of_____ and State of_____

agreeably to the Plans, Drawings and Specifications prepared for the said works by_____Architect , to the satisfaction and under the direction and personal supervision of_____Architect , and will find and provide such good, proper and sufficient materials, of all kinds whatsoever, as shall be proper and sufficient for the completing and finishing all the_____

_____

and other works of said building mentioned in the_____

_____Specifications, and signed by the said parties, within the time aforesaid for the sum of_____

_____Dollars.

Second.—The said part_____ of the second part do____ hereby for_____ heirs, executors, administrators or assigns, covenant, promise and agree to and with the said part_____ of the first part,_____ heirs, executors, administrators or assigns, that_____ the said part_____ of the second part,_____ heirs, executors, administrators or assigns, will and shall, in consideration of the covenants and agreements being strictly executed, kept and performed by the said part_____ of the first part, as specified, will well and truly pay, or cause to be paid, unto the part_____ of the first part, or unto_____ heirs, executors, administrators or assigns, the sum of_____ Dollars, lawful money of the United States of America, in manner following :

First payment of $_____

Second payment of $_____

Third payment of $_____

Fourth payment of $_____

Fifth payment of $_____

when the building_____ is all complete, and after the expiration of_____ days, and when all the Drawings and Specifications have been returned to_____Architect

Provided, That in each case of the said payments, a certificate shall be obtained from and signed by_____

_____Architect , to the effect that the work is done in strict accordance with Drawings and Specifications, and that he_____ considers the payment properly due ; said certificate, however, in no way lessening the total and *final responsibility of the Contractor ; neither shall it exempt the Contractor from liability to replace work, if it be afterwards discovered to have been done ill, or not according to the Drawings and Specifications, either in execution or materials ; and,* **Provided further,** *that in each case a certificate shall be obtained by the Contractor , from the clerk of the office where liens are recorded, and signed and sealed by said clerk, that he has carefully examined the records and finds no liens or claims recorded against said works, or on account of the said Contractor ; neither shall there be any legal or lawful claims against the Contractor , in any manner, from any source whatever, for work or materials furnished on said works.*

AND IT IS HEREBY FURTHER AGREED, BY AND BETWEEN THE SAID PARTIES:

First.—That the Specifications and Drawings are intended to co-operate, so that any works exhibited in the Drawings, and not mentioned in the Specifications, or *vice-versa*, are to be executed the same as is mentioned in the Specifications and set forth in the Drawings, to the true intent and meaning of the said Drawings and Specifications.

Second.—The Contractor , at his own proper cost and charges, is to provide all manner of labor, materials, apparatus, scaffolding, utensils and cartage, of every description, needful for the due performance of the several works ; must produce, whenever required by Superintendent or Proprietor , all vouchers showing the quality of goods and materials used ; and render all due and sufficient facilities to the Architect , Superintendent or Clerk of Works, for the proper inspection of the works and materials, and which are to be under their control ; and they may require the Contractor to dismiss any workman or workmen who they may think incompetent or improper to be employed ; the workmen and Contractor being only admitted to the ground, for the purpose of the proper execution of the works, and have no tenancy. The Contractor shall deliver up the works to the Proprietor in perfect repair, clean and in good condition, when complete. The Contractor shall not sub-let the works, or any part thereof, without consent in writing of the Proprietor .

Third.—Should the Proprietor ,at any time during the progress of the said works, require any alterations of, deviations from, additions to or omissions in the said Contract, Specifications or Plans, he shall have the right and power, to make such change or changes, and the same shall in no way injuriously affect or make void the Contract ; but the difference for work omitted, shall be deducted from the amount of the Contract, by a fair and reasonable valuation ; and for the additional work required in alterations, the amount based upon same prices at which Contract is taken shall be agreed upon before commencing additions, as provided and hereinafter set forth in Article No. 6 ; and such agreement shall state also the extension of time (if any) which is to be granted by reason thereof.

Fourth.—Should the Contractor , at any time during the progress of said works, become bankrupt, refuse or neglect to supply a sufficiency of material or of workmen, or cause any unreasonable neglect or suspension of work, or fail or refuse to follow the Drawings and Specifications, or comply with any of the Articles of Agreement, the Proprietor or his Agent, shall have the right and power to enter upon and take possession of the premises, and may at once terminate the Contract, whereupon all claim of the Contractor , his executors, administrators or assigns, shall cease ; and the Proprietor may provide materials and workmen sufficient to complete the said works, after giving forty-eight hours' notice, in writing directed and delivered to the Contractor , or at his residence or place of business ; and the expense of the notice and the completing of the various works will be deducted from the amount of Contract, or any part of it due, or to become due, to the Contractor ; and in such case no scaffolding or fixed tackle of any kind, belonging to such Contractor , shall be removed so long as the same is wanted for the work . But if any balance on the amount of this Contract remains after completion in respect of work done during the time of the defaulting Contractor , the same shall belong to the persons legally representing him , but the Proprietor shall not be liable or accountable to them in any way for the manner in which he may have gotten the work completed.

Fifth.—Should any dispute arise respecting the true construction or meaning of the Drawings or Specifications, or as to what is extra work outside of Contract, the same shall be decided by Architect , and his decision shall be final and conclusive ; or in the event of his death or unwillingness to act, then of some other known capable Architect, or a Fellow of the American Institute of Architects, to be appointed by the Proprietor ; but should any dispute arise respecting the true value of any works omitted by the Contractor , the same shall be valued by two competent persons, one employed by the Proprietor , and the other by the Contractor , and these two shall have power to name an umpire, whose decision shall be binding on all parties.

Sixth.—No new work of any description done on the premises, or any work of any kind whatsoever, shall be considered as extra unless a separate estimate in writing for the same, before its commencement, shall have been submitted by the Contractor to the Superintendent and the Proprietor , and their signatures obtained thereto, and the Contractor shall demand payment for such work immediately it is done. In case of day's work, statement of the same must be delivered to the Proprietor at latest during the week following that in which the work may have been done, and only such day's work and extra work will be paid for, as such, as agreed on and authorized in writing.

Seventh.—The Proprietor will not, in any manner, be answerable or accountable for any loss or damage that shall or may happen to said works, or any part or parts thereof respectively or for any of the materials or other things used and employed in finishing and completing the said works ; or for injury to any person or persons, either workmen or the public, or for damage to adjoining property, from any cause which might have been prevented by the Contractor or his workmen, or any one employed by him against all which injuries or damages to persons and property, the Contractor having control over such work must properly guard against, and must make good all damage from whatever cause, being strictly responsible for the same. Where there are different Contractors employed on the works, each shall be responsible to the other for all damage to work, to persons or property, or for loss caused by neglect, by failure to finish work at proper time and preventing each portion of the works being finished by the several Contractors at date named in this Contract for completion, or from any other cause ; and any Contractor suffering damage shall call the attention of the Proprietor or Superintendent to the same, for action as laid down in Article No. 4.

Eighth.—The Contractor will insure the building to cover his interest in the same from time to time, as required ; and for any loss of the Contractor by fire the owner will not, under any circumstances, be answerable or accountable ; but the Proprietor shall protect himself by insurance to cover his interest when payments have been made to Contractor .

Ninth.—All work and materials, as delivered on the premises to form part of the works, are to be considered the property of the Proprietor , and are not to be removed without his consent ; but the Contractor shall have the right to remove all surplus materials after his completing the works.

Tenth.—Should the Contractor fail to finish the work at or before the time agreed upon, shall pay to or allow the Proprietor , by way of liquidated damages, the sum of dollars per diem, for each and every day thereafter the said works remain incomplete.

In Witness Whereof, *the said parties to these presents have hereunto set their hands and seals the day and year above written.*

Signed and sealed in presence of

Witnesses : _____

_____

Part of the
First Part. _____ { SEAL. }

_____ { SEAL. }

Witnesses : _____

_____

Part of the
Second Part. _____ { SEAL. }

_____ { SEAL. }

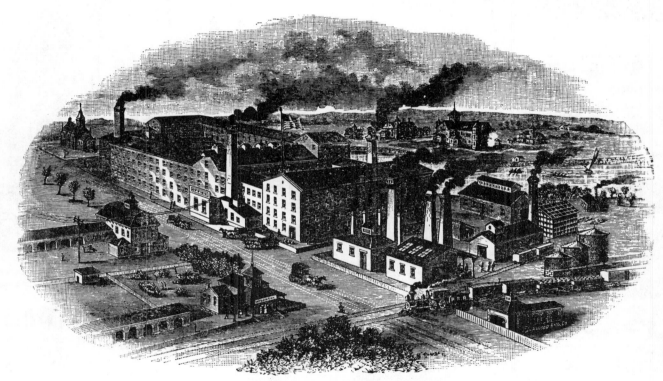

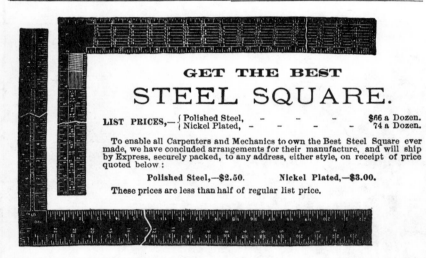

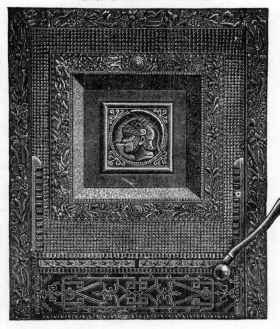

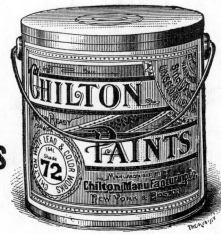

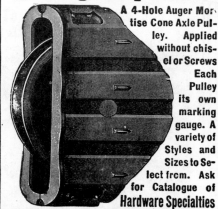
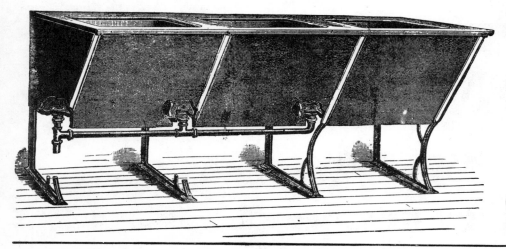

"SANITAS" TRAP.

PLUMBING
APPLIANCES.

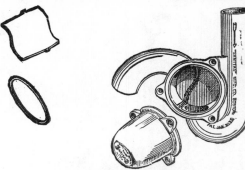

"SANITAS" TRAP OPENED.

These "Sanitas" Appliances are admitted by all authorities to be the best in the market. Used together they form the simplest, cheapest, and only perfectly safe sanitary system now known.

THE "SANITAS-- WASH-BASINS AND TRAPS,
Set in Tile-work.

The "Sanitas" Trap, whether vented or unvented, has shown itself when properly set to be capable of resisting indefinitely, siphonage, back-pressure, and all other adverse influences met with in plumbing.

The "Sanitas" Basin flushes out the pipes and keeps them clean.

THE "SANITAS" WATER-CLOSET.

———THE———
SANITAS M'F'G CO.,
BOSTON, MASS.

THE "SANITAS" WASH-BASIN.

———THE———
Niles' Patent
Locks and Knobs

MANUFACTURED BY THE
CHICAGO HARDWARE MFG. CO.,
CHICAGO, ILL.

GEO. J. WELLS,
    General Eastern Agent,
        P. O. Box 3514 Boston, Mass.

A. C. FARNSWORTH,
    General Pacific Coast Agent,
        109 California St., San Francisco, Cal.

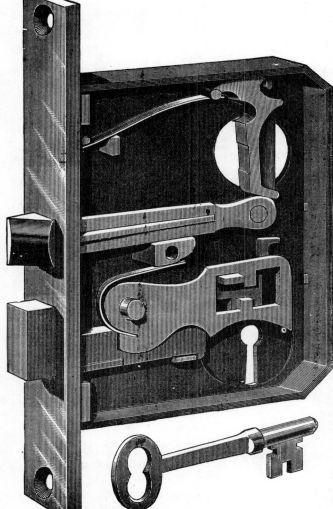

These Locks and Knobs are now acknowledged to excel all others, by having these merits:

EXTREME DURABILITY. There are no spindles in the knobs, no hubs in the locks, no washers, no knob screws, roses and escutcheons always combined.

QUICKLY PUT ON. About one-third the screws needed that other knobs require, and instant adjustment to any thickness of door.

KNOBS NEVER BIND. Each knob works independently, so that shrinkage of doors can never cause it to bind.

PERFECT FINISH. All bronze work has the highest finish— every part of the locks is perfectly fitted, and having the best hardware designer in this country, the newest and best designs can always be furnished.

☞ Drawings of any special designs will be furnished on application and to match any other style of architecture.

☞ **A full line of Hardware furnished to match any design or finish.**

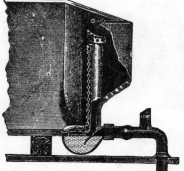

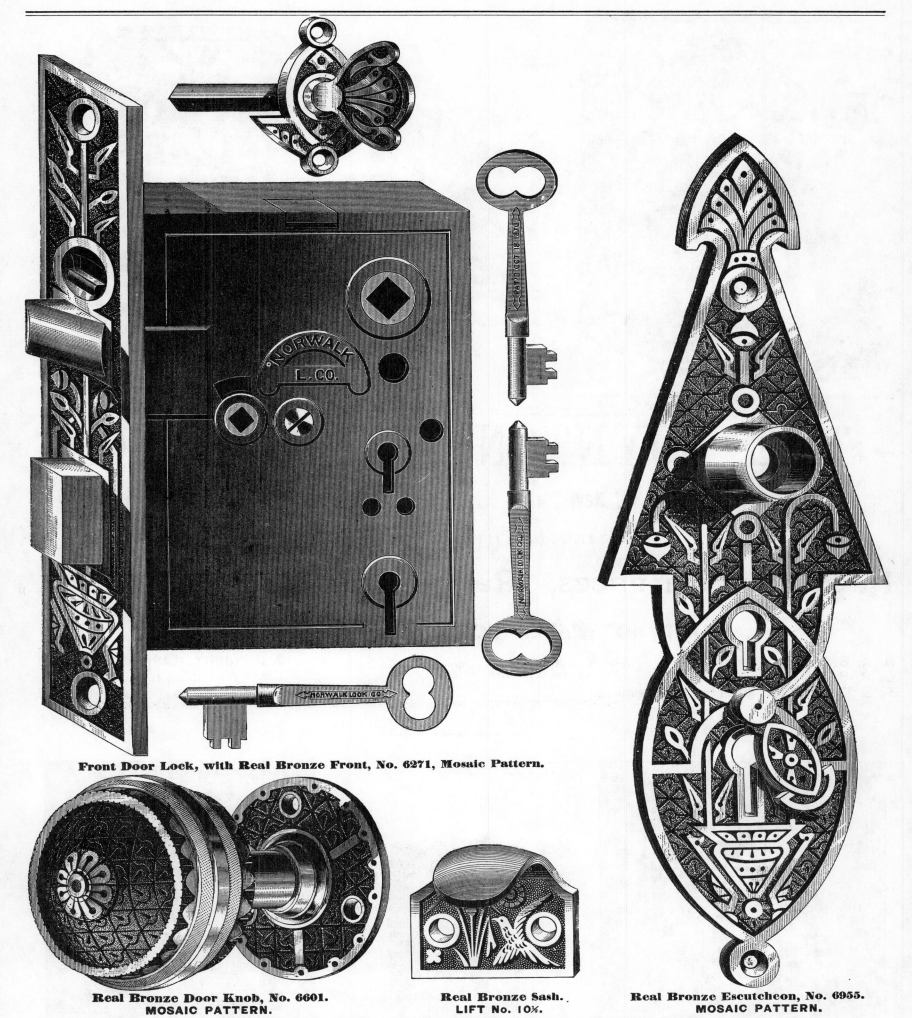

Front Door Lock, with Real Bronze Front, No. 6271, Mosaic Pattern.

Real Bronze Door Knob, No. 6601.
MOSAIC PATTERN.

Real Bronze Sash.
LIFT No. 10½.

Real Bronze Escutcheon, No. 6955.
MOSAIC PATTERN.

NORWALK LOCK COMPANY,
SOUTH NORWALK, CONN.,
Manufacturers of Door Locks, Knobs and Builders' Hardware.
NEW YORK OFFICE, No. 82 CHAMBERS STREET,

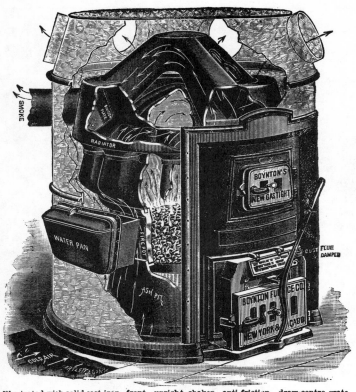

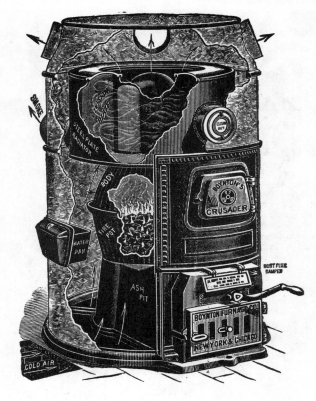
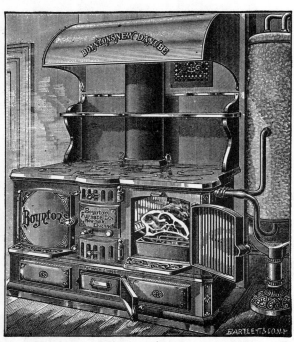

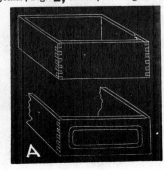

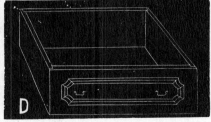
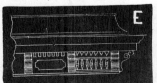
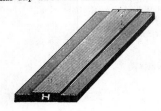

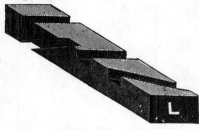
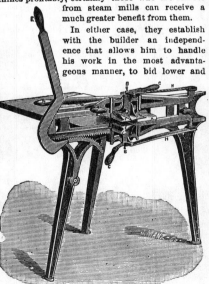

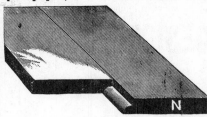

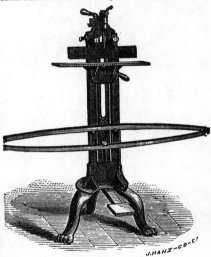

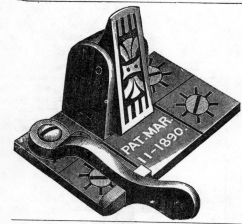
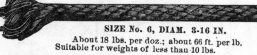
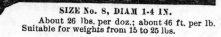
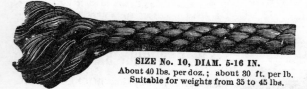

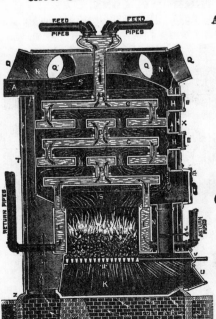

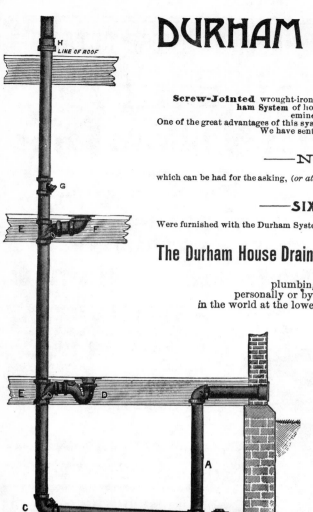
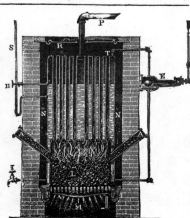

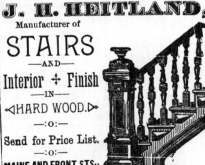
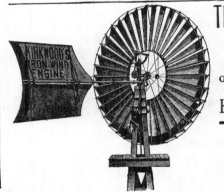

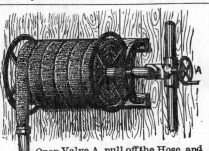

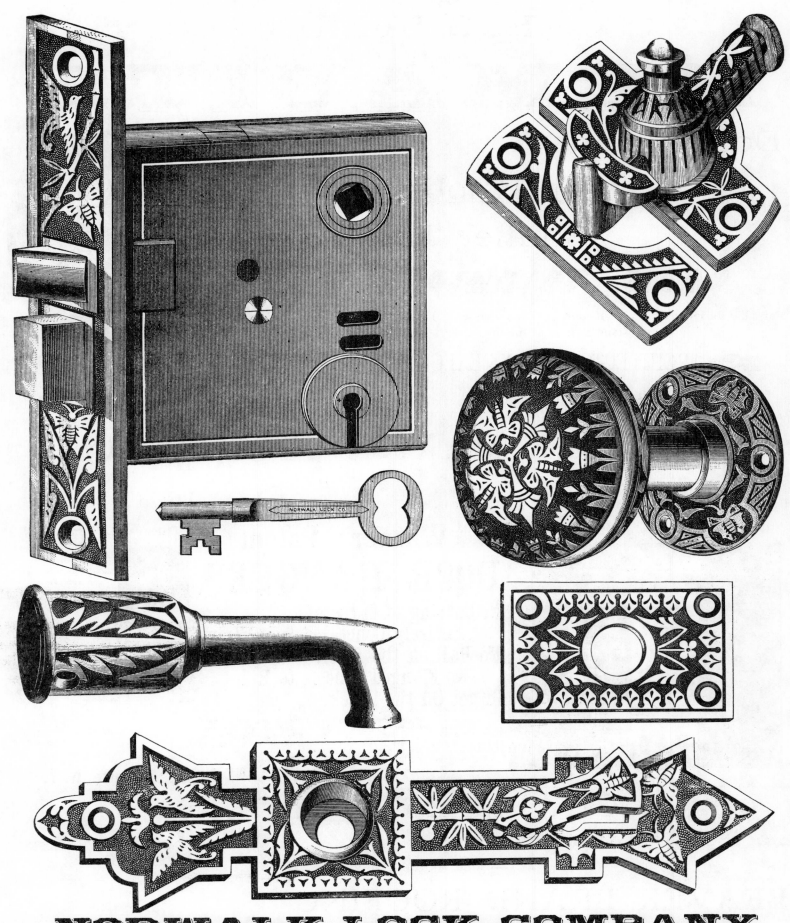

NORWALK LOCK COMPANY

MANUFACTURERS OF

DOOR LOCKS AND LATCHES, PADLOCKS AND KNOBS,

ORNAMENTAL BRONZE & OTHER BUILDERS' HARDWARE.

SOUTH NORWALK, CONNECTICUT, U. S. A.

NEW YORK OFFICE, 82 CHAMBERS ST.

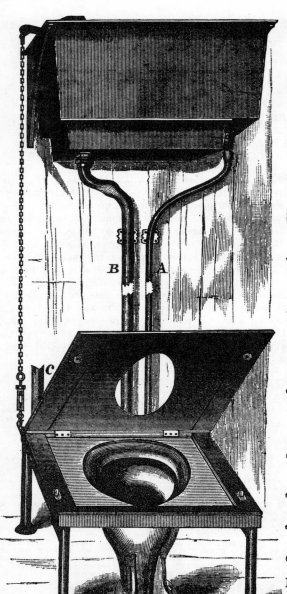

HARRISON'S
—PATENT—
DRIP TRAY SLOP-HOPPER,

WITH IMPROVED FLUSHING-RIM AND VENTILATOR.

ESPECIALLY ADAPTED FOR

HOTELS, PUBLIC BUILDINGS, OFFICES, STORES, TENEMENT HOUSES, RAILROAD DEPOTS, HOSPITALS, OR PLACES
WHERE PERSONS NEGLECT TO LIFT THE PULL OF AN ORDINARY WATER CLOSET.

SUPPLIED WITH WASTE-PREVENTING CISTERN, SEAT,
LEGS AND ALL ATTACHMENTS EXCEPT LEAD PIPE.

THE SUPPLY FROM CISTERN TO HOPPER SHOULD BE 1 1-4 INCH PIPE.

Drip Tray and Hopper one solid piece of earthenware, combining Urinal, Slop-Hopper and Water-Closet.

This Hopper is made self=acting by means of a very simple attachment to the seat.

When in use a small stream trickles down the back of the Hopper; after the seat is relieved, a large body of water is rap= idly discharged through the Flushing=rim, giving a very copious and cutting after=wash, thoroughly cleansing the Hopper and Trap.

PLUMBERS & ARCHITECTS WILL PLEASE DESIGNATE AS
HARRISON'S No. 4 HOPPER COMBINATION.

HARRISON'S
PATENT T HANDLE SELF-CLOSING
BASIN FAUCET.

FOR HOTELS, PUBLIC BUILDINGS, HOSPITALS AND APARTMENT HOUSES.

———

SIMPLE—DURABLE—RELIABLE.

We make a full line of Self=Closing Faucets on the same principle for Urinals, Kitchen and Butler's Pantry Sinks.

MANUFACTURED BY
CHARLES HARRISON & CO.,
NO. 16 WEST FOURTH ST.   NEW YORK.

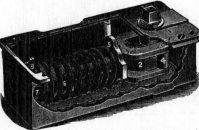

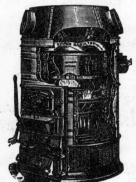

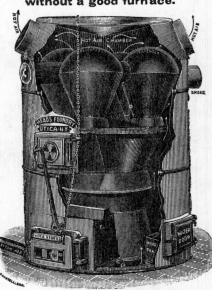

Design 87

Represents a popular style of cottage, painted with the following combination of colors:

First-floor Body,	No.	215
Second-story Body,	"	266
Trimmings,	'	259
Roof,	"	218

Design 87, Plate 30, Palliser's New Cottage Homes.

Design 59

Seaside Cottage with "Porte Cochère," roomy and cosy. Have employed the following colors:

First-floor Body,	No.	201
Second-story Body,	"	270
Trimmings,	'	229
Roof,	"	251

Design 27, Plate 10, Palliser's New Cottage Homes.

The selection of shades depends in a great measure on the neighboring surroundings.

Design 59, Plate 19, Palliser's New Cottage Homes.

·JOHN LUCAS & CO.·
PAINT, COLOR, VARNISH AND GLASS MANUFACTURERS
PHILADELPHIA & NEW YORK

Design 38, Plate 14, Palliser's New Cottage Homes.

Design 27

Small Modern Cottage, generally painted with any combination of three colors that harmonize.

Body color,	No.	216
Trimmings,	"	258
Roof,	"	240

Design 38

Modern Suburban Cottage, on the Queen Anne order of architecture. Illustrating the following colors:

First-floor Body,	No.	291
Second-story Body,	"	265
Trimmings,	"	O.W.
Roof,	"	211

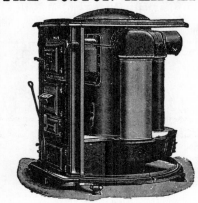

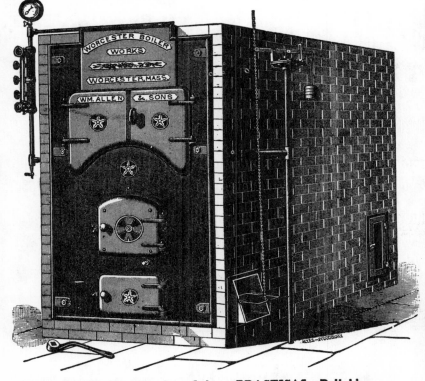

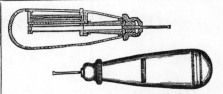

JOHN F. CARR,

Cabinet Woods,

CALIFORNIA REDWOOD LUMBER

◁AND FANCY SHINGLES,▷

ALL THOROUGHLY SEASONED

543 to 557 West 23d St.,

New York.

READ AND BE CONVINCED!

Experience has demonstrated that health and comfort are obtained only as sanitary conditions are carried into the heating of our buildings. Stoves are out of date and hot air furnaces proven not only unhealthful but absolutely dangerous. Hot Water Heating has therefore excited considerable interest.

Why? Because of its economical operation by virtue of the fact that water is the most rapid absorbent of heat, a larger per cent. being actually utilized and discharged, without perceptible loss, into apartments.

An ordinary 2-story cottage can be comfortably warmed by our **Improved Hot Water Heating Apparatus,** with the Bundy Radiator, for only

TWO HUNDRED AND FIFTY DOLLARS.

By using this apparatus you can dispense with one or two chimneys, which virtually reduces the expense below that of any other known system of heating.

BUNDY		HOT
The only Heating apparatus by which you obtain a pure, healthy atmosphere.	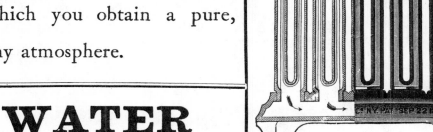	"It takes a heap of love to make a woman happy in a cold house."--F. W.
WATER		**RADIATOR.**

A. A. GRIFFING IRON COMPANY,

480 COMMUNIPAW AVENUE, - - - - - - - **JERSEY CITY, N. J., U. S. A.**

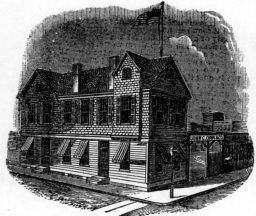

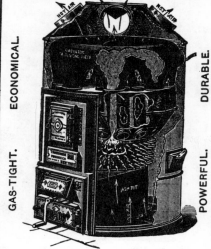
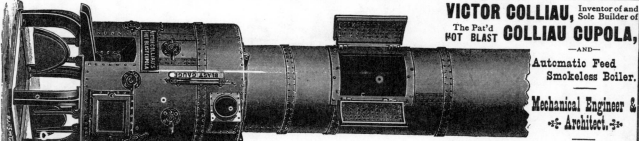

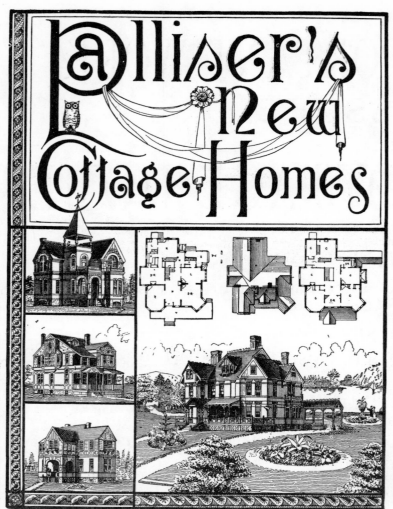
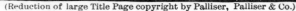

 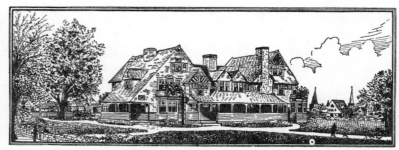 

PALLISER'S USEFUL DETAILS;

AN IMMENSE PRACTICAL WORK ON EVERY DESCRIPTION OF MODERN ARCHITECTURAL DETAIL.

FORTY PLATES, size of each 20x26 inches.

The cost of Drawing each Plate for Engraving is $35, and the Price for the whole Forty Plates published is put at the nominal sum of $2.

A few specimens of exterior details from these Plates are given below, reduced to one-sixth the size as given on Plates.

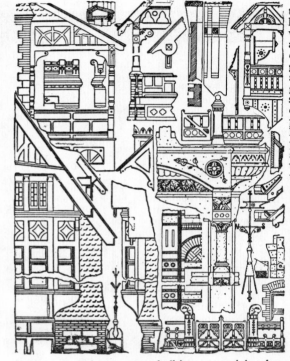

Each Plate is engraved and printed on tinted plate paper, so as not to soil by handling, and is a fac-simile of original Drawing without reduction, therefore just the same as if drawn by hand for placing in the hands of the mechanic for execution. They are given at a very large scale, none being smaller than ¾ inch to foot, and many larger and up to half full size; in fact, they are so plain that every mechanic and apprentice can readily understand them. That they are practical designs is evident, all the drawings having been built from, many of them duplicated several times over, and the thousands of letters received from mechanics the past two years have convinced the authors that this is the work they need.

PALLISER'S USEFUL DETAILS are published for the benefit of the builder, mechanic, and all people interested in the Building Arts. They embrace a variety of constructional Drawings for all classes of work—exterior and interior—pertaining to the erection of buildings of every description, and such as never before published. The designs shown are a free adaptation of the so-called Queen Anne and all other new and popular styles.

Each plate is worth ten times the price charged for the whole to any one requiring any ideas for the new, artistic, and useful, be it ever so little. If you wish to build a fence, a door, a mantel-piece, book-case, or any special features for outside or inside work, as gable finish, a porch, veranda, cornices, bay-window, or to finish up a dining-room or hall in any special style or manner, here are the ideas which will give the key to enable you to work out your problems; and, furthermore, it has been the aim of the author to fully prove to the mechanic that these new styles of exterior and interior construction and ornamentation, when properly understood, are no more expensive or difficult to execute than the ordinary jig-sawed, ginger-bread, box-like work that have had their day; to prove to the masses that the false ideas of ornamentation without constructional qualifications are as vulgar to the true mechanic as brass compared with gold to the goldsmith; to help those who are seeking to help themselves, and to promote a higher artistic feeling in connection with the every-day work of the mechanic, and to do the same without any more cost than if the old rates were followed.

Among the details given are for brick and stone work, water-tables, sills, belt courses, steps, window and door openings, cornices, chimneys, panels and other miscellaneous brick and stone work, including terra-cotta work of a large variety.

For exterior wood work; framing, giving plans, elevations or sections of same; water-tables, belts, gables, brackets, balconies, verandas, porches, door and window frames; towers, cupolas, ventilators, roofs, store fronts, steps and buttresses; balustrades for all kinds of balcony and veranda finish; wood fences in such style and variety never before dreamt of, but all very practical and elegant in their simplicity; barge boards, rafter feet and cornice in endless variety; overhanging projections, combinations of brick, stone and wood finish; dormer windows of different styles and finish, adapted to modern work; crestings, finials, front and outside doors, conservatories, plant cabinets, drive porches, finish for barns, out-houses, well-houses, summer-houses, grape arbor and other detail, too numerous to mention. For interior work will be found different styles of finish for every part, and which includes doors of almost every kind and finish; window finish, casings and architraves, base boards, chair boards, wainscoting, sideboards, side tables, hall stands, book-cases, tables, chairs, benches, pews and seats for churches; stands, drawers, wardrobes —all easy practical designs, such as the master mechanic can readily execute. Staircases, newels, rails, balusters, mantel-pieces, picture molding, wood and plaster cornices, centerpieces, brackets, beam and arch finish, wooden ceilings, wood finish for side walls, inlaid floors, bank counters, desks and office fittings; grocery, dry goods and drug store fittings. Also, a new, full and comprehensive method of

Stair Building and Hand Railing,

prepared expressly for this work. The easiest and simplest yet devised, having few lines and complications, hence can be readily understood. Every one of these stair problems is drawn to a scale of 1½ inches to the foot, and are such as the carpenter has to encounter in his every-day work, hence their usefulness.

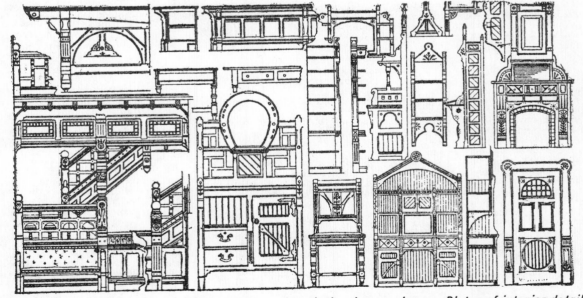

Above are given a few examples, reduced to one-fourth the size, as given on Plates of interior details.

Palliser's Useful Details is the first work of its kind ever published in this country and meets a real demand never before supplied. It is to the intelligent mechanic what the encyclopædia is to the student and journalist. Every Builder and Mechanic should possess it.

PALLISER'S USEFUL DETAILS is the best work of its kind ever issued, and at one-quarter the price of any previous attempt, and also contains twice as much material.

The ideas or designs need not be used as a whole. The parts being complete in themselves, they can be combined so as to produce different results. No matter what kind of a job you are called on to do, here are the ideas to help you out.

Mechanics, as a rule, say they cannot afford to be without this Book of Drawings, rather than they cannot afford to buy it, and all wish they had got it sooner.

When you look at the contents in detail, you will be surprised that so much can be given at so low a price. Only $2.00 for these 40 plates—only 5 cents each—which furnish the mechanic nearly eleven hundred ideas, and practical ideas that you want every day,

PALLISER'S useful DETAILS

An Immense Work.

ONE VOLUME.   BOUND IN FLEXIBLE COVER.   PRICE, ONLY $2.00, POSTPAID.

ADDRESS PALLISER, PALLISER & CO., 24 EAST 42D ST., NEW YORK.

CONTENTS

What the "Builder and Woodworker" says of this book:

These details are, without exception, the best and cheapest lot of working drawings that have been offered to the workman. The whole series of forty plates contain something like eleven hundred separate designs. Each plate is a fac-simile of the original drawing, without reduction, therefore just the same as if drawn by hand for placing in the hands of the mechanic for execution, and are so plain that every mechanic and apprentice can readily understand them.

"Carpentry and Building" says of it:

The plates are large and withal are crowded, as though space were valuable. This is in one sense an advantage, since so many more designs are obtained for the money expended. They are from the best examples of the popular modern styles which they represent, and the scales to which the drawings are made are unusually large ones for the purpose, some of them being less than ¾ inch to the foot. and many of the shapes being half full size, a feature which will be appreciated.

THE PALLISER SPECIFICATION BLANKS.

For Brick or Frame Buildings of every kind, in three different forms to suit cost of buildings.

Printed on one side of paper 9x14 in size, suitable for filling in blanks with pen and ink. Handsomely bound in paper cover with fastenings, etc., for pocket use.

Invaluable to *Builders* and those who design buildings, as by their use they will save hundreds of pages in writing and copying, besides having a more complete, full and practical specification than is usually written.

Those who write specifications will find a full reminder of everything requisite in the erection of such buildings they apply to, and parties not used to specifying for work will find them worth twenty times the cost.

These specifications are complete in every respect; blank spaces are left for everything that changes with the difference in class and cost of buildings, as sizes of timber and other material, in fact, *everything* not shown on plans.

Where the buildings are inexpensive and require no slate roofing, plumbing or heating, pages can be closed up or cut out, and by drawing the pen through a single word or by adding a word in writing, a desired change can be made.

PRICE LIST.

Any Architect, Builder or other person sending us an order for them amounting to $6, and wishing to be instructed in their use, can have one filled out—free of charge—for such a class of Building as he may designate; and we know of no reason why these practical and labor-saving Specification Blanks should not be in general use, as it is a fact that one becoming familiar with them can fully complete a set inside of two hours' time, while copies can be made in half an hour—at least such is the experience of ourselves and others. Very truly yours, PALLISER, PALLISER & CO., Architects, New York.

SOME OPINIONS OF THE PRESS.

The work of thoroughly experienced architects, complete in items, logical in arrangement, and amply provided with blank spaces for entering additional matters to suit the peculiarities of buildings.—*Carpentry and Building.*

In the department of plumbing and sanitary matters, we are glad to see details, embodying the design of thorough work, every particular being so arranged as to insure the dispersion out of harm's way of all sewer gas or noxious emanations.—*American Engineer.*

The first example within our knowledge of a complete set for brick buildings as well as those of wood, and it is high but deserved praise to say that with the proper amount of additional matter to suit the peculiarities of particular buildings, for which ample spaces are left, such specifications can easily be made as thorough and full as the most scrupulous architect need desire. The whole work shows throughout the hand of thoroughly experienced architects, and not only experienced in a certain class of work, but in a great variety of processes and modes of finishing.—*American Architect and Building News.*

A form for use in making contracts for building, being complete and practical specifications covering all essential points. Blank spaces are left for detail, which change with the difference in class and cost of houses, such as the sizes of timber and parts not shown on plans. Messrs. Palliser, Palliser & Co. have done the public, and mechanics especially, great service in preparing these specifications, which obviate a great deal of writing and tend to prevent errors by making all the points perfectly clear.—*Scientific American.*

Any one who means to build had better get them and read them than to trust to an impromptu manuscript.—*Springfield (Mass.) Republican.*

THE PALLISER BUILDING CONTRACT BLANKS, with Bond, 5 cents each, 40 cents per dozen, indorsed by all Building Journals, and by Architects, Builders and Attorneys at Law throughout the United States.

OFFICE OF
Palliser, Palliser & Co.,
ARCHITECTS,

ESTABLISHED 1877
AT BRIDGEPORT, CONN.

24 East 42d St., between Madison and 5th Avenues,
NEW YORK.

DEAR SIR,—If you have selected a design from some book or other publication that about meets your wants, we shall be pleased to furnish you for a reasonable compensation working plans and specifications for the same with any changes desired, but if you wish a specially prepared design and plans to meet your requirements we would refer you to the following :

It is desirable for parties who contemplate building to obtain the greatest amount of room, with the best architectural effect, for the amount of money expended, and to accomplish this they should secure the services of a competent architect, one who has made such things a study and pursuit for years, and has used every means to become familiar with it in all its detail. The parties for whom the building is to be erected should carefully study their wants, and give their ideas to the architect, to be worked out by him; he can then prepare a complete set of drawings, details and specifications. The proprietor knows just what he is going to have before the building is commenced, and he feels the assurance that there can be no misunderstanding with his contractor, as the architect's drawings and specifications serve as a mediator between the owner and contractor, to remind the former what to require, and the latter what his agreement is to perform.

Care should be taken by clients not to place too many restrictions on the architect—how he shall do this or that, and make a mere draughtsman of him; but after stating the price, it would be well to say what room is required, and give him your ideas on the matter; and you may be sure that everything will be added to the building which can be, internally and externally, that will enhance its beauty and usefulness.

When parties communicate with us with a view to obtain our services in preparing plans, etc., they will please give the following particulars, and any and all the ideas they have on the subject which they may deem of importance.

1. The amount you will expend on the building to make it complete in every particular. Do not state an amount less than you really intend to spend, as by so doing you may be disappointed, as some of our clients have been heretofore on account of their understating the amount they were willing to expend, with the idea that it was sure to run up above the amount they named. A lady client of ours instructed us that her house and barn must not exceed $10,000 in cost, and the actual cost by contract was $9,500, and she was disappointed and would have been glad to have had it better finished and more elaborate work and would willingly have paid $15,000, and believed at the start that it would run up to that figure before it was finished, her friends having informed her that architects' estimates were always increased in actual execution by about one-half.

2. Prices of labor and material in your locality for cash; also state how you intend to have your work done, by contract or how, or would you give it proper personal attention yourself, and sharp business management in buying the material and getting the work done according to advice and suggestions that we could give as to purchase of some of the materials and doing the work; give character and ability of contractors in your locality that you are likely to employ; are they mechanics and workers, thorough, pushing, wide-awake business men and close buyers for cash, or are they bound to buy in the local market and pay whatever some one chooses to ask, who gives them credit, and are unable to buy elsewhere?

3. Nature of ground, size and shape of lot, grade of ground and in which direction the building will front, also principal side. The best way is to send a rough draft of the lot, with points of compass, and indicate roughly where building is to be placed, something like this:

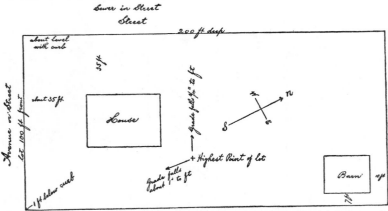

4. What material will be used in construction? Wood, brick or stone? Give full particulars where material can be obtained, and state which can be had most conveniently and economically for the several purposes. What is your preference for foundations and also for underpinning?

5. Particulars of other buildings near it, if any.

6. Number and what rooms are required on each floor; heights of ceilings and number of floors; also give particulars of any special disposition to be made of any of the rooms on account of scenery, views, or otherwise.

7. What the building and rooms are to be used for.

8. From which direction are your most severe winds and storms.

9. Give particulars of locality and character of the grounds and surroundings, and any special circumstances to be considered in the design, and in the location and arrangement of rooms.

10. What improvements are required, such as heating, hot and cold water, bath, gas, water closets, etc.

11. Outside finish—porches, tower, bay-window, verandas, etc., etc.

12. Have you any public water works? Do you require cisterns to receive water from roof, or what provision must be made for water service? Also give full particulars of drainage. Can yours connect with a sewer in the street or must a cesspool be provided, and state whether the ground has a bottom of sand, gravel, hard-pan or clay.

13. What fence and outbuildings are required?

14. Name any work and materials you wish to do or supply, so that they may be mentioned in specifications.

Write your name and address legibly, giving your post-office, county and State, and write your own name at the bottom of your letters.

After receiving particulars, anything that will interfere with the proper arrangement of the rooms, and the carrying out of a suitable design, will be brought to your notice, and we shall correspond with you until everything will harmonize. We do not wish to send out designs when we think they will not give satisfaction.

Correspondence invited from those who contemplate building, which will always receive our prompt and careful attention.

When we are employed by parties at a distance we make preliminary sketches of floor plans, and usually with this we send a small free hand sketch of the elevations. These we send to the client, and they are returned with whatever alterations, corrections and suggestions he makes. Then we make the changes suggested as far as proper and send again to the client for final approval if necessary, and when our sketches show just what is wanted by our client to meet his necessities and desires, we make the working plans, detail drawings and specifications, etc., as required for the builders to work from. Parties who wish to employ us should not wait until the last moment, but should open correspondence with us two or three months, or even more, before they wish to commence building.

Our charges for services are for full working plans, all detail drawings for exterior and interior work and fittings, specifications and forms of contract, two and a half per cent on cost of erecting and completing building, and, where parties are unknown to us, one-quarter of said charges usually accompanying the order for preliminary sketches, and as a guarantee of good faith.

In addition to above rates, one per cent is charged when elaborate sketches and perspective in line or color are required to be made previous to making full working plans; also one per cent additional when there is a large amount and variety of elaborate interior wood work and fittings to design in detail for first-class dwellings, mansions, etc.

For preparing complete bills of quantities of materials, a charge of three-quarters per cent is made.

For superintendence, one and one-half to three per cent, according to the requirements, or by the visit by special agreement for inspecting the work to see whether contractor's payments are due or not, and that he is fulfilling the conditions of the contract.

When required, we furnish our client with a competent and reliable clerk of works to be constantly on the ground superintending the construction, and which is very necessary in the case of large or intricate buildings.

For designs in detail of Furniture and Interior Decorations, ten per cent on cost.

For buying material and appliances required in building and furnishing, such goods in all cases being bought at the best wholesale trade rates, a charge of five per cent is made.

For appraising and valuing, charges are made according to time occupied and circumstances.

Traveling expenses and surveying in all cases are charged in addition to above rates.

Charges are based on the total cost of actual execution and payment of full value, but previous to ability to arrive at the proper and full cost, the approximate intended cost is used as the base on which to reckon charges.

It is our constant aim to please our clients, and we usually succeed. Our long practice has convinced us that it is quite as easy to satisfy parties with our designs when we never see them, as in any other way. When parties correspond with us in regard to procuring designs, we are always prompt in answering their inquiries; but ofttimes people have written us simply to get our ideas and not pay for them. To all such we would say that our time is valuable, and we sincerely wish they would not trouble us. We mention this fact because we have received scores of letters, and answered them, when the parties really never intended to employ us, but simply steal our ideas. Now our ideas are for sale, and by this means we live, and it is a pleasure as well as a livelihood to assist people to build artistic, convenient and comfortable homes. Perhaps if architects were rich—they seldom are—it would be sufficient compensation to them to assist people as far as possible with ideas; but as they are not, they are obliged to combine pleasure and profit in a way it is seldom done except in architecture.

When you want a lawyer, do you ask all the attorneys you know to make a "bid," and then employ the cheapest? Do you not rather look for the attorney whose skill, knowledge of the law and personal character insure thorough and honest effort in your interest? Level-headed business men seek the best legal talent; in their judgment the best is the cheapest, and it should be just the same in regard to the employment of architects, yet many think that the least they can get a design for is so much made. This is a great mistake, and is admitted by all intelligent men. It is impossible to get anything for less than its value, and at the same time have it prove satisfactory. It is but a very small design that will occupy a week's time in its study, and the proper preparation of the drawings and specifications.

We shall be very glad to hear from all persons who intend to build, and wish our services, and we will serve them faithfully.

Our aim is to please our clients, and to give just as much for their money as possible.

It may seem a curious fact, but to design a small cottage, and get the most for a limited cost, is a much harder study than to design a house to contain so many rooms, and have this and that, where we are not limited to cost.

Our drawings are made on vellum, so that they will stand wear and tear; are thoroughly lettered, figured, and made plain as daylight. Also, any one can understand our full-size working drawings. The specifications are always made complete in every particular, and are furnished in duplicate, for builder and proprietor, as are also our forms of contract; and all instructions are given our clients in the most complete way to enable them to have the design properly executed, and their building affairs satisfactorily conducted.

To those who need our services, we would say that our aim at all times is to produce what will in every way give satisfaction, and our services, advice, etc., are rendered in full confidence that they will do so.

You will do us a favor by showing this book, or speaking of it to your friends and any one in your locality who intends to build or is otherwise interested. We have the honor to be yours most respectfully,

PALLISER, PALLISER & CO.,

ARCHITECTS.

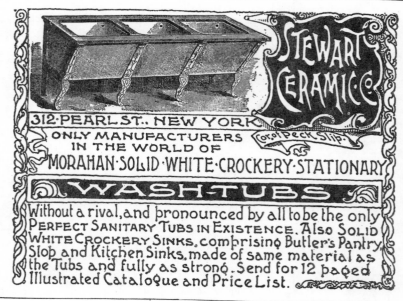
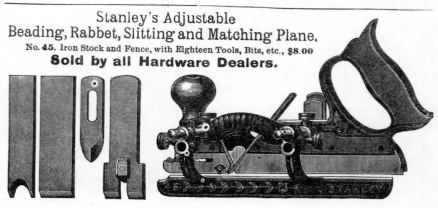

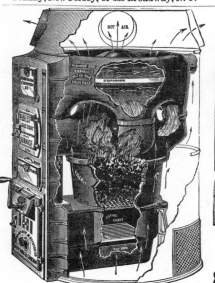